The Works of Peter Schott, 1460-1490, Vol. II

UNC | COLLEGE OF ARTS AND SCIENCES
Germanic and Slavic Languages and Literatures

From 1949 to 2004, UNC Press and the UNC Department of Germanic & Slavic Languages and Literatures published the UNC Studies in the Germanic Languages and Literatures series. Monographs, anthologies, and critical editions in the series covered an array of topics including medieval and modern literature, theater, linguistics, philology, onomastics, and the history of ideas. Through the generous support of the National Endowment for the Humanities and the Andrew W. Mellon Foundation, books in the series have been reissued in new paperback and open access digital editions. For a complete list of books visit www.uncpress.org.

The Works of Peter Schott, 1460-1490, Vol. II
Commentary

MARIAN L. COWIE AND MURRAY A. COWIE

UNC Studies in the Germanic Languages and Literatures
Number 71

Copyright © 1971

This work is licensed under a Creative Commons CC BY-NC-ND license. To view a copy of the license, visit http://creativecommons.org/licenses.

Suggested citation: Cowie, Marian L., and Murray A. Cowie. *The Works of Peter Schott, 1460-1490, Vol. II: Commentary*. Chapel Hill: University of North Carolina Press, 1971. DOI: https://doi.org/10.5149/9781469657288_Cowie

Library of Congress Cataloging-in-Publication Data
Names: Cowie, Marian L. and Cowie, Murray A..
Title: The works of Peter Schott, 1460-1490, vol. II : Commentary / by Marian L. Cowie and Murray A. Cowie.
Other titles: University of North Carolina Studies in the Germanic Languages and Literatures ; no. 71.
Description: Chapel Hill : University of North Carolina Press, [1971] Series: University of North Carolina Studies in the Germanic Languages and Literatures.
Identifiers: LCCN 63063888 | ISBN 978-1-4696-5727-1 (pbk: alk. paper) | ISBN 978-1-4696-5728-8 (ebook)
Classification: LCC PD25 .N6

TABLE OF CONTENTS

Preface IX
Errata et Emenda to Volume I XIII
List of Plates XV
Chronology I – Peter Schott's Life XVI
Chronology II – Schott's Letters and Poems to Summer 1481 XVIII
Chronology III – Schott-Hassenstein Correspondence . . . XX
Special Index – Alphabetical Index to *Lucubraciunculae* Items XXII
Notes to Volume I 361
    Introduction 363
    Lucubraciunculae. 417
    De mensuris syllabarum epithoma 688
    German letter to Anna Schott 694
Biographical Section 697
Appendices 773
Bibliography (including List of Abbreviations) 813
General Index 845

PREFACE

Since early 1963, when the first volume of this edition of Peter Schott's works went to press, we have had access to a number of primary and secondary sources not previously available to us. Results of research therein have not only enlarged our understanding of Schott, his period and his works but have also revealed gaps and misinformation in earlier data. Hence the material in this commentary volume supersedes any already published by us.

Some of the information about Schott and his time in the works of the Alsatians Dacheux, Grandidier and Schmidt (who do not always agree) we have been able to check with information in other secondary sources or in a few primary sources, such as university records of Bologna and Paris. Yet much of the information in these and other Alsatian works we have had to accept as it is, because the original sources of such information were destroyed in the Strassburg fire of 1870. For example, Schmidt, a prolific but not overly exact scholar who at times mixes fact with fiction, has delved into diverse, recondite fields of old Alsatian lore, untouched by other modern researchers, and thus has often the only information available.

To the best of our ability we have in this volume corrected mistakes in chronology made in the introduction to volume I. From additional data gathered on persons and topics mentioned by Schott we have been able also to rectify textual errors made in transcribing and in resolving abbreviations of the incunabulum, e.g., the passages discussed in N. 681 and N. 1077. We do not claim, however, to have found all errors either in the incunabulum or in volume I; nor do we claim to have recognized all the quotations – Biblical, classical or otherwise – in the original text.

To facilitate reference both from the text in volume I to the notes in volume II and from one note to another, there appear at the top of each page of notes in volume II several numbers: 1. the number of the page (and, if an item is concerned, of the item) in volume I to which the material on the page in volume II refers; 2. the number of the note beginning the page.

Pages in volume II continue numbering from volume I. Numbers of notes run consecutively from 1 to 1842.

Symbols and abbreviations appearing in this commentary volume are used as follows: (cf. also pp. 361, 813)

1. The symbol # preceding a number indicates an item in the *Lucubraciunculae*, e.g., #20 = item 20 of volume I.

2. An asterisk after a person's name indicates that there is an entry for that person in the Biographical Section of volume II.

3. A capital *N.* preceding a number indicates a note in volume II, e.g., N. 130 = note number 130. A small *n.* in a bibliographical reference refers to a note in a reference work.

4. A capital *P. (Pp.)* or small *p. (pp.)* refers to a page (pages) in volume I (e.g., p. xxi or P. xxii), unless otherwise specified.

5. An *f.* or *fol.* preceding a number or letter of the alphabet means "folio".

6. The abbreviation *par(s).* = paragraph(s).

7. *Luc.* = *Lucubraciunculae.*

All Biblical references are to the Vulgate, and the abbreviations used for the books of the Bible are those listed in the Vatican edition of the Vulgate, 1929, page xv.

For the composition of bibliographical references, cf. the first page of the bibliographical section.

Notes to an item form a unit and are preceded by a heading which gives the date of composition and the place of origin for the item. In order that Schott's material may be more easily accessible to those unfamiliar with Latin, the first note for each item is an English summary – or in some cases an English translation – of its contents. The second note is often a discussion of the date, or of the addressee, or of the relation the item bears to other parts of Schott's works. So far as possible, repetition of subject matter has been avoided by cross references. Where notes of several paragraphs are concerned, reference is sometimes made to a single paragraph within the note, e.g., N. 16, par. 2. Notes of considerable length, *viz.*, the note on benefices (N. 130), are divided into sections 1, 2, 3, etc., so that reference may be made to a specific paragraph in a certain section of a note, e.g., N. 130, 3, par. 2. In notes to the prose items each comment forms an entire note. In notes to the poems, however, where comments are often mere identification of abstruse classical allusions, one note may cover the comments to an entire page of text.

The biographical section contains entries for those persons mentioned in the Introduction and in the text of Volume I to whom we have found reference in at least one source other than Schott's works and whom we are sure of having identified. In some cases there are two or even three possible identifications, *viz.*, Heinrich Boyk and Johann Teutonicus. Those persons to whom we have no reference elsewhere or at whose identity we can merely guess are discussed only in the notes to the item mentioning them.

Persons discussed in the biographical section appear in alphabetical order, except in the case of rulers who appear in chronological order under the heading France, Hapsburg, popes, and the like.

For well-known persons such as popes, emperors, kings of France, etc. only minimal information appears in the biographical section.

Legal authorities and glossators or commentators on civil and canon law are not included in the biographical section. Information about them is readily accessible in articles on "Canon Law," "Decretals," "Corpus iuris canonici," "Roman Law," "Law," in the *Catholic Encyclopedia*, the *Encyclopedia Britannica* and similar compilations; a few outstanding jurists, as for example Bartolus de Sassoferrato, appear in these compilations as individual entries. The exponents of civil and canon law are discussed by Sebastian Brant in his *Titulorum*, and the glossators of civil and canon law are listed in the same work on pp. 440ff. and 449ff. respectively.

The appendices to this volume contain among other material of interest copies of: 1. a manuscript letter[1] from Peter Schott to Friedrich von Zollern in the Strassburg archives; 2. two German translations by Schott of letters of state, as published by Hugo Holstein from the "Wimpheling Codex" over 80 years ago; 3. a manuscript copy of Schott's letter to his sister Anna which was made by Charles Schmidt and glued into his copy of the *Lucubraciunculae*; 4. the Strassburg decree permitting criminals condemned to death the solace of the Last Sacrament – as published by Wencker 250 years ago.

The general bibliography includes all material – books, periodicals, manuscripts – used, except the following: 1. such books, etc., which concern one individual or one topic; these are mentioned in the appropriate notes or in the biographical section; 2. concordances to classical authors and to the Bible or Vulgate; 3. general reference works valuable for background but having no pertinent information on any one subject touched upon in this volume; 4. modern reference works which merely copy material from older reference works.

---

[1] This letter and a second letter (mentioned in N. 2) have been published by Otto Herding, "Bemerkungen zu den Briefen des Peter Schott (1460-1490) anlässlich einer Neuausgabe," *Archiv für Kulturgeschichte*, XLVI (1964), 121ff.

It has been our privilege since May 1963 to work in *Bibliothèque nationale* at Paris; the British Museum; the *Carolina Rediviva* at the University of Uppsala; the city archives at Bruges, Deventer, Bologna and Strassburg; the theological seminary library at Salzburg; the Vatican Library; *Universitätsbibliothek* at Vienna; *Bibliothèque nationale et universitaire* at Strassburg; the Library of the University of Arizona; the episcopal library of the Tucson diocese. For the unfailing courtesy and patience of the many efficient staff members who helped us in these libraries we wish here to express our sincere appreciation. Our very special thanks are due to Messrs. Fischer, Hahn and Rot of *Bibliothèque nationale et universitaire* at Strassburg for allowing us the freedom of the stacks; to M. Hahn also for obtaining information on the present state of the *Rohraffen* mechanism in the Strassburg cathedral; to M. Wittmer, chief archivist of the Strassburg archives; and to Miss Prichard, interlibrary-loan librarian at the University of Arizona.

We wish also to thank M. Sabbe, the chief archivist of the *Archives Générales du Royaume* at Brussels, for his kindness in sending us information we requested.

To Professor John G. Kunstmann who first inspired us to undertake this edition and to whom it is dedicated we are deeply indebted for his painstaking reading of the final draft of volume II and for his invaluable suggestions.

The purpose of this edition is twofold: to increase our understanding of that rather neglected area, the late fifteenth century, and to ease the path of future investigators in the area. To those using the commentary we quote the injunction in the colophon of the *Lucubraciunculae*:

>Whatever be lacking, supply;
>Whatever be superfluous, delete;
>Whatever be crude, polish;
>Whatever be obscure, clarify;
>Whatever be incorrect, emend.

ERRATA ET EMENDA TO VOLUME I

P. x, l. 23	Middle Ages-Reformation-Volkskunde
P. xii, l. 26	"...Lucubraciunculae..."
P. xv, l. 13	Goetz
P. xvi, l. 28	At other times the ę seems...
P. xvii, l. 24	exclamation
P. xx, ll. 29-30	Cf. N. 47 for corrections.
P. xxi, l. 38	*Delete the comma after "exposed".*
P. xxiii, l. 2	letters or poems
P. xxiii, l. 26	Claus in 1500
P. xxiii, l. 30	Peter Schott (1427/34-1504)
P. xxiv, l. 2	1477/78
P. xxv, l. 7	In 1473
P. xxv, l. 13	Codrus
P. xxv, ll. 15-18	*Cf. chronology I for corrections.*
P. xxvi, ll. 12-16	*Cf. chronology I for corrections.*
P. xxvi, ll. 37-43	*Cf. chronology I for corrections.*
P. xxvii, l. 41	Emerich
P. xxx, ll. 28f.	He was thus one of the first to contend that the *Imitatio Christi* (i.e., *De contemptu Mundi*) was...
P. xxxi, l. 22	Goetz
P. 6, ll. 35f.	Emerich
P. 51, l. 32	Thesaurarij etc. Capituli
P. 91, l. 34	reuerendissima Paternitas tua exequi
P. 99, l. 2	Metamorphosis
P. 99, l. 35	omnes [omnem] priscorum
P. 118, l. 15	Fridericum
P. 120, l. 36	morbos
P. 121, l. 20	arbitror
P. 127, l. 22	Principium itaque actionum
P. 134, l. 8	Reuerendissimi Domini Augustensis
P. 155, l. 30	Forniani [Formiani]
P. 161, last line	perandi [peraudi] Oratoris
P. 164, l. 6	divinorum
P. 171, l. 38	Iacobus Mug senior
P. 173, l. 36	Reuerendissimam Vestram
P. 176, ll. 5f.	Ludouicus Aquilanus Episcopus
P. 190, l. 20	quid et quomodo et...

P. 190, l. 30	quomodo tibi id quod
P. 198, l. 7	obsenio [obsonio]
P. 204, l. 12	Folio CXVIa
P. 213, l. 14	#198 To those who attended... first mass
P. 234, l. 31	haberi racionem...
P. 240, l. 25	video
P. 246, l. 34	#221...clerics' hair
P. 251, l. 40	quando nam obligent?
P. 252, l. 30	#224 Reply to above by Johann Rot
P. 267, l. 19	Alcreos [Alcaeos]
P. 268, l. 10	Nempe [tuos *or* tui]
P. 271, l. 5	Torinna [Corinna]
P. 272, l. 15	Te si
P. 277, l. 17	*Delete* [auricomo].
P. 280, l. 11	Archiuum [Argiuum]
P. 289, last line	Bacchum Lyeum dixerunt
P. 296, l. 31	Rex [Res] gestae
P. 300, ll. 33f.	Folio CLXXIIIIa *precedes* 'Temnit et odit'.
P. 306, #281	Poem on the siege of Rhodes
P. 311, l. 4	Petre
P. 319, l. 31	annum [annulum]
P. 321, l. 16	fallitur
P. 332, l. 2	I. Letters...
P. 347, ll. 28-34	Cf. N. 1815 for corrections.
P. 349, l. 12	[anachorita]
P. 352, l. 15	πασίφη
P. 352, last line	Barbara in el ut Daniel

For other corrections, cf. Otto Herding, *op. cit.*, 114-116.

LIST OF PLATES

(plates follow p. XXV)

5. Strassburg, *ca.* 1500
6. Strassburg Coat-of-arms to *ca.* 1523
7. Map of Alsace, *ca.* 1450
8. Cloister of New St. Peter at Strassburg

CHRONOLOGY I

CHRONOLOGY OF PETER SCHOTT'S LIFE

10 July 1460 – born at Strassburg (N. 57-N. 58)

Ca. 1465 – Johann Müller appointed his tutor (#297, p. 315)

Ca. fall 1465 or spring 1466 – fall 1470 – with Müller at Dringenberg's school in Schlettstadt (N. 92)

End 1470 or beginning 1471 – ca. fall 1473 – with Müller at the university of Paris; A.B. degree in 1473 (N. 95)

Late 1473 – spent 3 months at home (N. 95)

End of 1473 or beginning 1474 – trip with Müller to Italy (N. 95)

Spring semester 1474 – late September 1478 – with Müller at the university of Bologna (N. 95 and N. 96)

Late September 1478 – precipitate departure with Müller for Strassburg because of plague in Bologna (N. 96 and N. 190)

Fall 1478 – fall 1479 – at home in Strassburg; first contact with Geiler (p. xxvi and N. 95)

Fall 1479 – ca. mid-September 1480 – at the university of Bologna (N. 95 and N. 96)
Spring 1480 visit to Ferrara
Summer 1480 finished the poem "De tribus Iohannibus" (N. 1578)
by 7 September received doctorate in civil and canon law

Ca. mid-September 1480 – sudden exodus with Hassenstein and other German students for Ferrara because of student uprisings in Bologna (N. 609)

Fall 1480 – March 1481 – university of Ferrara (N. 96)

March 1481 – May 1481 – visit to Rome (N. 96)

May 1481 – stop in Ferrara on return from Rome (N. 96)

End of May 1481 – June/early July – to Strassburg via Venice (N. 96)

July 1481-12 September 1490 – in Strassburg

Summer 1481 – early spring 1482 – composed *Epithoma* and sent it to Hassenstein (N. 47); began collecting Geiler's aphorisms for the "Imitaciunculae" (p. xxvii and N. 114)

22 April 1482 – installed as canon of New St. Peter at Strassburg (N. 116)

Summer (?) 1482 – visit with Schott, Sr., to Nicholaus von Flüe in Switzerland (N. 826)

21 December 1482 – ordained priest (N. 119)

End 1482 or beginning of 1483 – first visit of Hassenstein to Strassburg (N. 101)

2 February 1483 – celebrated first mass (N. 119)

Fall 1484 – plan for graduate study in theology at Paris cancelled (N. 121)

Summer 1485 – second visit of Hassenstein (N. 101)

Late July 1486 – with Geiler and Rot in Dillingen for the coronation of Friedrich von Zollern as bishop of Augsburg (N. 811)

Mid-1487 – third visit of Hassenstein (N. 101)

January 1488 – treatise on Christian life composed for Hassenstein (N. 849)

6 September 1488 – edition of Gerson's works with "Compendiosa laus Gersonis" as the introduction (N. 136)

9 August 1490 – edition of Thomas von Strassburg's commentary on the Sentences of Peter Lombard (N. 138)

6 September 1490 – report of being ill during the previous night (#156, p. 172); last dated letters (#156 and #157)

12 September 1490 – death (N. 57-N. 59)

CHRONOLOGY II
CHRONOLOGY OF SCHOTT'S LETTERS AND POEMS TO SUMMER 1481

LETTERS

p. 357	to Anna	Bologna	28 February 1476
#235	to Gesler	Bologna	26 December 1477
#8	to Schott, Sr.	Bologna	very early 1478
#6	to Schott, Sr.	Bologna	1 April 1478
#7	to Schott, Sr.	Bologna	2 May 1478
#9	to Rot	Bologna	15 September 1478
#10	to Brant	Strassburg	12 December 1478
#12	to Maeler	Strassburg	17 April 1479
#11	to Geiler	Bologna	fall 1479
#173	to Müller	Bologna	fall 1479
#14	to Geiler	Bologna	30 January 1480
#15	to Maeler	Bologna	12 March 1480
#16	to Rot	Bologna	12 June 1480
#17	to Maeler	Bologna	29 June 1480
#240	to Geiler	Bologna	summer 1480
#242	to Gossenbrot	Bologna	summer 1480
#13	to Geiler	Ferrara	20 December 1480
#18	to Geiler	Ferrara	6 March 1481
#19	to Maeler	Ferrara	25 May 1481

POEMS*

#234	Schlettstadt	spring 1470
#270-#276	Bologna	1474-1480
#280	,,	,,
#285-#286	,,	,,
(#282-#284 ?)	,,	,,
#266	Italy	1474-spring 1481
#277	,,	,,
#289	,,	,,
#236-#239	Bologna	1477
#243	,,	,,
#244	,,	,,
#278	,,	,,

#268-#269	Bologna	1477-1480
#279	”	”
#290	Strassburg or Basel	fall 1478
#241	Bologna	early 1480
#281	Bologna	late summer 1480
#287	Ferrara	March 1481
#288	Ferrara	May 1481

* For the few poems not by Schott, check Special Index, p. XXIV.

CHRONOLOGY III

CHRONOLOGY OF SCHOTT-HASSENSTEIN CORRESPONDENCE

LETTERS

#25	to Hassenstein	Strassburg	5 September 1481
#170	to Hassenstein	Strassburg	October 1481
[#189	to Ladislaus	Strassburg	Winter 1481/1482]
#169	to Hassenstein	Strassburg	Winter 1481/1482 (after #189)
#37	to Schott	Ferrara	20 May 1482 (answer to #169)
#36	to Hassenstein	Strassburg	16 November 1482
#106	to Schott	Hassenstein	10 April 1487
#108	to Schott	Hassenstein	10 August 1487
#107	to Hassenstein	Strassburg	10 September 1487 (answer to #108)
#109	to Hassenstein	Strassburg	5 February 1488
#144	to Schott	Venice	16 May 1490

POEMS

#236	to Hassenstein	Bologna	1477
#237	to Schott	Bologna	1477
#238	to Hassenstein	Bologna	1477
#239	to Schott	Bologna	1477
#285	in defense of Schott	Bologna	1474-1480
#286	in defense of Schott	Bologna	1474-1480
#289	to Schott	Italy	1474-1481
#287	to Schott	Ferrara	March 1481
#288	to Schott	Ferrara	May 1481
#265	to Hassenstein	Strassburg	Summer 1481-Spring 1482

OTHER WRITINGS

Epithoma	to Hassenstein	Strassburg	Summer 1481-Spring 1482
#297	Oration for Schott	Strassburg	Winter 1482/1483
#110	Treatise on Christian life for Hassenstein	Strassburg	beginning 1488

SPECIAL INDEX

Alphabetical Index to *Lucubraciunculae* Items (Numbers are item numbers)

LETTERS

I. From Schott to:

Adelsheim, Gottfried 184, 185
Agricola, Rudolf 65, 78
Barbus, Marcus (Cardinal St. Mark) 85
Biel, Gabriel 136
Bondorf, Conrad 226
Brant, Sebastian 10
Caraffa, Olivier (Cardinal Neapolitanus) 163
Cardinal, A 160
Cluniaco, Ferricus de (Cardinal St. Vitalis) 158
Faculties of theology and law at Heidelberg 210, 211
Friend, A 190, 191, 193
Friesenheimer, Daniel (Augustinian Provincial) 209
Geiler von Kaysersberg, Johann 11, 13, 14, 18, 20, 21, 34, 48, 61, 99, 104, 114, 119, 124, 125, 133, 135, 137, 168, 240, (199, 200, 203, 204, 206, 207?)
Gesler, Johann 235
Goetz, Johann 157
Gossenbrot, Sigismund 171, 142
Groshug, Eucharius 181, 182
Hagen, Jacob 45
Halewin, Gualter van 94
Hassenstein, Bohuslaus von 25, 36, 107, 109, 169, 170
Hoffmann von Udenheim, Crato 154
Imola, Hieronymus Count de 159
Innocent VIII, 81, 167
Keller, Johann 134
Kemel, Emerich 32, 186, 187
Klitsch von Rixingen, Johann 79, 96, 102, 188
Ladislaus Vesprimensis (189?)
Laudenburg, Johann 143
Leontarius, Conrad 126
Louis XI of France 50, 51
Maeler von Memmingen, Vitus 12, 15, 17, 19, 23, 24, 26, 27, 29, 31, 39, 43, 46, 47, 55, 59, 62, 68, 69, 72, 74, 75,

                    76, 77, 86, 92, 93, 97, 98, 100, 101, 118, 121,
                    128, 141, 179, 180, (191?)
Malleolus, Paul 146, 148
Manlius Britonoriensis, Antonius 73
Meiger, Johann 87
Moser, Heinrich 95
Müller, Johann 54, 60, 63, 84, 103, 151, 152, 153, 155, 156, 173,
                    174, 175, 176, 177
Neguiler, Johann 64
Occo, Adolf 139, 150
Ortwin, Johann (suffragan bishop) 165
Premonstratensians, The 195
Ribysen, Theodoricus 70
Riedner, Johann 56
Rochefort, Guillaume de 49
Rot, Johann 9, 16, 28, (192, 213?)
Rupeforti, Guillermus de cf. Rochefort
Rusch, Adolf 117, 130, 183
Schott, Peter Sr. 6, 7, 8
Scriptor, Johann 58, 178
Sixtus IV 53, 161
Spangel, Pallas 142
Widmann, Johann 22, 33, 41, 44, 66, 67, 88, 111, 112, 115, 116, 129,
                    131, 132, 138, 140, 145, 147, 149, (190?)
Wimpheling, Jacob 82, 90, 91, 113, 120, 122
Wolf, Thomas Sr. 30, 35, 38, 40, 42, 57, 172
Zanctivis, Hieronymus de 71
Zollern, Friedrich von 83, 105, 123, 127, also Appendix B

II. to Peter Schott from:

Friesenheimer, Daniel 208
Hassenstein, Bohuslaus von 37, 106, 108, 144
Ortwin, Johann 164, 166
Wimpheling, Jacob 89

III. from other persons to others:

Caraffa, Olivier, to the Magistrates of Strassburg 162
Hassenstein, Bohuslaus von, to Geiler 292, 293
Lampertsheim, Thomas, to Sixtus IV 52
Leontarius, Conrad, to Wimpheling 291
Simmler, Johann, to Wimpheling 294

POEMS

I. by Peter Schott for:

Agricola, Rudolf (written at request of Adolf Rusch) 245
Bartolomaeus Favensis 277
Erlebach, Georg 266
Geiler von Kaysersberg, Johann 241
Hassenstein, Bohuslaus von 236, 238, 265
Heinrich 269
Hennenberg, Heinrich von 130
Matthias I of Hungary and Beatrice of Naples 243
Maximilian, King of the Romans 263
Rusch, Adolf 130
Schoolmasters and Schoolboys of Strassburg 246-264
Schott, Martin (302?)
Wimpheling, Jacob 244, 279
Zollern, Friedrich von 252, 256

II. to Peter Schott by:

Gallus, Jodocus (for Schott's fellow canons) 295
Hassenstein, Bohuslaus von 37, 237, 239, 285, 286, 287, 288, 289
Heinrich 268
Reuchlin, Johann 290
Wimpheling, Jacob 2, 3, 4

III. Miscellaneous poems by Peter Schott:

234, 267, 270-278, 280-284, 299

IV. Miscellaneous poems by others:

Gallus, Jodocus 296
Leontorius, Conrad 291
Wernher, Adam 298
Wimpheling 299, 300

ITEMS CONCERNING CANON AND CIVIL LAW

I. by Peter Schott

163, 209, 210, 211, 212, 215, 217, 218, 220-223, 225-229, 231

XXIV

II. by others:

Biel, Gabriel (and Peter Schott) 222
Caraffa, Olivier 163
Friesenheimer, Daniel 208
Rot, Johann 213, 224, (216?)
Simmler, Johann 214
Wimpheling, Jacob (219?)

ORATIONS

I. by Peter Schott to:

Cassetta, Salvi, General of the Dominican Order 194
Priests officiating at funeral services 196
Those present at his first mass 198
Those attending the entombment of Diether von Isenburg(?), archbishop of Mainz 197

II. by Bohuslaus von Hassenstein to:

Strassburgers 297

PETITIONS

I. by Peter Schott to:

Innocent VIII 80
Sixtus IV 230

MISCELLANEOUS ITEMS

I. by Peter Schott

Aphorisms from the sermons of Geiler von Kaysersberg 233
Eulogy of Gerson 232
Treatise on Christian Life 110

II. by others

Trithemius, Johann – excerpt from the *Liber* 5
Wimpheling, Jacob – introduction 1, conclusion 301

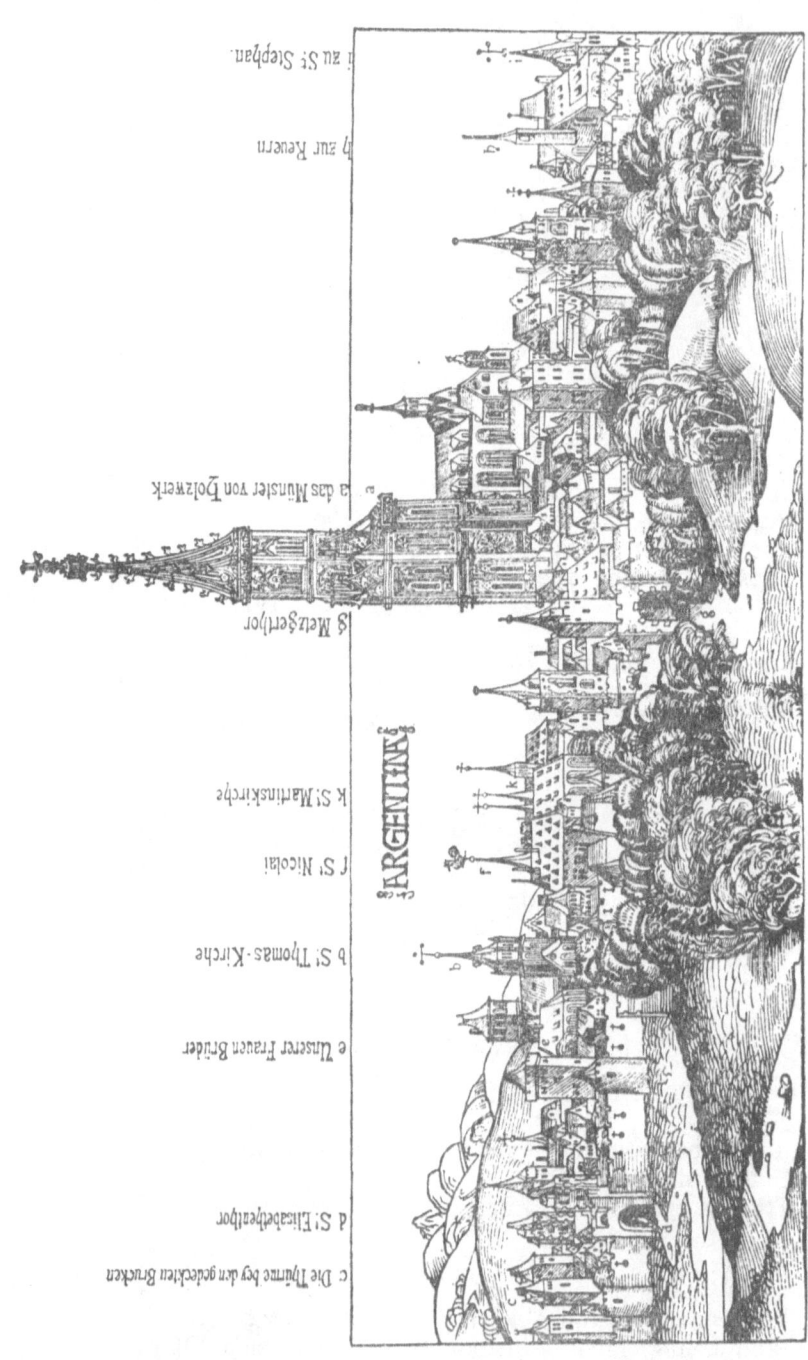

plate 5. *Strassburg, ca.* 1500.

plate 6. *Strassburg coat-of-arms to ca.* 1523 (Cf. *N*. 1643).

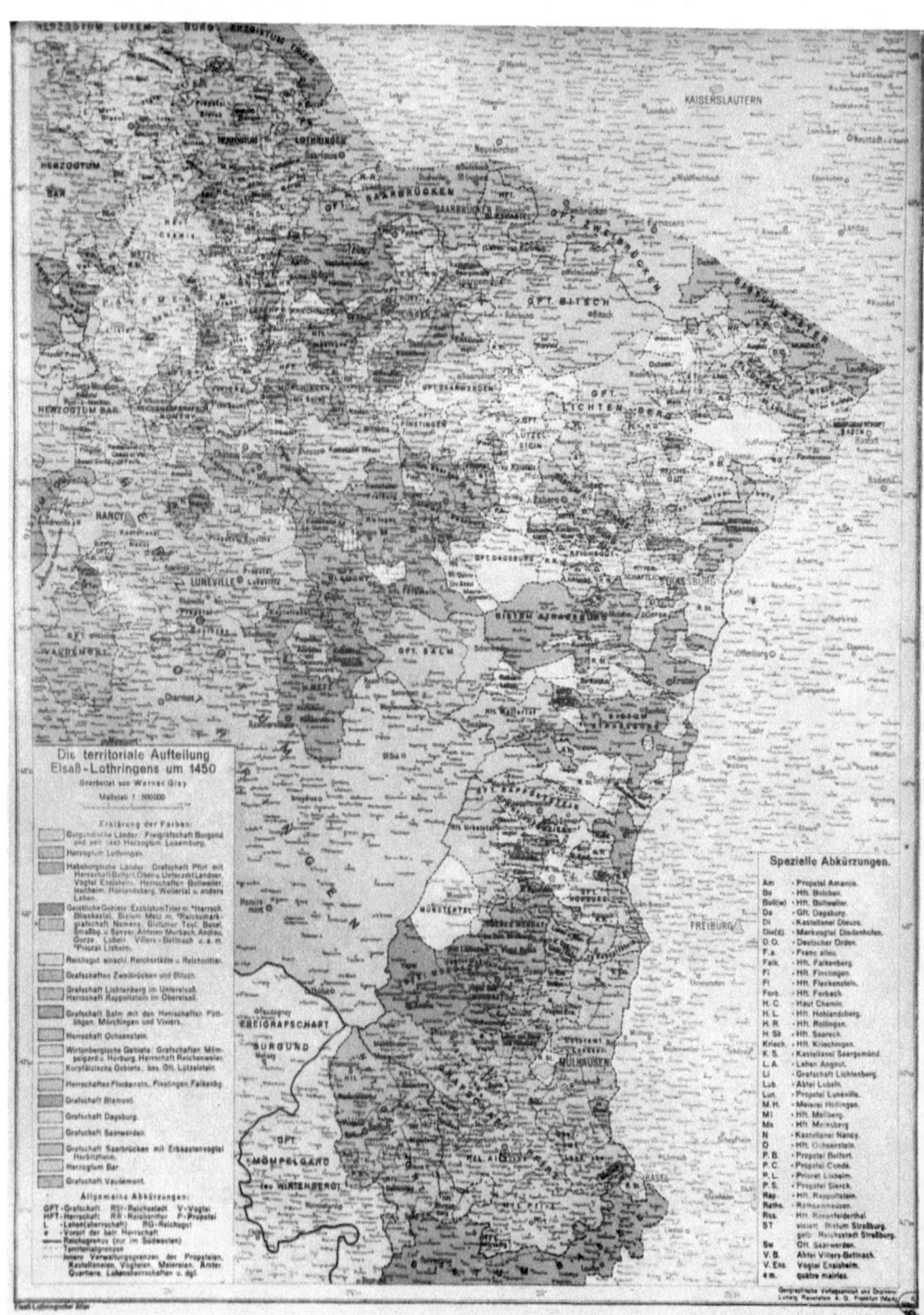

plate 7. Map of Alsace, ca. 1450.

plate 8. Cloisters of New St. Peter at Strassburg (Cf. N. 117, last paragraph)

NOTES TO VOLUME I

P. = Page in volume I

N. = Note

= Item number

* indicates that the person is discussed in the biographical section.

Abbreviations of classical writers and works are for the most part those used in *Harpers' Latin Dictionary*, vii ff.

For the form of bibliographical references, see p. 813.

For other abbreviations, for other symbols, for the composition of the notes, see p. X.

P. xi   N. 1

INTRODUCTION

1. Peter Schott
There was a later humanist, a teacher at Ghent, named Peter Schott, who flourished *ca.* 1530-1540. He is mentioned by A. Bömer, *Die lateinischen Schülergespräche der Humanisten,* Part II, 113, 119, 127 (= *Texte und Forschungen zur Geschichte der Erziehung und des Unterrichts* ..., I [Berlin, 1897]). This may be the same Schott whose words in praise of Seneca's style are quoted by W. A. Edward, *The Suasoriae of Seneca the Elder* (Cambridge University Press, 1928), x.

2. in order that all of Schott's works might be available ... volume
To the number of Schott's extant works is to be added a letter which we discovered in the Strassburg archives during the summer of 1964, a year after the text volume of Schott's works had been published. Investigating an entry in the *Inventaire* (IV, 105B): "Pierre Schott. 1486 2 lettres à Frédéric II, évêque d'Augsbourg," we identified one letter[1] as a handwritten copy (lacking the salutation) of *Lucubraciunculae,* #83, written by Schott 30 March 1486 to Friedrich von Zollern* (cf. Appendix C). The other letter we found to be a hitherto unpublished letter[1] of 28 February 1486 from Schott to Zollern. It is not Schott's original letter but a handwritten copy and lacks the salutation. A reproduction of this letter along with transcription and explanatory notes appears in Appendix B of this volume. Although the letter contains little new information, it does underline Schott's unflagging efforts to secure a proper benefice for his beloved master Johann Müller* (cf. N. 527).

Here must also be mentioned Schott's German translations of two letters of state from Milan. These are preserved in the "Wimpheling Codex" (cf. Appendix D) and in 1899 were published along with the original letters by Hugo Holstein in his article "Neue Mitteilungen. Alsatica," from which the texts appearing in the appendices of this volume have been taken (cf. Appendices E and F).

The first translation is of a letter written in Latin 27 November 1478 by Duchess Bona and her young son Duke Giovanni Galeazzo Maria Sforza to the city of Zürich. The letter decries as unjust the declaration of war by Zürich and its confederates against the Lombards on 19 November 1478, but warns that the Lombards will defend their cause. (In the winter skirmishes of the war which ensued the Lombards were defeated, and peace, mediated by Louis XI, was made at Pentecost 1479).

How the letter came into the hands of Peter Schott one can only conjecture. It is known that his father Peter Schott, Sr., reported to the Strassburg city council on a meeting of the confederates at Zürich in 1478 (*Inventaire [Brucker]*, I, 102); the meeting may well have concerned the war against the Lombards, and at the time or later the Zürich magistrates may have given Schott, Sr., a copy of the Milan letter which he then handed for translation into German to his son (at home for a period in late 1478 before returning to Bologna).

---

[1] Cf. note 1; page XI.

P. xi   N. 2

The second translation is of a letter written in Italian 27 June 1481 from Duke Giovanni to the Strassburg magistracy. He requests that a master architect from the Strassburg cathedral be sent to Milan to advise on the strength of the pillars necessary to support the proposed vast dome of the Milan cathedral. At Strassburg the letter was, no doubt, handed to Schott, Sr., as director of the board (*fabrica*) in charge of cathedral construction and repairs (N. 76), and he had young Peter (just home from Italy) prepare a German translation.

Schmidt ("Notices...P.S.", 248) accounts for the request from Milan by assuming that Schott, Jr., had stopped in Milan on his way home from Italy in 1481 and had been presented to the duke, that the duke through him learned of Schott, Sr.'s, position in Strassburg. Whether or not Schmidt's assumptions have any basis in fact, it is quite obvious that Duke Giovanni was prompted to write to Strassburg by the *fabrica* of the Milan cathedral which shortly before the date of the letter on 14 June had chosen two members to effect the procurement of a Strassburg master builder (cf. Latin text of the *fabrica* minutes in Holstein, *op. cit.*, 80).

A request to Strassburg at this period for help in matters architectural needs no explanation other than that the spire of the Strassburg cathedral was considered the quintessence of architectural genius. During the construction of the spire, 1277-1439, students from everywhere had come to study under Strassburg master builders. Indeed it was to distinguish these masters and their students from all others elsewhere that the Order of Free Masons was founded at Strassburg in 1452 by the master builder Jodok (Jost) Dozinger von Worms; until 1620 Strassburg remained the center of the order (cf. Grandidier, *Über die Entstehung des Frei Maurer Ordens*).

Because Strassburg delayed sending the master builder to Milan, Duke Giovanni on 19 April 1482 directed a letter in Latin to Peter Schott, Sr., who was mayor of that year, and requested that the matter be expedited (text of the letter in *Inventaires ... St. Thomas*, 346; also in Holstein, *op. cit.*, 82; cf. Appendix G). If Schott, Jr., rendered this letter into German, his translation is not extant.

The matter was concluded the following year when the Milan cathedral *fabrica* contracted with the Strassburg master builder Johannes Nexemberger von Graz for the construction of the dome (Holstein, *op. cit.*, 83). Neither of the Milan letters mentioned above asks for a specific builder, yet Strassburg records claim such was the case, although they do not agree upon the name; it is possible that the envoy bringing the letter from Milan delivered the request verbally. Strobel (460) gives the name as Johann Niesenberger who is no doubt identical with Nexemberger; Schmidt (*op. cit.*, 248) gives the name as Conrad von Strassburg; and the explanatory note beside the picture of the Milan cathedral in the *Musée de l'Oeuvre de Notre Dame* (cf. N. 76) gives the name as "probablement Conrad Vogt." The Milan episode is mentioned also in Schadäus' preface (no pagination) and in Dacheux, *Fragments*, III, 143.

3. the letter to Anna has been twice printed
The letter has actually been printed three times. Weislinger published his copy of the original in 1749; Dacheux (*Réf.*, 425) reproduced Weislinger's copy and Dreher (XVIII, 9, n. i) reprinted the text from Dacheux (cf. pp. xxif. and N. 51, N. 53).

Since volume I of this edition went to press, we have found Schmidt's handwritten transcription made in 1855 from the original letter. The small manuscript is pasted onto a blank rear folio in the undamaged copy of the *Lucubraciunculae* which is now at the *Bibliothèque nationale et universitaire de*

364

P. xi   N. 3

Strasbourg, but which was previously in Schmidt's library and, according to the notation on the title folio, once belonged to a monastery: "Lieber Bruder Scottus pertinet ad monasterium SS. Mart. Marcellini et Petri." Schmidt included in his manuscript the comment Anna wrote at the end of the original letter and added two comments of his own in French: 1) that Anna had pasted the letter on the inside cover of her copy of Vincent de Ferrara's *Sermones de Sanctis*, a gift from her brother, which was formerly in the library of the monastery of St. John but at the time (1855) was in the *Bibliothèque de Strasbourg*; 2) that the copy of the letter published by Weislinger is inaccurate. This remark appears also in Schmidt's *H.L.*, II, 9, n. 20. For a reproduction of Schmidt's manuscript, cf. Appendix A.

4. Two other works, no longer extant, ... written by Peter Schott.
To the lost works by Schott should be added a poem "Andree apostoli laudes carmen breve" which is listed among Schott's works by Trithemius, *Cathologus*, f. 55b.

It is possible that Schott wrote two other works: the "doctrina de accentibus grecis" which he sent to Bohuslaus von Hassenstein (#107, p. 117) and a biography of Nicholaus von Flüe* which he promised to complete for Hassenstein (#107, p. 118). See also the works mentioned in N. 5.

5. A commentary in Latin ... inserted ... into a book of sermons
Both Weislinger (681) and Schmidt (*H. L.*, II, 29, n. 78; cf. also his note appended to the handwritten copy of the letter to Anna and N. 3) identify the lost book of sermons as St. Vincent de Ferrara's *Sermones de Sanctis* (sermons on the saints celebrated throughout the year) and describe the items Anna had pasted into it. In addition to her brother's letter inserted on the inside cover there were four items at the end of the volume:

1) Schott's Latin commentary written in his own hand and containing explanatory notes on John 13:17. On the last leaf of the commentary Anna noted "Disz buch hat min bruder doctor Schott geben mir."

2) A handwritten Latin letter of unknown origin [by Schott?] dated 1490 and giving religious counsel. At the end appeared the words "Iacobus Sturm manu propria" and Anna's explanation "Jacop Sturm hat disz geschrieben in sein x jor," meaning that young Jacob had copied the letter when he was 10 years old, i.e., in 1499. As Schmidt notes, Weislinger (553) mistakenly published this as a letter composed by Jacob Sturm*; obviously, Sturm who was born in 1489 could not have written it in 1490.

3) A copy of Geiler's sermon to the Strassburg synod of 1482.

4) An unidentified exposition on the psalms [by Schott?].

6. A vocabulary of names of instruments and implements
Cf. #25, p. 33.

7. Scholars have ... misquoted material from the Lucubraciunculae
Compare Goldast's printing of folios XXXVIbff. (reproduced in Appendix I) with #65. Compare also such misinterpretation of material in the *Lucubraciunculae* as is discussed in N. 62, N. 249 and N. 550.

Furthermore, scholars have without evidence made erroneous statements about Schott, his father and Geiler. For example, virtually every detail concerning Schott and his writings in Holstein ("Mitteilungen," 78) is

365

P. xi   N. 7

incorrect. Confusing Schott with his father, Hartmann (42, n. 3) makes the statement that Peter Schott, the humanist, was the grandfather of Jacob Sturm.* Wuttke in his recent Geiler article for *NDB* (VI, 150f.) has erred in saying (a) that Geiler was persuaded by "his pupil Peter Schott" to accept the Strassburg cathedral chair, newly established and financed by Schott; and (b) that from 1478 to 1486 Geiler preached in the church of St. Laurentius (cf. N. 80). Zacher (22, 27) terms Schott Geiler's "pupil" and "secretary." Cf. also the errors discussed in N. 13 and N. 19.

An example of both misinterpretation of material in the *Lucubraciunculae* and of erroneous statements is found in two pages of Schmidt (*H. L.*, II, 32 and 33) where of eleven statements made by Schmidt – seven of which concern material in the *Lucubraciunculae* – four are mere assumptions without any basis in fact and seven are completely erroneous. A brief discussion of Schmidt's statements follows (page references are to Schmidt's work):

P. 32, ll. 2ff. Schmidt avers that it was Kerer himself who in #21 told jokes at Wildbad to spice the Schotts' dinner, whereas it was someone sent by Geiler and Kerer.*

P. 32, ll. 8f. There is no record that the Schotts "from time to time" visited the castle at Wasselonne to see Ottilia Schott* (wife of Zeisolf von Adelsheim, Sr.*). Only once does Schott speak of a visit to Wasselonne, in a letter to Zeisolf von Adelsheim, Jr.* (nephew to Zeisolf, Sr.). Cf. # 185, p. 203.

P. 32, ll. 9f. Gottfried von Adelsheim,* the doctor of law and *praepositus* of Wimpfen, was not Ottilia Schott's brother-in-law, but her nephew by marriage.

P. 32, ll. 12-14. Schott does not say in #63 of November 1484 that he has been in Basel and has heard Johann Heynlin.* Certainly he did not, as Schmidt avers, at that time attend the ceremony at which Brant* received his licentiate in law, for Basel matriculation records (Wackernagel, I, 138) give the date of that occasion as 1483.

P. 32, ll. 19-22. So far as can be learned from Schott's correspondence, Bishop Friedrich von Zollern* did not invite Schott "à plusieurs reprises" to visit him.

P. 32, ll. 24ff. There is no mention in the *Lucubraciunculae* of a visit (or visits) to Gabriel Biel.* In his letter of August 1489 (#136) Schott accepts Biel's invitation to ceremonies in Tübingen on condition that Geiler go also and that his parents give him leave. As indicated in N. 1025, it seems that Schott did go to Tübingen rather than, as Schmidt infers, that his parents opposed his going because of his health, "de plus en plus chancelante." There is no evidence in the *Lucubraciunculae* that Schott's health became progressively worse; indeed, at this time it was the health of his father (still serving his term as mayor) which would have kept Schott from going to Tübingen.

Pp. 32f., n. 94. Trithemius, *Cathalogus*, folio 55, does not give the year of Schott's death as 1490, but as 1491 (N. 161). It is the excerpt from Trithemius, *Liber* in the *Lucubraciunculae* (#5) which gives the year as 1490.

P. 33, ll. 9f. There is no proof that Hassenstein brought "nombreux manuscrits" from his trip to the Near East, although he may very well have.

P. 33, l. 13. Hassenstein's oration on Schott, as explained on p. xxiii (also N. 62 and N. 63), is not a funeral oration.

P. 33, n. 95. Here Schmidt states that Schott's epitaph was still in existence at New St. Peter at the time of writing (*ca.* 1878/9), whereas other nineteenth-century sources, including Horning who wrote extensively about the history of New St. Peter, say the epitaph disappeared in 1791 (N. 57) and quote one of the copies of the epitaph made before 1791.

P. xii   N. 8

P. xii

8. All acclaimed him as the first Alsatian humanist
The designation "first" is always suspect. Schott was not the first Alsatian of the fifteenth century to be deeply interested in the classics or in the Renaissance, nor was he the first Alsatian to study in Italy. Alsatians are inscribed in the *Acta bonon.*, for instance, as early as 1295, when there were at least four students from Alsace and one from Strassburg at Bologna.

9. Leo Dacheux in his excellent biography...
The one drawback to Dacheux' work is the lack of an index of any kind. Quotations from the *Lucubraciunculae* appear throughout the Geiler biography, but most of them are in the section on pp. 286-427. The Latin text of Schott's items is quoted in entirety or in part in the notes, and selected passages are translated in the discussion.

10. Charles Schmidt in a series of articles ... Histoire littéraire...
"Notices sur les humanistes strasbourgeois. II Pierre Schott," *RA* (1857), VIII, 241-256, 308-321, 337-352. *H. L.*, II, 2-35.

11. the disastrous Strassburg fire of 1870
Cf. p. xxii and N. 56.

12. Vulpinus (Renaud) published in an article...
JbGElsLotr, X (1894), 37-61. Vulpinus has brief introductory remarks and a few footnotes. He does not give the Latin text, nor does he explain why he omitted four of Schott's letters to Geiler (#34, #48, #135, #137). His German verse translation of the poem "De tribus Iohannibus" (*ibid.*, 57-61) is in the elegiac metre of the original.

13. Wolfgang Stammler ... has two sentences on Schott...
Von der Mystik zum Barock, 56: "Da kehrte 1488 der Kanonikus Peter Schott (gest. 1492) aus Italien, wo er sich den juristischen Doktorhut erworben hat, in das Thomas=Stift zurück und brachte neues Latein, neue Schriften, neue Gedanken von dort mit. Das Kapitel von St. Thomas nimmt nunmehr den jungen Humanismus in seine Obhut." These sentences are repeated in the second edition (1950), p. 65. From the *Lucubraciunculae* it is apparent that Schott returned from Italy in 1481; that he became canon of New St. Peter in 1482; that he was never a canon of St. Thomas; and that he died in 1490. GGr^2, I, 419 and Erhard, III, 280, say that Schott became canon in 1488.

14. Georg Ellinger ... refers to Schott...
Geschichte der neulateinischen Literatur Deutschlands. I. Italien und der deutsche Humanismus, 411.

15. single studies on Schott published since 1900...
The pages for the articles mentioned are: Hammer, *ZfdP* (LXXVII, 1958), 361-371; Cowie, *Kunstmann-Festschrift*, 141-155, and *SP* (LVIII, 1961), 483-495.

P. xiii   N. 16

P. xiii

16. *the free imperial city of Strassburg*
The higher ground at the confluence of the Ar and the Breusch with the Ill (whence some say derive *Elsass, Alsace*), near the point where the Ill flows into the Rhine, has since prehistoric times been a strategic site favored for settlement. The encircling network of river arms and swamps, which were later drained by canals, made the area easily defendable; it was a natural crossroads of main east-west and north-south travel routes; and it was situated in an abundant land. To the north and south stretched the broad, fertile Rhine valley; to the west rolled the foothills of the scenic Vosges towering in the distance; and to the east across the Rhine rose the sharp heights of the Black Forest. The waters teemed with fish and the forests abounded in game. Here grew the city we know as Strassburg or Strasbourg.

Through the centuries the city has had many names, the earliest of which Argenta, Argentilla or Argentos (*ar*=water, cf. Aar; *gen*=water, cf. Genoa, Geneva) was probably of Celtic origin. To the Romans the city was known as Argentorate or Argentoratum. According to some authorities this name comes from the German dialect of the Vangiones; Ptolemy, however, claims that the city was so called because of the silver mines found by the Romans in the area. Ptolemy's explanation gave rise to the names Silberina, Silberstadt, Argentoracum and Argentina, the last mentioned being the one favored by the Alsatian humanists and the early printers. The name Strateburgum, from which Strassburg is derived and which means the fort at the crossroads, came into use during the early Middle Ages. In former times the inhabitants of the city, too, had many names; e.g., Argentoracenses, Tribores, Tribaces and Argentinenses.

The first known inhabitants of the city were Celts. Then German tribes, mainly the Tribochi, pushed across the Rhine and mingled with the Celts. At the time of Augustus, when Strassburg was made one of the posts of the defense line (*limes*) against German tribes east of the Rhine, artisans and merchants from Italy and the East and legionaries from every part of the Roman empire were added to the already heterogeneous population. At the time of Ptolemy (*ca.* 140) Strassburg was the headquarters of the eighth Roman legion.

During the *Völkerwanderung* Strassburg lay directly in the path of barbarians invading Gaul and in 357 was the scene of Julianus' victory over the Alemanni. After the withdrawal of the Roman legions from northern Europe at the end of the fifth century, the city was laid waste and deserted by most of its inhabitants. From the ruins rose the medieval city which became one of the most important trade centers on the main artery of travel between Italy and northern Europe and which in the age of Charlemagne boasted a cathedral unparalleled along the Rhine. By 1444 Strassburg had an estimated population of 17,000 to 18,000 and was exporting Alsatian wines to points as distant as England.

In 1262 Strassburg succeeded in casting off the rule of the bishops and became a free city of the Holy Roman Empire (a status it lost 400 years later on its capitulation 1681 to Louis XIV). In the mid-fourteenth century, after a prolonged struggle to break the power of the nobility in whose families the chief offices of the city had become virtually hereditary, a democratic government was formed under a rather flexible constitution (*Schwörbrief*) which with minor revisions, mostly linguistic, remained in effect until 1790 (when Strassburg sank to the level of a provincial capital and the first popularly elected mayor took office). The government of the free imperial city of Strassburg was considered exemplary. Erasmus called it "a monarchy without tyranny, an aristocracy without factions and a democracy without strife."

In the latter part of the fifteenth and early years of the sixteenth centuries, before the turmoils brought on by the Reformation, Strassburg enjoyed its period of greatest efflorescence. This was the Strassburg which Aeneas Silvio Piccolomini termed the "German Venice" and which Bohuslaus von Hassenstein praised as superior to all its neighbors in natural and human resources (#297, p. 315). This was the Strassburg of Peter Schott.

Cf. Borries, 70-74. Dacheux, *Réf.*, Appendix X. Dollinger, 9-13. Glöckler, I, 6f., 37. Hertzog, viii, 40. Rapp, 36. Rathgeber, *Strassburg*, 5. Spach, *Zunftwesen*, lff. Specklin, 9, 85-88 (text of *Schwörbrief*). Wittmer-Meyer, Introduction, *passim*. Cf. also N. 69.

17. Strassburg... became a leading center of humanism...
By the mid-1490's Strassburg had the intellectual atmosphere for which Schott had longed on his return from Italy in 1481. Not only had a younger generation of Strassburgers been schooled in the *humaniora*, but also scholars from elsewhere had been attracted to the city. Among the better known humanists active in Strassburg during the decade before and the decade after 1500 may be mentioned Thomas Wolf, Sr.,* Johann Müller,* Andreas Hartmann,* Sebastian Brant,* Thomas Wolf, Jr.,* Philip von Endingen,* Beatus Rhenanus,* Johannes Pauli, and Hieronymus Gebweiler. All of these men had received the best training possible at the time and many had studied in Italy. Some were jurists; others were writers; Rhenanus and Gebweiler were schoolmasters; Wolf, Jr. was the first Alsatian archeologist. A number of them were canons of the collegiate churches St. Thomas and New St. Peter, both of which were centers of learning.

Geiler must be included here. Geiler the humanist has always been overshadowed by Geiler the mystic, the reformer, the renowned preacher. Yet he was well versed in the classics; he was greatly concerned with education; he collected a magnificent library; he prodded his younger contemporaries to edit manuscripts and write history. In short, he had all the attributes of a humanist. He was also responsible for Brant's return, as well as for Rhenanus' and Gebweiler's coming to Strassburg.

Wimpheling, too, belongs to the Strassburg humanists although he was never for any lengthy period resident in the city. It was he who founded the Strassburg humanistic society, "Sodalitas Litteraria Argentinensis," as is attested by the words of a contemporary "ipse Jacobus fundamenta iecit." Just when the society began is not known; it was in existence when Celtis visited Strassburg at the turn of the century and in full bloom for Erasmus in 1514.

18. first great humanistic gymnasium
In the late fifteenth and early sixteenth centuries, elementary and secondary education was provided by the schools of the cathedral, the three collegiate churches and the monasteries. There were also schools operated by private individuals where fundamentals were taught, such as that of Johann Uttenheim, "Buchbinder und Leermeister." Among the institutions noted for their excellence were those of St. Thomas, New St. Peter, the Dominicans, the Franciscans and the Hermits of St. William. Some schools offered advanced studies and had outstanding teachers; e.g., Heinrich von Wesmail was professor of theology at the Dominican school in 1481; Conrad Bondorf* lectured on Scotus at the Franciscan school in 1484 (#54, p. 59) and became lector there in 1489. (Cf. N. 123 and N. 480).

P. xiii   N. 18

When the schools were disrupted by the economic and religious upheavals accompanying the Reformation, new means of training the young became necessary. In 1528 the Strassburg government formed a committee of three members – *Stettmeister* Jacob Sturm,* *Altammeister* Nicolaus Kniebs and Jacob Meyer from the *Dreizehner* – to organize a system of public education. Separate schools for boys and girls were established, and in 1531 the school at St. Thomas was taken over by the city as a secondary school. This school was moved in 1532 to the abandoned Franciscan monastery, the income from which was allotted to the headmaster, and then moved to its permanent home in the buildings of the former Dominican monastery which dated from 1228. In 1538 this first Protestant Gymnasium, named the Johann Sturm Gymnasium for its first rector, was formally opened. The university founded 1566 completed the Strassburg educational system.

The learned Dr. Johann Sturm (1507-1589) was brought to Strassburg by Jacob Sturm to be headmaster or rector of the Gymnasium and held that post until his death. Johann Sturm was not a member of the Strassburg Sturm von Sturmeck family but belonged to an unrelated family of Sturms from Sleida in the Eifel area. Like Dringenberg,* Agricola* and Erasmus, he had been trained by the Brethren of the Common Life (cf. N. 88). He studied at Louvain and Leyden, then at the university of Paris, where he met Jacob Sturm. For his outstanding contribution to education he was knighted by Emperor Charles V.

After having been ravaged by fire in 1860, the Gymnasium buildings were rebuilt as they had been originally. The *Temple Neuf*, the old monastery church adjoining the Gymnasium, was destroyed in 1870 but subsequently restored. Today, as one walks along the narrow street between the Place Kléber and the Place Broglie, one may see youngsters crowding through the gates of the "Jean Sturm Gymnase Protestant."

Cf. *ADB* XXXVII, 21-38. Engel, *Schulwesen*, 39f.; (this work has a list of schoolmasters). Engel, *Les commencements...*, *passim*. Hasse, II, 163ff. Hertzog, viii, 144ff. Kindler von Knobloch, *Buch*, 365ff. Truttmann-Burg, 189ff.

19. As Archer Taylor... remarks...
The statement quoted from Taylor, *Problems*, 47f., is true. Taylor, however, goes on to say that Schott was Geiler's nephew and ward. Now the Schott and Geiler families were not related, and Schott, Sr., a wealthy man, outlived his son by 14 years. Evidently Taylor has confused Peter Schott with Peter Wickgram who was Geiler's nephew as well as successor in the cathedral chair at Strassburg and whose education, along with that of his brother Conrad, Geiler supervised. Taylor also states that the *Lucubraciunculae* is a collection of letters written by Schott from Italy to Geiler. This is not quite correct; of the 303 items in the *Lucubraciunculae* 20 are letters to Geiler and of these only 5 were written from Italy, the others were written in Strassburg or at the baths (cf. N. 106).

J. G. Müller's article on Geiler in Wetzer-Welte, V,191, has the rather ambiguous clause: "Peter Schott, der unter Geilers Obhut erwachsen..." which is correct only in the sense that Schott from his eighteenth year was greatly influenced by Geiler and that Schott, Sr., largely at Geiler's urging, allowed his son to study theology and enter the Church.

20. The first... edition of the Lucubraciunculae...
Cf. P. Butler, *Newberry Library Check List of Books printed during the Fifteenth Century* (Chicago, 1924), 5. *Catalogue of Books printed in the XVth Century now in the British Museum* (London, 1908), I, 96. J. G. T. Graesse, *Trésor*

P. xiii   N. 20

de livres rares... (Dresden, 1865), VI, Part 1, 315. L. Hain, *Repertorium bibliographicum* (Stuttgart, 1831), II, 296, no. 14524. M. Maittaire, *Annales typographici...* (Amsterdam, 1732), IV, Part 2, 666. G. W. Panzer, *Annales typographici* (Nürnberg, 1793), I, 342. R. Proctor, *An Index to the Early Printed Books in the British Museum* (London, 1898), no. 409. J. A. S. Riegger, *Amoenitates literariae friburgenses* (Freiburg i. B., 1779), 187f. C. Schmidt, *Histoire Littéraire de l'Alsace...* (Paris, 1879), II, *Index bibliographique*, 34.

21. Margaret Stillwell... lists seven copies... in the United States.
Incunabula in American Libraries (New York, 1940), 453: "Copies: CHSL, HEHL, IoSL, LC, LC (T), NewL, PhF(W)L." The third edition (1964), edited by F. R. Goff, notes (p. 552) copies also at Bryn Mawr and Yale.

P. xiv

22. Devise of Martin Schott
The devise at the end of the *Lucubraciunculae* (cf. p. 324, plate 4) differs from the devises in Martin Schott's* other printings which feature Martin's coat-of-arms, an unmistakable head of cabbage with curling leaves, and his initials M. S. (cf. the coat-of-arms copied by Schmidt from Luck's *Wappenbuch* in the Schmidt material, Appendix A). This head of cabbage appears with the initials I. S. in the devises of Martin's son Johann,* although Johann used also his grandfather Mentelin's coat-of-arms.

The devise in the *Lucubraciunculae* which looks like a flowering tree with roots exposed is identical with the design in the coat-of-arms of Schott, Sr., as it appears in Straub's 3 reproductions (Appendix L), *viz.*: in the description of the altar donated to Sts. Margaret and Agnes (cf. N. 84), in the copy of Schott's epitaph (cf. N. 57) and in the copy of the memorial plaque to Zeisolf von Adelsheim* and his wife Ottilia Schott.* The use of this coat-of-arms in the *Lucubraciunculae* may have been meant as a tribute to both Schott, Jr., and Schott, Sr.

Some secondary sources agree with Straub in their portrayals or descriptions of the coat-of-arms of Schott, Sr., others give it as a cabbage of varying appearance. It is possible that the latter sources are confusing the coats-of-arms of the several branches of the Schott family, each of which had its own coat-of-arms as has already been noted in the case of Martin Schott. Because the cabbage appears so frequently in these coats-of-arms, the question has been raised as to whether the original Schotts of Alsace or Strassburg were gardeners. Friese's surmise, however, that the Schotts who were gardeners in Strassburg in the sixteenth century were descendants of Schott, Sr., is incorrect, for the latter had only the one son Peter, Jr., who was unmarried.

Cf. *ADB*, XXXII, 405. Friese, II, 105. Hertz-Barach, 4 and *Tafel* II. Hertzog, vi, 203. Kindler von Knobloch, *Buch*, 331, no. 402. Pastorius, 186. Ristelhuber, 113f. Ritter, *Histoire*, 69. Schmidt, *H. L.*, II, 2, n. 2 and "Notices... P.S.," 241, n. 1; 242. Straub, 84, 85, 86.

23. On folios... are lacunae. These represent Greek quotations...
The folios mentioned are to be found on pp. 18, 72, 99, 118, 159, 190, 289, 296. The lacuna on p. 101 represents two words omitted in the quotation from Priscian (cf. N. 729).

24. Martin Schott had no Greek type.
Greek typography developed in Italy during the late fifteenth century and was not introduced north of the Alps until sometime after 1500. Prior to that time, printers in Strassburg and elsewhere in northern Europe coped with Greek quotations by leaving lacunae where they occurred, by rendering them in Latin or Gothic type, or by reproducing them rather unsatisfactorily with wooden blocks into which the Greek words had been cut. This process known as xylography (cf. N. 45) was tried at Mainz as early as 1468 and was first used at Strassburg by Johann Grüninger in his 1497 edition of Wimpheling's *Isidoneus germanicus* and in his 1498 edition of Brant's *Varia Carmina*. The first edition of Erasmus' *Collectanea* at Paris in 1500 has lacunae as does the 1506 edition of Schott's *Epithoma* by Hupfuff at Strassburg. In 1511 and 1512 Mathias Schürer at Strassburg was still rendering Greek words in Latin type.
    Cf. A. Appelt, *Studies in the Contents and Sources of Erasmus' Adagia* (diss. University of Chicago, 1942), 131. Bogeng, 453-462. Linckenheld, 169, 171, 174. R. Proctor, *The Printing of Greek in the Fifteenth Century* (Oxford, 1900), 138, 139f. D. B. Updike, *Printing Types, their History, Forms and Use* (Cambridge, 1922), I, 236, n. 1.

25. Martin Schott may have intended to have Greek written in... never entered...
Copies of the incunabulum seen at Paris, Strassburg, Vienna, the British Museum and the Vatican libraries have the original lacunae.

26. the word 'priora'... line three of Wimpheling's epitaph (cf. p. 10)
No other copy of the incunabulum seen has this word.

27. as Thomas Vulpinus says...
Cf. Vulpinus, 37.

28. These were collected... by Geiler von Kaysersberg and Jacob Wimpheling.
Because Wimpheling edited the incunabulum, he is generally given sole credit for collecting Schott's works. To show that Geiler not only shared in the task, but may indeed have instigated the project of publishing the works, we quote his letter of 28 January 1494 to Reuchlin:*

> Eximie doctor, si quas apud te Domini Petri Schotti tenes epistolas, eas mihi mitteri digneris. Colligere enim undecunque nitor, et multas iam collegi ac in unum volumen redigere statui imprimendum.
>   Aiunt enim illi qui earum rerum habent peritiam eas collectu fore dignas atque divulgatione. Ego plane non intelligo, ideo neque iudico, sed peritis aestimatoribus credo, praesertim si tuo quoque iudicio congruerint, quod non parum ponderis afferet.
>   Vale. Ex Argentina VI ante festum purificationis Beatae Mariae M.CCCC.LXXXXIIII. (From *Epistolae illustrium virorum ad Reuchlinum* [Tübingen, 1514], fol. e; text also in Geiger, *Briefwechsel*, 38, and Dacheux, *Réf.*, 424, n. 1).

29. work... finished sometime before 1498... to have been printed in Basel
For Wimpheling's statement, cf. his *Epitome rerum Germanorum*, cap. 57; also Schmidt, *H. L.*, II, 34.
    That the *Lucubraciunculae* was ready for publication in 1494 and had

P. xiv   N. 29

been offered to the printer Johann Amerbach in Basel is indicated by a passage in Leontarius'* letter of 19 November 1494 to Amerbach:

> Deinde cum sciam ad huc duo apud te imprimenda extare opera vnum praestantissimi doctoris Ioannis Reuchlin, scilicet Capnion vel de verbo mirifico, alterum epistolarum disertissimi quondam doctoris Petri Scotti Argentinensis, te etiam atque etiam rogatum esse cupio, ut si impressa sint, uel alterum illorum mihi per hunc servum meum transmittas, qui tibi pecuniam praeste adnumerabit. (From Hartmann, 42).

Another indication that the *Lucubraciunculae* was ready for publication in 1494 is to be found in Trithemius' two works the *Liber de scriptoribus ecclesiasticis* and the *Cathalogus illustrium virorum*, The *Liber* was published 1494, but the manuscript was already finished by 1492, as Trithemius observes in the introduction. The item on Schott in this work (f. CXXVIb) is identical, except for the date of Schott's death (cf. N. 161, N. 164), with Trithemius' item on Schott in the *Lucubraciunculae* (#5). The *Cathalogus* was published 1495; the item on Schott therein (f. LVb) differs somewhat from that in the *Liber* (cf. N. 161) and ends with the statement: "cuius [Schotti] vitam mores et ingenium iacobus vimphelingus descripsit." It appears then that the item for the *Lucubraciunculae* was excerpted from the *Liber* soon after the publication of the latter or perhaps even before, because it was customary to circulate one's manuscripts among friends for comment and criticism (cf. N. 309). Trithemius' statement quoted above from the *Cathalogus* may mean that Trithemius had seen Wimpheling's introduction to the *Lucubraciunculae* (#1) or possibly the manuscript of the *Lucubraciunculae* before writing the item in the *Cathalogus*.

30. Geiler and Wimpheling included writings of others... pertinent...
Cf. the works not by Schott in the Special Index of this volume. The short poems #298-#300 have no connection at all with Schott and were perhaps put in at the end of the collection as fillers.

31. It was not possible to assemble everything... as Wimpheling observes...
For Wimpheling's observation, cf. #301, p. 322. Bohuslaus von Hassenstein mentions orations composed by Schott in Italy, none of which is extant; cf. also Notes 2, 4 and 5.

P. xv

32. Correspondence... the only remnant is Reuchlin's invitation in verse...
Cf. #290, p. 311. Geiger, *Reuchlin*, 78, states that of Reuchlin's* poetic works – a number of poems and a book of epigrams – only this invitation seems to have survived.
   For Schott's statements about Reuchlin in a letter to Brant,* cf. #10, p. 18.

33. Geiler writes to Reuchlin...
For the full text of the letter, cf. N. 28.

34. The item with the earliest date is a letter to Johann Gesler...
The letter of 26 December 1477 to Gesler* (#235) is also the earliest extant

P. xv N. 34

Latin writing by Schott, while the German letter of 28 February 1476 to Anna Schott (pp. 357f.) is the earliest extant writing of any kind by Schott. The letter to Gesler was placed by the editor in the poetry section, because it accompanied copies of poems which Schott and Hassenstein had composed (#236-#239). Two other letters (#240 and #242) are likewise in the poetry section because Schott enclosed them with copies of the poem "De tribus Iohannibus" (#241) sent to Geiler and Gossenbrot.

35. The last dated item is a letter... to Johann Goez
To be exact, the letter to Johann Goez* (#157) is the last dated piece of Schott's correspondence. The item with the latest date is the document for a sale of onion seed grown in 1490 (#228), which was signed and sealed before the magistrate 5 November 1490. It was written by Schott at the time the contract was made, probably at seeding season, but was not legally processed until late fall when the seed was delivered.

36. For the most part, the items are chronologically arranged...
Items not in chronological order fall mainly into one of these categories:

1) Those which have dates giving only the year; cf. ##8, 11, 47, 125.
2) Those dated by movable feasts; cf. ##67, 98, 99, 101, 112, 131, 132, 135, 145-148.
3) Those with dates before the kalends of January; cf. N. 218.
4) Those forming units; cf. #36 and #37, N. 34, N. 278.
5) Those with typographical errors in dates; cf. N. 251 and N. 893.
6) Those without any date.

37. Wimpheling wrote... heading for each item...
There are no headings for the following items: ##49, 89, 106, 144, 183, 187, 200-207, 235, 264, 292, 293.

P. xvi

38. First letters of words... Initial letters in capitals
For difficulties in determining the meaning of abbreviations, cf. N. 342, N. 181, N. 681. Cf. also N. 1077, N. 1155.

P. xix

39. Interesting forms are... saguin- for sanguin-
According to Forcellini, III, 327, very often *n* preceding *s* and other consonants is omitted: *meses* for *menses*, *cosul* for *consul*, *quoties* for *quotiens*, *laterna* for *lanterna*, *ligula* for *lingula*.

40. a Greek accusative ending: Peana
This is just one example of the many Greek accusatives. There are also a number of Greek plurals.

41. the German phrase 'einer grieben'
Cf. N. 1549.

42. *De mensuris syllabarum epithoma... The first edition*
Cf. *Catalogue of Books... in the British Museum*, I, 166. Graesse, *Trésor*, VI, Part 1, 315. Hain *Repertorium*..., II, 296, no. 14525. Maittaire, *Annales*..., IV, Part ii, 728. Panzer, *Annales*..., I, 384. Proctor, *Index*..., 765. Stillwell, *Incunabula* ... (^{2}1940), 453; (^{3}1964), 552. For bibliographical data, cf. N. 20.

43. *third edition... was printed by Mathias Hupfuff at Strassburg*
This edition, copies of which we have seen at the *Bibliothèque nationale et universitaire de Strasbourg* and at the British Museum, is a *contrafaçon*, i.e., the text is identical line for line and page for page with the text of the first edition. Hupfuff, however, has left lacunae for Greek words and instead of Latin type has employed broad Gothic type which makes the letters seem crowded. One may assume that the second and fourth editions of the *Epithoma* are also *contrafaçons* since the practise of copying previous editions was common during the early days of printing; cf. the editions of Gerson's works (N. 136, par. 6).

Hupfuff inserted four poems in his edition. After the title are a distich by Johann Adelphus:

> Parva solet magnum torrens superare fluorem
> Coetera per breuibus sic preit et istud opus.

and a tetrastich by Gangolf Steinmetz*:

> Qui cupis Interpres vatum genialis haberi
> Atque supercilio condere digna gravi
> Proxima qui phoebo conari versibus optas
> Hijsce rudimentis perdidicisse potes.

After the colophon: "impressum per Mathiam Hupfuff Civem Argeñ. Anno salutis humane MCCCCC.VI," appear Petrarch's poem to Mary Magdalene at St. Baume (cf. biographical note on Geiler) and a poem of 100 lines "Ad diuam Mariam magdalenam Errantium specularum Udalrici Zasii historicon" by Ulrich Zasius.

44. *copy of the first edition... Free Library of Philadelphia... Widener...*
The quotation below is from a letter of 31 July 1962 by Ellen Shaffer, Rare Book Librarian of the Free Library of Philadelphia:

"The book is not in the Widener Branch and has not been for many years. The story back of it is that in 1899 P. A. B. Widener, the wealthiest Philadelphian of his day, gave his residence at Broad and Girard Avenue to the Free Library of Philadelphia (of which he was a Trustee) to be used as a branch library. With the gift he included Walter Arthur Copinger's personal collection of incunabula, 500 volumes in number, which his agent had just purchased in England. For many years the incunabula remained in the old Widener home which had become a branch of the Free Library. However, in 1949 when the Rare Book Department was opened in the Central Library at Logan Square, the Copinger-Widener collection was at that time brought into this Department and has remained with us ever since. The old Widener home was later sold by Free Library and is now used as an office by an engineering firm. The name has been retained, and the Free Library's Widener Branch is now located at 2531 W. Lehigh Avenue, but has no rare material as our rarities are now concentrated in this Department. Mr. Goff has promised that the forthcoming Stillwell census will make clear that the incunabula are no longer at the Widener Branch."

In his 1964 edition of Stillwell, Mr. Goff lists this copy of the *Epithoma*

P. xix   N. 44

as being in the Free Library of Philadelphia, Copinger-Widener Collection. He lists also a second copy in the United States at Yale.

P. xx

45. *Greek proper names... written in by hand... lacunae for Greek words.*
Since writing these comments, we have seen other copies of the first edition of the *Epithoma* and these copies have the identical Greek entries. The Greek was therefore not entered by hand but was printed by xylography, as Proctor (*Printing of Greek...*, 138) says, cf. N. 24.

46. *Indeed, the arrangement of the sub-headings... is... highly confusing.*
For examples of the confusion, cf. p. 347: *I ante C, Genitiuus in icis* and N. 1815 thereto, also p. 350: *O ante R, decor decoris* and N. 1820 thereto.

47. *When the Epithoma was written is not known...*
That the *Epithoma* was written for Bohuslaus von Hassenstein is certain. In poem #265 Schott remarks that he must needs obey Bohuslaus' commands and has therefore sent recently to Bohuslaus, who, deeply involved in composing verses, is desirous of knowledge in metrics, a notebook – meagre in scope but useful – on words, position and syllable quantity. This description very nicely fits the *Epithoma*.

It seems likely that Schott composed the *Epithoma* soon after his return in the early summer of 1481 to Strassburg, because Hassenstein, left in Italy and suddenly deprived of Schott's constant companionship and advice to which he had in six years of association grown accustomed, would have felt very keenly the need of a guide like the *Epithoma*. The date of composition would probably be during the period: summer 1481 and April 1482, before Schott became canon at New St. Peter (N. 116). We may be sure that the *Epithoma* was composed while Hassenstein was still in Italy (i.e., before the end of 1482); the rumor Schott mentions in his poem (#265) about Hassenstein's having produced new poems which he (Schott) has not seen could very easily travel from Ferrara to Strassburg but could only with great difficulty travel from Bohemia to Alsace; Hassenstein himself complains (#106; cf. N. 813) that few persons go from Bohemia to Alsace.

48. *Schott... asked Agricola about spellings and derivations...*
Cf. #65, pp. 71f.; N. 568.

49. *his two letters of 1486... Wimpheling had composed a work on prosody...*
In #90 and #91 Schott answers the questions asked by Wimpheling in #89.

Wimpheling's pamphlet of 12 leaves *De arte metrificandi libellus* was published at Strassburg in 1505 by Mathias Hupfuff and is said to have been printed in 1496 without Wimpheling's consent. Some authorities claim it was composed by 1484; Knod places the probable date of its composition in the late 1470's (Cf. Schmidt, *H. L.*, II, 324; Knod, "Bibliographie," 473).

Reuchlin* wrote a work on prosody which was published along with two similar works by other writers 1501 in Strassburg under the title *Vocabularius breuiloquens cum arte*.

P. xx   N. 50

50. Epithoma... the work of an amateur
As indicated in N. 47, the *Epithoma* in the form we have it was not meant to be a finished work for publication.

P. xxi

51. German letter to Anna Schott... the only example of his German writings
The letter to Anna is the only extant example of Schott's original writings in German; for his German translations, cf. N. 2. and Appendices E and F.

52. He... wrote German letters... as is indicated by... a note of 1486...
Cf. #77.

53. The letter to Anna... Weislinger claims to have copied 'von Wort zu Wort'
Schmidt says Weislinger's copy is inaccurate, cf. N. 3.

P. xxii

54. One may question the dialect term 'fierd'...
Schmidt's copy has "freid," cf. Appendix A.

55. Whether the original manuscript had commas... is not known...
Schmidt's copy has commas, colons, semicolons but no virgules, cf. Appendix A.

56. Much source material... and many secondary sources... have perished...
Following are some reasons for the loss of primary and secondary source material. The wonderful cathedral library, a treasury from the eighth century of rare manuscripts and a storehouse of early printed books, was sold after the Reformation by the Protestant canons to many different buyers during the period 1584-1597. Remnants are now in the Bern public library and in the Vatican. The well-stocked libraries of Old St. Peter and New St. Peter vanished without a trace, as did excellent private libraries like Geiler's which had been willed to his successors in the chair of cathedral preacher.
Conquering armies carried off materials as booty and not all of these materials had the happy fate of the "Wimpheling Codex" which was carefully preserved by the Swedes at Uppsala (cf. Appendix D). A serious fire ravaged the archives in 1686. The city hall "Pfalz" and the city chancery were pillaged in 1789 at the time of the French Revolution. The city library with its priceless collection of manuscripts and incunabula was completely destroyed in the conflagration started by bombs in 1870 during the Franco-Prussian war. In number of losses this was the worst disaster of all.
Cf. Grandidier, *Essais*, 361-363. Rathgeber, *Schätze*, 177. Schmidt, *Bibliotheken*, 14. Schneegans, "Pfingstfest," 238.
A sad comment appears in the introduction to volume I of Dacheux, *Fragments*. In 1868 a committee under the auspices of *la société pour la conservation des monuments historiques d'Alsace* prepared to publish all the manuscript chronicles of Alsace but was unable to raise the necessary funds. Two years later the manuscripts disappeared forever, except for parts of the *Chronik von Königshoven* which were being printed in Leipzig at the time.

In World War II the *Bibliothèque nationale et universitaire de Strasbourg* was gutted by flame bombs and considerable losses of material were suffered, but the real treasures were safely hidden away.

From the latter part of the nineteenth century on Alsatian scholars have been diligently publishing older material of all kinds and since 1870 have even restored as much as possible of the old chronicles by painstakingly piecing them together from references and quotations in other works. So great is this commendable zeal for preservation of the past that not only may a work appear as single editions in both French and German or as part of a collection, but an excerpt from the work may appear as a book or an article under a different title. Because Alsace during the period 1871-1945 has come alternately under German and French rule, the names of writers and editors often vary from the German to the French form, e.g., Jean Jacques (Johann Jacob) Meyer, Charles (Karl) Schmidt, Louis (Ludwig) Schneegans, Lucien (Luzian) Pfleger. The result is that the bewildered investigator finds himself constantly confronted with the same material in different guise.

57. Copies of Schott's epitaph
The original epitaph in the Zorn chapel of New St. Peter (N. 117) disappeared in 1791 during the Reign of Terror when the church was being used by the army as a magazine. Texts of the epitaph published since are taken from copies made before 1791, *viz.*: the copies of Reichard, Weislinger, Grandidier and Friese (cf. below).

Schmidt (*H. L.*, II, 33, n. 95) has the text of the epitaph but gives no source. Except for omission of periods and the spelling of three words (*huius, linguae, Susannaeque*), the text agrees with Weislinger's text which is discussed by Schmidt in n. 94, beginning on page 32. Following the text Schmidt makes the statement: "Cette inscription existe encore dans l'église catholique de S. Pierre-le-jeune". That is, Schmidt says that, at the time he was writing (*ca.* 1878/79), the epitaph was still in New St. Peter. Perhaps the negative *n'* was omitted before *existe*. In any case, Schmidt's statement must be discounted (N. 7), for Horning, the historian of New St. Peter, not only says that the epitaph was lost after the French Revolution but tells of the new epitaph placed in the Zorn chapel at the time of restoration in 1891 (N. 143); this epitaph we have seen.

There is no way of ascertaining whether the four above-mentioned copies of Schott's original epitaph were transcribed from the original or taken from transcriptions. One could expect Reichard, the genealogist of old Strassburg families, to have made a fairly exact transcription from the original, but unfortunately we have his text only in Straub's copy which was made from the genealogical manuscripts of Reichard before their destruction in the fire of 1870. Grandidier may have transcribed his text directly from the original. Weislinger and Friese infer that they did so, but they disagree on the location of the original; Weislinger says he visited Schott's tomb in New St. Peter 21 March 1749 and saw the epitaph set into the wall above the tomb, while Friese describes the epitaph as hanging on a pillar ("an einem Pfeiler aufgehängt"), a description supported by Horning's statement (*Festschrift*, 35) that the broad indentation on the pillar at the right of the street entrance to the Zorn chapel marks the place of Schott's epitaph.

Reichard's copy (made in the early sixteenth century; copy in Straub, 85; cf. Appendix L):

PETRO. SCHOTTO. ARGEN. DIVI IVNIORIS
PETRI AEDIS CANONICO PRESBYTERO

P. xxii   N. 57

INNOCENTISSIMO IVRISCONSVLTO ET
ORATORI POETAEQVE. DOCTO. PETRI SCHOT
TI SENATORIS SVSSANNAEQVE FILIO PIEN
TISSIMO. AMICI MESTI POSVERE.
MOR. ANNO. C̄HRI M.CCCC.LXXXX.
II ỸD. SEP̃TEB
(Schott and Cöllen coats-of-arms)

Weislinger's copy (*Armamentarium*, 780; published 1749):
PETRO SCHOTTO. ARGEN. HUJUS. DIVI. PETRI. AEDIS.
CANONICO. PRESBYTERO. INNOCENTISSIMO. JURIS.
CONSULTO. ET. ORATORI. POETAEQUE. CLARISSIMO.
AC. GRAECAE. LINGUE. DOCTO. PETRI. SCHOTTI. SENATO-
RIS. SUSANNEQUE. FILIO. PIENTISSIMO. AMICI
MESTI. POSUERE. VIX. ANN. XXXII. M. II. D. III. MORT.
ANNO. CHRI. M.CCCC.LXXXX. II. YD (Die 13.) SEPTEMB.

Note Weislinger's interpolation in the last line. He read the year as M.CCCC.LXXXXII and the day as the Ides (13) September instead of two days before the Ides (12) September, as is evident from his words: "Hieraus sehen wir, dass der junge Herr Schott gestorben seye, den Herbst Monat Anno 1492, seines Alters 32 Jahr. 2. Monath und 3 Tag. Folglich ist sein Geburths Tag gewesen 10. Julii 1460."

Grandidier's copy (*Mélanges*, 352 and *Nouv. oeuvr.*, II, 490; Grandidier published works during the 1780's, but the two mentioned remained in manuscript until 1897-1900):

Petro Schotto Argentinensi, hujus divi junioris Petri aedis canonico, presbytero innocentissimo, jurisconsulto et oratori, poetaeque clarissimo ac graecae linguae docto, Petri Schotti Senatoris Susannaeque filio pientissimo, amici mesti posuere. Vixit annos XXXIII, mens. II, die. III, mortuus an. Christi M.CCCC.LXXXX. secundo ydus Septembris.

Friese's copy (II, 105; published 1791):

Petro Schotto Argent. hujus Divi. Petri
Aedis Canonico Presbytero innocentissimo juris
Consulto et Oratori poeteque Clarissimo ac
Graece Lingue Docto. Petri Schotti Senatoris,
Susanneque Filio pientissimo amici mesti
posuere. Vix. Ann. XXXII. M. II. D. III.
Mort. MCCCCXC. II Sept.

Friese omitted *Yd*. before *Sept*. in the last line, but corrected his error in a footnote on the same page as the epitaph.

Comparison of the four copies yields the following data:

1) Reichard's copy lacks words and phrases present in the other three; it does not give the number of years, months and days Schott lived as do the others.

2) Weislinger and Friese give Schott's age as 32 years, 2 months and 3 days; Grandidier gives it as 33 years, 2 months and 3 days.

3) Weislinger, Grandidier and Friese agree on the number of months and days Schott lived after his last birthday, viz. 2 months and 3 days.

4) Discounting Weislinger's interpolation and misinterpretation, all versions agree on the year of Schott's death as 1490 and on the day of his death as 2 days before the Ides of September.

379

P. xxii N. 57

Counting the days at each end in the Roman fashion, we can calculate Schott's day of death as 12 September and his day of birth as 10 July. Note that Weislinger, by not counting the day at each end, arrived at the same date for Schott's birth.

The positive evidence obtained from the copies of Schott's epitaph is that his birthday was 10 July and that he died 12 September 1490.

58. These errors and discrepancies have... become cumulative.
The above statement is best exemplified by the disagreement of secondary sources on Schott's age, the year of his birth, the year of his death and the cause of his death. Most disagreement stems from the four sources mentioned below, which were either incorrect or were misinterpreted.

1) The copies of Schott's epitaph, as already noted in N. 57, do not agree on his age.

2) The biographical items on Schott in Trithemius, *Liber* (f. CXXVIb), *Cathalogus* (f. LVb) and subsequent editions of the two works give the date of Schott's death as 1491. This date was corrected to 1490 in Trithemius' item for the *Lucubraciunculae* (cf. N. 160).

3) The phrase "annos nondum tres et triginta natus" is used by Wimpheling in the conclusion to the *Lucubraciunculae* (#301, p. 322) when speaking of Schott's youth. Wimpheling is stressing the fact that Schott had not yet reached the traditionally accepted age of maturity, i.e., 33, a third of a century, or – according to some authorities – the age of Christ (cf. *DW*, VI, 2038; *Cath. Ency.*, III, 738). In other words, "not yet three and thirty years old" was a stock phrase and was not necessarily meant to be taken literally.

4) Specklin gives the date of Schott's death as 1491 and his age as "not over 30 years," and in a melodramatic account which would do credit to a modern detective novel claims Schott died of poison in a drink handed him by the provost's cook:

> Anno 1491 war ein gelehrter thumbherr, als man nit finden möchte, zum Jungen S. Peter, nit über 30 iahr alt, Peter Schott genant. Der hub an auss gottes wort alle laster zu straffen, verwarff den gekaufften ablass, so ohne reu und besserung des lebens kaufft wurde, verwarff auch des pabsts ansehen, der sich über Christum wolle setzen, die ehre gehoere Christum zu, der uns mit seinem leiden und sterben ablass erworben hatte, wer solches mit warem glauben annehme. Als er aber etliche geistliche missbrauch, darneben der geistlichen gottlos leben auch angriffe, wardt er in drey stunden todt, dan ihme mit gifft vergeben wurde, als er einsmals mit dem probst asse, dessen koechin ihm solches in einem trunck soll zugereicht haben. ("Collectanea," 287)

Dacheux (*Réf.*, 421, n. 3) terms this account "une calomnie posthume" and Schmidt (*H. L.*, II, 33, n. 94) calls it "un récit de fantaisie." Certainly there is no evidence that Schott opposed the sale of indulgences; on the contrary, he once asked that a sale of indulgences be announced (#207; cf. also N. 2206). Neither is there evidence that he felt the pope considered himself above Christ. Schott did, however, condemn the practice of clerics' holding multiple benefices (cf. p. xxx and N. 133, par. 3) and gave his opinion (#217) on such clerical practices as the use of funds received from the Church to support concubines.

In assessing the reliability of Specklin's account, it must be kept in mind that Specklin was a militant Lutheran of the sixteenth century and used the lives and works of pre-Reformation men of integrity like Geiler and Schott to bolster arguments for his own religious persuasion. This was customary among post-Reformation writers, both Lutheran and Catholic (e.g., Flacius Illyricus and Weislinger); the Lutherans saw in Geiler and Schott forerunners of the Reformation, the Catholics saw in them proof that there were enlightened, responsible members of the clergy before the Reformation.

In later secondary sources Schott's age varies from 31-34, the year of his birth from 1457 to 1460, the year of death from 1482-1499 (extremes like 1499 may, of course, be typographical errors). The majority of writers followed Trithemius' sketches on Schott in the *Liber* and *Cathalogus*; some obtained their data from one or other of the epitaph copies, several even repeating Weislinger's error; others took Wimpheling's comment literally; a few accepted Specklin's story, notably Stöber (*Neue Alsatia*, 281), Horning (*Festschrift*, 36, and other works) and Ristelhuber (115) who suggests the cook may be a personification of the plague. Most writers in the past 80 years have quoted Schmidt (*H. L.*, II, 4, and "Notices... P.S.," 241f.) who gives Schott's dates as 1458-1490. It is noteworthy that Dacheux (*Réf.*, 286ff.) who did considerable research on Schott, arrives at the correct conclusion that Schott was born 10 July 1460 and died of the plague 12 September 1490.

Curious inconsistencies appear in data given by the same writer; e.g.: Adam (24) has Schott's dates as 1459-1491/92 and his age as 31; Cave (*Appendix*, 1693) has the dates as ca. 1459-1491, the age as 31. Schmidt, as noted above, gives the dates as 1458-1490, but in his "Notices... P.S." (339) he remarks that Reuchlin was 2 years older than Schott, although the accepted dates for Reuchlin are 1454/55-1522, and in *H. L.* (I, 19) he sets the time of composition of Wimpheling's poem to the Virgin in 1492, yet lists Schott as one of those who composed verses lauding this poem (cf. #279 and N. 1701 and N. 1702).

59. almost the only reliable source on Peter Schott... the Lucubraciunculae
Data about which later secondary sources disagree, *viz.*: when Schott obtained his baccalaureate degree at Paris, when he returned from Italy after receiving his doctorate, why he was prevented from going to Paris for further study in 1484, etc., can be established by comparing evidence in the *Lucubraciunculae* with information from university records and a few other reliable sources (cf. N. 92, N. 95, N. 121).

By such comparison – along with the positive information from the copies of the epitaph – can also be determined Schott's age, the date of his birth, the date of his death and the cause of his death. (Cf. N. 57 and N. 58 for disagreement on these vital statistics).

1) The date of birth. Trithemius' item in the *Lucubraciunculae* (#5) gives the date of Schott's death as 1490; this date was corrected from 1491 to 1490 when the item was excerpted from the *Liber* (cf. N. 161) and is the date given by all copies of the epitaph (N. 57). Trithemius' item (#5) also has the information that Schott died in his thirty-first year, i.e., after his thirtieth birthday. Three copies of the epitaph agree that his birthday was 10 July. Accordingly, the date of his birth was 10 July 1460. There is no evidence for a date of birth earlier than 1460; rather there is evidence to support this date.

In the letter to his father, written shortly before 1 April 1478, which sets forth arguments for remaining longer in Italy, Schott speaks of himself at one point as needing time to mature in years, body and knowledge, and at another point as being too young and too slight for his years to attempt completing the doctorate in both laws (#8, p. 13f.). These arguments sound reasonable coming from a lad who would not mark his eighteenth birthday until the following July. Six months later, on 15 September, he writes in much the same vein to Rot: the extension of time for study granted by his parents is, he says, greatly to his advantage because of his age and the voluminous amount of material to be assimilated for the degree in both laws (#9, p. 17). Again these statements sound reasonable from one who had passed his eighteenth birthday just 2 months previously.

The close friendship between Schott and Hassenstein began in the first days of their association at Bologna, when they were both in their early teens. Usually boys at this stage of adolescence have their best friends in their own age group, and there is no indication that these two boys were different from others. When Schott crossed the Alps into Italy and matriculated at Bologna in early 1474 (N. 95), he was in his fourteenth year; as Dacheux says (*Réf.*, 287, n. 2): "Schott aurait eu treize ans passés en partant pour l'Italie en 1473-74." Hassenstein's date of birth is given as 1460/1462, but the most likely year for his birth is 1461, for in a poem written shortly after he returned from his odyssey in August 1491 he tells us that he has passed his thirtieth birthday: "transcendi aetatis bis tria lustra meae" (Potuček, xi). That he was the younger of the two friends is clear from his words "Is [Schott] me Bononiae adolescentulum adolescens unice diligebat et observabat" (*ibid.*, 55). If, like Schott, he arrived at Bologna during the first half of the year 1474 (even though the first entry for him in the *Acta Bonon.* is 1475), he was in his thirteenth year when he met Schott.

2) Date of death. From evidence in the *Lucubraciunculae* Schott died shortly after 6 September, the date on which his last dated letters were written (#156, #157). The only item by Schott with a later date is the legal document (#228) which, as already noted (N. 35), was prepared by Schott but not legally processed until 5 November 1490. None of the undated letters, poems, or other items has references warranting a date later than 6 September 1490. The copies of the epitaph agree that he died on 12 September 1490. Cf. also N. 1123.

3) Cause of death. There can be no doubt that Schott died of the plague. His first reference to the 1490 outbreak of plague in Strassburg occurs in the letter of 30 August to Johann Müller; he writes that he has not yet decided to leave Strassburg, for it seems safer to stay at home, and that he is taking remedies daily (#152, p. 166). On 3 September he writes again to Müller that he is not going to the baths although he had hoped to persuade his parents that he should go "praesertim hoc Autumni tempore" (#155, p. 171). In the last letter to Müller 6 September he observes that one reason for his difficulty in getting guarantors for Müller is the absence of friends because of the plague: "alij mei... ob pestem absentes: id agere non potuerunt"; and speaking of himself he says he was bathed in perspiration the previous night, has been bled and feels better that day (#156, pp. 171f.).

That there was a severe epidemic of plague in Strassburg during the latter part of the year 1490 is confirmed by sources other than Schott's writings. According to Jodocus Gallus'* elegiac (#295) Schott died when savage plague was raging in the city: "dum pestis atrox ferit Vrbem." In mid-August the city council, which had the right to arrange religious observances, ordered small processions in all churches to ward off the plague ("fur den Sterbott"), and on 20 October the council ordered a great procession with *Ammeister* and council participating (cf. Pfleger, "Gottesdienste," 37; Stenzel, "Gerichte," 234). It might also be mentioned here that farther north in Heidelberg the university closed its doors on 25 June because of the plague and did not reopen until 2 February 1491 (cf. Toepke, xli; 397, n. 1).

Jacob Wencker (1668-1743), archivist of Strassburg, who made extracts from various Strassburg archives (since lost), has in his *Archivi* (428

P. xxii N. 59

and 632) two passages on Schott. The first reads: "Petrus Schottus filius obierat peste infra VIII Nativitat. Marie quae fuit 12 Septembris anno 1490. In cujus locum in canonicum Sti Petri Junioris assumptus est Comes Henricus de Werdenberg"; that is, Schott died of the plague 12 September 1490 and was succeeded as canon of New St. Peter by *Graf* Heinrich von Werdenberg (cf. N. 130, last paragraph). The second reads: "[Schott] mortuus Argentinae et in Ecclesia S. Petri sepultus, sub Friderico Imper. III et Innocentio Papa VIII anno Domini 1490 Indictione nona aetatis suae 31." That this passage is almost identical with that at the end of Trithemius' item (#5) may be coincidence in use of formulae, or it may indicate that Wencker quoted from the item; in either case, the archivist's stamp is given to the date of Schott's death as 1490 and his age as the thirty-first year.

Taking into account all the above evidence, the conclusion must be that Schott was born 10 July 1460 and died of the plague in his thirty-first year on 12 September 1490, a conclusion in which Dacheux concurrs.

P. xxiii

60. Details of his boyhood and other data... Hassenstein's oration
Biographical material for the period before 1477 is found in #9, where Schott reminisces about student years at Paris, in #178, where he speaks briefly about his study at Paris and his early years at Bologna, and in the poem #287, p. 310.

For Trithemius' item, cf. #5; for Wimpheling's introduction, cf. #1; for Hassenstein's oration, cf. #297 and N. 1751.

61. Trithemius gives the date of death... does not mention the day and month
Cf. N. 59.

62. scholars have erred in... funeral oration
E.g., *ADB*, XIX, 49: "Gedächtnissrede"; Ristelhuber, 114f.: "son éloge funèbre"; Schmidt, *H. L.*, II, 33: "un éloge funèbre."

63. Bohuslaus speaks of Schott as being alive...
#297, p. 321: "hunc quem praesentem intuemini: cuius mentem sensusque et os cernitis..." (cf. N. 101, par. 3).

Ryba (iv) suggests that the oration was merely an exercise written at the time Schott received his doctorate and that it was never delivered; he does not say on what evidence he bases this assumption.

64. Trithemius' details... accepted as true... knew the facts.
Cf. N. 161.

65. The Schotts... were an old and important patrician family
The fact that the Schotts of Strassburg were patricians, not nobles, was a deciding factor for the career of Peter Schott, Sr., because as a patrician he was eligible for membership in the guilds and hence also eligible to hold the office of mayor (cf. N. 69; Schott family in Biographical Section; Appendix L of this volume).

P. xxiii   N. 66

66. *A manuscript on genealogy... Claus...*
The reference is to the lost Hertz manuscript, excerpts of which are in Straub (81, note). Another Claus Schott served on the city council in 1500 (Straub, 83); he may be Schott's cousin "Vetterclaus" mentioned in #20, p. 29.

67. *Last record of the family... 1554*
From 1179 to 1554 the Schott family is documented regularly in Strassburg records. After Sebastian Schott who appears in an entry of Straub (84): "1554 Sebastian S. Dreier auf dem Pfennigturm" (cf. Appendix L), there are only two Schotts mentioned: an Augustin Schott, "Gärtner" (Kindler von Knobloch, *Buch*, ii, 331), who in 1587 lived in the *Schottengasse unter Wagnern*, now called *Impasse des Jardiniers*, and an Odele Schott, prioress of Sts. Margaret and Agnes, whose tripart painting of the Crucifixion in the convent church had the Schott coat-of-arms and the inscription:

> Othila Schottin Priorin
> Zu S. Margaretha und S. Agnesen
> in Strassburg Anno 1611.   (Straub, 87).

She is probably identical with the Odele of another Straub entry (80) who is noted as having entered the same convent as Anna Schott and whose name appeared on a tablet incorporated into a frieze in 1661 at St. Etienne.

68. *Bernard Hertzog... lists the Schotts... extinct before his time.*
Hertzog (1537 – after 1592) was writing in the latter part of the sixteenth century.

69. *Not only was he on the city council...*
As mentioned in N. 16, Strassburg had set up a democratic form of government in the mid-fourteenth century. Because the internal organization of the several bodies changed from time to time, descriptions of the government vary. The government at the time of Peter Schott, as described by Dacheux (*Réf.*, Appendix, X), operated, in brief, as follows:

The chief magistrate or mayor, called *Ammeister* or *magister scabinorum*, was elected for a term of one year by the 20 guilds from their membership, which admitted artisans, burghers and patricians, but no nobles; hence no noble could hold the office of mayor. As secondary presiding officers with the mayor were four *Stettmeister* who were elected annually by the nobles for a term of 3 months each.

The highest governing body was the city council or grand council, *grosser Rat*, presided over by the mayor and composed of 31 members: 20 plebes, *Schöffen*, elected by the guilds (10 being changed annually) and 10 nobles (including the *Stettmeister*) elected by the nobles.

The second highest governing body, the so-called permanent magistracy, consisted of three chambers, the members of which served for life: a) the chamber of the XIII or *Dreizehner*, presided over by the mayor and composed of 4 nobles, 4 former mayors (*Altammeister*) and 4 plebes. This chamber had charge of foreign affairs and the army. b) The chamber of the XV or *Fünfzehner*, presided over by a member chosen from the floor and composed of 5 nobles and 10 plebes. This chamber administered internal affairs, the constitution and finances. c) The chamber of the XXI or *Einundzwanziger*, composed of men distinguished for ability and service who had been twice elected to the city council and were members of the XIII and XV. This chamber served in an advisory capacity.

The body of 300 magistrates, *Schöffen* or *scabini*, presided over by the mayor and composed of 15 members from each of the 20 guilds, convened at the call of the city council and was seldom assembled.

The small council, *kleiner Rat*, presided over by the *Altammeister* who had just served and composed of 6 nobles and 11 plebes, controlled affairs concerning wills, succession, possession, servitude, etc.

Cf. the description of the Strassburg government in the fifteenth century by Borries (70-74), which differs in details from that of Dacheux. Cf. also Bernegger, *passim*. Pastorius, *passim*. Piton, I, 157. Spach, *Zunftwesen*, 1ff.

70. *1470 to 1490 he served four terms as mayor...*
Schott, Sr., was elected mayor 1470, 1476, 1482, 1488. When the official year of the Strassburg government began and terminated we do not know; it seems not to have corresponded to the calendar year. Did it correspond to the indiction year (cf. N. 164)?

71. *In 1483... he had the... Schwörbrief... rewritten.*
Sources do not agree on the years for the various versions of the *Schwörbrief* to Schott, Sr.'s, time: Hertzog gives 1382, 1416, 1482; Specklin gives 1332, 1371; the Straub entry on the revision made during Schott, Sr'.s, term as mayor gives the year 1483, but this revision as quoted by Weislinger ends with the words: "und wir Peter Schott der Ammeister... geben auf den heiligen Weihnacht abend Anno 1482."

Cf. Hertzog, viii, 59-61, 70-72, 82-86. Specklin, 9, 85f. Straub, 81, Weislinger, 334.

72. *Strassburg... an influential member of the confederation of Rhine cities*
The beginning of the confederation (*Basse Ligue, niedere Vereinigung*) was the *League Decapolis* formed 1353 by 10 free imperial cities of Alsace: Mülhausen, Colmar, Münster, Türckheim, Kaysersberg, Schlettstadt, Obernai (Oberehnheim), Rossheim, Hagenau, Weissenburg. In succeeding centuries the number of members varied as original members quit and others of the free imperial cities of Alsace (Strassburg, Landau, Seltz, Hagenbach) joined the union; but the confederation existed until the French Revolution.

The city of Basel and the Swiss cantons were close allies of the confederation. It was to demonstrate how quickly Zürich could bring aid to Strassburg that a party of stout-hearted boatmen left Zürich with a pot of hot porridge before sunrise on 21 June in the critical year of 1476 and at sunset bore the pot of porridge – still warm – triumphantly ashore at Strassburg. The hundredth anniversary of this amazing feat (Zürich is a day's drive from Strassburg by auto) was commemorated by Fischart in his poem *Das glückhaft Schiff von Zürich* (1576).

In 1474 the confederation along with its close allies (the Swiss cantons and the city of Basel) formed a 10-year league with other states of the upper Rhine against Charles the Bold* (cf. N. 74). Among the members of this league were Bishop Ruprecht of Strassburg, Bishop Johannes of Basel, Archduke Sigismund of Tyrol* (because of his holdings in upper Alsace), Duke Reinhardt of Lorraine and sundry landed nobles of Alsace; for some years Emperor Friedrich III and Louis XI of France also joined the league. This is the league referred to as *foederati* and *confoederati* in the *Lucubraciunculae*.

P. xxiii   N. 72

Cf. #26, p. 35; #28, p. 36; #34, p. 41; #55, p. 60; #149, p. 163; #170, pp. 190f. (gives names of confederates). *Cambridge Medieval History*, VIII, 210ff. Hertzog, ii, 121. Schöpflin, *Histoire*, 14-22. Stenzel, "Politik," 53. Cf. also N. 74.

73. Schott, Sr.,... had to go on diplomatic missions... son lamented... absence
For these diplomatic missions, cf. biographical note on Schott, Sr. The son mentions the father's absence #25, p. 33; #26, p. 35; #28, p. 36; #149, p. 163; #169, p. 189; #170, p. 190.

74. Conflicts with Charles the Bold
When Charles the Bold* in 1467 succeeded his father Philip the Good as duke of Burgundy, the most powerful duchy in Europe, he set out to realize his three predecessors' dream of recreating old Lotharingia, the middle kingdom of 843, by annexing the territories lying between his southern possessions (Burgundy and Franche Comté) and his northern possessions (among which were Luxemburg, Brabant, Flanders and Holland). For ten years he overran his neighbors and terrorized the upper Rhine. Emperor Friedrich was too weak to check him. Even the mighty Louis XI, assiduously consolidating and expanding his kingdom, saw in his relative Duke Charles not only a formidable rival for territory but, through Charles' alliance with the English, a grave threat to France itself.

Charles' first opportunity of gaining a foothold on the left bank of the upper Rhine came in May 1469 when Archduke Sigismund of Tyrol,* of the "ever-empty purse," who needed money for his war with the Swiss, mortgaged his lands of the Sundgau, the Breisgau and Pfirt in upper Alsace to Charles for 80,000 gold guilders. Believing that the mortgage would never be paid because of traditional Austrian penury, Charles sent Peter von Hagenbach as governor (bailiff, *Landvogt*) into these lands. By exorbitant taxation and outrageous conduct Hagenbach soon antagonized the people to the point of revolt, and when protests to Charles fell on deaf ears, riots broke out.

In July 1473, at the death of Duke Nicholas of Lorraine, Charles began maneuvers to dispossess the rightful heir Reinhardt and to claim the duchy of Lorraine for himself, thus gaining another part of old Lotharingia.

With a view to stopping Duke Charles' encroachments on the empire by making him a powerful ally, Emperor Friedrich met him 20 September 1473 at Trier. Marriage between Friedrich's son Maximilian and Charles' daughter Mary, the most sought after heiress in Europe, was discussed. Charles, eager for a royal title, was to be created King in Burgundy, as well as King of the Romans, and to be guaranteed the succession as Holy Roman emperor. Agreement on details, however, proved impossible, and Friedrich, frightened by Charles' arrogance and power, fled by night across the Rhine.

In the same year (1473) Charles caused consternation in Alsace by marching south into the mortgaged lands. Archduke Sigismund, dismayed at Charles' growing might, repented his bargain and redeemed his lands with money which was loaned by Basel and Strassburg and for which Louis XI stood surety.

In the spring of 1474 Hagenbach, who had been imprisoned by the infuriated people of the Breisgau, was tried before an assembly (*Malesitz*) of delegates from the Rhine league (cf. N. 72) and Breisach; he was condemned to death and beheaded. The people's joy at their deliverance merged with Easter celebrations and expressed itself in the chant sung even by children:

P. xxiii   N. 74

Christ is risen, the governor has been captured,
Let us rejoice!
Sigismund will console us, Kyrie Eleison!

Hagenbach lived on in folksong and legend as the prototype of the wicked governor and became the model for Gessler in Schiller's *Wilhelm Tell*. His execution was commemorated by Wimpheling in a poem of 1474.

Charles the Bold responded to the execution of Hagenbach by opening hostilities. For three years the league fought Charles on battlefields in Alsace and Lorraine until in 1477 at Nancy, on 5 January (a day long celebrated in Alsace) the golden age of Burgundy came to an abrupt end with the slaying of Charles and the decisive victory of the league. Duke Reinhardt became master of his lands, although he had to borrow 44,000 florins from Strassburg to pay for Swiss aid, a debt not paid until 1622; Louis XI received Piccardy and the duchy of Burgundy; Maximilian and Mary of Burgundy were wed; and Alsace, as so often throughout its history, began repairing its war damages. Strassburg which had had 500 foot soldiers and 300 cavalry at Nancy suffered considerable loss in lives and property; yet despite the 156,000 florins spent outright on the war and the money lent to Dukes Reinhardt and Sigismund, there had been no special levy, a fact which gives some indication of the prosperity of the city and the healthy state of the public treasury.

Cf. Calmette, 185, 189, 258f. Dacheux, *Fragments*, III, part iv, "La chronique strasbourgeoise de Jacques Trausch," 12-25 (best chronicle account of the Burgundian wars). Dacheux, *op. cit.*, II, 462f. Friese, 90f. Hertzog, ii, 120-126, viii, 140. Anon., "Peter von Hagenbach, das historische Urbild von Landvogt Gessler in Schillers Wilhelm Tell," *Elsässische Monatsschrift für Geschichte und Volkskunde*, I (1910), 632. Rapp, 37, 40. Reuss, *Meyer*, 98ff. Tritheminus, *Ann. Hirs.*, 481-496 *passim*.

75. Schott, Sr., was one of the two commanders...
Cf. note on Schott, Sr., in Biographical Section.

76. the committee called 'fabrica' which managed finances... of the cathedral.
The term *fabrica*, fabric – literally, building and, in ecclesiastical usage, the church building – came to mean not only the administrative building of the church but also the body which cared for the church buildings.

In the late Middle Ages the *fabrica* of the Strassburg cathedral was one of the richest in France and Germany. The city council named the collector of revenue of the *fabrica* and appointed the three directors from the permanent magistracy; that is to say, the laity, not the clergy, controlled the revenues and administration – a situation unusual at that time. Originally control had been in the hands of the bishop, but at the death of Bishop Walter von Geroldseck in 1263 it had passed to the canons of the cathedral chapter, because disputes between bishops and the city had impeded construction of the cathedral. In 1290 the canons had requested the city council to assume the responsibility. (Cf. Grandidier, *Essais*, 38-44 *passim*; 409-413).

The Gothic building of the *fabrica* (*Frauenhaus, Maison de Notre Dame*), parts of which date from the thirteenth century, was completed 1347. It stands beside the bishop's palace in the cathedral square and originally housed not only the administrative offices and the treasury of the cathedral, but also the workshops, studios, storerooms and equipment needed by the artisans. In the great beamed hall on the main floor assembled the masons and stone cutters at whose head was the master builder; here, too, from its founding until 1620 met the grand chapter of the Order of Free Masons. In 1580 was added a new wing of the same Gothic style as the old building. (Cf. Schadäus, 106-110).

Today the *fabrica* building, restored and expanded in 1931 to include adjoining houses of historical interest, is the *Musée de l'Oeuvre de Notre Dame*, said to be the most beautifully arranged museum in France. The building complex with its two elegant circular staircases, its finely proportioned rooms and historic windows is a museum piece in itself. The exhibits, some of which are unique, have been strategically and artistically displayed to show both them and their surroundings to full advantage.

77. Strassburg cathedral

On the site of the present magnificent cathedral there once stood a grove sacred to the Tribochi god of war. The Romans felled the grove to make place for their temple to Mars (Hercules?). In the fourth century the first bishop of Strassburg erected on the ruins of the Roman temple a cathedral which was destroyed by barbarians 406-407. Its successor, the renowned cathedral begun by Clovis 504 or 507, had stood five centuries when in 1007 it was struck by lightning and gutted by the ensuing fire. Eight years later the ground was cleared for the Romanesque structure which forms the core of the present cathedral. In 1176 the Gothic style of architecture supplanted the Romanesque for the remainder of the construction. The great spire, rising like a tall taper of stone lace and dominating the landscape for miles, was built 1277-1439. The projected second spire was never begun, although detailed plans for it were drafted; these may be seen in the *Musée de l'Oeuvre de Notre Dame*.

The sacred spring, a deep well used successively by the Tribochi and the Romans for cleansing sacrifices and sanctified for baptism by St. Remigius, was to be seen in the cathedral until 1696 when it was covered; in 1776 it was sealed.

Like so many cathedrals, the Strassburg cathedral is dedicated to the Virgin and is known as *Notre Dame, Unser Frauen Münster*. Until the Reformation the cathedral and its square were the center of the city, the heart of the diocese and an integral part of everyday life. During the centuries of its construction voluntary workers from all over the diocese cut and carted great stones from the quarry; these helpers were served free meals, and they as well as those who contributed money were given special indulgences. During annual festivals people from the city and the diocese came in procession to the cathedral; in times of rejoicing or calamity people gathered in the cathedral square; here the army assembled before proceeding to battle. The *Schwörbrief* was read annually in the bishop's garden. Vendors had booths in the square and outside the cathedral porticos. The mayor held audience in the nave, and people going to and from market used the cathedral aisles as thoroughfares.

The cathedral sculptures reflect the religion, history and character of the people. The *Reuterlein auf der Säulen* is said to be the statue of a miller, the first person to bring stone from the quarry for the transept. Three horsemen represent Clovis, Dagobert and Rudolf von Habsburg; a horseman representing Louis XIV was added 1824. The *Rohraffe*, the cock on the great mechanical clock and the animal groups (depicted as marching in a funeral procession and celebrating mass on the pillars by the choir) express the boisterous humor and satiric irony so inherent in medieval piety.

One comment on the effect of the Reformation on the cathedral: *Die kleine Münsterchronik* has for the period 1475-1496 31 entries concerning cathedral additions, renovations and repairs; for the period 1516-1530 it has

P. xxiii N. 77

16 entries concerning damages from the Peasant War, abolition of the cross, the mass, etc., but not one entry about repairs or additions.
Cf. Dacheux, *Fragments*, I, Part i, *passim*. Haug, *passim*. Grandidier, *Essais*, *passim*. Schadäus, *passim*. Schneegans, *Sagen*, 1-11. Specklin, 9. Cf. also N. 78, N. 80, N. 1326 (par. 12), N. 1333-N. 1338.

P. xxiv

78. the great organ renovated
The first organ, the work of an unknown maker, was donated to the cathedral by the knight Ulrich Engelbrecht 1260. The second organ - built by Gunzelin von Frankfurt - burned 1298 in a fire that ravaged cathedral and city. The third organ – installed 1327 – was damaged by fire in 1384 and restored as well as enlarged in 1385, probably by Conrad von Rotenburg. The inner workings of this organ were rebuilt by Krebs von Anspach 1489, renewed 1714-1716 by André Silbermann, furnished with additional keys and pipes by Wegemann 1833-1844, remade in the romantic style 1893 and completely restored by Roethinger 1935. The exterior, however, has remained virtually unchanged since the fourteenth century.
Cf. Dacheux, *Fragments*, II, 468. Gass, *Orgues*, 6. Haug, 133. Grandidier, *Essais*, 64. N. 1333.

79. he brought Geiler to Strassburg... to be cathedral preacher
The date for Geiler's arrival in Strassburg, as noted in the *Errata*, should be 1477/78; cf. note on Geiler in Biographical Section.
According to Hertzog (113) and Grandidier (*Essais*, 69), Schott, Sr., was already at that time a director of the cathedral *fabrica* ("praefectus fabricae majoris ecclesiae;" cf. Schöpflin, *Alsatia*, 668), although Schadäus (109) does not list him as such until 1481.

80. Among his many gifts to the Church is the beautiful pulpit...
For other such gifts made by Schott, Sr., cf. N. 84 and note on him in Biographical Section.
Because the regular pulpit in the cathedral nave had been removed during the strife between the orders and the lay clergy (N. 955, par. 3), it is said that Geiler first preached in the cathedral crypt and then – on account of his increasing congregation – preached from a pulpit in the north transept or from a wooden pulpit in the nave. Some accounts, however, claim that from his arrival in 1477/78 to 1486, when the new pulpit was installed, Geiler preached in the chapel of St. Laurentius. Yet this chapel may not have been usable for services during those years, because it was not completed until 1494-1505, though apparently begun years before under Schott, Sr.'s, supervision. When Geiler came, there was evidently only an altar to St. Laurentius in the cathedral; this is mentioned as early as 1077 and served as the parish altar, but its location in the cathedral is disputed. Wuttke has just recently further confused the issue by saying that from 1478 to 1486 Geiler preached in the church of St. Laurentius. Surely, after laboring to restore cathedral preaching of which the Strassburgers had long been deprived (N. 955, paragraphs 3ff.), the administrators of the cathedral would not have allowed Geiler, the first incumbent of their new cathedral chair, to hold preaching services outside the confines of the cathedral for eight years!
Cf. Barth, *Handbuch*, 1440, 1450. Laguille, 366f. Pfleger, "Münster-

kanzel," 377. Piton, 322. Winckelmann, "Kulturgesch.," 278. Wuttke, *NDB*, VI, 150f.

Largely at his own expense Schott, Sr., had the intricately carved stone pulpit made for Geiler by the cathedral master architect Hans Hammer. The screen alone is said to have cost 18 florins. Haug calls the pulpit "un des plus ravissants chef-d'oeuvres du mobilier flamboyant." It stands against the base of the third pillar on the north side of the nave.

The lusty humor characterizing many a cathedral ornament (cf. N. 77) found expression in two small figures near the ramp of the pulpit: a lewd little monk just touching the skirt hem of the demure little nun kneeling beside him. This "groupe immodeste" was removed in 1764.

Cf. Barth, *Handbuch*, 1440, 1458. Dacheux, *Fragments*, I, 15, 65; III, 143. Grandidier, *Essais*, 63, 270f., 273. Haug, 131f. Pfleger, "Münsterkanzel," 377. Piton, I, 322. Rathgeber, *Gottesmänner*, 12. Specklin, 287. Winckelmann, "Kulturgesch.," 278; "Nachträge," 308.

81. interest in the renaissance music of the day
Cf. #42, p. 48. Sixtus IV encouraged improvement in church music and established the Sistine choir. During the last quarter of the fifteenth century, music and the style of singing in cathedrals along the Rhine was greatly influenced by the great composer-musician Conrad von Zabern, teacher and preacher at Heidelberg, who was born in 1450 and died during the papacy of Sixtus IV. His book on the teaching of singing was written 1474. He is known to have written also a treatise on the instrument called monochord.

82. authority on herbology... considerable reputation
Cf. #107, p. 117; #134, p. 152; #138, p. 155; #154, p. 169; #177, p. 198.

83. Anna entered the convent of St. Margaret... probably in 1471.
Anna actually entered the Dominican convent of St. Agnes which stood outside the city walls of Strassburg. Attempts to reform the convent in 1465 had met with considerable resistance: the prior of the Dominican monastery had the convent gates barred to reforming sisters, and the wife of *Stettmeister* Theobald von Müllenheim, who was visiting her daughter, was locked inside. To settle affairs and effect reform of the convent, it was necessary for the general of the Dominican Order Marcialis Auribelli, to come to Strassburg. Cf. N. 689, par. 4.

In 1475 when Charles the Bold* was threatening Alsace (N. 74), the city government set up a committee of 8 men, one of whom was Schott, Sr., to plan additional defenses. To make way for new fortifications, the committee ordered that buildings lying outside the city walls be razed. Among the condemned buildings were those of St. Agnes and of other religious institutions. Permission to level them was obtained from the pope and the work of demolition began 8 November 1475 (Dacheux, *Fragments*, III, 18).

The nuns of St. Agnes were transferred to the Dominican convent of St. Margaret within the city. *Stettmeister* Theobald von Müllenheim and Friedrich Bock* opened the city gates to them; Rudolph von Endingen* and Schott, Sr., conducted them to St. Margaret. From that time on the convent was known as Sts. Margaret and Agnes although later documents not only refer to it simply as St. Margaret, but also apply the name St. Margaret to the former convent of St. Agnes. The convent was under the special protection of both Sixtus IV and Innocent VIII and enjoyed visits of such dignitaries as Salvo de Casseta,* general of the Dominican Order, 1482; Cardinal Raymond Peraudi,* 1502 and 1504; Emperor Maximilian, 1507. Records mention Anna Zorn* as prioress to 1511, Margredt Sturm as custodian 1498 and Odele Schott as prioress 1611 (cf. N. 67).

That the early days of the St. Agnes nuns at St. Margaret were perhaps not too pleasant may be inferred from Schott's words in his letter of 28 February 1476 to Anna (p. 358): "Even if you are now in another convent, may God give you joy and grace and grant that I may find you happy and well in body and spirit." To Schott's letter Anna appended the following note (cf. Appendix A): "My dearly beloved brother Peter wrote me this letter from Bologna in the first year that we of St. Agnes came to this convent of St. Margaret."

The date when Anna entered St. Agnes is not known, but from the statements of Peter and Anna quoted above, it is clear that she was in that convent long enough before its demolition to feel herself a part of it. In Straub (81) is an entry: "1471 Margret Schott nun at Sts. Margaret and Agnes of Strassburg." Since the only Margred Schott* mentioned in records is Anna's eldest sister, who was twice married, the given name may be an error for Anna.

Cf. Barthelmé, 147, 190. Bussierre, 21-28. Dacheux, *Fragments*, II, 463; III, 18, 220; IV, 173. Gass, *Blätter*, 19-20; *Dominikanerinnen*, 14. Meyer, *Reformacio*, 126, 140. Straub, 80, 81, 82, 87.

84. She was apparently prioress... an altar in her name...
The prioress was Anna Zorn* (N. 83, par. 3).

The elaborate wooden altar donated by Schott, Sr., to the convent Sts. Margaret and Agnes 1494 in honor of his daughter, "der Ehrwürdigen Muther Anna [Schott]" cost 200 Rhenish florins. It stood in the upper choir of the convent church and displayed the Schott and Cöllen coats-of-arms. The intricate carving of its panels, which were painted and gilded, depicted scenes from the Nativity.

85. Her Latin work on the Passion of Christ has been lost.
For other works by Anna Schott, cf. the note on her in the Biographical Section.

86. The only son... was to follow in his father's footsteps...
Only after much persuasion on the part of Geiler, Anna, Peter and very likely Müller, did Schott, Sr., give up the idea of a public career for his son. Peter did not feel that he was physically fitted for such a career (#18, p. 27), nor, after observing his father's exhausting and thankless work as a public official, did he want any part of it. In a letter of October 1481 he observes to Hassenstein that if nothing else were impelling him to choose a quiet life, the example of his father's life would be more than enough to do so; and he wishes Hassenstein might just for one day watch the ceaseless stream of importunists who besiege his father (#170, p. 190).

87. their constant concern for his health... restricted his activity...
Schott was not physically robust, as he himself intimates in two statements: 1) "pro etate graciliori" (#8, p. 14) when speaking of the need for more time to complete his doctorate in both laws; and 2) "ad quas nec corpore nec animo satis idoneus essem" (#18, p. 27) when speaking of his distaste for a public

P. xxiv   N. 87

career. That he had periods of illness we know from his letters (#42, p. 47; #43, p. 48; #63; #66; #68, p. 76; #78, p. 84; #99, p. 110; #104, p. 114; #112, p. 132; #156, p. 172), but none of his contemporaries was free from bouts of illness and many of them suffered from some kind of chronic complaint; e.g., Schott, Sr., had kidney or bladder stones, Geiler had kidney trouble and Wimpheling had dyspepsia.

Despite rather delicate health, Schott had amazing powers of endurance and sustained energy, as is attested by the concentration with which he devoted himself to study in Paris and Italy (#297, 316ff.), the number of his compositions, the large correspondence, his editing and cooperation with Geiler, his legal work, his assistance to Schott, Sr., the time spent with *famuli*, etc.

The exaggerated solicitude of his parents, though loving and well meant, amounted in actuality to domineering interference which almost blighted his life. Though out of filial devotion and piety he never openly rebelled, he often complains to his friends of the restrictions imposed by parental solicitude. Cf. pp. xxvi; xxvii; #8, p. 14; #9, p. 17; #17, p. 26; #18, p. 27; #20, p. 29; #25, p. 33; #28, p. 36; #54, pp. 59, 60; #58, p. 63; #60, p. 65; #73, p. 80; #136, p. 154; #144, p. 159; #156, p. 172; #170, p. 190; #177, p. 197.

The following passage from his letter to Antonius Manlius* perhaps best expresses how patiently he endured the constricting bonds of parental love: "All is well with me here at home so far as worldly blessings are concerned except that I am wracked by this one problem of being managed by my parents with overmuch indulgence and affection – more than I would wish – to such a point that they are adamant against my leaving home, though I have been panting this long time to return to my studies. I am very much torn with longing to go, yet knowing how attached they are to me, I shall definitely not upset them or leave unless they are willing; and so I am compelled to remain in Strassburg..." (#73, p. 80).

88. the school at Schlettstadt... alumni many famous Alsatians
1) Schools of the Brethen of the Common Life

Because the schools established by the Brethren of the Common Life in the Lowlands influenced Alsace directly through Dringenberg* and indirectly through Thomas à Kempis,* Agricola,* Biel,* Erasmus, *et al.*, a few words should be said about them here. The first school was founded at Deventer by Gerhard de Groot (1340-1384) who had studied at Paris with Gerson* and at Cologne. Wishing to share the large number of manuscripts he had collected, he gathered his friends around him. This was the origin of the Brethren of the Common Life (*Brüder vom gemeinsamen Leben, fratres et clerici vitae communis*, also called *canonici regulares, Kugelherren, Kappenbrüder, blaue Brüder, Hieronymianer, Gregorianer, Gerhardini*). They took no vows, but lived together under the rules of the early Christians. They copied and illustrated manuscripts which they sold for the support of their foundation and directed a school open to all desirous of profitting from their learning and free to indigent scholars (who were even supplied with books).

Unfortunately all records of the early school have been lost, not as in the case of Strassburg through disasters but through disinterest, and few details are available in the Deventer city archives. The Brethren apparently took over the cathedral Latin school, first mentioned in 1311, but according to tradition founded in 765. From the archives we learn that Cardinal Nicolas de Cusa, an alumnus of the school, gave the city in 1469 a grant of 4800 gold Rhenish florins to support 20 poor scholars in a *tehuis* or *burse*. From Rudolph Agricola's* congratulatory letter to Alexander Hegius (†1498) we learn that Hegius, who was Erasmus' teacher, became rector of the school in 1483. It was Hegius who introduced Greek into the curriculum. The present Alexander Hegius Gymnasium is a descendant of the Brethren's school.

Imbued with humanistic ideals from their experience at the Brethren's school at Deventer, students and alumni went forth to establish foundations of the Brethren. Johann Hämmerlin (Thomas à Kempis), for example, established the foundation on Mount Agnes, near Zwolle, where he was serving as preacher; it was under him that Dringenberg* studied. The foundation at Windesheim was begun by Florentius Radewyns as a result, it is said, of his death-bed promise to de Groot. Foundations were established up the Rhine at Marienthal in the Rheingau, at Butzbach and as far south as Swabia, where Gabriel Biel* was instrumental in founding new houses. The movement spread northward as far as Rostock and eastward as far as Kulm in Silesia and Poland. It died out during the Reformation.

Cf. *Cambridge Med. Hist.*, VIII, 787ff. Dacheux, *Réf.*, 442f. Dorlan, *Notices*, 94-99; "Nouv. études," 338f. Heimbucher, II, 552-560. Obermann, 10-21. Röhrich, I, 83. ter Kuile, 5-11. Velden, 142, 209, 260.

2) The school at Schlettstadt

Schlettstadt in the fifteenth century was, like Strassburg, a free city of the empire; it too had a democratic form of government, was an important trade center and a member of the Rhine confederation. In Schlettstadt developed the finest Latin school in the upper Rhine area.

There is no certain date for the founding of the school; a schoolmaster is mentioned in 1420. First a private (*Pfarrschule*), then a public school, it became famous under Ludwig Dringenberg who arrived as headmaster in 1441 and taught several generations of Alsatian leaders. He is credited with introducing humanistic studies into Alsace and with improving conditions for teachers, whose salaries were raised in 1459. The curriculum included Bible reading, catechism, oral Latin and the reading of Latin authors.

Wimpheling, an alumnus of the school, says that the *Doctrinale puerorum* of Alexander de Villa Dei (thirteenth century) was used there for 40 years or more. This was the most popular Latin grammar of the day; there were 49 editions in the fifteenth century and 15 editions in Strassburg alone to 1516. When Hermann Torrentinus wrote a commentary to the *Doctrinale* in 1509 and presumed to improve it, he was accused of heresy! The arrangement of the *Doctrinale* is much like that of modern Latin grammars: declensions, conjugations, uses of cases, etc. The explanations are in Latin prose, the rules and examples in leonine hexameters for easy memorization, as there were no individual texts for each pupil. Dringenberg did not follow the grammar slavishly, but used it as a basis for his teaching.

Crato Hoffmann* succeeded Dringenberg as headmaster in 1477 and remained at the school until his death 1501. He continued the humanistic tradition and introduced more Latin authors (Cicero, Suetonius, Ovid) and Greek. He was particularly interested in Petrarch, Lucan and Sallust and obtained copies of their works from the printer Johann Amerbach* of Basel, whose two sons Bruno and Basilius were his pupils. One of his pupils, Jacob Spiegel, Wimpheling's nephew, at one time secretary to Maximilian I, says of Hoffmann: "festive severus et severe festivus, litteras cum sanctis moribus edocebat," a statement which Knepper suggests could be the motto for Alsatian school humanism.

Hoffmann's successor was Hieronymus Gebweiler. He was headmaster from 1502 to 1509 when he went to teach in Strassburg. In his *Chronik* he comments on the training received in the school: "so die Jugent nicht nur allein in gueten Kinsten und lateinisch Buchstaben, sondern auch in christlichen tugenten underwissen und gelert..." He describes his thirty

P. xxiv   N. 88

boys as being "Teitsche Graffen und Freiherren, Riter, Edel und Unedel. Auch andrer fromer Leüt Kinder."

Johann Sapidus (Hans Witz) was the next headmaster (1509-1525); under him the school deteriorated as the conflicts attendant on the Reformation reached Schlettstadt. When the last headmaster Caspar Stüblin left for the university of Freiburg in 1558, the school was taken over by the Church and became a Jesuit school. Its valuable library now forms part of the Schlettstadt city library.

During its heyday, the school was housed in a building beside the church of St. Georg; this building was still standing and was city property when Glöckler was writing (ca. 1879). The city paid the teachers and provided the headmaster with quarters, wood and light. The headmaster also received certain emoluments from the church, because he and his pupils led the singing in services. Each pupil paid 10 shillings a year tuition. The school day began at 4 a.m. and ended at 9 p.m. There were 11 hours of study, including lectures and *exercitia*. The usual period for completing the school course seems to have been 6 years. The city also provided a *deutsche Schule* for "hantwerckknecht und andre personen, so ungevarlich uber zwelff jar alt sint und sust kinder, die nit geschickt sint in lateinisch schul zu gon."

Among the noted alumni of the Schlettstadt Latin school (not mentioned above) were: Peter Schott, Jodocus Gallus,* Johann Müller,* Johann Hugo, Johann Meier, Beatus Rhenanus,* Jacob Pavo, Sebastian Murrho, Johann Torrentinus, Jacob Delphin, Florentinus Hund, Eitelwolf von Stein (cf. N. 90).

Cf. Anon., "Aus dem neuen deutschen Reichsland Schlettstadt," *Illustrierte Zeitung*, (Leipzig, 1872, No. 1496, 155). Dacheux, *Réf.*, 443-448. Dorlan, *Notices*, II, 94-122; "Nouv. études," 339. Freundgen, 110. Gény, 25-28. Gény-Knod, ii, 23. Glöckler, I, 338. Knepper, *Schulwesen*, 236, 237ff., 240f, 278, 357. Röhrich, I, 78-108. Strüver, 7-23, 26-28, 46, 49, 55, 61-63.

89. Whether Wimpheling had already left Schlettstadt...
In a letter to his nephew Jacob Spiegel, Wimpheling says that he himself remained at Schlettstadt into his twelfth year: "In domo paterna sub Heidelbergensi Ludovici Dringenbergio apud scholas triviales ab infantia in duodecim aetatis annum permansi" (Dorlan, *Notices*, ii, 102). Since the accepted year of his birth is 1450, he must have left Schlettstadt in 1461/62 although Knepper (*Wimpheling*, 132) gives the year of his leaving as 1463.

90. Brant... was probably still in Schlettstadt
Though not mentioned in the list of alumni of the Schlettstadt school, it is quite certain that Brant* was at the school with Schott (cf. note on Brant in Biographical Section).

91. he translated the Alsatian proverb... extemporaneously
Cf. #234 and N. 1550-N. 1552. Schott at the time was not yet ten years old, says Wimpheling in the heading to the poetic translation.

P. xxv

92. After completing the course at Schlettstadt...
Since Schott was in Paris by 4 January 1471 (N. 95), he must have left

P. xxv   N. 92

Schlettstadt in late 1470, after having been there about five or six years. He was at that time in his eleventh year. As noted in N. 89, Wimpheling was at Schlettstadt into his twelfth year, but there is no reason to suppose that the precocious Schott needed to stay there that long, especially when he had Müller to tutor him.

93. the University of Paris...
The medieval university was an independent community exercising criminal and civil authority over everyone within its bounds – teachers, students, artisans, tradesmen, servants, etc. There was no distinction between teaching and learning; one began by learning, then combined learning and teaching and often spent a period teaching before returning to the outer world. The several levels in the training program resembled those of the guilds; a *scholaris* (apprentice) attached himself to a master and became in turn *baccalaureus* (journeyman), *licentiatus* (a term indicating he was admitted to the teaching ranks) and master (the title which he received after having obtained the licentiate and which his master conferred upon him).

The four faculties – theology, medicine, law and arts – included both teachers and students. The faculty of arts was the first or basic faculty through which one passed before specializing in one of the higher faculties. Students were admitted to the arts faculty at about age 12. The period for obtaining the bachelor of arts varied, according to the university and the aptness of the individual, from about 2 to 3 years; that for obtaining the master of arts varied from about 2 to 3 1/2 years. The largest of the higher faculties was law, because practically every church and village needed lawyers; theology was considered the highest faculty and a doctorate in theology the crown of all learning.

To protect themselves against extortion and injustice from citizens of the university towns and to promote fraternal association, scholars from outside early banded together in societies known as nations, guilds or universities. These came to exercise considerable influence and gave the medieval university its democratic character.

European universities of the late Middle Ages and early modern period were modelled on the university of Paris and the university of Bologna, each of which had special features.

The community of scholars which became the university of Paris during the years 1150-1170 (but had no written statutes until 1208) developed from the cathedral school and the monastery schools on the *Ile de la Cité*. Instruction was under the authority of the cathedral chancellor. Each of the higher faculties was headed by a dean. The arts faculty was headed by a rector who was elected by the members of faculty; in time the rector became the chief official of the university. The arts faculty was divided into four nations, with a proctor or procurator at the head of each nation. University affairs were settled in congregations of the four faculties by a majority vote, the vote of the arts faculty being determined by the majority vote of the nations.

The school of legal studies at Bologna which was recognized as a university toward the end of the twelfth century developed independently of the Church. Students of the university, being preponderantly law students and often career men returning for advanced study, were more mature than those of other universities. A college of doctors in each faculty had charge of examinations and granting of degrees within the faculty. Other university affairs were virtually controlled by the nations, inasmuch as they elected the rector in whom was vested criminal and civil authority over the university community. Originally there were two nations, the *Ultramontani* for

P. xxv   N. 93

scholars from north of the Alps and the *Citramontani* for scholars from south of the Alps, but later there were four or more nations including one for the native Bolognese.

The *Ultramontani* or German nation had special privileges by virtue of immunities and privileges granted to foreign scholars by Barbarossa in 1158. The German nation had two procurators, whereas other nations had but one. The two procurators, not the rector, had jurisdiction over members of the nation, and members took the oath of obedience to the procurators, not to the rector. The procurators were elected annually on 6 January and kept records of the fees paid by the members, of the possessions of the nation, etc.

Cf. *EB*, XXVII, 750ff. Hertzog, viii, 144ff. Kibre, *Nations*, 29, 34, 36f.; *Privileges*, 47. Paulsen, "Gründung" and "Organisation," *passim*.

94. Paris... study of law... subjects in the philosophical faculty
To be exact, Schott was enrolled in the arts or philosophical faculty at Paris (N. 93, par. 2) and could not devote himself principally to the study of law. Technically he could not become a student of law until he had received his A.B. degree.

95. In 1473, having received his A.B. degree at Paris... Bologna
The year when Schott received his A.B. degree was 1473, as noted in the *Errata*.

There is no record of the date when Schott arrived at Paris, or of the day in 1473 when he received his A.B. degree; nor is there a record of the date when he matriculated at Bologna. Approximate dates can, however, be established by collating various bits of information.

That Schott with his tutor Müller came to Paris at the end of 1470 or in the first days of 1471 is apparent from an entry for Müller in the *Liber procuratorum nationis Alemanniae (Auct.*, III, 161f.) which states that at a university meeting on 4 January 1471 the "Alemannia" nation (for all students from the empire, from Britain and from other non-French areas north of the Alps) had two points of business, the first being to receive two bachelors from other universities, one of whom was "Johann Molitoris de Rastadt d. Spirensis bac. Erforden."

Documental evidence that Schott received his A.B. degree at Paris during the year 1473 is also to be found in the above-mentioned *Liber procuratorum... (Auct.*, III, 224). The minutes of a meeting of the "Alemannia" nation on 13 January 1473 list among the names of those recommended for the baccalaureate degree "rigorose temptati":

> Dominus Petrus Schot, provisor provintiae, dyocesis
> Argentinensis cuius bursa valet xi soliis.

(For the phrase "provisor provintiae" in the quotation above, cf. N. 1764). It may well have been the latter part of 1473 when the degree was conferred. From Schott's comment of 15 September 1478 to Rot that it was five years since the two of them had studied together at Paris (#9, p. 16) and from data discussed below, it appears that Schott was in Paris as late as mid-September 1473 and probably until later.

To determine the approximate date of Schott's matriculation at Bologna we have the following data:

1) After leaving Paris Schott and Müller spent three months in Strassburg before going to Bologna (#297, p. 317).

2) The academic year at Bologna began the first of November and ended in mid-August (#9, p. 15). One may assume that the spring semester began about mid-April.

3) The earliest entry for Schott or Müller in the records of the German nation at the university of Bologna is [January] 1475 (*Acta bonon.*, in the section called *Annales*, 220). The entry for Schott reads:

> Dominus Petrus Schot de Argentina solvit solidos XIIII.
> doctor utri. iuris et canonicus S. Petri iun. Argentinensis.

That for Müller reads:

> Dom. Joh. artium doctor de Rasteten

Note that the above entries give the degrees earned later from Bologna and, in Schott's case, his subsequent position. The addition of such information to the entries makes it difficult to determine the academic level and position of unknown persons at the time of their first becoming members of the nation. A second entry for Schott in this section (228) is for the year 1480:

> Item a domino Petro de Argentina (ad emendum calicem) II grossos.

There are no entries in this section for Schott in the period 1476-1479, although we know from his letters that – except for his Strassburg sojourn 1478-1479 (N. 190) – he was in Bologna during those years. Since there are only two entries for Müller (*viz.*, 1475 and 1476, the latter because he was elected procurator that year) and three entries for Hassenstein (*viz.*, 1475, 1476, 1480) although he was at Bologna until 1481, it seems that entries for old members of the nation were not always made annually.

In the section of the *Acta bonon.* called *Instrumenta* (403) is a notation for 1477 which mentions Schott as one of the witnesses to the inventory of the nation's possessions when at the end of their term as procurators Müller and his co-officer handed over those possessions to the incoming procurators:

> ... presentibus... domino Petro Sotth de Argentina scolaribus Bononie... testibus.

Entries in the *Acta bonon.* were apparently made only once a year on or after 6 January, the date when the procurators of the nation were elected (N. 93, par. 7) and fees from old and new members of the nation were collected. This means that names of students who had matriculated for the preceding spring semester, as well as the names of those who had matriculated in November for the current academic year, would not be entered until January.

4) Schott himself says he had been studying law at Bologna for almost a complete five-year period when he was forced to leave because of plague: "ibi quinquennium fere integrum legibus indulsi: peste coactus in patriam me contuli" (#178, p. 199). We know that he came home after 15 September 1478 (N. 190); therefore, he evidently would have completed a full five-year period at Bologna if he could have remained through the winter semester beginning in November 1478.

From the above data it appears then that Schott, having received his A.B. degree at the university of Paris, left Paris in late 1473, that he spent three months in Strassburg, that he proceeded to Italy at the end of 1473 or beginning of 1474 and that he matriculated at the university of Bologna for the spring semester of 1474. Dacheux (*Réf.*, 287, n. 2) observes that Schott departed for Italy 1473-1474 and elsewhere (296) gives 1474 as the year of Schott's first trip to Italy.

Schmidt mistakenly states that Schott went to Paris in 1473 ("Notice... Brant," 8) and left Paris 1476 (*H. L.*, II, 5). Knod also errs (*ADB*,

XXXII, 406, and *Studenten*, No. 3397) in saying that Schott obtained his A.B. degree from Paris in 1475.

96. During the winter of 1479... returned to Bologna
These statements are not quite accurate. Schott's movements from 1478 to 1481 are somewhat difficult to trace, not only because of the paucity of letters for that period, but also because of problems in the dates of these letters: *viz.*, the date of #17 as printed in the incunabulum is incorrect (N. 251) and the date of #11 has no day or month (N. 201).

From examination of all available information, the following sequence can be established:

1) Home to Strassburg after 15 September 1478 (#10, N. 190)
2) In Bolgona again by fall 1479 (N. 201)
3) Visit to Ferrara spring 1480 (#17, p. 26; N. 244)
4) Abrupt departure from Bologna September 1480 (#71, p. 77; N. 607, N. 609)
5) In Ferrara September 1480 to March 1481 (#13, #18, N. 609)
6) In Rome March 1481 to May 1481 (#18, p. 27; #19)
7) Stop in Ferrara May 1481 (#19)
8) Via Venice to Strassburg by July 1481 (#19)

97. several months in Ferrara
The University of Ferrara, one of the most celebrated universities of Europe, had its beginnings in 1135 when the cathedral of Ferrara was built; it received its charter from Boniface IX in 1391. During the latter part of the fifteenth century it offered courses in all existing faculties and numbered no less than 51 professors and lecturers. With the decline of the D'Este family which had fostered art and learning in Ferrara, the university also declined and has been noted in later times chiefly as a school of medicine.

98. see the 'eternal city' before... captured by the Turks
Cf. #18, p. 27, and N. 261.

99. In Bologna Schott made lasting friendships... among his friends were...
In the letter to Heinrich Moser* (#95, p. 107) are named some of the friends at Bologna. Others were Hassenstein's tutor Ladislaus,* Ulrich Fronsperger,* Heinrich Georg Erlebach, Johann Weschbach.*

100. The... affection between Bohuslaus and Schott... composed intricate verses
For the plan of the two to enter the priesthood together and spend their lives in work and study, cf. N. 302.

For the poems composed to one another, cf. #236-239, #265, #285-289; #287 tells of their study together; cf. also N. 1720 and N. 1723.

101. Bohuslaus... made several trips to Strassburg... delivered his oration...
Bohuslaus von Hassenstein made 3 trips to Strassburg: late 1482 or early 1483, 1485 and 1487.

The visit of 1485 is mentioned twice in Schott's letters. On 28 September 1485 he writes to Vitus Maeler* (#72, p. 79): "My *dominus* and very dear brother Bohuslaus von Hassenstein was with me for some days and bade me greet all of you in his name." On 28 October 1486 he writes to Heinrich Moser* (#95, p. 107): "Bohuslaus, now archchancellor of Bohemia, visited me again last year." Since the latest letter to Maeler preceding that of 28 September was written 28 May (#69), Hassenstein must have been in Strassburg during the period June to September.

That the visit of 1485 was not the first is indicated by Schott's statement to Moser: "Bohuslaus visited me again." The first visit would have been in late 1482 or early 1483, after Hassenstein had received his doctorate in canon law at Ferrara 26 November. Mitis, Cornova and Knod believe Hassenstein, on finishing his studies in Italy, returned to Bohemia via Strassburg. Certainly that was his intention when he wrote to Schott from Ferrara, 20 May 1482 (#37, p. 44): "I shall see you sooner than you may expect." His tutor Ladislaus* may have accompanied him at this time, for Schott, writing in the winter 1481/82 to Ladislaus at Ferrara (#189, p. 208), enjoins him to keep his promise of visiting Strassburg. Hassenstein may have arrived in Strassburg for the Christmas season 1482 and attended Schott's consecration as priest on 21 December. He may have been present for Schott's first mass 2 February 1483. He must have been a guest at some of the functions held in honor of Schott during the period: late December and early 1483, and it is logical to assume that he delivered his oration on Schott (#297) at one of these functions.

The visit of 1487 is alluded to twice in the Schott-Hassenstein correspondence of that year. On 10 August Hassenstein writes (#108, p. 118) that from the time he left Strassburg he has sent Schott only one letter and even that, through the negligence of Bernard Adelmann,* has failed to reach Strassburg. This fact he laments, because in the letter he had described "omnem vite mee condicionem." In the answer to Hassenstein's letter of 10 August, Schott on 28 August (#107, p. 117) says that he does not yet know whether the things he sent not long after Hassenstein's departure from Strassburg have arrived in Bohemia. The only other correspondence of 1487 between the two friends is Hassenstein's brief note of 10 April (#106) which states merely that he is well and has no news. This note is obviously not the undelivered letter referred to above and must have been written before Hassenstein's visit. Accordingly, Hassenstein left for Strassburg sometime after 10 April and returned home before 10 August.

102. society of Strassburg humanists
Cf. N. 17.

103. At Bohuslaus' urgent request, Schott... (to end of paragraph)
Information about Bohuslaus von Hassenstein's public career at court is in the biographical note on Hassenstein. Wimpheling in his *De integritate* (xiii) recommends to his pupil Jacob Sturm* the reading of Schott's treatise on Christian life (#110): "contra tales gelidos et indevotos tu teipsum armabis ex Petri Schotti opusculo de vita Christiana ad Bouslaum Bohemum praesertim"; also in the codex prepared for Jacob Sturm, Wimpheling included the text of section 3 of the treatise (cf. contents of "Wimpheling Codex," Appendix D).

Hassenstein's letter to Schott on the eve of his departure for the Near East tells of the places he intends to visit (cf. #144, dated 16 May 1490; N. 1056).

P. xxvi   N. 104

P. xxvi

104. Schott's years in Italy were interrupted...
Cf. N. 190. It is clear that Schott came home after mid-September 1478, but it is not entirely clear whether during the period from fall 1478 to fall 1479 there were two sojourns in Strassburg or only one (cf. N. 201).

105. Question... whether the son should complete the doctorate in laws...
Cf. #8, and N. 176.

106. confidential letters to Geiler... Italy
Viz., #11, #13, #14, #18, #240.

107. extra Lenten foods permitted by the bishop's new decree...
Cf. #14, p. 22; N. 224. The bishop of Strassburg at this time was Albrecht von Bayern.*

108. predilection for theology which would allow... 'quiet life'...
Cf. N. 121, par. 2, and N. 255.

109. notation in the Acta... degree of doctor...
The *Acta Bonon.* (220) gives Schott the title of "doctor utriusque iuris"; information on the dates when the degree was conferred is found in the manuscript records of doctorates conferred by the faculty of law at Bologna. "Liber secretus iuris caesarii (1378-1512), Primus Liber," f. 170b:

    Petrus Schottus d'Argentina 7 Sept. 1480

"Liber secretus iuris pontificii I (ab anno 1377 ad annum 1528)," f. 148a:

(a) die prima Septembris Dispensatum fuit cum domino petro de argentina ...ad examen.
(b) Examinatus doctoratus fuit dominus petrus de argentina praesentatus per dominum Io. de Salla... insignia doctoratus rendedit... d. Johannes de salla.

Cf. also Knod, *Studenten*, 507f.

110. probably in the early months of 1481 – an outbreak of hostilities...
The outbreak of hostilities between the university nations at Bologna occurred in September 1480, cf. N. 96, N. 607, and N. 609. In the letter to Hieronymus de Zanctivis (#71) Schott apologizes for having been unable to pay his professor personally.

111. he stopped in Rome... first tonsure... in Venice to buy books...
Cf. #19, and NN. 263f.

112. He fretted because his books did not arrive... no one... knew Greek.
The books which had been sent off before Schott left Venice arrived in

P. xxvi

Strassburg sometime in the fall. Cf. #24, p. 32; #25, p. 33, #170, p. 190; N. 263.
 In 1485 Schott was still the only one in Strassburg who knew Greek (#73, p. 80).

P. xxvii

113. he was far from idle... assisted his father... heard lectures...
In 1481 begins the long sequence of Schott's letters to Maeler, concerning benefices for friends (#23, #26, #29); Schott may at this time have already been acting as procurator.
 There are many references to assisting his father (#25, p. 33; #26, p. 35; #28, p. 36; #169. p. 189; #170, p. 190). He wrote letters in his father's name (#193, #186, #201) and translated official letters into German (N. 2). The imperial procurator for fiscal affairs commissioned both Schott and his father to attend to a certain matter of state (#134).
 Schott tells Hassenstein (#25, p. 33) that he is hearing sermons. These may have been sermons not only by Geiler but by other preachers and by teachers in the schools of Strassburg (cf. N. 18). In 1484 Schott attended the lectures of Conrad Bondorf* at the Franciscan monastery school (#54, p. 59).

114. he jotted down from Geiler's sermons the aphorisms... "Imitaciunculae"
Schott may have added to his collection of Geiler's aphorisms through the years. Schmidt ("Notices... P.S.," 255) claims that the manuscript of the "Imitaciunculae" (#233) was found among Schott's papers after his death. The influence of Geiler's pithy phraseology, so marked in these aphorisms, is apparent in the vivid similes Schott uses in the "Treatise on Christian life" (#110, pp. 122, 124, 128).
 There were others besides Schott who made notes on Geiler's sermons. Rathgeber (*Gottesmänner*, 16) lists: Jakob Biethen von Reichenweyer who took down "Arbor humana" ("Der menschliche Baum"); Jacob Other, Geiler's former *famulus* and friend; Johann Pauli; Peter Wickgram, Geiler's nephew; Susanna Hörwart, a nun of the Magdalene convent (*Reuerinnen*), where Geiler preached weekly as confessor to the convent.

115. he wanted a 'quiet life'... to enter the priesthood
Cf. #170, p. 190, and N. 255. While they were students together in Italy, Hassenstein had urged Schott to become priest (#36, p. 43) and planned to enter the priesthood himself (cf. N. 302).

116. In 1482 he became canon of New St. Peter
1. Schott was not the first of his family to become a canon in Strassburg. Schöpflin (*Alsatia*, 668) mentions a Conrad Schott who was canon at St. Thomas in the thirteenth century.
 To obtain the canonicate at New St. Peter in April 1482 Schott had to secure a papal *gratia* (#73, p. 80), because April was one of the months when the pope had the right to fill vacant benefices (N. 130), and securing a papal *gratia* involved the use not only of money but of every possible influence. How many letters on behalf of Schott were written, we do not know; there are, however, five in the *Lucubraciunculae*: Schott's letter soliciting support from Kemel (#32), the letters written by Schott in the name of the Strassburg magistracy to solicit the support of persons in-

fluential at Rome (#158- #160), the letter written by Schott in the name of the Strassburg magistracy recommending him to the pope (#161); cf. N. 1143. Schott's statement in #100, p. 110, that he owed his canonicate to Thomas Wolf, Sr.,* no doubt means that Wolf – himself a canon of New St. Peter – used his influence in persuading the chapter to accept Schott's *gratia*; indeed, Wolf may have been the chapter's nominator and may have nominated Schott as candidate for the vacant benefice, a move which would cause the chapter to honor the *gratia* with better grace (cf. N. 130, par. 2).

The election and installation ceremony at which Schott was formally inaugurated as canon was probably very much like that described as being used at New St. Peter in 1450 (see N. 1134).

It should be noted that after Schott's death in September 1490, the chapter elected Graf Heinrich von Werdenberg to succeed in the canonicate – September being a month when chapters could fill vacancies, but Werdenberg was unable to hold the canonicate against other more influential claimants (cf. N. 130, last paragraph).

2. The following paragraphs contain a brief description of what the position of canon in Schott's day entailed.

A canon enjoyed certain rights and privileges. In return he had duties to perform, some of which were general duties performed by all canons and some of which were special duties connected with his canonicate.

A year of residence was necessary before he was free to obtain leave of absence and to use his income for study at a university, or for pilgrimages, or for trips to Rome (even though these might be in the chapter's interest). When in residence, he was allowed six weeks holiday per year to go to the baths or to travel; however, he could not take his holiday during a period when he had special obligations to fulfill in the church or choir. After three years of residence he was entitled to quarters in one of the chapter's canonical houses, or, as in some wealthy chapters, to an individual house. There is no evidence that Schott ever lived in a canonical house belonging to New St. Peter. Except for the months he spent in the canonical house of Wolf, Sr. (cf. #40, p. 47; N. 404), during the latter's absence, Schott seems always to have made his home with his parents (cf. N. 1022).

A canon was expected to attend all chapter meetings and regular church services. He had his place in the choir, where strict rules were enforced for entrance, for seating according to rank, for remaining in place, for preserving silence, for not leaving without permission and so on. Church services included special masses and ceremonies, such as the *anniversarium* (cf. N. 144, par. 5ff.). Unless excused by a superior, a canon was obligated to attend canonical hours in the choir; this duty is mentioned in several items of the *Lucubraciunculae* (#216, p. 236; #217, p. 237f.; #222, p. 250; #298, p. 321; #205 is an excuse for non-attendance; cf. also N. 1401, and N. 1451).

He had to participate in processions. In Strassburg on major feast days, such as Pentecost, the secondary chapters marched in procession to the cathedral where they joined the grand chapter at the entrance and proceeded inside. After services they returned in procession to their own churches. On the feast of the Holy Sacrament all the regular and secular clergy marched with banners and relics through the city. In times of great public weal or woe the city council ordered special religious processions and masses, as for example in 1482 when there was unusually bad weather; in 1488 when Maximilian was captive in Bruges; in 1490 when the plague raged. Robes for various functions were prescribed.

For the first three years a canon at New St. Peter did not receive the full income from his benefice; until 1452 he paid 1/9 of the income per annum to the chapter, thereafter he paid 40 Rhenish florins. In addition to his income from his benefice, each canon received annually a proportionate amount of grain and wine from chapter lands. He also received the so-called weekly bread prebend of 15 (sometimes more) loaves of bread, baked 3 times a week in the chapter's bakery, and a share of: a) daily distributions in the choir for attendance at divine services, b) offerings from burials, special masses or anniversaries, c) special distributions on feast days.

Cf. Dacheux, *Réf.*, 408. Horning, "Stift," 24, 53: Pfleger, "Gottesdienste," 37. Schmidt, *Chapitre*, 53, 114-117, 121-127.

117. New St. Peter
In Schott's time the collegiate church of New St. Peter, so-called to distinguish it from Old St. Peter (N. 132), ranked third in importance among the churches of Strassburg; the cathedral being first, then the three collegiate churches in order of importance: St. Thomas (N. 337), New St. Peter and Old St. Peter.

New St. Peter began in the early eleventh century as a monastery, replacing the Merovingian church and hospital of St. Colombo which had been destroyed by Hermann of Swabia. For almost half a century it stood outside the city walls. In 1031 it became a collegiate church and was consecrated in 1050 by Pope Leo IX on a visit to his native Alsace; the dalmatic left by Pope Leo as a memento was in existence until the beginning of the eighteenth century. The Romanesque church has an unusual system of buttressing. Its bell tower burned in 1337 and was rebuilt in Gothic style.

The largest of the chapels, the Zorn, which is really an integral part of the north nave, was added probably in the fourteenth century. A recent architectural congress of France classed the chapel as one of the finest examples of thirteenth and fourteenth century Gothic. During the restoration in 1889 tombstones from the nave and other parts of the church were placed on the walls of the chapel.

In 1300 when Gerhardt, archbishop of Mainz, visited Strassburg, the chapters of St. Thomas and New St. Peter united with the grand chapter of the cathedral in sharing the costs of the visit. This union continued throughout the struggle against the bishops (cf. N. 16, par. 5) and to the Reformation.

New St. Peter, though small, was a rather wealthy foundation. Wine from its vineyards filled the cellars, and grain flowed into its granaries from lands scattered about Alsace. Apparently the chapter leased some of its lands, for Markgraf Christoph of Baden* is documented as paying the chapter 240 florins rent in 1480. The foundation supported 15 canons by 1450; its number of vicars varied from 14 to 31; in 1511 it still had 40 benefices. The canons were drawn preferably from noble or patrician families, and minors were eligible for canonicates. The school served minor canons and children of parishioners, as well as of the poor, and sent its talented scholars to French, Italian or German universities at the foundation's expense. The richly endowed library contained rare manuscripts and 200 incunabula; works helpful for preaching were outnumbered by works on liturgy, law and history.

Some officers in a collegiate chapter were:

1) The *praepositus* (provost, *Probst, prévôt*), the head of the chapter, had charge of administration and represented the chapter in external affairs. He was invested by the bishop and in turn invested chapter members.
2) The *decanus* (dean, *Dechant, doyen*) maintained discipline and as confessor of the chapter had the spiritual care of the canons and vicars.
3) The *thesaurarius* or *custos* (treasurer, *Küster, trésorier*) had charge of the treasure, i.e., the relics, ornaments, vases, cups, etc.

4) The *scholasticus* (schoolmaster, *Schulmeister, écolâtre*) presided over instruction of minor canons, pupils of the choir, children of parishioners and paupers.
5) The *cantor* (cantor, *Sänger, chantre*) directed singing for services and gave musical instruction to minor canons and pupils of the choir.
6) The *portarius* or *portenarius* (porter, *Pförtner, aumônier*) distributed alms at the church door and received strangers and the poor.
7) The *camerarius* (*Kämmerer*) had charge of grain.
8) The *cellarius* (*Kellermeister*, cellérier) administered the wine cellars.
9) The *dapifer* (*Tafelmeister, maître de la table*) had charge of the refectory and meals.
10) The *pincerna* (*Mundschenk, bouteiller*) administered wine culture and distribution of the wine ration.
11) The *procurator capituli*, procurator of the chapter.

There were other minor officers, such as the *bacularius* who cited before the chapter those members infringing on rules; the *plebanus*, a vicar who served as parish priest; the *summissarius*, a vicar in charge of high mass; the *animissarius* in charge of masses for the dead; the baker, cook, etc. Sources do not always agree on the duties of an officer, e.g., the duties of the *camerarius* are also defined as having charge of books and garments and sounding bells for services. Not every chapter had all the officers mentioned, and in many chapters one member might hold several offices.

After the Reformation the church of New. St. Peter was used alternately by Catholics and Lutherans or stood vacant until it was permanently taken over by the Lutherans in 1561. (Thereafter the Catholic parish of New St. Peter built its own New St. Peter outside the old city.) During the Reign of Terror the army used the church as a magazine and so badly damaged it that it was no longer fit for services. The interior was virtually ruined; the tombs had been ripped open, the corpses robbed and the bones tossed back into the earth. Rebuilding inside and out since that time and the restoration, finished in 1891, have left the church usable but decidedly unattractive. The beautiful main portal and the quiet cloister alone are unspoiled; the cloister presumably looks much the same as it did after the restoration in 1500 (which was financed by Wolf, Sr.) although the frescoes have vanished (Plate 8). Across the narrow street to the left of the main facade, where once were chapter houses and gardens, stands the very modern Hotel St. Pierre-le-Jeune which was opened in 1964.

Cf. Barth, *Handbuch*, 1397-1403. Dacheux, *Fragments*, IV, 134. *Strassburg Chronik*, II, 730. Grandidier, *État*, 12-15; *Mélanges*, 341ff. Hertzog, viii, 113f. Horning, *Kirche, passim*; "Stift," *passim*; *Jung-St.-Peter, passim*. Schmidt, *Chapitre*, 53ff., 114-127 *passim*. Stein, 5-120 *passim*. Straub, "St. Pierre," *passim*.

118. an entry in the records of the Strassburg bishopric... reads...
Cf. Meister, 131. The 24 florins paid by Schott were the fees payable upon taking possession of a benefice (cf. the fees paid for Müller, #156, p. 171).

119. In December... he was ordained... celebrated his first mass...
Schott was ordained 21 December 1482 (#30, p. 38; #36, p. 43) and celebrated his first mass on 2 February 1483 (#39, p. 45; #40, p. 46). Cf. N. 341.

P. xxvii   N. 120

120. Having completed more than a year... income from prebends...
The terms prebend and benefice are used interchangeably. Technically, however, prebend meant the monthly or yearly income from a benefice, while benefice meant: a) a church office and its income, or b) the property supplying the income, or more fully, c) the lifetime right granted by a church authority to a cleric of drawing income from specified church properties in return for certain services (cf. N. 116, pars. 5ff.).

121. Schott prepared in the fall of 1484... end of the cherished dream...
Few priests and clerics of Schott's time were trained theologians. Those who had studied at universities were mainly lawyers. For this reason earnest churchmen stressed the need for masters and doctors of theology in church positions. According to a letter of Johann Rot* to Geiler 30 May 1493, there were at that date only three bachelors of theology and one master of theology in the entire Strassburg diocese (cf. Dacheux, *Réf.*, Appendix viii).
As priest, Schott felt keenly the lack of sound training in theology, and spoke of himself as being ignorant of sacred writings (#64, p. 70). Even before he considered entering the priesthood, he inclined toward theological studies, "ad quas natura mea est inclinacior" (#13; cf. also #18), and it had been his desire on receiving his A.B. degree to continue study under the noted theologian Johann Scriptor* at Paris instead of going to Bologna for law studies as his father wished (#178, p. 199). Soon after his return from Bologna in 1481 he began planning to go away for theological studies. In October of that year he wrote to Hassenstein that he would wait until winter was past when his parents could bear his absence more easily (#170, p. 190). On 16 November of the following year he wrote again to Hassenstein, "When I have completed my year of residence in the canonicate of New St. Peter...I shall study theology" (#36, p. 43). On 5 March 1484 he wrote to Müller of his frustration and his parents' continued opposition to his going away (#54, p. 60). When his parents consented to his entering the University of Paris in the fall of 1484, he made all arrangements for his stay there (#58, #60, #176, N. 510, N. 518) and was ready to leave by the end of August.
After the poignant letter to Müller (#177) telling about last minute cancellation of plans because of Müller's message that plague was raging in Paris and about postponement at least for the winter, there are but two references to studying theology: writing to Müller 30 November 1484, Schott repeats the statement that his parents insist he stay at home for the winter (#63); and writing to Manlius* 6 October 1485, he explains that he has not gone away because of his parents and will not go until they wish him to (#73, p. 80; cf. N. 87). The time for realizing this dream never came. Had death not come so early, Schott might well have gone to Paris later in his career.
There is no evidence that illness prevented Schott from leaving for Paris in 1484 – the reason Knod gives (*ADB*, XXXII, 406f., and *Studenten*, #3397). It is true that Schott mentions being troubled by "gravedo et pituita," when writing to Müller on 30 November 1484 (#63), but there is no mention of this difficulty in letters of earlier November or in the letter to Müller (#177) at the time the trip to Paris was definitely postponed, in the late summer (N. 1257).

122. His collaboration with Geiler... continued... (to end of paragraph)
From Schott's remark, "Omnia te duce... secundet coepta nostra" in the

405

P. xxvii   N. 122

letter of 22 July 1481 (#20, p. 29), it seems that the collaboration may have begun soon after his return from Italy.

For information on adulteration of coinage, cf. #168, and N. 1197.

For usury in lending and selling grain, cf. #168; #213 (a case involving such usury stated by Johann Rot*); #214 and #215 (opinions on the case by Simmler* and Schott); N. 1431-N. 1442, *passim*.

For description of abuses, cf. #187; N. 1326-N. 1338.

For the case of the Last Sacrament given those condemned to death, cf. #187, #210- #212, N. 1325.

P. xxviii

123. Both he and Geiler were instrumental (to end of paragraph)
Improvements in school curricula bore fruit. The first lectures in history to be delivered anywhere are said to have been given in Strassburg. By the beginning of the sixteenth century the school of New St. Peter had developed sufficiently advanced training to employ the distinguished Johann Gallinarius as rhetorician. Hieronymus Gebweiler came from the Schlettstadt school to direct the Strassburg cathedral school in 1509. Ottmar Luscinius, the first Greek teacher in Strassburg, came after 1510.

Schott's school poems are #246- #264; cf. N. 1606.

Plans to use the income and buildings of St. Christian abbey, then in a state of decline, for a secondary school and to appoint a staff of secular clerics who were highly trained theologians and jurists came to naught, because Bishop Albrecht* – though very much interested in the project – could not bring himself to make a final decision. Very similar plans were put into effect in 1531 under the leadership of Jacob Sturm* who was greatly influenced by Geiler and Wimpheling (cf. N. 18).

Cf. Dacheux, *Réf.*, 45ff., 451-454. Knepper, *Schulwesen*, 305, 341. Schmidt, "Notices... P.S.," 317f. Varrentropp, 221ff. Zacher, 47f.

124. In an early poem to Bohuslaus... (to end of paragraph)
The poem to Bohuslaus is #238; the letter to Occo* is #150; the poem commemorating the victory over Charles the Bold* is #244; the elegiac on Agricola's* death is #245 (cf. also N. 562).

Writings of Schott on the theme of German nationalism, not mentioned, are: the epithalamium to Matthias I* of Hungary and Beatrice of Naples (#243), the asclepiad on the captivity of Maximilian* (#263), the two poems against Germans who repudiated their heritage (#270, #272).

Though not a chauvinist, Schott like other Strassburgers was proud of his native city, its history and its importance in military and commercial affairs of the empire. In a letter to Johann Scriptor* (#178) he praises the fruitfulness of the soil, the abundance of wildlife and the healthful climate; in his encomium of Strassburg (#254) he extolls not only natural abundance but also the city's mighty walls, its dedicated leadership and splendid cathedral; in the poem on Maximilian's captivity (#263) he lauds the part played by the Strassburg contingent of the imperial army in effecting the king's release.

125. Schott, like Geiler... took in boys... cleverly phrased admonition...
For a list of Geiler's *famuli*, cf. N. 279. For Schott's *famuli*, cf. the letters to Johann Klitsch von Rixingen*: #79, #96, #102, #188; the references to Klitsch and Gangolf von Steinmetz* in #146, pp. 160f.; #148, p. 162;

P. xxviii   N. 125

#176; #177, pp. 197f. Cf. also the letter to Ribysen* (#70 and N. 606). Klitsch and Steinmetz are the only ones of Schott's *famuli* whose full names are known and who have been identified. Cf. Dacheux, *Réf.*, 341ff.; Knepper, *Schulwesen*, 185, 320, 358, and *passim* for discussions of *famuli*. The admonition quoted is from #79.

P. xxix

126. Gangolf von Steinmetz... furnished... biographical material... poem by him
Clauss ("Geiler," 487) claims Rhenanus'* biography of Geiler is based principally on Steinmetz' verbal accounts and Geiler's own notes in a calendar. For Steinmetz' poem in the third edition of the *Epithoma*, cf. N. 43.

127. As an authority on civil and canon law, Schott... (to end of paragraph)
Cf. #231, for the opinion on declaration of war by the bishop of Spires; #227, for the betrothal or marriage of an eleven year old girl; #226, for the regulations about diet; #208 and #209, for the case of the stolen confession.

128. the case of the homeless Clingenthal sisters...
Cf. #49-#53, #85 and the account of the Clingenthal sisters in the Biographical Section.

129. One of Schott's greatest services to Strassburg... Geiler's remaining...
The fact that the post of cathedral preacher at Strassburg remained virtually unconfirmed by the pope from 1478 to 1489 (N. 955, par. 6) naturally made offers of good posts elsewhere (N. 963) seem very attractive to Geiler.

Biel's* response to the question whether Geiler should remain in Strassburg was as follows: "All circumstances considered, I deem it expedient and advisable that he remain in the post to which he has been called and that he do not yield to the subtle wiles of Satan which under the guise of good deeds are intent upon blighting the fruit of God's Word" (#222, p. 251). Five of Schott's letters to Geiler concern this question: #61, #99, #114, #124, #125; the most masterful of these is #125. Cf. also Schott's words to Friedrich von Zollern,* bishop of Augsburg, about not keeping Geiler in Augsburg (#123, p. 141; #127, p. 147).

130. obtaining benefices
1. In the latter part of the fifteenth century, obtaining benefices was a highly complicated system involving chapters, pope and emperor and employing trained procurators in every bishopric and a corps of solicitors and procurators in the Roman *Curia*. Sixtus IV in 1482 limited the corps in the *Curia* to 100 and granted to these the rank of papal officials.

Originally, when vacancies occurred in cathedral or chapter benefices, candidates were nominated and elected by chapter members to fill the vacancies. All too often, however, because opposing factions failed to agree on a candidate, the chapter became involved in protracted and costly litigation. As a deterrent to such friction and its deleterious effects, the chapter of the Strassburg cathedral in 1318 inaugurated the system of election by rotation, i.e., the candidate for the first vacancy was nominated by the eldest chapter member, the candidate for the second vacancy by the provost, the candidate for the third vacancy by the next eldest member, the candidate for the fourth vacancy by the dean and so on until every member had had his turn of nomination by order of age or rank, when the procedure began over again. This system was adopted by St. Thomas in 1353 and by New St. Peter in 1450 (for a description of the formal election procedure at New St. Peter in that year, cf. N. 1134).

As a further deterrent to friction, the St. Thomas chapter ruled in 1367 that a candidate must furnish two guarantors who pledged to pay costs of any litigation or damages arising from the candidate's taking possession of the benefice. This procedure was also adopted by other chapters. In Schott's time the number of guarantors at Old St. Peter – and no doubt at other Strassburg collegiate churches – was four, two of whom had to be clerics, the other two, laymen (cf. #153, p. 167; #155, p. 170; #156, p. 171). Yet no amount of precaution could forestall litigation; for example, the case of Engelhard Funck* vs. Thomas Wolf, Jr.,* over a canonicate at St. Thomas was in litigation at Rome for five years (cf. N. 334); Johann Kerer* was involved in litigation over a vicarate in the Strassburg cathedral (#86, p. 95); after Schott's death his canonicate at New St. Peter was hotly contested for six years (cf. this note *infra*).

At first a candidate needed only to be a cleric, but in time certain provisions for qualification were established, e.g., that the candidate must be at least seven years old and of legitimate birth, that he must not have committed a major crime or have too many benefices, that he must belong to the artisan or merchant classes. The higher ecclesiastical positions became restricted to knights, patricians and nobles (cf. #80-#82 and N. 661).

2. The emperor had the right in every chapter of the empire to dispose of the first benefice becoming vacant after the day of his coronation. This right, *ius precium primarium*, was first used in the thirteenth century and was approved by the Council of Basel 1438. Maximilian began exercising the right when he became King of the Romans in 1486; in that year he issued 1540 *preces primae* (*preces primariae* or *preces regales*) and in 1508 he issued 612. If the chapter refused to accept his candidate, the emperor could employ a powerful weapon – that of withholding the revenues of the foundation. For example, Friedrich III gave *preces* for a canonicate at St. Thomas to the secretary of the imperial chancery, Christian Kolbeck von Freisingen, but the chapter had already elected Albrecht Wigersheim before the *preces* arrived and refused to withdraw him in favor of Kolbeck, whereupon Friedrich caused all revenues of the chapter to be confiscated from the time Wigersheim was installed until the chapter finally capitulated nine months later and accepted Kolbeck.

It was possible for a chapter to win the contest with the emperor. In 1474 *praepositus* Albrecht von Bayern* (later bishop) nominated Nicolaus Kuhn as candidate for the vacant benefice of *cantor* in the Strassburg cathedral chapter, while Friedrich III gave his *preces primae* for that benetice to Sixtus Scharffenecker. After five years of litigation, the Roman *Curia* declared in favor of the chapter's candidate.

Johann Müller* became canon at Old St. Peter on the strength of *preces primae* secured at Schott's instigation by Bishop Friedrich of Augsburg from Maximilian (#83, p. 91, and N. 680), but considerable electioneering was necessary in persuading chapter members to accept Müller (#153, and N. 1108; #155, and N. 1113).

3. From early centuries the pope had the right to recommend candidates for vacant benefices. With time these papal recommendations, which were virtually commands, developed several forms, such as 1) the general *provisio* for any benefice in any place and the special *provisio* for a particular benefice; these *provisiones* were usually granted to a favorite; 2) the *gratia apostolica* for a specific benefice; this was introduced by Innocent

IV and could easily be obtained by anyone through favor or money; 3) the *gratia expectativa* for a specific benefice while the incumbent was still living; this came into use during the Great Schism.

The Council of Constance stipulated 1418 that the chief offices in the chapter were to be filled by the chapter itself; other benefices were to be filled alternately by pope and chapter. Nicholas V decreed 1448 that the pope should have disposition of all benefices becoming vacant in uneven months, *menses papales* (February, April, June, August, October, December), and the chapter should have disposition of benefices falling vacant in even months, *menses ordinariorum* (January, March, May, July, September, November). It should be noted that *preces primae* of the emperor were not restricted, but were effective in all months, as Schott points out (#185, p. 204). Nicholas V also decreed that the reigning prince of the realm should have a voice in choosing candidates for the highest church offices, such as archbishop or bishop (cf. N. 674).

If a chapter did not accept the pope's candidate, the pope could resort to his most powerful weapon – that of excommunication. In 1504 the chapter of New St. Peter in Strassburg which had elected Jacob Wimpheling to the post of *summissarius* balked when Julius II demanded that the post be given to the candidate of his choice and was excommunicated for disobedience. Even though the chapter did not retain Wimpheling but accepted the pope's candidate, the ban of excommunication was not lifted until 1512. Wimpheling was the cause also of bringing excommunication on the chapter of St. Thomas. On the strength of his two *gratiae expectativae* which he had obtained from two popes for a summissariat at St. Thomas, the chapter supported his candidacy when such a post became vacant, but Leonard Bellendrin who had among his *provisiones* for various benefices in the Strassburg diocese one for a summissariat at St. Thomas claimed the post and was supported by Johann Burckard.* When the chapter protested that Bellendrin, being the natural son of a priest, was according to decrees of the Council of Basel ineligible, Burckard used his influence with the pope to have the chapter excommunicated.

Persons holding papal recommendations might thus contend for the same benefice. In 1449 Bishop Ruprecht of Strassburg who had procured a *provisio* for a canonicate at New. St Peter claimed a vacant canonicate at that church, but Paul Munthart who had a *provisio* of an earlier date for the same canonicate demanded recognition of his prior claim. When the bishop appealed to the pope, the chapter of St. Thomas, of which Munthart was canon, supported Munthart's claim as did city officials. At this point, apparently, the bishop withdrew from the contest, because his name does not appear in lists of New St. Peter canons, while Munthart became not only canon but later *praepositus* of New St. Peter.

Despite the stipulation of the Council of Constance that the chief offices were to be filled by the chapter, these were not secure from outside meddling. After Friedrich von Zollern resigned his post as dean of the cathedral chapter in Strassburg, the chapter waged a six-year losing battle with the pope to maintain the right, guaranteed by its age-old statutes, to elect its dean from the ranks of its own canons (cf. #167, and N. 1188).

Emperor and pope could come into conflict over their rights to supply candidates for benefices. On 21 September 1486, a few months after Maximilian's coronation as King of the Romans, Innocent VIII forbade German bishops to honor Maximilian's *preces primae* unless approved by the Holy See. Few if any of the *preces* were approved until Innocent, needing support from both the emperor and Maximilian in his war with Naples and Hungary, revoked the order of 1486 on 9 June 1489 and on 30 November of that year began approving the *preces*. Johann Müller was one of the holders of *preces* affected by this altercation between emperor and pope (cf. N. 799).

4. Candidates with royal or papal recommendations did not have to appear before the chapter at all. They could appoint a procurator to take office for them and collect revenues, without forfeiting any privileges; absentee canons, for example, took their turns at nominating. The practice of absenteeism thus defeated the original purpose of benefices, which was that the incumbents do specific parts of the work for which the chapter was responsible. This purpose was further defeated by such resident benefice holders who had been foisted upon the chapter and who either had no training for their posts or took no interest in the affairs of the chapter.

To protect themselves the chapters set up regulations requiring holders of benefices to be in residence in order to draw revenues, but little could be done in the face of privileges granted by pope and emperor. The result was that residence requirements became a formality of one year, or, in some chapters like that of Old St. Peter, were altogether discontinued.

In a letter to Geiler, 30 May 1493, Johann Rot* relates his conversation with Heinrich von Hennenberg* during the course of a walk. Hennenberg described the new cathedral library and the increased space for its goodly number of books. In answer to Rot's question whether there were many learned men in the chapter to make use of these books, Hennenberg replied that 40 years previously on his entry into the chapter there had been many members noted for their scholarship, but now, because of papal *gratiae* which compelled the chapter to accept anyone, there were very few. Rot then suggested means of improving the situation by designating 20 of the better benefices for trained theologians who were doctors, licentiates, or at least bachelors of theology. Hennenberg, however, felt such a program would be difficult to confirm at the Roman *Curia*.

5. Absenteeism gave rise to plurality of benefices. A keen benefice hunter could acquire a number of really fat prebends, especially if he sought them personally in Rome, "the smithy," Schott comments somewhat bitterly, "where these are forged," and where a Strassburg benefice could be more easily obtained than in Strassburg itself (#73, p. 80), because it was difficult for local chapters to get ahead of the "rabid jaws of the *Curia*" (#177, p. 198). There were those like Geiler and Schott who recognized the evil in the heaping of benefices, but were unable to curb so universally accepted and so lucrative a practice. Neither Geiler nor Schott ever held more than one benefice, and Schott (#73, p. 80, and #74, p. 82) declared he never wanted more than one. Wimpheling satirizes multiple benefices in his humanistic drama *Stylpho*: the titular hero, a benefice hunter, acquires 4 *gratiae*, and another character "de astutiis curtesan" has a host of benefices. One of Brant's* fools off to Narragonia is the holder of many benefices (*Narrenschiff*, 30: "von vile der pfrunden").

It was quite usual to have three or more benefices. The worthy and philanthropic lawyer Johann Simmler* was canon and *scholasticus* of Old St. Peter, canon and *portarius* of New St. Peter, canon and dean of St. Thomas, rector in Herlisheim. The *bon vivant* Thomas Wolf, Sr.,* was canon and provost of Old St. Peter, canon and *cellarius* of New St. Peter, canon of St. Thomas, canon at Basel, canon at Worms, rector of Rheinbischoffsheim in Baden. Perhaps the most ardent and proficient Alsatian benefice hunter of the day was the papal protégé in Rome Johann Burckard* who by currying favor, by good hunting tactics and by successful litigation acquired not only a long list of benefices but also achieved the rank of suffragan bishop. By contesting the post of dean at St. Thomas over a period of years, he made life so unpleasant for Johann Simmler that Simmler finally resigned (Dacheux, *Réf.*, 124). In 1496, after 6 years of litigation, Burckard, through intervention of Cardinal St. Praxedis, won Schott's canonicate which had also

P. xxix   N. 130

been sought by Georg von Gemagen, Lucas Schlegel and Gottfried von Adelsheim* (the last named had *preces primae*, #185); the candidate elected by the chapter of New St. Peter, Heinrich von Werdenberg, evidently withdrew early in the contest when opposed by claimants with *gratiae* and *preces*.

Cf. Dacheux, *Réf.*, 98-153, Appendix viii. Hofmann, I, 134ff. Horning, "Stift," 23. Meister, 131, 151. Santifaller, 23, 585. Schmidt, *Chapitre*, 44-52, 278; *H. L.*, I, 48. Stein, 13. Straub, *Geschichtskalender*, 279.

P. xxx

131. His tireless efforts... for... Müller... elected as canon...
Cf. N. 527; #151- #153, #155, #156.

132. Old St. Peter in Strassburg
The church of Old St. Peter was founded in the year 60 A.D. by St. Maternus. In 1398 the chapter of St. Michael at Rheinsau moved to Strassburg and was given the parish church of Old St. Peter, hence the two patron saints for the foundation and the name Sts. Michael and Peter. In 1454 the foundation supported 20 canonicates and 15 chaplaincies. At the time of Peter Schott, Old St. Peter ranked third in importance of the three collegiate churches of Strassburg (N. 117).

Cf. Barth, *Handbuch*, 1342-1350. Büheler, 44. Grandidier, *État*, 15f.

Today the church houses two faiths, the Lutheran in the old nave and the Catholic in a new wing.

133. Schott had no patience with plurality of benefices... (to end of paragraph)
For the refusal to act as procurator to the multiple-benefice holder recommended by Friedrich von Zollern,* cf. #105. The epigrammatic comment on Maeler's many benefices is in #76, p. 83.

Schott warned Gottfried von Adelsheim, Jr.,* against forcing the chapter of New St. Peter to honor his *preces primae* (#185).

References to plurality of benefices: #1, p. 9; #46, pp. 50f.; #55, p. 61; #59, pp. 64f.; #69, p. 76; #73, p. 80; #74, p. 82; #76; #98, p. 109; #105, p. 115; #128, p. 148; #179, p. 200; #185, pp. 203f.; #197, p. 213; #216, p. 236; #301, p. 322.

134. Schott was active in publishing
The item on Schott in Trithemius' *Cathalogus*, folio 55b, mentions the works of Gerson* edited by Schott and has the notation thereafter, "alia quoque nonnulla edidit, que ad noticiam meam non venerunt," which implies that Schott edited more than one or two works. Unfortunately Schott did not, like Wimpheling, put his name to his editions. It is very likely that he edited the Flach* publication of Thomas à Kempis'* *Imitatio Christi* (N. 137) and perhaps one or more works of Chrysostomus (#203). In 1489 he was working with Adolph Rusch* on an edition of Vergil, when Rusch died (#130, p. 151; N. 1003).

135. Influenced by Geiler... with Müller's help... eulogy of Gerson...
Geiler is said to have been inspired to become a theologian by the life and works of Jean (Johann) Charlier de Gerson.* Some of his sermons are based

on Gerson's works: the *Trostspiegel* is a version of Gerson's *De consolatione in mortem amicorum*; the *Passion des Herrn Christi* is an adaptation of a similar work by Gerson; the *Guldene Regel* which he preached to the Strassburg Magdalenes is a translation and reworking of a work by Gerson. On his trip through France at the time when he visited St. Baume, he stopped at the monasteries of the Carthusians at Avignon and of the Celestines at Lyons, to which Gerson had willed his works, and at considerable expense had copies of the works made for himself. Cf. Dacheux, *Réf.*, 337, and Pfleger, "Geiler," 195; also biographical note on Geiler.

While Müller was in Paris, he collected for Schott and Geiler as many of Gerson's works as he could find (#60, p. 65; #176, p. 196).

Schott's eulogy to Gerson – "compendiosa laus Johannis de Gerson" (#232) – and his poem "de tribus Iohannibus" (#241) were considered his best writings and are sometimes listed separately in older literary histories; e.g., Cave, 118; Eysengrein, 176; Gesner, 552, and *Bibliotheca instituta*, 566. Trithemius, *Cathalogus*, f. LVb, and *De script. eccl.*, f. CXXVIb; *Universal= Lexikon*, XXXV, 1038. The section on St. John the Divine (#241, pp. 274f.) appears in Rupprich, 76ff. (Cf. p. xxxi, N. 12, N. 141).

136. Gerson's works... published in one volume of three parts
A complete copy of Schott's edition of Gerson,* *Opera*, is in the Vatican Library; parts 1 and 2 are bound together, part 3 is bound separately. The date when the edition was finished is given at the end of part 3 as 6 September 1488: "finiunt opera... 1488. Idus vero mensis Septembris octavo." There is no mention in the edition of the printer, the editor, or the place of printing. From bibliographical sources we know that Johann Prüss* printed the edition at Strassburg. The works, some of which are poems, are arranged in 99 sections through the three parts. The first part contains "tractatus fidem et potestatem ecclesiasticam concernentes" (sections 1-23); the second part contains "opera moralia" (sections 24-52); the third part contains "tractatus ad mysticam nam seu contemplationi accomodatos" (sections 53-99). Cf. Schott's description of the arrangement, #232, p. 261, and N. 1526.

Mention should be made of several somewhat extraneous but interesting items which were placed at the beginning and at the end of the edition. Before the first part proper opens, there appear in order: 1) an alphabetical list of Gerson's works in the edition: 2) a letter of 1 January 1416 written at Constance by Gerson to his brother, the prior of the Celestines at Lyons, whose name is also Johann (Jean) de Gerson; 3) a poem alluded to by Gerson in the above letter; 4) Schott's "compendiosa laus" (#232) which serves as the introduction to the edition; 5) the table of contents of the three parts.

At the close of the edition, after Gerson's last work which is a tract on the "Song of Songs," there appear in order: 1) a statement by Gerson's brother that Gerson died a few days after completing the above-mentioned tract, his swan song; 2) a long epitaph to Gerson; 3) the epitaph from Gerson's sepulchre; 4) a letter by Gerson's brother, concerning Gerson's works; 5) a contemporary list of Gerson's works: "annotatio opusculorum Johannis cancellarij parisiensis quorum multa deperierunt: de multis incertum est si et ubi superfuit...;" 6) additions to the above list: "Subscribuntur per me iacobum de ceresio tituli quorundam opusculorum domini mei Johannis cancellarij parisiensis cum quibusdam opusculorum annotationibus pro domino oswalo de domo maioris carthusie vbi iam pars posita est... 1429;" 7) a letter written after Gerson's death by the archbishop of

Lyons, Amadeus de Talaru,* to Gerson's brother: "Venerabili patri fratri Johanni de gerson priori celestiorum lugdunensis in omnibus singularissimo;" the archbishop comforts the sorrowing brother and speaks words of high praise about chancellor Gerson.

After Schott's death, Wimpheling, while living at the monastery of the Strassburg Hermits of St. William (cf. Truttmann-Burg, 198, and N. 616), completed – probably at Geiler's instigation – the Schott-Geiler edition of Gerson's works by preparing for publication the fourth part. This along with the three parts, which Prüss had printed in 1488, and with an introduction by Wimpheling was published at Strassburg by Martin Flach, Jr., in 1501. According to the colophon at the end of the edition, the printing was finished on 1 March 1501: "Finit quarta pars operum Johannis gerson: que prius non fuere impressa: Iam verbo prodeunt feliciter ex officina Martini flacci iunioris Argen. exactissima Mathie Schürer Sletstatini consobrini eius opera kal. Martij anno 1501."

An edition of the fourth part, which was published by Mathias Schürer in collaboration with Flach: "quarta pars operum Johannis Gerson prius non impressa... III Cal. Martii anno 1502," is mentioned by Riegger (*Amoen.*, 74) and by Schmidt (*H. L.*, II, 332). This we have not seen.

From examination of various early editions of Gerson, the following facts emerge:

1) The 1488 edition of three parts printed by Prüss at Strassburg does not resemble a 1483 edition of Gerson's works by J. Koelhoff at Cologne. Some of the items are the same, but the organization is entirely different. This means that the Schott-Geiler collection of Gerson's works represents an independent effort. Schott himself observes (#232, p. 261) that the works in the edition were collected "non sine singulari labore" and Wimpheling in the introduction to the 1501 edition of four parts states that the texts in the fourth part are unpublished works collected in Paris and other places in France (cf. N. 135; Dacheux, *Réf.*, 337; Schmidt, *H. L.*, II, *Index bibliographique*, 374; Stöber, *Aberglauben*, 87).

2) The 1488 edition of three parts by Prüss was reproduced in subsequent editions (*contrafaçons*): a Basel edition of 1489 by Nicolaus Kessler, a Nürnberg edition of 1489 by Georg Stuchs, a Strassburg edition of 1494 by Martin Flach, Sr.,* all having exactly the same Gerson texts in exactly the same order, the same index, table of contents and Schott's "compendiosa laus."

3) The 1501 edition of four parts by Martin Flach, Jr. reproduced the first three parts directly or indirectly from the 1488 Prüss edition. Flach's 1501 edition in turn was reproduced by Johann Knoblouch at Strassburg in 1514 and by Johann Parvus and Franciscus Reynault at Paris in 1521.

137. Schott states that the De contemptu Mundi... not by Gerson
As noted in the Errata, the wording here should be: "Schott states that the *De contemptu Mundi* (i.e., *Imitatio Christi*) is not included among the works of Gerson*... He was thus one of the first..."

The question of who wrote the *Imitatio Christi* was long debated, some scholars claiming Gerson as the author, others Thomas à Kempis.* The edition of the *Imitatio Christi* by the Jesuits (Antwerp, 1664; p. 14) attributes the work to Thomas à Kempis and mentions among the five witnesses to his authorship Geiler, Trithemius and Schott. The passage concerning Schott reads: "Quinto Petrus Schottus Argentinensis Canonicus qui vixit tempore Thomae à Kempis in fine Vitae Joannis Gersonis... operibus ejus praefixae...," there follows a quotation of the lines from the *Luc.* (#232, p. 262) "Alij tractatus/ qui sibi... non sunt operibus suis inserti." The *Dictionnaire de théologie catholique* published 1920 states (VI, 1327) that Thomas à Kempis is now accepted as the author and gives bibliography for writings on the question. The *Encyclopedia Britannica* (XIV, 333f.) calls the "Contestation" over the author "probably the most considerable and famous controversy that has ever been carried on over a purely literary question," and concludes that Thomas à Kempis is the author.

In 1487 Martin Flach, Sr.,* published the four books of the *Imitatio Christi* under the name of Thomas à Kempis along with a short tract by Gerson; the title of the edition is: *Tractatus de imitatione Christi. Cum tractatulo de meditatione cordis.* On folio I is the notation: "Incipit liber primus fratris Thome de Kempis canonici regularis ordinis sancti Augustini. De imitatione Christi et de contemptu omnium vanitatum mundi." On folio LXXVII where the Gerson work of 18 chapters begins is the heading: "Tractatus de meditacione cordis magistri Johannis Gerson". It is very likely that Schott edited this edition. In 1489 the edition was reprinted: *De imitatione Christi... Item Joh. Gerson de meditatione cordis* (Argentina, 1489); no name of a printer is indicated.

Schmidt, *Bibliotheken*, 103, says that Adolph Rusch* printed an edition of the *Imitatio Christi*. We have not seen this. It is possible that it was the same as Flach's edition, or *vice versa*.

138. his edition of Thomas von Strassburg's commentary...
The edition was probably on the press as early as February 1490, for Schott in his letter of 21 March 1490 to Pallas Spangel* (#142) speaks of two *scripta* in the process of printing.

As we learn from volume two (cf. *infra*) of this very beautiful two-volume edition, entitled *Acutissimi Thome de Argentina scripta super quattuor libros sententiarum*, it was completed by the printer Martin Flach, Sr.,* on 9 August 1490. There is no mention of the editor.

At the beginning of the first volume is a letter from Pallas Spangel to Martin Flach, which congratulates Flach on the excellent and correct printing of the first two *scripta* and promises that other works of Thomas will be sent. The letter is without date, but it must have been written sometime after 21 March 1490 when the first two *scripta* were being printed (cf. Schott's letter mentioned above) and well before 9 August 1490 when the edition came off the press. (The text of the letter is to be found in Ritter, *Histoire*, 78.)

In the second volume, following book IIII, is the colophon of Martin Flach, Sr.; "Acutissimi materiarum theologicalium resolutoris Thome d'Argentina prioris generalis ordinis fratrum heremitorum sancti Augustini scripta super quattuor libros sententiarum per Martinum flach Argentine diligenti prehabita examinatione impressa finiunt. 1490." At the end of the volume, after the tract "Modus legendi abbreuiaturas in utroque iure...," is a passage giving the day and month when the printing was finished: "Finit liber plurimorum tractatuum iuris impressus argentinae Anno dni. M.CCCCXC. Finitus in vigilia Laurentij," i.e., on the eve of the feast of St. Lawrence, which is celebrated on 10 August.

Karl Hartfelder in his article on Spangel (*ADB*, XXXV, 32f.) attributes the editing of this edition to Spangel.

139. He seems to have worked closely with... Adolf Rusch... text Rusch wanted
In the letter to Rusch* (#130, p. 150), written 26 May 1489, Schott observes that he has been busy with the illustrations for the forthcoming edition of Vergil (cf. N. 134, and N. 1003). While at Bologna, he asked Rot* to deliver a message to Rusch about a book the latter wanted (#16, p. 25).

P. xxx   N. 140

140. Some later critics... Schmidt... early poems composed in Italy...
Cf. Schmidt, "Notices... P.S.", 343 and *H. L.*, II, 19, 27. Cf. also N. 381.
The early poems composed in Italy are: #236- #239, #243- #244, #266, #268- #289.

P.xxxi

141. encomium to Strassburg... three-part poem "De tribus Iohannibus"...
The encomium to Strassburg is #254; the "Carmen annale," #257; "De tribus Iohannibus," #241. The last mentioned poem was written at Geiler's request; Schott mentions its lack of classical allusions in the letters to Geiler and Gossenbrot (#240, #242). Cf. N. 12; N. 135, par. 3; N. 1576.

142. In the summer of 1490... plague in Strassburg... Schott died of plague...
Cf. N. 59, 3. The letter of 6 September 1490 to Goetz is #157.

143. three copies of his epitaph... Zorn chapel of that church
For the copies of Schott's epitaph, cf. N. 57.
When the Zorn chapel was restored (cf. N. 117, par. 3), a simple stone with a German inscription to replace Schott's lost epitaph was put on the wall to the left as one enters the chapel from the street. Horning (*Stift*, 5) mentions the new epitaph as having been put in the chapel in 1591, an obvious misprint for 1891, because he also states that the original disappeared after the French Revolution. The new epitaph reads:

>   Peter Schott
>   Dem hochgelehrten
>   Stiftsherrn
>   Von Jung St. Peter
>   Dem frommen Sohn
>   des Ammeisters Schott
>   Dem Freunde Geilers
>   von Kaisersberg
>   †1490 im 32. Lebensalter.

It will be noted that the age is given as 32 years (cf. N. 58).

144. Schott's friends... mourned his early death... (to end of paragraph)
Bohuslaus von Hassenstein wrote to Geiler shortly after his return from his odyssey in August 1491 and expressed his grief over the news of Schott's death (#292). A year later, in a letter of 11 September 1492 to Geiler, Hassenstein says his grief for Schott is unabated (#293, p. 313), and in a letter of 16 March 1507 he writes Geiler that the memory of Schott's friendship is and will always be with him, and that it comforts him in adversity (Potuček, 119; cf. copy in Appendix J of this volume).
    In a letter of 4 September 1499 to Johann Sslechta, Hassenstein writes in tribute to Schott:
    "Quod ad Petrum Schottum, cuius in litteris tuis meministi, attinet, scito magnum virum fuisse: peritissimum divine humaneque iuris, neque a studiis mansuetioribus abhorruisse: fide autem innocentiaque tanta, ut nequaquam nostro seculo natum diceres. Is me Bononiae adolescentulum adolescens unice ipse et diligebat et observabat, carminaque saepenumero ad me scribebat, et nostra vicissim accipiebat: deinde cum uterque nostrum

P. xxxi   N. 144

ad suos rediisset, frequens inter nos commercium literarum fuit, magis tamen earum, quae nostrum mutuum amore testarentur, quam quae eloquenciam prae se ferrent." (Potuček, 54f.). Sslechta's reference to Schott mentioned in the above passage may have been prompted by the first edition of the *Lucubraciunculae* which had appeared in 1498.

Among the last items of the *Lucubraciunculae* are statements about Schott's untimely death by Leontarius* (#291), Simmler* (#294), Gallus* (#295) and Wimpheling (#301, p. 322).

One may imagine the grief of the Schott family and especially of the parents at the loss of the only son to whom they had been so close and to whom they had looked for comfort in their advancing years. The family – probably Schott, Sr. – gave money to New St. Peter for celebrating an *anniversarium* (anniversary mass) in honor of his son. Originally such a ceremony was to be held on the anniversary of a loved one's death, but because there were at times conflicts with major feasts or previous commitments, the chapter was allowed to chose another date. Some chapters held the *anniversarium* within a month of the date of death, others within 11 months. In the case of New St. Peter there seems to have been no specified period, and ceremonies were held on the same date for several members of a family. Cf. Stein, 102; Wetzer-Welte, I, 867f.

Following are the texts of three *anniversaria* (from Straub, 81, 83), the first for Schott and his parents; the second for Schott, Sr., his wife Susanna, his son Peter and his own parents; the third for the parents of Schott, Sr., Schott, Sr., himself and his wife.

1) "Anniversarium Dni Petri Schotti V.J.D. Confratris nostri ad div. Petrum Juniorem, et progenitorum ipsius celebratur ad divum Petrum Juniorem Argentinae 3 Idus Junij id est 11 Junii."

2) "1504 8. Aug. Obijt Dnus Petrus Schott olim magister Scabinorum Argentinae, Anniversarium Dni Petri magistri Scabinorum, Susannae eius uxoris, Petri Schotti J. V. Doctoris eorum filii confratris nostri ad Divum Petrum Juniorem, viventium nunc et progenitorum ipsius celebr. ad Divum Petrum Jun. Argentinae 3 Idus Junij." (11 June)

3) "Anniversarium Dni Jacobi Schotten et Ottiliae eius uxoris, nec non Petri filii et vxoris eiusdem celebratur 8 Calendarum maij ad Div. Petr. Jun. Arg." (24 April)

The text of the *anniversarium* for Schott is also in Horning, *Festschrift*, 39, n. 2.

P. 9   #1   N. 145

LUCUBRACIUNCULAE

P. 9

#1. INTRODUCTION BY JACOB WIMPHELING Soultz, 27 July 1498

145. Summary Peter Schott of Strassburg devoted himself from an early age to liberal arts and sciences. He learned the rudiments of grammar and dialectic in Schlettstadt under Ludwig Dringenberg. He then studied philosophy and the theories of Duns Scotus in France; and finally in Italy he learned oratory, poetics, history, cosmography, Greek and both civil and canon law. His like would be hard to find in our century, although in former times Germany produced many great scholars.
   Schott's life was decorous and blameless. Of an equable disposition, unassuming and temperate, he was kind to all, devoted to his parents and devout toward God. He wrote elegant poems which are free from all frivolity, and in his letters he vied in style with Cicero. He shared his knowledge with all who sought information from him. The reader will profit from a perusal of his works.

146. Primum enim in patria nostra... in Galijs... apud Italos... optime didicit.
For the school at Schlettstadt, cf. N. 88; for the universities of Paris, Bologna and Ferrara, cf. N. 93, N. 97. For the dates of Schott's study at the several schools, cf. pp. xxivf., N. 92, N. 95, N. 96.

147. Quamuis Rhabanum olim sortita sit Germania... tum profundos.
The Hrabanus referred to may be either Hrabanus Maurus,* one of whose poems was published by Wimpheling in 1503, or Hrabanus,* bishop of Spires, who is mentioned in #80. The other scholars named are in order: Heinric Boyck,* Johann Teutonicus,* Albertus Magnus,* Thomas von Strassburg,* Udalricus Argentinensis.*

148. Fuit eciam in Petro... innocentissima vita... (to end of paragraph)
In his tribute to Schott (cf. N. 144, par. 3), Bohuslaus von Hassenstein* speaks of Schott's *innocentia*. In fact, much of Wimpheling's introduction is reminiscent of Hassenstein's oration (#297, pp. 315ff.; cf. N. 1751).

149. neque inflauit Senatoria Patris dignitas
For the importance of Schott, Sr., to Strassburg, cf. p. xxiii and the biographical note on him.

150. Prebendas ecclesiasticas cumulare... vnam... sibi sufficere aiebat...
For the practice of plurality of benefices, cf. N. 130,5; N. 133. Schott twice states that he wanted no more than one benefice (#73, p. 80; #74, p. 82).

P. 9 #1 N. 151

151. ecclesie/cuius erat Canonicus
Schott was canon of New St. Peter, cf. p. xxvii, N. 116 and N. 117.

P. 10

152. Ex pago Sulce prope Mollisheym
Dacheux (*Réf.*, 430) gives the modern name of the town as Soultz-les-Bains. Jacob Wimpheling's uncle, Ulrich Wimpheling, with whom Jacob lived after his father died, was priest at Soultz.

#2. EPITAPH FOR PETER SCHOTT BY JACOB WIMPHELING [after 12 September 1490]

153. Summary Death has snatched away Peter Schott who was an ornament to our fatherland. Strassburg gave him life, Schlettstadt the first rudiments of grammar, France logic. In Italy he learned civil and canon law. Cicero, Quintilian and Livy were well known to him, as was the Greek language. From his tender years he was exemplary in behavior and character.

154. Argentina sibi vitam... Italia terra docet.
Cf. N. 146.

155. priora (line 3)
This word is very carefully printed by hand at the end of line 3 in the copy of the *Lucubraciunculae* belonging to the Newberry Library. It does not appear in other copies we have seen, and spoils the hexameter by adding an extra measure.

156. Historiae Vates (line 8)
The reference seems to be to Livy, in whose works Schott was interested (cf. #183).

#3. DISTICH BY JACOB WIMPHELING [after 12 September 1490]

157. Summary (translation) A crow lives so many ages, so many ages a stag. Schott died before his day; our fatherland sorrows.

P. 11

158. Saecula tot cornix... ceruus
Wimpheling may be referring to an ancient tradition which has come down to us in a Hesiod fragment preserved by Plutarch "De oraculum defectu:" a crow lives 9 generations of man, a stag attains the age of 4 crows, a raven the age of 3 stags, a phoenix the age of 9 ravens. Cf. Anthon, 1054.

#4. DISTICH BY JACOB WIMPHELING [after 12 September 1490]

159. Summary (translation) You who pass the tomb of Peter Schott, say at least, "May your rest be sweet, Peter."

#5. ITEM ON PETER SCHOTT FROM JOHANN TRITHEMIUS, DE ECCLESIASTICIS... (1494)

160. Summary Peter Schott of Strassburg, canon of St. Peter in that city, was well versed in divine Scriptures, in both civil and canon law and in the humanities. He was a renowned philosopher, rhetorician and poet, excelling in genius and outstanding in life and conduct. His chaste and polished works commend him to posterity: a charming poem in elegiac verse on Saints John the Baptist, the Evangelist, and Chrysostom;*a eulogy to Johann Gerson;* letters and poems in various metres. He died at Strassburg and was buried in the church of St. Peter, during the reign of Friedrich III and the papacy of Innocent VIII, in the year 1490, in the ninth indiction, in the thirty-first year of his life.

161. This item is taken from Trithemius, *Liber*, f. CXXVIb. The only deviations from the original (other than orthographical) are: a) omission of *li.i*, i.e., one book, in three places, *viz.*, after *carmine elegiaco, gerson, epistulas elegantissimas*; and b) the date of Schott's death as 1490, which was corrected from 1491 by Martin Schott,* Geiler, Wimpheling, or perhaps one of Schott's immediate family.

For comparison, Trithemius' item from *Cathalogus*, f. LVb, is quoted below:

> Petrus Schot argentinensis presbyter et canonicus sancti petri in argentina: vir in diuinis scripturis exercitatum habens ingenium: in utroque iure doctissimus: atque in ceteris humanitatis artibus valde eruditus: philosophus rhetor. et poeta celeberrimus: ingenio excellens: vita et conuersatione maturus. honestus. et praeclarus. Scripsit tam metro quam prosa quedam pulchra opuscula: quibus memoriam sui posteris commendauit. De sanctis iohanne baptista: euangelista: et chrysostomo: scripsit instructum et delectabile opus carmine elegiaco li. i. Diuersorum carminum li. i. Epistularum ad diuersos li. i. Andree apostoli laudes carmen breue. Laudes iohannis de gerson ante primam eius operum partem impressas. Alia quoque nonnulla edidit: que ad noticiam meam non venerunt. Moritur sub frederico imperatori tercio. Anno domini Mill. CCCC.XCI. Indictione IX. Etatis sue anno XXXI. Argentine in ecclesia sua sancti petri sepultus: cuius vitam mores et ingenium iacobus vimphelingus descripsit.

It will be noted that the item quoted above from the *Cathalogus* contains information not in the item from the *Liber*, *viz.*, a poem to Apostle Andrew; the edition of Gerson's works and other editions not seen by Trithemius; Wimpheling's note on Schott. Cf. N. 29, par. 3.

Since Trithemius was the first writer of his age to publish biographical dictionaries, it seems to have become customary to excerpt his biographical items for editions of an author's works; Mitis has Trithemius' item on Bohuslaus von Hassenstein at the beginning of *Bohuslai... Lucubrationes*. Later writers of biographical dictionaries repeated Trithemius' information; e.g., Cave, Eysengrein, Fabricius, Gesner, Moréri, Pantaleon.

162. Canonicus sancti Petri ibidem
Schott was canon of New. St. Peter (cf. p. xxvii and N. 116).

163. De sanctis Iohanne Baptista... Laudes Iohannis Gerson
Cf. N. 135, par. 3.

P. 11   #5   N. 164

164. Moritur... Anno domini M.CCCC Nonagesimo. Indicione nona.
That is, Schott died 1490 in the ninth indiction. The indiction is said to have been instituted by Diocletian or by Constantine as a fiscal period of 15 years at the commencement of which property taxes were reassessed. In the Middle Ages the use of the indiction was continued as a 15 year cycle of time calculation. It was reckoned by formulae, one of which is:

> Si tribus adjunctis Domini diviseris annos
> Ter tibi per quinos, indictio certa patebit.

According to the formula: "if to the year of our Lord one adds 3 and divides the sum by 15, the remainder will be the year of the indiction." When the remainder is zero, the indiction year is the last or fifteenth in the cycle.

As already mentioned (N. 161), the date of Schott's death which was given as 1491 in the original Trithemius' item was corrected to 1490 when the item was excerpted for the *Lucubraciunculae*. The indiction year, however, remained unchanged. Applying the formula, we find that the ninth indiction is 1491, while 1490 would fall in the eighth indiction. Now Wencker's second passage on Schott (quoted N. 59, 3, par. 2) – like the Trithemius item (#1) – gives Schott's date of death as 1490 in the ninth indiction. Do we then assume that the person or persons correcting the date in the *Lucubraciunculae* erred in not changing the year of the indiction and that Wencker, not familiar with the indiction, copied an earlier error? Or do we assume that the indiction year in Strassburg was different from that used by Trithemius? There were, in fact, 3 indiction years, each beginning at a different time: the Greek indiction, used in some parts of western Europe, began 1 September; the imperial or Caesarian began 24 September; the Roman or pontifical began 25 December or 1 January. If the Strassburgers used either the Greek or pontifical indiction, the date of Schott's death, 12 September 1490, would be in the ninth indiction; and if Trithemius reckoned according to the imperial indiction, 12 September 1491 would also be in the ninth indiction.

165. Consummatus... ne malicia mutaret intellectum eius.
Cf. Sap. 4:11, 13. Trithemius also paraphrases these passages from *Liber Sapientiae* in his account of Albrecht Ernst von Sachsen who in 1482 at the age of 18 became archbishop of Mainz and died 2 years later: "et ne malitia temporum, ut fieri solet, intellectum eius depravaret, sublatus est" (*Ann. Hirs.*, II, 514).

P. 12

#6. TO PETER SCHOTT, SR. Bologna, 1 April 1478

166. Summary On the Saturday after Easter, the courier Laurentius Grave called in Bologna on his way to Rome, but said nothing of his errand except that it concerned Schott, Sr. He promised that the merchant Laurentius Hertzog would come to Bologna soon. The latter's arrival is being eagerly awaited by both Schott and his "magister" Johann Müller*, because they hope he will bring an answer to the letter Schott dispatched to his father via Jacob Dedinger.*

167. The only letters to Schott, Sr., are #6-#8. Chronologically #8 (undated) is the first. In both #6 and #7 Schott mentions that he and Müller

P. 12   #6   N. 167

are expecting the answer of Schott, Sr., to a letter, the contents of which – alluded to in #7 – tally with those of #8.

168. Si vos et vestri valetis...
To his father, Schott uses the formal form of address, the second person plural. For Schott's views on the formal form, cf. #9, p. 15, and N. 184.

169. Fuit apud nos die Sabbati post Pascha... Laurencius Graue tabellarius
In 1478 the Saturday after Easter was 28 March. Until the Reformation the term "Sabbath" meant the seventh day of the week; only thereafter was the term applied also to the first day of the week, Sunday.

We have found information in no other sources on the courier Laurentius Grave. He is most likely the "other" Laurentius of #29, p. 37, and may be the courier mentioned #15, p. 24; #39, p. 46.

170. in negocijs vestris
The business Grave was to transact in Rome may have been the confirmation of Geiler's appointment as cathedral preacher in Strassburg (cf. N. 955, par. 6).

171. Laurencium Hertçog mercatorem... ut consilium vestrum intelligam...
The merchant Laurentius Hertzog seems to have travelled between Strassburg and Rome. He frequently carried letters from Schott to Maeler and is mentioned in #24, p. 32; #25, pp. 33, 34; #26, p. 34; #29, p. 37. We have found no other information about him.

Hertzog was presumably to bring a letter from Schott, Sr., in answer to Schott's letter of sometime in March (#8). Both Schott and Müller were anxious to know the father's decision about the son's stay in Italy (cf. N. 176).

172. dominus Ioannes Sartoris
Johann Sartoris may be identical with Johann Laudenburg* of #143.

#7. TO PETER SCHOTT, SR.   Bologna, 2 May 1478

173. Summary The money sent by Schott, Sr., via Johann Meyger* has been gratefully received. Both Schott and Müller are awaiting the answer to their letter as Penelope awaited Ulysses. Müller in particular will not rest easily until they know the father's decision. (Cf. N. 167).

174. honorandum mihi Magistrum... de nobis sedeat
Aside from his concern for his pupil's career, Müller needed for his own sake to know the decision of Schott, Sr. As tutor, his plans depended on those of Schott. Should Schott return to Strassburg, Müller would have to make arrangements for his own future.

P. 13   #7   N. 175

175. Viuam enim vocem quam mortuam... energie
Cf. Hieronymus, *Ep.*, 53. 2 (Migne XXI, 541).

#8. TO PETER SCHOTT, SR. [Bologna, before April 1478]

176. Summary Persuaded by Müller to inform Schott, Sr., about his own sentiments concerning further study in Italy, Schott explains that there are three courses open: a) to return, as his father seems to expect, to Strassburg in September with a degree; b) to visit Strassburg before completing his studies and come back to Italy for further work; c) to remain in Bologna for a longer period until he is mature enough and fully prepared to take the doctorate in both civil and canon law, then return home when the work is completed.
    The first course Schott considers inadvisable. He has understood all along that his father wished him to become doctor of both laws; to cover the field of civil law alone takes five years of study, and he has as yet had very little time to devote to the intricacies of canon law. Moreover he feels he is still too young and underdeveloped for his years to be taking a doctorate. The second course is possible, but he himself prefers the third as best for his work and for development in body and mind. (For date, cf. N. 167.)

177. prouectiorem etatem... defuerit
This passage and the passage in the next paragraph of the text: "Plane et iuuenis sum et pro etate graciliori..." (p. 14) are the only references in the *Lucubraciunculae* to Schott's age, for which cf. N. 59, par. 4.
    Schott's lack of physical robustness is implied in the phrase "pro etate graciliori" just quoted; for further discussion on the subject, cf. N. 87, par. 2.

P. 14

178. legalissimus ille Imperator Iustinianus
That is, the pandects of Justinian which with the glosses and commentaries were the texts for civil law.

179. ut eam quam terciam viam proposueram complecti velitis
This third course was the one Schott, Sr., allowed his son to follow; in the letter of 15 September 1478 to Rot (#9, p. 17) Schott says he has received parental permission to remain longer in Italy.

180. quia hactenus aeris temperiem et habuimus... speramus
Schott is reassuring his over-solicitous parents that the Italian climate has not been unhealthy for him or Müller; in both #6 and #7 he mentions their well-being. For the many references to the parents' solicitude, cf. N. 87. Bohuslaus von Hassenstein observes that Schott was never ill in Italy (#297, p. 320).

181. Auunculamque Nostram
The maternal aunt may be Margrede von Cöllen whose picture was placed

P. 14   #8   N. 181

beside that of Susanna von Cöllen in the church of St. Nicholas in Undis (cf. biographical note on Schott, Sr.).

The original has "Auunculamque N." The N. according to Traube, 206ff., always indicates a form of *noster*; according to Capelli, it has a multitude of meanings; and according to Du Cange, it is used in place of a proper noun, as our X. Ten of the eleven occurrences of N in the *Lucubraciunculae* were resolved as some form of *noster*: viz., #159, p. 174; #160, pp. 174f.; #197, p. 213; #189-#193; #219, p. 242. Cf. N. 1147, N. 1150, N. 1151.

P. 15

#9. TO JOHANN ROT Bologna, 15 September 1478

182. Summary Schott is writing during the recess between semesters. He explains that his letter of six months ago has not reached Rot,* because – under the impression Rot had left Strassburg for Paris – he had sent it to Paris. He comments on the absurdity of the formal form of address, which contrary to logic and historical usage treats one individual as though he were many. He reminisces about professors and courses with Rot at Paris five years previously and observes that a thorough grounding in arts is necessary for advanced studies. He had hoped that Rot, on receiving the master's degree, would also study law. His parents have extended his time of study for the doctorate. There is war in Italy and plague in Bologna.

183. Sex ampliusve menses acti sunt... facturum te mihi significaueras...
Rot had apparently left Paris for Strassburg early in 1478 and had not returned to Paris as he had intended; in the letter of 26 December 1477 to Gesler* at Paris, Schott sends greetings to Rot (#235). Whether Rot spent any time at the university of Paris from late 1477 to June 1480 when he became curate at Dambach (#16, p. 24) is not known.

The holiday between academic years at Bologna was from mid-August to beginning November.

184. vnicum videlicet hominem pluratiuo numero... duplicatis nomine appellare?
Despite his aversion to the formal form of address, Schott uses it in addressing his father and exalted persons like kings, popes, cardinals and papal nuncios. To others he uses the second person singular. He remarks that Hassenstein addresses even the king of Bohemia familiarly (#171, p. 192; cf. Potuček, 23f., 42ff.). In two letters of 1482 to papal nuncio Kemel *(#32, #186) he uses the formal form of address, but in the letter of a later date (#187) he uses the familiar form, indicating that in the interim he has become better acquainted with Kemel. It is rather curious to find the venerable suffragan bishop Ortwin* and the Augustinian provincial Friesenheimer* addressing Schott with *vos*, while the much younger Schott addresses them as *tu* (#164-#166, #208, #209). In a letter to Maeler* there is a shift from the familiar form in the letter to the formal form in the postscript (#29, p. 37). The editorial "we" appears in #40, p. 46 *(nostre)*, #139, p. 155, and #265, p. 298.

That the humanists' deviation from accepted usage was daring is illustrated by the sharp criticism directed against a versifier of the time who had the temerity to write: "Unum vosamus falso, vereque tuamus." Cf. Schmidt, "Notices... P.S.," 342.

P. 16   #9   N. 185

P. 16

185. de quorundam praeceptorum mihi plurimum... venerabilium...
One of Schott's professors at Paris was Johann Scriptor von Kaysersberg*
(#58); another may have been Johann Heynlin a Lapide,* who is mentioned
in a letter to Müller (#63, p. 69).

186. Nonnumquam tortuosis dialetice nodis certantes... reducendis intenti...
Cf. Hassenstein's words about Schott's aptitude in solving the knottiest
problems of dialectic, #297, p. 316.

187. vel ipse Carneades homo portentuosa memoria
Carneades, distinguished philosopher of Cyrene and pupil of the Stoic
Diogenes, founded the New Academy at Athens. He was noted for his
prodigious memory and his powers of reasoning. On one occasion he was
ordered by Cato the Elder to leave Rome, because his two speeches, one in
favor of justice and one against it, had excited Roman youth in philosophical
speculation.

P. 17

188. meum sit: Parentum meorum voluntatem audire...
As he had requested in his letter to Schott, Sr., Schott was allowed to remain
in Italy for an extended period of time to finish his doctorate in both laws
(cf. #8 and N. 176). Unfortunately, fate in the shape of plague forced him
to interrupt his study and return to Strassburg a short time after this letter
was written.

189. De rebus bellicis quae Italiam fere totam commouerunt
In 1478 Italy was torn by civil and foreign wars. As a result of the vicious
conspiracy of Hieronymus de Im(m)ola* (Girolamo Riario; N. 940, N. 1147)
and the Pazzi to murder the Medicis, Sixtus IV was at war with Florence, as were
Naples and Siena. France was at war with Milan. Cf. Raynaldus, 1478, par. 1.

190. qui iterum ob pestis metum: nullorum aduenarum... aduentu
The plague which had virtually isolated Bologna must have worsened, for
shortly after this letter was written (15 September) Schott and Müller
departed the city and made for home, reaching Strassburg in time for Schott
to go to the baths (#10, p. 17). They obviously planned only a short visit in
Strassburg and an early return to Bologna, at least in time for the beginning
of the winter semester in November. Otherwise Müller would certainly not
have left behind his precious books and his long shirt (#173), items indispensable to a serious and impecunious scholar.
   While at home, however, something happened to make Müller's return
to Italy uncertain. Perhaps Schott, Sr., doubted his son's further need of a
tutor, or perhaps Müller was already being considered by his prince, *Markgraf*
Christoph I of Baden,* as candidate for the post of canon and dean at Baden-
Baden and as tutor to the heir apparent, Jacob,* then about seven years of
age (N. 211). Writing at Strassburg in late 1478 to Scriptor, Schott says he
is about to depart for Italy, but "we" are not sure whether Müller will be
going along (#178, p. 199); and writing a little later on 12 December 1478

at Strassburg to Brant,* Schott mentions the prospect of seeing Brant and other friends in Basel soon on his way through to Italy, but makes no mention of Müller's accompanying him (#10, p. 18).

When – after exasperating delays – Schott did return without Müller to Italy in the fall of 1479 to complete his doctorate (N. 201), one of his first tasks was to ship Müller's books and shirt (#173, and N. 1232).

#10. TO SEBASTIAN BRANT Strassburg, 12 December 1478

191. Summary A sojourn at the baths has delayed Schott's answer to Brant's welcome letter; however, Schott did not need Brant's admonition to cherish their friendship begun in childhood, because he prizes the love of those who, like Brant, further the "humaniora". He has great admiration for Johann Reuchlin* and wishes he might study Greek under him. He would have written his reply to Reuchlin's letter in Greek, had he not feared making blunders. Brant is to convey greetings to Reuchlin and others in Basel. Schott hopes to pass through Basel shortly on his return to Italy.

192. ego voluptatis balnearis gracia absens
1. The modern Europeans, north of the Alps, who crowd the numerous spas for the 21-day course of treatments for rheumatism, bronchial ailments, stomach disorders and so on, are following a tradition going back to prehistoric times when the tribes sought out the hot, cold, sulphur or other mineral waters. The Romans, too, took great interest in the curative springs, as the many remains of their bath installations testify. Enthusiasm for spas did not wane in the Middle Ages. Charlemagne built his palace-fortress and his beautiful chapel at Aachen on the slope above the hottest mineral waters in central Europe, reputedly his favorite spring.

During the late Middle Ages, almost everyone took his annual cure at a spa. Even criminals, excluding murderers or highwaymen, were granted sanctuary while undergoing the regimen of the baths. Thomas Murner's humorous satire *Badenfahrt* gives a vivid contemporary description of the various types of baths, the prescribed regimen and the rigorous, often painful procedures for stimulating circulation. In the *Lucubraciunculae* 24 items mention baths.

According to the old bath calendars which took careful cognizance of the phases and conjunctions of the moon, the times propitious for baths were those when the moon was waning and when it was in conjunction with the Ram, Scorpion, Cancer or Pisces; the times unpropitious were those when the moon was full or when it was in conjunction with the hot signs – Leo, Gemini, Capricorn and Virgo (cf. N. 275). In England the best months for baths were April and May; the second best were August and September. On the upper Rhine the best month was July, often called bath month (*Bademonat, mois des bains*).

2. The period for a stay at a spa was three weeks to a month, and once the regimen was begun, it could not be interrupted without possible ill effects; for example, Johann Müller* who had just started treatment could not leave even though his presence in Strassburg was almost mandatory to effect possession of the long desired canonicate. Johann Simmler,* who was apparently near the end of his treatment, returned at considerable risk to himself in order to support Müller's candidacy (#153, p. 167; #155, pp. 169f.). The strenuous regimen could be fatal, as it was in the case of Adolf Rusch* who died of an infection contracted at Baden-Baden (#130, p. 151).

The bath regimen was under medical supervision, and noted physicians

P. 17   #10   N. 192

like Johann Widmann* wrote treatises on the relative curative powers of well known springs for different ailments. In addition to the many kinds of natural waters (*thermae ferales*), there were available artificial baths of every sort: hot baths, cold baths, steam baths, herb baths, oil baths, even lye baths. These were accompanied by brisk rubbing, scraping, switching and pummeling of the body to induce perspiration. Blood-letting and internal purging were prescribed, which in conjunction with profuse perspiration drew off humors. Diet was restricted and forbade newly laid eggs and spiced or heavy foods, such as rich pastries, rich meat and fowl.

To uphold the morale of those subjected to the regimen, it was customary, Schott tells us (#240, p. 273), to send them gifts; one also entertained them on their return home. Gifts of books, jokes, poems were sent; gifts of food had to be in keeping with the diet prescribed for the particular patient. Amusements, such as dinner parties, story telling, gaming, reading, helped while away the time. There were even bath songs; one of these begins:

Aussen Wasser, innen Wein,
Lasst uns alle fröhlich sein.

3. Strassburgers frequented Baden-Baden, fashionable then as now, about 35 miles from Strassburg. The Romans had called this spa *Aurelia Aquensis* and had built luxurious bath houses to utilize the hot waters flowing from the 29 springs. These waters are good for the treatment of rheumatism, gout, paralysis, neuralgia, skin diseases and internal complaints like kidney stones and uric acid.

A favorite spa of the Schotts was Wildbad, a natural warm spring, in Württemberg on the banks of the rushing Entz, at a point where the river has cut a narrow gorge between towering hills. The hills are mentioned by Schott (#13). The popularity of Wildbad may be judged by the fact that when the village burned in 1525, most of the 23 buildings destroyed were hostels. The curative properties of the spa's warm waters, which contain considerable sulphur, mineral salts and sodium, were described by Johann Widmann* and other physicians, and were recommended for people suffering from kidney and liver ailments, stomach and bowel troubles, cramps, gout, etc. Cf. N. 706.

Johann Müller seems to have preferred the popular baths at Zellerbad on the Neckar, near Tübingen. Zellerbad, like Wildbad, is said to have been first improved by the Romans. Its waters contained alum, copper and some sulphur.

The waters most favored by Friedrich von Zollern* were those in the gorge of the Tamina in Switzerland, where bathers were let down by ropes into the warm water and often stayed in – eating and drinking – for eleven hours.

Cf. Bäumer, *passim*; Bonatti, 453, 587. Dreher, XIX, 75. Fricker, 389-429. Grandidier, *Oeuvr. hist.*, V, 64. Hatt, *Ville*, 348. James, *Baths*, 123ff., 142-144. Martin, *Badewesen*, 70-83, 144-195. Thorndike, I, 738. Zeiller, 91, 95, 155, 373, 420f., 674f.

References to baths in the *Lucubraciunculae*: #20, p. 29; #21, p. 30; #22, p. 31; #25, p. 33; #34, p. 41; #44, p. 49; #45, p. 50; #57, p. 62; #67, p. 75; #88, p. 96; #104, pp. 113f.; #117, pp. 136f.; #119, p. 138; #129, p. 149; #130, pp. 149ff.; #131, p. 151; #132, pp. 151ff.; #133, p. 152; #135, p. 153; #151, p. 165; #153, p. 167; #155, pp. 169ff.; #156, p. 172; #240, p. 273.

References to bath gifts: #21, p. 30; #67, p. 74; #45, p. 50; #117, p. 137; #119, p. 138; #130, p. 150; #155, p. 169; #240, pp. 273f.

P. 17   #10   N. 193

193. abineunte etate...
Cicero *De Oratore* i. 21. 97. The phrase appears also in #221, p. 247; #232, p. 260. Brant and Schott were both Strassburgers, of about the same age; they were at Schlettstadt together. Cf. N. 90.

P. 18

194. Nil ego contulerim iucundo sanus amico.
Horace *Sat.* i. 5. 40ff.

195. Isocrates scribit...
Cf. N. 23. The passage from Isocrates *Demonicus* 2, seems to fit the length of the lacuna and the context: "Not all eternity can blot out the friendship of good men." (G. Norlin, *Isocrates with an English Translation* [London, 1928], I, 4).

196. Quod ad litteras Magistri Johannis Reuchlin... pertinet...
Schott is evidently alluding to a statement made by Brant. The fact that he discusses Reuchlin and sends greetings to Reuchlin via Brant: "Ei me plurimum commendes velim," indicates that Reuchlin must have been in Basel in late 1478. Yet Geiger (*Reuchlin*, 18ff.) asserts that Reuchlin went to the law school at Orléans at the beginning of 1478, took his bachelor of law there in 1479 and did not return to Germany until 1481.

The exact time when Schott and Reuchlin became acquainted is uncertain. They probably knew one another at Paris, for Reuchlin with his princeling *Markgraf* Karl von Baden* seems to have arrived in Paris in early 1473; he was already at the university when Louis XI issued his ultimatum against Nominalism on 1 March 1473 (Geiger, *op. cit.*, 9f.); and Schott did not leave until late 1473. They did not meet in Italy, because Reuchlin's first trip to Italy was in 1482; by that time Schott was at home in Strassburg. Cf. N. 1731.

197. Legi etenim in Hesiodo hanc sentenciam...
Cf. N. 23. The lacuna is 1 1/2 lines long (cf. plate 2, p. 19). The following passage from Hesiod *Theogony* 84f., would fit space and context: "All the people look towards him while he settles causes with true judgments." (Translation from H. G. Evelyn-White, *Hesiod, the Homeric Hymns and Homerica* [London, New York, 1914], 85).

198. ego vero ipso praeceptore... vel famulatu contenderem...
Schott is being facetious, for the son of a wealthy patrician would scarcely assume the duties of a *famulus*; his admiration for Reuchlin and his interest in Greek were, however, genuine.

199. propediem vos coram videbo: vel Bononiam: vel Patauium petiturus
Having been at home since early fall, Schott was planning to return to Italy in December of 1478. Basel was on the direct route from Strassburg to Italy, and he would have an opportunity of seeing Brant and other friends.

If the plague had not abated in Bologna, Schott apparently meant to stop at Padua. The legal school at Padua, celebrated from the eleventh

427

P. 18   #10   N. 199

century, had at the end of the thirteenth century incorporated other faculties and become a flourishing university. In the number of foreign students attracted to its courses, particularly in civil law, Padua was rivalled only by Pavia. The University of Pavia, founded in 1374, traced its beginnings to a ninth-century law school and enjoyed during the fifteenth century an especially brilliant period.

#11. TO JOHANN GEILER VON KAYSERSBERG Bologna, [November or December] 1479

200. *Summary* Schott is grateful for the precepts sent by Geiler, which demonstrate Geiler's interest in the salvation and happiness not only of all mankind, but in particular of Schott. He will obey Geiler's admonitions to avoid vices which swarm about him like bees, to cultivate love – without which all things are nothing – and to set forth on the path of virtue.

201. *Date.* This is the first of Schott's letters to Geiler. It was written at Bologna on the same day, says Schott, when he received Geiler's letter with the precepts, but he does not indicate the day or month; at the close of the letter he gives only the year 1479. Item #10 (preceding this letter) was written from Strassburg 12 December 1478, and in that item Schott tells Brant he hopes he will see him and other friends in Basel very shortly on his way to Italy. Item #12 (following this letter) was written also from Strassburg 17 April 1479; in that item Schott tells Maeler his parents are talking about delaying his return to Italy until the beginning of the new academic year, i.e., November 1479.

The placement of this letter, #11, from Bologna between two letters from Strassburg gives the impression that Schott returned to Bologna sometime after 12 December 1478 and came home again before 17 April 1479. Was this actually the case? Was the plague still raging in Bologna or was there a new outbreak? Was Schott called home because of illness in the family? Or is the order of items in the *Lucubraciunculae*, as in other instances, incorrect?

The probability is that Schott's departure in December was postponed, that his departure was still being postponed in April 1479, that he did not return to Italy until the beginning of the academic year in November 1479, that item #11 was written in November or December 1479 and that the order in the incunabulum is incorrect. Dacheux (*Réf.*, 287) assumes that Schott's second trip to Italy was delayed until the end of 1479.

202. *Que ad me praecepta misisti...*
The precepts which Geiler sent to Schott may have resembled the *Monita* he wrote for Friedrich von Zollern, for which see Appendix H.

P. 20

203. *Apes mihi nescio quas commemoras...*
Bees seem to have been a common symbol for vices, cf. the title of John Mandeville's book, *The Fable of the Bees or private Vices, Publick Benefits* (London, 1714).

204. *charitatem ut habeam. Sine illa... nihil haec omnia.*
Cf. I Cor. 13.

205. quam leui momento/uili delectaciuncula commutamus
Cf. Gn. 25: 27-34.

206. in dextrum elementi Samij ramum
The reference is to the Samian letter, "littera Pythagorae Y ('γφιλόν),"
with which Pythagoras is said to have been the first to compare the forks
in the path of life, the right fork being the way of virtue, the left being the
way of vice.
   Cf. Ausonius *Edyll* 12, "De litteris monosyllabis Graecis ac Latinis."
K. E. Georges, *Ausführliches Handwörterbuch*, II, (Hannover, Leipzig, 1918),
2108. Lactantius 6.3.6. Epigram attributed to Vergil, "Littera Pythagorae
discrimine secta bicorni Humanae vitae speciem praeferre videtur...,"
Caecilii Lactantii Firmiani opera omnia..., ed. C. M. Pfaffius (Leipzig,
1739), 708. Riegger, *Amoen.*, 119. Persius 3. 56.
   Johann Rot* had a mural representing the two ways in the form of a Y
painted in the St. Laurentius chapel of the Strassburg cathedral (cf. #143,
p. 158; N. 1049 and N. 1052).

207. Hic enim non secus atque cautes Marpesia
Marpessa is a mountain on Paros, where the celebrated Parian marble was
quarried. Cf. Vergil *Aen.*vi.471.

#12. TO VITUS MAELER Strassburg, 17 April 1479

208. Summary Schott has little news and no letters from Maeler to answer.
Johann Müller is now dean at Baden-Baden. Schott's return to Italy may
be postponed until the beginning of the next academic year. He is eager for
news of friends.

209. communem amicum nostrum kilianum Herbipolensem
Kilian of Würzburg has not been identified.

210. domino Christofero Augustensi
This may be the person of the *Acta bonon.* entry (217): "1472 Cristoforus
Herb. Aug. dioc."

211. honorando mihi Magistro Ioanne... inter Badenses presbyteros...
Johann Müller had accepted the post of canon and dean of the collegiate
church at Baden-Baden. Apparently he had begun seeking a post when he
and Schott did not return to Bologna for the academic year beginning in
November 1478 (N. 190) and, since he was a native of the principality of
Baden, was offered the benefice at Baden-Baden, then the capital of the
principality. He must have been confirmed in the benefice sometime before
2 February 1480, the date when he resigned the benefice at Dambach (N.
239), for it was customary to retain one benefice until another had been
confirmed. The post at the "first" church of Baden-Baden was, however,
not so exalted as the title might indicate. The income was very little and
tenancy depended upon the whim of *Markgraf* Christoph I;* also in Müller's

P. 20   #12   N. 211

case the post included the thankless but responsible task of being tutor to young Jacob von Baden,* the heir presumptive. Cf. N. 526.

The church at Baden-Baden has been many times devastated by war or fire and as many times restored, the last restoration having been 1952-1956. It now serves as the parish church of Baden-Baden. On its site once stood, so says tradition, a chapel which had been erected early in the Christian era on the ruins of a Roman temple and which in the seventh or eighth century was enlarged into an unpretentious church. In the first half of the twelfth century *Markgraf* Hermann V of Baden began a parish church, and 200 years later *Markgraf* Bernard II,* the sainted Bernard, set about converting this church into a collegiate church. His plans, realized in 1453 by his son Jacob I, provided benefices for 22 chapter members – 12 canons and 10 vicars, the authority for selecting these members being vested in the *Markgraf*. The first *praepositus*, Bernard, a son of Bernard II, served until 1475.

P. 21

212. domini Ioannis Vueschbach
Johann Weschbach.*

#13. TO JOHANN GEILER   Ferrara, 20 December 1480

213. Summary Schott rejoices over his father's decision that he study theology and is deeply grateful for Geiler's influence in shaping this decision. Now by applying himself diligently to the kind of study for which he believes himself best fitted, he can obey both his father and Geiler. He has not yet been to Rome because of the plague there.

214. Chronologically this item belongs after #17. Cf. N. 218 at the end of this item, where the date is discussed. The matters touched upon in the item are elaborated in #18.

215. diuinis litteris incumbam... ad quas natura mea est inclinacior
As already mentioned in N. 121, par. 2, Schott had wanted to study theology at Paris after receiving his A.B. degree.

216. Super his quae mihi Rome perficienda... a Parentibus mea incepta est
Schott is doubtless referring to the delayed papal confirmation of Geiler's appointment as cathedral preacher, a post which Schott's parents had worked hard to establish (cf. N. 955, par. 6).

217. Ex Ferraria
When in September 1480 trouble developed between the two nations of the university at Bologna, Schott with Hassenstein and other friends joined the exodus of the *natio Germaniae* from Bologna and went to the university of Ferrara (cf. N. 609).

Schott had wanted to spend the winter of 1480-1481 studying in Rome (#17, pp. 25f.), but a violent outbreak of the plague in Rome forced him to cancel his plan. He remained in Ferrara until early March 1481 before going to Rome (#18, p. 27; N. 252 and N. 261). The stay in Rome was brief, for by 25 May he had returned to Ferrara and was about to leave for home (#19, p. 28).

218. ad xiij kalendas Ianuarias... M.cccc.lxxx.
Is the date of this letter 20 December 1479 or 20 December 1480? In the case of dates before the kalends of January, it is doubtful whether the writer means December of the year given or of the previous year. There are eight items in the *Lucubraciunculae* with such dates: #13, #30, #64, #78, #82, #126, #197, #235. Examination of the items shows that Schott meant December of the year given.

1) Item #13 was written 13 days before the kalends of January 1480. Wimpheling, or Martin Schott,* or whoever arranged the items, interpreted the date as 20 December 1479, because the letters immediately preceding are dated 1479 and those succeeding are dated early 1480. The contents, however, are like those of #18, written 6 March 1481, in which Schott repeats much of what is said in #13: he is happy about his father's wish that he study theology; he has not yet gone to Rome because of the plague there; he will attend to certain business for Geiler and his parents when he goes thither. Hence #13 must have been written shortly before #18, and its date must be 20 December 1480; chronologically it belongs after #17.

2) Item #30 was written 10 days before the kalends of January 1482. The arranger interpreted the date as 23 December 1481, because the letters preceding are from late 1481 and those succeeding from early 1482. Schott's own statements in the letter prove, however, that the date must be December 1482: a) He tells Wolf* that the latter's young nephew has been desperately ill with a cough and has been moved from Theobald Fuch's* home to the home of Johann Hell (Onheim).* This information is subsequent to that of the letter, #35, written 5 November 1482, in which Schott notifies Wolf that the child has a bad cough and is being cared for by Theobald Fuchs. b) Schott mentions his having been consecrated priest two days previously and his uncertainty of the day when he is to celebrate his first mass. We know the consecration took place in December 1482, because Schott wrote Hassenstein 16 November 1482 that he was to be consecrated during the coming Christmas season (#36, p. 43) and we know Schott celebrated his first mass in February 1483, because he wrote Maeler 4 February 1483 that he had been saying mass for the past three days (#39, p. 45). Item #30 is therefore out of order and should chronologically follow #38, which was written 21 November 1482.

3) Item #64 was written 10 days before the kalends of January 1485. The arranger interpreted the date as 23 December 1484, since the letters preceding are of late 1484 and those following of early 1485. There is no evidence in the text to indicate in what year Schott wrote the letter.

4) A note appended to #78, the letter of 8 December 1485 to Agricola,* explains that the letter was returned three days before the kalends of January 1485, because Agricola had died before it could be delivered. In this instance there is absolutely no doubt that the date in the note is 30 December 1485, for not only is the note appended to a letter of early December 1485 but Agricola is known to have died in late 1485.

5) Item #82 was written three days before the kalends of January 1486. The arranger interpreted the date as 30 December 1485, since the letters following are dated early 1486; the items preceding are undated. The content of the letter gives no clue as to the year when Schott wrote the letter.

6) Item #126 was written ten days before the kalends of January 1489. The arranger interpreted the date as 23 December 1488, since the letters preceding are of 1488, those following of early 1489. Although there is no evidence in the letter to indicate the year when it was written, the fact that after Schott's death, Leontarius,* the recipient of the letter, laments his friendship with Schott as having been very brief (#291) suggests the year 1489.

7) Item #197, the epitaph for the entombment of Diether von Isenburg,* archbishop of Mainz, gives the day of the entombment as 16 days before the kalends of January 1483. We have found no other reference to the day when the archbishop, who died 7 July 1482, was laid in his tomb. The carved stone tombs for nobles and prelates were a long time in making, and it was not unusual for several years to elapse between death and entombment.

8) Item #235 was written 7 days before the kalends of January 1477. No comparison with dates of other items is possible because this item, the letter to Johann Gesler at Paris with which Schott sent from Bologna copies of his own and Hassenstein's poems (#236-#239), is placed in the poetry section, following Schott's earliest poem, written in 1470, and preceding item #240, written in 1480 (cf. N. 1574). That the date of the letter must, however, be 26 December 1477 (cf. N. 1559) is apparent from the allusion (in one of the poems sent to Gesler, #238) to the defeat of Charles the Bold at Nancy which occurred 5 January 1477).

From the foregoing, it appears that in 5 of the 8 examples (#13, #30, #64, #82, #126), where comparison with dates of other items is possible, the arranger interpreted dates before the kalends of January as December of the previous year, not as December of the year given. It also appears that in the 4 examples (#13, #30, #78, #235), where dates can be determined from the content of the items and from other information, Schott means December of the year given.

Evidence to support interpreting dates before the kalends of January as December of the year given is in the *Epithoma*. Wimpheling's introduction to the *Epithoma* (p. 332) was written 27 November 1500. Johann Schott's* colophon (p. 354) has the date of publication as nine days before the kalends of January 1500. Since Wimpheling could not have produced an introduction in 1500 for a work published 1499, the year in the colophon must be 1500. The date for the publication of the *Epithoma* is therefore 24 December 1500. All bibliographical works give the date as 1500.

An authority for interpreting dates before the kalends of January as December of the year given is Professor B. L. Ullman. In a personal interview, Prof. Ullman told how he had corrected an error based on the misinterpretation of such a date. In his dissertation *The Pseudo-Ciceronian Consolatio* (University of Chicago, 1910), 7, Evan T. Sage, attempting to establish the date of the *Consolatio*, states that "Lipsius had pronounced his opinion [on the work] as early as January 1583," but according to Prof. Ullman, the work was not published until later in 1583. Mr. Sage's claim is based on the date of a letter by Lipsius (Iustus Lipsius, *Epistularum selectarum centuria prima miscellanea* [Antwerp, 1603], No. 99, p. 118), "XIV Kal. Ianuar. MDLXXXIII," i.e., 14 days before the kalends of January 1583. This date Prof. Ullman reads as December 1583 not as December 1582. His interpretation is verified by the date of another letter by Lipsius (*ibid.*, No. 79, p. 94) written "XVI Kal. Ianuar. MDLXXXIV," i.e., 14 days before the kalends of January 1584. Here the date must be December 1584, because in the letter Lipsius refers to the deaths of Sigonius and Guillemus, both of whom died during the year 1584.

On the basis of the above evidence, we have interpreted all dates before the kalends of January in the *Lucubraciunculae* as December of the year given.

P. 22

#14. TO JOHANN GEILER Bologna, 30 January 1480

219. Summary Geiler is admonished to take time for relaxation, especially during Lent when there are extra demands on his energies, and to partake of the Lenten foods now allowed by the bishop's dispensation. Italian preachers make great display of their learning, but give little evidence of piety. Geiler, on the other hand, who is a true sower of the Gospel, devotes his efforts, without ostentation, to producing fruit.

220. te: rebus arduissimis et diuinis omelijs... sollicitam illam mentem...
An omnivorous reader as well as an indefatigable student and worker, Geiler imposed upon himself a strict daily regimen, probably much like that he recommended to Friedrich von Zollern* in the *Monita* (cf. Appendix H). He ate but twice a day and drank little wine. During Lent, when in addition to his regular duties he preached a daily Lenten sermon, he fasted each day and followed an even stricter regimen, which he described thus:

> De mane surgo secunda vel tertia hora et studeo quid predicare velim et hoc usque sextam. Hora sexta predico. Hora septima rescribo que predicavi. Hora octava lego primam, tertiam, sextam horas. Nona celebro. Decima dico nonas et versperas. Undecima prandium. Duodecima modicum movendo dico quindecim gradus. Prima dormio unam vel duas horas. Tertia hora quero materiam predicabilem. Quarta dico completorium. Sexta dico matutinas et post sextam et septimam aliqualem recreationem sive motionem vado dormitum. (Cf. Dacheux, *Réf.*, Appendix vi, pp. lxixf. "Modus vivendi tempore quadragesimali doctoris Jo. Geyler de Keysersberg, ut retulit.")

In the introductory words to the *Monita*, Geiler reveals himself as a man who has conquered strong passions by rigid self discipline. His face as seen in contemporary pictures is that of an ascetic (cf. reproductions of pictures of the young Geiler in Freher, 98, and Rathgeber, *Gottesmänner*, frontispiece; of the elder Geiler in Dacheux, *Réf.*, frontispiece, and Könnecke, 33). Beatus Rhenanus* describes Geiler as "tall in stature, having curly hair, gaunt in appearance, frail but physically healthy and, except for a kidney complaint, subject to no illnesses" (Riegger, *Amoen.*, 68 and 100ff.).

221. remittendum enim esse nonnumquam animum: laxandasque curas
Geiler expresses the same thought in a sermon heard by Schott (cf. #233, p. 265, section 23 of the "Imitaciunculae").

222. omnium sapientissimus Socrates... nos vegeciores reddi
Valerius Maximus viii. 8. ext. 1.

223. ut laborem tute exigas... exegi paciaris...
That Schott dares to indulge in a bit of humor at Geiler's expense here and in the passages of the following paragraph ("benigna principis indulgencia"

P. 22   #14   N. 223

and "plus maceracioni corporis studeas... superesse") indicates how close was the friendship between the two at this time.

224. lactis et butiri concesso nunc edulio... benigna principis indulgencia...
At his confirmation as bishop of Strassburg, which was before 11 November 1478, Albrecht von Bayern received from Sixtus IV the dispensation allowing use of milk and butter during Lent to such persons in the Strassburg diocese who paid a stipulated sum in taxes to the bishop. Geiler considered this dispensation an infraction against ancient discipline and never forgave Albrecht for using it; even in his funeral oration for Albrecht he condemned it. Yet such a dispensation was not without precedent. One of the 300 articles of the Waldenses allowed butter and eggs on fast days. A gloss discovered by Schott permitted lard and fats on days when meat was forbidden (#226). The use of butter and eggs on fast days was granted to the dioceses of Trier and Cologne in 1344, and to the Swiss cantons Luzern, Schwitz and Zug in 1456. In 1468 Bishop Hermann of Constance received permission for the people of Überlingen to substitute butter and other dairy products on fast days for the prescribed olive oil which had to be imported and was not only expensive but difficult to obtain.

Nor was the tax exacted by Bishop Albrecht on milk and butter unusual. The so-called butter towers of Rouen and Chartres were built with money collected from similar taxes. The tax money in Strassburg was to be sent to the pope for alms, but Albrecht used at least part of it for restoration of the episcopal palace at Zabern, which had been badly damaged during the Burgundian wars, and for buying instruments of war, "tormenta quae Bombardas vocant." The fun-loving Alsatian folk was soon joking about butter-canons, "Bombardas butiri, lingua sua Anckenbüchssen."

Cf. Dacheux, *Réf.* 38, 483. Grandidier, *Oeuvr. hist.*, IV, 369. Hertzog, iv, 114f. *Inventaire (Brucker)*, II, 78. Specklin, 237, 298. Xavier Udrey, "Archivalien aus Orten des Amtsbezirks Überlingen," *ZGORh*, n. f. XXII (1907), 169. Wimpheling, *Cat. ep.*, 114.

225. Nisi forsitan Stoica illa sentencia...
The reference may be to: a) the Stoic maxim "to live according to nature," i.e., nature uncorrupted by human society; cf. Seneca *De vita beata* viii. 2: "Idem est beate vivere et secundum naturam"; *De ira*, iii. 15; *Ep.* xxii. 7, lxvi, lxx, lxxi; Lipsius, *Manductionis ad stoicam philosophorum*, 200, 203; b) the Stoic doctrine that health and other goods of this life are subordinate considerations; c) Seneca's idea that the body is but a fetter of the soul and only when freed from the body, does the soul begin its true life.

226. contra monicionem Hieronymi: mediocre bonum/ maiori praeferres
Cf. St. Hieronymi "Adversus Jovinianum," i, Migne, XXIII, 234. For a discussion of *bonum, summum bonum*, cf. Seneca *Ep.* lxvi, lxx, lxxi.

227. populum autem quotidiana doctrina fouere...
According to the statutes governing the cathedral chair at Strassburg, the cathedral preacher was obligated to preach daily during Lent (cf. N. 955, par. 5). Rathgeber (*Gottesmänner*, 15f.) says that the services began at midnight and lasted until six or seven o'clock in the morning. Geiler adhered to this custom for a time, then changed the hours to begin at six o'clock in the morning (cf. N. 220).

228. cum eos praedicatores intueor quibus Italia... fauoribus... tuentur
To some Italian scholars of the late fifteenth century, humanism meant breaking away from convention and orthodox religion; they strove to be supermen and encompass all learning. For them Christianity lost its force and became even a source of jest. Schott is perhaps referring to preachers who were this type of humanists.

229. utpote hereticum a populo vitandum monet
Cf. Tt. 3:10.

230. Euangelij seminator
Mr. 4:14.

231. Sapiencie religionisque columen
Cf. close to #240 and N. 1574.

#15. TO VITUS MAELER Bologna, 12 March 1480

232. Summary Schott is worried about his friend Friedrich Büchsner* who, on the spur of the moment and without proper preparation, has rushed off to Rome. He asks Maeler to take care of him. He thanks Maeler for a favor.

233. Quod in rebus... Parentes meos et filium cum sororibus... moderaberis.
Maeler's favor to the Schotts is not explained. Several months later, on 29 June 1480 (#17) Schott in his own name and in that of his parents thanks both Maeler and Nicolaus Barbitonsor (cf. N. 244) for their efforts on the Schotts' behalf, but does not say what the efforts concerned. Perhaps special prayers or masses were said at Rome for the Schotts, and the written record of these services was to bear the names of the Schott family members, possibly also the papal seal.

234. Dominum Fridericum Buchsener... porrectus est...
Friedrich Büchsner* may have accompanied Schott from Alsace to Bologna in the fall of 1479.

235. Laurencius hominem nouit
Possibly Laurentius Grave or Laurentius Hertzog. Cf. N. 169, par. 2, and N. 171.

236. de barbacianis meis quinternis quatuor... praestancia Imperatoris...
The four booklets of five pages were most likely commentaries by the famous professor of law at Bologna, Andreas Barbatia, which Schott had lent to Maeler. Among the books sent to Müller were several by Barbatia (#173, p. 194; cf. N. 342, par. 2).

P. 24   #15   N. 237

237. Georgius Vngarus sodalis noster
Georgius Ungarus.*

#16. TO JOHANN ROT   Bologna, 12 June 1480

238. Summary Müller has written Schott about resigning the benefice at Dambach and being succeeded by Rot.* Schott is sorry that Müller no longer has ties in the Strassburg diocese, but is happy that Rot has a post. He charges Rot to be a good pastor to the flock committed to him. He sends a message to Adolph Rusch.*

239. praeceptore meo... te sibi in cura Tambachensi successisse...
Johann Müller had been permanent vicar at Dambach since 18 August 1470 and resigned the post 2 February 1480 after he had become dean of the collegiate church at Baden-Baden (N. 211) in the diocese of Spires. Evidently Rot's appointment was not quickly confirmed; 5 November 1480 is the date given in records. Rot kept the benefice until 3 August 1482, when he accepted a post in Strassburg. Cf. Barth, *Handbuch*, 247-252; #12, p. 20; N. 1278.

Dambach was one of the many benefices in the Strassburg diocese controlled by the cathedral chapter (cf. Wuerdtwein, 58, 243).

240. gregem pascere ... in ... campos quos Elisios.
Cf. Gn. 37:12; Is. 40:11; I Cor. 9:7; Jo. 21:15ff. Cf. N. 381.

241. Vticensis ipse Cato integritate vite...
Cato Uticensis, great grandson of Cato the Censor and friend of Cicero, is said to have possessed integrity and steadfastness so great that nothing could swerve him from what he considered to be the true course of liberty and justice.

P. 25

242. Pacem aiunt Italis esse...
The war between Sixtus IV and Florence was concluded sometime in 1480. Cf. N. 189.

243. Adelphum virum honestissimum... librum rerum memorabilium...
We have found no work by the title *Liber rerum memorabilium* in lists of early printed books. If Rusch printed such a work, there is no trace of it. Was he perhaps in search of a manuscript copy of Xenophon's *Memorabilia*?

#17. TO VITUS MAELER   Bologna, 29 June 1480

244. Summary Schott is putting in writing what he had expected to say personally to Maeler, if Maeler had come to Bologna as planned. He expresses thanks on behalf of himself and his parents to Maeler and Nicolaus Barbitonsor for their services. His parents have agreed to his spending the winter in Rome, and he would like to know not only about courses in Rome but also about the possibility of staying with Maeler. He has recently been in Ferrara,

P. 25   #17   N. 244

where he was handsomely welcomed by Johann Weschbach.* There has been trouble between Walter Halewin* and the beadle; the lady Margarita Jacoba and daughters are well and are keeping Maeler's belongings safe for him.

245. Plane rem egisti: et mihi et vtrique Parenti meo quam gratissimam...
The favor Maeler did the Schotts is mentioned in #15 (cf. N. 233).

246. Quem cum tardatum esse ex margarita Pavonis audirem...
Maeler had been delayed at the university of Pavia (cf. N. 199) and had not been able to come to Bologna.

247. insignitum pocius quam adhuc incinctum
Schott did not receive his doctorate in laws at Bologna until several months after writing this letter; that is, he was writing in June and took the degree in September. At this time he seems to have been considering the possibility of finishing his degree at the university of Rome where Maeler may have obtained his doctorate in canon law. The university of Rome had developed from the earlier *Schola Palatina* or *Studium Curiae*.

P. 26

248. Mirum enim est... quorum sum in potestate
The reference is to Schott's overly solicitous parents (cf. N. 87).

249. Fui ante exactos aliquot dies Ferrarie... saluum mansit.
It has been taken for granted that this entire passage refers to incidents and persons in Ferrara. Yet there is no basis for this in Schott's words. He says, to be sure, that he was in Ferrara "some days ago" and was handsomely greeted by Johann Weschbach. He goes on to say, however, that he believes Weschbach is well (i.e., at the time of writing), a statement which indicates that the "some days ago" was quite some time ago, perhaps during the break between the winter and the summer semesters. On the other hand, in mentioning "domina Margarita: Iacoba/ et filie sue," Schott is very definite about their state of health, for "they are well." Unfortunately, there are no records of trouble between a beadle named Dominicus and Halewin over the slaying of the latter's *famulus*, or of the beadle's being deprived not only of his office but being banished as well; nor is there any record of Halewin's whereabouts at the time (we know he and Schott were at Bologna together; cf. #94, p. 105, and it is very likely that he left Bologna for Ferrara when other students of the empire left in September 1480). There is likewise no record of "domina" Margarita Jacoba and her daughters. One can therefore not offer evidence to prove that it was Bologna where the above-mentioned fracas took place and that it was in Bologna where Maeler's effects were stored at the home of "domina" Margarita Jacoba. But neither should one state as fact that Schott is writing about Ferrara, nor postulate that because Maeler's effects are mentioned, Maeler attended the university of Ferrara; one should also not romanticize about Hassenstein's odes to the mysterious Carlotta as having been composed to one of "domina" Margarita Jacoba's daughters in Ferrara (cf. biographical note on Hassenstein).

According to Kibre (*Nations*, 58), the beadle at Bologna – and no doubt at Ferrara as well – was a personage of considerable importance. He

P. 26   #17   N. 249

was elected by the rector and councillors. His duties included (1) announcing disputations, lectures, festivals and books for sale, (2) assisting the rector on all public occasions and (3) attending all processions for private or public examinations. He was reimbursed for his services by the students and took up two collections during each academic year; students were forbidden to deprive him of his just due.

250. Nicholao barbitonsori...
This Nicolaus has not been identified. Barbitonsor appears as a surname in Weissenborn, *Akten der Erfurter Universität*, III, 13, but here it is probably the title given a papal chamberlain, "custos interioritus cubilis" or "cubicularius secretus," who was a person of influence and often a nephew or favorite of the pope (cf. Hofmann, I, 161).

251. Anno a natali Christiano M.cccc.lxxxi
The final *i* of the year is a typographical error. The contents of the letter show that it was written in June 1480. Schott mentions his not yet having his degree and his tentative plans for spending the following winter in Rome. We know that he received his doctor of laws from Bologna in September of 1480 (N. 109), that he was prevented from going to Rome in the winter of 1480/81 by the plague there (#13; #18, p. 27) and that he visited Maeler in Rome during Lent – Easter was 22 April – in 1481. Furthermore, by the end of May 1481 Schott was ready to leave for Strassburg (#19, p. 28) and by 22 July 1481 he was at home (#20). Cf. N. 96.

#18. TO JOHANN GEILER   Ferrara, 6 March 1481

252. Summary Schott is happy that he may now with his father's consent pursue a career in theology which has always been his first love and which Geiler's example has convinced him to be the proper career. Though Geiler may deny it, Schott knows he influenced the father's decision. Schott had never felt himself either physically or mentally fitted for the career for which his father intended him. Theology, however, will enable him to lead the quiet life he desires. He is not yet certain whether he will enter the priesthood. The trip to Rome has thus far been delayed, first because of the plague there during the winter and then because he preferred to spend the pre-Lenten season in Ferrara. In Lent he will certainly betake himself to Rome. (Cf. N. 214).

253. quam natura mea semper amplecti cupiebat
Cf. N. 121, par. 2.

254. ut ita dicam ansam oblatam esse videbam
Cf. Cicero *Laelius de amicitia* 59: "tamquam ansas ad reprehendum;" Stoett, 866, p. 331, "ansam praebere alicui," to offer opportunity for something to someone.

255. Tranquille inquam vite et quiete... (to end of paragraph)
I Tm. 2:2. By quiet life Schott does not mean an idle existence, but a life of service through study and learning, as exemplified by Geiler, in contrast

to the hectic life of a public official, as exemplified by his father. While at home from Italy during the period fall 1478 – fall 1479 (N. 96), he had had opportunity to observe Geiler and had become more averse to the public career for which his father was grooming him.

He was familiar with Cicero's and Horace's views on the value of "life exempt from public haunts" and was at this time reading Isocrates (#10, p. 18; #20, p. 29) who expresses preference for such a life in *Antid.* 151. For other references to this subject, cf. #32, p. 40; #36, p. 43; #95, p. 106; #125, p. 146; #169, p. 189; #170, p. 190; pp. xxvi; N. 86; N. 115; N. 302, N. 1772.

P. 27

256. ad quas nec corpore nec animo satis idoneus essem...
Cf. N. 87.

257. An ego occasionem: tam breuem tam optatam tam insperatam... amitterem?
Terence *Eunuchus* iii. 604. Schott's words after this quotation echo the rest of the speech in the play. The implication is that just as Chaerea pretended to be a eunuch in order to gain access to his beloved's chamber, so Schott has feigned devotion to law in order to gain a career in theology.

Terence's works were readily available to Schott: Hain (II, 398f.) lists 12 editions published by 1481, and Hawkins (15f.) lists an edition by Rusch* in 1470. Schott may also have seen Terence's plays performed on the new "Terence stage," popular after the death (1471) of the antihumanist pope, Paul II, and promoted at Ferrara by Duke Ercole D'Este (cf. W. Stammler, *Deutsche Theatergeschichte* [Leipzig, 1925], 18, 19).

258. nec monachum futurum... nec sacerdocij culmen conscendam...
Although Schott says he has not considered becoming a priest, Bohuslaus von Hassenstein was urging him to do so (#36, p. 43). Cf. N. 302.

259. Non enim sciencie vitam accomodare... sed vite scienciam...
These words might well be the motto of dedicated fifteenth-century humanists and of Schott.

260. Romae que nomine tuo agi oportet: vbi... exequar.
Schott had been in Ferrara since the fall of 1480 (cf. N. 609). His visit to Rome had been postponed for some time. Apparently he was to make inquiries at Rome about the delay in papal confirmation of Geiler's post in the Strassburg cathedral (cf. N. 955, pars. 6f.).

261. In quadragesima illuc me conferam: ut si a Turcis capienda...
This letter was written 6 March which in 1481 was Shrove Tuesday, i.e., the day before Lent began; Easter was 22 April. Schott did go to Rome during Lent as he intended; this we learn from his next letter to Maeler (#19).

The reference to the possible capture of Rome by the Turks was no idle jest. In August 1480, Sultan Mohammed II, having failed to conquer Rhodes and to defeat Matthias* of Hungary, had turned on Italy. He moved into Apulia and captured Otronto. Italy was panic-stricken and Sixtus IV prepared for flight from Rome. In 1481, presumably after the date of this

P. 27   #18   N. 261

letter, Mohammed died and the Turks were driven from Italy. Cf. Rodocanachi, 44; Trithemius, *Ann. Hirs.*, II, 510.

P. 28

#19. TO VITUS MAELER   Ferrara, 25 May 1481

262. Summary Schott expresses his gratitude for Maeler's kindness to him while he was in Rome and cautions Maeler to wrap the document of his first tonsure carefully in a sealed letter so that it will reach Strassburg intact. Ladislaus* and Bohuslaus send greetings. Schott expects to leave the next day for Strassburg via Venice.

263. patriam petam per Venecias
Schott's main purpose in going to Venice was to buy books (#24; #25, p. 33), because Venice was a very important book mart. In the three decades following 1469 when Johann von Speyer (†1470) set up the first Venetian printing press – continued by his brother Wendelin until 1477 – Venice became the world capital for printing and the book trade. Between 1470-1480 there were in Venice no fewer than 50 typographers whose names are known today; many of them were Germans. Indeed, Venice at the time had a large and powerful colony of German merchants and a big German exchange (*Fondaco dei Tedeschi*), where Germans from any part of the empire could meet countrymen, hear and send news, dispatch or receive goods. Cf. Barge, 98-102; Brown, 17-28.

From Venice Schott shipped not only the books he had just bought in Venice but also those books he had used at Bologna and Ferrara. Three years earlier he had shipped Müller's books from Bologna via Venice, for this route was apparently safer (#173, p. 193). Schott's books left Venice before he did, but did not arrive in Strassburg until sometime in the fall (#170, p. 190; N. 1204), although he expected them much sooner. Already in August he mentioned the delay in their arrival (#24) and in September he said if the Strassburg merchants returning from the Frankfurt fair did not bring his books, he would consider them lost (#25, p. 33).

264. Instrumentum de prima tonsura mea... preuenire possit.
Schott evidently believed that the record of his first tonsure, if enclosed in a letter bearing the seal of an official of the Roman *Curia*, would be surer of reaching Strassburg than if sent in less imposing guise. Cf. #23 and N. 292.

Bearers ran the risk not only of being robbed but of having their goods confiscated at various custom and military barriers. For example, copies of the apostolic petitions sent by Maeler to Schott were taken from the bearer by soldiers (#92, p. 103). On one occasion Schott, dispatching a purse as a gift to Rome, comments that an empty purse will be more likely to reach its destination than a full one (#191, p. 209).

Bearers themselves were not always trustworthy, as in the case of the bearer who failed to deliver eight florins for Gangolf in Paris (#63, p. 69; N. 547). For references to caution in the choice of bearers, cf. #26, p. 35; #71, p. 78; #92, p. 104; #93, p. 105; #95, p. 107; #150, p. 163; #235, p. 266.

Letters, though they had no monetary value, did not always reach the addressee. Sometimes they did not arrive as quickly as desired. To ensure one's information and to expedite it, one therefore sent letters with similar information by different messengers. This explains almost identical letters in the *Lucubraciunculae* such as #26 and #27, #146 and #148, #63 and #177.

265. Dominus Ladislaus et Dominus Bohuslaus...
Cf. N. 217, par. 1.

#20. TO JOHANN GEILER Strassburg, 22 July 1481

266. Summary Schott cannot join Geiler at the baths in Baden-Baden, because he is accompanying his parents to another spa. He would like to send Geiler wine from the Schott cellar but fears heat might damage it en route. He is undergoing a phase of uncertainty when he seems to be afraid of everyone. He awaits Geiler's letter, because Geiler appears to know what is best for him, and he will follow Geiler's counsel.

267. vereor ne posthabitis Argentinensibus... numquam reuertereris
Since Geiler's post as cathedral preacher was not yet confirmed and his salary was small, there was real cause for the Strassburgers to fear that he might accept a better post elsewhere (cf. N. 955, par. 6, and N. 963).

268. alias in thermas quas nosti Parentes comitabor... Vinum... vellem voto...
That Schott and his parents went to the baths at Wildbad is apparent from the next letter to Geiler (#21) which is written from that spa. Geiler was at Baden-Baden, as is evident from the fact that Schott sends greetings to Johann Müller (cf. close of #20) who was at that time in Baden-Baden (cf. N. 211).
The wine would have been sent as a bath gift. For the popularity of baths and the custom of sending bath gifts, as well as for descriptions of Wildbad and Baden-Baden, cf. N. 192.

269. cum eo duce nunc viuas regaris ve...
The *duce* referred to is Christoph I,* reigning *Markgraf* of Baden.

270. Verum Epistola... non erubescit.
This quotation is from Cicero *Ad fam.* v. 12. A similar statement is in Isocrates *Philip* 81: "I have expressed myself more boldly to you than others." Cf. Martial x. 64. 5: "non tamen erubuit lascivo dicere versu."

271. Omnia enim te duce... coepta nostra.
This may be a reference to some cooperative project planned by Geiler and Schott.

272. Vetterclaus suadet... pignora luetis.
Vetterclaus (German for Cousin Claus) is probably Claus Schott.* His

facetious warning that he will not go surety for Geiler and party, if they squander their money, may well refer to gambling, a vice Geiler abominated and condemned (N. 1326). Schott, too, spoke against gambling (#254, p. 288; #255, p. 290) and Wimpheling mentions gambling in the list of vices by which inheritances are lost (#301, p. 323).

Because of the second person plural in *prodigatis* and below in *vestra* and *negligatis*, it may be assumed that Geiler was accompanied by his mother Anna Zuber* (cf. N. 285) who is mentioned elsewhere as travelling with him (#61). It is also possible that Johann Kerer* who is mentioned at the end of the letter is included in "you."

273. Elisabet vestra orat... comes nauis Rhenum traijecerit.
Elisabeth fears that the dog which was evidently meant to remain in Strassburg has swum the Rhine after the ferry which carried Geiler and his mother across. Elisabeth may be identical with the solicitous housekeeper or servant of #61 (p. 67). Dacheux (*Réf.*, 297) identifies Elisabeth as "without doubt also a relative;" Schmidt (*H. L.*, I, 355) as "the old housekeeper;" Vulpinus (43) as "Geiler's sister," although to our knowledge there is no record of the name of Geiler's sister. It is possible but not very probable that Elisabeth is Kerer's housekeeper, the "Elisabeth aus Merdingen" mentioned in his will (Beckmann, 11); she may have accompanied Kerer to Strassburg and remained in Geiler's home.

274. Dominum Doctorem Rectorem Friburgensem
That is, Johann Kerer, professor at Freiburg and rector of that university in 1481.

275. Domina insanit... fortunari membra...
The *domina* here is the moon. According to the *Thesaurus Linguae Latinae*, V, 1932, as the sun is considered masculine (*dominus*) so the moon is considered feminine (*domina*); and according to Thorndike, I, 113, "The moon is a moist planet and therefore female." In English the designation of the moon as "Lady Moon" is age-old; Thorndike, I, 727, quotes a twelfth century prayer (Edgerton 821) which begins, "O lady Moon, free me...;" Bishop, I, 68, speaks of "Lady Luna."

Astrologers claim that the moon rules the head of man. "Luna governs the bulk of the Brain or nerves, the Bowels, the Bladder, the left Eye of a man, the right of a Woman," says Middleton, 183. Cf. also 'Al-Kabīsī 'Abd al-'Azīz ibn 'Uthman, *Alcibitu ad magisterium iudicorum astrorum isagoge, Commentario Ioannis Saxonii dederata* (Paris, 1521), 2, 4; Bishop, I, 68; Bonatti, 453, 587; Cardano, folios 44, 49, 68.

In August, while Geiler would still be at the baths, the moon is in conjunction with Virgo who is connected with powers of darkness, such as Freia, Venus, Frau Holle, Proserpine, Hecate, Artemis. During the dog days of August, Ceres becomes the fury Erinnys or Canicula who brings plagues, epidemics, hydrophobia and madness (cf. F. Nork, "Der Festkalender" in J. Scheible, *Das Kloster*, VII [Stuttgart, 1847], 500f.). It should be noted that *Canicula* is another name for the dog star Sirius.

Belief in astrology was common to all classes of society. There are references to astrology in Geiler's sermons, and Wimpheling in a letter to Geiler 1503 describes the activity of monk astrologers (cf. Knod, "Wimpheling," 240).

P. 29   #20   N. 275

For other references to astrology, cf. #112, p. 133; #177, p. 198; #239, pp. 271f.; #266, p. 299; #286, p. 309; N. 895, N. 1267, N. 1570, N. 1719.

276. Magistrum meum Charissimum in arce Badensi...
Johann Müller was at this time in Baden-Baden (cf. N. 211).

P. 30

#21. TO JOHANN GEILER Wildbad, 7 August 1481

277. Summary Not only the Schotts, but also the maid servants, were convulsed with laughter at the witty stories and jokes sent by Geiler and Kerer.* Susanna von Cöllen requests that Geiler preach in Strassburg on Assumption Day; then permission to extend his holiday for visiting his native haunts will be more willingly granted.

278. This item is chronologically out of order. Its date is later than that of #22 to Widmann (22 July 1481) and that of #23 to Maeler (26 July 1481). In some cases letters written to the same person at about the same time are grouped together; e.g., #20 and #21, #23 and #24, #36 and #37, #49-#53, #104 and #105, #106-#110, #111 and #112. Cf. N. 34 and N. 36.

279. si Nicholao tuo credi oporteat
Dacheux, (*Réf.*, 409), identifies this Nicholaus with Schott's cousin Claus Schott,* the "Vetterclaus" of #20; Zacher (27) identifies him as one of the *famuli* or *familiares* whom Geiler took into his home and helped educate until they were ready for the university. It is possible that Claus Schott was Geiler's *famulus*.

Other *familiares* of Geiler were: Ottmar Luscinius, later the first Greek teacher in Strassburg; Jacob Other; Christoph von Haus (de Domo), later canon at Spires; Theodorich Gresemund; Geiler's two nephews Peter and Conrad Wickgram; Eucharius Henner (Gallinarius), a licentiate in law, whom Geiler had known since his Freiburg days and who accompanied Geiler on four trips. Cf. Dacheux, *Réf.* 517; Riegger, *Amoen.*, 119.

Zacher (25) includes among Geiler's *familiares* Gangolf Lützelstein or Steinmetz,* but from evidence in the *Lucubraciunculae* it is clear that Gangolf was Schott's protégé and studied in Paris under Schott's auspices; he was receiving his master's degree in late spring 1490. Perhaps after Schott's death, Geiler helped Gangolf in his studies for the priesthood. We know he became Geiler's secretary. Cf. #60, #63, p. 69; #146, p. 160; #150, p. 112; #174, p. 195; #176; #177, p. 197; p. xxix; N. 126.

280. domino Doctori de Friburgo
Johann Kerer enjoyed social functions; he is said to have possessed a keen sense of humor and an ironic wit.

281. qui omelijs et scomatibus suis coenam nostram... condiuerit
The jokes and stories were sent by Geiler and Kerer from Baden-Baden by a messenger, perhaps the Nicholaus mentioned above (N. 279), and were meant

P. 30   #21   N. 281

as a kind of bath gift for the Schotts. On one occasion Schott sent riddles and a poem to Rusch* at the baths; the tripart poem "De tribus Iohannibus" was sent to Geiler at the baths. At the end of this item, Schott mentions a gift being sent to Geiler. Cf. N. 192, 3, par. 3.

    Because Geiler was noted for his wit and clever *bons mots*, the collections *Margarita facetiarum* and *Scommata*, published in one volume at Strassburg 1508, are generally attributed to him. Although his nephew and successor Peter Wickgram denies Geiler's authorship, Wimpheling who worked closely with Geiler lists the collections among Geiler's works. Knepper in his discussion of the collections (*Sprüche*, 160-176) quotes from them 7 selections which are identical with aphorisms 2, 3, 6, 8, 10, 25, 31 in the "Imitaciunculae" (#233), which Schott took down from Geiler's sermons and translated into Latin. The passage in this letter, #21, is definite evidence that Geiler collected witty and pithy sayings. Cf. Alfonsus (the edition of *Margarita facetiarum* and *Scommata* mentioned above). Riegger, *Amoen.*, 75, 128ff. Vollert, 53.

282. montibus et quidem pluuia stillantibus... and below *siluestribus penitus occluderemur rupibus*
For a description of Wildbad, cf. N. 192, 3, par. 2.

283. ut qui omnio aquis excoriandi essemus
For the rigorous regimen of the baths, cf. N. 192, par. 5.

284. ut in solennitate beatissime genitricis dei: Assumpcione... exhibeas
The statutes governing the chair of the cathedral preacher at Strassburg required that the preacher deliver sermons on the eve and on the day of every feast day of the Virgin (Wencker, *Arch.*, 432, and N. 955). Hence it was quite in order for Susanna von Cöllen to suggest that Geiler preach on Assumption Day, which is celebrated 15 August and in 1481 was on a Wednesday, even though the day came during Geiler's holiday.

285. Deinde si natalem vestram patriam visitare sit animus...
The word *vestram* seems to indicate that Geiler's mother Anna Zuber* was with him at the baths; it could not refer to Kerer whose birthplace was Wertheim near Würzburg. Apparently Geiler and his mother were planning to visit Kaysersberg and vicinity, where Geiler was reared and his mother was born. To make this trip Geiler would need an extension of his annual holiday, because he would have spent at least 3 of the 4 weeks allotted him at the baths. Cf. N. 192, 2, and N. 955, par. 5.

#22. TO JOHANN WIDMANN Strassburg, 22 July 1481

286. *Summary* Schott expresses his deep gratitude to Widmann for restoring Susanna von Cöllen who has been gravely ill. He describes the improvement in her condition since Widmann saw her and ordered treatment, and he asks whether it be advisable for her to go to the baths as planned.

287. This letter should follow #20 (cf. N. 278) which was written on the same day.

288. domino Iohanni Vuidman in Baden
The distinguished physician Johann Widmann* was at this time serving as personal physician to *Markgraf* Christoph I von Baden.*

289. Ingenui siquidem (ut Cicero noster ait) est animi...
Cf. Cicero *Ad fam.* 2. 6. 2.

290. dum apud vos diebus proxime exactis esses
Is *vos* a misprint in the incunabulum for *nos*? I. e., had Widmann been in Strassburg a few days before this letter was written to see the Schotts or his own parents? If the latter is true, then Widmann's parents must have left their home in Maichingen (Württemberg) some time previously and settled in Strassburg. Although there is no mention of them elsewhere in the *Lucubraciunculae*, they may even have been good friends with the Schotts. This would account for the close friendship between Widmann and the Schotts. Widmann himself did not come to live in Strassburg until about mid-1483.

291. Ad balneas seu thermas in Valtbrun: vnacum genitore meo
Schott's parents were obviously planning a sojourn at the baths of Wildbad, for on 7 August Schott writes to Geiler from Wildbad (#21) and on 5 September he tells Hassenstein that he has been at Wildbad (#25, p. 33).

Since the name Waltbrunn or Waldbronn does not appear on any maps, old or new, of southwestern Germany or Alsace and is not mentioned in any accounts we have read of spas, the conclusion is that Waldbronn must be another name for Wildbad, as is intimated by Zeiller in the description of Wildbad in his mid-seventeenth century chronicle (420f.). Waldbronn may mean natural springs, as does Wildbad. For information on baths, cf. N. 192.

#23. TO VITUS MAELER Strassburg, 26 July 1481

292. Summary The record of Schott's first tonsure has arrived in Strassburg. He sends Maeler* money and commissions him to take care of certain business. He will be diligent in watching for vacant benefices. Cf. N. 278.

293. Formatum meum recoepi
Schott's record of his first tonsure was dispatched from Rome some time after 25 May 1481 (cf. #19, p. 28).

294. De vacancijs diligens ero: quamquam aliquot dies non... profuturum...
This passage indicates that Schott may have begun his work as procurator shortly after his home-coming; in succeeding letters of 1481 to Maeler, there are commissions for benefices (#24, #26, #27, #29). The expected absence from Strassburg is a reference to the sojourn at the baths in Wildbad (#21).

P. 32   #23   N. 295

295. Nemo ex hijs eger est: qui beneficia ampla possideat.
Similar humorous comments about the good health of benefice holders occur in #24; #60, p. 66; #63.

#24. TO VITUS MAELER Strassburg, 24 August 1481

296. Summary Schott is well but somewhat bored, because the books which were shipped from Venice before he left that city have not yet arrived. There is no present prospect of vacant benefices. Via the bearer of this letter, he is commissioning Maeler to take care of a small matter. He does not know whether the letter and money sent earlier have been delivered to Maeler.

297. libris careo: nondum enim ad me venerunt... ante me Venecijs abierint
Cf. N. 263.

298. per Laurencium Mercatorem
Laurentius Hertzog (cf. N. 171).

#25. TO BOHUSLAUS VON HASSENSTEIN Strassburg, 5 September 1481

299. Summary If the books from Venice do not arrive from the Frankfurt fair, Schott will consider them lost. He describes his life at home and speaks of future plans for himself and Bohuslaus which are approved by Geiler. He is sending a manuscript on names of instruments for Bohuslaus' appraisal, as well as gifts for Bohuslaus and his tutor Ladislaus.

P. 33

300. per Laurencium mercatorem
Laurentius Hertzog, mentioned also below. Cf. N. 171.

301. libros meos qui nondum venissent... nisi ex Nundinis Franckpfordensibus
Cf. N. 263.
    The fairs held in major centers were direct descendants of fairs popular in Roman times. During the early Christian era fairs were fostered by churches on great feast days, such as the anniversary of dedication, and tolls were collected from nomadic artisans and merchants who sold wares to the people gathering for the celebration. After the crusades, fairs became increasingly important, and eventually their control passed from the Church. Cities bought from heads of state the rights previously sold or given by church authorities.
    The Frankfurt fair seems to have attracted numbers of Strassburgers. An entry in the Strassburg records for 1473 (*Inventaire*, III, 106) reports the attack of the robber knight Dietrich von Hoh-Geroldseck on a boatload of people going to the fair. *Pfalzgraf* Friedrich* was asked by the Strassburg magistracy to effect the release of those held captive. Cf. N. 1524, also N. 802.

P. 33   #25   N. 302

302. Ego mi Bohuslae rem nostram ita paro: ut quasi perfecerim...
Here and in several passages following in this letter, Schott refers to his and Hassenstein's plan to enter the priesthood and spend their lives working and studying together, a plan of which Geiler approved (the plan is also referred to in #36, p. 43; #170, p. 190). They did not expect to begin this association in the immediate future; as Schott says, it might be one or three years. Their hopes were dashed, however, because for some unknown reason Hassenstein's two elder brothers prevented him from becoming a priest (cf. Potuček, vi), although as the youngest son in a noble family he should – according to the usual practice of the time – have entered the Church.

303. Deus inicium esto et finis
Ap. 21:6.

304. in re familiari quae nobis... Patrem praesentem iuuo... vices absentis...
For Schott's assistance to his father, cf. N. 113, par. 2.

305. me Doctores plerique: Beginalem doctorem vocent...
The Begines or Beghards, named after their founder Beghart, were wandering bands of mendicants, women or men, who wished to live a simple and pious life, without adhering to the rules of an order. They first appeared in the Netherlands at the end of the twelfth century and spread up the Rhine. They were considered *personae non gratae* by both regular and secular clergy, particularly in later centuries when they acquired the reputation of being hypocrites, because outwardly they observed Christian ethics but privately led riotous lives. Geiler said the Begines were to be shunned like devils. Cf. Heimbucher, II, 639f.; Schmidt, "Beginen", *passim*; Wimpheling, *Diatriba*, chap. xiii.

During his first months at home, Schott was dubbed *beginalis doctor*, perhaps because he seemed to have no foothold and showed more interest in religion than in jurisprudence for which he had been trained.

306. Patrem moneo... ut ab impedimentis publicis abstineat... ipsa odiosa...
Schott had no taste for a public career like his father's (cf. N. 86 and N. 255).

307. Nollem subito exasperare Parentes meos: sed paulatim lenire.
Cf. N. 87, N. 302.

308. Fui in thermis in Vuiltbaden... Prior Ratisponensis...
While he was at Wildbad in August 1481, Schott met Johann Nigri* from Regensburg, a friend of Hassenstein. Nigri is mentioned #36, p. 44, as having been in Strassburg and #106, p. 116, as having written Schott.

309. Mitto ad te Codicillum... nomina instrumentorum...
This work is not extant (cf. p. xi) and according to Schmidt, "Notices... P.S.," seems never to have been published. For other lost works by Schott, cf. N. 4 and N. 5.

It was practice among scholars to send copies of their works and also works or letters of others to learned friends for perusal and criticism. Schott

P. 33   #25   N. 309

sent riddles and poems to Rusch (#130) who had sent him poems (#117). His poem "De tribus Iohannibus" he sent to Geiler (#240) and to Gossenbrot (#242) who also received others of Schott's writings (#171, p. 191). Groshug sent Schott compositions (#181, p. 201). Gesler who had sent poems to Schott received the poems written by Schott and Hassenstein (#235). Occo borrowed compositions by Schott and others (#139) and returned a work of Schott (#150, p. 164). Wimpheling sent a poem in praise of Schott to the latter (#244) and sent copies of his *De triplici candore Marie* to Schott and other friends (N. 1701). Moser sent Schott a funeral oration (#95, p. 107).

P. 34

310. dominum Ladislaum: per Laurencium Mercatorem... Vlricum Fronsperger...
For Ladislaus of Veszprém,* cf. N. 101, par. 3. Laurentius Hertzog (cf. N. 171) carried Schott's gifts to Ferrara. Ulrich Fronsperger* was a fellow student and friend of Schott and Hassenstein.

311. Hic qui has litteras... studiosus ut spero bonarum litterarum.
It is not known what young Alsatian is referred to, perhaps a *famulus* of Geiler who had studied in the Lowlands with the Brethren of the Common Life (cf. N. 88) and was now to continue his education at Bologna or Ferrara.

#26. TO VITUS MAELER Strassburg, 9 September 1481

312. Summary Maeler is requested to expedite a matrimonial case and to procure a *gratia expectativa* for Martinus Lauri; because the bearer of this letter is unknown to Schott, money for Lauri will be sent by Johann Burckard* who is to be in Rome by 1 November. Schott has not heard of any vacant benefice in Strassburg.

313. Sane per Laurencium Hertzog mercatorem causam Matrimonialem... misi...
Laurentius Hertzog (N. 171) was already on his way to Rome with details about the matrimonial case, which is mentioned again in #27 and #29. Nothing is known of the case.

314. Martinus Lauri de Vingen... graciam expectatiuam... in forma pauperum
We have found no information in other sources about Martinus Lauri de Vingen, who, Schott tells us, was a priest of sufficient training but poor from the diocese of Constance and who wished Schott to procure for him a *gratia expectativa* for a benefice in the Strassburg diocese (also mentioned #27, p. 35, and #29, pp. 36, 37), but decided against it. He may be identical with Martinus, the parish priest of St. Thomas, mentioned in #202.

It is possible that Lauri originated from a village named Fingen, now no longer existing, for there is a village near Constance named Anderfingen; indeed, the ending-*fingen* occurs in several place names of the Constance and Baden-Württemberg area.

The legal term for entitling persons with no means to sue or to be defended in court without payment of fees is "in forma pauperis." The variant used in this passage, "in forma pauperum," must mean that for a *gratia* thus obtained the fee would be waived.

315. ad aliquod beneficium eciam curatum... monasterij sancti Stephani
The convent of St. Stephan is listed by Wuerdtwein (62) among the institutions in the Strassburg diocese whose benefices were controlled by the Strassburg cathedral chapter, certain chapter members having authority to fill certain benefices, e.g., the *custos* appointed the chaplain of the altar of St. Stephen. Cf. N. 437.

St. Stephan in Strassburg, which began as a Benedictine convent and changed to the rule of St. Augustine, was founded in the seventh century by Adalbert, brother of St. Odile, on the site of the Roman castle inside the city walls. Adalbert's daughter Amalia was the first abbess. Confirmed by Childeric II († 720) and by Lothar in 845, the convent came under the dominion of the bishop of Strassburg in 1003. Records mention only one abbess in the fifteenth century, Dorothea von Ratzemhusen 1492. Cf. Barth, *Handbuch*, 1487-1501; *Gallia Christiana*, V (Paris 1731), 843, 846.

316. Pater meus rarissime est domi... nihil praeter voluntatem eius...
During the year 1481 Schott, Sr., attended the *Nürnberg Tag*, at which members of the empire decreed to assist Friedrich III in his war against Matthias of Hungary* (cf. N. 623). He was also a delegate to the meetings of the league (N. 72) concerning the Richard Püller affair (cf. N. 358). While his father was absent, Schott carried on his father's work (cf. N. 113), but he did not undertake decisions about his own future, such as plans for going away to study.

#27. TO VITUS MAELER Strassburg, 15 October 1481

317. Summary This letter and the promised 16 florins are being delivered by Johann Burckard.* Maeler is to secure for Martinus Lauri von Vingen a *gratia expectativa* for a post at St. Stephen convent. There has been no word from Maeler about the matrimonial case. Johann Müller* visited Schott three days previously.

318. Schripsi ad te diebus superioribus...
The content of this letter is almost identical with that of #26. Evidently Schott did not trust the bearer of #26 to deliver the message to Maeler (cf. #264). For notes to cases mentioned in this item, cf. notes to #26.

319. Magister Iohannes Muller... apud me esset
Müller was at Baden-Baden (cf. N. 211).

#28. TO JOHANN ROT Strassburg, 20 October 1481

320. Summary Schott's reason for not visiting Rot is not illness but preoccupation with his father's affairs, both when the latter is at home and when he is away.

P. 36   #28   N. 321

321. domino Ioanni Rot in Tambach Curato
Rot had succeeded Müller in the Dambach benefice in early 1480 (cf. #16 and N. 239).

322. ita me parentum onus... ad se nectit
Cf. N. 87 and N. 113, par. 2.

323. Pater grauedinosus abijt Legatus ad Foederatos
Cf. N. 358.

324. Soror filium enixa: apud nos... agit
The sister may be Ottilia, the only one of Schott's three married sisters who did not live in Strassburg. Ottilia's son Lucas von Adelsheim died in 1505.

325. Magister Iohannes Muller... sanus a me recessit.
Müller's visit was mentioned in the letter of 15 October to Maeler (#28; cf. N. 319).

#29. TO VITUS MAELER   Strassburg, 4 November 1481

326. Summary Maeler is asked to obtain the *gratia expectativa* for Martinus Lauri by some means other than *in forma pauperum*. Schott awaits the dispensation in the matrimonial case. He recommends the bearers; both are friends and neighbors of the Schotts and would like to be employed in Rome.
   In the postscript Schott advises Maeler to drop proceedings for both the *gratia expectativa*, because Lauri does not believe it will help him obtain a benefice, and the matrimonial case, because it presents difficulties.

327. Scripsi ad te vir optime/ diebus... exactis...
Cf. N. 318. For notes on the cases mentioned in this letter, cf. notes to #26.

P. 37

328. Nondum redijt ad nos Laurencius mercator... cum altero Laurencio...
The first person referred to is Laurentius Hertzog; the second may be Laurentius Grave (cf. N. 170 and N. 171).

329. Hos qui ad te litteras has ferunt... intelligant
Nothing more is known about the two messengers.

330. scribo ad vos praesentibus... Valete
Schott uses the formal form of address to Maeler in this postscript, perhaps for the benefit of the messengers. For Schott's opinion on the formal form, cf. #9, p. 15, and N. 184.

P. 37 #30 N. 331

#30. TO THOMAS WOLF, SR. Strassburg, 23 December 1842

331. Summary Schott reports on the litigation in Rome between Wolf's young nephew and ward, Thomas Wolf, Jr.,* and Engelhard Funck* over the canonicate at St. Thomas (to which the chapter of St. Thomas had elected young Wolf). Schott suggests that Wolf, Sr., let the Roman tribunal handle the case and avoid personal interference. The child Thomas has been seriously ill but is recuperating and is being cared for in the home of Johann Hell* (called Onheim). Schott has been consecrated priest; he is not yet sure when he will celebrate his first mass and whether it should be an occasion of pomp and ceremony or a simple service; he asks Wolf's advice on the matter.

P. 38

332. This is one of five letters written to Wolf, Sr., while he was in residence at Worms as cathedral canon. The letters in chronological order are: #35, #38, #30, #40, #42, #57. For a discussion of the date of this item which is "before the kalends of January," cf. N. 218.

333. Consolar te exulantem vt quereris Doctor praestantissime...
Thomas Wolf, Sr., had been at Bologna with Schott and, according to Schott, was responsible for Schott's obtaining the canonicate at New St. Peter (#100, p. 110; N. 116, par. 2). During Wolf's term of residence at Worms, Schott lived in Wolf's canonical house (N. 404).

334. Quod ad rem Thome nostri attinet...
The Thomas mentioned is the child canon of St. Thomas, Thomas Wolf, Jr., namesake, nephew and ward of Thomas Wolf, Sr., and godson of Schott. The affair concerning young Thomas is the case of litigation brought against the child canon by Engelhard Funck,* lawyer at Rome.
At the death of Johann Hell,* canon and dean of St. Thomas, in 1481, Jacob Hagen* was nominated by Wolf, Sr., to the vacant canonicate, but in the following year 1482, Hagen resigned the canonicate in favor of young Thomas. The latter's claim to the benefice was, however, contested by Engelhard Funck, who held a *gratia apostolica* for a benefice at St. Thomas. As counselor for young Thomas, Wolf, Sr., appointed Johann Burckard,* procurator at the *Curia* in Rome. Litigation dragged on for five years; at one point in 1484 Funck even cited Schott to appear at the *Curia* (#55), although Schott had no official connection with the case. After much expense, worry and correspondence, the court in 1487, probably soon after 7 July (#100, N. 1229), decided in favor of young Thomas.
The case is explained in detail in item #74,; it is mentioned in items: #55, p. 61; #75, p. 82; #86; #93; #100; #172.

335. Tum quia vt virum noui: Epistolis non cedit... in lite... cum Rot...
Engelhard Funck, obviously an avid and relentless benefice hunter, had early in the year of 1482 caused Johann Rot considerable expense by starting a case of litigation against him over a benefice at St. Thomas, as Schott tells us, and only withdrew claim to the benefice after repeated letters from officers of the chapter. This benefice, which Rot seems not to have been able to hold against other claimants, must have been an exceedingly juicy

plum, because Vitus Maeler* also competed for it until advised by Schott to desist. Cf. #179, N. 1277, N. 1278.

336. Prepositum et Decanum sancti Thome
The *praepositus* of St. Thomas at this time was Christopf von Uttenheim*; the dean was Johann Simmler*.

337. sancti Thome
St. Thomas, a collegiate church since 1031, was second in importance only to the cathedral (cf. N. 117). It was a very wealthy foundation; hence its 26 canonicates and 26 vicarates were considered prize benefices. Until the Reformation it played a leading role in the religious and social life of Strassburg. It is now an important Protestant church of Strassburg.
Cf. Barth, *Handbuch*, 1503-1513. Grandidier, *État*, 11f. Schmidt, *Chapitre, passim*. Schneegans, *Église, passim*.

338. Quamobrem honestius... eum per auditorem Rote compesci...
Schott advises that Funck be dealt with by the *Rota Romana*, the high tribunal at Rome which decides contentious cases, and that Wolf refrain from personal interference.

339. Dominum Theobaldum Fuchs... Dominum Ioannem Onheim... Otiliam eius...
I. e., Theobald Fuchs*; Johann Hell,* called Onheim. Otilia may be the latter's housekeeper or sister.

340. nudiustercius sacrum presbiterij ordinem... nondum decreuimus.
Schott was, according to his own statement here, ordained 21 December 1482; in #39 (p. 45) he tells us that he celebrated his first mass on 2 February 1483.

341. Verum vnum est... consilio tuo... sententiam tuam significes.
As *praepositus* of Old St. Peter, Wolf would be well versed in protocol. Thus it is logical that Schott should put questions to Wolf about the manner in which his first mass ought to be celebrated. Wolf's answers are mentioned in #40 (p. 46) when Schott reports on the celebration of his first mass. This event is the subject of #198. Cf. also N. 401.

342. Bartolum super C et super prima parte...
The original has *Bar. super C...* The abbreviation *Bar.* occurs seven times in the *Lucubraciunculae*: f. 17b (#30, p. 39), f. 123a (#209, p. 217), f. 127a (#212, p. 224), twice on f. 135b (#217, p. 237), f. 146b (#226, p. 254), f. 148a (#229, p. 256) and each time it obviously indicates a legal glossator. In this edition the abbreviation has been interpreted as referring to the great glossator Bartolus de Saso; however the abbreviation for Bartolus given by Cappelli is *Bart.* which occurs once in the *Lucubraciunculae* on f. 148a (#229, middle of last paragraph on p. 256). The abbreviation *Bar.*

P. 39   #30   N. 342

according to Cappelli refers to the prophet Baruch, an interpretation which does not fit the occurrences in the *Lucubraciunculae*. Were both *Bar.* and *Bart.* used as abbreviations for Bartolus in the fifteenth century? Brant's *Titulorum...* has *Bar.* (442) and *Bart.* (446), but unfortunately Brant does not explain who is meant. Seckel (I, 317, n. 14) mentions two occurrences of *Bar.* which he says refer to the glossator Bernardus (the accepted abbreviation for whom is *Ber.*).

It is possible that Schott and Brant used the abbreviation *Bar.* to designate their celebrated elder contemporary, the jurist Andreas Barbatia (Barbazza) Siculus who taught law at Bologna in the 1470's. Whether Schott studied under Barbatia is not known, but he did have copies of Barbatia's works and sent three works by Barbatia to Müller. Cf. #15, p. 24; #173, p. 194; N. 236.

#31. TO VITUS MAELER Strassburg, 26 February 1482

343. Summary Schott sometimes wishes he and Maeler could exchange places so that their mutual affection and cooperation might be evident. [I. e., Schott feels he is always asking favors of Maeler and is unable to do anything in return.]

#32. TO EMERICH KEMEL Strassburg, 5 April 1482

344. Summary Kemel is requested to add his recommendation to those recommendations being presented to the pope on behalf of Schott for a certain prebend. Schott declares that he has been prompted by neither ambition nor avarice to seek this benefice, but solely by the desire to serve God in peace and quiet, removed from the hue and cry of public life.

Immediately after hearing Kemel's speech in Strassburg, the city officials decided to bestow upon him such honors as are usually reserved for princes; only Kemel's precipitate departure prevented carrying out the plan.

345. fratri Emerico de Kemel: ordinis fratrum minorum de Obseruancia
Emerich Kemel belonged to that faction of the Franciscan Order called Observants who adhered to the original strict rule of poverty and were violently opposed to the Conventuals, the Franciscan faction which had come into existence during the fourteenth century and which maintained that the Franciscan Order like other orders should have the right to hold property. After Martin V in 1430 granted the Conventuals the right to hold property, the friction between the two factions increased to such a point that Eugene IV by the Separation Bull of 1446 recognized independence of the two from one another, although they both remained within the order. Cf. "Friars Minor," *EB*, VI, 281-302.

346. domui nostrae dum Argentine essetis
Kemel apparently was guest in the Schott home during his stay in Strassburg (cf. N. 351). Note that in this letter and in #186 Schott uses the formal form of address to Kemel, while in #187 he uses the familiar form (cf. N. 184).

347. in causa quadam praebendali... meipsum eciam commendare dignemini.
The "prebendal case" refers, of course, to the canonicate at New St. Peter which Schott obtained in spring 1482 (cf. xxvii and N. 116, 1).

348. huic nuncio nostro... ad Sanctissimum...
The messenger was probably carrying to the pope the letter of recommendation from the Strassburg magistracy (#161) and the letters to other dignitaries whose support Schott solicited (#158, #159, #160). Cf. N. 1143.

349. parentem meum iam in Magistratu summo vrbis nostre constitutum...
Schott, Sr., was mayor of Strassburg in 1482.

350. Id sane polliceor: quod neque ambicioni... negociosis commercijs...
Schott's declaration that he desires the benefice not because of ambition but in order to lead a life removed from secular business is true. He never tried to accumulate benefices; on the contrary, he speaks repeatedly against this vice (N. 133) and in letters to Müller and Maeler states that he never wanted more than one benefice (#73, p. 80; #74, p. 82). His interest in a "quiet life" is spoken of elsewhere (cf. N. 255).

351. Nondum vllus vobis honor... a re publica nostra consueuerunt.
Kemel came to Strassburg in early 1482 while on tour to preach Sixtus IV's crusade against the Turks and to sell indulgences for supporting it; he also assisted in drafting statutes for the Knights of St. John of Jerusalem at Strassburg. His precipitous departure may have been occasioned by special orders from Sixtus IV, bidding him to proceed to Basel for the trial of Andreas Zamometič, archbishop of Carniola, whose campaign to reactivate the council of Basel and to dethrone Sixtus had gained considerable support and who was being held at Basel. Kemel was present at the trial and at the execution of Andreas which took place 4 May 1482 (cf. p. 735).
    Cf. *Anal. Francisc.*, II, 457, 481. *Bullarium*, III, 807, 813. Grandidier, *Chevaliers*, 58.

#33. TO JOHANN WIDMANN Strassburg, 5 July 1482

352. Summary Schott is sending books which Widmann has bought. He describes the symptoms of his brother-in-law's fever and asks Widmann's advice.

353. Sororius meus eadem febre laborat
Sachse, 409, gives for *sororius* the meaning of brother-in-law. It is not known which of Schott's brothers-in-law is referred to here.

354. Sabbato post Vdalrici
St. Udalrich's day, 4 July, fell on Friday in 1482; the Saturday (cf. N. 170) following was therefore 5 July.

#34. TO JOHANN GEILER Strassburg, 1 August 1482

355. Summary Schott misses Geiler who is at the baths. The carriage requested will fetch Geiler and his mother on 11 August. Schott, Sr., has been summoned to a conference of the league in Oberbaden, where it is hoped peace can be negotiated.

356. cum balnearum gracia secesseris...
Geiler may have been at Baden-Baden, although there is no indication in the text as to what baths he was visiting. For the popularity of baths, cf. N. 192.

357. Pollicitus est mihi Procurator fabrice... nomine Patris absentis...
Schott, Sr., was a director of the cathedral *fabrica* (cf. N. 76), which evidently was responsible for transportation of the cathedral preacher. In his father's absence, Schott had made arrangements with the procurator of the *fabrica*. The procurator at the time may have been Conrad Hammelburger whose name with the titles of procurator of the *fabrica* and vicar of the grand chapter appears among the executors of Jacob Reiffsteck's will (cf. Dacheux, *Réf.*, 359, n. 1). Geiler would be expected to return to Strassburg to preach before and on the next feast of the Virgin (N. 284) which here is Assumption Day, 15 August. In 1482 the Sunday preceding the holiday was 11 August.

358. Absens autem est genitor meus... bellum efficient.
The conference at Oberbaden (presumably the town of Baden in Switzerland, northwest of Zürich) was called to deal with the case of Richard Püller von Hohenburg which was threatening to cause war between Strassburg and Zürich.

Richard Püller, described by Trithemius as "vir bellicosus et inquietus," was the last male descendant of the Hohenburgs, an Alsatian family belonging to the Hohenzollern *gens*. In 1474 he was banned from the Strassburg diocese by Bishop Ruprecht for sodomy and fled to Zürich, where he was received with honor and made a citizen, not because of his own wealth – for he had depleted his estates in an abortive quarrel with *Pfalzgraf* Friedrich I – but because his wife Sophie Bock was the heiress of wealthy Hans Conrad Bock, former mayor (*Altammeister*) of Strassburg. Sophie, however, had separated from Püller and returned to her father's home in the city of Strassburg.

When Bock died in 1480, Püller claimed his wife and her inheritance, but she appealed to Strassburg for protection and was made a citizen in her own right. When Püller through the magistrates of Zürich asked for a safe conduct to Strassburg, Strassburg refused to allow him within its gates and sent to Zürich a letter he had written some years before in which he had promised to enter a religious order and repent. Püller disclaimed the letter. Zürich with an eye to the inheritance continued to support Püller and demanded a reconciliation between husband and wife. After much correspondence failed to settle the dispute, members of the league (N. 72) sent delegates to a meeting in Oberbaden 1480, where Bern tried vainly to mediate between the two cities.

In 1481 strained relations reached the breaking point when Zürich captured and imprisoned two Alsatians (Caspar Bockel and Rudolf Voltz) on their way as pilgrims to Einsiedeln. Fruitless meetings of delegates followed at Luzern and Zürich. In 1482 Zürich informed Strassburg by

letter that she was preparing to march on Strassburg. The league intervened and called a meeting at Einsiedeln which ended in failure as did a second meeting at Oberbaden in August. Finally at a third meeting in Strassburg a settlement was reached: Zürich agreed to convict Püller for his crimes and Strassburg agreed to pay 8,000 guilders. Peace was signed at Zürich on 23 September 1482. On the same day Püller along with his servant who had been involved in his crimes was burned at the stake outside the gates of Zürich.
 Cf. *ADB*, XII, 671. *Code hist.*, II, 209ff. Dacheux, *Réf.*, 301, n. 1. *Inventaire*, III, 106; IV, 59. Reuss, *Meyer*, 36, 108f. Saladin, 297f. Stenzel, "Politik," 18f.; Strobel, 383ff.

359. hominem perlepidum...
Not identified.

360. Dominam commatrem meam/ matrem tuam
Commater: Baxter, 89 = godmother; Sachse, 409 = *gevater*. Cf. the medieval proverb: "Commater dantis manui manus accipientis" ("Gebende Hand und empfangende Hand sind nahe Verwandte").
 Since the word *Domine* below in the last sentence of the paragraph in the text refers to Geiler's mother, the conclusion must be that *Dominam commatrem meam* likewise refers to her and that *matrem tuam* is therefore in apposition to *commatrem*. There is no evidence that Geiler's mother Anna Zuber* was Schott's godmother; indeed, the Geilers and the Schotts apparently were not known to one another until Geiler became a preacher. Hence *commatrem* here has the meaning of "courtesy aunt;" cf. French *commère*.

361. Domine et matri Fridrichen
For *Domine*, cf. N. 360 above. *Matri Fridrichen* may refer to "Domina Veronica Friderichen" mentioned in Geiler's will (cf. Dacheux, *Réf.*, 304, lxxiii) or to Agnes von Werdenberg, the mother of Friedrich von Zollern,* or to the mother of Friedrich Büchsner.*

#35. TO THOMAS WOLF, SR. Strassburg, 5 November 1482

362. Summary Schott thanks Wolf for all his kindnesses. The nephew Thomas Wolf, Jr.,* has been very ill with a cough but is recuperating under the watchful care of Theobald Fuchs* and the Schotts.

363. This is the earliest in the series of letters written to Wolf at Worms (cf. N. 332).

364. Humanitatem et incredibilem in me... omni ex parte demonstras...
As mentioned in N. 116, par. 2, Schott attributed his canonicate to Wolf's efforts. While Wolf was in Worms, Schott lived in Wolf's canonical house (cf. #40, p. 47, and N. 404). What specific favors of Wolf are referred to here can only be conjectured.

P. 42 #35 N. 365

365. Et ipse Thomas Canonicus... in re timeamus.
The child Thomas Wolf, Jr.,* nephew of Wolf, Sr., and canon of St. Thomas (cf. N. 334), was at this time living in the home of Theobald Fuchs,* *scholasticus* of New St. Peter. For a later report on the child's illness, cf. #30, p. 38.

#36. TO BOHUSLAUS VON HASSENSTEIN Strassburg, 16 November 1482

366. Summary Because there has long been no word from Hassenstein, Schott is not sure whether the former is still in Italy or has returned to Bohemia. Schott is to be consecrated priest during the Christmas season and expects to go off for theological study when his year of residence as canon of New. St. Peter is ended.

367. This letter and #37 from Hassenstein to Schott are placed together, though not in chronological order; cf. N. 36 and N. 278, and chronology III (Schott-Hassenstein correspondence).

P. 43

368. prorsus ignoro: domum ne redieris... operam impendas.
When Schott wrote this letter, Hassenstein was still at Ferrara, where he obtained his doctorate in canon law ten days later, 26 November 1482 (Pardi, *Titoli*, 60). Thereafter he returned to Bohemia via Strassburg (cf. N. 101, par. 3).

369. Magistri Valentini de Ponte
Unidentified.

370. Magnificatorem rerum vestrarum Pium secundum...
Aeneas Sylvio Piccolomini who was Pope Pius II (1458-1464) wrote *Historica Bohemica (Austriaca).*

371. Iohannes ille Canonicus Eistetensis
Unidentified. Riegger, *Anal.*, 198, mentions a venerable and worthy Johann Gretzer, canon of Eichstätt.

372. Ego iam per dei graciam... sim suscepturus.
Schott is referring to his having begun a theological career and his impending consecration as priest (N. 340), a station which Hassenstein had urged him to attain. The two sentences: "Sed vide vt et... quid dico," are probably a reference to the plan of the two friends to spend their lives working and studying together (N. 302).

373. Vbi annum residencie compleuero... Theologie operam dabo.
Schott's year of residence at New St. Peter would be completed in April 1483 (cf. N. 116), and he would be free to leave his post. For the fate of his dream to go away for theological studies, cf. xxvii and N. 121.

374. Per Nurenbergam... comodissime mittere posses.
Schott seems to have had connections with book dealers in Nürnberg (cf. #202).

375. Aut per patrem Iohannem Nigri Priorem...
Schott had met Johann Nigri,* a friend of Hassenstein's, at Wildbad in the summer of 1481 (#25, p. 33).

#37. TO PETER SCHOTT FROM BOHUSLAUS VON HASSENSTEIN [Ferrara], 20 May 1482

376. Summary In answer to Schott's letter asking about his health, Hassenstein composes a poem in which he describes his grave illness and his recovery. He hints that he may be seeing Schott sooner than the latter anticipates.

377. Cf. N. 367: This letter may be the reply to #169, Schott's letter of early 1482, or to one of several other lost letters Schott wrote at the time.

378. Venetos hostes nobis imminere
Venice was at war with Ferrara in 1483 (Raynaldus, 1483, pars. 6ff.); apparently at the time of this letter war clouds were already threatening.

379. patire calamitatem intueri.
The calamity in his homeland of which Hassenstein speaks may be the disturbances in economic, religious and political circles of Bohemia and elsewhere caused by the Hussites. For other references to the Hussites, cf. #107, p. 118; #109, pp. 120f.; #232, p. 260; #238, p. 270; #239, pp. 272f.; Hassenstein's letter of 16 March [1507] to Geiler, Appendix J; N. 828.

380. Litteras trinas a te recepi... edoceri cupis.
In late 1481 or early 1482 Hassenstein had been seriously ill and his tutor Ladislaus* had informed Schott of the illness (cf. #169). Schott had then written to both Ladislaus (#189) and to Hassenstein (#169).

381. Viuo: licet nostre forsan... Flegetonta videntem.
Because Christianity is clothed with classical garb – e.g., Virgin Mary is the goddess mother unfurling the heavens (*Olympum*), Cornova (250) terms this poem an outrageous combination of Christian truth and heathen lies, though admitting such practice to be common to almost all former poets. He judges from the viewpoint of his age, without considering that neither Hassenstein nor any fellow humanist believed it in the least blasphemous. Schmidt (H. L., II, 19) also objects to this practice. Other examples are: "Elysian fields" for heaven (#16, p. 24), *Sator* for God (#288, p. 310), the examples in N. 1576.

382. Ex eo tempore/ quo Daniel... Petrus accelerat...
Neither of these persons who carried letters from Hassenstein in Ferrara to

Schott in Strassburg has been identified. It is possible that they were Schott's nephews, Daniel and Petrus Müg (sons of Maria Schott* and Florencius Müg*), who may have been studying at Ferrara.

383. Videbo te cicius: quam speras forte.
This is a hint that Hassenstein intends to visit Strassburg after completion of his studies in Ferrara. Cf. N. 101., par. 3.

P. 45

#38. TO THOMAS WOLF, SR. Strassburg, 21 November 1482

384. Summary Schott suggests that Wolf* take time from his work for proper recreation, especially because of the plague in Worms. The dean of New St. Peter has recently been installed.

385. Cf. N. 332 for the series of letters to Wolf at Worms.

386. Tamen nonnumquam remittere seueritatem... prudentissimi viri consueuerunt.
For a similar passage, cf. #14, p. 22.

387. in loco (vt aiunt) pestilenti...
The wording is reminiscent of Jr. 42:22.

388. Longeuum Patrem
Cf. Vergil *Aen.* iii. 169; ii. 529.

389. decanus noster possessionem adeptus in octaua Martini.
"Noster" indicates that Schott is speaking of the dean of New St. Peter, of which Wolf was also canon. The dean who took office was probably Jacob Hagen.* The date of his installation was 4 November, St. Martin's Day being 11 November.

#39. TO VITUS MAELER Strassburg, 4 February 1483

390. Summary Schott congratulates Maeler on his new accessions. He reports that he himself has entered the priesthood and has celebrated his first mass. He bids Maeler secure a *gratia expectativa* for Johann Müller.

391. accessionibus tuis amplissimis... gratulor
The reference concerning Maeler's acquisitions may be to Maeler's new rank as papal official which Sixtus IV granted in 1482 to the 100 solicitors and procurators of the Roman *Curia*. This new rank may have carried the title solicitor of apostolic letters which we know Maeler received in 1482 (Hofmann, II, 197) and by which Schott addresses Maeler in June 1483 (#43). The reference may also be to the deanship mentioned below in this letter, for –

P. 45   #39   N. 391

although Schott does not address Maeler with the title "Decanus Iuncensis" until March 1484 (#55, N. 486) – it is possible that already in early 1483 Maeler was in the process of acquiring the deanship. Hämmerle lists for Maeler the benefice of priest at St. Moritz (Augsburg) in 1483 and Knod a benefice in the Trent diocese.

392. Ego iam diuino munere summum sacerdocij culmen... mitto.
Cf. N. 340.

393. Decanatui tuo...
Sleumer defines *decanatus* as a district composed of several parishes with a dean at its head. Cf. N. 391.

394. nec frustra decipieris etc.
Cf. Terence *Heaut.* 725-729.

P. 46

395. Duos aureos Renenses... huic Laurencio... tradas.
The two gold florins were mentioned in #31. The bearer of this letter may have been either Laurentius Hertzog or Laurentius Grave (N. 170, N. 171).

396. Magistrum Iohannem Muller... gracia expectatiua... Argentine non est.
From this time on Schott repeatedly asks Maeler's help in securing a benefice for Müller (cf. N. 527). Müller was in Baden-Baden when this letter was written (N. 211 and biographical note on Müller).

397. Ad collacionem Episcopi... Petri iunioris Argentinensum...
The three highest collegiate chapters of Strassburg had united in the fourteenth century (cf. N. 117, par. 4). A *gratia expectativa* (N. 130) addressed to the united chapters would presumably be valid for a benefice in any one of the chapters.

398. nouum creari Pontificem summum...
There may have been rumors that Sixtus IV († 1484) was ill, or perhaps Schott was just making plans for the future.

#40. TO THOMAS WOLF, SR. Strassburg, 1 March 1483

399. Summary Schott is grateful for Wolf's advice on the celebration of his first mass and tells about the guests invited on that occasion. He is busy attending social functions in his honor. Wolf's full granaries await him.

400. Cf. N. 332.

401. Prudenter quidem solennitati... consuluisti... grata nobis fuit.
Schott had asked Wolf's advice in the letter of 23 December 1482 (#30, p. 38). For the date of Schott's mass, cf. N. 340. Cf. also N. 341, N. 184.
      Evidently Wolf had suggested a number of relatives and friends be

invited to the celebration, but since his letter was somewhat late, the Schotts, who seem to have disliked elaborate functions, had already invited only the few who could not be excluded, *viz.*, all the canons and vicars of New St. Peter, several priests, six to eight relatives. Obviously Schott's immediate family and his closest friends, such as Geiler and Rot (and perhaps even Hassenstein, cf. N. 101, par. 3), though not mentioned, also attended. Cf. #198 and N. 1378.

P. 47

402. obruens me obstrepencium turba... inter epulas etenim hec dictabam
The many social functions held in honor of Schott are mentioned in #190, pp. 208f.

403. granaria tua plena te opperiunt... Dominum Laurencium Hell...
For the grain received by benefice holders from the chapter, cf. N. 116, last paragraph. Laurentius Hell* was a cousin of Thomas Wolf, Sr.

404. domum tuam quam incolo.
During Wolf's absence in Worms, Schott lived, at least part of the time, in Wolf's canonical house which belonged to St. Thomas and which Wolf had occupied apparently since 1479. In 1484, according to Schott's letter of 6 July 1484 (#57, p. 62), the house became the residence of the boy canon Thomas Wolf, Jr. This house, demolished in our century, was built sometime before 1276 and through the centuries bore various names: "Zum Hanap," "Zum Napfe," "Zu dem Nope," "Zu dem Stouffe," "Zum roten Hahn" and "Sturmhof." Wimpheling, Erasmus and Calvin are said to have stayed here, and Johann Sturm, the first director of the Strassburg gymnasium (N. 18), lived here from 1554 until his retirement in 1581 and perhaps until his death in 1589. Cf. N. 505.

#41. TO JOHANN WIDMANN Strassburg, 25 May 1483

405. Summary Schott forwards letters to Widmann and expects Widmann's arrival in Strassburg soon. He sends greetings to Johann Müller.

406. Ioanni Vuidman: Phisico principis Badensis
Cf. N. 288.

407. Soror mea
Possibly Ottilia Schott.*

408. Magistrum Iohannem muller
Cf. N. 396.

#42. TO THOMAS WOLF, SR. Strassburg, 31 May 1483

409. Summary Schott has been ill. He is glad that Wolf may soon return

P. 47   #42   N. 409

from Worms, and Susanna von Cöllen is looking forward to Wolf's contribution to church services in Strassburg.

410. Cf. N. 332.

411. Quamquam te ex infirmitate nostra turbari... Medicus sperabamus.
Schott's illness is mentioned in #43, p. 48. The physician attending Schott was probably Widmann, cf. N. 405. For remarks on Schott's health, cf. N. 87.

412. gaudeo residencie tue terminum aduentare...
Wolf came home to Strassburg in September 1483 only for a visit and did not leave Worms permanently until August 1484 (#57, p. 62). His term of residence at Worms was almost 2 years (#35, #57).

P. 48

413. Canonici nostri; praeter Prepositum...
Schott is doubtless speaking of the chapter members of New St. Peter (cf. N. 389) where Wolf was a fellow canon. The *praepositus* was Conrad Munthart.*

414. quod sperat te inter tam compositos... concentores... sis executurus.
This statement implies that the cathedral at Worms had especially well trained singers and that Wolf himself had a good voice.

415. Breue est quod me tibi precipere... extricari valet.
There is no other mention in the *Luc.* of Wolf's involvment in secular affairs, against which Schott warns here. Certainly Wolf as a man of considerable wealth had many secular transactions connected with his private estates. Such transactions Schott must have noted while living in Wolf's home; also Wolf's non-celibacy was common knowledge (cf. biographical note on Wolf).

416. et funem ut Hieronymus docet non soluat...
The passage in St. Jerome alluded to has not been identified.

#43. TO VITUS MAELER Strassburg, 9 June 1483

417. Summary Schott has been seriously ill, but is now recovering. He discusses the Ottobeuren case before the city of Strassburg and announces that Johann Müller may have become canon and dean at Pforzheim.

418. tam graui et molesto morbo decubuerim...
The illness mentioned to Wolf on 31 May must have worsened soon thereafter (#42). For Schott's health, cf. N. 87.

419. De causa Abbatis in Ottenburn...
Nothing is known of this case which is also referred to in #46, p. 51; #59, p. 65; #62, p. 68. Nicolaus Roeslin,* abbott of the Benedictine abbey Ottobeuren in Bavaria, was evidently the defendant. The plaintiff was the woman – whose name is not given – mentioned #59, p. 65. In order to be tried in the city courts of Strassburg, the case must have been a civil case and may have concerned a dispute over money or property. The plaintiff may have been a Strassburg citizen since the case was tried in Strassburg, or the court in the district where the dispute arose may have referred the case to Strassburg for arbitration (cf. the case of procurator Rot vs. the Dunzenheims #162, p. 180, which was referred to another city).

420. Consules vrbis nostre nihil acturos...
The term *Consules* refers to members of the Strassburg city council; cf. *consulibus* #162, p. 176, and *consulatus* #228, p. 255. Cf. also N. 69.

P. 49

421 dispensacione/ in causa quadam Matrimoniali...
We have found no information on this case.

422. Laurencio presencium latori
The bearer was probably Laurentius Hertzog or Laurentius Grave (N. 170, N. 171).

423. Magister Iohannes muller Canonicatum... Decanatum in Pforçheim...
This is the only mention of the post in Pforzheim. It is quite possible that Müller was prevented from securing the canonicate and deanship by *Markgraf* Christoph von Baden* who later thwarted attempts to acquire for Müller a proper benefice at Strassburg, because he feared Müller might resign as tutor of the young heir apparent of Baden (cf. #175). Cf. N. 211 and N. 526.

424. Nona die Iunij.
Schott here uses the modern system for dates; normally he uses the Latin.

#44. TO JOHANN WIDMANN Strassburg, 16 August 1483

425. Summary The Schotts are greatly distressed over Widmann's illness and offer to do anything in their power to help him. Widmann is to send a message with the provost's carriage which will be returning from the baths to Strassburg.

426. Prepositus ecclesie nostre ad balnea vestra diuertit...
It is not clear whether the *praepositus* of the cathedral or of New St. Peter is meant. If it is the *praepositus* of the cathedral – which is more likely since Widmann was not connected with any church in Strassburg and since "nostr-" was applied to the cathedral by all Strassburgers – then the person in question is Johann, duke of Bavaria.* If it is the *praepositus* of New St.

P. 49   #44   N. 426

Peter, then the person is Conrad Munthart* who is mentioned in May as suffering from tertian fever (#42, p. 48). The baths referred to are those at Baden-Baden, as is indicated by "vestra," for Widmann was at the time in Baden-Baden (cf. N. 288).

P. 50

#45. TO JACOB HAGEN Strassburg, 22 September 1483

427. Summary Schott sends Hagen,* who is at the baths, a gift of small game birds and best wishes for a salubrious holiday. He reports that the ranks of those in the choir at New St. Peter are much diminished and that Thomas Wolf, Sr., who has been in Strassburg is about to return to Worms.

428. muneribus huiuscemodi balneacioni accomodatis... hec nostra volatilia...
For information on baths and gifts sent to friends at baths, cf. N. 192. Small game birds were permitted on the diet of those undergoing the bath regimen.

429. ut adaquacionem hanc tuam: prosperam et salubrem...
The term *adaquatio*, from *adaquor*, means the stay at a watering place.

430. Tu fac ut termis indulgeas... diem vnum aut alterum... deesse...
The bath regimen of three weeks to a month once begun had to be completed if one wished to profit and not suffer any ill effects from it (cf. N. 192).

431. Ad eam etenim penuriam Canonicorum numerus...
The chapter members were either away or were just not attending services, because Hagen, who was presumably dean and hence in charge of discipline, was absent. Cf. N. 389.

#46. TO VITUS MAELER Strassburg, 20 October 1483

432. Summary Schott congratulates Maeler on his honors, emoluments and benefices but warns against the danger of too much ambition and too close involvement in the business of the *Curia*. Johann Müller with the heir apparent of Baden has gone to Paris.

433. honoribus... ac emolumentis/ accesionibusque...
For the complete list of Maeler's benefices, cf. his biographical note. Cf. also N. 133.

P. 51

434. Magister Iohannis muller cum primogenito principis Badensis Parisius...
Young Jacob of Baden* whom Müller had been tutoring since 1480 was now ready for university work. Just as Müller had accompanied young Schott to Paris, so he was now supervising Jacob there. Cf. N. 211 and N. 526.

#47. TO VITUS MAELER Strassburg, [early December] 1484

435. Summary Schott asks Maeler to secure for Johann Klein* of Plienswiler a *gratia expectativa* for a post as chaplain in the church of St. Richardis Abbey at Andlau. This is to be done as soon as possible, and the money for expenses will be sent later.

436. Scripsi non multos ante dies... litteras tumultuarias...
The letter referred to is #62, written 24 November 1484, in which Schott introduces and fully explains the case of Johann Klein.* The date of the present item should therefore be about 1 December. Klein is mentioned also in #68, #69, #72. Cf. N. 264, pars. 2f.

437. Ad Collaciones ecclesie Argentinensis... Sancte Richardis in Andelo...
Wuerdtwein, viii, 61, lists St. Richardis abbey among those institutions whose benefices were controlled by the chapter of the Strassburg cathedral; he names also the chapter members having power of assigning the benefices. Cf. N. 315.

The abbey of St. Richardis, belonging to the Benedictine Order, was founded as a *collegium* for noble women in 880 by Empress Richardis, wife of Karl III (the Fat). The empress served as the first abbess. In 881 the abbey came under the jurisdiction of Pope John VIII. Only the abbess was required to take the vow of chastity; other members could return to the world at any time. Barbara von Knobloch was abbess 1480-1493. The abbey church had 13 chaplaincies.

Cf. Barth, *Handbuch*, 65f. *Gallia Christiana*, V (1731), 880. Rieple, 122ff., 144. Wuerdtwein, viii, 87.

438. et ceterorum
Cf. *Errata et Emenda*. The original has *etc*.

439. Iohannes Vueschbach... Vtinam dominus dirigat pedes... in viam pacis.
Johann Weschbach* was a colleague of Maeler. The pious wish is reminiscent of Lc. 1:79.

#48. TO JOHANN GEILER Strassburg, 7 February 1484

440. Schott requests Geiler's aid in persuading Friedrich von Zollern,* dean of the cathedral, to help settle the case of Udalrich Stromeyer, Jr.,* against Thomas Wolf, Jr.,* who has injured Udalrich.

441. gracia et pax
Rm. 1:7; I Cor. 1:3; II Cor. 1:2; Gal. 1:3.

442. Iniuriam illatam Vdalrico Stromeyer iuniori
It is not known what injury was done Udalrich, son of Udalrich Stromeyer, Sr.;* perhaps there had been a fight between Udalrich and the boy canon

P. 52   #48   N. 442

Wolf, who was at this time 9 years old. It is quite possible that Udalrich was a cathedral choir boy, since he insists upon having the opinion of "domini sui," the dean, before settling the case.

443. Pater illius/ qui facinus perpetrauit.,, ei compater.....
The father of young Thomas Wolf, Schott's godson, was a brother of Thomas Wolf, Sr.,* but there is disagreement in secondary sources as to his Christian name and his vocation; cf. biographical note on Johann Wolf.

444. Quod ad Casparem organistam pertinet...
Caspar's name does not appear among the cathedral organists mentioned by Gass, *Orgues*, 31. Nothing is known of Caspar or of the affair alluded to.

445. tercia ante Apolloniae...
St. Apollonia's Day is 9 February. Other items dated by fixed feasts are: # #96, 100, 114, 138, 151, 152.

#49. TO GUILLAUME DE ROCHEFORT [Rhentingen, before 30 August 1483]

446. Summary Schott, writing in the name of the Clingenthal sisters* who have been forcefully expelled from the Clingenthal convent and are subsisting in dire poverty at Rhentingen, asks Rochefort* (Rupefort), the chancellor of France, to intercede with Louis XI on their behalf.

447. Note that this item lacks a heading by Wimpheling (cf. N. 37). This item and #50 and #51 are chronologically out of order; for the date of their composition, see N. 450 below. The editor Wimpheling may have placed them here purposely because he considered the five items #49- #53 to be a unit (cf. N. 278).
   The *Luc.* contains six letters concerning the case of the Clingenthal sisters: three of the letters (#49- #51) solicit aid from Louis XI; two (#52, #53) solicit aid from Pope Sixtus IV; one (#85) asks Marcus Cardinal of St. Mark to receive the sisters into the Dominican Order.

448. Sororum a Clingenthal minoris Basilee eiectarum
For details about the case of the Clingenthal sisters, cf. Biographical Section: "Clingenthal Sisters."

P. 53

449. accessiones successusque vestros: tam egregie tanquam digne...
Rochefort* had but recently been appointed chancellor of France by Louis XI.

450. christianissimus Francorum Rex
The king of France referred to here is Louis XI (1461-1483). From evidence in the three letters #49-51, which were delivered simultaneously (N. 451),

it is clear that the date of their composition must have been some time before the death of Louis on 30 August 1483.

1) The statements concerning the French king's well-known piety, his liberality to the Church, the many new religious foundations established and the many churches restored during his reign (#51, p. 56) could apply at this time only to Louis XI, for his son Charles VIII who succeeded him in the latter part of 1483 was but six years of age.

2) Guillaume de Rochefort is congratulated on recent honors and promotion (#49, p. 53); this is a reference to his appointment as chancellor by Louis XI in 1483.

3) The expulsion of the sisters from Clingenthal is spoken of as having been quite recent (*diebus nuper exactis*, #50, p. 54). We know that this event took place in late 1482 or early 1483, because Glöckler (496) says the sisters began their work at Clingenthal 13 January 1480 and Schott says they were at Clingenthal nearly three years (#53, p. 58).

Apparently the death of Louis prevented any aid being granted to the sisters by the French crown; at least none is mentioned in records, and the plight of the sisters as described in #52 and #53 a year later has not changed.

451. litteras deprecatorias mittunt: generosi fratres Comites... non reddere
Counts Han and Wecker von Lyningen,* who had given the sisters refuge in Rhentingen (diocese of Metz), appealed – in a letter written by Schott (#50) – to Louis XI for aid to the destitute nuns. The sisters themselves – in a letter also written by Schott (#51) – besought Louis to lighten their overburdened lot. These two letters were sent off at the same time as the present item to Rochefort at Paris to be handed by the latter to his sovereign.

#50. TO THE KING OF FRANCE [Rhentingen, before 30 August 1483]

452. Summary Schott, in the name of Counts Han and Wecker von Lyningen,* asks Louis XI to aid the indigent Clingenthal sisters.*

453. For the chronological order and the date of this item, cf. N. 447 and N. 450.

454. pro Sororibus a Clingenthal eiectis
Cf. N. 448.

455. Christianissimo Francorum Regi
Louis XI (cf. N. 450).

456. dominus Guillermus de Rupeforti
Guillaume de Rochefort.*

#51. TO THE KING OF FRANCE [Rhentingen, before 30 August 1483]

457. Summary Schott, writing for the Clingenthal sisters,* asks Louis XI to take pity on their plight.

P. 55 #51 N. 458

458. For the chronological order and date of this item, cf. N. 447 and N. 450.

459. Sorores a Clingenthal propulsarum... Regem Francorum
Cf. N. 448 and N. 450.

460. Ex litteris generosorum... Comitum de Lyningen... Guillermi de Rupeforti
Reference is made here to the letter written by Schott for the counts of Lyningen* (#50) and to the letter written to Guillaume de Rochefort* (#49); cf. N. 451.

P. 56

#52. TO POPE SIXTUS IV FROM LAMPERTHEIM Rhentingen, 17 February 1484

461. Summary Thomas Lampertheim,* confessor to the indigent sisters ejected from the convent of Clingenthal,* petitions Sixtus IV to grant the sisters a share of the money which is collected from the annual sale of indulgences in Rhentingen on the Feast of the Annunciation and which by order of Sixtus has for some years been divided among several orders.

462. Cf. N. 447. This letter and #53 were written at the same time. Cf. N. 466.

463. Pro Sororibus in Rhentingen petuntur...
Cf. N. 448.

464. Domino Sixto quarto
Sixtus IV was pope from 1471 to 13 August 1484. It is not known whether he granted the sisters the funds for which Lampertheim asked; cf. N. 473.

465. Frater Thomas Lampertheim
Thomas Lampertheim (Lamparter)* had been confessor to Anna Steelen, prioress of the persecuted nuns, and hence took a personal interest in their plight. He brought them to Rhentingen and served as their confessor. One may suppose, since Lampertheim was a close friend of Geiler, that Geiler learned from him the details of the case and was appalled at the treatment of this small group of devout women. It may have been Geiler who influenced Schott and later Christopf von Uttenheim* to support their cause which officially concerned the bishopric of Metz since Rhentingen belonged to that diocese.

P. 57

466. Comites de Lyningen qui eciam... scribunt
Counts Han and Wecker von Lyningen,* who had appealed to Louis XI the previous year for aid to the nuns (#50; cf. N. 451), evidently wrote to the

pope at this time, too, and very likely had Schott compose the letter for them as he had before.

467. in festo Annuncionis glorissime Virginis
The Feast of the Annunciation is 25 March.

468. xiiij kalendas Marcias...
The year 1484 was a leap year, hence any date before the kalends of March adds one day when translated into our system of reckoning and the date here is 17 February instead of 16 February.

P. 58

#53. TO POPE SIXTUS IV Rhentingen, 17 February, 1484

469. Summary Schott, writing in the name of the sisters expelled from Clingenthal,* describes the almost unendurable conditions under which they are existing at Rhentingen and entreats Sixtus IV to take pity on them.

470. Cf. N. 447 and N. 462.

471. Sarracenus aut Thurcus his moueri potuisset. Sed omnia... Romae.
For caustic remarks similar to Wimpheling's here: that this letter would have moved an infidel but only money talks at Rome, cf. #73, p. 80, and #177, p. 198; also N. 624.
     The proverb *Sed omnia venalia Romae* is probably based on Juvenal *Sat.* iii, 183. Cf. Riley, 311, 312; *Oxford Dictionary of English Proverbs*, 39; *Oxford Dictionary of Quotations*, 549a.

472. Sororum ex Clingenthal eiectarum
Cf. N. 448.

473. necessitatem nostram: quam propter obedienciam... nos passe sumus.
The plight of the nuns was a direct result of their obedience to Sixtus IV's orders. In 1480 Sixtus had given the Dominican provincial Jacob Stubach the task of reforming the rebellious convent at Clingenthal in the diocese of Basel. To initiate the reform Stubach had brought 15 Dominican nuns from the convent of Engelspforten at Gebweiler to Clingenthal (Barthelmé, 114f.), but the Clingenthal convent refused to be reformed and cast out the 15 nuns who had been brought in. The expelled nuns were thus victims of circumstances and political intrigue (cf. "Clingenthal Sisters" in Biographical Section); they had a right to expect help from Sixtus; however, he died about six months later, without – so far as can be ascertained – having done anything to alleviate their misery.

P. 59

474. Rhentingen xiiij kalendas Marcij...
Cf. N. 468.

#54. TO JOHANN MÜLLER Strassburg, 5 March 1484

475. Summary Schott's plan of studying theology at Paris is still being deferred and meanwhile he is attending Conrad Bondorf's* lectures on Duns Scotus. Though sometimes disheartened by his parents' growing opposition to his going away, he will expend every effort to make good use of the opportunity for realizing his plans when it presents itself.

476. Magistro Ioanni Muller: Collegium Burgundie Parisius incolenti...
Müller had gone with his charge young Jacob von Baden* to the university of Paris the previous fall (#46, p. 51). Cf. N. 211.
The "Collège de Bourgoinge," where Müller and no doubt young Jacob were living and which stood near the Premonstratensian priory, was founded 1329 by Jeanne de Boulogne, wife of Philip the Long, Duke of Burgundy, as a residence for 20 Burgundian scholars. Its site was later occupied by the faculty of medicine. Cf. Lincy, 171.

477. perinde triumphare inter tuos...
What honor Müller received from his fellows at this time is not certain. It may be that he became professor of arts in 1483, although Schott does not address him with that title until April 1486 (#84, p. 92).

478. Nycholao Grummel
Nicholaus Grummel or Grymmel is unidentified. He is mentioned #177, p. 198, as returning to Paris in the fall of 1484. He may have been a Strassburger – possibly even a former *famulus* of Schott or Geiler – who was studying at the university of Paris.

479. cum mihi Parisiensis adhuc schola differatur
Schott had planned to go away for theological studies when his year of residence as canon of New St. Peter was completed in spring 1483 (#36, p. 43). Cf. N. 116, N. 121, p. xxvii.

480. Interea ad Minores quartum Scoti... ab Doctore Conrado Bondorffer...
The Franciscan monastery at Strassburg had a good secondary school (N. 18, par. 1) of which Wimpheling speaks highly (Knepper, *Schulwesen*, 68f.). That it could offer lectures by so well-known a scholar as Bondorf vouches for its quality. Bondorf was lecturing on the fourth book of Johannes Duns Scotus' commentaries. Schott had studied Duns Scotus under Scriptor* in Paris (#58, p. 63, "doctor subtilis;" cf. N. 510).

481. quia Parentes magis... nituntur: et quia te abiturum intelligo
For the exaggerated parental solicitude Schott endured, cf. N. 87. Schott had wanted very much to be in Paris while Müller was there. He knew that Müller was at this time planning to leave for Orléans with his charge (#55, p. 61).

482. nobiscum dies et ducere et concludere...
Schott is referring to his attempts to secure for Müller a post in Strassburg, cf. N. 527.

483. Domino meo Marchioni Iacobo... Magistro Mathie: et Iohanni Iorger...
Jacob von Baden,* the eldest son and heir of *Markgraf* Christoph*; Matthias Kolb;* Johann Jörger.*

484. Soror Otilia: et filia eius... uxor Martini Sturm: Magdalena...
The persons mentioned are: Schott's sister Ottilia Schott*; her daughter Ottilia von Cöllen,* wife of Martin Sturm* and mother of Jacob Sturm*; Old Magdalena, possibly an aged servant or housekeeper of the Schotts.

#55. TO VITUS MAELER Strassburg, 19 March 1484

485. Summary Schott tells of the imminent expiration of the league and his hopes for continued peace. He congratulates Maeler on the successful reform of the Franciscan monastery at Ulm and mentions possible reform of the Franciscans at Strassburg. He reports that Johann Müller is in Paris and that he himself has been cited to the Roman *Curia* by Engelhard Funck* in the case of litigation of the latter with Thomas Wolf, Jr.*

486. Decano Iuncensi
The post of dean mentioned here may be the *decanatus* of #39, p. 45. *Iuncensis* may be the Latin for Jungingen, a town just north and west of Ulm in the diocese of Augsburg, Maeler's home diocese.

487. Erunt forsitan plura quam optemus... quarta Aprilis.
The league Schott mentions is no doubt that formed in 1474 by the Rhine confederation, the Swiss, etc. against Charles the Bold* (cf. N. 72). Schott's fears that hostilities might break out after the league was dissolved were apparently groundless, for there is no record of troubles between Sigismund, Archduke of Tyrol* (the prince of Austria mentioned in the text), and the Swiss or the Rhine confederation at this time.

488. in Reformacione conuentus Minorum Vlmensium
Many monasteries and convents which had resisted change through the centuries heeded the insistent call of Sixtus IV for reform. There were, of course, some like the Clingenthal convent (cf. Biographical Section "Clingenthal Sisters") where all attempts at reform failed.

The Franciscan monastery at Ulm and the nearby Franciscan convent of St. Clara seem to have accepted reform in January 1484 only after the intervention of *Graf* Eberhard von Württemberg and of the Dominicans. Cf. *Anal. Francisc.*, 489. Barthelmé, 110. Loë, 47.

Maeler was involved in the reform of these foundations perhaps because of his post as dean of Jungingen (N. 486). The letters which Schott requests Widmann to give the Franciscan monastery at Tübingen for delivery to Ulm (#115, p. 135) may have been meant for the Franciscan monastery at Ulm.

489. quamuis nescio quid moliantur Prouincialis... adhuc sit intentata.
There was obviously a reform of the Strassburg Franciscans proposed, but we have found no further information about it. The provincial of the Franciscans in upper Germany at this time was Georg Summer;* the episcopal *conservator* for the Strassburg diocese was Thomas Wolf, Sr.*

490. Ioannes Muller Parisiensem rursus cum discipulis suis...
Müller probably had spent the holiday between semesters in Baden-Baden. Since Schott speaks of Müller's "pupils," it is possible that not only Jacob* but also one or more younger sons of the *Markgraf* returned with Müller to Paris, or perhaps Schott had sent Müller one of his protégés.

491. Aurelianensem ut audio propediem/ legum Imperialium gracia... petiturus.
The university of Orléans, the beginnings of which date back to the first half of the thirteenth century, was endowed with university privileges by Clement V in 1305. During the fourteenth century its reputation for legal studies was unsurpassed in Europe. In the fifteenth century it was preeminent in civil law, as Paris was in canon law (Geiger, *Reuchlin*, 18).

492. Citatus sum heri ad Curiam Romanam ex parte Engelhardi Funck...
Engelhard Funck* who was contesting the canonicate at St. Thomas, held by Thomas Wolf, Jr.,* was evidently under the impression that Schott was guardian as well as godfather to young Thomas. Nothing more is said of Schott's being cited to the *Curia*. For details of the case, cf. N. 334.

493. Doctoris Thome Vuolff tibi cogniti
That Maeler and Wolf, Sr., knew one another is evident from statements in Schott's letters #62, p. 68 and #100, p. 110. They may have been at Bologna at the same time; Wolf came to Bologna in 1470 and Maeler took his doctor of arts there in 1473.

494. Decreueram scribere domino Iohanni Vueschbach... praebendis onustam...
It appears that Johann Weschbach,* whom Schott evidently considered a competent collector of benefices, had asked Schott to act as procurator for him in Strassburg.

#56. TO JOHANN RIEDNER Strassburg, 18 May 1484

495. Summary Schott congratulates Riedner* on his appointment. Johann Müller, in Paris with the heir apparent of Baden, has his own Greek psalter with him; Riedner may, however, easily procure a copy of the psalter from Bohuslaus von Hassenstein* who has the original.

496. professori Iohanni Riedner in Ingelstat... Accessionibus tuis...
The congratulations refer to Riedner's professorship at the university of Ingolstadt whither the peripatetic poet had come 4 March 1484.
　　The university of Ingolstadt was founded in 1459 by virtue of a bull of Pius II which had been requested by *Herzog* Wilhelm von Bayern, but lectures did not begin until 1472. In 1800 it was transferred to Landshut and in 1826 to Munich.

497. Magister Iohannes noster nondum doctor
Johann Müller was already a doctor of arts, but he did not yet have the doctor of law for which he was working.

498. Tu a domino Bohuslao copiam facile impetrabis: qui originale habet.
Hassenstein possessed a magnificent library (cf. Biographical Section: Hassenstein). Riedner, Hassenstein and Schott had been fellow students at Bologna. Their continuing friendship in later years is attested by this letter and by Hassenstein's letters to Riedner, three of which are printed in Mitis' work on Hassenstein (Fabricius, *Bohuslai*, folios 55-57) and one of which is printed in Potuček (126f.).

#57. TO THOMAS WOLF, SR. Strassburg, 6 July 1484

499. Summary Schott reports that his father is having an escort provided for Wolf's* return to Strassburg. He and his parents will be in Wildbad for a time. He has taken possession of a house in Wolf's name; Wolf's former house is now occupied by Wolf, Jr.*

500. Cf. N. 332.

501. Accelerare residencie tue terminum...
Wolf's residence as cathedral canon of Worms was almost terminated, cf. N. 412.

502. Quod ad satellitem et equos pertinet... ut petisti.
Schott, Sr., in his capacity as director of the cathedral *fabrica* (N. 76) was providing an official escort for Wolf, an officer of the bishop, *conservator episcopus* (#55, p. 61). It is not clear whether the escort belonged to the city or to the bishopric; since the *fabrica* was controlled by the city, either the city or the bishopric could be responsible for the safety of episcopal officers. The names of two official escorts of the city of Strassburg are known: Johann Falckner (#63, p. 69) and Udalrich Elhart (*Inventaire* [*Spach*], III, 407).

503. in profesto Bartholomei...
That is, St. Bartholomew's Eve or 23 August.

504. cum parentibus thermas in Vuiltbaden petemus
For details about spas, Wildbad, types of baths, cf. N. 192.

P. 62   #57   N. 505

505. De curia quondam domini Theobaldi Fuchs... consecutus est...
The canonical house may have become vacant because of Fuchs'* death; at any rate, he is not mentioned in the *Luc.* after this date. We learn from this passage that the house formerly occupied by Fuchs has been allotted to Wolf, Sr. (who also succeeded Fuchs in the post of *scholasticus* at St. Thomas), and that the house heretofore occupied by Wolf, Sr., has been allotted to Wolf, Jr. Apparently Schott had taken possession of the new residence in Wolf, Sr.'s, name and was holding it until the latter's return. For information on the house Wolf, Sr., had occupied since 1479, cf. N. 404.

P. 63

#58. TO JOHANN SCRIPTOR Strassburg, 30 August 1484

506. Summary Schott writes that he expects to be attending the University of Paris for theological study and asks Scriptor* for letters of recommendation. If Scriptor's house at the Sorbonne is vacant, Schott requests the privilege of occupying it and of leasing any furniture therein. Schott has not forgotten his commission to secure a benefice in Strassburg for Scriptor, but the opportunity has not yet presented itself.

507. This letter should chronologically succeed #60 in which Schott tells Müller that he will be asking Scriptor for letters of recommendation.

508. Doctori Ioanni Scriptoris ecclesie Moguntinensis concionatori...
Johann Scriptor who had taught Schott at Paris was at this time occupying the post of cathedral preacher in Mainz. For information on such posts, cf. N. 955. Cf. also N. 930.

509. Equidem si recte meministi... abire paterentur.
For other references to Schott's plan for theological study in Paris, cf. p. xxvii and N. 121; cf. also N. 87, par. 4.

510. Neque enim sublimiorem gradum desidero... ut scriptis Doctoris subtilis...
It was apparently not Schott's intention at this time to achieve the highest possible degree of learning, the doctor of theology (N. 93), but to become thoroughly versed in theological lore.
   Doctor subtilis is the epithet applied to Johannes Duns Scotus whose works Schott had studied under Scriptor and about whom Schott had recently been hearing lectures by Conrad Bondorf (#54, p. 59). For other such epithets, cf. #232, p. 261, and N. 1537.

511. tamen si tu me et prouisori Collegij: et ceteris... (to end of paragraph)
The college mentioned here and later in the paragraph is the Sorbonne (N. 522), where Scriptor was for years professor of theology, served for a term as prior and was allotted a house. We do not know who was *provisor* of the Sorbonne in 1484; according to Gabriel (87), Johannes Lhuillier held that highest office of the college in 1478 and apparently in 1481.

512. In re mihi per te commissa... ad eam occasio.
When in Strassburg a year previously, Scriptor had evidently commissioned Schott to obtain a benefice for him.

#59. TO VITUS MAELER Strassburg, 20 August 1484

513. Summary Schott congratulates Maeler on his new post as *praepositus* of St. Vitus in Freising, but warns against the evil of accumulating too many benefices. The Ottobeuren case is still pending. To the bearer of this letter, a Strassburger who has studied at Erfurt, Maeler is requested to give any aid needed.

P. 65

514. nihil prodesse homini... animae vero sue detrimentum pati.
Mt. 16:26. Mr. 8:36.

515. Causa Ottenburnensis adhuc indecisa pendet...
Cf. N. 419.

516. presencium exhibitorem... Erfordie didicit... in vrbe nostra filius.
This Strassburger has not been identified. The university of Erfurt, like that of Cologne, a union of religious schools, was founded 1389.

#60. TO JOHANN MÜLLER Strassburg, 23 August 1484

517. Summary Müller is gratefully thanked for his efforts in collecting works of Gerson for Schott and Geiler. Schott is sending his *famulus* Gangolf von Steinmetz* ahead to Paris and requests that Müller care for the boy until he himself arrives. Müller's precocious little nephew was recently at the Schott home. With considerable disgust Schott relays a message from the chaplain at Baden-Baden that Müller should be less stern with the young *Markgraf* Jacob.* There is a possibility that Müller may be able to secure a certain post soon to be vacant at Strassburg.

518. This is the first of four letters (in chronological order #60, #176, #177, #63) to Müller on the subject of Schott's going to Paris for theological studies. For other references, cf. p. xxvii, also N. 121.

519. ut nouis illis officijs/ qui tam solicitus Cancellarij scripta conquisi eris
Müller had been collecting in Paris works of Jean Charlier de Gerson,* former chancellor of the university of Paris. Cf. N. 135 and N. 136.

520. premitto puerum meum Gangolifum... ut vel in Collegio Camerista... famuletur
Schott was sending his *famulus* Gangolf von Steinmetz* to Paris ahead of the

P. 65   #60   N. 520

date when he himself intended to leave. It is probable that Gangolf had finished all available training in Strassburg, and Schott wished him to spend the months before the opening of the academic year at the university preparing for future courses by studying grammar. Until Schott's arrival Gangolf was to earn his keep as a *famulus* to Müller or to some other professor, or as a *camerista* (apparently a kind of janitor, cf. p. 196 and p. 198) in a college. The eight Rhenish florins to be deposited for Gangolf with Müller were to be used only in case of dire need. Cf. N. 125 and N. 547.

521. *Ego vix tandem Parentibus persuasi...*
Cf. N. 373, N. 479.

P. 66

522. *inter collegas Sarbonenses hospes admitti desiderarem...*
The Sorbonne, the most celebrated college of the university of Paris, was founded by Robert de Sorbonne *ca.* 1257. It attracted students from all over Europe, particularly from the Holy Roman Empire. Because the theological faculty of the university of Paris held its disputations in the Sorbonne college hall, that faculty was popularly known as the Sorbonne faculty.

523. *Impetrabo eciam a Magistro nostro Ioanne Scriptoris commendicias litteras*
Schott wrote to Scriptor for letters of recommendations a week later, cf. #58.

524. *Nepotem tuum ex fratre... apud nos nuper vidi...*
We have not found any information on Müller's young nephew or on his brother.

525. *dominus Iacobus Capellanus Illustris principis Badensis...*
Jacob, chaplain to Christoph I of Baden, may be identical with Jacob Keller* who is mentioned #103, p. 113.

526. *ne seueriorem tristioremue praecoeptorem agere... anxijsque erumnis.*
Christoph I,* *Markgraf* of Baden, and his wife Ottilie von Katzenellenbogen, feared Müller was being too harsh toward their eldest son and heir, thirteen year old Jacob,* who had been in Paris with Müller for a year. Schott, having been under Müller's tutelage from early boyhood until his nineteenth year, bitterly resented the treatment accorded Müller by the rulers of Baden during the years Müller bore the onerous but thankless responsibility of being tutor to Jacob. Not only did Christoph control Müller's post as dean of Baden-Baden (N. 211, N. 613), but he several times stood in the way of Müller's obtaining a good benefice, because he was afraid that if Müller had an independent income, he would not continue as tutor to Jacob. Christoph refused, for example, to confirm a post of preacher voted to Müller by the chapter at Baden-Baden and prevented Müller's receiving a benefice at the Strassburg cathedral (#63; N. 550; #175, p. 196). It may well be that Christoph ruined Müller's prospects of becoming canon and dean of Pforzheim

in early 1483 (#43, p. 49; N. 423). Had Müller lived to see how Jacob as archbishop of Trier confounded everyone by his erudition, he might have felt his efforts and sacrifices had been rewarded.

527. Vtinam liber esses: et Magister Iohannes Rot et ego... sed frustra.
From February 1483 (#39, p. 46) until 5 September 1490, when in Müller's name he took possession of the canonicate at Old St. Peter (#156, p. 171), Schott was trying to release his former tutor from bondage to Christoph I of Baden* by securing an adequate benefice for Müller, as is attested by the many references to his efforts: #39, p. 46; #60, p. 66; #62, p. 68; #63, p. 69; #69, p. 76; #72, pp. 78f.; #74, p. 82; #75, p. 83; #77, p. 84; #83, p. 91; #86, p. 94; #87, pp. 95f.; #103, p. 113; #151-#153; #155-#156; #174, p. 195; #175; #177, p. 198. Cf. p. xxx, N. 2, end of par. 1, and N. 704.

As an example of Schott's constant vigilance on Müller's behalf may be cited two letters to Friedrich von Zollern. On 28 February 1486 (Appendix B) just five days after the death of Johann von Werdenberg, bishop of Augsburg, while Friedrich's election as his successor was still rumor, Schott requests that Friedrich be mindful of Müller; this was a hint that Friedrich should obtain for Müller *preces primae* from Maximilian who would be empowered to issue such *preces* from the day of his imminent coronation (N. 130). This request was repeated 30 March 1486 (#83, p. 91) as soon as Schott heard that Friedrich had been elected bishop by the Augsburg chapter (cf. N. 680 and Appendix B).

Schott knew that Müller was weary of teaching and tutoring (#87, p. 95), that he longed for peace (*loc. cit.*; #73, p. 80) and wanted time to devote to study. Schott also knew that the income from Müller's benefices – the post as dean at Baden-Baden and the two small posts as chaplain – was insufficient to support even a man of such simple needs, who asked only to be supplied with food and clothing (#87, p. 95), and that Müller's tenancy of the post at Baden-Baden depended entirely upon the whim of Christoph I (N. 613). Schmidt's observation, therefore, that in denouncing plurality of benefices Schott made an exception of Müller (*H. L.*, II, 16) is ill taken, for Müller certainly could not be considered a benefice hunter in the sense that he was waxing fat from prebends.

To obtain a proper benefice for Müller was, however, difficult, because he was poor (cf. N. 802), of neither noble nor patrician birth, and a diffident, impractical scholar, incapable of currying favor or publicizing his worth. When the canonicate at Old St. Peter fell vacant, Schott used every possible means to secure it for Müller (#151-#153, #155, #156), even though he himself was already ill before possession was effected. Indeed, the extra effort and energy expended at this time may have been partially responsible for his falling prey to the plague.

528. Magister Iohannes Rot
Johann Rot* had resigned the post of vicar at Dambach in August 1482 to become lay curate at the chapel of St. Laurentius in the Strassburg cathedral.

529. ut si beneficium quoddam in ecclesia maiori... in mense ordinariorum vacet
This benefice, mentioned repeatedly (#62, p. 68; #63; #72, #86, p. 94; #175, p. 196; #177, p. 198; Appendix B), was that of perpetual vicar in the Strassburg cathedral. Its vacancy had been anticipated for over a year when the aged incumbent Gregorius Stuckmann* died 26 September 1485.

#60   N. 529

Although September was a month when chapters had the right to fill vacancies (N. 130), a holder of a *gratia expectativa* may have obtained the benefice (cf. N. 612). In any event, despite the efforts of Schott, Maeler, Friedrich von Zollern and others, Müller did not obtain it (#86, p. 94; N. 698).

The vacancy of this benefice was being anticipated in 1484 when the *praepositus* of Baden-Baden refused to approach Christoph I and request Müller's release, for fear of bringing down Christoph's wrath upon his own head (#175, p. 196).

The members of the cathedral chapter having power to appoint the holder of this benefice were the *praepositus* (at this time Johann VI, *Herzog von Bayern*)*, the dean (at this time Friedrich von Zollern) and the *portarius* (possibly Ludwig, *Graf* von Zweybrücken).

530. domini Nycholai zeis Sletstatini amici tui
Nicholaus Zeis of Schlettstadt may be the *praepositus* of the Baden-Baden church and the "dominus noster Nycholaus" mentioned in #175 (p. 195 and p. 196, respectively). We have no other information about Zeis.

531. virum venerabilem Magistrum kolb...
Matthias Kolb.*

#61. TO JOHANN GEILER Strassburg, 8 November 1484

532. Summary Schott urges Geiler to let the Strassburgers know where he is and how he and his mother are faring, because rumors are current that Geiler is seeking another post and because friends are worried about his and his mother's safety, particularly since the plague is raging.

533. quod sub pretextu diuersionis/ discessionis dissimulaueris deliberacionem
Since Geiler's post as cathedral preacher in Strassburg had not yet been confirmed (N. 955, par. 6), the cathedral chapter and *fabrica* members had good cause to fear he might be seeking a post elsewhere (N. 963). Indeed, he might have actually been in Basel at this time to look over the position of cathedral preacher then vacant, but later in the year filled by Johann Heynlin à Lapide* (#63).

534. Nam cum te vniversus populus/ quem... frustraris: desideret
Geiler never minced words in attacking the sins besetting his people; yet crowds flocked to hear him, as is evident from Schott's statement here and elsewhere (#99, p. 109; #125, p. 145) and from the fact that – because of increasing attendance – Geiler had to move his services from the altar of St. Laurentius or, as some say, from the crypt into the cathedral nave (N. 80).

535. in primis tamen ministra tua... noctes insomnes se ducere queritur.
Cf. N. 273.

536. De genitricis eciam tue successu soliciti sumus...
Cf. N. 272.

537. Dominum Decanum post duos... dies visuros nos speramus.
The dean mentioned is Friedrich von Zollern, dean of the Strassburg cathedral.

538. ut pastore carentes: mercenarios passim errabunda vagacione... sequantur.
Cf. Mr. 6:24; Mt. 9:36; Jo. 10:12.

#62. TO VITUS MAELER Strassburg, 24 November 1484

539. Summary Schott presents the case of Johann Klein* and asks that Maeler procure for Klein a *gratia expectativa.* Johann Müller who is in Paris with Jacob,* heir apparent of Baden, would like some sort of a benefice in Strassburg, and Maeler is requested to advise on ways and means; there is possibility of securing a benefice in the near future. The Ottobeuren case is still unsettled.

P. 68

540. Iohannes Klein de Pliensvuiler: presbiter Argentinensis diocesis... (to end of paragraph)
This letter should chronologically precede #47 (cf. N. 436). For comments on the benefice for Klein, cf. N. 437.

541. Magister meus Iohannes Molitoris... (to end of paragraph).
Schott is referring to his former tutor Johann Müller in Paris with the heir of Baden (N. 526). The benefice which might be available for Müller is mentioned earlier, cf. N. 529. Cf. also N. 527. Müller's request that Maeler's aid in obtaining a benefice be enlisted is mentioned #177, p. 198.

542. Causa Ottenburensis adhuc indecisa pendet...
Cf. N. 419.

543. Dominus Prepositus sancti Petri senioris Doctor Thomas Vuolff...
Cf. N. 493.

P. 69

#63. TO JOHANN MÜLLER Strassburg, 30 November 1484

544. Summary Schott explains that Müller has had no word, because his previous letter was not delivered to Müller but returned to Strassburg. His parents insist that he remain at home at least for the winter; he therefore requests Müller to watch over Gangolf von Steinmetz. The expected vacancy in the cathedral is not yet available, but there may be a possibility of securing the benefice in Baden-Baden which Johann Heynlin à Lapide resigned when called to be cathedral preacher at Basel.

545. This is the fourth and last letter to Müller about Schott's plan to study theology in Paris (cf. N. 518); its content is almost a brief summary of #177 (N. 264, par. 4).

P. 69   #63   N. 546

546. littere ad Nanseyum vsque... prosperioribus ut spero auibus
The letter taken, by Johann Falckner, an official escort of Strassburg, as far as Nancy and then returned to Schott, was doubtless #177, in which the reasons for Schott's not coming to Paris are explained in detail. It is being re-sent with hope of better success (*prosperioribus auibus,* cf. *bonis avibus,* Ovid *Fasti* 1.513; Riley, 40) in reaching its destination. Cf. N. 264, par. 4.

The Johann Falckner mentioned may be identical with Johann Falckner who was bailiff of Willstett in 1478 (*Inventaire,* IV, 56) or possibly with a Johann Falckner (†1512) of Basel who studied at Erfurt in 1456 and at Basel 1460-1461 (Wackernagel, I, 13).

547. Tu interim pueri curam vel modicam habe ne pereat... (to end of paragraph).
Schott had sent ahead to Paris his *famulus* Gangolf von Steinmetz (cf. N. 520), expecting to join him later. Apparently the bearer entrusted with delivering 8 Rhenish florins for Gangolf in Paris (#60, p. 65) had kept them, and Adolph Rusch,* incensed by such dishonesty, took upon himself the task of writing the bearer an abusive letter which would make him produce the money.

548. In re tua: nondum soluit nature debitum... spes nos bona tenet.
Cf. N. 529. For *soluit nature debitum,* cf. *Harpers',* 515, under "debitum."

549. Magistro Vito Romam scripsi... viam graciarum experiri.
Schott is referring to his letter written 24 November to Vitus Maeler (cf. #62, p. 68, and N. 539).

550. Quamquam eciam audiuerim Magistrum vestrum de Lapide... conijciunt.
The post held by Johann Heynlin à Lapide* in Baden-Baden was that of canon and preacher at the collegiate church (N. 211). When he resigned to become cathedral preacher at Basel, Müller would evidently have been elected by the Baden-Baden chapter to succeed him, had *Markgraf* Christoph I* not refused his consent (#175, p. 196). Cf. N. 526 and N. 527.

Schmidt (*H. L.,* II, 30), without apparent foundation, cites this passage as proof that Schott was in Basel 1484 and heard Heynlin preach there.

551. Cum hec scriberem: grauedo et pituita mihi admodum molesta erat...
Cf. N. 87.

552. Commenda me domino Illustri: et Magistro Mathie.
The persons referred to are Jacob of Baden* and Matthias Kolb.*

#64. TO JOHANN NEGUILER Strassburg, 23 December 1485

553. Summary Schott regrets that he has not been able to compose for Neguiler* the poem requested on the ship of St. Ursula. He has expended much time and effort, but has achieved nothing.

554. Chronologically this letter should follow #79 (cf. N. 218).

555. de nauicula diue Vrsule non lucubrauerit,.. quidam Carthusiensis...
According to legend, St. Ursula and her 11,000 maidens started on their pilgrimage to Rome by sailing on 11 triremes from Britain up the Rhine to Basel. From that point they continued on by land. Returning by the same routes, they were attacked and slaughtered by Attila's Huns at Cologne. Ursula had at first been spared as a prospective bride for Attila, but when she refused that honor, was transfixed by an arrow. Immediately on her expiration, heavenly hosts resembling the 11,000 maidens appeared and utterly routed the Huns. The grateful people of Cologne buried the martyrs and raised a church to St. Ursula. The feast day of St. Ursula and the 11,000 maidens is 21 October. Cf. Baring-Gould, XII, 535-556. Grandidier, *Oeuv. hist.*, V, 73. Hauck, XX, 354. Stadler, V, 616-624.

It is said that the British Virgin Islands were named in 1493 by Christopher Columbus to honor St. Ursula and her 11,000 virgins.

The cult of St. Ursula and her 11,000 maidens seems to have been particularly popular in Strassburg because of the following legendary incident. On the return trip down the Rhine one of Ursula's close friends, St. Aurelia, is said to have become so ill that she had to be put ashore at Strassburg, where she later died. Her bones were discovered in 1460. The church built in her honor during the eighth century was in 1471 incorporated into St. Thomas.

Three companions, who were put ashore with Aurelia: Saints Einbeth, Worbet and Vilbeth, were buried in Old St. Peter and had a cult of their own. Their feast day is 17 September. (Barth, "Kult," *passim*).

In Germany, especially along the Rhine and in Swabia, during the latter part of the Middle Ages were founded confraternities or guilds for both men and women called "Skiffs of St. Ursula." These were under the direction of monks, usually Carthusians. At Strassburg, in 1480, such a skiff was "laden" with 6,455 masses; 3,550 psalters; 20,000 rosaries; 4,025 penitential psalms; 180,000 prayers on the Passion; 76,000 corporal punishments, and so on. Its sail, the veil of St. Ursula, was composed of 11,000 Paternosters. Those who "sailed" in the skiff were provided with special indulgences from the pope. In processions members of the confraternities carried a boat, the symbol of their organization, through the streets. Cf. Baring-Gould, *loc. cit.*

It should be noted that the Carthusian monastery founded 1474 at Strassburg bore the name "St. Ursula Schifflein."

Which of the St. Ursula ships – the saint's original ship, the confraternity, or the Strassburg monastery – the Carthusian Johann Neguiler asked Schott to celebrate in verse is not clear from the text. There was seemingly no dearth of compositions to St. Ursula's ship during this period in Strassburg. Ritter, *Histoire* (13, 85, 138) informs us that Heinrich Knoblochtzer printed 13 works entitled *Sanct Ursulenschifflin* between 1481 and 1484; Bartolomeus Kestler in 1497 printed with music the poem *Ursula Schifflein* by Johann Gosseler (Gesler*); Johann Grüninger in 1499 printed *Sankt Ursullin Schifflein*.

556. quia scripturis sanctis (quarum ego sum imperitus)...
Schott's protestation of ignorance in theological writings is a bit like Shakespeare's "little Latin and less Greek." Schott had taken courses in theology at Paris and at Bologna; he was just not thoroughly versed in the field. Cf. N. 121.

P. 70 #64 N. 557

557. praeceptum Horacij et Quintiliani... edicio ne precipitetur...
The words of Quintilian (*Ep. ad Tryph.* 82), "Usus deinde Horatii consilio, qui in arte poetica suadet, ne praecipitetur editio," express a recurrent theme of Horace *Ars poetica*.

#65. TO RUDOLPH AGRICOLA Strassburg, 18 February 1485

558. Summary Schott expresses his great admiration for Agricola.* Since hearing the high praise of the Italians for Agricola, he has wished to meet him and has tried to acquire his writings. Now that Agricola is in Heidelberg the wish to make his acquaintance may be fulfilled. As a first step toward this goal Schott makes bold to initiate correspondence and to request that Agricola clarify certain troublesome problems of spelling, derivation and accent.

559. This is the first of two letters to Agricola, the second being #78 which was written 8 December 1485 and was never read by Agricola, for he had died the previous month; Schott's elegiac on Agricola's death is #245. Compare the text of the present item with that printed by Goldast in *Philogoricarum epistularum...* (Appendix I of this volume).

P. 71

560. Si Epistolarum genus illud est praecipuum... ipsorum intersit
Cf. Cicero *Fam.* ii.4.1.

561. nec dextera dextram (ut aiunt) contigerim
So far as we can ascertain there is no classical or German expression exactly like this. Vergil has *dextram tetigisse* (*Aen.* vii. 266) and *data dextera* (*Aen.* iv. 307) which Servius explains as "foedus amicitiarum". *Manum dare* is a common Latin phrase, and the custom of giving or raising the right hand in greeting is age-old. Perhaps Schott is here translating a peculiarly Alsatian proverb, as he does on another occasion (cf. #119, p. 138, "quod secundo foeceris...," and N. 932).
Although Schott was at Bologna during the years of Agricola's second Italian sojourn, 1475-1478, the paths of the two did not cross. From his letters it appears that Agricola spent these years mostly in Pavia and in Ferrara at the court of Duke Ercole d'Este.

562. honestissimarum arcium tuarum: quamplures et eos... mirari et extollere...
In the scholarship of Agricola, Schott and other German humanists saw proof that the Germans could produce eminent scholars to command the respect of all, even of the boastful Italians. In this connection Ludwig Geiger (*ADB*, I, 152) says of Agricola: "...in ihm wurde zuerst, und vielleicht klarer und schärfer als in einem seiner Nachfolger, der Gedanke lebendig, dass den Deutschen, die nach Italien gingen, eine höhere Aufgabe obliege, als nur für sich gelehrte Kenntnisse zu erwerben, die nämlich, das Gelernte für das Vaterland zu verwerthen, um von ihm den Vorwurf der Unbildung und Verachtung der Wissenschaft abzuschütteln und das 'barbarische Deutschland' berühmter und glänzender zu machen, als Italien selbst. Er ward nicht müde, mit lebhaften Worten Andere zur Erfüllung dieser Pflicht zu

ermahnen und selbst an der Verwirklichung des Gedankens zu arbeiten."
Erasmus contended that Agricola could have been the first in Italy, had he not preferred Germany (cf. Hartfelder, *Briefe*, 4).

563. dum Ferrarie tercium ante annum agerem...
Agricola had left Italy in 1478. Schott was in Ferrara several times: briefly in the spring of 1480; during the period fall 1480 to spring 1481; in May 1481 (N. 96).

564. quam sperarem tanto policiorum litterarum principe... liberandamque fore
Cf. similar phraseology in the elegiac on Agricola #245.

565. Itaque et tunc libellos/ qui in manus meas... excribere curaui...
Some of Agricola's translations from Greek to Latin which are known to have been completed by 1481 and which Schott could have copied are: Lucian's *De non facile credendis delationibus (1479)*, Plato's *Axiochus* (ca. 1480), Isocrates' *Demonicus* (ca. 1480). Schott had access to the Greek text of the *Demonicus*, for he quotes from it in a letter to Brant, 12 December 1478 (#10, p. 18). One may assume that editions of Agricola's works were exhausted almost immediately; otherwise Schott would not have spent valuable time making manuscript copies of them.

566. Tandem Argentinam reuersus... Thoma Vuolfio... Adelpho Rusco... declinent.
That Thomas Wolf, Sr.,* and Adolph Rusch* were friends of Agricola is apparent from Agricola's letters to Rusch (Allen, 31f.).

The wording of this sentence in the text, i. e., the phrase "tandem Argentinam reuersus" and the tenses of "intellexissem" and "coepisse," seem to imply that Agricola had already been teaching in Heidelberg when Schott returned from Italy in 1481, although it is generally accepted that Agricola's Heidelberg activity did not begin until 1484.

In the chronological table of Agricola's correspondence as arranged by Allen (313-315), one notes that Agricola visited Heidelberg in early 1482 and came to teach there 2 May 1484. One also notes that in the period late 1480 to early 1484 there are only two letters, both of uncertain dates. The first, written from Cologne, is dated 19 October but lacks the year. To this letter Allen has assigned the year 1480, because in the text the death of Agricola's father is mentioned. The exact date when the latter died is, however, not known; indeed, the only known fact about his age is that he was in charge of a monastery for 36 years after Agricola's birth, the date of which is given as 1442/43/44; Seidlmayer in his article on Agricola in *NDB* (I, 103) gives Agricola's birth date as "1444 (1443?)." Allen has reckoned Agricola's year of birth as 1444, because that is the year given by Peutinger who was closely associated with Agricola during the last years of the latter's life. If one reckons instead with the year 1442 or 1443, the date of the letter from Cologne might be 1478 or 1479. The second letter lacks dating of any kind and is assumed by Allen to have been written during the winter 1481/82 at Gröningen.

Except for several months during 1479 spent in Dillingen at the call of the bishop of Augsburg Johann von Werdenberg,* there is no exact information on Agricola's movements from 1479 to the second half of 1481 when

P. 71   #65   N. 566

at the behest of the city of Gröningen he went to the court of Maximilian at Brussels. Is it not possible that during this period he might have spent a semester or more in Heidelberg?

567. *te Heidelberge iam coepisse purgare et linguas... verbosas inepcias...*
Cf. N. 564.

568. *Quia igitur argumentum querebam... visum fuit super his...* (to end of paragraph).
It was quite usual for humanists to exchange information about spelling, accent, quantity, derivation, etc. of Greek and Latin words. Agricola wrote to Alexander Hegius to answer questions on difficult words (*ADB*, I, 153); Heinrich Bebel wrote to Reuchlin for advice on spellings, etc. and received a reply (Erhard, III, 206); Johann Müller wrote to Reuchlin* for information on Greek forms (Geiger, *Briefwechsel*, 22); Wimpheling asked Schott about accents in poetry (#89-#91) and about spelling (#113); Johann von Laudenburg asked Schott about spelling (#143). This exchange of information involved minute but necessary details. Quintillian (*Inst.* I. 4.6) warns against scorning elements of grammar as insignificant matters. Cf. p. xx.

569. *Vilibus in scopis... flagicium ingens.*
Horace *Sat.* ii.4.81-82.

P. 72

570. *quum in hymno quopiam canimus. Os/ lingua/ mens/ sensus... charitas.*
Goldast (Appendix I) interpolates *Ambrosii* after *hymno.quopiam*.
According to the *Liber Usualis* (235), every Sunday at terce are sung the verses:

> Nunc Sancte nobis Spiritus, Unum Patri cum Filio
> Dignare promptus ingeri nostri refusus pectori.

and immediately thereafter on solemn feasts, such as the first Sunday of Advent, Christmas, etc., is sung the hymn mentioned by Schott, the text of which is:

> Os, lingua, mens, sensus, vigor
> Confessione personent:
> Flammescat igne caritas,
> Accendat ardor proximos.
>
> Praesta, Pater piissime,
> Patrique compar Unice
> Cum Spiritu Paraclito
> Regnans per omne saeculum. Amen.

571. *Flammascat an flammescat legendum sit... labasco et ingrauesco.*
Schmidt ("Notices,... P. S.," 340) claims Schott as one of the first to perceive barbarisms which had been introduced into Christian hymns. Other scholars who applied themselves to correcting hymns and to establishing as pure texts as possible in that age were Wimpheling and Johann Adelphus in Alsace, Heinrich Bebel in Swabia, Jodocus Gallus* for the bishop of Spires.

Schott's questions on the spelling of inceptive or inchoative verbs show his meticulous care for detail. Since he did not have at his command modern reference material and definitive editions of Latin works, he could not determine: (a) whether *flammescat* was derived from the verb *flammare*, in which case *flammascat* would have been correct, or from the noun *flamma*, the correct derivation; (b) whether *labasco* was derived from the verb *labare*, the correct derivation, or from the adjective *labes*; (c) whether *ingravesco* was derived from the verb *gravare*, or from the adjective *gravis*, the correct derivation.

Even with the help of present day scholarship, the spelling of inceptive verbs is confusing, and no single reference work we have seen discusses the problem. The following conclusions may be drawn: inceptive verbs derived from verbs of the first, second and fourth conjugations and from *io* verbs of the third conjugation have the endings *asc-*, *esc-*, *isc-* and *isc-*, respectively. Otherwise there seems to be no set pattern for spelling; e.g., *tremiscere* from *tremere* (3), *alescere* from *alere* (3), *mitescere* from *mitis*, *evanescere* from *vanus*, *irascere* from *iratus*, *gemnescere* from *gemma*, *vesperascere* from *vesper*.

572. charitatem dico grecam arbitreris an latinam?
Caritas derives from Latin *carus*.

573. Et si grecam: qua deductione... deriuetur.
The lacuna in the text is for an omitted Greek word or words (cf. p. xiv). What Schott originally wrote can only be surmised; perhaps he was asking how *charitas* could be derived from the noun χάρις, χάριτος or from the verb χαίρω. Goldast (Appendix I) fills the lacuna with a phrase involving χάρις.

574. Sin latinam dumtaxat: cur ab his... aspiretur?
Schott and his contemporaries may be forgiven their confusion about the Romans' use of "h," for the practice varied from age to age. The early Romans rarely used the letter, even before vowels, and avoided it in conjunction with consonants. Later there was a period when "h" was used to excess. Cf. Cicero *Or.* 48.160; Gellius ii.3.1-4; Quintilian *Inst.* i.5.19-20; Catullus' biting epigram lxxxiv, *de Arrio*. For a good discussion of the subject and for pertinent quotations from classical writers and others, cf. E. H. Sturtevant, *The Pronunciation of Greek and Latin* (Chicago, 1920), 69-74.

575. Auctor per c scribendum sit semper?
Cf. *Harpers'*: "*auctor* (incorrectly written *autor* or *author*);" Menge: "*auctor* (*augeo*)."

576. Lachrime et Pulcher... aspiracionem paciantur?
Cf. *Harpers'*: "*lacrima* (archaic *lacruma*... old form *dacrima*):" "*pulcher*... and less correctly *pulcer*... (for *polcer*, root *polire*...);" and Walde-Hofmann: "*pulcher*, Etymologie unsicher." For Cicero's statement about the spelling of *pulcher*, cf. *Or.* 49.

577. Euxenia: vel vt quidam contendunt Enxenia: idonea... xenijs.
The question here seems to be whether late Latin terms may be used in

place of classical. *Strena* and *xenium* are classical Latin words meaning respectively: "New Year's gift" and "presents made to guests" (cf. *Harpers'*). *Enxenium* is a medieval Latin word meaning "gift" (*munus, donum*); spellings *exenium* and *exennium* also occur (cf. Du Cange). *Euxenium* is not listed in standard Latin or Greek dictionaries or in any medieval vocabularies we have seen. Is this word a case of confusion between *eu* and *en*, or is it a late Latin derivative from Greek εὔξενος meaning "hospitable, kind to strangers?"

578. Et si quid de morticinis habes: quo accentu proferantur... obtinuerint?
The accent in *morticin-* is on the third syllable, the vowel of that syllable being long while the vowel of the second syllable is short. Reuchlin in his *Vocabularius breuiloquens...*, published three years after Schott wrote this letter, states that the penultimate syllable of *morticinum* is long.

In the second part of his question concerning *morticinis* Schott is apparently asking what the basic meaning of the word is. Most classical and medieval dictionaries which we have consulted define *morticinus, a, um* as "dead, of or belonging to an animal that has died" and *morticinum, i, n.* as "corpse, carcass, carrion." Sleumer adds a special meaning of the plural noun "reliques of the saints." The *Thesaurus Linguae Latinae* (VIII, 1577,B) gives for the adjective also the meaning "sinful," and for the masculine, feminine and neuter forms of the noun the meanings respectively "an offensive person," "mortal flesh," "sin."

#66. TO JOHANN WIDMANN Strassburg, 1 March 1485

579. Summary Schott is very ill with tertian fever. Because he does not fully trust any doctor in Strassburg, he writes an exact description of his condition and asks that Widmann come, if he think it necessary. Susanna von Cöllen sends Widmann's wife an *Agnus Dei* to aid in childbirth. (Cf. N. 893 and N. 888).

580. Numquam mihi non molesta fuit absencia tua... et calamitosa...
After leaving the service of Christoph I of Baden, Widmann had for a time been city physician in Strassburg. He was now professor of medicine at the University of Tübingen.

581. Tercianis laboro febribus: pro quibus pellendis... confiderem.
This bout of tertian fever lasted almost 7 weeks (cf. #68, p. 76); it is mentioned #78, p. 84 and #112. Cf. N. 583, N. 647.

582. Secunda post dominicam Inuocauit... (next paragraph) die sancti Mathie
Schott describes events on four consecutive days from Monday, 21 February, to Thursday, 24 February. In the year 1485, *Invocavit* (the first Sunday of Lent) came on 20 February, and the feast of *Cathedra Petri* (St. Peter's Chair at Antioch, 22 February) was on the next Tuesday. The day designated as "secunda post Inuocauit" which was followed by *Cathedra Petri*, "sequenti die: qua colebatur festum Cathedre beati Petri," must have been Monday, 21 February. The day after ("postera die") *Cathedra Petri* was

P. 73   #66   N. 582

Wednesday, 23 February, and the feast of St. Matthew the Apostle (24 February) was on Thursday.
In this passage the designation of Monday, 21 February as "secunda post Inuocauit" is concrete evidence that when reckoning dates Schott counted both the *terminus a quo* and the *terminus ad quem*.

583. Aperueram quindecim antea diebus venam Epaticam... Cephalicam...
Schott states here that two weeks before he became ill, he had been bled from the hepatic vein and that when he became ill, he was bled from the cephalic vein. The hepatic vein, beginning behind the head of the pancreas, drains blood from the stomach, intestines and pancreas and divides into right and left branches in the porta of the liver. Since it was regular medical practice to perform the operation of bleeding – in cases of acute diseases – on a vein some distance from the organ affected and since both pancreas and liver are affected by malarial fevers like ague, tertian fever, etc., Schott apparently had symptoms of tertian fever several weeks before he suffered the severe attack. The cephalic vein in the forearm just below the bend of the elbow is the vein from which patients are usually bled.

584. per quendam Phisicum: qui Argentinam nuper venit
The physician mentioned is no doubt "Magister Leonhardus" of #112, p. 132, i.e., Leonardus Wirt.*

585. Tu qui me intus et in cute nosti...
Cf. Persius 3.30: "te intus... novi;" *Oxford Dictionary of English Proverbs*, 345; Riley, 195; Stevenson, III, 30; Tilley, T246. Schott uses the quotation also in #117, p. 137.

586. hic tuus affinis intra octauum ad nos rediturus
Widmann's relative (unidentified) did not return to Strassburg until 14 March (cf. #112).

P. 74

587. vxori tue matrone honestissimae...
This is first mention of Widmann's wife; for other references to her, cf. the sketch of Johann Widmann in the Biographical Section.

588. mittit ei Agnum dei: qui... pericula plurima auertere creditur.
The image of the *Agnus Dei* and that of the pregnant Virgin which Susanna von Cöllen sent to Widmann's wife on another occasion (#111, p. 131) were birth charms such as have been popular since earliest times. J. P. Frank (*System einer vollständigen medizinischen Polizey* [Mannheim, 1788], IV, 635f.) tells about birth charms sold under the auspices of the Church: mendicant monks sold "Nikodemus Brödchen" to pregnant women to ease childbirth pain; at Maria Einsiedeln were sold "Muttergotteskäpplein" with labels on which were written in French, Romansch and German the words: "Gegenwärtige Mutter-Gottes-Käpplein seynd in d. einsiedl. Gnaden Capell, wider allerlei Teufels-Künsten, Zaubereyn u. Krankheiten, wie auch für die Gebährende geweihet, und haben das Gnadenbild berührt"; each label carried a seal

P. 74   #66   N. 588

portraying the Virgin flanked on the right by a monk, on the left by a warrior. Cf. N. 1039, par. 2.

#67. TO JOHANN WIDMANN [Wildbad], 16 May 1485

589. Summary The Schotts at the baths have enjoyed the game birds sent by Widmann.* They expect to return to Strassburg the following day unless Widmann considers it advisable for Schott, Sr., (whose arthritic knee has improved) and for Susanna von Cöllen (who has not fully recovered) to remain longer at the baths. Widmann is requested to reply immediately or come in person.

590. This item belongs chronologically after #68. Cf. N. 278.

591. Pro his quae nobis... donasti volucribus... cum insanas nequaquam iudicaremus
Widmann had sent game birds as a bath gift. Since he was a physician, he would have sent only such birds as could be allowed in the diet of those undergoing the bath regimen. For the popularity of baths, bath gifts, diet, etc., cf. N. 192.

P. 75

592. Respondebis: vel si tibi vacet ad nos diuertere
The Schotts were quite likely at Wildbad (N. 192, 3) which is about 35 miles from Tübingen – near enough to allow Schott to have a message delivered to Widmann in Tübingen and receive an answer within a day's time.

593. Prepropere secunda post Exaudi
In 1485 *Exaudi*, the sixth Sunday after Easter, came on 15 May.

#68. TO VITUS MAELER Strassburg, 14 April 1485

594. Summary Schott fears his letters recommending Johann Klein* for a *gratia expectativa* have not been received by Maeler. He urges Maeler not to delay in procuring the necessary documents; the money will be sent as soon as the amount needed is known. He attributes his peevishness to the tertian fever from which he has been suffering nearly seven weeks.

595. Binas ad te litteras pluresue superioribus diebus scripsi
The two letters mentioned are #62 and #47 (cf. N. 436).

596. super collacionibus Episcopi... sancte Richardis in Andelo
Cf. N. 437.

597. ne paciaris signaturam: et datarij notam diucius differi
Haste was necessary to forestall anyone else seeking the same post, for evidently the first *gratia* to have signature and seal of the *Curia* had priority.

P. 76 #68 N. 598

P. 76

598. quod iam septem ferme hebdomadibus tercianas passus
The first mention of this bout with tertian fever was 1 March (#66); cf. N. 581.

#69. TO VITUS MAELER Strassburg, 28 May 1485

599. Summary Maeler is to refrain from doing anything more about the *gratia expectativa* for Johann Klein* until further notice. Klein has been provided with a curateship in the diocese and may not desire the *gratia*, and Schott does not wish Klein to become ensnared in plurality of benefices. Schott will ascertain whether Müller is interested in a *gratia expectativa*; all attempts to secure him a post in Strassburg thus far have been in vain. If Maeler is acquainted with Emerich Kemel* at Santa Maria de Araceli, he is to deliver to Kemel the message that both Schott and Geiler are anxious to settle the matter about which Schott has written Kemel.

600. pro illo cuius nomen desideraueram graciam expectatiuam... prouisum fuisse...
The benefice acquired by Johann Klein in May – a month when chapters had authority to dispose of benefices (N. 130) – was confirmed by September (#72, p. 79); it may have been the perpetual vicarate at Zellweiler, (cf. Biographical Section).

601. Nollem enim sine cause eum pluribus Beneficijs irretiri.
Schott's words here are an indirect thrust at Maeler who was accumulating fat benefices.

602. Interea forsitan a Magistro Ioanne Molitoris... multa conemur.
Cf. N. 541.

603. si fratrem Emericum ordinis Minorum in Ara celi nosti... cupit
"Brother Emerich" is Emerich Kemel* to whom Schott had in Geiler's name written some weeks earlier about flagrant abuses in Strassburg and who had been requested to collect for Geiler opinions of noted authorities on such abuses (#187).
Santa Maria de Araceli, built 595 on the site of the temple to Jupiter Capitolinus on the Capitoline Hill, served as a Benedictine monastery and was known as Santa Maria in Capitolo until the thirteenth century. In 1252 by mandate of Innocent IV it became the official seat of the order of the *Fratres Minores de Observantia* (cf. N. 345). Its buildings were restored 1464 by Cardinal Caraffa and reconstructed 1798.

P. 77

#70. TO THEODORICUS RIBYSEN Strassburg, 15 June 1485

604. Summary Schott thanks Ribysen* for his unfailing help to a protégé at Spires and asks that Ribysen make sure the boy does not miss the boat which is to carry him down river with free passage as far as Mainz and perhaps as far as Cologne.

P. 77   #70   N. 605

605. Theodorico Ribysen Sexprebendario Spirensi
Ribysen* (referred to as "Magister Theodoricus" #154, p. 169) was one of the six non-noble members (*sexprebendarii*) of the Spires cathedral chapter whose benefices were equal in rank to those held by nobles; cf. N. 661, par. 3.

606. Commendacionem pureri mei... (to end of paragraph).
It appears that the boy in question had been studying at Spires and was now to be sent for further training to a school down the Rhine, possibly the school of the Brethren of the Common Life (cf. N. 88) at Windesheim or Deventer. This protégé or *famulus* of Schott may have been Johann Klitsch,* for Schott's first extant letter to him (#79) was written about six months later. Cf. N. 125, also p. xxviii.

#71. TO HIERONYMUS DE ZANCTIVIS   Strassburg, 25 June 1485

607. Summary Schott apologizes to Zanctivis,* his former professor at Bologna, for not having paid his fees. Because of clashes between the student nations, he had to leave Bologna suddenly and could not attend to the matter himself. Instead he gave money to Professor de Sala* with the understanding that Sala would pay all Schott's outstanding debts. He did not discover until much later that Sala had failed to reimburse either Zanctivis, or Professor Dolpholis,* or the university secretary, who not only confiscated Schott's belongings but dunned him repeatedly. With this letter Schott is sending a gold ducat, which he hopes the professor will accept in the spirit it is offered, and asks that the bearer be given a signed receipt to settle the matter officially.

608. Domino Ioanne Sala... promotore meo...
Sala headed the committee presenting Schott for the doctorate of laws in September 1481 (cf. N. 109).

609. propter perniciosas ea tempestate Germanis a Maluicijs paratas insidias
The name *Malvicii* may have been applied to the *Citramontani* (Italian nation) or to the native Bolognese students at the university of Bologna (cf. N. 93). From the thirteenth to the sixteenth centuries, there were periodic outbreaks of violence between the *Citramontani* and the *Ultramontani* (German nation); according to accounts, outbreaks in 1491 and following years were particularly severe, and the outbreak in 1562 caused the entire German nation to migrate to the university of Pavia (*Acta bonon.*, xxxff.; Kibre, *Nations*, 35).

Although accounts do not mention the outbreak in September 1480, it must have been quite violent to cause Schott to leave without taking time to settle his university debts. The German nation seems to have migrated to Ferrara; at least there is little doubt that Hassenstein – who was enrolled at Bologna for the year 1480 (*Acta bonon.*, 228) – and his tutor Ladislaus accompanied Schott to Ferrara.

An examination of contemporary university of Bologna records shows that the exodus of students of the German nation at this time was considerable and that the effects of this exodus were felt for some years thereafter. The "Liber secretus iuris pontificii," I, for each of the years 1475-1479, lists names of graduates in various months throughout the year. In 1480 the last entries are for 11 September, the month Schott received his doctorate;

P. 77 #71 N. 609

in 1481, entries begin with August and end 25 October. Not until 1483 are there again entries throughout the year. The *Acta bonon.* which every January listed new scholars (N. 93) has 36 entries for 1480, 16 for 1481, 19 for 1482, none for 1483, 7 for 1484. The largest entries thereafter – 27 for 1487 and 28 for 1489 – do not equal the number for 1480.

It is possible that *Malvicii*, as a special appellation for a student faction, derived from Malvezzi, the name of a prominent and influential Bolognese family, a branch of the Medicis. The introduction to the *Acta bonon.* (xxxiii) mentions "senator Pyrro de Malvezziis 1533." The original manuscripts of the *Acta bonon.* which had been lost in 1796 (when the French occupying Bologna suppressed the university) were found in 1825 and bought by Josepho Maria Malvezzi de Medici. They were still in the possession of the family in 1887 when the edition was made.

P. 78

610. Verum ut et ego nuncij fidem probem: et apud me super ea re cercior sim
Bearers were not always trustworthy (cf. N. 264).

#72. TO VITUS MAELER Strassburg, 28 September 1485

611. Summary Schott urges Maeler to investigate possibilities of securing for Müller one of the two Strassburg benefices left vacant by the death of Gregorius Stuckmann* on 26 September. The provincial of the Hermits of St. William whom Maeler had recommended to Schott has died en route. Hassenstein* has spent considerable time with Schott in Strassburg. Johann Klein,* installed in his benefice, needs no *gratia*.

612. Obijt apud nos... Gregorius Stuckman... pro Magistro Iohanne muller...
Despite the fact that Stuckmann, the *decrepitus* of #63, died in September, a month when chapters had the right to fill vacancies (N. 130), his perpetual vicarates at the cathedral and at St. Thomas seem to have been allocated to holders of *gratiae expectativae*. Since, however, these *gratiae* had been issued by Sixtus IV who had died the previous year († 12 August 1484), the new pope Innocent VIII was expected to revoke them in order to issue his own; hence the need for Maeler to be on the alert in securing the vicarate at the cathedral for Müller (cf. N. 529, also N. 527).

613. Sacerdos diocesis Spirensis. Duas Capellanias... a quo amouibilis est.
As a native of Rastatt and as dean of Baden-Baden, Müller belonged to the diocese of Spires; and his two small chaplaincies may have been in that diocese. If so, it would account for Schott's not knowing anything about them. The only other mention of them is in #174 (p. 195), where Schott asks Müller for the titles of the two benefices even though Müller had apparently vacated them.

From this passage we learn that Müller's deanship at Baden-Baden was an *officium manuale*, i.e., a benefice which the one who controlled it might take from the incumbent at any time. In this case control rested in Christoph I,* *Markgraf* of Baden, as ruler of the principality. Thus Müller was completely at the mercy of Christoph (cf. N. 527).

P. 79   #72   N. 614

P. 79

614. Et audio eum (Laurencius est nomen eius)... personaliter Romam pecijsse.
The Laurentius who held a *gratia expectativa* for the vacant benefice at St. Thomas and was making sure of securing that benefice by interceding personally at the *Curia* might possibly be Laurentius Hell.*

615. domino Leonardo de Egloffstein...
Leonhard von Egloffstein,* like Weschbach, was a fellow student of Schott at Bologna.

616. venerabilem patrem Vuilhelmitarum Prouincialem... in itinere mortem...
The provincial of the Hermits of St. William mentioned here may have been Johann Russ, who is noted in the *Inventaire* (II, 119) as being prior of the Strassburg monastery and provincial in 1482.
    There were 18 monasteries of the order of St. William in Germany; its members adhered to the Rule of St. Benedict and were followers of St. William of Maleval (William the Great) who became a hermit in 1153. (These Hermits of St. William are not to be confused with the Knights of St. William of Aquitania).
    The church of St. William at Strassburg was built in 1300; in 1302 the Hermits founded their monastery there (cf. Friese, *Merkwürdigkeiten,* 146f.). In the second half of the fifteenth century the monastery was plagued by disorders to such a degree that the prior Jacob Messinger had to complain personally at Rome and that in 1490 the city magistrates had to intervene (Schmidt, *H.L.*, I, 27, n. 80). It may have been to investigate these disorders that the provincial was en route.

617. Dominus meus et frater carissimus Bohuslaus de Hassenstein... fuit.
Cf. N. 101.

618. De illo Iohanne klein de quo sepe scripsi... desiderat.
Cf. N. 436, N. 599, N. 600.

#73. TO ANTONIUS MANLIUS BRITONORIENSIS Strassburg, 6 October 1485

619. Summary Schott reminisces about studies and discussions with Manlius,* his teacher of Greek at Bologna. He explains that consideration for his parents keeps him in Strassburg where there is little intellectual stimulus and where he is the only Greek scholar. In response to Manlius' request to procure for him a Strassburg benefice, Schott answers he would very much like to see Manlius in Strassburg and has recommended him, but the surer way to secure a benefice in Strassburg is to seek it at Rome, the smithy where benefices are forged. By way of news he mentions that the emperor is preparing a campaign against Matthias* of Hungary and that Müller is in Paris with his pupil Jacob of Baden.*

620. Anthoni non solum memor sum praeceptorum tuorum... in grecorum litteris...
In #76, Schott refers to Manlius again as "praecoeptorem meum in litteris

grecis." Dallari, however, does not list Antonius Manlius Britonoriensis as a teacher of Greek at Bologna. For 1474/75 Dallari has no entry for Greek; for 1475/76 Greek is listed but no instructor is mentioned; 1476/77 and 1477/78 Greek was taught by Magister Antonius de Cesena; 1478/79 and 1479/80 both Greek and Latin were taught by Antonius de Cesena (Dallari, 95-110).

It is possible that Antonius Manlius Britonoriensis is identical with Antonius de Cesena, although so far as can be ascertained the former had no connection with Cesena. It is also possible that Manlius taught Greek either privately or as part of his law courses and thus was not officially listed as a teacher of Greek.

P. 80

621. Equidem inter meos saluus sum... nisi ipsi velint.
This passage is translated in the last paragraph of N. 87. For the many references to Schott's hopes of studying at Paris being deferred, cf. p. xxvii, N. 121.

622. apud nostros... vbi amplior est epulis atque armis locus quam litteris.
Schott's cutting remark that in Strassburg there is more room for banquets and arms than for letters is one of the best known passages of the *Luc*. A couplet expressing a similar thought appears in a letter to Johann Bolzheim, published in Ottomar Nachtigal's *Progymnasmata graecae litteraturae* (Strassburg, 1521):

> Doctrina vacuis est urbs Strasburgia mater,
> Doctis atque bonis esse noverca solet.
>
> (Cf. Engel, *Schulwesen*, 21)

623. Imperator tamen mense superiori in vrbe nostra fuit... (end of paragraph)
The sporadic attempts of Emperor Friedrich III to oppose the aggression of Matthias Hunyadi (Corvinus),* king of Hungary, lasted from 1481 until Matthias' death in 1490. In 1481 at Nürnberg an assembly of representatives from all states of the empire had decreed that each state should contribute to the emperor's forces; Schott tells how the emperor in the fall of 1481 sought favor with Strassburg and incited the states of the empire against Matthias (#170, p. 190). Strassburg promised to send the emperor 76 cavalry and foot-soldiers, but later refused to supply them and made instead a cash settlement.

In 1485 the situation became critical when Matthias occupied Vienna and took up residence there. At the assembly of the imperial states in Frankfurt 20 March 1486, the states decreed to unite with the emperor and Maximilian against Matthias. A week later, 27 March, Maximilian reported that a sizable army was promised.

As already indicated, Strassburg seems to have taken little interest in the emperor's war against Matthias. Further indication is a querulous letter of 2 November 1488 from Friedrich to the Strassburg magistracy, in which he objects to a Strassburg political publication as uncomplimentary to him and intimates that the magistrates should prevent any more of such being printed because an imperial state should preserve the dignity of the empire:

Uns lanngt an wie die hañdlung des mutwilligen unpillichen Kriegs,

493

P. 80   #73   N. 623

so der Künig von Hungern, on all ursach über hoch glübd, eyde und verschreibung, gegen uns und unsern erblichen lannden gebrauchet, in der Statt Straszburg in schrifft gedruckt und unnser etlicher massen schimpfflich darinne gedacht werden sülle. Nu wisset jr in was gestalt wir lanng jar und zeit von den Türken und demselben Künig von Hungern mit Krieg swerlichen angefochten, und wie die allein auf uns und unnser erbliche lannd gelaitet und von meniclich darinne verlassen seien...

(Schmidt, *Bibliotheken*, 146f.)

Cf. Chmel, 724, 725. Reuss, *Meyer*, 70. Strobel, 386. See Schott's poem in praise of Matthias' exploits #243. For the fate of Hungary after Matthias' death, cf. biographical note on Vladislaus, king of Bohemia. Cf. also N. 1596.

624. *sed prebendas tibi apud nos/ facilius tu in vrbe... Vbi et ego... paraui.*
Schott's description of Rome as the smithy where prebends are forged is reminiscent of his statement a year earlier that it is difficult to get ahead of the *Curia's* rabid jaws in securing benefices (#177, p. 198). Manlius seems to have followed Schott's advice to seek prebends in Rome, where he himself had secured his (i.e., by *gratia*), for Manlius was in that city two months later (#76, p. 83). For other references to Schott's benefice, cf. N. 116, N. 130, N. 630.

625. *Iohannes Muller Magister meus nunc Parisiensem... quamuis quietam mallet.*
Cf. N. 526 and N. 527.

P. 81

#74. TO VITUS MAELER Strassburg, 14 October 1485

626. *Summary* Schott urges Maeler to send information on the state of the case of litigation brought by Engelhard Funck* against Thomas Wolf, Jr,* and to continue trying to secure Johann Müller a benefice.

627. *Longioribus te nuper allocutus sum... conducibile fore sperare possim.*
Since mentioning the case of Engelhard Funck* against Thomas Wolf, Jr., to Maeler in March 1484 (#55), Schott had apparently written frequent letters about it. (For a brief discussion of the case, cf. N. 334.) Further letters to Maeler mentioning the case are: #75, #86, #93, #100.

628. *viro tam bene de me merito*
The person in question is Thomas Wolf, Sr., guardian and uncle to young Thomas mentioned above. For Schott's indebtedness to Wolf, cf. N. 364.

629. *Engelhardum Funck substitutum Magistri Heinrici Schonleben...*
Funck* was a co-worker or representative of Heinrich Schönleben* in Rome. Sleumer defines *substitutus* as "Mitarbeiter," "Helfer," "Amtsvertreter."

630. Ego vero Beneficia ecclesiastica plura non moror. Vnicus est... Muller...
Schott was not interested in more than one benefice; as he states in #73, p. 80, he never wanted more than one. His one concern at this time is to get a proper benefice for Müller (cf. N. 527).

#75. TO VITUS MAELER Strassburg, 24 October 1485

631. Summary Schott asks Maeler to do anything he can for the bearer of this letter, Leonhard Sturm, a relative and good friend, who is coming to Rome as a pilgrim. Maeler is requested to purchase copies of certain petitions delivered before the pope which are on sale in Rome and to give them to Sturm who will pay for them and deliver them to Strassburg. Schott wishes to be kept informed about the case of Funck* vs. Wolf* and about the possibility of a benefice for Müller.

632. Ipsum quoque virum affinitate et amicicia... christiane deuocionis causa.
The bearer of this letter, the Benedictine Leonhard Sturm, was Schott's relative by marriage; i.e., Schott's niece Ottilia von Cöllen had married into the Sturm family. He is mentioned #76, p. 83 and #86, p. 94. His visit to Rome for the sake of piety and devotion is, Schott observes ironically, quite out of the ordinary, but cf. N. 761. We have no further information about Leonhard.

633. super statu cause inter Engelhardum Funck et Vuolff iuniorem...
Cf. N. 334.

634. Audio oraciones quamplures habitas coram Pontifice maximo...
It is not known what these petitions made before the pope concerned. Perhaps Schott was interested in their format which may have resembled that of the petition to Pope Innocent VIII which he composed in 1487 (#80).
The copies requested are mentioned in #76, p. 83; #86, p. 94; #92, p. 103. It was spring of the next year before Schott had copies and these were sent by Sturm not Maeler; the copies sent by Maeler were confiscated (cf. N. 264). A second lot sent by Maeler reached Strassburg in June 1487 (#101).

635. Domino Leonardo de Egloffstein... quid in Magistri Iohannis...
Cf. N. 615, N. 527.

#76. TO VITUS MAELER Strassburg, 3 December 1485

636. Summary The request for copies of petitions delivered before the pope is repeated. Having heard from Johann Weschbach* how deeply imbued Maeler has become with the spirit of the *Curia*, Schott reminds Maeler of their student days, when he would have been satisfied with a benefice of 40 florins income, and warns against cupidity and the evil of multiple benefices.

P. 83   #76   N. 637

637. Scripsi ante menses duos per... Leonardum Sturm... et desideraui oraciones
Cf. #75, N. 632, N. 634.

638. Ioannes noster Vueschbach... Comitem Osualdum de Dyrstein... Sigismundi
Johann Weschbach* may have been at this time procurator for Archduke Sigismund* of Tyrol and hence was travelling in the company of the latter's councilor Oswald von Dyrstein.*

639. Memini quum non semel aut iterum... quadraginta aureos annuos.
Cf. p. xxx for partial translation of this passage.

640. Non possumus Christo seruire: et Mammone.
Mt. 6:24. Lc. 16:13.

641. Dominum Leonardum de Egloffstein... dominum Antonium Britenoriensem
Cf. N. 615, N. 624.

P. 84

#77. TO VITUS MAELER [Strassburg], 17 March 1486

642. Summary Schott explains that he has written the news of Alsace in the vernacular, lest Maeler forget his native tongue among things Latin. Johann Müller is rector of the university of Paris.

643. The index to the *Lucubraciunculae* (p. 326) has "eidem," i.e., Vitus Maeler, as the recipient of this item, which was evidently a note Schott enclosed with six letters that had been returned undelivered and were being resent to Maeler; hence the date of March 1486 among items of December 1485.

644. Magistrum meum Ioannem Molitoris
Cf. N. 541.

#78. TO RUDOLPH AGRICOLA Strassburg, 8 December 1485

645. Summary Schott's intense joy over Agricola's* answer to his letter raised him from bed when he was so stricken with tertian fever that his parents despaired of him. He has been prevented from acknowledging Agricola's letter earlier, first because of his illness and then because Agricola was in Italy. He hopes Agricola may pay Strassburg the long anticipated visit so that he may show his devotion. He is thankful that Agricola has reached home again safe and sound. The postscript tells that this letter was returned by the bearer, Thomas Wolf, Sr.,* 30 December 1485, because Agricola had died before it could be delivered. (Cf. N. 559).

646. qui me tuis tam peritis et suauibus litteris non solum edocueris...
Agricola's answer to Schott's letter of 18 February 1485 is not extant. It is mentioned as having already been written in Agricola's letter of 27 March 1485 to Adolph Rusch*: "Respondi litteris tuis, itidem litteris doctissimi hominis Petri Schotti, quas litteras arbitror tibi redditas esse" (Hartfelder, *Briefe*, 31). Writing again to Rusch on 13 April 1485, Agricola sends greetings to Schott and Wolf: "doctissimo uiro Petro Schotto, item Thome Uuolfio honestissimis et amantissimis uerbis meis saluta" (*ibid.*, 32). The fact that Agricola took time to answer Schott's letter so soon after he received it and the tone in which he writes of Schott to Rusch would seem to indicate that he did not consider Schott's questions "absurdities."

647. febricitantem me forte tempestate illa... magna leticia mirarentur
Schott took ill of tertian fever very soon after writing to Agricola on 18 February. In his letter of 1 March to Widmann* (#66, p. 73) he says he has already had four recurrences of fever and in his letter of 14 April to Maeler (#68, p. 76) he mentions that he has been suffering from fever for almost seven weeks. Agricola's letter probably reached Schott at the end of March or in early April. For comments on Schott's parents' overly solicitous care for his health, cf. N. 87.

648. foecit absencia tui: qui priusquam vires reciperem: Romam pecijsses
The exact date of Agricola's departure with Dalberg from Heidelberg for Rome is not known, but it was after 13 April, the date of Agricola's letter to Rusch (N. 646). He was in Rome by 30 May (letter to John Agricola, Allen, 315).

649. Dominus Thomas Vuolfius... Adelphus noster Ruscus
Cf. N. 566.

650. deo diuisque (ut Plautum imiter) ago gracias... te exemerunt
A paraphrase of Plautus *Cap.* 922-924:

> Iovi disque ago gratias merito magnas
> Quom te redducem tuo patri reddiderunt,
> Quomque ex miseriis plurimis me exemerunt.

651. Plangebam ego maximopere vicem tuam... (to end of item)
Agricola became ill of fever on the return journey from Rome and was left behind by Dalberg and the rest of the party at Trent, where he wrote his last two extant letters – both to Dalberg – on 4 August and 1 September (Allen, 316). Some time thereafter he left Trent and reached Heidelberg; the exact dates are not known. His fever persisting, he sent for his friend and countryman, the physician and humanist Adolph Occo,* then at Augsburg. Unfortunately, Occo did not arrive in Heidelberg until a day after Agricola's death (Hartfelder, *Briefe*, 9), which, according to Seidlmayer (*N D B*, I, 103), occurred 27 October 1485; Hartfelder does not give the date of Agricola's death, but alludes to it indirectly when mentioning honors bestowed by *Pfalzgraf* Philipp II* on Occo 19 November 1485 as having been conferred "also bald nach Agricolas Tod."

P. 85   #78   N. 651

If Agricola died on 27 October, it is strange that news of his death did not reach Strassburg before 8 December. To be sure, communication was slow, yet Schott tells of a letter which travelled from Strassburg to Rome in seven days less two hours (#100, p. 111).

652. Relate... ad tercium kalendas Ianuarias M.cccc.lxxxv
For a discussion of dates before the kalends of January, cf. N. 218.

#79. TO JOHANN KLITSCH Strassburg, 10 December 1485

653. Summary Schott chides his protégé Johann Klitsch* for not writing either to parents or to him and suggests that letters be sent via the Müg* brothers in Antwerp. Klitsch is encouraged to fulfill the hopes of parents and friends for his future. (Cf. N. 125 and N. 606).

654. Vidi mense superiori litteras Andree comitis tui... me cerciorem reddas.
Klitsch may be the protégé who was to board ship at Spires for the journey down the Rhine (cf. #70 and N. 604, N. 606 thereto). Andreas (mentioned in #96) was no doubt another of Schott's protégés or former *famuli*; no further information on him has been found. Both boys were probably at one of the schools operated by the Brethren of the Common Life (N. 88) – possibly at Deventer or Windesheim – in the Lowlands, since mail was to be sent from Antwerp.

655. Antvuerpiam ad Florencium: ad Ludouicum Mugen mercatores Argentinenses
The Strassburg merchants Florentius and Ludovicus Müg* (note German plural ending in "Mugen") apparently had a depot at Antwerp. Florentius was Schott's brother-in-law, having married Merga (Maria) Schott.*

656. Spes enim quam de te coepi: confidenciam... gloriam parabis eternam.
Cf. pp. xxviiif. for translation of this passage; cf. also N. 125.

657. Parentes tuos et Magistrum Thomam...
Nothing is known of Klitsch's family. *Magister* Thomas may be Thomas Lampertheim – whom Schott calls *Magister Thomas* (#125, p. 146) – or a schoolmaster at New. St. Peter.

658. Saluere te iubet Genitrix mea: quae te vehementer diligit...
Susanna von Cöllen seems to have taken a very personal interest in her son's *famuli*.

P. 86

#80. TO POPE INNOCENT VIII [early 1487]

659. Summary The undersigned have heard a rumor that His Holiness' predecessor Sixtus IV, importuned by a faction of canons, agreed to exclude from canonicates in certain cathedral churches, particularly Spires, those not of knightly birth. The undersigned cannot believe that the Holy See could agree to such exclusion, because the same Holy See formerly granted Bishop Rabanus of Spires the right to appoint to canonicates worthy scholars not of knightly birth. Nobles and knights are indeed worthy of holding canonicates, yet distinguished scholars are not unworthy to do so. Should His Holiness feel that scholars are not to be considered on the same basis as knights, then at least a certain percentage of scholars should be included. If, however, nobility of birth be the criterion, it follows that the nobler the more acceptable and even simple knights should be excluded. May His Holiness, therefore, deign to end the misunderstanding and affirm that scholars are to be accepted.

(Signed)
The Holy Roman Emperor in Germany; cities; states; senates and republican states; canons and prelates of collegiate churches; twelve universities of Germany.

660. This undated petition to be delivered before Innocent VIII (N. 634) with its accompanying undated letter to Innocent (#81) and the letter of 30 December 1486 to Wimpheling (#82) concern the restriction of canonicates in cathedral chapters to nobles and knights. From internal evidence it is obvious that the letter to Wimpheling was written before the petition or the letter to Innocent VIII and that the latter two items must have been written therefore sometime in 1487, possibly early in the year. In the *Luc.* arrangement the items are out of order in relation to one another – their proper order being #82, #80, #81 – and also out of order in relation to other items, their place chronologically being after #97 of 10 December 1486 (cf. N. 218).

From the letter to Wimpheling three points are clear: that certain factions were bringing pressure on Innocent VIII to decree that canonicates in cathedral chapters be restricted to knights and nobles; that Wimpheling had requested Schott to compose a document setting forth arguments against such restriction; that Schott, not in possession of all the facts and not sure what type of document was desired, wrote an outline of the arguments in his letter to Wimpheling and expected Wimpheling to draft the document. On receipt of Schott's letter, however, it seems Wimpheling must have decided that the document should be composed by Schott, who then wrote the petition (#80) and the letter (#81) to Innocent VIII. The outcome of the case is not known.

661. Fama volat... membra et Canonicos non debeant assumi.
The primary qualification for appointment to high ecclesiastical offices was illustrious birth. Education was secondary. The regulations for membership in the college of cardinals, for example, as set down by the councils of Constance and Basel, required that only one-third of the members be university graduates.

It was general policy in Germany for cathedral chapters to bestow canonicates almost exclusively on nobles and knights. In the three most important cathedral chapters – those of the archbishop-electors at Cologne, Mainz and Trier – no commoner could be admitted. To become canon at Mainz or Trier one had to be at least a knight. To become canon at Cologne one had to be, according to the bull of Sixtus IV issued 1474, of legitimate birth and of noble ancestry through five generations (i.e., *seize quartiers* in heraldry). Of the Cologne chapter Innocent VIII once said with pride that it surpassed all chapters in Germany in nobility of birth.

There were, however, a few cathedral chapters which did not stress noble birth above everything else. Lübeck required only that its candidates be of legitimate birth. Spires and Wimpfen am Neckar divided benefice holders into three classes: the first class consisted of nobles; the second consisted of six commoners – hence the term *sexprebendarius* – whose benefices were equal to those of the first class (cf. Theodoricus Ribysen, #70); the third consisted of nobles and commoners whose benefices were 1/2 the value of those in the first and second classes.

Cathedral chapters were havens for younger sons of the nobility. Canonical lists show that for generation after generation the same families sent their sons, often several at a time, to the same chapter. In the Strassburg cathedral chapter, for instance, two uncles of Friedrich von Zollern had held canonicates before him, and the brothers Heinrich and Berthold von Hennenberg held canonicates simultaneously.

Collegiate chapters, too, emphasized illustrious birth. New St. Peter in Strassburg which preferred nobles and patricians in canonical elections is an example of this practice.

Cf. Horning, "Stift," 24, Kisky, 8-15. Wetzer-Welte, XI, 792 (*Stift*).

662. papam quartum... obrutam indulsisse
Note feminine ending on *obrutam*; the original has *obrutā*, the final *a* of which may be a misprint for *u*.

663. Rabanus Spirensis quondam ecclesie Episcopus... bonos et doctos viros
Bishop Rabanus* at the beginning of the fifteenth century had obtained papal permission to admit scholars of lowly birth as canons into the cathedral chapter at Spires (cf. N. 660). Successors of Rabanus shared his zeal for learning so that by the end of the fifteenth century the chapter was noted as one of the most scholarly in Germany and its library known for its excellence (cf. #122). Noble canons of the chapter not only honored humanists but had close contact with them; Georg von Gemmingen, for example, was a friend of Reuchlin,* and prebends were allotted to men like Wimpheling who later (as did Jodocus Gallus*) held the cathedral chair of preacher. Canon Thomas Truchsess had a celebrated private library containing all genres of literature (Schmidt "Notices... P.S.," 337). It is no wonder that the chapter and Wimpheling were appalled at the prospect of a papal decree directed against them.

664. Ibique Crucifixi patrimonio vti... equaliter cum eis percipere.
Schott here makes a telling point. Since church funds come from all the faithful, they should not be used to support only a small favored group.

665. Sacroromanus Imperator... Duodecim Germanie Vniversitates
The first signature on the petition would have been that of Emperor Friedrich III. By *Vrbes* Schott perhaps meant the free imperial cities; by *Civitates: Senatus et Respublice* he perhaps meant to distinguish between states which were ruled by bishops or princes and those which had republican governments of one type or another.

The twelve German universities existing at that time were, according to Paulsen ("Gründung," 251-278): Prague, founded 1348; Vienna, 1365; Heidelberg, 1385; Cologne, 1388; Erfurt, 1389; Leipzig, 1409; Rostock, 1419; Greifswald, 1456; Freiburg, 1456; Basel, 1456; Mainz, 1476; Tübingen, 1476. It may be noted that Paulsen omits from this list the university of Ingolstadt which began instruction in 1472 and which was more likely than Prague one of the twelve universities Schott had in mind.

#81. TO POPE INNOCENT VIII [early 1487]

666. Summary We know that opinions of the Holy See are the result of long and serious deliberation. We also know that factions soliciting decrees from the Holy See unashamedly suppress facts. On hearing a rumor that persons swollen with pride in their noble blood are striving to usurp canonicates in cathedral churches, we have made bold to explain that such usurpation is not only contrary to the Christian religion but also pernicious to German churches. (Cf. N. 659, N. 660 and N. 661).

667. (cui christi Vicarius possidet)
What is the construction of *cui*? Is it archaic spelling for the indefinite *qui* used as an expletive – "surely," or the archaic form of *cuius* (in which case one must assume that *possidet* here governs the genitive), or a misprint for *cum* in the sense of "inasmuch as?" The assumption that *possedit* (which is written out in full in the incunabulum) is a misprint for *praesidet* would not only explain *cui* as the dative (of the relative pronoun) after *praesidere* but would also make good sense.

#82. TO JACOB WIMPHELING Strassburg, 30 December 1486

668. Summary Schott deplores his inability to fulfill Wimpheling's request that he compose a document setting forth arguments against restriction of canonicates in cathedral churches to nobles and knights. He outlines the divisions and arguments of such a document and suggests that Wimpheling who is in possession of all the facts draft the final document. (Cf. N. 660, N. 661).

669. Ceterum/ quod subuerebaris: dum nobiscum esses... lacerare videreris.
In his many quarrels about every kind of subject Wimpheling was notoriously vehement and ill-tempered.

670. quod in perniciem ouium paliata dolositas erexisset
Cf. Mt. 7:15.

671. Ex Argentina tercia kalendas Ianuarij... M.cccclxxxvi.
For dates before the kalends of January, cf. N. 218.

P. 90   #83   N. 672

#83. TO FRIEDRICH VON ZOLLERN Strassburg, 30 March 1486

672. Summary Schott congratulates Friedrich* on his election as bishop of Augsburg and particularly the diocese of Augsburg on obtaining a worthy bishop. He warns against listening to blandishments of courtiers and recommends adherence to Geiler's precepts. He asks that Friedrich secure from Maximilian *primae preces* for Müller and use his influence in having the cathedral chair at Strassburg confirmed.

673. This item and Schott's manuscript letter of 28 February to Friedrich von Zollern (Appendix B) treat the same matters. The manuscript letter precedes chronologically the present item. Cf. N. 2 and notes to Appendix B.

674. Domino Friderico electo Augustensi Episcopo... et ope sis prouectus.
The date when Friedrich von Zollern was unanimously elected bishop by the Augsburg cathedral chapter is given as 31 March 1486, yet Schott already knew of the election and was writing this letter on 30 March 1486. Is it possible that the date of the election was 13 March instead of 31? Since the former bishop Johann von Werdenberg (Friedrich's uncle) had died 23 February, one might suppose the chapter election was held very soon thereafter, perhaps even before 13 March, as by 28 February there already were rumors of Friedrich's election (Appendix B).
  Friedrich received the first news of his election in Frankfurt, where he had been since at least 16 February, the date when Maximilian was created King of the Romans; the official news reached him in Aachen, where he was representing the elector of Brandenburg at Maximilian's coronation on 9 April (cf. biographical note on Friedrich von Zollern).
  Election by the chapter did not, as indicated in Schott's letter, automatically make Friedrich bishop of Augsburg. Because bulls issued by Sixtus IV on 1 July 1478 and 15 March 1480 decreed that both pope and emperor were to decide upon episcopal candidates in a great number of bishoprics, including Augsburg, and because Nicholas V had previously ruled that heads of state had a voice in the choice of bishops, Friedrich had to be accepted by Pope Innocent VIII, Emperor Friedrich III (Friedrich's godfather), Maximilian as King of the Romans (referred to in the text as "Regie Maiestatis"), the electors of the empire as advisors of the emperor and the lesser princes concerned, for to the bishopric of Augsburg belonged Swabian, Frankish and Bavarian lands.
  The electors, with the exception of *Pfalzgraf* Philipp,* recommended Friedrich to the emperor and presumably to Maximilian. The lesser princes favoring Friedrich belonged to the Hapsburg faction: Sigismund von Tirol,* Eberhard von Württemberg,* the bishops of Bamberg and Eichstätt. Those opposing Friedrich belonged to the Wittelsbach faction: Georg (*der Reiche*) von Landshut; Albrecht, Christoph* and Wolfgang* von München; Otto von Neumarkt. Thus five Bavarian dukes opposed Friedrich, although the ruling duke and elector of Bavaria Albrecht III (*der Weise*) was, as noted above, for him. The Wittelsbachs cast their votes for their relative Johann von Mosbach, canon and *praepositus* of the Augsburg cathedral chapter.
  Although Schott implies that approval of all temporal powers had been obtained, there must have been difficulties, because not until 12 May did the cathedral chapter of Augsburg send two of its canons to Rome for official confirmation by the pope of Friedrich's election as bishop. This confirmation was received 14 June; yet the official date recorded at Rome for Friedrich's election is 21 June 1486 (Eubel, II, 98). Friedrich was

P. 90   #83   N. 674

crowned at Dillingen 21 July (N. 811). The total cost of *provisio*, etc. for his becoming bishop was over 3550 florins.
     Cf. Dacheux, *Réf.*, 370. Hofmann, I, 279. Steichele, 115ff. Zoepl, 483.

675. qui vel ignorans accersiri: et inuitus vocari...
This passage seems to imply that Friedrich was unaware of being considered as candidate for bishop of Augsburg and was an unwilling victim of politics.

676. molestari ab onere: et operibus/ quae ipsum in se Episcopatus nomen...
In this paragraph Schott discusses the heavy responsibilities of a bishop in the light of St. Augustine's definition of *episcopatus* in *De civitate Dei*, xix (Migne, XLI, 647): "Apostolus... exponere voluit quid sit episcopatus: quia nomen est operis non honoris. Graecum est enim... vocabulum quod ille qui praeficitur, eis quibus praeficitur supertenuit, curam eorum scilicet gerens."

P. 91

677. te hortor: ut omnia gubernes: et moderere... si te audies.
Cicero *Ad Fam.* ii.7.

678. quae Iesu Christi sunt: quam quae sua: aut mundi
Cf. Ph. 2:21.

679. In summa breuibus habeto... Doctore Iohanne de keisersberg... confirmasti.
While Friedrich was still a student at Freiburg, Geiler had written for him precepts (*Monita*, cf. Appendix H) and at the time of Friedrich's accession Geiler composed *Monita quaedam J. Geileri ad Fridericum electum Augustanum in aditu episcopatus*. Schott may have been thinking of the early precepts or of Geiler's repeated warnings to Friedrich, during the years of their association in Strassburg against yielding to the temptations of the easy life which was Friedrich's by right of birth and wealth.
     Geiler had opposed Friedrich's becoming bishop, because such a position involved not only embroilment in the intrigues of secular and ecclesiastical politics but also exposure to worldly pomp and luxury. When Friedrich learned of his election, he wrote in great perturbation to Geiler, who answered with a very frank letter stating among other things: "Just count your horses and mind the falcon, never visit your diocese or extirpate vices, do not dispense revenues to the poor – they belong to the poor, do not make ordinations if you wish to be like the bishops of our time. If you do not wish to be like them, but wish to be a phoenix, a phenomenon among bishops, it were better you had never been born."
     Dacheux, *Réf.*, 365, 394. Dreher, XVIII, 27f. Zoepfl, 487.

680. supplicacionem nomine Magistri et didascali mei... facultas fuerit...
Maximilian was to be crowned at Aachen a few days after the date of this letter and Friedrich was to be present at the ceremony (N. 674, par. 2). From the day of his coronation Maximilian would have the right of granting

P. 91   #83   N. 680

preces primae (N. 130,2). Hence Schott urges Friedrich to obtain at the first opportunity *preces primae* for Müller for a canonicate in Old St. Peter at Strassburg.

In his letter of 28 February (Appendix B) Schott had hinted that Friedrich obtain these *preces*. Schott, Sr., too, was anxious that Friedrich not forget Müller: Johann Rot* in a letter to Friedrich relays a message from Schott: "Rogat dominus D. Schot ut memor sis commendationis mgri Io. Molitoris, quia eum genitor suus tibi commendavit, cum tecum esset Francofordiae" (Dacheux, *Réf.*, App. IV).

Friedrich must have acted quickly, because Müller's *preces primae* were issued 7 May 1486 at Cologne (Santifaller, 623) and were in Baden before 21 July 1486 (#174, p. 195). Such prompt action was a tribute to the Schotts as well as to Müller, for whom Friedrich had vainly tried to secure a post in the Strassburg cathedral (N. 529). In July 1487 Schott writes to Müller (#103, p. 113) that the royal *preces* should soon be confirmed by the pope in Rome. Confirmation was, however, not secured until much later, because the pope was refusing to recognize Maximilian's* *preces* (N. 130,3, par. 6). Finally in 1490 when Müller was in Rome, he with Maeler's help received confirmation and informed Schott of the fact (#153, p. 167; N. 1099). By virtue of these *preces* Müller became canon of Old St. Peter in September 1490. Cf. N. 527.

681. reuerendissima Papa terrae
As noted in the *Errata*, this phrase should read *reuerendissima Paternitas tua*. The incunabulum has *Pa. t.* The accepted reading for *Pa.* is *Papa*; for *t.* there are many readings. When we discovered that *preces primae* were imperial and not papal favors, it became obvious that the correct reading had to be *Paternitas tua*, a phrase abbreviated as P.T. elsewhere in the incunabulum (cf. folios LXIIb and LXXVIIIb). P. for *paternitas* appears in the abbreviation for the phrase *vestra paternitas* four times on folio LXXXXVIIa and twice on folios LXXXXVIIb and LXXXXVIIIa.

682. Nec eo minus si quid ad Predicacionis officium... honestum fuerit.
This passage seems to indicate that Friedrich had not yet resigned as dean of the Strassburg cathedral (indeed, it was customary to keep one benefice in hand until another was confirmed), even though Strassburg statutes demanded that the dean be in residence. Schott is thus urging Friedrich both as dean and as newly elected bishop to use his influence in hastening the confirmation of Geiler's position as preacher of the Strassburg cathedral (cf. N. 955, par. 6).

Zoepfl's interpretation of this passage as a hint from Schott that Friedrich should resign the canonicate in the Strassburg cathedral chapter does not seem applicable. Friedrich had held this canonicate since early youth; furthermore the canonicate had nothing to do with the cathedral chair; indeed, the chair was finally confirmed in 1489, two years before Friedrich at Geiler's request resigned the canonicate in favor of Hoyer von Barby (cf. N. 1188).

P. 92

#84. TO JOHANN MÜLLER Strassburg, 15 April 1486

683. Summary Schott has long been trying to secure a benefice for Müller and if ever he should have the opportunity of nominating a canon or co-canon (one he doubts will ever come to him, since sexagenarians are still waiting their turn) he would nominate no one but Müller.

684. Quod a me petis: quid sit non ignoras... quoad hoc caput agimus.
Apparently Müller has been complaining about Schott's lack of success in securing a benefice for him. (For Schott's persistent efforts to do so, cf. N. 527.) The perpetual vicarate at the Strassburg cathedral had recently been sought in vain (cf. N. 529).

685. Neque enim ego mihi tantum vite promitto... nominandi in Canonicum sors
For the method of nominating candidates to vacant canonicates or other benefices, cf. N. 130, 1.

686. Verum ne me Antigonum insimules: si ego ad eam sortem peruenero...
Antigonus Doson (†220) was said always to be about to give someone something but never did.

#85. TO MARCUS, CARDINAL OF ST. MARK [Zabern], 22 May 1486

687. Summary Schott, writing in the name of Bishop Albrecht,* requests Cardinal Marcus Barbus* to have the Clingenthal sisters* and their present abode of Obersteigen accepted into the general chapter of the Dominicans so that the sisters may enjoy privileges of a recognized convent. (Cf. N. 447 and N. 448.)

688. domino Marco: Cardinali sancti Marci: ac Patriarche Acquilegiensi...
This appeal may have been directed to Marcus Barbus because he had been appointed cardinal in charge of German affairs (cf. biographical note on him).

689. Sorores quamplures ordinis Sancti Augustini... Predicatorum de Observancia
The sisters had come originally from the Dominican convent at Engelspforten; some of them may have after their expulsion from Clingenthal become Augustinian nuns or they may have accepted Augustinian nuns into their group. At Obersteigen the sisters were under the the supervision – though not accepted members – of the Dominicans of Strict Observance.

This monastic, ascetic group of Observants within the Dominican Order had come into being at the end of the fourteenth century after difficulties had arisen in maintaining balance between the two divergent groups – the monastic canonical and the clerical apostolic, both of which were provided for in the rule of St. Augustine adhered to by the Dominican Order. To restore monastic observances which had declined Raymond de Capua in 1390 ordered that a monastery of strict observance be established in each Dominican province.

Basel seems to have spearheaded the reform in southwestern German

P. 93   #85   N. 689

lands and was the center of the observant faction. The Dominican monastery at Colmar belonged to the Strict Observance (#141, p. 156).

The Strassburg Dominicans were opposed to reform and resisted by all means at their command any efforts to reform them (cf. biographical note on Johann Ortwin; N. 83, par 1; and N. 1546).

690. in nemoribus se ad tempus recipientes... anno superiori tradidimus...
The sisters had first been given shelter by the counts of Lyningen in the parish of Rhentingen near Metz (N. 451). Then in 1485 Christoph von Uttenhein* bought an old monastery at Obersteigen (in the rugged hills near Wasselone about 15 miles northeast of Strassburg) and gave it to the sisters.

P. 94

#86. TO VITUS MAELER Strassburg, 24 May 1486

691. Summary Schott is pleased that Maeler recognizes the dangers in plurality of benefices. He is sorry their attempt to procure a benefice for Müller has failed. Copies of the petitions delivered before the pope have not yet arrived. Maeler is to report on the status of the case Engelhard Funck* vs. Thomas Wolf, Jr.*

692. Quod in eis scribebas: monitis meis te aurem...
This is a reference to Schott's warnings against cupidity and plurality of benefices in #76 (p. 83).

693. Operam quam pro Magistro meo... frustra factum fuisset
Combined efforts of many friends had failed in securing for Müller the benefice of perpetual vicar at the cathedral at Strassburg (cf. N. 529).

694. Scribis eciam te mittere aliquas Oraciones: verum nullas recepi.
Cf. N. 631 and N. 634.

695. de statu cause/ quam Engelhardus Funck mouit Thomae Vuolf... (end of paragraph)
Cf. N. 334.

P. 95

696. Et inter tela Martis et Apollinis hoc est bellorum et estus
The wars referred to were probably 1) that of Archduke Sigismund* of Tyrol against the Venetians which began 1486 and ended with victory for Sigismund in 1487, and 2) the particularly bloody war between the Lombards and the Swiss league. Cf. Trithemius, *Ann. Hirs.*, II, 529f.

697. Dominum Leonardum Egloffstein... dominum Anthonium praecoeptorem grecum
Cf. N. 615, N. 620 and N. 624.

506

P. 95   #86   N. 698

698. Causam domini Doctoris Kerer de Friburgo: super Vicaria in ecclesia...
Nothing is known about a case of litigation against Kerer over a vicarate at the Strassburg cathedral. The pope did create Kerer a vicar in Strassburg (Dreher, XX, 30), but the name of the church and the time are not given. The disputed vicarate may be the one Schott tried to secure for Müller (cf. N. 529).

#87. TO JOHANN MEIGER (Meyger) Strassburg, 29 May 1486

699. Summary Meiger* is requested to support Müller's candidacy for a vacant perpetual vicarate in Andlau which Johann Rot* has had to refuse.

700. Iohanni Meiger: Rectori in Bliensvuiler...
Johann Meiger was also a fellow canon of Schott at New St. Peter. Note that *Bliensvuiler* is spelled *Pliensvuiler* #47, p. 51; #62, p. 68; #68, p. 75.

701. Vicaria quedam perpetua in Andelo... Magistri Iohannis Muller nunc Parisius...
The perpetual vicarate at Andlau was probably in the convent of St. Richardis (N. 437). Müller did not obtain this benefice, and there is no further mention of it.

702. iampridem pertesum se esse laboris Gymnastici... cum nulla gratitudine
Cf. N. 526 and N. 527.

703. Domino Andree concanonico tuo
I.e., Andreas Hartmann von Eppingen,* fellow canon of both Meiger and Schott and vicar general of the bishop.

P. 96

704. Indubitatum est siquidem mihi... si ipse ea pocietur: consecuturum.
In this passage and in the passage above in the text (p. 95), "Qui quam ad huiusmodi Beneficium esset idoneus... probatissimus pollet," Schott pays tribute to Müller's character and ability.

#88. TO JOHANN WIDMANN [Strassburg], 6 July 1486

705. Summary Schott's parents are about to go to Wildbad and would like to meet Widmann's wife there and Widmann himself if possible, because they wish to consult him about strange miscarriages suffered by their daughter Ottilia and their granddaughter Ottilia von Cöllen.

706. thermas vestras ferales. Illuc... vxor quoque tua... reuisere eos velis
The terms *balnea feralia, balnea ferina, balnea ferarum* indicated baths of pure, natural spring waters (cf. "Baden Ferino," #132, p. 152 and "Balneo Ferarum," #133, p. 152); the terms *thermae ferales, thermae ferinae* indicated warm baths of pure, natural spring waters and both of these terms were

P. 96   #88   N. 706

applied to Wildbad (cf. Zeiller, 420; Geiger, *Briefwechsel*, 361, note to "thermas illas ferinas"). Schott calls these baths at Wildbad "vestras" (your), because they were situated in Württemberg, near Tübingen, where Widmann was serving as personal physician to the reigning prince. It is possible that Widmann also served as spa physician at Wildbad; he wrote a tract on the properties of its waters. For a discussion of baths, their popularity, etc., cf. N. 192. For Widmann's wife, cf. N. 587.

707. sororem meam de Adeltçheim: et filiam ipsius... quoddam monstrum...
Both Ottilia Schott* and her daughter Ottilia von Cöllen* seem to have given birth to hydratiform moles – a mass of cysts developing out of the bag in which the fetus grows – a condition about which apparently little is known even today. The same phenomenon seems to have occurred two years later (cf. #111, p. 131).

708. Domini Iohanni Sifridi significa... eum beneuolencia complecti.
Johann Sifrid * may have been spending his holiday at Tübingen or Wildbad.

#89. TO PETER SCHOTT FROM JACOB WIMPHELING Spires, 26 July 1486

709. Summary Wimpheling requests Schott's opinion, supported by references and quotations, on the question whether – as certain of his associates maintain – "common syllables" in words like *tenebrae* and *cathedra* must always be pronounced long in prose.

710. Note the absence of a heading by Wimpheling (N. 37). This item and Schott's two letters (#90 and #91) following concern questions of syllable length.

711. Petro Schotto... praeceptori suo semper venerando
The term *praeceptori* here does not mean "teacher" in the sense that Wimpheling studied under Schott; it means some one from whom it is possible to learn; in other words the term is used as a complimentary form of address to a person highly respected. Cf. Schott's salutations in #137 to Geiler and in #30, #35, #172 to Thomas Wolf, Sr.;* Schott's reference in #136, p. 154 to Biel;* Friesenheimer's* salutation in #209 to Schott; also *praecoeptoribus* below in this item (p. 97).

P. 97

712. communes sillabas: puta Tenebre/ Cathedra... produci oportere.
"Common syllables" are those which can be either long or short (cf. Diomedes ii. "De communi syllaba"). The syllables under discussion in this item are the antepenults of the examples quoted, i.e., of *tenebre* and like words. Normally a short vowel followed by two consonants becomes long by position, (cf. Quintillian i.5.28, ix.4.86 and Diomedes ii. "De accentibus"), but – as Schott demonstrates by examples from the classics and quotations from grammarians in #90 and #91 – a short vowel followed by two consonants, one of which is a mute, the other a liquid, is short in prose and – depending upon the metre – may be either short or long in poetry. Therefore the con-

tention of Wimpheling's associates that such syllables are always long in prose, is incorrect. Cf. Schott's words, p. 333 (*Epithoma*, V, *secunda*).

713. Ego aliquid in eo putabam me effoecisse: at nihil profoeci.
Wimpheling is referring to his work on prosody (cf. N. 49).

714. Tu quoque mei esto memor... acceptabilissimam victimam.
I.e., Wimpheling wishes to be remembered when Schott saying mass offers the host.

#90. TO JACOB WIMPHELING Strassburg, 20 August 1486

715. Summary Schott gives examples to prove that in *tenebrae* and like words the antepenult is short; he explains why the *e* of *cathedra* is short. (Cf. N. 710 and N. 712).

716. sentencia Marci Celij Quintiliani... Nihil inquit peius est his... perdocent.
Cf. Quintilian *Inst. orat.* i.1.8. Modern editions of Quintilian have *peius est iis*, cf. Butler, *The* "Institutio...," I, 22; Radermacher, I, 9; Spalding, I, 23; for *falsam scienciae* (below in this passage) the same three editions have *falsam sibi scientiae*, and for *peritis* Butler and Radermacher have *partibus*, but Spalding has *peritis* which seems to be the better reading.

717. Itaque Tenebras/ latebras/ Celebres... testes sunt... Et spes (p. 99)
The passages cited are: Lucan i.542, vii.177 and 552, ix.674; Ovid *Met.* xv.154; Vergil *Geor.* iii.401; Juvenal vii.3,47, 203. As noted in the *Errata, Metamorphos.* – the abbreviation used in the incunabulum – should be resolved into *Metamorphosis*.

718. Cathedra quod e breuem habeat... est breue.
I.e., *cathedra* is originally a Greek word and in the Greek spelling its antepenult has an epsilon, which is a short vowel; hence the *e* of *cathedra* is also short.

#91. TO JACOB WIMPHELING Strassburg, 23 September 1486

719. Summary Schott quotes from Diomedes, Priscian and Quintilian pertinent passages to prove that in words like *tenebrae* the antepenult is always short in prose and may be either long or short in poetry, depending upon the exigencies of the metre. He appends a list of examples from classical poets. (Cf. N. 710 and N. 712, also Appendix I).

720. Quoniam priori Epistola tua me oraueras...
Schott is probably referring to #89 although it is possible that Wimpheling

P. 99   #91   N. 720

on receipt of #90 had written a second letter requesting more information and proofs.

721. *nihil tum de soluto stilo: super quo non inquisieras*
The double negatives *nihil* and *non* make the *quo* clause positive: "about which you had asked," for Wimpheling had indeed asked about syllable length in prose style (*soluto stilo*). Double negatives occur again in the text below (p. 100): "quibus si non credatur: nescio quid in Grammatica solidum...," where *non* makes *nescio quid* mean "nothing."

722. *sed et omnes [omnem] priscorum aetatem*
Cf. *Errata*. Goldast (Appendix I) has *omnem*, as has Lurwig, 82.

723. *quae producenda erant: correpta per Sistolem...*
Systole: A syllable which is regularly long may sometimes be shortened in verse for metrical purposes (cf. Diomedes ii. "De metaplasmis").

P. 100

724. *Num faciliora opera: excusasset Priscianus illud Virgilij?*
We have been unable to locate the phrase "faciliora opera" in Vergil, and so far as we can ascertain, Priscian does not cite it as an example. Schott apparently quotes the phrase to demonstrate a combination of syllables which cannot be fitted into dactylic hexameter without poetic license. Of the eight syllables only one is naturally long, i.e., the *or* of the comparative (Priscian *Partitiones* 46); the *i* preceding it is short and cannot be lengthened (*Idem, Inst.* iii.8, 13); natural stresses are on *fa, or* and *op*. Hence the poet would have to lengthen an unstressed short syllable, i.e., employ diastole, or ignore the elision, i.e., employ hiatus; hiatus with a short final vowel is rare, but does occur in Vergil (cf. *Aen.*i.405).

725. *Ponite spes sibi quisque...*
Vergil *Aen.* xi.309. The quotation is used by Priscian to illustrate his comment (*Inst.* i.40) that *s* loses its force as a consonant: "S in metri apud vetustissimos vim suam frequenter amittit," a comment Schott paraphrases.

726. *ut M. Cicero dixit: sed ad verborum libertatem spectet.*
Cf. Cicero *De Or.* i.16, 70; iii.44, 173.

727. *ut Horacius ait: arbitrium est et vis et norma loquendi.*
Horace *Ars Poetica* 72. Modern editions have, instead of *vis*, *ius* or *jus*.

728. *Loquatur igitur Diomedes... In trissillabis...* (to end of paragraph, p. 101)
The three selections from Diomedes: "In trissillabis... ut Latebre/ Tenebrae," "Si penultima posicioni... Tenebre/ latebre," "Et tenebres... sillaba offertur" are from *Art. Gram.* ii. "de accentibus" 2.

Between the words "Hec si" and "posicione longa" of the first selection the full text of Diomedes is as follows: "Haec si natura longa fuerit, in-

510

flectitur, ut Romanus Cethegus marinus Crispinus amicus Sabinus Quirinus lectica si vero eadem paenultima posicione longa fuerit" (Keil, I, 431).

729. Accedat et Priscianus... Trissillabe vero... accentum. ut Latebrae/ Tenebrae
Priscian "De Accentibus Liber" ii. The lacuna after *Trissillabe vero* is not for omission of Greek (N. 23) but for the two Latin words "et tetrasyllabae." The text of the passage from Priscian as quoted here is slightly different from that as edited by Keil (III, 521): "Trisyllabae namque et tetrasyllabae sive deinceps, si paenultimam correptam habuerint, antepaenultimam acuto accentu proferunt, ut Tullius Hostilius/ nam paenultima si positione longa fuerit acuetur, antepaenultima vero gravabitur ut Catullus/ Metellus, si vero ex muta et liquida longa in versu esse constat, in oratione quoque accentum mutat ut latebrae tenebrae."

730. Auditur itaque Quintilianus... Euenit ut metri quoque... versus Heroicus
Quintilian *Inst. Orat.* i.5.28. The edition by Radermacher (I, 32, 1.6) does not have *ut* following *Euenit*.

731. Carmina probatiua prescriptorum
N.B. the different heading Goldast has here (Appendix I).
1) Virgil *Georg.* iii.401.
2) *Aen.* iii.195.
3) *Aen.* iii.232.
4) *Aen.* viii.244. Incorrectly cited in the incunabulum as iij.
5) Horace *Ep.* i.15.31. Schott cites this Epistle as "Maenius, ut rebus" which was formerly considered the beginning of a separate epistle but is now considered as a continuation of *Ep.* i.15 (lines 26ff.), cf. E. C. Wickham, *Horace* (Oxford, 1903), II, 247.
6) Juvenal *Sat.* vii.47.
7) *Sat.* vii.203.
8) *Sat.* vii.3.
9) Ovid *Met.* i.216.
10) *Met.* i.388.
11) *Met.* i.593.
12) *Met.* xiii.696.
13) *Met.* xv.154.
14) *Ars Amatoria* ii.392.
15) *Ars Amatoria* ii.620. Incorrectly cited in the incunabulum as iii.
16) Lucan *Pharsalia* i.542.
17) *Pharsalia* iii.714 and 735.
18) *Pharsalia* iv.192.

19) *Pharsalia* vii.177 and 552.
20) Martial *Epigrammata* xiii.62. The thirteenth book of Martial's epigrams used to be called *Xenia*, (cf. N. 577 and N. 734).
21) Claudian *Stilich.* ii.136f.

#92. TO VITUS MAELER Strassburg, 5 September 1486

732. *Summary* Schott reports that the copies of papal petitions which Maeler sent have been confiscated by soldiers. He commissions Maeler to obtain *sub rosa* a marriage dispensation for a couple who have been married more than ten years and have just discovered that they are related in fourth degree. Johann Müller with his princeling has returned to Baden-Baden.

733. *Quamuis enim Oraciones a te mihi beneuolencia... a militibus ereptas*
Cf. N. 634.

734. *quam apophoretis accumulare non praetermitterem...*
Apophoreta is the title of book xiv of Martial's epigrams; the term means gifts which guests at banquets received to take home, especially at the Saturnalia.

735. *Sunt Argentine duo Iohannes et Elizabeth... in quarto gradu affinitatis...*
The case of marriage between these unidentified persons related in the fourth degree is mentioned #93, p. 105; #97, p. 108; #101, p. 111. The last item noted reports that one of the couple has died.

Canon law on consanguinity as modified by Innocent III (1198-1216) permitted marriage between persons related beyond the fourth degree. The computation of degrees of consanguinity in canon law, however, was much more restrictive than that in civil law, for in canon law step-relatives, godparents and relatives by adoption were counted as blood relatives. It is therefore easy to understand how one might be unaware of relationship. Cf. "Arbor Affinitatis" and "Declaracio affinitatis" in *Corpus Iuris Canonici*, I, 1431ff.

736. *ignorancia iuris non facti*
Legal proverb (cf. *Dictionary of Latin and Greek Quotations*, 161; *Oxford Dictionary of English Proverbs*, 217; *Oxford Dictionary of Quotations*, 321a).

737. *Pecunia apud me est deposita... nuncius hic portare abnuisset.*
The messenger was evidently afraid that money might be taken from him, cf. N. 264.

738. *Quo et dispensacionem per Poenitenciariam... per Cameram... foro contensioso...*
The *Poenitenciaria Apostolica* was the papal court which dealt with matters concerning confession, indulgences and matrimony. The *Camera Apostolica* was the papal ministry of finance. We have been unable to discover what kind of court is meant by *forum contentiosum*; the term appears also #214, p. 228; #215, p. 233.

739. *Magister Iohannes Molitoris... cum Domino... in arcem Badensem*
Johann Müller had now been three years at the university of Paris with his charge Jacob of Baden* (cf. N. 527, N. 541).

P. 104   #93   N. 740

#93. TO VITUS MAELER Strassburg, 28 September 1486

740. Summary Maeler is rebuked for not reporting on the litigation of Engelhard Funck* vs. Thomas Wolf, Jr.,* concerning which Schott has repeatedly requested information. Thomas Wolf, Sr.,* is himself writing to Maeler about the case. Would Maeler when answering Wolf's letter please be good enough to attest Schott's constant diligence in the case, lest Wolf doubt that Schott has ever mentioned it. By another messenger Schott will send money and more details on the matrimonial case.

741. super controuersia/ quae inter Engelhardum Funck et Thomam Vuolf iuniorem
Schott had requested reports on this case in October 1485 (#74) and in May 1486 (#86) and perhaps in letters not extant. For details of the case, cf. N. 334.

P. 105

742. per quendam fraterum ordinis sancti Vuilhelmi... super dispensacione...
The brother belonging to the Order of the Hermits of St. William (N. 616) has not been identified. For the case of consanguinity, cf. N. 732 and N. 735.

#94. TO WALTER DE HALEWIN Strassburg, 25 October 1486

743. Summary Schott congratulates Halewin* on his post in the bailiff's office at Bruges and on his marriage. Their association at Bologna is commented upon and more frequent correspondence to keep the fire of friendship burning is suggested.

744. domino Gualtero de Halevuin: Equiti aurato...
The term *eques auratus* or *miles auratus* (knight of the golden spurs) is applied to the knight who had undergone the ceremony of being dubbed knight. According to Dreher (XVIII,39) the term applies to the knight who had been dubbed at the Holy Sepulchre in Jerusalem.

745. his tuis amplissimis accessionibus ... generis nobilitate conscenderis ...
In being appointed to the staff of the bailiff of Bruges, Halewin was following a tradition of the Halewin noble family, many of whose members from the thirteenth century on served as bailliffs or other functionaries to the counts of Flanders.

746. (sextus enim nunc annus euolutus est: quo te non vidi)
Schott means (N. 582, par. 2) he has not seen Halewin since 1481. It is possible that after finishing his studies in Italy Halewin stopped in Strassburg on his way to Flanders to visit Schott. Such a visit would explain why Schott sends Halewin greetings from the senior Schotts and family at the close of the letter: "Et me meosque tibi..." (p. 106).

P. 105   #94   N. 747

747. ut cum hos fratres probatissimos viros: te conuenturos intelligerem...
The brothers referred to may be the Strassburg merchants Florentius and Ludovicus Müg* who apparently had a depot at Antwerp (N. 655) and would have cause to visit Bruges, the capital of Flanders and at that time an important English Channel seaport.

748. bene/ prospere/ ac feliciter euenerit...
Cf. Cicero *Mur.* 1 and Livy 31.5 (from *Harpers'*, 667, under "evenio").

P. 106

749. amorem nec tempore nec loco dirimi... et distanciori loco segregamur.
For similiar thoughts about the durability of friendship, cf. Isocrates *Dem.* 2; Cicero *Laelius de Amicitia* 76, 85; Christy, I, 417, 29; *Dictionary of Greek and Latin Quotations*, 289; *Oxford Dictionary of English Proverbs*, 33.

#95. TO HEINRICH MOSER Strassburg, 28 October 1486

750. Summary Schott, happy to have learned of Moser's* whereabouts, congratulates him on his marriage and on his success as a lawyer. Schott explains his laxness in returning to Moser the funeral oration lent him and gives news of fellow students at Bologna.

751. Heinricus de Hevuen: nobilis ac praestantissimus... Decanus
I.e., Heinrich von Hewen.*

752. Dominus Ioannes de Seckingen Eques auratus
I.e., Johann von Seckingen;* for *eques auratus*, cf. N. 744.

753. ego autem Ecclesiasticus: quietem petens: ab omni strepitu...
Schott's preference for a quiet life is discussed in N. 255.

P. 107

754. Oracionem hanc funebrem: quam a te comodato... nisi certis.
Although Schott does not say so definitely, the author of the oration may have been Moser. Moser may also be the Heinrich who composed the poem #268 and to whom Schott addressed the poem in reply #269. For the custom of sending compositions to friends, cf. N. 309.

755. De consortibus... Bohuslaus... Fridericus Bussener... Vdalricus Buck
For a discussion of Hassenstein's* trips to Strassburg, cf. N. 101. It is almost certain that Friedrich Büchsner* came with Hassenstein to Strassburg, for his home was in Alsace (cf. N. 819, par. 3).
    We have found no record of Ulrich Buck. He may be the Ulrich Bock (cousin of Friedrich Bock*) who was drowned at Ghent in 1488 during the Flemish campaign (cf. biographical note on Friedrich Bock). Nor have we found any record of Buck's charge, young Duke Albert. He may have

been the son of Ludwig (†1476), Duke of Bavaria and count of Veldenz, a younger brother of the great *Pfalzgraf* Friedrich; this Ludwig fought on the side of Archbishop Diether von Isenburg.* Cf. Bauch, 94; Wuerdtwein, 399; Raynaldus, 1481 (paragraph 24).

#96. TO JOHANN KLITSCH Strassburg, 10 September 1486

756. *Summary* Schott bids his protégé Johann Klitsch* to be diligent in his studies and to write letters in Latin, not in the vernacular. Money will be sent Klitsch from Cologne. (Cf. N. 125 and p. xxviii. This letter should chronologically precede #93.)

757. *scribis: et id amplius quam sperabam: barbare aut... saltem latine*
Schott is emphatic about Klitsch's writing in Latin, because he wants the boy to learn and practice Latin. Schott was certainly not averse to the use of the vernacular; he himself wrote letters in German (cf. #77 and the letter to his sister, p. 357).

758. *Tui quoque ut audio... Andreas... Ioannes successor aput me tuus...*
Cf. N. 654 and N. 657. Of Klitsch's successor Johann, another of Schott's protégés, nothing is known; he is mentioned in #102 as joining Klitsch.

759. *Dominica post Natiuitatis gloriosissime virginis*
The feast of the Virgin's birth is 8 September; in 1486 the Sunday thereafter fell on 10 September. Note that this item and #98-#101 are dated from feasts and are not in chronological order. Cf. N. 36.

#97. TO VITUS MAELER Strassburg, 10 December 1486

760. *Summary* To Maeler's care is commended the venerable bearer of this letter who is making his first trip outside his homeland by going on a pilgrimage to Rome in hopes of leaving his mortal remains among the relics of the saints. Money has been sent for the matrimonial dispensation.

761. *Romam petit: istic inter sanctorum exuuias/ membra sua... compositurus.*
Pilgrimages to Rome were made by people from all classes and it was not unusual for elderly persons to make the pilgrimage with the intention of being laid to rest in the eternal city.
    To accommodate the hosts of pilgrims coming to Rome, each major nation had its own national church with hostel attached. The German church which with its church-hostel-hospital complex covered considerable ground is documented in 1399 as *Beata Maria Alemannorum* (or *Teutonicorum*) *de Anima* (or *Animarum*) and was later known as *Santa Maria de Anima*. In 1499 one of its officers, Johann Burckard,* received papal consent to raze the church and build a new one. One-third of the money collected from the sale of indulgences during the jubilee year 1500 at Cologne was donated by Cardinal Raymond Peraudi* to complete the *fabrica* of the new church. In

P. 108   #97   N. 761

1518 Maximilian I issued a mandate placing the church under the protection of the empire.
    Anima members during our period other than Burckard were Vitus Maeler,* Johannes von Brandis,* Berthold von Hennenberg.* Among the visitors registered at the *Anima* were Albrecht bishop of Strassburg,* Udalrich von Fronsperger,* Leonardus Egloffstein.* In 1491 Johann Müller* was buried there.
    Liber confrat., 20-26, 83ff., 247. Nagl, 21-28 *passim*. Schmidlin, 28, 105, 125, 135, 193.

762. opis indiguam
Cf. Paul. Nol. *Carm.* 27.4; 16. 196 (from *Harpers'*, 935, *indiguus*).

763. misi vna aureos Renenses decem... in causa quadam Matrimoniali...
Cf. #92 and N. 735.

#98. TO VITUS MAELER Strassburg, 18 March 1487

764. Summary Addressing Maeler by all his titles, Schott, as a close friend of long standing, bids him take care of his well-being not only in body but especially in soul. Information about a case and news of the hostilities in Italy are requested.

765. Nullam tam stabilem ac firmam amiciciam esse putant... non paciatur.
A similar thought is expressed in #94, p. 106; cf. N. 749. For the phrase "detrimentum patiatur," cf. "detrimentum pati," Mt. 16:26.

P. 109

766. fac mi Doctor: mi Preposite: mi Decane... et si quid sit aliud...
The list of titles and the words following are a veiled warning against the dangers of multiple benefices.

767. Cerciorem me facito: ecquid in negocio tibi pridem credito...
This may be a reference to the case of marriage between parties closely related (cf. N. 735).

768. Super statu Italie: quem nouis tumultibus moueri audio...
The war between Archduke Sigismund and the Venetians was still in progress (cf. N. 696).

769. ipsa dominica Oculi... Anno M.cccc.lxxxvij.
Oculi, the third Sunday of Lent, fell on 18 March in the year 1487. Cf. N. 759.

#99 TO JOHANN GEILER Strassburg, 27 May 1487

770. Summary Geiler is away and the preaching bell is silent. Knowing

P. 109   #99   N. 770

how close Schott is to Geiler, people are plying Schott with questions as to Geiler's whereabouts and the date of his return, to such an extent that Schott, plagued by his own grief over Geiler's absence, asks Geiler either to return or let Schott join him. From Bishop Friedrich of Augsburg has arrived a letter for Geiler to be opened by none other than the addressee. Schott pleads the case of the Strassburgers whom he fears Geiler may be planning to desert. He sends greetings to Brother Sebastian.*

771. dum festis diebus/ consuetum eris campani sonum... frequenciam populi...
According to the regulations of 1478 for the cathedral preaching chair, the bell was to be rung for every preaching service in the cathedral (cf. Wencker, *Arch.*, 432; N. 955 and Appendix K).
   Schott's reference to the absence of the throngs who normally crowd to hear Geiler and to the amount of questioning he is enduring on Geiler's account indicate how much the Strassburgers appreciated Geiler's sermons (cf. N. 534).

772. adeousque paternum in me amorem tuum/ omnes perspexisse videntur
Geiler's affection for Schott was apparent enough to be commented upon in later chronicles; cf. *Chronik von Maternus Berler* (114): "D. Petrum Schott libett Geiler von Keysersberg."

P. 110

773. superuenit Magister Iohannes Rot... nisi tibi ipsi sit redditurus
Since Johann Rot* was parish priest for the cathedral and perhaps taking Geiler's place at certain functions, he would be among the first to know of the letter sent by Friedrich von Zollern* via official channels of the Augsburg cathedral chapter and messenger. There can be little doubt that this letter is the one of 23 May 1487 offering Geiler the cathedral preacher's chair at Augsburg (Stenzel, 77). The Augsburg messenger Johann has not been identified.

774. dolor/ qui me prorsus turbat...
It is not quite clear whether Schott means physical pain or worry caused by Geiler's absence and possible resignation of the Strassburg post; item #101 written about two weeks after the present item makes no mention of any illness; cf. N. 805, however.

775. Vnum id memori corde seruato... experiencia perdidicisse.
The vivid description of a ship tossed at sea may be based on actual experience, for it is not unlikely that Schott saw a storm on the Adriatic when he was in Venice or that during his years in Italy he spent holidays on either the Adriatic or Mediterranean coasts. He was, of course, familiar with Rhine floods and their danger to navigation, as well as with descriptions in the classics of storms at sea.
   In this metaphorical passage Schott entreats Geiler not to desert Strassburg where he is so sorely needed. It is not quite clear, however, for which position Geiler might desert Strassburg. Certainly in the spring of 1487 Geiler was considering the chair at Augsburg cathedral which he knew Friedrich von Zollern wished him to inaugurate, for the two friends must have discussed the offer before it became official on 23 May of that year

(cf. N. 901). Yet the offer from Augsburg does not explain Geiler's extended absence which had already been so long that by the end of May, when Schott was writing this item, the Strassburgers were deeply concerned. Geiler was not and had not been at that time in Augsburg. This fact we know from several sources: 1) the official letter from the Augsburg chapter to Geiler on 23 May was sent to Strassburg (#99, p. 110); 2) in his letter to Friedrich von Zollern on 23 August (#105) Schott makes no mention of Geiler's having been or being at the time in Augsburg, although he asks that when Geiler does come he not be kept too long; 3) Geiler actually left for Augsburg on or after 19 September (#123 and N. 947). Nor was Geiler spending an overly long holiday at the baths in spring 1487; in fact, he did not go to the baths that year until sometime in July, as we know from #104.

The only explanation for Geiler's absence and Schott's apprehension at this time is that Geiler had answered a call elsewhere, perhaps to Basel. The cathedral chapter there may have already been casting about for a successor to Johann Heynlin à Lapide,* who resigned in the fall of 1487, and have again approached Geiler whom they had apparently wanted as preacher in 1484 before Heynlin was offered the post (N. 533 and N. 963).

776. *Fratrem Sebastianum saluere iube: et ad preces inuita.*
Geiler paid periodic visits to the Alsatian hermit *Frater* Sebastian,* whom he had known from early childhood; indeed, it is said his grandfather first took him to Rohrtal to meet Sebastian (Wittmer, "Flüe," 170).

777. *Deus cor et pedes tuos dirigat in viam pacis.*
Cf. Lc. 1:79.

778. *Dominica Exaudi… M.cccc.lxxxvij.*
Cf. N. 759. *Exaudi*, the sixth Sunday after Easter and the first Sunday after Ascension came in 1487 on 27 May.

#100. TO VITUS MAELER Strassburg, 7 July 1487

779. *Summary* This letter of commendation for Thomas Wolf, Sr.,* is being delivered with a letter from Wolf, himself. Maeler is urged to help Wolf, Sr., – to whom Schott owes his canonicate and who had been *in loco parentis* to him – in every way possible with the case of litigation against the nephew Thomas Wolf, Jr.* The postscript tells that this letter made the journey from Strassburg to Rome in the record time of seven days less two hours, but was returned unused because the bearer did not need it.

780. *Litteras recipis: viri Insignis… Thome Vuolff.*
It would seem that on receipt of Schott's letter #172 (NN. 1228 f.), Wolf, Sr., hastened instructions to Rome for concluding the case of litigation against his young nephew and ward. For details of the case, cf. N. 334.

781. *cuius opera et cura: quam vnicam possideo prebendam: fuerim adeptus.*
Cf. N. 116, par. 2.

782. *Quamuis enim ipse tibi sit: non mediocri amicicia carus...*
Cf. N. 493.

783. *Sabbato post visitacionis Marie... M.cccc.lxxxvij.*
The feast of the Visitation is 2 July; in 1487 the Sabbath, i.e., Saturday (N. 170), after the feast was 7 July. Cf. N. 759.

#101. TO VITUS MAELER Strassburg, 15 June 1487

784. *Summary* Schott thanks Maeler for the papal petitions sent him. He asks that proceedings for the matrimonial dispensation be conducted very quietly, because one of the parties has died. Johann Müller and his princeling are in Padua.

785. *At si tibi eas referrem gracias... quas ad me dedisti oraciones.*
Cf. N. 634.

786. *Quod prius super dispensacione in causa Matrimoniali impetranda...*
This case had been pending since September 1486 (cf. N. 735).

787. *Magister Iohannes Molitoris Patauium... et Venetos dispulerit.*
Schott's fears that Johann Müller* and his young pupil Jacob of Baden* would be unable to remain in Padua because of the war between Archduke Sigismund* and Venice (N. 696) were justified. Apparently the two were in Ferrara by sometime in early 1487, for Müller received his doctor of laws there in May several weeks before Schott wrote this present letter (cf. N. 797).

788. *secunda post corporis Christi... M.cccc.lxxxvij.*
Corpus Christi is 11 days after Pentecost which in 1487 was on 3 June, hence the day after Corpus Christi was 15 June (N. 582). Cf. N. 759.

#102. TO JOHANN KLITSCH Strassburg, 14 March 1487

789. *Summary* Since another protégé of Schott's will be joining Johann Klitsch* and give news verbally, Schott writes but briefly. Johann's parents bid him be frugal and can send at the most five pieces of gold; however, Schott and Johann Rot* have obtained for him some money from the estate of *Magister* Georius and of this Johann is to receive one gold piece now, more later. (Cf. N. 606. This item should chronologically precede #98).

790. *Quia Iohannes meus successor tuus/ vel ante hunc... ad te venturus est...*
Cf. N. 758.

P. 112   #102   N. 791

791. Parentes tui bene habent... aureos tibi mittere
Cf. N. 657.

792. effoecimus: ut ex largicione Magistri Georij... aliquid consequaris.
Perhaps this unidentified *Magister* Georius like Johann Simmler,* Johann Kerer,* Johann Hell* and other philanthropic clerics had willed money to be used for educating impoverished young scholars.

793. vel per fratres Canonicos Regulares missurus
Canonici regulares is another term for Brethren of the Common Life (cf. N. 88). The probable import of Schott's statement is that he might send money to Klitsch with Brethren travelling down the Rhine to Windesheim or Zwolle in the Lowlands (N. 606).

794. Disce: et Deum time.
Cf. Dt. 6:24; 10:12. Schott's injunction doubtless implies the thought that "the fear of the Lord is the beginning of wisdom" (Ps. 110:10).

795. Socios/ praesertim iuuenem Magistri Melchioris ama...
Klitsch's fellow student may have been a protégé of Melchior Kungsbach.*

#103. TO JOHANN MÜLLER Strassburg, 30 July 1487

796. Summary Schott, his parents and Johann Rot* congratulate Müller on attaining the degree of doctor of laws. With the added prestige from the degree and with the *preces primae* – when confirmed – Müller should have very good chances of obtaining the hoped-for canonicate. The money from the sale of Müller's furniture in Paris which Schott was holding for fees for that canonicate has been claimed by Jacob Keller* as belonging to young Jacob of Baden.*

797. Iuris vtriusque Doctori: Magistro Iohanni Muller... tanquam fratri...
This is the only time Schott addresses Müller as "brother;" perhaps the term here is meant to imply that Müller is now a fellow lawyer.

P. 113

798. Primum ego tibi ob adeptum honorem gratulor...
Müller had received his doctor of laws at Ferrara on 17 May 1487.

799. Confirmabuntur ut spero: aliquando preces Regales... sine comodo.
The *preces primae*, which Friedrich von Zollern* had obtained for Müller from Maximilian, and other such *preces* issued by Maximilian were awaiting papal confirmation (cf. N. 680. Cf. also N. 130, 2 and 3).

800. si quid eciam in ecclesia tua vacaret (tuam/ spe nomino)...
Müller's *preces primae* were for Old St. Peter, referred to here as "your

P. 113   #103   N. 800

church." Perhaps it seemed that being a poor commoner he might have better chances of securing a canonicate in the least important of the three collegiate churches in Strassburg (N. 117); also Schott's close friend Thomas Wolf, Sr.,* was *praepositus* of that church and could be expected to use his every influence. Cf. N. 527, also N. 680.

801. Addidi quoque Magistrum Mathiam Kolb... per Argentinam... patriam pecijsse
Mathias Kolb* with his pupils passed through Strassburg on his way from Paris to his native Posen during Lent. Like Müller he probably was poor and had to act as tutor to wealthy young students. Easter being 15 April in 1487, he had probably left Paris after the end of the winter semester.

802. domino Iacobo keller miseram... eidem in Nundinis nostris tradidi...
Jacob Keller* is probably identical with Jacob, the chaplain of Christoph I* of Baden (#60, p. 66); he had come to Strassburg for the annual fair which was held 15 July (cf. N. 301). That he demanded the money realized from Müller's furniture in Paris as belonging to young Jacob of Baden gives some indication of Müller's poverty (cf. N. 526).

803. et vbi e re vestra fuerit: focos laresque paternos foeliciter reuisere
Müller and young Jacob were at home in Baden by May 1488 (#118, p. 138).

#104. TO JOHANN GEILER   Strassburg, 31 July 1487

804. Summary   Schott and Johann Rot* expect to dine with Geiler and Kerer,* who are at the baths, on the following Thursday when Schott can be allowed to expose himself to the sun safely after treatment taken for his illness. Geiler is requested to make reservations at a suitable inn. When they are together, they can discuss further plans for holidaying.

P. 114

805. effoecit valitudo mea: non vsque quaque prospera... post euacuacionem...
Schott may have had a slight case of the disease, possibly a variety of typhus, which reached epidemic proportions by fall of 1487 and continued into 1488 (Krieger, 93). Schott could have had treatment either by bleeding or purging, for *evacuatio* has both meanings.

806. Vbi conuenerimus: consultabimus... an Balnearum... zum Vngemach...
There is no indication which baths are meant, possibly Baden-Baden, where Geiler and Kerer had spent a previous bath holiday together (#20); Schmidt (*H. L.*, II, 31) believes the inauspiciously named inn "Trouble" was in Baden-Baden. For the popularity of baths, the usual period for a course of baths, etc., cf. N. 192.

#105. TO FRIEDRICH VON ZOLLERN   Strassburg, 23 August 1487

807. Summary   Schott regrets that he cannot accept Bishop Friedrich's

P. 114   #105   N. 807

commission to serve as procurator in a case involving plurality of benefices. Geiler, believing that Friedrich has been pressured by Sigismund Bruschenckner* into asking Schott, is also against the latter's serving as procurator. The case has therefore been put into the hands of another procurator. Friedrich is entreated not to detain Geiler too long at Augsburg; the Augsburgers should be content to have a good bishop and the Strassburgers should be allowed to have at least a good preacher.

P. 115

808. Litteras tuas Antistes optime... quibus mihi causam domini Viti scribe...
There is no record of a Vitus Scriba in the Augsburg diocese. *Scriba* need not be a name, however; it can mean a secretary. Is it possible that Vitus Maeler is the one seeking another benefice? He belonged to the Augsburg diocese and held several benefices in that diocese.

In commissioning Schott to be procurator, Friedrich, as Geiler so shrewdly concluded (p. 115 *infra*), may not have wished the *dominus* Vitus to secure the benefice; Schott's aversion to heaping of benefices being well-known, Friedrich could anticipate his reaction. Friedrich himself was not in a position to refuse outright a request to help secure the benefice, for he held a number of benefices and as bishop could not easily divest himself of them, however much his conscience might prick him.

809. delatum est negocium ad dominum Benedictum... perficiet.
The procurator Benedict has not been identified.

810. Paternitate tua: cui vni equo anoim... saltem bono predicatore.
In this passage Schott pays tribute to both Friedrich and Geiler. The quip that the Strassburgers should be allowed at least a good preacher is, however, something less than a tribute to Bishop Albrecht of Strassburg* whom neither Geiler nor Schott considered a good bishop.

The Strassburgers are spoken of as belonging to Friedrich (*tui*), because Friedrich had been dean at Strassburg cathedral and still held a cathedral canonicate (N. 682). Cf. N. 901.

811. Confidenter scribo: quod foecit... humanitatis tua... in Tillingen...
Geiler, Schott and Rot* had stayed in Dillingen when at Friedrich's invitation they attended his coronation there 21 July 1486 (#174, p. 195); cf. #256, N. 674 and N. 1645.

The charming little town of Dillingen on the Danube is about 25 miles from Augsburg. In 1258 *Graf* Hartmann V of Dillingen, who had been bishop of Augsburg since 1248 and was the last male heir of his line, willed a major portion of his estates, including the town of Dillingen with the great family castle, to the cathedral of Augsburg. As relations between the bishops and the free city of Augsburg grew more and more strained, Dillingen became the refuge and finally the episcopal seat of the bishops of Augsburg and remained so until secularization in 1802. The old castle, the seminary (descendant of the sixteenth century university) with its ornate church, well-preserved medieval buildings and an atmosphere unspoiled by industry make Dillingen today worthy of a visit.

P. 115   #105   N. 812

812. quam Pater omnipotens dirigat in viam salutis eterne
Cf. Ac. 16:17.

P. 116

#106. TO PETER SCHOTT FROM BOHUSLAUS VON HASSENSTEIN Hassenstein, 10 April 1487

813. Summary Bohuslaus attributes his silence not to lack of affection, or to negligence, but to the fact that so few persons from his area journey to Strassburg. He professes his friendship and mentions having heard recently from the prior at Regensburg about Schott's friendship for himself. He sends small gifts, for which Schott is to be grateful.

814. Note the absence of a Wimpheling heading (N. 37). Shortly after writing this letter Hassenstein apparently visited Schott in Strassburg (cf. N. 101). Items #106- #110 are out of chronological order in relation to other items because they form a unit in the Schott-Hassenstein correspondence (Chronology III); further, #107 being the answer to #108 should, of course, succeed the latter.

815. Magister Iohannes ordinis Predicatorum: Prior Ratisponensis... scripsit. Johann Nigri reported to Hassenstein either conversations he had held with Schott – perhaps at the baths as in 1481 (#25, p. 33) – or sentiments Schott had written to him.

#107. TO BOHUSLAUS VON HASSENSTEIN Strassburg, 10 September 1487

816. Summary Schott thanks Hassenstein for letter and gifts. With the bearer of this letter he is sending flower seeds, books and knives. He does not know whether the things which he sent via a Nürnberger shortly after Hassenstein's departure or two letters, one of which accompanied a work on Greek accents, have reached Hassenstein. Editions of Plato in translation are available in Strassburg and will be sent if Hassenstein has not yet acquired them. Schott will try to compose precepts for guiding Hassenstein as royal secretary at the Bohemian court even though he feels himself inadequate for the task. Nicholaus von Flüe* has died; he is described as he appeared when Schott and his father visited him. Schott finds the Hussite tracts sent by Hassenstein insidious. (Cf. N. 814).

817. domino Bohuslao de Hassenstein: Regio secretario...
Hassenstein served for a time as secretary to Vladislaus II,* King of Bohemia (cf. biographical note on Hassenstein).

P. 117

818. semina nonnullarum herbarum florumque... ad te mitto
Cf. p. xxiv and N. 82.

P. 117 #107 N. 819

819. Michaelis istius... Eselbergum Nurenbergensem... Fridericum quoque tuum
The unidentified Michael may have been a retainer of Hassenstein.
The Nürnberger Eselberg may have been a Nürnberg printer or bookseller with whom Schott had connections (cf. #202), or he may be identical with the poet Elbin von Eselsberg.
"Fridericus" is no doubt Friedrich Büchsner* who – having accompanied Hassenstein to Alsace – remained behind to visit his parent(s). He was in Strassburg again the following February (#109, p. 120).

820. Quarum alteras/ comitabatur doctrina de accentibus grecis
This work on Greek accents may have been written, like the *Epithoma*, by Schott for Hassenstein. Cf. N. 4.

821. omnes libri Platonis: per Florentinum quempiam nuper translati...
It is not clear whether Plato's works translated by an unidentified Florentine were published in Strassburg.

822. Ad litteras tuas... petis... ut tibi praescribam: quid tibi... accessurus...
Hassenstein's injunction that Schott compose for him precepts is in #108, p. 119. For the precepts, cf. "Treatise on Christian Life," #110, pp. 122-130.

823. nequaquam imparem ei: qua penus Hannibal delirare dixit Phormionem...
Cf. Cicero *De Or.* 2.18.75.

824. in quem tendas: et in quem dirigas arcum: ut Persius ait
Cf. Persius 3.60.

825. Quandoquidem omnia... diligentibus Deum: in bonum cedant.
Cf. Rm. 8:28.

826. Fratrem Nycholaum e vita discessisse... abbreuiato contextu: quaesit...
The revered hermit Nicholaus von Flüe had died in March 1487. Compare Schott's description of Nicholaus here, as he looked when Schott and his father visited him in 1482 (date from Wittmer, "Flüe," 171), with the description by Pantaleon (*Prosopographiae...*, Part ii, 459f.): "Erat is ueneranda facie homo, procerae staturae, capillo nigro cum canitie interserta, barba tenui et diuisa, colore castaneo, corpore macilento, sed uoce uirili et tarda praeditus. Veste utebatur simplici et oblonga, pedibus et capite nudus erat... Homines ad se uenientes benigne et laeto uultu alloquebatur, atque eos ad uirtutes et pietatem adhortatus est."

P. 118

827. Eius tibi... diu quaesitam aliquando mittam... asseuerare nolim.
In the incunabulum the lacuna of about 8 spaces following *Eius tibi* is apparently for a Greek feminine noun, possibly the accusative singular of the word for biography, βιογραφία. Cf. N. 4 and N. 23.

828. Misisti ad me tractatus quosdam: plenos profecto subdolis... certum esse.
For other references to the Hussites, cf. N. 379. Ryba (iii) maintains that Hassenstein received his early schooling from the Calixtines or Utraquists, a moderate faction of the Hussites which believed the faithful should receive communion of both bread and wine "sub utraque specie." Schott therefore had reason to feel that Hassenstein had sympathies at least with this faction of the Hussites. That Hassenstein abominated the Taborites, the radical faction of the Hussites which caused revolts and wars, is evident from the passage "Praeterea nos posse refers" and the verses following in his poem to Schott (#239, pp. 272f.).

829. quas salutasti soror eiusque filia: eorumque coniuges... Doctor keisersberg...
Hassenstein had sent gifts not only to Schott's parents but also to his sister Ottilia Schott and her husband Zeisolf von Adelsheim, to Ottilia's daughter Ottilia von Cöllen and her husband Martin Sturm and to Geiler. Hassenstein was very fond of Geiler; cf. the three letters he wrote to Geiler (#292, #293 and Appendix J) and the references to Geiler in the Schott-Hassenstein correspondence (#108, p. 120; #144, p. 159 and N. 1740).

830. Fridericum eciam: et Stephanum saluere iube.
Note *Errata*. The persons referred to are Friedrich Büchsner, mentioned above in the text (p. 117) and Stephan Piso.*

#108. TO PETER SCHOTT FROM BOHUSLAUS VON HASSENSTEIN
Hassenstein, 10 August 1487.

831. Summary Hassenstein regrets that the one letter he has written since his departure from Strassburg has not been delivered because of the negligence of Bernhard Adelmann.* He describes in detail his activity as a gentleman farmer and overseer of the Hassenstein estate. He would be content to grow old in this rural activity, but he must leave to take a post in the royal secretariat. For guiding his path at court he entreats Schott to compose for him precepts. (Cf. N. 814).

832. ex eo tempore/ quo tecum Argentine fui... Bernardi mei Adelmanni...
Hassenstein had been in Strassburg sometime between mid-April and late August 1487 (cf. N. 101). Bernhard Adelmann, a former fellow student at Ferrara and at this time canon in Eichstätt, had failed to have a letter (either left with him or sent to him by Hassenstein) delivered to Schott.

833. Quoniam ut ait ille: huiusmodi hominem: minime male cognitantes sunt.
Cf. Cato *De agricultura* iv.3-4.

834. Quod si adesses: et me inter Tyturis Coridonesque meos... cerneres...
Tityrus is the name of a shepherd in Vergil *Ecl.* i and viii.55; Corydon is the name of a shepherd in Vergil *Ecl.* ii and *Aen.* iv.307.

P. 119   #108   N. 835

835. O fortunatos nimium: bona si sua morint... qua Poeta ille... cecinit.
The quotation is from "that poet the greatest of all," Vergil *Geor.* ii, 458-460.

836. Ceterum utcumque se hae res habent: ego non magnopere... consenescam.
Hassenstein seems to have taken an interest in managing the estate efficiently and according to the most advanced methods. At one time he requested Johann de Pibra to send him surveyor's instruments, "quaedam ad mensuras agrorum sylvarumque pertinentia" (Potuček, 81).

837. nisi Fratrum dissensio quos in mutuam perniciem aliquantulum... pellicio
Hassenstein's two elder brothers were involved in a dispute with one another and with Hassenstein over family property (Potuček, vi).

838. eciam atque eciam rogo: ut ea de re exiguum ad me libellum conscribas...
Cf. N. 822, also N. 817.

P. 120

839. Parentes cum Filia et Nepte... Fridericus te magnopere saluere...
Cf. N. 829, N. 819 and N. 830.

#109. TO BOHUSLAUS VON HASSENSTEIN Strassburg, 5 February 1488

840. Summary Friedrich Büchsner* has arrived with a letter from Hassenstein demanding the promised precepts before Schott has put them into final form and polished the style. In order not to delay Büchsner's return to Bohemia, Schott is sending the treatise in rough draft. He comments at length on the insidious snares laid by Hussite heresies. He finds the idea of scholarly Hassenstein armed for military "foolishness" vastly amusing. (Cf. N. 814).

841. sed paruulis intellectum dat Dominus
Cf. Ps. 118:130; Mt. 11:25.

842. De his quae Hereticorum doctrinam complectuntur... (to end of paragraph)
For other references to the Hussites, cf. N. 379, also N. 828.

843. Habet enim insidiosus ille venator: animarum et recia... Bernardus ait.
The reference is to St. Bernard's description of the devil whose snares are gold and silver and whose arrows for wounding souls are wrath, envy, etc. (cf. St. Bernard, *Meditationes Piissimae,* xii, 33).

844. ut dum morbos Prelatorum sanare velint...
Cf. *Errata.*

P. 121   #109   N. 845

P. 121

845. (ut dicit Apostolus) Heresis ut cancer serpat.
St. Paul was called "the Apostle," *Apostolus.* For the quotation cf. 2 Tm. 2:17, also Ovid *Met.* ii.825f.

846. Atqui accepi: tibi arma parari... foeliciorem in armis speras M. Cicerone
Potuček (xiii) suggests that Hassenstein was to participate in the Silesian campaign of King Vladislaus.* Whether he actually did so is not known. For the reference to Cicero and arms, cf. Cicero *Ad fam.* xii.13.16; also *Fragmenta* ii.5.6 and *Ad Quintum fratrem* i.1.30.4.

847. Haud bene conueniunt: nec in vna sede morantur: Mars et Calliope.
We have not been able to locate the author of these one and one-half lines of verse. Did Schott compose them to fit this passage?

#110. TO BOHUSLAUS VON HASSENSTEIN, A TREATISE ON CHRISTIAN LIFE [Strassburg, January 1488]

848. Summary (preliminary remarks) Schott explains: a) that the style of the treatise is straightforward and lacking embellishment of any kind, b) that he has composed such precepts as would apply to himself since he and Hassenstein share like ideas and interests, c) that he has drawn his subject matter mainly from Geiler's teachings.

849. Date Since Büchsner took the treatise with him on his return to Bohemia in early February, the time of its composition may be placed in January 1488, or end of 1487.

850. praecipue ab exhortacionibus Iohannis Geiler de keisersberg... eruditus
Schott may well have drawn on the fund of admonitions he heard from Geiler in his constant association with that master of wit. He may also have used the precepts which Geiler had sent him in Italy and of which we know three (#11): to resist vices swarming about like bees; to have love; to follow the path of virtue. He seems to have been familiar, too, with the *Monita* (Appendix H) composed by Geiler for Friedrich von Zollern,* for there are similarities between the treatise and the *Monita* (e.g., N. 863, N. 865, N. 868, N. 871-873), although the *Monita* are more practical and more tersely couched than the precepts of the treatise. Graphic examples appearing in the treatise are reminiscent of Geiler and of the "Imitaciunculae" (#233) based on Geiler's sermons (cf. for example the simile of the whirlpool, p. 122, and the two similes of the sick man refusing medical help, p. 124 and p. 128).

P. 122

851. SUMMARY OF 1) QUAM EGRE MORES....
It is exceedingly difficult to adhere to one's ethical code when one is living among those adhering to a different code, unless one is strong enough to influence them rather than be influenced by them. This is about as easy as

P. 122   #110   N. 851

trying to save some one from a whirlpool while one clings to a steep, slippery bank. If you must go to court (N. 817), be in it but not of it and leave before it corrupts you.

852. eum qui picem tangit: inquinari ab ea solere
Cf. Sirach (Ecli.) 13:1: "Qui tetigerit picem inquinabitur ab ea." Wander, III, 1200, 15: "Wer Pech angreifft, der besudelt sich." Stoet II, 1794.

853. in igne medio versantem: non ardescere.
This is a reference to the story of Shadrach, Meshach and Abednego in Daniel 3.

P. 123

854. SUMMARY OF 2) CHRISTIANUM DECERE...
To clarify what is meant by Christian ethics and to give Hassenstein definite guide posts, Schott – speaking as a Christian and priest to a fellow Christian – outlines, in the pages following, points of Christian wisdom which he expects Hassenstein to take to heart.

855. non summis (ut aiunt) labris a te contingi
Cf. Seneca *Ep.* 10.3.

856. SUMMARY OF 3) DE FIDE...
Living faith, which having captivated the mind expresses itself in meditation and works, is the best medium for achieving salvation.

857. iustus ex fide viuit
Cf. Rm. 1:17; Gal. 3:11; Heb. 10:38.

P. 124

858. Eciam si cor nonnumquam tangitur
Cf. I Rg. 10:26; Horace *Ars poetica* 98; Lucretius iii.909.

859. SUMMARY OF 4) VT EQUANIMITER SUSCIPIAMUS...
Whether we are visited by prosperity or adversity, we should neither boast nor complain since God is meting out our fate in His eternal wisdom.

P. 126

860. diligentibus illis Deum... omnia tam secunda... in bonum operata fuissent
Cf. Rm. 8:28.

861. SUMMARY of 5) VT ET NOS COOPEREMUR...
We shall have learned to seek not our own glory but that of God when we do a good work anonymously for its own sake.

P. 126 #110 N. 862

862. Que est autem opera nostra: quam Deo debemus?... et Prophete.
Cf. Mt. 22:37-40.

P. 127

863. Tum vero comperiemus nos gloriam nostram non quere... peracturos fuisse.
One of the main points of Geiler's *Monita* is doing the good deed which you know you should (cf. *Monita* LVIII, Appendix H).

864. SUMMARY OF 6) VITAM ORDINANDAM ESSE...
One must follow a regular daily routine of alternating prayer and work. One must pray in all humility, concentrating with all one's mind and all one's strength on the content of the prayer.

865. quisque sibi viuendi modum: consilio prudentis... transgrediatur...
Cf. Geiler's *Monita*, LVI (Appendix H), also "Imitaciunculae", 23), 24), p. 265.

866. id quod Anthonium heremitam Angelus edocuit... operacioni succederet
St. Anthony was instructed in a vision by an angel to apply himself to manual work, then leave it for prayer and return again to work. Cf. Butler, *Lives of the Saints*, I, 104, 106.

867. Principium itaque actionum singulis diebus... Thome Abbatis offeramus.
Cf. *Errata*. The incunabulum has *principiñ itaque actionū*; a better reading of the phrase than that given in the text of this edition is the one above, where one assumes that the final letter of the first word is a typographical error for *u*.

Thomas, the abbot, who advised that the day be begun with prayer, has not been identified. He may possibly be identical with Thomas "abbas Mauriniacensis," a contemporary of St. Bernard, who resigned his post as abbot and returned to his original monastery at Colmar.

868. Non autem eam Oracionem puto: quae verbis conficitur... Deum eleuatur
In his *Monita*, LVI (Appendix H) Geiler is emphatic about giving full attention physically, mentally and spiritually to the business at hand, whether prayer or work.

869. corde contrito et humiliato (quod deus non despiciet)
Cf. Psalm 50:19

P. 128

870. quicquid talium perseueranter Orauerimus: id nobis dandum fore
Cf. Mt. 7:7; 10:19; Lc. 11:9.

871. SUMMARY of 7) OPERACIO QUALITER SIT AGENDA...
When working we must not hurry or day-dream but devote our entire atten-

tion to completing the task to the best of our ability. After the period set for work we return to prayers, for which there is a wide variety of material so that we may vary their daily content: e.g., God, the saints, prophets, patriarchs, apostles, martyrs, Virgin, Christ's Passion, angelic chorus, Trinity. At other times whether we partake of food or yield to sleep or are at leisure we must act with thought and purpose because everything we do is part of God's plan.

872. Operacio etenim: nisi attento fiat animo: parum ab ocio differt... ocium.
Cf. *Monita*, LVI (Appendix H), also "Imitaciunculae," 24)-27), p. 265.

873. opera nostra integra esse debere: ut scilicet quicquid... perficiamus
Cf. *Monita*, LVIf (Appendix H).

874. videlicet/ ut septem tibi superant... suscipias
alemosinas=eleemosynas. Who are the seven most magnificent princes of heaven (?), dispensing alms daily?

875. Sicque non agemur ut equus et mulus: quibus non est intellectus...
Cf. Ps. 31:9

876. SUMMARY of 8) PLUS LABORIS ESSE IN SERUICIO...
Our life on earth is a never-ending war and whether we will or no, we must fight either in the service of God or in that of the Devil. To serve God, though difficult, is twice as easy as to serve the Devil.

877. An ignoras: miliciam esse vitam hominis super terram?
Cf. Jb. 7:1; also Büchmann, 296.

878. ipse tortor/ occultum: ut ait ille: flagellum quaciens
Cf. Juvenal xiii, 195. *Ille* refers to Juvenal.

879. Siquidem quietem nusquam inuenire possit,.. Deo: qui eius saciacio...
Cf. St. Augustine, *Sermo CLVIII*, 7: "cultus gratuitus Dei, Qui solus animum satiat..." (Migne, XXXVIII, 565) and *In Psalmum* CII, 10 (Migne, XXXVII, 1324f.). The noun *satiatio* used by Schott in paraphrasing St. Augustine's words and an obvious derivative from *satiare* does not appear in any dictionary or word-list we have seen.

880. quod iugum Christi: suaue et leue super se tollens: sustinere...
Cf. Mt. 11:29-30.

881. nequaquam tamen ut Apostolus monet: condigne sunt... palmam...
For the quotation from St. Paul (*Apostolus*, cf. N. 845) concerning the "sufferings of this present time," cf. Rm. 8:18. The passage following the quotation, concerning the athlete competing on the race course for the palm of victory, is doubtless based on I Cor. 9:24-27; cf. also Heb. 12:1f.

882. suis solummodo occupacionibus singulis deducentur: quibus... sufficient
Cf. Mt. 6:34.

883. adeousque certe id magnum est Christi: quae menti: ut... sperarent
The syntax of this passage is obscure. What is the construction of *quae menti*? (The incunabulum has these words spelled out in full.) What is the subject of *sperarent*? Since the passage occurs at the end of the recto side of the folio and the beginning of the verso side, is it possible that the printer omitted words or lines of the text?

P. 131

#111. TO JOHANN WIDMANN Strassburg, 8 March 1488

884. Summary Schott describes his father's acute kidney (or bladder) trouble and reports that his sister Ottilia Schott,* wife of Zeisolf von Adelsheim,* has suffered a miscarriage. His mother is sending Widmann's wife an image of the pregnant Virgin. (This item, #115 and #116 form a unit).

885. Ille siquidem ab eo tempore/ quo primum harenam perpessus... vidimus.
Schott, Sr's, condition is referred to again in #115, #116 and #140, p. 156.

886. Soror vero mea... iam iterum immaturum foetum... monstri adiacentis...
Cf. N. 707.

887. Vxori tue mater imaginem virginis pregnantis mittit...
Cf. N. 587. The image of the pregnant Virgin was, like the *Agnus Dei* of #66 (p. 74), a birth charm (cf. N. 588).

#112. TO JOHANN WIDMANN Strassburg, 14 March 1485

888. Summary Having not as yet received Widmann's comments on his letter written 13 days previously, Schott describes the developments in his tertian fever and lists the ingredients of a syrup prescribed by Dr. Leonhard Wirt.* Should Widmann accompany the Württemberg delegation to Strassburg after Easter, the Schotts will be happy to see him. The postscript tells of the arrival of Widmann's relative with Widmann's letter. Schott is grateful for Widmann's solicitude and recommendations. He will postpone taking the medicines prescribed until the moon changes, unless his condition worsens. (Cf. #66 and N. 893).

889. *Magister Leonhardus*
I. e., Leonhard Wirt,* the *quendam physicum* of #66, p. 73.

890. *Recipe syrupi acetosi cum radicibus... mistis et fac haustus.*
In the incunabulum *Recipe* is abbreviated ℞ the symbol still used in prescriptions. All ingredients of the syrup, as noted below, have properties for alleviating ills connected with tertian fever.

Syrupi acetosi refers to a syrup made from sugar, water and vinegar boiled together; this was good for tertian and other fevers, so the herbal written by Beck (xlix: "Acetum grece oxi oder oxos") and published in Strassburg 1528 tells us.

Radicibus mese, i.e., the roots of a species of hemp (*cannabis*); cf. *Thesaurus Linguae Latinae*, V.viii, 854: "mesos,e; mesa; meson – Pliny: laudatissima est cannabis e medio genere quae mesa vocatur." According to Beck, xc, "Canapus" taken in a mixture with hysop and other herbs helps reduce the humor which brings on pestilence.

Aque ysopi: hysop, in addition to its use in the mixture noted above, may be boiled in wine as a potion for aches of stomach and bowels (cf. Beck, ccccxxvii, "Ysop").

Aque endiuie: of endive only the leaves when green are used. It helps, Beck tells us (clxvii, "Endivia"), the heart when sick with heat and livers when hot; syrup of endive is good for jaundice and tertian fever.

891. *Aiunt consiliarios generosi Comitis tui/ Argentinam venturos... pascha.*
Representatives of southwestern states of the empire may have held a conference at Strassburg in 1485 after Easter (3 April) to discuss the aid they were to send the emperor in his war against Hungary (cf. N. 623) or to make plans for the emperor's visit in September (#73, p. 80). The reigning prince of Württemberg, to whom Widmann was physician and who founded the university of Tübingen where Widmann was professor, was *Graf* (later *Herzog*) Eberhard *der Bärtige*.*

892. *Dominam honestissimam coniugem tuam... puerperium salubre agat.*
Cf. N. 587. It was for the awaited birth mentioned here that the *Agnus Dei* (#66 and N. 588) was sent.

893. *secunda post Letare... M.cccc.lxxxvij.*
This item although dated 1487, the day after the fourth Sunday in Lent, is placed with items of March 1488. One should thus infer that the editor considered the year when the item was written to be 1488 and that 1487 is a typographical error for 1488. Yet none of the items of March 1488 (#111 of 8 March, #113 of 11 March, #115 of 24 March), despite the fact that two of them are written to Widmann, mentions the tertian fever which had prostrated Schott for several weeks. Nor is there any mention of the fever in the two letters of March 1487 (#102 and #98) or in the one letter of March 1486 (#83).

In spring 1485, however, several items mention the fever (#66, #68; cf. also #78, N. 581, N. 583, N. 647) and one of these, #66 of 1 March, not only is written to Widmann, but describes the fever from its beginnings. That this letter of 1 March is the one referred to in #112, our present item, as having been written 13 days previously is evident from an examination of the dates of *Letare* in the years 1485-88. In 1488 *Letare* came on 16 March, in 1487 on 25 March, in 1486 on 5 March, in 1485 on 13 March. In 1485 *secunda post Letare* would have been 14 March (cf. N. 582) which is exactly 13 days after 1 March.

Additional evidence that the present item was written 14 March 1485 is to be found by comparing its contents with those of #66. In #66 Schott says he has suffered the fourth paroxysm of tertian fever and is expecting the fifth that night; in #112 he says he has had the ninth paroxysm and for two days thereafter was dangerously ill, but at the time of writing he is feeling better. Reckoning the paroxysms of fever as lasting 3 days, one can see that the time between 1 March and 14 March fits the course of the fever. Furthermore, Widmann's relative is mentioned in but 2 items of the *Luc.*, i.e., #66 and #112. In the earlier item he is mentioned as carrying Schott's letter to Widmann and as expecting to return to Strassburg with Widmann's answer; the second letter reports that his return is anticipated and its postscript reports his arrival with Widmann's answer. Also the imminent birth of the Widmann baby mentioned in #66 is referred to in #112.

894. cuidam Magistro profecturo in Tubingen
This person is identical with *Magister* Caspar mentioned at the end of the letter. He has not been identified.

895. presertim cum instet incensio lune
The reference here seems to be to the conjunction of the moon with a fiery planet. From 21 February to 21 April the moon is in Leo and Aries; it is therefore dry and causes many deaths; in addition, its conjunction with Aries afflicts the head. The moon in itself causes cramps, convulsions, colic, stomach aches, diseases of the bladder and affects recurrent diseases such as ague. Cf. Bishop, I, 68; Cardano, f. 44, f. 49; Middleton, 186, 195. For other references to astrological beliefs, cf. N. 275.

#113. TO JACOB WIMPHELING Strassburg, 11 March 1488

896. Summary The spelling *idololatrarum*, Schott explains, was not a slip of the pen on his part but is the correct form according to the Greek from which it derives; the spelling *idolatrarum*, though common, is incorrect. The case of the lady recommended by Wimpheling has been settled by Schott, Sr. Wimpheling is urged to persuade Theobald von Mülnheim to resume study of the arts.

897. idolatrarum quasi graecae discipline contrarium verbum respuam
The Greek noun is εἰδωλολατρεία. Souter (181) suggests that the shortened spelling *idolat-* can hardly be earlier in origin than the sixth century, though manuscripts of authors preceding that century often have that spelling. Schott himself uses the shortened form (*idolatras*) in #221, p. 248 (cf. N. 1472).

P. 133   #113   N. 898

898. Causam matrone quam mihi commendatam foecisti: ego apud Patrem... tribuit.
We have found no information on the lady in question or on her case, which probably concerned civil affairs in Strassburg, since Schott, Sr., who was mayor in the year 1488 settled it.

899. Ceterum Theobaldum de Mulnheymo... homine praesertim nobili: et Argentinensi.
This passage exemplifies Schott's zeal in promoting the study of arts among Strassburgers. For Schott's interest in education, cf. p. xxviii.

P. 134

#114. TO JOHANN GEILER Strassburg, 21 November 1488

900. Summary Schott reports that the Strassburg cathedral chapter has granted Bishop Friedrich's petition to allow Geiler a second extension of his leave but with the proviso that it be the last extension. Johann Rot* has agreed to replace Geiler at Augsburg and will leave for that city as soon as Geiler returns but not earlier because he is supplying for Geiler in Strassburg. Only some of the books Geiler requested have been sent to him. Everything concerning Geiler's home and furnishings has been attended to; his mother is well and awaiting his return. (This item should follow #124, cf. N. 909).

901. Peticioni tue vel pocius Reuerendissimi Domini Augustensis paruit...
Cf. *Errata.* According to the regulations governing the Strassburg cathedral chair, Geiler might not be absent from his post without permission of the chapter dean (cf. N. 955, par. 5), and had a month's leave annually. Geiler had already spent more than the allotted time at Augsburg (N. 951) and Friedrich von Zollern* himself had requested the chapter to extend the leave a second time.

Bishop Friedrich wanted Geiler to leave Strassburg and initiate the chair of cathedral preacher at Augsburg which he was founding (cf. N. 955, par. 2). He had offered Geiler the post in a letter of 13 May 1487 (cf. N. 773), and Geiler had spent some time in Augsburg during the fall of 1487 (#105, p. 115). In the fall of 1488 – at the time the present item was written – Geiler had already been in Augsburg for two months, having left Strassburg on or immediately after 19 September with Schott's letter of that date to Friedrich (#123, p. 141). According to Braun (III, 114), Geiler preached almost daily from Michaelmas to Innocents' Day in the Augsburg cathedral and, according to a contemporary account quoted by Steichele (I, 137), did not leave for Strassburg until 17 January 1489:

"Am sambstag post octavam Epiphanie ryt Dr. Kaysersperg gen strasburg wan die von Strasburg hetten gar vil Brief geschickt... [und] hetten sin unwillen das er so lang was onerlaupt."

On 28 January Schott wrote to Bishop Friedrich to thank him for returning Geiler (#127).

This letter and #124 also from Schott to Geiler can doubtless be numbered among the "gar vil Brief" sent from Strassburg to Augsburg. The Strassburgers had very nearly lost Geiler to Basel in the early months of 1488 (#125; N. 962) and feared they might now lose him to Augsburg, for their cathedral chair remained unconfirmed (N. 955, par. 6). Hence the

P. 134   #114   N. 901

entire cathedral chapter assembled to decide whether Geiler should be granted further leave, although as mentioned above only the chapter dean needed to give his decision. In addition there were present Johann Simmler* as official of the bishop and Schott - perhaps as spokesman for Geiler or representative of his father, who was director of the *fabrica* (N. 76) and in that year also mayor.

During the following summer before 13 August 1489 (#136) Geiler was again in Augsburg and apparently again stayed longer than expected, but since the Strassburg cathedral chair had in the meantime been confirmed and Geiler formally installed as preacher (N. 955, par. 6), the Strassburgers were not unduly worried.

902. *Miseros nos: qui cum terra sine aqua simus... stertimus in vicijs.*
Cf. Ps. 106:35; Ps. 142:6. Cf. Cicero *Ad Fam.* vii.24.1; Tilley, 917.

903. *In sexternionibus tibi missis... expediciorem foeci.*
These booklets are mentioned in #124, p. 143, as about to be sent to Geiler. The term *sexternio* does not appear in dictionaries or vocabulary lists; it is probably related to *sexternus*, a book of six pages as *quaternio* is related to *quaternus*, a book of four pages (cf. DuCange, VII, 465; Baxter, 344, 387). Schott uses the term *quinternus*, a book of five pages, in #15, p. 24.

904. *Super domo tua ac suppellectili... a domino Christiano: et famulo tuo...*
In accordance with the stipulations for the cathedral chair (1478), Geiler was provided with "ein ersam hus" (Appendix K; N. 955, par. 5); whether he also received furniture is not known. Schott, Sr., is known to have given Geiler a bed (Dacheux, *Réf.*, 510).

The Christian referred to may be Christian von Uttenheim who was a nephew of Christoph von Uttenheim* and a great friend of Geiler. He is also mentioned in #124, p. 143, and #137, p. 154. Dacheux, *op. cit.*, 408, suggests Christian may be a relative of Geiler. He must have had an income of his own to support the *famulus* and himself.

Geiler's *famulus* is unidentified; for the names of some of his *famuli*, cf. N. 279.

905. *praeterquam pane... e pistrino datur... aureos quatuor... Matri tue...*
A benefice holder received weekly rations of bread from the foundation's bakery (N. 116.) The four gold coins from the *fabrica* (N. 76) which Christian gave to Geiler's mother Anna Zuber* were probably part of Geiler's salary.

906. *ecquid/ ancillam tibi conduci velis... Sed age: mentem tuam declara.*
Schott is having a bit of fun at Geiler's expense over the prospect of a maid servant in Geiler's house, for Geiler bitterly condemned non-celibacy among clerics, and the *Corpus iuris canonici*, Decret. I, dist. xxxiii, warns against maid servants, even though they be blood relatives.

907. *Suasi Magistro Iohanni Rot: ut tibi succedat... vices tuas hic ageret?*
Johann Rot,* who was preaching for Geiler during Geiler's absence, was a secular cleric as stipulated by the charter of the Strassburg cathedral chair, namely that the person supplying for the preacher must be – like the preacher himself – a secular cleric. Cf. Appendix K and N. 955, par. 5.

908. dominus de Hennenberg ne desideres rogat...
Heinrich von Hennenberg,* vice dean of the Strassburg cathedral chapter, served as acting dean after Friedrich von Zollern left in 1486. For the long battle to fill the post of dean, cf. #167, p. 186 and N. 1188.

909. ipsa die presentacionis beatae Marie virginis
The Feast of the Presentation of the Virgin is celebrated 21 November. This item is therefore out of order; it should chronologically succeed #123 and #124. Cf. N. 36.

#115. TO JOHANN WIDMANN Strassburg, 24 March 1488

910. Summary The Schotts are grateful for Widmann's prompt diagnosis of Schott, Sr.'s, ailment and for the medicine sent. Widmann's opinion of Dr. Andreas Oudorp* and his advice on Ottilia Schott's* difficulties are requested. He is asked to give the accompanying letter to the Franciscans at Tübingen for delivery to those at Ulm. (Cf. N. 884).

911. periculum Genitoris mei intelligeres
On 8 March Schott had written Widmann a detailed description of his father's symptoms (#111).

912. scribet tibi Andreas Phisicus: Doctor omnium iudicio non indoctus
Andreas Oudorp is mentioned again in #116.

913. Simulque de Sororis accidenti: vbi vacauerit scribes... vxorem...
Cf. N. 884, N. 707, N. 587.

914. Litteras his iunctas: nisi pigeat: in conuentum Minorum apud vos...
The Franciscans at Ulm were reformed with the help of Vitus Maeler in 1484 (#55, p. 61 and N. 488).

915. Tabellario Pater duodecim plappardos numerauit.
The "plappardi" are also called *blaffardus, blappart, blaphart, plappert* and *plaphardus* (#213, p. 226). For their relative value, cf. Appendix N.

#116. TO JOHANN WIDMANN Strassburg, 30 April 1488

916. Summary If words were adequate to express proper thanks to Widmann, Schott would gladly exhaust the papyrus of Egypt! Schott, Sr., is suffering acutely from his kidney (or bladder) ailment. The condition is described in detail. When Widmann comes to Strassburg during his holidays, he can assess the condition himself. The Schotts are sending a gift of gold to Widmann's wife, who has a new baby. (Cf. N. 884 and N. 910).

P. 136 #116 N. 917

917. purgatus est... per Magistrum Andream leniter
I. e., Andreas Oudorp,* who is mentioned in #115.

918. Attamen quia te in vacacionibus: ad nos diuersurum scripsisti...
Widmann evidently planned to come to Strassburg when the spring semester at the university of Tübingen closed.

919. Vxoris tue matrone honestissime puerperio gratulamur...
Cf. N. 587. It was for the birth of this baby that the figure of the pregnant Virgin was sent (cf. #111, N. 887).

#117. TO ADOLPH RUSCH Baden, 5 May 1488

920. Summary Schott thanks Adolph Rusch* for the poem sent as a bath gift and describes his condition under the bath regimen, to which he attributes both his poor penmanship and the inelegance of his letter.

P. 137

921. atque (ut aiunt) intus et in cute nouissem
Cf. N. 585.

922. Rubere cutem: humoremque quem minus accomodum mihi credam stillare.
For rigor of the bath regimen, popularity of baths, bath gifts, cf. N. 192.

923. de licenciato quopiam adducendo... nisi doctorem Ioannem Muller...
Müller had received his doctor of laws in May 1487.

#118. TO VITUS MAELER Strassburg, 31 May 1488

924. Summary Schott, not at the moment hunting benefices [for others], is writing only for friendship's sake. He gives details about the release of Maximilian, King of the Romans, from captivity in Bruges and expresses fears about the emperor's possible vengeance on the people of Flanders. Johann Müller has returned from Italy to Baden.

P. 138

925. Ceterum si de bello ab Imperatore contra Flandrenses... (to end of paragraph)
Maximilian and Mary of Burgundy had been married five years (N. 74) when Mary was thrown from her horse and killed 1482, leaving their four year old son Philip (the Fair) as heir to the county of Flanders. It was natural that Maximilian should be regent until Philip became of age, but the Flemish, unwilling to have foreign intervention in their affairs, agitated to have Maximilian resign all rights of administration and have Philip declared ruling count of Flanders.
On 11 February 1488, Maximilian, en route to aid the dukes of

P. 138   #118   N. 925

Britanny and Orléans against Charles VIII, the king of France, stopped in Bruges to see his son. On entering the chateau, he was by ruse taken captive. The duke of Ghent who had abetted this rash act wanted to transfer the captive Maximilian to Ghent, but the people of Bruges disapproved and Maximilian himself entreated them not to surrender him to the unpredictable duke. There is some disagreement in sources as to where Maximilian spent the eleven weeks of his captivity in Bruges; according to information in the Bruges archives, he was in the "Hôtel de Jean Gros," one of the most luxurious houses of the city.

The emperor appealed to member states of the empire for help in freeing Maximilian and received enough contributions to raise a sizable force. Strassburg sent 100 cavalry, 100 foot soldiers and 4 "Schlangenbüchsen," for example, and the bishop of Augsburg, 100 foot soldiers and 6 cavalry. The army was at Aachen when the alarmed people of Bruges hurriedly freed Maximilian 18 May 1488. Despite letters of surety given by Maximilian, the emperor marched into Flanders and for over a year waged war against the Flemish. Peace was declared on 6 September 1489.

In this present item and in #121 Schott gives details we have not seen elsewhere about the strength of the imperial army, losses, etc. Cf. also Schott's poem on the captivity and release of Maximilian (#263) and notes thereto.

Cf. *Code hist.*, II, 215. *Corpus Chronicorum Flandriae*, IV, 63, 65, 531. Dreher, XIX, 74. Eheberg, I, 338f. Freher, 731ff. *Inventaire des Archives ... de Bruges*, VI, 289, 303. Laguille, Part I, 368, Reuss, *Meyer*, 71. Trithemius, *Ann. Hirs.*, II, 530f. Wencker, *Juris*, 30-34 (copies of documents concerning the campaign against Bruges).

926. *die Sabbati: post festum Ascensionis... die Dominica... die Lune*
In 1488 Ascension Day was 15 May; the Saturday (N. 170) following was 17 May; the Sunday and Monday thereafter mentioned further on in the text were 18 May and 19 May, respectively.

927. *Dominorum de Rauenstein: et de Beuri... ducibus Vuolffgango... de Baden*
The *domini* were probably Philipp von Ravenstein* and Albrecht III* (*der Weise*), the reigning duke of Bavaria. These two noblemen may have been chosen to sign with Maximilian documents of surety for the Bruges leaders, because both had interests in the Lowlands which would cause them to restrain the emperor from taking punitive measures against the Flemish.

Dukes Wolfgang* and Christoph* von München belonged to one of the minor lines of the Bavarian ruling house. *Markgraf* Christoph I* was the ruling prince of Baden; Albrecht* was his brother.

928. *Doctor Iohannes Muller: qui ex Ferraria ad te scripsisse... agit.*
Müller with his charge Jacob of Baden* had recently returned from Italy. His letter to Maeler from Ferrara may have concerned his *preces primae* (N. 680).

#119. TO JOHANN GEILER Strassburg, 19 June 1488

929. *Summary* Schott sends fresh herbs as a bath gift to Geiler. He also sends books to Hieronymus Brunschwig* and to a certain Father Jacob.

P. 138 #119 N. 929

He urges Geiler to beware the dangers and to obtain all possible good from the bath regimen.

930. concionatorique Iohanni de keisersberg: Predicatori...
Of the titles stipulated by the Council of Basel for a cathedral preacher (cf. N. 955, par. 1), Schott generally uses *praedicator*; this item and #58 have the only occurrences in the *Luc.* of *concionator*.

931. Ne sine donario viderer balneantem alloqui: volui vel hoc eruorum calato
For baths, and bath gifts, cf. N. 192. Geiler was probably at Baden-Baden, because he is asked to convey greetings to Müller who had just recently returned to Baden from Italy (cf. N. 928).
The bath gift to Geiler was a basket of herbs, called *erva* which dictionaries translate as "vetch"; Dacheux (*Réf.*, 409) uses the French term for "early vegetable (green peas)." The German equivalent of *erva* is *Wicke*, an herb which Alsatian herbologies of the time recommend in certain mixtures as good for kidney trouble (from which Geiler suffered). Cf. Fuchs, CCXVI; Bock, 233. For Schott's interest in herbology (cf. p. xxiv and N. 82).

932. ne quod in prouerbio est: quod secundo foeceris: tercio cogaris iterare
Cf. the Alsatian proverbs (Martin-Lienhart, II, 922): "Was sich zweit, dritt sich auch", "Was zweimal geschehn ist, wiederholt sich öfter". Cf. also *Oxford Book of English Proverbs*, 9, and Tilley, T. 175.

P. 139

933. tamen huiusmodi excoriacio: bilem mouet... ut et prudentem docere velim.
The severe regimen of the baths could be dangerous to patients (cf. N. 192), and Schott feared the strong-willed Geiler might impose excessively harsh demands upon his frail constitution (N. 220).
Schott's remark that he does not presume to teach the wise is an allusion to the proverb of the swine teaching Minerva. Cf. Cicero *Acad.* 1.5.18, *Ad Fam.* ix.18.3, *De Or.* ii.57; also Apperson, 620, and Riley, 249. Schott refers to the proverb again in #125, p. 144, and in #276, p. 305.

934. libellos duos: quorum alterum domino Hieronymo... Patri Iacobi Minori
The booklets sent as gifts to Geiler's companions were copies prepared by Schott and may have contained his own writings. The doctor of medicine Hieronymus is doubtless Hieronymus Brunschwig.* Pater Jacob may have been a Franciscan or his surname may have been Minor; if he was a Franciscan, he may be identical with Jakob Berman who is mentioned as being "guardian" of the Strassburg Franciscans and as attending a meeting at Terni in 1500 (cf. Eubel, *Minoriten*, 348, n. 727) and mentioned again as being vicar of the Strassburg Franciscan province and *custos* of Alsace in 1510 (Eubel *op. cit.*, 351, n. 729).

935. Nycholaum saluta... precipue Magistrum meum... si ex balneis redierit.
For Nicholaus, cf. N. 279. The baths from which Johann Müller might return while Geiler was at Baden-Baden are probably those at Zellerbad, where Müller took the course of baths in 1490 (#155, p. 169; cf. N. 1124)

and which he may have chosen for his holiday in order to get away from the castle and his duties as tutor at Baden-Baden itself.

936. Dominum Anthonium Licenciatum... Magistrum Georium: sodales tuos.
Neither of these persons who were with Geiler at the baths has been identified. *Magister* Georius is probably identical with the Georius mentioned #140, p. 156 and #149, p. 163; he is obviously not the same as the *Magister* Georius of #102 who died in 1487.

#120. TO JACOB WIMPHELING Strassburg, 7 July 1488

937. Summary Schott requests that Wimpheling give both counsel and letters of recommendation to Johann Goetz* who wishes to continue his studies at Heidelberg.

938. simul ad eos quos tibi doctrina... in Heydelbergensi gymnasio conciliauit ...litteras ei tribuas...
Wimpheling had taught many years at Heidelberg and his recommendation would carry weight with professors there. Goetz did continue his studies and received his A.M. in 1490 (cf. #157, p. 172, and biographical note on him).

#121. TO VITUS MAELER Strassburg, 18 August 1488

939. Summary Schott comments on the news Maeler had written about the intrigues against Hieronymus Im(m)ola* and Galeotti Manfredi.* He reports on the status of the Flemish campaign.

940. sediciones illas subdolas... in Hieronymum immole: ac alterum Fauenciae.
In April 1488 Hieronymus de Im(m)ola* (Girolamo Riario) was assassinated, and in May 1488 Galeotti Manfredi,* lord of Faenza, was slain (cf. N. 189, N. 1147).

941. virtutem nostrorum: qui regem suum: cuius captiuitatem... scripseram...
Schott had written about the capture of Maximilian at Bruges and his release in #118, p. 138. Cf. N. 925.

942. inter quos Albertus Marchio Badensis: necati sunt... ad octauum Idus...
Albrecht,* brother of Christoph I* of Baden, was one of the princes slain on 6 August 1488 (cf. #118, p. 138).

943. Magister meus dominus Doctor Iohannes Muller... in ecclesia Badensi...
Maeler may have been trying to obtain confirmation for Müller's *preces primae* (cf. N. 928) and had asked Schott for a list of Müller's benefices. It may be noted that the small benefices mentioned earlier are not referred to here (cf. #72, p. 78, and N. 613). Perhaps Müller had resigned them by 1488.

#122. TO JACOB WIMPHELING Strassburg, 6 September 1488

944. Summary Wimpheling is requested to assist Adolph Rusch,* the bearer of this letter, in securing the loan of certain parts of a dictionary in the Spires library.

945. partes quasdam Dictionarij: quas apud vos repositas nouit...
One of the editions ascribed to Rusch is the *Biblia latina cum glossa ordinaria Walfridi Strabo*, printed *ca.* 1480, but no individual gloss is listed among the books from his press. There is, however, some evidence that he may have published the glosses listed as #4282 in the *Gesamtkatalog der Wiegendrucke* (Leipzig, 1925). In a letter to Johann Amerbach,* Rusch requests that Amerbach do not print the "glossam ordinariam" (Strabo's ?), which according to rumor is about to go to press, because he (Rusch) has "circuiter centum Glosas quas retinui nesciente Koburger ut non ex tot exhaustus, verum ut dietim eciam aliquid pecuniarum pro quotidiana expedicione domus reciperem" (Hartmann, I, #11). This statement tells us that Anton Koburger, a Nürnberg printer (1464-1491), had a contract with Rusch for the sole rights of selling the glosses; it does not say that Rusch printed the glosses; it does imply that he did. Certainly the passage in Schott's letter is evidence that Rusch was assembling material for a gloss.

For the excellence of the Spires cathedral chapter and its library, cf. N. 663.

946. folium id quo in sermonibus Bernardi subsignatum his litteris...
What work Schott is requesting is not known, nor is it clear whether the work is by St. Bernard or by the Blessed Bernard II* of Baden. Perhaps Schott was collecting works of Blessed Bernard with the intention of having an edition of them published. Rot* and Geiler were also interested in these works: Rot asked Geiler to have a copy made of a homily by Blessed Bernard (#124, p. 143).

#123. TO FRIEDRICH VON ZOLLERN Strassburg, 19 September 1488

947. Summary Bishop Friedrich is entreated not to keep Geiler, the bearer of this letter, overly long at Augsburg, so that the Strassburgers, already bereft of the best dean, may not be said to have lost also their one remaining jewel. Susanna von Cöllen begs pardon for sending so meagre a gift as a nut; yet, since the bearer refused to be burdened with anything heavier, it seemed not amiss to send nuts to Swabia, where they are said to be eaten with gusto. The nut has wondrously curative properties when tasted. (This item should precede #114, cf. N. 909).

948. ne nobis Doctorem a Deo datum diucius subtrahere: conareris.
Cf. N. 901.

949. ut quibus praereptus sit Decanus optimus: ijdem... Predicator talis...
Friedrich von Zollern* had been dean of the Strassburg cathedral before becoming bishop of Augsburg, and Strassburg did not secure a new dean

until 1491 (N. 1188); the new dean could scarcely be described as *optimus*.
In #105, p. 115, Schott pays tribute to Geiler and to Friedrich (N. 810) in much the same vein.

950. tam exili munere nucis... in Sueuiam nuces mitti... (*to end of paragraph*)
We have only Wimpheling's words in the heading that the nut is marked with symbols of Christ's Passion. Perhaps the nut was a walnut which in popular tradition is said to contain the cross, the hammer and the nails of the Crucifixion. The walnut was used in sympathetic medicine: according to Beck (cclxxi), the kernel of the *Wellchnusz* or *nux usualis* when soaked in vinegar and eaten protects against the plague; it may also be wrapped in cloth and carried on the person as a protection.
    The walnut, native to the Orient, was brought to Gaul by the Romans and later presumably flourished on the slopes of the Black Forest and other Swabian heights. In "sending nuts to Swabia" Schott may be alluding to a popular local proverb with a meaning akin to "carrying coals to Newcastle" (cf. similar proverbs in Stoett, II, no. 2521, 478f.).

#124. TO JOHANN GEILER Strassburg, 25 October 1488

951. Summary Members of the Strassburg cathedral chapter are worried about Geiler's continued absence because of the effect on the congregation and because of the possibility of losing Geiler to Augsburg. Schott has helped persuade them, however, to yield to the requests of both Geiler and Bishop Friedrich of Augsburg for an extension of Geiler's leave. Schott is sending a document drafted by Johann Simmler* concerning the Strassburg cathedral chair, books – though not all Geiler requested – and a paper signed by Gabriel Biel.* Johann Rot* wishes a copy made for him of a homily by the Blessed Bernard* which is in Geiler's possession. (This item chronologically precedes #114, cf. N. 900 and N. 909).

952. presertim domini Heinrici de Hennenberg: qui vigilanciores... (to end of paragraph)
Cf. N. 908, N. 901.

953. Praesertim cum hic suus: interea luporum morsibus (ut aiebant) expositus
Cf. Jo. 10:12; Ac. 20:29; *Oxford Dictionary of English Proverbs*, 595; Jente, 42, 121.

954. Famulus te expectabit.
For Geiler's *famuli*, cf. N. 279.

955. Quoad sentenciam nostram: super erectione Officij predicacionis: mitto...
In the second half of the fifteenth century throughout the empire special chairs for cathedral preachers were being established as a result of the decree made by the Council of Basel in 1438 that in each cathedral church at the

earliest opportunity a canonicate becoming vacant should be given to a *magister* or *baccalaureus formatus* or licentiate in theology or philosophy who had spent ten years at a recognized university. (This decree was actually an extension of Innocent III's decree of 1215 which had stated that every cathedral should have capable men to assist the bishop in preaching, in hearing confession and in imposing penance). The Basel decree further stipulated that the cathedral preacher should be called *praedicator, concionator*, or *ecclesiastes*, that he was to have a suitable residence and income, that he was to preach once or twice a week. These special chairs were much sought after because they paid better than ordinary preaching posts and were considered positions of honor.

The archepiscopal cathedral at Mainz in 1465 was the first cathedral to set up a special chair for a cathedral preacher; among the early incumbents of this chair was Gabriel Biel.* Other cathedral churches followed Mainz' example: Basel in 1469, Spires in 1471, Strassburg in 1478; Würzburg was inaugurating its chair 1476-1477 when Geiler was called there; Augsburg began organizing its chair in 1486 as soon as Friedrich von Zollern became bishop. Papal confirmation was sometimes long in coming: Strassburg waited 11 years, and Augsburg did not receive confirmation until 1505.

In Strassburg, cathedral preaching had been for a long time under the auspices of the orders – the Dominicans predominating – and parish preaching had been under the auspices of the lay clergy, i.e., a regular cleric preached in the nave pulpit and a lay cleric preached at the altar of St. Laurentius (N. 80) which served the parish. Then arose the vicious quarrel – particularly fierce 1451-1457 at Strassburg – between the orders and the lay clergy over the burial tax, *ultimum vale* (cf. #225 and N. 1501), levied by the lay clergy on survivors of those buried by the orders in monastery cemeteries. Johann Kreutzer, or Creutzer (1418?-1468), doctor of theology and lay curate of St. Laurentius, supported by the bishop and the people, led the fight against the orders. The orders appealed to the pope who declared the tax an infringement on the privileges of the orders. A decision of the Strassburg city council (1455?) upheld the pope's declaration. Sustained now by both pope and city council, the orders became even more virulent in their attacks on the lay clergy, with the result that Kreutzer, having suffered all manner of abuse, was forced to leave Strassburg in 1456. To restore some semblance of order, the bishop discontinued cathedral preaching and the city council had the cathedral pulpit removed. For years there was no preaching in the cathedral.

In 1477 Susanna von Cöllen, aroused by this state of affairs and by the dissatisfaction of the people, persuaded her husband Schott., Sr., and his associates to take action. It was decided to set up a cathedral chair for a secular preacher. To raise the necessary funds, Schott, Sr., pledged 200 florins while Bishop Ruprecht (1477-1478), in concert with the cathedral dean *Graf* Johann von Helfenstein, arranged to discontinue the post of perpetual episcopal chaplain in the choir and transfer its income to the new chair. The incumbent episcopal chaplain Symphorien (Schimpfele) Ole resigned on payment of a considerable sum to which Schott, Sr., contributed; the annual payment of 40 florins from the defunct post was guaranteed at Rome and Geiler was chosen to be the first cathedral preacher.

The Strassburg charter of 1 April 1478 for the chair of cathedral preacher (Appendix K) had the following provisions. The dean and chapter of the cathedral had the sole right of naming the preacher. The preacher was to be worthy and learned, a licentiate or doctor of theology and a member of the secular clergy. He was to be on approval for two months – after Geiler's first sermon, the administrators of the *fabrica* (N. 76) determined to keep him at any cost. He was to be provided with a house near the cathedral

P. 143   #124   N. 955

and to have four weeks holiday annually; the rest of the year he might not be absent without permission of the dean and never in Lent, nor was he to be excused from preaching services except by permission of the dean. During his absence the preacher replacing him had to belong to the secular clergy. He was not obligated to attend choir (N. 1401). He was not to cause difficulties in the parish or for the curate of St. Laurentius. He was not to publish circulars or the like without authority of the dean. He was to render formal obedience to the cathedral chapter. His duties were to preach daily in Lent, every Sunday during the rest of the year, on feast days, on the eve of principal holidays and on all special occasions such as times of plague, war, bad harvests, visits of papal legates or of other dignitaries. (These special occasions would also include funeral services for bishops, as in the case of Bishop Ruprecht and Bishop Albrecht,* and the opening of the synod of 1482). For every preaching service the bell was to be rung.

Sixtus IV in a bull of 22 May 1479 confirmed the chair at Strassburg, but there were unfortunate mistakes or ambiguities in the wording of the bull which made it appear that Ole still held the post of episcopal chaplain and that his resignation was still to be secured; although the discontinuation of this post was mentioned, no definite measures for effecting such were stated. Thus the chair was not really confirmed at all. While the Strassburg cathedral chapter was attempting to rectify the misconceptions, the orders, dismayed at the appointment of a secular preacher to the chair, complained to Sixtus and obtained his bull of 12 February 1486 which demanded that Bishop Albrecht cease infringing on the prerogatives of the orders. Yielding to this demand would have endangered the chair, but Bishop Albrecht was not intimidated. The fight to secure papal confirmation of the chair lasted 11 years. During this period Geiler's status was unofficial and his income uncertain, the only sure money being that contributed annually by Schott, Sr. Hence it is small wonder that Geiler was tempted by offers to become cathedral preacher in Basel, in Augsburg, or elsewhere (cf. N. 963). Not until 7 July 1489 was Geiler formally installed with great ceremony by Heinrich von Hennenberg,* acting dean (cf. N. 908).

Geiler's successors in the post of cathedral preacher at Strassburg were his nephew Peter Wickgram who served 1510-1521; Simphorien Pollion, 1521-1523; Caspar Hedion, 1523-1549, who became in turn a Lutheran, Zwinglian and Calvinist; Protois Gebwiller, 1550-1559. During the years 1549-1550 and 1559-1561 there was no cathedral preacher. From 1561-1681 all cathedral offices were occupied by Protestants and from 1683-1764 by Jesuits.

Cf. Barth, *Kreutzer*, 186. Dacheux, *Réf.*, 23, 29-31. Falk, 3-6, 82ff., 84-86, 88-92. Grandidier, *Essais*, 69f., 274-280. Hertzog, iv, 113. Meister, 143. L. Pfleger, "Predigtwesen," 529-538. Rathgeber, *Gottesmänner*, 10. Schmidt, "Notices... P.S.," 250-252, 309f. Stenzel, 70, 77. Wencker, *Arch.*, 430f. Wimpheling, *Cat. ep.*, 110. Cf. also Appendix K.

What specifications different from those already discussed with Rome were in the document prepared by Johann Simmler* – probably in his capacity as an episcopal officer – is not stated, but it was not too many months thereafter (about the end of June 1489) that the pope confirmed the chair.

956. *Omeliam Beati Bernardi de qua scribis*: *non habet Magister Iohannes Rot...* Cf. N. 946.

957. *Cerciorem... faciam Matrem tuam*: *et dominum Chistianum... non adest...* Both Geiler's mother and Christian are mentioned in #114 as anticipating

P. 143   #124   N. 957

Geiler's return (N. 904 and N. 905). Christian may have been helping with the grape gathering on cathedral lands, from which Geiler would receive his allottment (N. 116, last paragraph).

958. Quod ad sexterniones pertinet tibi mittendos...
Cf. N. 903.

959. Et cartulam: quam subscripsit famatus ille theologus Gabriel Biel...
During Gabriel Biel's visit in Strassburg Schott and he participated in a question and answer exercise. One of the questions put by Schott was whether Geiler should resign his post in Strassburg (#222, p. 251; cf. p. xxix). It is possible that Biel's answer or even the entire exercise was contained in the *cartula* which Schott was sending Geiler.

960. Rogat litteris suis dominus Doctor Iohannes kauffman Iuris peritus...
This jurist has not been identified. He may be the Johann Kaufmann of "Rottwila" listed as enrolling at Heidelberg in 1459 and 1483 and at Tübingen in 1480 (Toepke, I, 299, 372; Hermelink, 32). Cf. also *Anal. Francisc.*, II, 487.

961. Ora... et sanctas Martires: atque Vdalricum.
By the "sacred martyrs" Schott may be referring to the 11,000 Virgins of Cologne whose feast had been celebrated 21 October, four days prior to the writing of this letter (cf. N. 555).
   St. Udalricus or Ulrich, bishop of Augsburg (955-973), who had been canonized in 993, was the patron saint of both the city and bishopric of Augsburg. It was quite fitting that Geiler who was at the time in Augsburg should address prayers to this saint. Cf. #267, poem on the collapse of St. Ulrich's church, and N. 1673.

#125. TO JOHANN GEILER [Strassburg, early] 1488

962. Summary Schott sets forth arguments against Geiler's accepting the post of cathedral preacher at Basel and refutes any arguments Geiler might offer for accepting.
   If it were not that the conditions in Strassburg, so improved under Geiler's husbandry, would revert to their former state once his hand were removed from the hoe, Schott would congratulate both the people of Basel on acquiring a preacher like Geiler and Geiler himself on securing a position worthy of him. The real issue to be decided, however, is which of the two involves more love for God and neighbor: to stay in Strassburg or to go to Basel.
   Strassburg, having the larger and more sinful congregation, has more need of sound guidance than Basel. It is possible that Geiler might accomplish much in Basel, but that he does not know. In Strassburg he has already accomplished incredible reforms and can do more. If Basel with an established cathedral chair and its own theological faculty has had to hunt afar for a preacher and found none, how will Strassburg with a cathedral chair still in its inception find a preacher to replace Geiler who is not at all ambitious? To be sure, those in power have long known Geiler's dissatisfaction with the unsettled state of the Strassburg chair, but for that very reason Geiler has

P. 143   #125   N. 962

a greater opportunity to exercise brotherly love and not allow temporal to outweigh eternal considerations. Should Geiler leave Strassburg, what about the confusion among the people and what about the stumbling block to those who had received his word that he would stay? Not only love for God but love for one's neighbor decide that Geiler shall remain in Strassburg. These are the sentiments of many who love Geiler. (Cf. p. xxix and N. 129, par. 2.)

P. 144

963. *Audiui praestantissime Doctor: te iterum ea perturbacione... afferebas.*
How many times Geiler had been tempted to accept promising positions elsewhere is not known, but from Schott's words here it appears that there had been numerous occasions; several of these may be identified in Schott's letters: #61 alludes to the period in the fall of 1484 when Geiler was considering a new post, very likely Basel (cf. N. 533); #99 concerns the offer at Augsburg and possibly Basel (cf. N. 775) in the spring of 1487; the present item discusses the offer (perhaps the third or even fourth) from Basel at the beginning of the year 1488 (N. 980); #124 and #114 refer to the offer at Augsburg during the period of Geiler's long stay there from September 1488 to January 1489 (cf. N. 901).

964. *is non sum: qui Mineruam: ut aiunt: sus docere debeam...*
Cf. N. 933, paragraph 2.

965. *et iam sarculo verbi vicia plura extirpasses... si sarculum retraheres...*
For the word *sarculum* cf. I Rg. 13:20; Is. 7:25; also Waddell, 93.

966. *qua profecto agricultura te retrospiciente*
Cf. Lc. 9:62.

967. *gratularer plurimum: condicionem status tibi dignam attigisse.*
Because the chair at Strassburg was as yet unconfirmed by the pope, Geiler was essentially still chaplain to the bishop (N. 955), whereas at Basel he would be cathedral preacher in fact.

968. *Sed quia caritas dei et proximi plus apud Christianum valere debet*
Cf. Mt. 22:36-40.

969. *viam veritatis doceas... veritatem/ non errores docencium*
Cf. Ps. 118:30 and Tt. 1:11.

970. *cor non tangit*
Cf. N. 858.

P. 145

971. *pro incredibili facundia tua*
It was Geiler's command of wit and satire that allowed him to castigate

hearers of any age or rank without their feeling rancor. It was also this command which drove points home. For a discussion of his story-telling ability and his eloquence, cf. Roeder, 23 and *passim*. Cf. also N. 281.

972. *An te vel auditorum poenitet? qui copiosiores sunt: quam vnquam... visi:*
Cf. N. 80.

973. *(ne de secretis dicam: quae solus Deus nouit)*
Cf. Mt. 6:6.

974. *in publicis consuetudinibus/ quas legi diuine contrarias... recenseam?*
For Geiler's reforms in civil and religious practises, cf. #187 and notes thereto.
     For desecration of churches, cf. #187; N. 1326, 11 and 12; N. 1333-N. 1337.
     For the long battle to obtain last rites for those condemned to death, cf. #187, p. 205; #210- #212; N. 1325; N. 1420.
     For masks used in revelries, cf. N. 1326, 11; N. 1337.

975. *Basilienses ad tam bene et firmiter institutum officium... panem frangit*
The cathedral chair of preaching at Basel had been established for 19 years. The chapter even provided the preacher with a personal library. The university of Basel from which Geiler received his doctorate was founded 1456. Strassburg waited until 1489 for confirmation of its preaching chair and until 1566 for a university. Cf. N. 955.
     For *panem frangit*, cf. Mt. 26:26; Mr. 14:22; Lc. 24:30; Ac. 2:42, 20:7; 1Cor. 10:16.

976. *pro negligencia eorum/ quos nosti: tantum et tantis impensis... redeat*
Schott's criticism is directed against the officers of the cathedral chapter who were lax in procuring confirmation of the chair from the pope, the orders in Strassburg who opposed the chair, the *Curia* and Sixtus IV. Cf. N. 955, par. 6.
     Among those who had instituted the chair with great expense and sacrifice were Bishop Ruprecht, Heinrich von Helfenstein, Schott, Sr. (cf. N. 955).

977. *Tu quem Christo viuere velle non dubito*
Cf. Ph. 1:21.

978. *De scandalo vt vereor multorum: praesertim eorum/ qui...*
For *scandalum*, cf. Rm. 14:13.

979. *Doctor Friburgensis Rector: et Magister Thomas Lamparter sufficiant.*
Johann Kerer* and Thomas Lampertheim* were very close friends of Geiler. Their opinion would bear much weight with him.

P. 146   #125   N. 980

980. Datum Anno domini M.cccc.lxxxviij.
It will be noted that in the close of this item, the place of origin is lacking (no doubt Strassburg) and both day and month of the date are lacking; the only positive information given is the year 1488. From the evidence available it is quite certain that the letter must have been written during the first half – probably the first months – of 1488.

    1. The item concerns the offer of the Basel cathedral chapter to Geiler in 1488 to succeed Johann Heynlin à Lapide* who had held the post of cathedral preacher since November 1484 (#61, N. 550) and had resigned in the fall of 1487 to enter the Carthusian Order. (Of all sources only Schmidt, "Notices... P.S.," 310, gives the year of Heynlin's resignation as 1488).

    2. From statements in the present item (first paragraph, p. 144; second paragraph, p. 145; first paragraph, p. 146) it appears as if Geiler had rather recently refused an offer from Basel (cf. N. 775) and had informed the Strassburgers of his refusal; it also appears as if the Basel chapter, after casting about in vain for a preacher, had again approached him.

    3. Of Schott's three other letters written to Geiler in 1488 – #119 of 19 June, #124 of 25 October, #114 of 21 November – none mentions the Basel offer; #119 makes no mention of any offer and both #124 and #114 concern the Augsburg offer.

    The present item could therefore not have been written later than mid-June 1488 and, judging from the activity of the Basel chapter and from the fact that its intent was to fill the post of preacher as quickly as possible, one may assume that the item was written in the first months of 1488.

#126. TO CONRAD LEONTARIUS   Strassburg, 23 December 1489

981. Summary In answer to a letter from Leontarius,* Schott writes that he will be very happy to inaugurate a friendship with Leontarius whom he has long greatly admired.

982. Conrado Leontorio Mulbronnensi... Cisterciensis Cancellario
Leontarius, writing after Schott's death to Wimpheling (#291), laments that his friendship with Schott was of so short duration and gives his appraisal of Schott.

P. 147

983. iuxta Aristidis sentenciam perpetuo duraturam esse amiciciam nostram
We have been unable to find the work with the sentiment of Aristides to which Schott refers.

984. Ex Argentina prepropere ad decimum kalendas ianuarij... M.cccc.lxxxix.
This item is chronologically out of order. For confusion about dates before the kalends of January, cf. N. 218.

#127. TO FRIEDRICH VON ZOLLERN   Strassburg, 28 January 1489

985. Summary The Schotts thank Bishop Friedrich for gifts. They are especially grateful to him for returning Geiler, the long awaited. Indeed, by so doing Friedrich has bestowed the greatest possible favor upon the Strassburgers. It is a pleasure to hear Geiler tell about Friedrich's fine work as a bishop.

986. Primum super muneribus: quae... quod ad te missa sunt...
The incunabulum has *ad te* although *a te* would seem more sensible. It is possible, however, that Bishop Friedrich had sent to the Schotts gifts which he himself had received.

987. Deinde quod nobis Doctorem reddidisti... beneficenciam videris...
Cf. N. 901.

988. dignacionis tue feruentissimum in salutem eorum çelum: studium... possint
Friedrich served his flock and his office well. For his accomplishments as bishop, cf. biographical note on him. Geiler was justly proud of him, even though at first he had opposed Friedrich's becoming bishop, for he knew what strength of character and effort it cost Friedrich to be a good bishop (N. 679). Dacheux expresses Geiler's feeling toward both Schott and Friedrich von Zollern very nicely by saying that as Schott was Geiler's model priest, so was Friedrich Geiler's model bishop (*Réf.*, 382).

P. 148

#128. TO VITUS MAELER Strassburg, 23 March 1489

989. Summary Schott warns Maeler against stressing temporal values rather than eternal. He feels he would be less a friend, did he not urge Maeler to take thought for his salvation. He asks for detailed information about violent disturbances in Bologna. Maximilian has called a meeting of all member states of the empire at Spires.

990. Quia profecto dies adueniunt... racionem reddere cogemur
Cf. Mt. 25:13; Rm. 14:10-12.

991. ut cum Dominus venerit: inueniat te paratum...
Cf. Mt. 24:44; Lc. 12:40; also Mt. 25:1-13.

992. Nam quam fluxa: quam caduca sit omnis mundi potencia
This passage sounds very much like a quotation, but we have been unable to find a source. Is this one of Schott's *bons mots*?

993. eos/ quos nos aliquando Bononie et florentes opulencia... (to end of paragraph)
In 1488 Bologna was torn by violence as a result of the abortive plot, headed by the Malvezzi family, to murder the entire Bentivoglio family which ruled Bologna with an iron hand. Giovanni Malvezzi and Giacomo Bargellini were condemned to death and in the disturbances that followed their execution there was much bloodshed in the city. Cf. James, *Bologna*, 60, and Muzzi, 137-149.

994. propediem conuentus omnium Principum et Oratorum vrbium... Spire...
We have no information on an assembly of the imperial states at Spires at this time. One purpose for the assembly may have been to discuss terms of peace with Flanders (cf. N. 925).

#129. TO JOHANN WIDMANN Strassburg, 24 April 1489

995. Summary Widmann is requested to reserve rooms for Schott, his parents and friends who will be arriving at the baths and are looking forward to seeing the Widmanns.

996. in thermis Ferarum cerciorem facias... ad Dominicam Cantate: illic sumus
The term *thermis Ferarum* (cf. N. 706) refers to the hot springs at Baden-Baden. Schott's letters #131, #132, #133 and #135 which were composed during this sojourn at the baths are written from "Baden," "Baden Ferino" and "balneo Ferarum."
The fourth Sunday after Easter, *Cantate*, was on 17 May in 1489.

997. Ceterum dominus Otto Sturm: cuius vxor... voluit ut eum tibi commendatum
The wife of Otto Sturm* has not been identified.

#130. TO ADOLPH RUSCH Strassburg, 14 May 1489

998. Summary Schott, busy with preparations for his sojourn at the baths, is writing in haste. He sends as bath gifts to Rusch riddles and a poem of his own composition. He complains of not having made much progress with illustrations for the edition of Vergil during Rusch's absence.
The postscript explains that Rusch, already ill, had read the letter at Baden-Baden before hurrying home to Strassburg, where he had died 26 May. The postscript ends with the poignant phrase "the last letter to him."

999. properacio mea efficit: qui iam nunc... balinearum petendarum gracia...
As announced in the preceding letter (#129) to Widmann, Schott with his parents planned to be in Baden-Baden by 17 May.

1000. Ceterum quae mea venacione assequutus sum... hec tibi dono mitto
Jokes and riddles were especially appreciated by persons undergoing the harsh regimen of the baths; Geiler and Kerer sent witty stories from Baden-Baden to the Schotts at Wildbad (#21); Reuchlin composed a riddle about shade or shadow at Wildbad (Geiger, *Briefwechsel*, 351). For customs connected with baths, cf. N. 192; for the custom of sending compositions to friends, cf. N. 309.

1001. Haud male conueniunt scirpi atque enigmata... tum mihi Phoebus erit.
The first three words of the riddle poem are reminiscent of the beginning

words in the two lines of verse "Haud bene conveniunt...," #109, p. 121; The description *monstrum Tetrum: informe: ingens* (lines three and four) is reminiscent of Vergil *Aen* iii.658 and iv. 181.

Non fuit: et non est... vel erunt, the first riddle, resembles the riddle quoted by Taylor, *English Riddles*, 40, no. 97, the answer to which is "tomorrow;" a similar riddle also quoted by Taylor (648) has the answer "age."

dum non est querimus omnes... querimur, the second riddle, is like the shadow riddle (ibid. 647): "If there is none, you are seeking it; if there is some, you do not take it."

Quod soli angustum est: aptum... plus satis esse tribus, the third riddle, has many parallels; its answer is "a secret;" a Danish parallel wants the answer "marriage" (ibid. 687; cf. also Apperson, 628 and *Oxford Dictionary of Proverbs*, 490).

1002. accipe alios versiculos... quibus puer... petebat in Choralium
Children of the poor received free instruction at monastery and collegiate schools; the more gifted were admitted to the ranks of choir pupils for further training (cf. Stöber, *Neue Alsatia*, 278). Judging from the case Schott mentions here, permission to enter the ranks of choir pupils at the cathedral had to be granted by the *scholasticus*, or perhaps by the dean (Heinrich von Hennenberg was both *scholasticus* and acting dean of the cathedral). The talented youngster for whom Schott wrote the little poem as a petition to Hennenberg may well have been one of his (Schott's) protégés.

1003. Icona argumentorum Maronis: non tam per desidiam... cessatorem.
With Schott's help, Rusch was preparing an illustrated edition of Vergil. So far as can be ascertained, the edition was not published posthumously. Cf. Ritter, 50.

1004. Appelles atque Lisyppus Alexandro: qui eis operam imperaret: caruerunt
On the artists preparing illustrations for the edition of Vergil Schott bestows the names of Apelles, a celebrated painter at the time of Alexander the Great, and the name of Lysippus, the only brass founder whom Alexander permitted to cast a statue of him. By implication then Rusch is likened to Alexander.

1005. me precoeptori meo vnice commenda
I. e., Johann Müller, at this time in Baden-Baden.

1006. ex inflammacione balnei aegrotans... tercia scilicet Rogacionum: mortem
Rusch apparently returned to Strassburg as Schott was en route to Baden-Baden, so the two never met again. Worried about Rusch's condition, Schott arranged for Widmann to treat Rusch (#135), but death intervened. For rigors of the bath regimen, cf. N. 192.

The day of Rusch's death, i.e., 26 May, was – Schott tells us – three days before Rogation Days. Rogations were special supplications – sometimes accompanied by religious processions – held at Eastertide, three weeks after Easter, three days before Ascension Day and in times of calamity. Here the

P. 151   #130   N. 1006

rogations before Ascension are meant, Ascension Day having been 28 May in 1489.

#131. TO JOHANN WIDMANN   Baden-Baden, 20 May 1489

1007. Summary The Schotts and Widmann's wife wish Widmann to join them at the baths.

1008. Coniunx tua matrona honestissima... se ab Abbate Hirsacensi nihil...
We are not told what items Widmann's wife (N. 587) was expecting from the abbot of Hirsau – who was at this time Blasius* – but it is possible that that Widmann had ordered herbs from the Hirsau monastery. Monasteries were repositories for herbs and herbology. Susanna von Cöllen received her supply of fuller's herb regularly from a monk in the Franciscan monastery at Barr (#154, p. 169).

1009. Ex Baden quarta post Cantate...
For the date of *Cantate* in 1489, cf. N. 996; for the method of reckoning dates, cf. N. 582, par. 2.

#132. TO JOHANN WIDMANN   Baden-Baden, 21 May 1489

1010. Summary Writing in the name of his parents and Widmann's wife, Schott again requests Widmann to come without fail to Baden-Baden.

1011. is qui attulit litteras tuas: famulus Doctoris Ludouici
Neither Doctor Ludovicus nor his *famulus* has been identified.

P. 152

1012. Ex Baden Ferino/ quinta post Cantate.
For "Baden Ferino," cf. N. 706, also N. 996 . For the date of *Cantate* in 1489, cf. N. 996, par. 2.

#133. TO JOHANN GEILER   Baden-Baden, 27 May 1489

1013. Summary The Schotts are enjoying their stay at the baths; they solicit Geiler's prayers.

1014. hanc nostram peregrinacionem...
Cf. Heb. 11:13; I Pt. 2:11.

1015. Ex Balneo Ferarum...
Cf. N. 706 and N. 996.

1016. Augustenses nonnulle nobiscum sunt: quarum vna soror... Georij Granser.
We have not been able to identify Georg Granser, his wife or his sister-in-law; all of them were Augsburgers whom no doubt Geiler knew.

#134. TO JOHANN KELLER Strassburg, 13 June 1489

1017. Summary Schott trusts that the preserved ginger he is sending will meet Johann Keller's expectations. He is sorry to have been absent during Keller's stay in Strassburg. Schott, Sr., bids Keller to be assured that he will do his best in the matter which Keller wished presented to the city of Strassburg.

1018. curaui ut at te conditum Zinçiber perferretur
Ginger, a rare and costly oriental spice at this period, was one of the spices sought by Columbus on his voyage in 1492. Also ground ginger mixed with water, egg-white and a little egg-yolk produces red ochre.
On ginger Beck (cccxxxiiii) has the following information: "Zinziber grece et latine... Serapio spricht daz dass sey ein gewechss... in Arabia... Galienus spricht das diss wurzel kumme uss India." Ginger, powdered or whole, is considered good for "den bösen magen der erkalt ist;" mixed with food, it cures syncope; mixed with vinegar it helps against night sweat; wine with ginger and anise is good for digestion and "für wehthunn des magens und gederms die von wind kummen."

1019. Ceterum quod mihi mandasti: ut cum Patre agerem... ciuitati nostri...
There is no indication what matter Keller, procurator of the imperial treasury, wished Schott and Schott, Sr., who was mayor 1488-1489, to bring before the city of Strassburg, perhaps imperial taxes or monies promised by Strassburg to Friedrich III for the Hungarian campaigns (cf. N. 623). That Keller should approach Schott on matters of state indicates how closely Schott worked with his father (cf. N. 113). We have found no information on Keller.

#135. TO JOHANN GEILER Baden-Baden, 28 May 1489

1020. Summary Schott is extremely worried about Rusch's condition. He has requested Dr. Widmann* to treat Rusch,* and Widmann is prepared to depart for Strassburg immediately if Rusch wishes him to come. Geiler is asked to sound out Rusch's feelings on the matter. (This item should precede #134, cf. N. 1023).

1021. Ceterum quoniam Adelphum Ruscum virum mihi probe carum... decumbere
Cf. postscript to #130, p. 151, and N. 998, also N. 1006.

1022. Atque in edes Patris mei/ per famulum significa: omnia... aperuimus.
According to Seyboth (177) and Piton (I, 32), the house where the family of Schott, Sr., lived stands at the corner of the *rue des Charpentiers* and the *rue Brulée*, just a block from the *Place Broglie*. It fronts on the *rue des Charpentiers* and juts out at an acute angle into the *rue Brulée*. Since Piton calls this house the home of Anna Schott, we may assume it was the family home until mid-1490, when – judging from Schott's instructions to Widmann* for finding the Schott house – the family apparently moved (#147).
The Schott home is mentioned also #190, p. 209, and #201.

P. 153   #135   N. 1022

The original home of the Strassburg Schotts may have been in the *Schottengasse*, later called *Almengässchen unter Wagnern*, now known as *Gärtnergässchen* or *impasse des Jardiniers*, where Schmidt (*Namen*, 152) records an Augustin Schott as living in 1587.

The *famulus* is unidentified; for Geiler's *famuli*, cf. N. 279.

1023. Ex balneo Ferarum Ipso festo Ascensionis
For *balneo Ferarum*, cf. N. 996, also N. 706. In 1489 Ascension Day came on 28 May. This item is out of order (cf. N. 36).

#136. TO GABRIEL BIEL   Strassburg, 13 August 1489

1024. Summary   Suspecting it might have a message for him, Schott has read Biel's* letter to Geiler who has gone to Augsburg and may be reached there. He thanks Biel for the invitation to accompany Geiler to the university ceremonies at Tübingen, when Biel's brother receives his licentiate, and he promises to accept if Geiler comes and if his parents can spare him.

P. 154

1025. votis tuis et quantum ad pecunias pertinet... inuitacioni tue.
In the year 1489 Biel was rector at Tübingen and may have invited Geiler to preach at the university commencement exercises. In that case the money mentioned would concern Geiler's fee and expenses. The name of Biel's brother who was to receive his licentiate at those exercises is not known; he may be identical with *Magister Gualterus* of #138 (cf. N. 1033).

Since his father was serving as mayor of Strassburg (1488 to 1489) and was not in good health, Schott felt he should not leave the city without the parents' consent. For Schott's devotion to his parents and their exaggerated solicitude for him, cf. N. 87.

Apparently Schott and Geiler did attend the ceremonies at Tübingen and were guests of the Widmanns*; at least Schott was in the Widmann home, cf. #138, N. 1031 and N. 1032.

#137. TO JOHANN GEILER   Strassburg, 25 August 1489

1026. Summary   Schott hopes that Geiler is already en route [from Augsburg] to Strassburg and will therefore not receive this letter. Yet if Geiler has decided to extend his absence, he must not delay too long, because all his orders pertaining to his house have been carried out by Nicholaus and because the stove – dry and resplendent in its coat of vermillion – may be offended at his tarrying. A neighbor of Geiler has died.

1027. quando in his quae per Nycholaum tuum fieri iussisti: nihil...
For Nicholaus, cf. N. 279.

1028. hospitem tuum: qui die Dominico... occidit: dominum Iohannem Landeck
Johann Landeck has not been identified.

P. 154   #137   N. 1029

1029. Commenda me maiorem in modum Reuerendissimo domino meo Augustensi
The person in question is Bishop Friedrich von Zollern of Augsburg.

1030. dominus Christianus
Cf. N. 904.

#138. TO JOHANN WIDMANN Strassburg, 31 October 1489

1031. Summary Schott sends a gift of herbs and seeds in thanks to the Widmanns* for their recent hospitality.

P. 155

1032. nos herbulas has/ vna cum seminibus: quas desiderasti: ad te mittere...
For Schott's interest in herbs, cf. p. xxiv and N. 82. The visit to Tübingen when Schott was guest at the Widmann home was no doubt on the occasion of the university commencement exercises there. Very likely Geiler was with him. Cf. N. 1024 and N. 1025, also #136, p. 154.

1033. Et me multis: praecipue Magistris nostris Gualtero Gabrieli... commendes
The two masters referred to are probably Gabriel Biel* and his brother who received his licentiate from Tübingen at the commencement exercises (cf. #136, p. 154, and N. 1025).

1034. In vigilia omnium sanctorum
I.e., on the eve of All Saints' Day, Hallowe'en.

#139. TO ADOLPH OCCO Strassburg, 1 December 1489

1035. Summary Schott threatens to lampoon Occo* with Catullian iambics unless he not only returns the letters and composition by Schott he recently borrowed but also as interest sends copies of works by himself or by others.

1036. Abstulisti a me nuper Epistolas virorum praestancium: et confictionem nostram...
For the custom of sending to friends works of one's own and of others, cf. N. 309. What composition of Schott's Occo borrowed is not stated. It is perhaps the *libellum* returned by Occo (#150, p. 164) in July 1490. The word *nostram* in the quotation above is undoubtedly the editorial "we" (cf. #265, lines 5f., and N. 1667).

1037. Alioqui Iambos... quibus Catullus amicam Forniani decoctoris... reflagitauit.
Cf. Cat. 41.4. The proper adjective in the above quotation is *Formiani*, cf. *Errata*.

#140. TO JOHANN WIDMANN Strassburg, 20 January 1490

1038. Summary Schott attributes to Providence Widmann's* fortunate escape

P. 155   #140   N. 1038

from a dangerous fire. Susanna von Cöllen thanks Widmann's wife for the fur cape made by the latter and requests that a silver emblem belonging to Widmann's wife be sent for insertion among prayer beads. Schott, Sr., is suffering from kidney (or bladder) stones; his condition is described in detail so that Widmann may diagnose and advise.

P. 156

1039. signum illud Argenteum vxoris tue... consuendum in seriem eorum circulorum... censeri solet.
Schott's reference to his having been in Tübingen may allude to his trip thither with Geiler for the university commencement exercises (cf. #138, N. 1031 and N. 1032).

The silver "signum illud" belonging to Widmann's wife (N. 587) which Schott could have brought back to Strassburg may have been a crucifix or perhaps one of the two gifts the Schotts had given her, i.e., either the *Agnus Dei* or the figure of the pregnant Virgin (#66, p. 74; #111, p. 131; N. 588). This object was to be inserted in a series of beads by which one keeps count of prayers. It seems that the beads and object were sent to Widmann's wife, for on 4 June 1490 (#147) Susanna von Cöllen requests the "circular prayers" so that she may chant for the health of Widmann's wife. In the following month, July 1490, Susanna sends "another computation of prayers" (#149, p. 163).

These "circular prayers" were prayer beads such as have been prized in many parts of the world as gifts of friendship. They may have indeed been rosaries, although Schott does not employ the term. It is not known precisely when rosaries were first used; according to tradition St. Dominic (1170-1221) received the rosary through revelation of the Blessed Virgin, but there is no contemporary evidence to support this tradition. Employment of the rosary for meditation and prayer was fostered by Sixtus IV and became general with the rapid spread of the *confraternitas* of the rosary, founded at Cologne in 1457 by Alanus de Rupe and Jacob Sprenger.* It is quite possible that at the time Schott was writing this letter (1490) the first Strassburg *confraternitas* of the rosary was being established under the influence of Sprenger who was then serving as Dominican provincial (N. 1382). That Schott's description of the "circular prayers" does not correspond with the appearance of the rosary as we know it today need not be surprising, for in the early years of its popularity many types of rosary, no longer recognized by papal authority, were in use.

1040. Pater diuino munere sanus est: quamquam nuper... nos mouit nouitas.
The condition of Schott, Sr., is mentioned several times (cf. N. 885).

1041. Scribit ad te domina Vrsula de Dunçenheim...
Ursula von Dunzenheim (probably a relative of Conrad Dunzenheim*) is mentioned in #154, pp. 168f., as being interested in herbs. It is quite likely that she was at this time trying to establish with Widmann an exchange of information concerning herbs.

1042. Item Magistrum Georium virum elegantem.
Cf. N. 936.

P. 156   #141   N. 1043

#141. TO VITUS MAELER Strassburg, 1 February 1490

1043. Summary Schott requests Maeler's aid for the prior of the Dominican monastery at Colmar who bears this letter and who has cases to put before the *Curia*. He sends greetings to Johann Müller.

1044. Priore Predicatorum Columbariensium de Obseruancia
Neither from Wittmer's obituaries of the Colmar Dominicans (*Obituaire*, 37, 61) nor from *Q.F. Domin.* (VII, 25, 33) is it clear whether the prior of Colmar who was carrying a letter from Schott to Maeler at Rome in February 1490 was Mathias Fanckel or Anton Pistor (Becker). Fanckel, a master of theology and doctor of canon law, was prior in 1484, but there are no data as to how long he held the office. Pistor became prior in 1482 between the dates 11 May and 8 October; on 20 February 1492 he was given the choice of monasteries; and in 1493, according to the archives of Colmar, he was prior. From the foregoing it appears as if Pistor held the post of prior at Colmar 1482-84 and sometime before 1493 was reinstalled.
For the Dominicans of Observance, cf. N. 689.

P. 157

1045. Precoeptorem meum Magistrum Iohannem Muller Decanum Badensem...
Johann Müller with his princeling Jacob of Baden* was at this time in Rome. He with Maeler's* help was trying to obtain papal confirmation of his *preces primae*; cf. N. 680.

#142. TO PALLAS SPANGEL Strassburg, 21 March 1490

1046. Summary Schott, in the name of the printer Martin Flach, Sr.,* requests Spangel* to send, as promised, copies of two works by Thomas von Strassburg* so that from them the texts being used for the edition of Thomas' commentary may be corrected.

1047. Hortatu tuo... agressus sum impressionem Thome nostri Argentinensis...
Flach and Schott were at this time cooperating on the edition of Thomas von Strassburg's commentary to the four books of sentences by Peter Lombard, Flach being the printer, Schott the editor. From the text of this item it is evident that Spangel urged the undertaking of such an edition. For a description of the two volume edition, cf. N. 138, also p. xxx.

1048. non verebor a doctissima illa praestancia tua desiderare... confingantur.
Spangel's letter, in which he praises the excellent work done on the first two *scripta* (mentioned by Schott here as in the process of printing at the end of March 1490) and in which he reaffirms his promise to send two other works by Thomas von Strassburg to Flach, appears at the beginning of the first volume of the Schott-Flach edition. Cf. N. 138, third paragraph.
Note the practice of obtaining the most correct reading possible by comparing all available versions of a text. This practice is mentioned in #203.

#143. TO JOHANN VON LAUDENBURG Strassburg, 24 March 1490

1049. Summary In answer to Laudenburg's* question whether the adjective derived from *theologus* ends in *-icalis* or *-alis*, Schott explains that neither of these endings occurs in good Latin; the correct ending is *-icus*.
Laudenburg is asked to verify the claim that he is one of the persons who has seen Conrad Bondorf's* copy of the papal bull permitting Franciscans the right to handle money. Laudenburg's statement will help in calming the storm of protest raised by the Franciscans against Johann Rot over the fresco Rot has had painted in [the St. Laurentius chapel of] the cathedral at Strassburg. The fresco, a representation of the narrow path to salvation and the broad way to perdition, portrays on the broad way every type and class of people, clerics not excepted; among the latter is a Franciscan carrying a purse. To this figure the Franciscans object, because, they say, its purse symbolizes an infraction of their rules as if the use of money were not permitted them, whereas, they maintain, it is in fact permitted them by an apostolic decree which they claim Laudenburg has seen.

1050. Queris a me: Theologicalis questio dici debeat... a Theologi deduci.
It was customary for humanists to exchange information on questions of grammar, spelling, derivation, etc. (cf. N. 568).

1051. Rescriptum Apostolicum bullatum: in quo eis Argenti... indulgeatur.
We have been unable to locate a papal bull stating specifically that Franciscans might be permitted the use of money. In bulls issued 1472-1479 Sixtus IV, the Franciscan pope, confirmed all privileges hitherto granted the Franciscans and also granted them freedom from episcopal jurisdiction and from tithing, as well as the privilege of having possessions. It was perhaps by a very broad interpretation of this latest privilege that Franciscans felt entitled to the actual use of money. Schmidt (*H.L.*, II, 17), equally unsuccessful in finding a papal bull specifically giving Franciscans the right to use money, believes Schott considered the bull spurious and wanted Laudenburg's confirmation of his suspicions.

1052. Magistrum Iohannem Rot... depingi iusserit in ecclesia... illud Ypsilon ...indultum.
According to Barth (*Handbuch*, 1450) Johann Rot had the fresco painted in the cathedral chapel of St. Laurentius *ca*. 1489 (N. 80). The Pythagorean or Samian letter "Y" which symbolizes the divergent paths of life is mentioned in #11, p. 20; cf. N. 206.
The outcome of the quarrel between the Franciscans and Rot is unknown (Schmidt, *H. L.*, II, 17), but the intense animosity exhibited is characteristic of the feeling between the lay clergy and the orders (cf. N. 955, paragraphs 3ff.), as well as of the enmity among the orders themselves. Dominicans in Spires, for example, had a Crucifixion painted in which Christ's one hand is nailed to the cross, the other is stuffing money into a money bag suspended from a Franciscan cord (Lindemann, 174, note 73).

#144. TO PETER SCHOTT FROM BOHUSLAUS VON HASSENSTEIN
Venice, 16 May 1490

1053. Summary Hassenstein, about to sail on his great voyage to the Near East, Egypt, Greece, Byzantium, and the Grecian Isles, writes in farewell to Schott. He had intended to visit India as well but has been dissuaded by merchants who say the route is not at all passable for Christians. He knows how hard it is for Schott to be left behind and he could wish for no greater boon than to have Schott's companionship. He would have written from Bohemia of his plans, had he not feared that Schott's parents, attached as they are to their son, might have been worried [presumably because at that point Schott could still have joined him]. (Note the absence of a Wimpheling heading, cf. N. 37).

1054. Grate mihi... sed gracius castissimum ipsum sacrificium: quod... offers.
I.e., Hassenstein wishes Schott, when saying mass, to remember him.

1055. quod de Nazareth et Galilea scribis: erunt mihi cure...
This may be a reference to the list compiled by Schott of places he and others wished to have explored (cf. #204).

1056. Statueram quidem Siria/ Arabia/ Egiptoque lustratis: Indos petere:
Two letters written by Hassenstein during his voyage tell of the places he visited: one of 5 November 1490 to Johann Sselnberck from Alexandria (Potuček, no. 18), the other of 16 April 1491 to Stephan Piso* from his ship off the southwest coast of the Pelopennesus near the city of Modon or Medoni or Methoni (Potuček, no. 19).

1057. sed scio que sit tuorum erga te pietas: et quam difficulter... vellem.
Hassenstein, having been for longer periods a guest in the Schott home, was aware of Schott's devotion to his parents and their solicitude for him, cf. N. 87.

1058. dum memor ipse mei: dum spiritus hos regit artus
Vergil, *Aen.* iv.336.

1059. ad te non sine... scripsisse. Totam domum... patrem meum Keysersberg.
The lacuna of about 13 spaces between *sine* and *scripsisse* doubtless represents a Greek word or phrase in the manuscript (cf. p. xiv, N. 23 and N. 24). The exact import of the Greek is somewhat difficult to guess – perhaps regret, heartache, longing, trepidation at what the journey might bring, excitement, or the like. Potuček (157, in his notes to no. 17) remarks that Ryba's suggestion (in an edition we have not seen) of the Latin word *praesagio* for the lacuna is inept.

    Hassenstein had been in the Schott household enough to become fond not only of Schott's parents but of other members of the Schott family; he had also grown to respect and love Geiler (cf. N. 829).

P. 160   #145   N. 1060

P. 160

#145. TO JOHANN WIDMANN Strassburg, 27 May 1490

1060. Summary Schott entreats Widmann* to come to Strassburg to attend Peter Reiffsteck,* canon of Old St. Peter, who is gravely ill. The patient, the patient's brother Jacob* and Schott's parents, as well as the dean of Old St. Peter, add their pleas that Widmann may come. The emolument will be liberal. (This item and #147 both concern the illness of Peter Reiffsteck).

1061. mittoque rogancia verba: ut est apud Horacium.
The passage in Horace to which Schott refers may be one of the following: *Ep.* i.9.2, i.1.62f.; *Sat.* i.9.63.

1062. Petri Reifsteck Canonici Sancti Petri seniores... Iabobi Reiffsteck
The Reiffsteck brothers Peter and Jacob were both canons of Old St. Peter (N. 132). Peter Reiffsteck apparently recovered from his severe illness mentioned in this letter, for he is most certainly the "fratrem" about whom Schott writes on 7 July (#149, p. 163); however Jacob fell sick in July (of the plague?) and died in August. It was Jacob's canonicate at Old St. Peter to which Johann Müller succeeded (#151- #153, #155).

1063. domini Decani ecclesie supradicte
Dacheux (*Réf.*, 359, n. 1) identifies the dean of Old St. Peter in the list of executors of Jacob Reiffsteck's will in 1491 as Nicolaus Reisner. Both Grandidier (*Nouv. oeuvr.*, II, 596) and Schmidt ("Notices... Wolf," 448) mention Johann Wolf* as being dean of Old St. Peter, but do not give the dates when he held that office. At the time Schott was writing the present letter, we do not know which of the two was dean.

1064. quarta ante Dominicam Penthecostes
In 1490 Pentecost Sunday was on 30 May; four days previous to Pentecost was therefore 27 May (cf. N. 582).

#146. TO PAULUS MALLEOLUS Strassburg, 4 June 1490

1065. Summary With this letter Schott is dispatching a letter sent to him from Andlau for speedy delivery to Malleolus.* These letters Schott has entrusted to the *orator apostolicus* who should reach Paris more quickly than any other messenger. Before departing from the university at Paris, Malleolus is asked to give counsel to Gangolf von Steinmetz* who is studying for the master's degree and to Johann Klitsch*; he is also asked to bring letters from Paris. Johann Rot* is now a Carthusian novice. (Cf. #148 and N. 1076; also N. 264).

1066. Paulo Malleolo Andeloensi Collegium Burgundie Parisius incolenti
Malleolus, a native of Andlau, was living at the *Collegium Burgundie*, where Müller had stayed (cf. #54 and N. 476).

1067. Mitto ad te litteras mihi per Andelahe creditas... Oratori apostolico...
The letter or letters from Andlau bore the sad news of Johann Meyger's* death. They were actually entrusted to the secretary of the papal ambassador Raymund Peraudi* for delivery to Malleolus, as we learn from #148 (cf. N. 1076) which was written to Malleolus two days later and sent by another messenger. Cf. N. 264, par. 4.

1068. rogo Gangolffi mei... et Iohannis Ryxingen: racionem habere velis...
The two students at Paris to whom Malleolus had been giving counsel were protégés of Schott, cf. pp. xxviiif., N. 125, N. 547.

P. 161

1069. qui Magistro Ioanni Rot communi amico nostro: nunc Carthusiensi...
Apparently there is an omission in the text here either before or after *qui* which as it stands is not the relative pronoun but rather an adverb meaning "as" or "for example." In #148 Malleolus is instructed to bring letters also from Johann Brockingen,* "whose master Johann Rot is becoming a Carthusian," perhaps some such information was omitted in this passage when the present item was printed in the incunabulum.

By 1492 Rot was evidently a full-fledged Carthusian, for in a letter to Johann Amerbach* on 30 May he signs himself as "Io. rot Karthus." (Hartmann, no. 27). The Carthusian Order was founded in the eleventh century by St. Bruno (born *ca.* 1030) at Chartreuse in the mountains near Grenoble. Its members followed the Benedictine Rule and lived as hermits in separate hermitages where they recited the canonical hours alone; they met thrice a day with their fellows in their church. They occupied themselves with "reading, prayer and the labour of their hands, especially writing of books." Their ascetic manner of life kept them free from the deterioration which plagued other orders; thus they were "never reformed, because never deformed" (*E.B.*, V, 432). Such an order would certainly have had appeal for scholarly men like Johann Heynlin (N. 980) and Johann Rot.

1070. prepropere sexta Penthecostes die... M.cccc.lxxxx.
The phrase "sixth day of Pentecost" indicates that at this period Pentecost like Easter was still an eight day celebration or octave, as ordered by the synod of Mainz in 813. That Pentecost Sunday was reckoned the first day of the octave is clear from a comparison of the dates of the present item and #148 which was written on Trinity Sunday, i.e., 6 June 1490, and in which Schott tells us that the present item was written "day before yesterday," i.e., 4 June; since Pentecost Sunday came on 30 May in 1490, the sixth day of Pentecost was 4 June. For Schott's method of reckoning dates, cf. N. 582.

#147. TO JOHANN WIDMANN Strassburg, 4 June 1490

1071. Summary Schott again beseeches Widmann* to come to the bedside of Peter Reiffsteck* and not to be deterred by the ambiguous letter of the dean. The patient himself and Schott's parents beg Widmann to come. Susanna von Cöllen bids Widmann bring the prayer beads she at one time gave to his wife so that she may chant for the latter's welfare. On reaching Strassburg, Widmann is to come to the Schott home, where he will find a welcome awaiting him. (Cf. #145 and N. 1060).

P. 161   #147   N. 1072

1072. litteris tam ambiguis domini Decani euocatus
Cf. N. 1063.

1073. rogat te Mater ut globulos nonnullos/ seu pocius circulos oratorios...
Cf. N. 1039.

1074. nullas edes petas priusquam nostras/ quibus olim Cantor... morabatur
Cf. N. 1022.

1075. sexta feria post Penthecosten
The sixth day after Pentecost would be the same date as the sixth day of Pentecost in #146 (cf. N. 1070).

#148. TO PAULUS MALLEOLUS Strassburg, 6 June 1490

1076. Summary Believing that the present bearer might possibly reach Paris before the party of Raymund Peraudi* to whose secretary letters for Malleolus* were entrusted, Schott repeats the information of those letters. Johann Meyger* has died in Baden-Baden; on his death bed he requested that Schott be commissioned to write of his passing to Malleolus and also to urge Malleolus to return home immediately. Malleolus is asked to bring letters from Gangolf von Steinmetz,* Johann Klitsch* and also from Johann Brockingen* whose master Johann Rot* is becoming a Carthusian. (Cf. #146 and N. 1065).

1077. credidi Camerario Raymundi: Oratoris Apostolici
The word "perandi" (cf. *Errata*) presented us with an interesting problem in transcription. Beginning with a small *p* and separated from "Raymundi" by a colon, it appeared to be a present participle modifying "Oratoris Apostolici," but there is no such present participle. In the transcription from the incunabulum, we therefore suggested the emendation "operandi" which would indicate that Raymund was performing the duties of an "orator apostolicus." Not until sometime after volume I of this edition was published did our investigation disclose that the full name of Raymund is Raymund Peraudi (later von Gurk) and that the word "perandi" of our text was in fact a misprint for his surname. The same misprint occurs, incidentally, in X. Mossmann, *Cartulaire de Mulhouse* (Strassburg, Colmar, 1886), IV, 404.

The secretary to Peraudi, mentioned as carrying letters to Malleolus, may have been Jehan Alujs or Loys – also called Crassus Calaber – whom Schmidt (*H.L.*, II, 111) names as Peraudi's secretary in 1491. Hieronymus Emser held that position in 1500.

P. 162

1078. A meis Gangolifo et Ioanne Ryxingen: a Iohanne... de Brockingen...
Cf. N. 1068 and N. 1069.

1079. Dominica Trinitatis... M.cccc.lxxxx.
Trinity Sunday is the first Sunday after Pentecost; in 1490 it came on 6 June (cf. N. 1064).

#149. TO JOHANN WIDMANN Strassburg, 7 July 1490

1080. Summary Friedrich Bibliopola, despite considerable effort, has been unsuccessful in securing for Widmann's golden apple a price within the range set by Widmann.* He requests that Widmann write Schott further instructions for the apple's disposition. As Widmann advised, Schott has given the three gold pieces left with him and the book to Friedrich. Susanna von Cöllen is sending Widmann's wife more prayer beads. Schott, Sr., is in Oppenheim attending a conference for regulating weights of gold coins. Jacob Reiffsteck* is convalescing.

1081. Fridericus Bibliopola
This Friedrich has not been identified. *Bibliopola* may indicate that he was a bookseller, or a publisher ("éditeur," Ritter, *Histoire*, 116). *Bibliopola* also appears as a surname.

1082. malum illud aureum
The significance, if any, of Widmann's golden apple is not known. Gold was considered to have healing properties, and an apple of gold may thus have been a proper article for a physician to have. Johannes Bohemus in 1520 mentions the custom of giving gilded apples "mit grünem Buchs verziert" as New Year's gifts (*Handwörterbuch des deutschen Aberglaubens*, IX, 908).

1083. Mittit Mater aliam oracionum supputacionem Coniugi tue
Cf. N. 1039 for the "computation of prayers"; cf. also N. 587.

1084. Pater Reipublicae gracia abest in Oppenheym: vbi conuentus...
Regulation of weights of gold coins was very necessary at this period because of speculation with foreign coins and debasement of currency values, cf. #168 and N. 1197

1085. Audio quoque dominum Iacobum Reiffsteck conualescere: cui fratrem...
Cf. N. 1062.

1086. Magistrum Georium ex me saluere iube
Cf. N. 936.

#150. TO ADOLPH OCCO Strassburg, 10 July 1490

1087. Summary Occo, who has complained about the medical profession's being a treadmill, is assured that the life of a priest is also one of unceasing labor. Occo is urged to write the history of the Germans and their achievements, a project he had recently discussed with Geiler and Schott at Strassburg. Schott is disappointed that his little book which he had sent to Occo for perusal has been returned without corrections; he hopes for Occo's comments later.

P. 163   #150   N. 1088

1088. Incuria nimirum baiulorum factum esse conijcio nonnullas... fuerint
Cf. N. 264.

P. 164

1089. Id quod Salvator ipse demandans: Negociamini inquit dum venio
Cf. Lc. 19:13.

1090. quod lucrifaciendis animabus... quotidiana perlustracione... praescribit
Schott is referring to the daily celebration of the mass.
    Cf. *Errata* for correction to *divinorum* in 1.6. of this passage.

1091. asinarie ut ita dicam mole
Cf. Mt. 18:6 and Mr. 9:41.

1092. Animis autem quis magis idoneus erit... (to end of paragraph)
If Occo ever composed the history of the Germans discussed here or any part thereof, nothing has survived; nor to our knowledge is there any mention of such a history in other writings. To what German accomplishments (falsely claimed by non-Germans) Schott is referring we do not know. The dispute over the identity of the inventor of movable type had already begun, and it is possible that Schott may have had the invention of movable type in mind as one of the accomplishments claimed by other nations.

1093. Libellum meum/ quem nudum remisisti... castigares.
Schott may be referring to the "confectionem" which Occo had borrowed (cf. #139). For the custom of sending compositions to learned friends for correction, cf. N. 309.

P. 165

#151. TO JOHANN MÜLLER Strassburg, 24 August 1490

1094. Summary Jacob Reiffsteck* is gravely ill and not expected to survive the night. If he should die, Müller has a good chance of succeeding him in the canonicate at Old St. Peter. Müller is advised to confer with Johann Simmler,* whose turn it is to nominate the candidate for the next vacancy at Old St. Peter, and who is presently at the baths in Hub near Baden-Baden. Should Müller hear of Reiffsteck's death, he is to come to Strassburg at once. (This is the first of five letters concerning Müller and the canonicate at Old St. Peter: #151-#153, #155-#156).

1095. Intelligo nescio quo vago rumore: te in Baden redijsse...
When last mentioned in early February of 1490 (#141, p. 157) Müller with his young princeling Jacob von Baden* was in Rome. At the time this letter was being written he had indeed returned to Baden-Baden, but – as we learn from #155, p. 169 – before the letter could be delivered, he had begun a course of baths at Zellerbad (N. 192, 3), a fact which complicated the procedure of obtaining his canonicate (cf. N. 1127).

P. 165   #151   N. 1096

1096. extrema egritudine laborare dominum Iacobum Reiffsteck... visurus
Cf. N. 1062. Jacob Reiffsteck died that night or soon thereafter, for Schott on 29 August (#152, p. 166) writes of going to Reiffsteck's funeral.

1097. Itaque cum Nominacio Canonici in ecclesia sanctorum Michaelis et Petri ad Magistrum Iohannem Symler pertineat
For the method of nominating candidates for vacant benefices, cf. N. 130, 1. Saints Michael and Peter were patron saints of Old St. Peter (N. 132).

1098. in thermis propinquis vobis zur Huoben
Zur Huoben was probably an inn at the hydropathic spa Hub (mentioned by Piton, II, ii, 12) at the entrance of the Neusatz valley in Baden.

1099. Nam precibus tuis nil credimus obstare... sigillum a Cancellario...
Müller had informed Schott that papal confirmation of the *preces primae* (N. 680) had been obtained, although Strassburgers returning from Rome later than Müller declared the contrary (#153, p. 167). From this passage it appears Schott had immediately drawn up documents necessary to guarantee Müller the first vacant canonicate at Old St. Peter (N. 132). These had been signed by Bishop Albrecht,* but had not yet received the episcopal seal, as Schott felt that Müller in person might secure the seal from the episcopal chancellor Gottfried von Quickener* for less money (perhaps because Müller was poor). When Müller did not appear, Schott solicited the aid of *Markgraf* Carl von Baden,* younger brother of Jacob von Baden* and *custos* of the Strassburg cathedral chapter, who got the seal for half price (#152, p. 165).

1100. vespere Bartholomei apostoli
I. e., the evening of St. Bartholomew's Day, 24 August.

#152. TO JOHANN MÜLLER Strassburg, 29 August 1490

1101. Summary Johann Simmler* strongly supports Müller's candidacy; the documents with the episcopal seal have just arrived from Zabern; the chapter of Old St. Peter meets within the hour. There Schott will accept the nomination in Müller's name and request possession of the benefice within five days. Friends (among them Schott, Sr.) to help Müller are not lacking.
Schott has not yet decided on a change of scene [because of the plague]; indeed it seems safer to stay at home and take daily medication. The funeral services for Jacob Reiffsteck* are about to be held in St. Thomas. (This is the second of five letters concerning Müller and the canonicate at Old St. Peter, cf. N. 1094).

1102. Gaudeo non habere te aduersarium Magistrum Iohannem Symler.
Cf. N. 1094. Simmler was so staunch an advocate for Müller that he returned prematurely from the baths (an unusual and at certain stages dangerous act, cf. N. 192) to support his candidacy; then he again sought the baths (#153 and N. 1109).

1103. processus tuus... Zaberniam misi... Cancellarius viginti pecijt.
Cf. N. 1099. Zabern (modern Saverne) – at the foot of the Vosges and about

P. 165   #152   N. 1103

20 miles from Strassburg – was, from the thirteenth century on, the official residence of the bishop of Strassburg. Of old Zabern only the parish church remains; the present episcopal palace dates from the eighteenth century. On a nearby lofty eminence overlooking the valley are the ruins of Hoh-Barr (Haut Barr), the bishop's fortress-palace, dating from the time of Barbarossa.

P. 166

1104. Restat ut post acceptacionem... possessionem tradant intra sex dies.
For election procedure, cf. N. 130 and N. 1134. Possession of the canonicate was not official until 5 September, there having been delay in securing necessary papers from Müller (cf. #153, #155).

1105. Et te cura: ne quid deterius contingat... tamen ocijssime.
Schott is referring here to the severe outbreak of the plague in 1490 (N. 59, 3). The medication he was taking might have been plague powders such as Susanna von Cöllen on one occasion sent to Müller (#177, p. 198).

1106. vocor ad exequias: domini Iacobi in ecclesia sancti Thome...
Jacob Reiffsteck,* being canon and *custos* of St. Thomas (N. 337) as well as canon of Old St. Peter, was being buried from the more important church where he held the higher office.

#153. TO JOHANN MÜLLER Strassburg, 1 September 1490

1107. Summary In considerable detail Schott describes how he, his father and Johann Simmler* campaigned among the canons of Old St. Peter to have Müller unanimously accepted. The chapter has promised possession of the benefice as soon as certain matters have been settled, such as 1) producing four guarantors – two of whom are laymen and two clerics; 2) taking the oath of allegiance to the chapter; 3) paying the fee for the canonicate; 4) informing Maximilian of the honoring of his *preces primae* for Old St. Peter so that he will not reissue such *preces* to another aspirant. Unless Müller can come to Strassburg immediately, he is to send a mandate giving Schott fuller powers as procurator than the old mandate allows, so he (Schott) may act as Müller's proxy in all matters. In case Müller has no notary readily accessible, Schott sends a draft of the five clauses which must be included in the mandate. (This is the third of five letters concerning Müller's canonicate at Old St. Peter, cf. N. 1094, N. 1101).

1108. octo enim successiue Canonici ambiendi... quod exemplo carebant (paragraph 3)
Jacob Reiffsteck had died in August, a month in which chapters did not officially have the right to fill vacancies, yet the chapter procedure of nominating was observed here (N. 130). In the case of a candidate who had *preces primae*, nominations apparently could proceed as follows. The canon whose turn it was to nominate the candidate for the vacant canonicate had the right to ignore the holder of the *preces primae* and name some one of his own choice. If, however, he was willing to honor the *preces* and pledge his support to the "royal" candidate, he was said technically to abstain from nominating, whereby he lost his turn to nominate and the second canon in or-

der was allowed to nominate. If the latter also abstained, then the third canon in order was allowed to nominate and so on to the last canon on the list.

There were at this time in Old St. Peter eight canons registered to nominate in turn; each of these eight had to be dissuaded from nominating in turn, and of his own free will had to pledge support to Müller, so that Müller might be unanimously elected, thus avoiding any possible wrangling or subsequent litigation, such as plagued the Wolfs (cf. N. 334). It was by eloquence, influence and respect for their judgment that the Schotts and Simmler won the chapter members. There was no coercion through fear of reprisals from Maximilian, a procedure Schott denounces in a letter to Gottfried von Adelsheim (#185, p. 204). Indeed, Schott comments that Müller's *preces primae* were the first in the Strassburg diocese to have been accepted with unanimous vote peaceably.

1109. Verum adiutus es beniuolencia... Magistri Iohannis Symler... redijt.
Cf. N. 1102. That Simmler used his considerable influence not only as canon of Old St. Peter but also as (acting?) dean of St. Thomas and episcopal official to support Müller was a tribute to the Schotts and Müller.

1110. Erat siquidem difficilius postremos auertere quam primos... egerunt
The canons whose names were at the end of the list of those empowered to nominate in turn were more difficult to win for Müller, because – presumably holding canonicates in no other church where they might have a turn at nominating – they felt if they gave up this unexpected turn, their chances of living long enough to have another were very slim. In an earlier letter to Müller Schott tells of sexagenarians who had never had a turn to nominate (#84, p. 92).

The period after *ut ceteri* does not end the sentence, for *ceteri* is the subject of *egerunt*. Apparently, when electing Reiffsteck's successor in his canonicate at St. Thomas, canons at St. Thomas who had won the chance of nominating by abstention of those prior to them on the list had refused to give up their turn.

1111. Equidem heri late declaraui: quis sis... promisi te recessurum...
Müller was relatively unknown in the city of Strassburg; it was therefore necessary for Schott to acquaint those concerned about the canonicate with Müller's qualifications, character, etc. Schott was particularly emphatic about the fact that Müller would be in residence and would carry his share of chapter duties; cf. N. 130, 5 for the deleterious effect of absenteeism.

1112. quatuor alios duos scilicet eccliasticos... Mandatum non habeo.
Requiring candidates for benefices to furnish guarantors was one method adopted by chapters to protect themselves from damages incurred through friction or litigation among contestants for a benefice (cf. N. 130, 1). Schott had held a mandate from Müller since at least 1487 (#103, p. 113) and had been acting as procurator for him since at least 1486 (#87, p. 95), but the mandate was not inclusive enough to cover all eventualities (#155, p. 169).

P. 167   #153   N. 1113

1113. de confirmacione precum istarum: per sedem Apostolicam... (in following paragraph) *bis ecclesia a Rege grauaretur...*
For details concerning Müller's *preces primae* from Maximilian, cf. N. 680. The chapter members of Old St. Peter stressed the necessity of informing Maximilian that they had obeyed the *preces primae* issued to Müller; since they were not convinced that these *preces* had really received papal confirmation, they feared Maximilian could reissue *preces primae* for their church to another aspirant who might obtain speedy papal confirmation, and thus burden their church with two royal candidates. Such reissues were perhaps not uncommon, considering that there were aspirants to benefices who held *preces primae* for several churches, as did Gottfried von Adelsheim, Jr. (N. 1313); if such aspirants did not use one or more of the *preces*, then Maximilian could give new *preces primae* for the church concerned to some one else.

P. 168

1114. Secundo ad solitum iuramentum... Tercio ad satisfaciendum iuxta...
For the procedure of installing new canons, cf. N. 1134. At the time of installation, chapter fees were payable; Schott paid 24 florins for his own canonicate (p. xxvii) and 29 for Müller's (#156, p. 171).

#154. TO CRATO HOFFMANN   Strassburg, 3 September 1490

1115. Summary Schott is flattered that Hoffmann* has asked him for medicinal information and herbs, but he does not claim sufficient knowledge to prescribe. He is enclosing descriptions of herbs, and he comments on the provenience of fuller's herb of which he will dispatch samples when available. He promises to compose an epitaph for Ludwig Dringenberg.* (Cf. p. xxiv, N. 82).

1116. Vrsulam de Dunçenheim matronam honestissimam
Ursula von Dunzenheim is mentioned in connection with herbs #140, p. 156. Cf. N. 1041.

P. 169

1117. Primo conscriptas acori condiciones...
Acorus, yellow lily, is described thus by Beck (xxi): "...Spatella/ Glaspatella/ oder Venerea... Galienus... sagt die Wurzeln von den gelen lilien mer krafft haben dann das krut oder die pluomen." Tea from the root is good for chills and pleurisy; the infusion of ground root boiled with vinegar – when strained and mixed with honey – is good for the liver.

1118. Doctor Thubingensis... Magistro Theodorico Argentine
I. e., Johann Widmann* and Theodorich Ribysen,* respectively.

1119. quae de puluere Materno tibi constent
As we have found no mention in herbologies of a powder by the name of *pulver maternus*, we are inclined to believe that Schott means a powder com-

P. 169   #154   N. 1119

pounded by his mother Susanna von Cöllen. It is quite possible that this powder is the same as that which Susanna sent to Müller during the plague epidemic in Paris in the fall of 1484 (#177, p. 198). If so, then Hoffmann's interest in the powder at this time (1490) is understandable because of the outbreak of the plague (cf. N. 59, 3). Hoffmann as the director of the school at Schlettstadt (N. 88) would be anxious about his charges.

1120. herbam Cardonis Benedicti... Herbam fullonum memini...
For *cardo Benedictus* Beck (cxvii) has the following information: "Bornwurtz... grece erigon sive erígéron... Galienus spricht das diss krauts natur sey uffthuon die verstopfften glider im leib und durchdringt und macht wol harnen." The plant flowers biennially in September, hence Susanna von Cöllen could expect a new supply of the herb to be sent her from Barr very soon. As Schott explains at the end of the paragraph this herb is sometimes called *herba fullonum* or fuller's herb; another name is *dispacus fullonum* or teasel. The spiney hooks of the teasel head have been used in fulling mills or wool factories since time immemorial for pulling up the nap on wool and felt; only recently have plastic substitutes been developed.

1121. Minorum Conuentus sancti Vdalrici prope Barr
The small Franciscan monastery of St. Ulrich near Barr in the hills was built in 1283. Here in 1480 was held the convention of Franciscans of the Strassburg diocese. The monks were driven from the monastery in 1543.
   Cf. *Anal. Francisc.*, II, 470. Barth, *Handbuch*, 102f.

1122. Sebastiano Apothecario... Conradum vxoremque eius. Item Coniugem tuam.
Neither the apothecary Sebastian, presumably of Strassburg, nor Conrad, who may have been a teacher at the Schlettstadt School, nor yet the ladies mentioned have been identified.

1123. Ludouicus Dringenbergius Vuestualus praecoeptor meus: cui epitaphion...
Schott died before he could keep his promise to write an epitaph for his former master at Schlettstadt, Ludwig Dringenberg. Only his preoccupation with Müller's canonicate at Old. St Peter and his own illness followed by sudden death (nine days after writing this letter, cf. N. 59, par. 8) could have kept him from paying his last respects to Dringenberg.

#155. TO JOHANN MÜLLER   Strassburg, 3 September 1490

1124. Summary Having just learned that Müller is at the baths in Zellerbad and fearing that earlier letters have not reached him, Schott repeats not only his injunction of the foregoing letter (that Müller send immediately a mandate giving him all powers necessary for effecting possession of the canonicate at Old St. Peter) but also the content of the clauses to be included in the mandate. The guarantors, the chapter, the money for fees – all are ready and waiting. In the postscript Schott adds that he has heard through a certain vicar about Simmler's* returning from the baths the next day to support Müller. Schott himself has not yet been able to gain his parents' approval on going to the baths, particularly in this fall season. (This is the fourth of five letters concerning Müller's canonicate at Old St. Peter; cf. N. 1094, N. 1101, N. 1107).

P. 169   #155   N. 1125

1125. Balneacio coepta ut salubrior sit... Cellense balneum petiuisses...
Cf. N. 1095. The chapter's readiness to give unanimous obedience to Müller's *preces primae* was, Schott believed, a bath gift from the Lord to Müller. For Zellerbad and the popularity of bath gifts, cf. N. 192. Cf. also N. 935.

P. 170

1126. Vix enim in tanta rerum ambiguitate... ut hac promissione contentarentur.
Cf. N. 1113.

1127. Quamobrem vellem: si non fuisset sanitati aduersum: teipsum personaliter praesenciam ostendisse.
Müller's presence in Strassburg would have facilitated matters. He could have vouched for the confirmation of his *preces primae*; the chapter members could have become acquainted with him; Schott would not have needed special powers to act as proxy, etc. Having just begun the regimen of the baths, however, Müller dared not interrupt it, a fact everyone involved in the election seemed to accept without question. For bath regimen, cf. N. 192, 2.

1128. Dominum doctorem Hieronymum meis verbis saluere iube.
I. e., Hieronymus Brunschwig.*

1129. Vicedecanus et Capitulum ecclesie sancti Petri senioris
The vice-dean of Old St. Peter has not been identified.

P. 171

1130. Magistrum Iohannem Symler... venturum se hodie Argentinam... (end of paragraph)
From the message sent to Schott by the chapter of Old St. Peter it appears that Johann Simmler – his interrupted regimen of baths now apparently completed – was returning to Strassburg on 3 September with the intention of nominating Johann Müller for the vacant canonicate. Perhaps Simmler feared that if he accepted the *preces primae* and abstained from nominating according to the plan described in #153, the other canons could not be trusted to do likewise (N. 1108). Judging, however, from the hurried proceedings (N. 1132 and N. 1133) when Schott in Müller's name took possession of the canonicate (#156, p. 171), the method of election had become immaterial.

1131. De balneis non est: quod a Parentibus sperem impetrare: praesertim...
Schott's parents seem to have felt it was unwise to go to the baths at this time of year when an epidemic of the plague was taking its toll everywhere (cf. N. 1105).

#156. TO JOHANN MÜLLER Strassburg, 6 September 1490

1132. Summary Müller's mandate has arrived on this date, 6 September.

Before its arrival, however, Schott, had heard that a certain legate planned to claim the canonicate before Müller could take possession – a dangerous situation which could explode into litigation. By pledging to deliver the mandate as soon as possible he had therefore persuaded the chapter to install him as Müller's proxy on the previous day, 5 September. He names the guarantors he has secured for Müller and mentions details about the canonicate still needing attention. He was very ill during the previous night, and his parents are worried. (This is the last of five letters concerning Müller's canonicate at Old St. Peter; cf. N. 1094, N. 1101, N. 1107, N. 1124).

1133. Perferebatur enim ad me properatum esse... litis conflatam fore.
Since the benefice fell vacant in August, a month when the pope had the right to fill vacancies, the claimant of the canonicate at Old St. Peter may have held a papal *gratia*. The chapter, faced with a possible dilemma of having both a royal and a papal candidate vying for the vacancy, hastened to install Müller (i.e., by proxy).

1134. Sicque factum est ut heri die Dominico post prandium... numerauerim.
Stein, p. 13, cites a contemporary description of the formal election procedure at New St. Peter in Strassburg in the year 1450; one may assume that the procedure at Old St. Peter in Schott's day was very similar. Before the assembled chapter, in the presence of the notary, the canon whose turn it was to nominate the candidate for the vacancy made his nomination and asked the chapter to allow the *electio* and *receptio* to proceed. Then the newly elected canon made a speech of acceptance and of thanks. Thereupon in the presence of the notary and several witnesses he was presented to the *praepositus* who was requested to authorize the election and invest the new canon. After formal investiture was effected by presentation of the canonical cap, the new canon took his oath before the assembled chapter, promised obedience to the dean and paid 10 guilders. Lastly the *praepositus* bade one of the canons show the newcomer his place in the choir and in the chapter seating (cf. N. 116, 2).

1135. Magister Melchior kungsbach: Dominus Petrus Mug... id agere non potuerunt.
Melchior Kungsbach,* Peter Müg, Jr.,* Jacob Müg, Sr.,* Eucharius Voeltsch* were Müller's guarantors; Kungsbach and Peter Müg being the two clerics, Jacob Müg and Voeltsch the two laymen (cf. N. 1107). Of the incident which had occurred two years previously and now prevented Schott, Sr., from acting as guarantor we know nothing. It had been difficult for Schott to find guarantors because many of those close to him were away at the fair – possibly at Frankfurt (cf. N. 301), or had left town on account of the plague (N. 1105). With the exception of Kungsbach, the guarantors were Schott's relatives by marriage.

1136. Supererit modo ut Notarijs multorum Actuum... pereat.
Schott's unfinished tasks in connection with Müller's canonicate may have included composing the letter to inform Maximilian that the chapter of Old St. Peter had obeyed the *preces primae* issued to Müller. It is, of course, possible that with the mandate Müller had sent absolute proof of papal

confirmation of the *preces*, in which case no letter would have been necessary (cf. N. 1113).

The terms "fructus" and "proventus grossi" concerned Müller's income from the benefice and sums of money paid quarterly by the chapter, or produce – such as grain, wine and fruit – apportioned by the chapter to benefice holders at the harvest season (cf. N. 116).

Obviously a year of residence was not mandatory for drawing income from benefices at Old St. Peter (cf. N. 130, 4), possibly because Old St. Peter, being the least important of the collegiate churches in Strassburg and its benefices being therefore less sought after, did not suffer too much from absenteeism. New St. Peter, as we know from Schott, required a year of residence (N. 373).

1137. Ego quidem hac tota nocte sudoribus stillaui... meliora sperens.
Symptoms of Schott's illness may have begun as early as 29 August when he mentions taking medication (#152, p. 166, and N. 1105). By 6 September, as he was writing this passage to Müller, he was really ill. Six days later, on 12 September he died (cf. N. 57-N. 59). The present item and the one following to Johann Goetz* are Schott's last dated letters.

#157. TO JOHANN GOETZ Strassburg, 6 September 1490

1138. Summary Having learned from Geiler of Goetz'* desire for a post in Strassburg, Schott informs Goetz that the parish priest of New St. Peter is leaving to become vicar in Zabernia Montana and will have to be replaced. If Goetz is interested in the post, he is to advise Schott within three weeks. The post is a good one and has formerly been held by such persons as the present prior of the Knights of St. John of Jerusalem and Melchior Kungsbach. (This is Schott's last dated letter; cf. N. 35).

1139. Magistro Iohanni Goeçoni Augustensi amico singulari
This is the Johann Goetz* whom Schott wished Wimpheling to recommend for advanced study at Heidelberg (#120, p. 139). It is likely that Goetz obtained the post of parish priest at New. St Peter, for he is known to have been a priest in Strassburg.

1140. Interea auxilio magistrorum Andree Hartmanni: et Iohannis Symler...
Andreas Hartmann* and Johann Simmler,* being episcopal officials, would have some jurisdiction over posts such as those of parish priests.

1141. Iacobus nunc Iohannitarum Prior
The prior of the Strassburg monastery of the Knights of St. John the Baptist of Jerusalem (Knights of Malta) has not been identified. The order had been in Strassburg for at least two centuries. In 1371 the Strassburg banker Rulmann Merswin gave to the order the island Grünenworth in the Ill river outside the city walls. Here was built the monastery "zum Grünenworth." In Geiler's and Schott's day this was a peaceful retreat, possessing a fine library particularly rich in the works of the mystics. In 1766 the monastery with its hospital became the district prison.

Cf. Barth, *Handbuch*, 1393-1397. Schmidt, *Chapitre*, 243.

P. 173　　#158　　N. 1142

#158. TO CARDINAL ST. VITALIS [Strassburg, 5 April 1482]

1142. Summary The cardinal's support is requested for the petition to be presented to the pope on behalf of Peter Schott, citizen of Strassburg. By granting his support the cardinal will be doing the entire republic of Strassburg a favor for which the Strassburgers will consider themselves most indebted to him.

1143. Date Items #158-#160 are letters written by Schott in the name of the Strassburg magistracy to solicit support in obtaining the papal *gratia* by virtue of which he became canon at New St. Peter in Strassburg, 22 April 1482. These items and #161 – the letter to Sixtus IV which accompanied the petition for the *gratia* – undoubtedly date from the same time as #32 – the letter of 5 April 1482 soliciting Kemel's support (cf. N. 343); indeed, all the items mentioned were probably sent with the same messenger to Rome; cf. N. 116, 1.

1144. Cardinali Sancti Vitalis
Ferricus de Cluniaco,* Cardinal St. Vitalis.

1145. Ad eius rei promocionem... Reuerendissimam Vestram Paternitatem quam...
Cf. *Errata.*

P. 174

#159. TO COUNT HIERONYMUS [Strassburg, 5 April 1482]

1146. Summary The count's intercession for Peter Schott, citizen of Strassburg, is requested when the petition for a *gratia* is presented to the pope. For this favor the city council and people of Strassburg will be greatly indebted. (Cf. N. 1143).

1147. Comiti Hieronymo N(ostro)
For *N*, cf. N. 181. The count in question is the favored nephew of Sixtus IV, Hieronymus de Im(m)ola* (Girolamo Riario). Cf. N. 189 and N. 940.

1148. que ut ad optatam cedat impetracionem...
The antecedent of *que* seems to be *peticio*. Is *que* perhaps a misprint for *qui*, referring to *Pape*? The latter reading would make better sense.

#160. TO A CARDINAL [Strassburg, 5 April 1482)]

1149. Summary The cardinal's support is requested for the petition which will be presented to the pope on behalf of a very learned man, dear to the Strassburgers. For such a favor the magistracy of Strassburg will be the cardinal's obedient servants. (Cf. N. 1143).

P. 174   #160   N. 1150

1150. Cardinali N(ostro).
For *N*, cf. N. 181. The cardinal to whom the letter is addressed may be Marcus Barbus,* Cardinal of St. Mark, who in 1471 was commissioned cardinal in charge of affairs in the Holy Roman Empire and Hungary.

P. 175

1151. sanctissimum Dominum Nostrum
The incunabulum has the abbreviation *D. N.*; here *N.* is obviously a form of *noster*, for Sixtus IV was indeed *dominus noster* to the church hierarchy (cf. f. LXXXXIXa, where *sanctissimi Domini nostri* is written in full; cf. N. 181).

#161. TO POPE SIXTUS IV [Strassburg, 5 April 1482]

1152. Summary The pope is requested to grant the petition presented on behalf of a very worthy man, distinguished by learning and high moral character. Should the pope favor their petition, the magistracy of Strassburg will be bound to the Holy See by even stronger ties than by the obedience they and their forebears have always shown. (Cf. N. 1143).

P. 176

#162. TO THE MAGISTRATES AND CONSULS OF STRASSBURG FROM OLIVIER CARAFFA
[Rome, before 17 October 1485]

1153. Summary Procurator Johann Rot* has disclosed to us how – having been falsely accused of libel by Elisabeth and Conrad Dunzenheim* and having learned that the Strassburg city council had ordered officers to seize him in his bed by night – he fled to Rome. He has with difficulty been restrained from prostrating himself before the pope to appeal for protection – an act which would involve public exposure of the entire scandalous affair. For the sake of avoiding litigation and keeping the peace, the city of Strassburg is requested to settle the case amicably between these its citizens.

1154. Date This item and the reply to it (#163) concern the libel case of Elisabeth and Conrad Dunzenheim against the procurator Johann Rot. The present item states the case from the side of Rot, the reply states the case from the side of the Dunzenheims and the city of Strassburg. The date of this item must be sometime before 17 October 1485, because one of the co-drafters of the item, Johannes de Aragonia,* cardinal of Aragon (N. 1155), died on that day.
    The reply (#163) must have been written shortly after the Strassburgers received the present item and must have borne the date 1485, as is evident from statements in the reply: 1) that the Strassburg magistracy was rendering prompt obedience to the communication from Rome (cf. the salutation and the first line thereafter, p. 177); 2) that the Dunzenheims had brought libel charges against procurator Johann Rot in the previous year when Conrad Dunzenheim was mayor of Strassburg (cf. p. 178). From Strassburg city records we know that Dunzenheim was mayor in 1484.

1155. Oliuier Episcopus Sabinensis... Aquilananus Episcopus Sacerdos
There are three co-drafters of this letter: 1) Olivier Caraffa,* Cardinal Neapolitanus; 2) Johannes de Aragonia,* Cardinal de Aragonia; 3) Ludovicus (cf. *Errata*) de Burses,* bishop of Aquila. Only after identification of the person who was bishop of Aquila in 1485, was it clear that the initial *L.* in the incunabulum was meant for the name Ludovicus and not as usual for the classical name Lucius.

1156. Magistrociuium et Consulibus Ciuitatis Argentinensis
I.e., to the mayor and the city council of Strassburg (cf. N. 420).

1157. Magister Iohannes Rot conciuis vester et familiaris noster
This Johann Rot* was procurator of the Strassburg ecclesiastical court and as such was well known at the *Curia* in Rome. He is not to be confused with the cleric Johann Rot* who studied with Schott at Paris and is mentioned so often in Schott's letters. The procurator Rot who was involved in the libel case with the Dunzenheims had a wife and children (#163, p. 179); he could, therefore, neither have served as preacher of the cathedral in Geiler's absence nor as parish priest in the cathedral chapel of St. Laurentius; he could not have been appointed episcopal vicar in matters of penitence. His character is not that of a man whom Geiler and Schott would have chosen as an intimate friend, or whom Friedrich von Zollern would have invited to attend his coronation, or of whom Schott would have written to Maeler: "si innocenciam/ mores/ et doctrinam viri nouisses" (#179, p. 200).

That there could be two Johann Rots with the title "magister" in Strassburg at the same time is not at all surprising, because both Johann and Rot were (and are) common names. Toepke (407) lists a Johannes Rot from Strassburg, cleric of the Strassburg diocese, as receiving the baccalaureate degree in 1495; this is obviously a different Johann Rot from the two mentioned above.

1158. Elisabeth de Dunçenheim... Conrado Dunçenheim Magistro Scabinorum
We have found no information about Elisabeth Dunzenheim, or of her relationship to Conrad Dunzenheim. The term "magister scabinorum" means mayor (cf. N. 69).

1159. Cognito quod a magnificencijs vestris preconi vestri... irrupcione
The late Latin *praeconus, i,* must have existed beside the classical *praeco, onis,* although we have not found *praeconus* listed in any lexicographical works.

As Schott remarks in the reply to this item (N. 1161), the incident of Rot's being almost apprehended in his own bed was pure fabrication. Strassburg did not accord such treatment to its citizens; indeed, its citizens received preferential treatment when involved in cases with foreigners (cf. #187, p. 206, and N. 1328).

1160. Ipsumque ad pedes sanctissimi Domini nostri
In 1485 the pope was Innocent VIII.

P. 177   #163   N. 1161

P. 177

#163. TO OLIVIER CARAFFA [Strassburg, 1485 (after the date of #162)]

1161. Summary Strassburg and the city council of Strassburg have been unjustly accused by the procurator Johann Rot,* and there was no neccessity of his fleeing Strassburg or of seeking help in Rome. In the previous year Conrad Dunzenheim* and his relative Elisabeth had come before the city council and told how Johann Rot had not only heaped execrable maledictions upon Elisabeth - calling her among other things a woman of loose morals, but had also termed Conrad a rascal and a good-for-nothing. When charged with such imprecations, Rot had denied having uttered them. The Dunzenheims then brought a libel suit against Rot and produced witnesses. They wanted Rot imprisoned until the case was ended, but the state considered that as a citizen with a wife and family living in Strassburg, Rot's oath that he would not remove himself or his family or his possessions from Strassburg was security enough. His story of being threatened with arrest in bed is pure fabrication. If the state had wished to arrest him, it could have done so at any time during the day. Indeed, had Rot been imprisoned, the present situation would not have arisen!

Obeying the injunction of the cardinal to bring about an amicable settlement, the magistracy approached the Dunzenheims with the suggestion of dropping the suit, but they feel their honor and reputation has without cause been too sullied not to demand full satisfaction. Therefore, if Rot agrees, the state of Strassburg proposes that the suit be tried at one of these three courts: Ulm, Colmar, or Schlettstadt, whichever Rot may choose. He is to come to the town chosen and remain there until the suit is ended. Thereafter, whatever the verdict, he may return to Strassburg without fear of the Dunzenheims, their adherents, or any one else in Strassburg. (Cf. N. 1153 and N. 1154).

P. 178

1162. Dominum vero Conradum de Dunçenheim: ea tempestate Magistrum Scabinorum
Cf. N. 1158.

1163. per Prothonotarium vrbis nostre diligentissime conscripta.
The clerk of the court was probably Udalrich Stromeiger, Sr.,* whose young son was involved in a scrape with the boy canon Thomas Wolf, Jr.; cf. #48, p. 52, and N. 442.

P. 180

1164. Quare si Magistro Iohanni in vno opidorum qua nominauimus... seclusis.
To our knowledge there is no record of this case in the Strassburg archives. It is possible that Rot withdrew his accusations made in Rome or that the case was tried in one of the cities specified.

#164. TO PETER SCHOTT FROM JOHANN ORTWIN [Strassburg, late 1481-*ca.* April 1482]

1165. Summary Johann Ortwin,* suffragan bishop of Strassburg, is sending a copy of Thomas Aquinas' *De Malo* and asks Schott to discuss the relative merits of Aquinas' and Scotus' answers to the question whether demons perceive man's thoughts.

1166. Date This letter, Schott's answer (#165) and Ortwin's second letter (#166) form a unit. It may be assumed that these letters date from the period late 1481 to April 1482 when Schott – fresh from Bologna and at loose ends – was attending sermons and lectures in Strassburg, before he obtained his canonicate at New. St. Peter (p. xxvii). Ortwin, a professor of theology, no doubt was lecturing at the Strassburg Dominican monastery (of which he was prior). The assumption that the letters date from this period is strengthened by the fact that Ortwin, though punctilious and pompous, does not address Schott as either canon or priest although he repeatedly calls Schott *doctor* and comments on the latter's learning.

Note that Ortwin in his letters uses the formal form of address, i.e., the second person plural, while young Schott replies with the familiar second person singular; cf. N. 184 and #9, p. 15.

1167. Iohannes Episcopus Mathoniensis... Ordinis Praedicatorum
Suffragan bishops were given titles of extinct bishoprics *in partibus infidelium*. Hence Ortwin, suffragan bishop of Strassburg, had the title of bishop of Matho (Modon, Medone, Methoni) in the Pelopennesus of Greece which was at that time in the hands of the Turks. (It was when anchored off the coast of Modon that Hassenstein on his odyssey composed a letter about his trip; cf. N. 1056).

1168. sancti Thome doctoris vobis transmittere scripta: in quibus veritatem...
The reference is to St. Thomas Aquinas, O.P. (*ca.* 1227-1274). Ortwin, being a Dominican, was a staunch supporter of Aquinas, i.e., a Thomist, and an adversary of Scotus, the Franciscan (N. 1170 below).

1169. testante Aristotele sumno philosophorum in duo decimo Methaphisice
Cf. Aristotle *Metaphisica* XII, iv, A and B.

1170. Quod autem Thomas Scotho sit cercior probant preinducta
Johannes Duns Scotus, O.F.M. (1265/75-1308), whose followers were known as Scotists, had disagreed with Aquinas (N. 1168) on many subjects, including the immaculate conception of the Virgin Mary; cf. N. 1702, par. 3.

1171. Infert enim sancta mater Ecclesia... adhesisse comprobantur.
The phrase *sancta mater Ecclesia* refers to the books of canon law. The term *corpus iuris canonici* was not used to designate canonical law until 1671 when an edition printed at Lyons carried that title.

Friedberg's 1959 unrevised reprint of *Corpus iuris canonici* (Leipzig,

P. 181   #164   N. 1171

1879) has several readings differing slightly with the quotation from *Decreti*, prima pars, dist. xx, c. i., as it appears in Ortwin's letter: for *videntur esse* Friedberg (Col. 65) has *esse videntur*; for *Plerique* Friedberg has *Plurimi*, but gives *plerique* as an alternate reading; for *comprobantur* Friedberg has *probantur*.

1172. Quis autem illorum duorum doctorum... testimonium dat sancta mater... Thomas Aquinas, argues Ortwin, speaks with the authority of the Church and canon law, because he was canonized (by John XXII on 18 July 1323). Also Innocent VI (1352-1362) declared it heresy to attack Aquinas' works: "he who dare assail it will always be suspected of error." Aquinas' epithets *doctor angelicus, doctor sanctus, doctor illuminatus et sublimis*, and *doctor universalis* reflect the reverent attitude toward him (cf. N. 1537).

P. 182

1173. Ideo hic mitto questiones sancti Thome de malo intitilatas Schmidt (*Bibliotheken*, 22) believes the copy of St. Thomas Aquinas, *De malo*, belonged to the library of the Strassburg Dominicans.

1174. et omnes qui vobis cohabitant I.e., Schott's family, for Schott lived with his parents (cf. N. 116, paragraph 7).

#165. TO JOHANN ORTWIN [Strassburg, late 1481-*ca*. April 1482, after #164]

1175. Summary In answer to Ortwin's request Schott has read Aquinas' work and summarizes his findings about the relative merits of Aquinas' and Scotus' words concerning demons perceiving man's thoughts: both Aquinas and Scotus agree that demons or bad angels cannot see the thoughts of man, but they disagree on the reasons for this phenomenon; Aquinas says demons are by nature incapable of seeing man's voluntary thoughts, while Scotus says bad angels are capable of seeing man's thoughts but are not permitted to do so. Schott then discusses implications in Scotus' statement: what about good angels, he asks, who are in perfect beatitude and not prohibited by evil nature, do they not see man's thoughts? Schott also questoins Aquinas' assumption that thoughts must be voluntary: what about evil thoughts, he queries, which come to us and, because we reject them, are not considered mortal sins; or what about thoughts we have in our sleep, which no one could assert are voluntary? Furthermore, he argues, even if one accepts the thesis that thoughts are voluntary, it is not clear why an angel – once God has moved man's will to think – cannot perceive the thought. Nor, he avers, is Aquinas' simile valid when he says that an angel can no more perceive man's thoughts than can a *praepositus* know immediately what action the king takes respecting a citizen; if the *praepositus* is present, Schott claims, he can perceive everything and just so must an angel present perceive man's thoughts. (This is the second of three letters between Ortwin and Schott on the same topic, cf. N. 1166).

1176. Recepi... questiones de malo doctoris Sancti Cf. N. 1172 and N. 1173.

1177. inter precipuos duarum theologicarum acierum Duces: ipse ego... nomine
Not having had advanced training in theology, Schott did not consider himself versed in theological writings (cf. N. 121, paragraph 2, and N. 556), certainly not enough to judge between the founder of the Thomists, Thomas Aquinas, and the founder of the Scotists, Johannes Duns Scotus (N. 1168 and N. 1170).

1178. quandoquidem eius in docendo auctoritatem extollis: cui Innocencius...
Cf. N. 1172.

1179. Imprimis siquidem quantum ego capio: beatus Thomas in eo loco/ quem... Scothus in quarto distinctione
Schott is referring a) to the passage marked by Ortwin in St. Thomas Aquinas, *De malo*, and b) to definite passages in Johannes Duns Scotus' works, probably the commentary on the four books of the Sentences by Peter Lombard, the so-called founder of scholasticism. *Sed dicit Magister* (below) refers to Scotus.

1180. In hoc itaque cum vtriusque mentem intuear...
From Schott's comments in this paragraph and the three paragraphs following, it is rather obvious that he cared little for the involved argumentation of scholasticism and felt no qualms in showing that both Aquinas' and Scotus' writings were often illogical and obscure. In the case of Aquinas such an attitude was indeed temerarious, especially since Schott was addressing his criticism of St. Thomas to Ortwin who was a zealous Thomist and a reactionary Dominican, as well as suffragan bishop of Strassburg.

1181. Quid ergo dicemus de angelis bonis? quos non est... tribuunt.
Thomas von Strassburg in his commentary on the four books of the Sentences by Peter Lombard discusses the question of whether angels can perceive the thoughts of man (1i. ii, dist. 7, art. 2; dist. 8, art. 8 to dist. 11). An angel knows our mind, says Thomas von Strassburg, for just as an angel has sense for the sensible, so he has intellect for the intelligible. St. Augustine's words, that it is not possible for an angel to see man's thoughts, pertain to intentions, affirmative or negative. As far as the nature of our acts and their obvious purpose are concerned, nothing prohibits an angel from knowing our thoughts. "Secunda conclusio est quod cogitationes nostras quantum ad affirmationes et negationes per se et determinate cognoscere non potest. Cognoscit tamen vt plurimum eas indirecte ex aliquibus signis in corporibus nostris apparentibus" (Schott's edition of Thomas de Argentina, *Scripta...*, I, folio D6 b).

#166. TO PETER SCHOTT FROM JOHANN ORTWIN [Strassburg, late 1481-*ca*. April 1482, after #165]

1182. Summary Ortwin sweeps aside Scotus' statements about angels' knowing man's thoughts. He attempts to answer Schott's queries with

P. 185   #166   N. 1182

scholastic arguments which only introduce extraneous issues and fail to settle anything. (This is the third of three letters on the same subject, cf. N. 1166).

1183. cum vtriusque Doctoris dicta nuclealiter intueor...
Ortwin is referring to the words of Schott who was *doctor utriusque iuris*.

1184. Si absolute permittatur quicumque Angelus etc.
In this paragraph and in each of the following paragraphs Ortwin takes up specific points in Schott's letter, pp. 183f.

1185. Item de mysterijs gracie... iuxta beatum Augustinum secundo super Genesi ad litteram.
Cf. St. Augustine, *De genesi ad litteram*, 2. 16-19.

P. 186

#167. TO POPE INNOCENT VIII [Strassburg, after 5 July 1488]

1186. Summary Schott, in the name of the chapter of the Strassburg cathedral, beseeches the pope to confirm the chapter's election on 5 July of Johann, *Freiherr* von Brandis,* to the deanship, a post vacant for two years. Should the pope have promised this post to another aspirant, the chapter requests that such a person be placed elsewhere, because – according to chapter statutes approved by preceding popes – the dean must be elected by the chapter from its member canons and must be in residence.

1187. Date The approximate date of this item is indicated by two statements in the item: that the post of dean had been vacant for two years and that the chapter had elected Johann Brandis to the post 5 July of the current year. Since Friedrich von Zollern,* the former dean, had left for Augsburg in 1486, the chapter must have elected his successor on 5 July 1488.

1188. Vacauit iam biennio... Decanatus dignitas in ecclesia nostra...
The post of dean at the Strassburg cathedral had remained vacant for two years, because both the Roman *Curia* and the cathedral chapter claimed the right to fill the vacancy. The chapter's election of Johann von Brandis did not end the contest, for the pope refused to confirm the election and insisted that the chapter accept his candidate Hoyer (Hieronymus), *Graf* von Barby Mulingen, even though Barby was not at that time a canon of the Strassburg cathedral.
Cf. N. 130, 3. Schmidt, "Notices... P.S.," 321. Stenzel, 86ff.
During the years of vacancy, the office of dean was administered by vice-dean Heinrich von Hennenberg,* a staunch supporter of Barby. In 1491, three years after the abortive election, the chapter was forced to yield and to install Hoyer von Barby as dean. That Barby was in every way unworthy of his office is evident from a scathing letter Geiler wrote to him. The text of the letter, the end of which is missing, is printed in Dacheux, *Réf.*, Appendix LXII-LXIX. In strong words Geiler denounces Barby for his sins, for keeping a mistress, for failing to restore order in the cathedral

chapter, for not having courage to do his duty and for deceiving Geiler himself. The last denunciation refers to the fact that Geiler – on the strength of Barby's promise that there would never be cause to regret the move – had urged Friedrich von Zollern to resign his canonicate at the Strassburg cathedral in favor of Barby (1491). This bishop Friedrich did, although it appears that before resigning he asked his brother in Nürnberg whether the latter desired the benefice for his sons. Cf. N. 682.

1189. suborta fuit non modica iurisdicionis illius (que ad Decanum pertinet)... Verum eciam cultus ipse diuinus...
The dean had charge of discipline of all personnel and was confessor to all benefice holders. Without a dean or with a dean who was not equal to his task, as in the case of Hoyer von Barby, the disciplinary and spiritual climate of a chapter could be very poor indeed.

1190. etiam si alicui per Sanctitatem Vestram de dicto Decanatu prouisum...
In this passage and again in the passage *et si cui prius prouidisset* below (p. 188) indirect reference is made to the papal candidate Hoyer von Barby.

1191. ut nullus in Decanum Argentinensis ecclesie recipiatur: nisi sit Canonicus dicte ecclesie; nobilis liber et ab vtroque Parente illustris...
The Council of Basel had stipulated that chief offices in chapters were to be filled by the chapters. This stipulation was one of the statutes of the Strassburg cathedral chapter, as Schott notes above. Further statutes of the chapter specified prerequisites for a candidate to the deanship, that he be a member canon in residence, that he be of noble lineage (cf. N. 661). It is possible that the pope refused to recognize Johann von Brandis as dean because he was of lower rank than Hoyer von Barby. Both Sixtus IV and Innocent VIII stressed lofty lineage in candidates for cathedral canonicates (N. 661).

#168. TO JOHANN GEILER [Strassburg, mid-1483]

1192. Summary Schott gives information received from knowledgeable relatives on abuses in trade and commerce. As a whole, Alsatian merchants are more honest and less prone to usury than their English, Danish, French, Italian or Swabian fellows. Indeed, almost all manner of abuses among merchants have already been attacked by Geiler, but there is still one detestable practice, that of lending and mortgaging grain, whereby many a wretched farmer is brought to ruin. Another vicious practice involving both merchants and money changers is that of coinage debasement.

1193. Date This letter was written probably in mid-1483, sometime after the items on the grain loans, which are mentioned here and which date from early 1483 (cf. N. 1432).

1194. Florencius Mug affinis meus
Cf. N. 655.

P. 188   #168   N. 1195

1195. alterum affinem meum
Schott is probably referring to Ludovicus Müg,* brother of the above-mentioned Florencius,* (N. 655). These merchants would be more likely to know about commercial practices in Alsace and neighboring states than would other relatives of Schott, such as Zeisolf von Adelsheim,* Martin Schott,* Wilhelm Bettscholdt.*

1196. aliquando Magister Iohannes Rot consuluit Magistrum Iohannem Symler et me... opiniones nostras
For Rot's statement of the case about grain graft, cf. #213; for Simmler's and Schott's opinions on the case, cf. #214, #215.

1197. in suppressione Monete: qui vbicumque Florenum vel nimio... subrogatur
Strassburg was surrounded by principalities (Baden, Württemberg, the Rhenish Palatinate, Lotharingia), each of which like Strassburg had its own coinage. That difficulties with exchange and the debasing of coinage were a constant problem is evident from the frequent references in sources to coinage and coinage regulations. An excerpt from the Strassburg archives for 1409 (Wencker, *Arch.*, 369ff.) mentions exchange problems, the minting of new coins and the setting up of regulations forbidding melting, selling or otherwise misusing coins; another excerpt (*ibid.*, 372ff.) concerns a conference on coinage at Frankfurt in 1433. An entry for 1482 in Specklin (286) describes the new Strassburg *creutzer* or *zweyling* struck in that year. Eheberg (I, 329-331, #131) cites the coinage regulations of 1484, some of which are briefly: silver may be smelted only by the minters; no one may collect large sums of coins for sending away, smelting, etc.; any suspicious money is to be reported to authorities; old coins no longer in use may be bought and smelted; no one may select heavier coins "die hie genge und gebe sint" for breaking or smelting. In 1490 Schott, Sr., attended a conference in Oppenheim to discuss regulating weights of gold coins (#149, p. 163). An entry for 1507 in Specklin (286) states that Strassburg obtained permission from Maximilian I to mint gold coins, then had the old gold coins discontinued and new ones struck. Cf. Appendix N.

P. 189

#169. TO BOHUSLAUS VON HASSENSTEIN [Strassburg, end 1481-very early 1482]

1198. Summary Having learned from Ladislaus* of Hassenstein's illness and having had three of his four letters returned, Schott is exceedingly anxious to hear from Hassenstein. He is staying at home as much as possible and avoiding involvement in public affairs which he abhors, preferring a quiet life; however, when his father is absent, he does help with domestic problems. He desires information on any books [recently] published which might interest him.

1199. Date Hassenstein's letter of 20 May (#37) – in which he tells of his recovery – is a reply to the present letter (or to a letter Schott wrote at about the same time as the present one). From comparison of contents and other information, it appears that this present letter must have been written during the period, end of 1481 and beginning of 1482: 1) Since the present item mentions Hassenstein's illness, it is certainly of a later date than #170 which was written *ca.* 20 October 1481 (N. 1204) and which makes no mention of the illness. 2) Since in the present item Schott speaks of being uncertain of his future, he must have been writing before there was any indication of his obtaining a canonicate at New St. Peter – negotiations for which began at least as early as 5 April 1482 (N. 116, 1). Potuček (App. 3) suggests the beginning of 1482 as the date of this letter.

The editor of the *Lucubraciunculae* placed the two letters to Hassenstein – #169 and #170 – together, though chronologically #170 should preceed #169. Cf. N. 367.

1200. ad me scripsit Ladislaus presbiter Vespriminensis
Ladislaus'* letter to Schott is mentioned in #189, p. 208.

1201. Ab eo enim tempore/ quo me in familiaritatem acriorem admisisti...
The friendship of Schott and Hassenstein may have begun as early as 1474 (cf. N. 59, par. 6).

1202. negocia forensia penitus declino... quas absente Patre libens suscipio
For Schott's preferring a quiet life, cf. N. 86 and N. 255. For his assistance to Schott, Sr., cf. N. 113.

#170. TO BOHUSLAUS VON HASSENSTEIN [Strassburg, *ca.* 20 October 1481]

1203. Summary After a time of depression because he missed Hassenstein and because he was deprived of his books, Schott now feels happier at home. He describes in detail the exhausting life of his father as a man of public affairs and declares that this example of a public career is enough to make him desire a quiet life. He hopes when the winter is past to go away for advanced study. He urges Hassenstein to study diligently and to suggest plans for their life together. Schott, Sr., has left this day to act as delegate for Strassburg at the conference of the league which has been called to discuss the quarrel between Strassburg and Zürich. The emperor is fomenting war against Matthias of Hungary.*

1204. Date Various details in this letter indicate that it was written in the fall of 1481 on or before 20 October. 1) Grain harvest and vintage are over. 2) Schott's books which were still unaccounted for in early September when he wrote to Hassenstein (#25, p. 33) have arrived. 3) Susanna von Cöllen who was ill in the summer (#22, p. 31) is restored to health. 4) On the day Schott is writing, Schott, Sr., has left to attend the conference of the confederates: "Abijt hodie Pater meus legatus pro Republica nostra"; almost the same wording without "hodie" appears in the letter Schott wrote to Rot* on 20 October (#28): "Pater abijt Legatus ad Foederatos"; hence the present item must have been written either before or on the same day as the letter to Rot. Cf. N. 1199, paragraph 2. Potuček (138) suggests the date "1481. exeunte."

P. 190   #170   N. 1205

P. 190

1205. libris quoque meis carere coactus
The books mentioned here and in the paragraph following "libris meis/ qui vix tandem appulerunt" had been shipped from Venice in June. Cf. N. 263.

1206. Patrem animo pacientem magis esse voluit: atque in rem nostram... sed eciam laudat.
Schott believed that his father, wearied by his own thankless labors, was becoming reconciled to the idea of his son's not following him in a public career.
The phrase *in rem nostram* above, *quem erga me remque nostram* (p. 189), and two passages (p. 190): *Tu modo fac animo constanti sis...te mecum habere*, and *quid in rem nostram* refer to the cherished plan of Schott and Hassenstein to work and study together. Cf. N. 302.

1207. Patri obsequor: et presencia mea... opitulor... mihi continget.
For other references to Schott's assistance to his father, cf. N. 113. For other references to the overly solicitous attitude of Schott's parents, cf. N. 87. For the fate of Schott's plan to study theology abroad, cf. N. 121.

1208. clarius ad te quid et quomodo et vbi discam perscribam.
Cf. *Errata*.

1209. Si nihil me ad quietem hortaretur/ vita Patris satis... impelleret...
Cf. N. 86 and N. 255.

1210. quid cum... incoeperis: quomodo tibi id quod ago placeat
Cf. *Errata*. The lacuna of about 11 spaces (4 of which are at the end of a line and 7 of which are at the beginning of the next line on folio CVIIb) between *cum* and *incoeperis* was doubtless left for one or even two Greek words in the manuscript (cf. p. xiv, N. 23 and N. 24). Potuček (167, in his notes to App. 2) suggests εὐτραπηλία which is used by Cicero *Ad Fam.* vii.32.1.

1211. Patria nostra sano quidem aere... frumenta et vina solito cariora... parum ferax
The year 1481 had been healthful in the sense that there was no outbreak of the plague such as had been brought on by Rhine floods in 1480, and even though the harvests of 1481 were poor, they were enough to insure against famine such as had prevailed the previous year. Cf. Dacheux, *Fragments*, III, v, 241; Strobel, II, 385; Trithemius, *Ann. Hirs.*, II, 512.

1212. Pacem nostram Imperator solicitat... Vngarorum Regem cogere contendit.
For the protracted period of trouble between Friedrich III and Matthias Hunyadi* (Corvinus) of Hungary, cf. N. 623.

P. 190   #170   N. 1213

1213. Item cum RepublicaThuricensium non omnino sincera... iniuriam nostris a Thuricensibus factam.
Delegates from the confederated Rhine cities, their close allies and states belonging to the league formed in 1474 (N. 72) were holding another meeting in an attempt to settle the quarrel between Strassburg and Zürich over the Richard Püller affair (N. 358).

P. 191

1214. nos studeamus (quoad eius fieri poterit) meliorem partem Marie imitari
Cf. Lc. 10:42

1215. ut ad ea quae diligentibus se Deus promisit adipiscenda: digni...
Cf. Jc. 1:12; 2:5. Dt. 5:10; 7:9.

1216. Heinricum Sancti Georij Bononie tabernarium
This person has not been identified.

#171. TO SIGISMUND GOSSENBROT [Strassburg, late 1478]

1217. Summary Schott considers himself unworthy of Gossenbrot's* high praise and of the appellation "lux," which in his opinion only men like Hassenstein deserve. He will strive to store up knowledge and virtue, the only solaces of old age; for such a goal Gossenbrot, who combines service to his country with scholarship, has set an example unparalleled among the ancients.
The Schotts cannot but marvel at the wonderful craftsmanship of the gift Gossenbrot made for them: a cross so intricately carved that it might be a second Daedalean labyrinth.

1218. Date The few tenuous clues to the date of this letter seem to point to the early part of the period (fall 1478 to fall 1479) which Schott spent at home, before returning to Bologna (N. 190): *viz.*, the student-like avowal to concentrate all efforts on learning; the comments on *lux*, indicating that Schott may well have sent his and Hassenstein's early poems (#236- #239, composed by late 1477) for criticism to Gossenbrot, who, it is to be noted, also received a copy of "de tribus Iohannibus" (#242) in 1480; the complete absence of references to Strassburg activities or Schott's later interests.

1219. Bonum nimirum tunc esse felicius: ex sentencia philosophorum Principis ... extiterit.
Cf. Aristotle *Metaphisica* xii.3. A-B.

P. 192

1220. O lux Dardanie o spes fidissima... expectate venis?
Vergil *Aen*.ii.281-283.

1221. solem Asie Brutum appellat. Stellasque... Comites.
Horace *Sat*. i.7.24-25.

585

P. 192   #171   N. 1222

1222. Quorum ego exempla secutus Bohuslaum illum lucem... vocitaui.
The opening line of Schott's epigram to Hassenstein (#236) is "O lux Bohemorum."

1223. Vratislauo Bohemorum Rege quam familiarissime vtatur
Hassenstein addresses Vladislaus II* of Bohemia as "Maiestas Tua" and "tu" in letters (cf. Potuček, 23f.). For Schott's opinion about use of the formal plural, cf. #9, p. 15, and N. 184.

1224. Nimirum tocius regni futurus illustrator: cum... Plato arbitretur...
The reference in connection with Hassenstein to Plato's thesis in the *Republic* that those states are happiest which are ruled by men of wisdom seems to imply that even as a student Hassenstein expected at some time to serve a term of office in the Bohemian government. Cf. biographical note on Hassenstein.

1225. Conabor etenim pro mea virili: sciencias virtutesque scrutari: certum habens: sola hec senectuti viaticum praeferre.
This passage is reminiscent of Cicero *De Senectute* 9 and Quintilian *Inst. Or.* i.1.19. Cf. a similar passage in Hassenstein's oration (#297, p. 316).

1226. M. Varronem doctissimum virum fuisse legimus.
Marcus Terentius Varro, celebrated Scholar and contemporary of Cicero, wrote *De Rustica* and *De lingua Latina* and collected the comedies of Plautus.

1227. Tu amborum desiderio patrie regimen... vna tecum adduxisti.
For Gossenbrot's services to Augsburg, his scholarship and his retirement to Strassburg, cf. biographical note on him.

P. 193

#172. TO THOMAS WOLF, SR. [Strassburg, *ca.* 7 July 1487]

1228. Summary Having planned to be absent from the city with his mother and having tried vainly to see Wolf, Sr.,* personally, Schott writes that it is urgent Wolf give the lawyer in Rome, Johann Burckard,* instructions for the case of litigation between Engelhard Funck* and Thomas Wolf, Jr.,* because the case – deferred until the following Monday – is nearing its end and there is strong possibility of a favorable verdict. (For other references to this case, cf. N. 334).

1229. Date The case of litigation mentioned as being near its end was settled in 1487 (N. 334). It appears that the information in this letter caused Wolf, Sr., to send posthaste to the *Curia* in Rome a letter of instructions to Burckard and a letter soliciting Maeler's aid, as well as a letter from Schott commending Wolf to Maeler (#100). Since #100 was written 7 July 1487, the date of the present item may be assumed to be on or prior to that day. Cf. N. 780.

1230. Mitto ad te Doctor ornatissime: registrum... quid agere oporteat.
The unidentified document probably concerned the case of litigation. One can safely conjecture that the details about the progress of the case in Rome were sent by Vitus Maeler* whom Schott had repeatedly asked to sound out information on the case (#55, #74, N. 626, N. 627). Any communication from the procurator Johann Burckard* would have been addressed to Wolf, Sr., as the young client's uncle and guardian, who had engaged Burckard.

1231. A me nil dictum velim: sed liberior sim quam deceat... audenciam tribuit
Perhaps Schott felt he had written somewhat peremptorily to Wolf, his senior canon and *cellarius* at New St. Peter, as well as *praepositus* at Old St. Peter.

#173. TO JOHANN MÜLLER Bologna, [November 1479]

1232. Summary Trying to get Müller's books to him as quickly and safely as possible, Schott has succeeded in making arrangements for shipment from Bologna to Germany via Venice. In addition to all the books requested by Müller, Schott has sent books he has purchased for Müller (the titles of which are listed in the letter). He has also sent Müller's long shirt which he so badly wanted. Schott tells of friends at Bologna and bids Müller write, for he misses their daily talks. He is devoting his whole attention to canon law.

1233. Date Five undated items to Müller, #173- #177, are placed together here though they are not in chronological order. The present item must have been written very soon after Schott's return to Italy for the academic year beginning in November 1479 (cf. N. 190 and N. 201).

1234. magis e re tua fuerat: saluos eos vehi: quam cum periculo... Venicijs...
There was danger of losing books in shipping. Part of Hassenstein's priceless library was destroyed by fire in transit (cf. his biographical note). When Schott shipped his own books from Venice to Strassburg, he considered them lost because of long delay in arriving (N. 263, par. 2).

1235. Mercatorem Vuolff kammerer... Mercatoris Anthonij de Matugliano... fratrem
None of the three merchants named – Anthonius de Matugliano in Bologna and his brother in Venice, or Wolf Kammerer in Venice – has been identified. They were all no doubt book sellers and book agents, and Kammerer may well have belonged to the large German merchant colony in Venice (cf. N. 263, par. 1).

1236. Transmitto autem tibi libros... domini Prepositi Surburgensis.
Following is the list of books purchased and sent to Müller by Schott.
1. A Greek dictionary which because of its rarity cost two ducats
2. A tract on irregular forms, presumably in Greek grammar
3. A Bible

P. 194   #173   N. 1236

4. *Racionale diuinorum*, the full title of which may have been *Rationale divinorum officiorum* by Guillemus Durandus († 1296)
5. The works of Terence with Donatus' commentary
6. Cicero's letters
7. *Liber de homine*, possibly the *De homine* of Galeottus Marcius,* professor at Bologna while Schott and Müller were there, for whom Schott wrote a defense (#278).
8. Johannes Duns Scotus, *Opus Oxoniense*, which contains his questions and commentaries on Aristotle and on Peter Lombard's four books of the *Sentences*
9. *Mamotrectus* or *Mammotrectus super Bibliam*, a popular compendium to the Bible and related subjects, particularly useful to schoolmasters.
10. *Sala de consti... de Iudicijs etc.*, legal commentaries by Giovanni Gaspara della Sala,* who was Schott's *promotor* for the doctorate in laws (cf. N. 109 and #71, p. 77).
11. *Barbacia de pactis etc... verb. obliga.*, legal commentaries by Andreas Barbatia (cf. N. 236 and N. 342, par. 2).
12. *Argonauticon cum reliquis etc.*, possibly a collection of medieval romances, containing a version of the *Argonautica* (a Greek epic written by Apollonius Rhodius and translated freely into Latin by Varro Atacinus or the Latin epic of the same title by Valerius Flaccus).
13. *In sermones Horacij etc.*, one of the several commentaries to Horace (*sermones* meaning his *Satires* and *Epistles*).
14. Hesiod
15. Rules of syllable quantity
Included in this shipment of books were items evidently not meant for Müller: two texts of the *Digesta* of Justinian's *Corpus Iuris* "domini Doctoris Vuolf" and a copy of Terence with Donatus' commentaries "domini Prepositi Surburgensis." Since we have been unable to find in lists of early printed books editions of the above works by Thomas Wolf, Sr.,* or Jacob Dedinger,* we may assume either that the books belonged to Wolf and Dedinger and had perhaps been used by Schott and Müller, or that Schott had been commissioned by Wolf and Dedinger to buy the books, as Schmidt says (*H. L.*, II, 10).

1237. Socios nobis habemus dominum Georium... quendam alium Pannonium.. The "we" no doubt refers to Schott and Hassenstein. The first Hungarian friend mentioned is Georgius Ungarus*; the second is probably Stephan Piso.*

1238. Commentarios Abbatis Siculi... totus Canonibus incumbo... The bibliophile Venetian edition of which Schott was so proud was the commentaries on the Decretals of Gratian by Nicolas de Tudeschi, *abbas siculus*, a famous glossator in canon law, to which Schott was now devoting himself.

#174. TO JOHANN MÜLLER [Strassburg, shortly before 21 July 1486]

1239. Summary Müller, about to leave Paris for Baden-Baden, is assured that Schott will care for his baggage when it reaches Strassburg, and that his arrival is eagerly anticipated. Schott is ready to depart with Geiler and Rot* for Dillingen whither they have been invited by Friedrich von Zollern* to attend the latter's coronation as bishop of Augsburg. Müller's *preces primae* which are now in Baden-Baden are to be sent to Schott for processing.

P. 194   #174   N. 1239

Müller is again asked to give the titles of the chaplaincies he has resigned. Schott sends messages to Gangolf von Steinmetz* at Paris.

1240. Date Cf. N. 1233. The date of this letter is indicated by Schott's reference to his imminent departure for Friedrich von Zollern's coronation which took place 21 July 1486 (cf. N. 674, also N. 811).

P. 195

1241. Supreme insuper quas hodie recepi: vasis cuiuspiam... subsecuturum.
Müller with his charge, Jacob of Baden,* had been at the university of Paris and possibly that of Orléans since the fall of 1483.

1242. Precinctus equidem sum profectioni ad aelectum... accersiuit.
In a letter of 10 June to Friedrich von Zollern, Geiler writes that he, Rot and Schott are coming to the coronation (cf. Dacheux, *Ref.*, Appendix XXXXVIII).

1243. in execucione primariarum precum... quamprimum praesentari
For the *preces primae* which Friedrich von Zollern obtained for Müller from Maximilian, cf. N. 680.

1244. tibi puerum Gangolifum commendatum perseuerare... venire paret.
Gangolf von Steinmetz had been studying in Paris since late summer 1484, when he had been sent ahead to await Schott's arrival (cf. N. 520). The passage concerning Gangolf's parents' decision to let him buy shirts in Paris rather than send him shirts already made from Strassburg is a commentary on the relative price of goods in Strassburg and Paris and on the cost of shipping between the two cities. In Strassburg today everything is still more expensive than in Paris.

1245. Magister Iohannes de Creyçnach: qui te vnice diligit
We have not found information about a Johann Creuznach (Kreuznach, Kreutzer?) who might be identical with the person mentioned here, except a notation in *Q.F. Domin.*, X (1914), 1, about a "Fr. Joan. de Crucenach" who in 1487 was to go to the monastery at Weissenburg after the death of his mother.

1246. titulos altarium Capellaniarum tuarum ad me perscribere... oportet...
Cf. N. 613. Schott wanted to make sure that there was no possibility of trouble about securing for Müller a canonicate in Old St. Peter. For his long-term efforts to help Müller obtain a benefice worthy of him, cf. N. 527.

#175. TO JOHANN MÜLLER [Strassburg, December 1484]

1247. Summary In a conversation with Schott, the *praepositus* of Baden-Baden Nicholaus Zeis* spoke of *Markgraf* Christoph's* great affection and esteem for Müller. Schott would rather the *Markgraf* valued Müller less highly, because this affection has damaged Müller; *viz.*, when the chapter of

589

the collegiate church at Baden-Baden preferred Müller as candidate for the post of [lay] preacher, the *Markgraf*, fearing he would lose Müller as tutor to his eldest son Jacob, refused his consent; and when the dean of Strassburg would have recommended Müller to a vacant benefice in the Strassburg cathedral, Christoph again stood in the way.

1248. Date Cf. N. 1233. In this letter Schott writes Müller recent information as to why he (Müller) was not elected to the post of preacher in the collegiate church at Baden-Baden. We know that this post had been vacated before 30 November 1484 (N. 550) and that Müller was being considered seriously as candidate on that date (#63, p. 69). Hence the date of the present item must be soon after 30 November.

1249. Prepositus Badensis vir praeclarus: nuper mihi... (to end of paragraph) The *praepositus* of the Baden-Baden church and the "dominus noster Nycholaus" mentioned in the following paragraph of this item appear to be identical with Müller's friend Nicholaus Zeis of Schlettstadt (#60, p.66; N. 530).

The consent of Christoph I, as head of state, was necessary – according to the Bull of Nicholaus V in 1448 (N. 130, 3) – to effect Müller's election as preacher at Baden-Baden (cf. N. 526 and N. 527). Since the collegiate church at Baden-Baden was the family church of the ruling family and as such the chief church not only of the capital but also of the principality, the lay preacher of the church, even though his emolument were small, would hold a position of eminence second only to that of a cathedral preacher.

1250. Eciam in ea causa de qua tibi sepe prescripsi... obseruare vellet.
The benefice which the dean of the Strassburg cathedral Friedrich von Zollern,* Schott, Sr., Johann Rot* and Schott, Jr. wanted to secure for Müller was that of perpetual vicar in the cathedral. As noted in N. 529, the benefice was not vacant until the following year.

1251. horret animus meminisse: quam ego tunc turbatus fuerim.
Schott was quite naturally perturbed because his hopes for Müller had again been dashed. Perhaps, too, he – as a citizen of a free imperial city – was appalled at the power of an absolute ruler over his subjects.

#176. TO JOHANN MÜLLER [Strassburg, soon after 23 August 1484]

1252. Summary Schott has much to tell Müller but expects to discuss things with him in person when he arrives in Paris. Both Schott and Geiler are deeply grateful to Müller for his efforts in collecting works of Gerson. Schott is sending ahead Gangolf Steinmetz,* his *famulus*, whom he commends to Müller's care and for whom he is having eight florins deposited with Müller. (Cf. N. 518).

1253. Date Cf. N. 1233. This letter must have been written very shortly after #60 of 23 August 1484. Indeed this letter is a briefer version of #60 and may have been sent by another messenger at the same time, as in the case of #146 and #148 (cf. N. 1076).

P. 196   #176   N. 1254

1254. Sollicitudine tua atque beneuolencia quam in perquirendis Cancellarij scriptis... graciam habeamus.
Cf. N. 519.

1255. Mitto vel forte premitto ad vos puerum meum Gangoliphum... contribui.
Cf. N. 520.

#177. TO JOHANN MÜLLER [Strassburg, beginning September 1484]

1256. Summary Schott had already sent off his baggage and was himself about to depart for Paris when Müller's letter arrived with the news of a severe epidemic of the plague in Paris. His parents, fearing for his health, would not listen to his pleas but insisted that he stay at home, at least for the winter. He speaks with pathos of his frustrated hopes, his bitter disappointment. He is particularly worried about his *famulus* Gangolf von Steinmetz* and entreats Müller either to take the boy himself or see to it that he is placed in a college where he can work and study. The boy's clothes are being brought to Paris, and Schott will send money when Müller writes what the situation is. In answer to Müller's request Susanna von Cöllen is sending the powders which have proved quite an effective remedy against the plague in Strassburg. Schott promises to write Maeler for advice on obtaining the *gratia* which Müller desires. There is a possibility of Müller's securing the post, previously mentioned, at the Strassburg cathedral. (Cf. N. 518).

1257. Date Cf. N. 1233. This letter was written in late summer of 1484 when Schott was ready to leave for Paris and realize the long-cherished plan of studying advanced theology. In the text he mentions not yet having heard who the new pope is (p. 198). Since Innocent VIII was elected on 28 August 1484, we may assume that this letter dates from about the beginning of September, before the news of the election had time to reach Strassburg.

P. 197

1258. inter offam et os multa interueniunt
Cf. Büchmann, 215. Taylor, *Proverb*, 13, 42, 50. Tilley, T 191. Wander, III, 196, 12; 775, 233 and 234.

1259. Georius reuersus a te
This person has not been identified.

1260. quo quisque procumbit: eo ipsum propellere
Cf. Wander, IV, 1707, 3.

1261. tuis litteris... quas Misnensis ille tabellarius... Medicis vel Astronomos
A messenger from the town of Meissen brought a second letter from Müller in which Müller evidently reported opinions of physicians and astrologers about the state of the plague in Paris.

1262. tempori parendum: et e rerum condicione sumendum consilium
Cf. Wander V, 552, 663. Riley, 458.

P. 197   #177   N. 1263

1263. puerum meum... is ut recte coniecisti: idcirco praemissus a me est...
Cf. N. 520.

P. 198

1264. Magister Mathias
Mathias Kolb*

1265. pro pane atro et obsonio vili... in alciora conscendere deberet.
Cf. *Errata.* The regular fare of poor students was dark bread supplemented by fish, vegetables, fruit, and other common foods.
    Schott did not believe in pampering his *famuli*. A little hardship, provided they had food, shelter and an opportunity to study, was evidently, in his opinion, salutary for them.

1266. Nycholaus Grymmel
Nicholaus Grymmel or Grummel (cf. N. 478).

1267. Pulueres tamen ut petisti Mater tibi mittit... contagio hec Iunonis pestifere expertes sumus.
Is there an omission of a verb or phrase after *hec*? At least a colon or period must be supplied.
    Cf. N. 1119. Iunonis pestifere may refer to *stella Junonis* or Venus, which is said to cause death from stomach, liver and intestinal ailments, also to cause death from cancer, fistulas, lichens, poisons and troubles stemming from excess or deficiency of moisture (Ptolemy *Tetrabiblios* IV. 9). For other references to astrology, cf. N. 275.

1268. In impetrandis gracijs... cum Magistro Vito habebo... Possit.
Schott kept his word to write to Maeler about a *gratia* for Müller; cf. #62 (p. 68) of 24 November 1484 and #63 of 30 November 1484. Apparently Müller thought the time opportune for obtaining *gratiae*, because Sixtus IV had died 13 August 1484 and the new pope could be expected to issue his own *gratiae* and perhaps to rescind those of his predecessor. Cf. N. 612.
    Schott's bitter comment that it is difficult to get ahead of the voracious jaws of the *Curia* in snatching a benefice at Strassburg collegiate churches is very like his caustic advice to Anthonius Manlius* about a year later to seek Strassburg benefices in Rome (#73, p. 80; N. 624).

1269. Sed id de quo scripsi antea in ecclesia maiore... vacacionem attingere.
If the benefice in the cathedral should fall vacant in a month when chapters had the right to fill vacancies, Müller would have a good chance, Schott believes, of securing it. For details concerning this benefice, cf. N. 529. Cf. also N. 527.

#178. TO JOHANN SCRIPTOR [Strassburg, before 12 December 1478]

1270. Summary Schott realizes more and more how well he was taught by Scriptor* and what a fine example Scriptor has set. He expresses his

P. 198   #178   N. 1270

gratitude to Scriptor and tells of his disappointment at not having been able to return to Paris after taking his A.B. there, for he had hoped to earn his doctorate under Scriptor; his parents, however, wished him to go to Bologna. Having spent almost five years studying at Bologna, he has had to come home because of the plague there. He is about to return to finish his course, but it is uncertain whether Müller will accompany him. He wishes Scriptor might settle in Strassburg, where he would enjoy the temperate climate, the beauty of the city and the company of learned scholars. In fruitfulness of the glebe, in abundance of birds, fish and wild game Strassburg is second to none.

1271. Date This letter seems to have been written sometime before that of 12 December 1478 to Brant (#10). In the present letter Schott tells Scriptor he is about to return to Italy, but is uncertain whether Müller will accompany him. In the letter to Brant Schott says he expects to stop in Basel very soon on his way to Italy, but he does not mention Müller at all, as he doubtless would if Müller were to be with him, for Brant was exceedingly fond of Müller. Also in the letter to Brant Schott mentions the possibility of going to Padua, a possibility not mentioned to Scriptor.

P. 199

1272. Equidem agnosco nunc clarius: quam ex re mea fuerit... coronari.
In reminiscing to Johann Rot* about studies in Paris, Schott has high praise for the solid grounding in fundamentals received there (cf. #9, p. 16). We learn from this passage that as an undergraduate Schott had the desire to do advanced work in theology and perhaps even become a doctor of theology (cf. N. 121); "et militare et coronari" (cf. 2Tm. 2:3-5).

1273. ibi quinquennium fere integrun legibus indulsi: peste coactus in patriam me contuli... quoque in Italiam diuertat
Cf. N. 95, 4 ; N. 190. Müller may also have studied under Scriptor.

1274. Te ego virorum optime: vellem aliquando in... patria habitantem...
In 1483 Scriptor visited Strassburg (#58, p. 63) and in 1484 asked Schott to help him procure a benefice in Strassburg (*ibid.*, p. 64).

1275. virorum doctorum atque bonorum frequens consorcium... atque virtutes
The more mature Schott in 1485 felt somewhat differently about the company of scholars in Strassburg, cf. N. 622 and #73, p. 80.

1276. Si feracitatem glebe queris: si volatilium... secunda est.
For other examples of Schott's love for his homeland, cf. N. 124, also p. xxviii.

#179. TO VITUS MAELER [Strassburg, early 1482]

1277. Summary Because one should consider friends' welfare as one's own, Schott tells Maeler he is wrong to contest Johann Rot's* possession of a benefice at St. Thomas, which – having little income – can be of no value to him, whereas Rot has already had considerable expense on account of the benefice. It is not for Schott's or Rot's sake, however, that Maeler should desist, but because the *praepositus* and dean of St. Thomas wish him to do so. If Maeler could but know what sterling qualities Rot has, he would of his own volition withdraw. Much as Schott would like to have Maeler in Strassburg, he knows this benefice is too small to draw Maeler thither.

1278. Date This letter and #192 concern the same benefice at St. Thomas, #192 being the earlier item, written when the benefice first fell vacant and chapter officers were considering Johann Rot as a very promising candidate, the present item having been written after the chapter had given Rot possession of the benefice but before papal confirmation had been received. The earliest possible date for #192 could be after 20 October 1481 when Schott wrote Rot at Dambach letter #28 which contains no reference to any benefice whatsoever. A later date for #192 seems, however, more feasible, as is indicated below.

On 26 February 1482 Schott promised to notify Maeler of any good benefice coming vacant in Strassburg (#31), but he mentioned no previous try on Maeler's part to secure a Strassburg benefice. We may therefore assume that the benefice at St. Thomas fell vacant after the above date, perhaps immediately thereafter at the very end of February or in April, both of which months were papal months when holders of *gratiae* could legally claim vacancies (N. 130, 3); vacancy in these months would explain why Rot's possession of the benefice was so vigorously contested. Indeed, since there is no record of his being a prebendary of St. Thomas, it is very likely that he could not defend his possession against all claimants and finally withdrew.

There is also no record of the date when Rot was appointed parish priest of the Strassburg cathedral, but it must have been long enough before 3 August 1842 – the date when he resigned his post at Dambach (Barth, *Handbuch*, 247f.) – to allow time for papal confirmation, as no benefice was relinquished until another was absolutely assured. Quite possibly the benefice of parish priest became vacant in a month when chapters had the right to fill vacancies – perhaps in May or at the latest in July – because there seems to have been no opposition to Rot's taking possession of that benefice.

The time then of Rot's somewhat protracted and unfortunate experience with the benefice at St. Thomas would seem to have been during the period: end of February to May 1482. The date of #192 and of the present item would accordingly be in this period.

P. 200

1279. Amicorum gracia omnia vel arduissima honeste posse suscipi... dispendium
For such definitions of friendship, cf. Aristotle *Ethica Nicomachea* viii.3; ix.4 and 6. Cicero *De Amicitia* 44, 80 and *De Finibus* ii. 72. Cf. also Christie I, No. 16, p. 402, and No. 63, p. 405. Tilley, F 690.

1280. nisi amico totus adsis: atque eius rem non secus agas: ac propriam
Cf. Lv. 19:18: "Diliges amicum tuum sicut teipsum."

1281. dominorum Prepositi et Decani ecclesie sancti Thome
I. e., Christoph von Üttenheim* and Johann Simmler,* respectively.

1282. Plane non dubito quin si innocenciam/ mores/ et doctrinam viri... nouisses
This passage is a fine tribute to Johann Rot.

1283. magnopere cuperem te aliquando in vrbe nostra habitare... diuerteres
Obviously Schott did not consider the benefice, *beneficiolum* as he calls it, worth writing about to Maeler, but Maeler had seemingly already begun to accumulate benefices. It is not known what benefices Maeler held by early 1482; not until 4 February 1483 is any of his benefices named in Schott's letters (#39, p. 45).

1284. Magnis impensis consecutus est possessionem Iohannes noster.
Cf. #30, p. 38, and N. 335.

1285. Tu per graciam suam: tuam ut aiunt purgare potes
Cf. Plautus *Amphitruo* 940-945.

1286. Quod si se tutum aduersus... decem Aureorum absens perciperes.
In this ironic comment on benefices *in absentia* Schott is telling Maeler it were better if he (Maeler) turned over to Rot – in case Rot could not hold the benefice at St. Thomas – some little benefice of his from which he could still draw ten guilders *in absentia*.

#180. TO VITUS MAELER [Strassburg, after 14 April and before 28 May 1485]

1287. Summary To Maeler's complaint that Schott has rebuked him, Schott replies that because he did not know Maeler's whereabouts, it was Maeler's obligation to write, and that they should not allow the friendship begun during their student days to cool. He warns Maeler against the dangers of association with those whose chief aim in life is acquisition of material goods.

1288. Date At the end of this letter Schott mentions the death of Nicolaus Kagen* en route from Rome. That Kagen was in Rome apparently in 1485 is attested by the *Liber confrat.* (80) which among entries of the year 1485 has an undated entry for Kagen. It appears then that this letter may have been written in 1485, probably after 14 April – when Schott complains that his letters to Maeler have been returned and he is not sure where Maeler is (#68) – and before 28 May, when he acknowledges a hurried letter from Maeler (#69).

1289. quod ad me scripsisti lacessiri te a me... ut nisi lacessam
Cf. the wording of the passage in Cicero *Ad. Fam.* 12.20.

P. 201   #180   N. 1290

P. 201

1290. Nam si idem velint amici: tam vere amici sunt: cum ut bene velint: ambo laborant.
For similar thoughts, cf. Aristotle, *Ethica Nicomachea* ix. 4,6; viii.3.

#181. TO EUCHARIUS GROSHUG [Strassburg, date unknown]

1291. Summary Groshug has sent Schott a book of eulogies which Schott is keeping longer than he should in order to study them more carefully.

1292. Date There is no evidence in the letter to indicate a possible date of composition.

1293. Euchario Groshug Iohannite
I. e., Eucharius Groshug,* member of the Order of the Knights of St. John the Baptist of Jerusalem, for which cf. N. 1141.

1294. hoc Eulogiorum volumen... tantas laudes: cum quibus parum... haberem
For the practice of sending works to friends for perusal and criticism, cf. N. 309. Apparently, at least one of Groshug's eulogies concerned Schott.

1295. Euestigio enim contrarie voluntatis testacionem... Paulus iurisconsultus monet
We do not know from what work of Paulus Iurisconsultus* Schott is quoting.

P. 202

1296. ut Demostenes ait: erubescere nos eciam cum vere laudamur decet
Cf. Demosthenes 270.2.

#182. TO EUCHARIUS GROSHUG [Strassburg, date unknown]

1297. Summary Schott thanks Groshug for a favor and promises to repay in kind.

1298. Date There is no evidence in the note to indicate when it was written, nor is there anything known about the matter referred to.

#183. TO ADOLPH RUSCH [Strassburg, fall 1478-26 May 1489]

1299. Summary Schott asks for the loan of Livy's works and promises to return them along with the works of Tortellius. (Cf. N. 37.)

1300. Date Schott's association with Rusch probably began during the months he was at home from Bologna – fall 1478 to fall 1479 (in 1480 he was searching Bolognese libraries for a work Rusch wanted [#16, p. 25]) and lasted until Rusch's death in May 1489. There is no clue in this note to indicate the time of its writing.

1301. Titem Liuium Romane historie principem... Tortellio
These works were doubtless from Rusch's library, for there is no record that Rusch published an edition of Livy or of Johannes Tortellius Arretinus.*

#184. TO GOTTFRIED VON ADELSHEIM, JR. [Strassburg, late 1489 or early 1490]

1302. Summary Schott writes to comfort Gottfried von Adelsheim, Jr.,* on the death of his father, Gottfried von Adelsheim, Sr.* Not only family and friends, but also people of the Rhine area and of all Germany mourn the loss of one who was outstanding in military and civil life. The immediate family's grief should be assuaged by the knowledge that Adelsheim, Sr., attained an age and high honors not granted to many.

1303. Date When Gottfried von Adelsheim, Sr., died is not known, but since he was very prominent in public affairs of Strassburg and is documented often in Strassburg records until into the year 1489, he must have died in late 1489 or early 1490.

1304. Equitis aurati
Cf. N. 744.

1305. eiuscemodi virum vita functum esse... ornamenta et dignitatum...
For the many honors and services of Gottfried von Adelsheim, Sr., cf. his biographical note. It may have been at Adelsheim's funeral that Schott delivered his address thanking priests who officiated at a burial service (#196).

1306. principes subinde duos victoriosissimos
Gottfried, Sr., had served *Pfalzgraf* Philip and the *Graf* von Württemberg, either Ulrich or his son Eberhard.

1307. Zeisolfus Patruus tuus, eiusque Coniunx soror mea
Zeisolf von Adelsheim, Sr.,* was the brother of Gottfried, Sr., and the husband of Ottilia Schott.*

1308. id quam maximam consolacionem M. Cicero putat: in ore... habere
That is to say, Gottfried von Adelsheim, Sr., had, like Scipio, attained such heights that he could have asked for nothing more in this life except to live forever. Cf. Cicero *De Amicitia* iii.10. Cf. also *De Senectute* x.33; xix.71; xxiii.82, 84, 85.

#185. TO GOTTFRIED VON ADELSHEIM, JR. [Strassburg, spring or summer 1490]

1309. Summary While visiting at the Adelsheim estate, Schott has learned that Gottfried von Adelsheim, Jr.,* is in residence at Wimpfen and on the strength of *preces primae* wishes to try for a benefice at Strassburg, falling vacant in a chapter month. Since his talk with Adelsheim Schott has heard nothing about confirmation by the pope of Adelsheim's *preces* and has therefore done nothing about a benefice for Adelsheim. He explains, however, that *preces primae* are valid in both chapter and papal months and that Adelsheim can perhaps acquire a benefice in Strassburg with his *preces* more easily than a holder of a *gratia expectativa* or than a candidate nominated by the chapter. Yet it is not advisable to force chapters into accepting *preces*, for intimidation is not the door by which one should enter the communion of Christ. If Adelsheim would prefer some one else to act as procurator, Schott will gladly step aside.

1310. Date For reasons listed below, this letter appears to be of a later date than the preceding letter to Adelsheim (#184) and was probably written in spring or early summer 1490. 1) Adelsheim is addressed in this letter as *praepositus* of Wimpfen, a title not mentioned in #184. 2) Also mentioned in this letter is the expected papal confirmation of Adelsheim's *preces primae* which could not have been expected until sometime after 30 November 1489 when Innocent VIII began recognizing Maximilian's *preces primae* (cf. N. 130, 3).

1311. Fuimus nudiustercius in Vuasselnheim apud Zeisolfum fraterem tuum Zeisolf von Adelsheim, Jr.,* elder son of Gottfried, Sr.,* and brother of Gottfried, Jr., had inherited the family estate and castle of Wasselonne or Wasselnheim in the Vosges foothills midway between Strassburg and Zabern.

1312. te in presenciarum confluencie residentem bene valere The name *Confluentia* is applied to a town at the confluence of rivers, e.g., Coblenz (*Confluentes*) in Germany and Coblenz in Switzerland. Here the name seems to apply to Wimpfen (N. 661, par. 3) at the confluence of the Schefflen with the Neckar, where Adelsheim had apparently not long before become *praepositus*.

1313. apud nos Beneficium/ quod vigore precum regalium sperare possis Adelsheim held two *preces primae*, one for St. Thomas and one for New St. Peter, and when Schott died (not long after this letter was written), tried for Schott's canonicate at New St. Peter; cf. N. 130, 5, and biographical note for Adelsheim.

1314. expectans apostolicus... nominatus a Canonico... non tam iure quam metu...
For the various types of *gratiae*, cf. N. 130, 3. For the election procedure in chapters, cf. N. 130, 1. For the procedure at Old St. Peter with Müller's *preces primae*, cf. #153 and N. 1108.

1315. si non ero ipse idoneus alios per teque... ea agere paciar
It appears that Adelsheim had become *praepositus* at Wimpfen since his talk with Schott (mentioned above in text) and that at the time of writing, Schott – not in sympathy with Adelsheim who is obviously a benefice hunter – would rather not be procurator for him, even though Adelsheim was so to speak in the family.

#186. TO EMERICH KEMEL [Strassburg, early 1482, before 5 April]

1316. Summary Kemel* is assured that the official escort he requested will be ordered by Schott, Sr. He need only specify whether he wishes five or more men and whether these are to be armed or unarmed.

1317. Date That the date of this letter is sometime in the early months of 1482, before 5 April, is indicated by the following: 1) Schott addresses Kemel with the formal form as in #32 of 5 April 1482, whereas in #187 of late 1484 or early 1485 he addresses Kemel familiarily (cf. N. 346). 2) From #32 we learn that Kemel had been in Strassburg on official business earlier in 1482 and had been obliged to depart hurriedly (N. 351). 3) Schott, Sr., must have been mayor to be able to speak for the city magistracy in providing Kemel with an escort; his term of mayor in 1482 (N. 70) is the only one of his four terms which will fit the time of both 1) and 2) above.

#187. TO EMERICH KEMEL [Strassburg, during the period: end of 1484 to 21 February 1485]

1318. Summary Writing for Geiler who is exceedingly busy, Schott enumerates a number of abuses (about some of which Kemel while in Strassburg had desired information) and requests Kemel to assemble and send to Strassburg opinions of outstanding authorities on such abuses so that Geiler, strengthened by these authorities, can continue his campaign for reform with greater assurance.
First Schott reports on the case of the Last Sacrament for those condemned to death. If Kemel had postponed his departure from Strassburg four days, he would have seen with his own eyes the unanimous verdict of the Heidelberg theologians and jurists: that to those condemned to death, provided they be penitent and desirous of it, the Last Sacrament must in nowise be denied.
The most flagrant abuses about which Geiler would like opinions are the following: restriction of the amount of money a person may retain on entering a monastic order; unequal laws for citizens and non-citizens in respect to theft and murder; prohibition against the willing of gifts to religious institutions or causes; safe conducts protecting holders of such from standing trial for violations of law; taxes imposed on the clergy for necessities of life; the infamous *Rohraffe's* disturbance of religious services; the mayor's holding audience in the cathedral during divine services; buying and selling in the cathedral porticos; people's use of cathedral aisles as thoroughfares and their carrying pigs, chickens, bundles through the cathedral; boisterous cavorting of choir boys during the Christmas season; the law allowing bakers from outside the city to sell their bread in Strassburg only on Sunday at the time of divine services; market days held on holy days. (Cf. N. 37).

P. 205   #187   N. 1319

1319. Date One section of this letter deals with the case of the Last Sacrament for those condemned to death; other items dealing with the case, in chronological order, are: #212, Schott's opinion ; #210, the first letter to Heidelberg; #211, the second letter to Heidelberg. The present letter is the latest in time of the four items; it was written after the verdict from Heidelberg reached Strassburg and before the decree granting the condemned the Last Sacrament was passed; the date of the decree is 21 February 1485. From the sequence of events leading to the decree (N. 1325) the approximate dates of the four items can be established: the first half of the year 1484 for Schott's opinion (#212); mid-1484 for the first letter to Heidelberg (#210); late fall 1484 for the second letter to Heidelberg (#211); the end of 1484 or early 1485 (i.e., before 21 February 1485) for the present item (#187).

Dacheux' inference (*Réf.*, 46) that Schott wrote the first letter to Heidelberg in 1482 and that in the same year Kemel refused to commit himself on the case before learning the verdict from Heidelberg is incorrect, as can be ascertained by perusing the known facts in the case (N. 1325). For the first letter to Heidelberg Wencker (*Arch.*, 432) gives the date "*ca.* 1483."

1320. patri Emerico Kemel: ordinis fratrum Minorum de Obseruancia... tibi
Cf. N. 345. Note the familiar form of address used by Schott to Kemel; in the interval between the two earlier letters to Kemel (#32 and #186) and the present letter Schott has become intimate with Kemel (cf. N. 184).

1321. Iohannis de keisersberg in ecclesia Argentinensi praedicatoris regij
Regij here means "*principal*," "first"; cf. Maigne D'Arnis, col. 1899: *regius – praecipuus, primarius.*

1322. Nosti vir praeclarissime çelum eius... doctoris... peruicaces induerunt.
This paragraph is an excellent characterization of Geiler the reformer, or as he called himself, the "fearless clarion which never ceased despite cannon balls and bullets and which death alone could silence" (Dacheux, *Réf.*, 31). In his zeal to root out evils of all kinds he was no respecter of person, rank, tradition, law or power.

1323. propter emulos eos: qui ut caseum habeant... non verentur vocem
The reference is to Geiler's enemies, especially the religious orders who had from the very beginning objected to the establishment of the cathedral chair for a lay preacher (N. 955, par. 6) and opposed his every move for reform. Note the allusion to Aesop's fable of the fox and the raven.

1324. super quibus peritorum et quorum fidem inconcussam... responsum ad nos
It should be noted that the opinions which Kemel was to collect from authorities did not arrive in time to affect the passing of the Strassburg decree about the Last Sacrament for the condemned. Three months after the decree was passed (21 February 1485), in a letter to Maeler (#69, written 28 May 1485) Schott sends a message to Kemel that both he and Geiler desire "de quo ei prius scripsi" be expedited. Since the opinions also concerned issues other than that of the Last Sacrament, Schott and Geiler were anxious to have them as support in effecting other reforms.

1325. In primis igitur in causa eorum qui vltimo supplicio plectendi...
Denial of the Last Sacrament to criminals condemned to death was an old custom, widespread in the Middle Ages. In Strassburg those criminals condemned to be hanged were taken before execution to the chapel "Zum elenden Kreuz," where they – if they so desired – were allowed to confess, were shown the Host and cautioned of their approaching end. Those condemned to be drowned received the same preliminary rites at St. Martin's before they were precipitated into the Ill from the *Schindbrücke*, now called *Rabenbrücke* or *Pont des Corbeaux*.

In 1482 Geiler began agitating to have such criminals allowed the Last Sacrament, and the issue was on the agenda of the Strassburg city council on 29 November of that year:

An. 1842. 5. post Catharinae
Item, den verurteilten Lüten das Sacrament zu geben.
Erkant, man soll es betrachten, Völtsch und Trachenfels.

(Wencker, *Arch.*, 433; cf. Appendix K).

Because of strong opposition, particularly from the religious orders (cf. N. 1420) who maintained that administration of the Last Sacrament to criminals indicated absolution from their crimes (cf. also N. 1430), the council apparently shelved the issue.

In 1483 Geiler sent to Mayor Maternus Trachenfels a formal request that criminals condemned to death be granted the Last Sacrament and a Christian burial ("Cedula Dr. Johannis Keiserspergij ad Consulem Maternum Trachenfels Anno 1483;" text in Wencker, *loc. cit.*). Unfortunately the exact date of the letter is not known, but it was doubtless this letter which caused the issue to be brought before the council again on 14 December 1483:

An. 1483. 2. post Luciae.
Item, der armen verurteilten Lüt halb, Inen das Sacrament
zu geben und die geistl. begrebde zuzulossen

(*ibid.*)

The council dared not, however, on its own authority abolish so firmly rooted an old custom which was not only exceedingly controversial but also involved canon rather than civil law. Six days later, on 20 December 1483, the council voted to maintain the status quo:

Eod. Sabbati Vigil. Thomae Apli.
Erkant, Lot es bliben wie harkommen, also das Sacrament
zeigen, und... der begrebde halb lot bliben wie erkant.

(*ibid.*)

At this time, i.e., end of 1483 or beginning of 1484, Geiler and the city council no doubt appealed to Bishop Albrecht* to give his decision on the issue, but he, too, was loath to assume sole responsibility and empowered his vicar to solicit opinions of experts in the Strassburg diocese, among them Schott. When the opinions were read, there was such disagreement on the issue that no verdict was possible. The bishop then had the opinions, along with a letter written in his name by Schott, sent to the dean and to the faculties of theology and law at the university of Heidelberg for a verdict. Several months having elapsed without word from Heidelberg, Schott wrote again in the bishop's name, urging the necessity for immediate action. Then, probably very near the end of the year 1484, came the unanimous verdict from Heidelberg that the Last Sacrament could not be denied those condemned to death.

With such powerful support the bishop hesitated no longer in re-

P. 205   #187   N. 1325

questing the city council to abolish the old law, and on 21 February 1485, "secunda post Invocavit Anno 1485," the council passed the decree permitting the Last Sacrament to criminals condemned to death (cf. Appendix K).
        Specklin claims (286): "der rath befragte sich bey drey hohen Schulen," yet according to the decree itself, it was Bishop Albrecht who appealed to "Gelerten in den Hohen Schulen." Wimpheling (*Cat. ep.*, 118) says that advice was sought "a praeclaris universitatibus." Schott implies, however, that only one university was consulted when he states that the Strassburgers have chosen the university of Heidelberg because of its superiority to other universities in the land (#210, p. 219), and in his letter to Kemel he mentions only the verdict from Heidelberg (#187, p. 205).
        Cf. Dacheux, *Réf.*, 45-49; text of decree, 49. Schmidt, "Notices... P.S.," 319. Cf. Schöpflin, *Alsatia*, 341. Specklin, 286. Wencker, *Arch.*, 433f., 631f., 633-639; text of decree, 434. Wimpheling, *Cat. ep.*, 118.

1326. Sed sunt et alia... petit eximius ille doctor... corroborarique.
Following is a list of abuses which Geiler attacked, but which are not mentioned in this letter, either because reform had already been effected or because they were not paramount at the time.
1. The lack of provision for the poor, especially in periods of famine
2. Graft in grain loans (#168, p. 188, #213-#215)
3. Devaluation of currency and suppression of coins (#168 and N. 1197)
4. Exclusion of syphilitic patients from hospitals
5. Lechery of the clergy, both lay and regular, male and female
6. Houses of prostitution
7. Gambling; articles 7-9 of the "21 Artikel" Geiler read before the Strassburg city council in 1501 deal with this vice.
8. Drunkenness
9. Permitting children and able bodied adults to beg for a living
10. Cheating widows of their property; article 6 of the "21 Artikel" notes this.
11. Unseemly behavior on holy days. For example, after services on Ash Wednesday masks mounted on poles, draped with ash-covered rags in mockery of the *Hungertuch* on the altar, were carried about the city. On Pentecost peasants dressed as for carnival and wild masked figures, such as the lewd "wild Weip von Geispoltzheim" (article 16 of "21 Artikel") rioted through the streets.
12. Desecration of holy places. One flagrant practice which Geiler particularly abhorred and caused to be abrogated in 1482 was the riotous vigil on 29 August (St. Adelphus Day, the anniversary of the dedication of the cathedral) when people from all the Strassburg diocese thronged into the cathedral to spend the night. In earlier centuries it was customary for pilgrims to keep vigil before the tombs of the martyrs, as preparation for communion; and to strengthen the pilgrims through their long hours of prayer an early director of the *fabrica* gave money for wine to be provided in the St. Catherine chapel. By the second half of the fifteenth century the vigil had degenerated into a night of revelry, likened by Wimpheling to orgies of Bacchus and Venus. There was eating, drinking, dancing, singing of profane songs and general gross misconduct. The altar became a buffet; a great cask in St. Catherine's chapel furnished free wine; sleepers were rudely roused by pricks from pins and iron-tipped staves.
        Cf. Brant, *Narrenschiff*, 87, 91, 434, 438. *Code hist.*, I, 119. Dacheux, *Réf.*, 38, 51-55, 60-62, 66, 82-89, 91f., 94. Enders, 658. Geiler, "21 Artikel" (Dacheux *Réf.*, V-XXXIII); *Predigen über das Narrenschiff*, folios 180f., 330. Glöckler, 335f. Grandidier, *Essais*, 72-75, 281; *Oeuvr. hist.*, 365-369. Hatt,

Ville, 418-435. Hertzog, 114f. Laguille, 365f. Lauffer, 38-46. Ritter, "Geiler," *passim*. Schmidt, "Notices... P.S.," 312f., 314ff.; *H. L.*, I, 174. Schneegans, "Pfingstfest," 197, 204ff., 228, 240. "Sermo Doctoris Peter Wickgram contra levitatem sacerdotum" in Geiler, *Sermones*, fol. 144. Specklin, 283, 285f., 288, 292, 297f., 300. Stenzel, *Chronik*, 64. Wimpheling, *Cat. ep.*, 117f. Winckelmann, "Kulturgesch.," 267-270, 280, 285f. Zacher, 49ff.

The bibliography above concerns the abuses discussed both in this note and in the text of the present item, pp. 206f. Special bibliography for specific abuses appears in other notes to this present item, *viz.*, N. 1333-N. 1338.

1327. Statuto ciuitatis Argentinensis cauetur: quod intrans religionem.
This law is mentioned in articles 1 and 2 of Geiler's "21 Artikel" and in his *Haas im Pfeffer*, where he comments bitterly that if a girl enters a convent, she loses all her inheritance except 200 florins, whereas if she is "ein bübin," she retains everything (Dacheux, *Réf.*, 51).

1328. Iterum Statuto cauetur quod Ciuis Argentinensis occidens peregrinum...
Article 18 of Geiler's "21 Artikel" demands that the slaying of a foreigner by a citizen and rape be more severely punished. The preferential treatment accorded by law to Strassburg citizens when involved with foreigners applied not only to cases of mayhem or theft. In the case of Sophie Bock, the city of Strassburg protected her and her inheritance even to the point of war with Zürich (cf. N. 358).

1329. xxx solidos: qui sunt prope tres florenos Renenses
Solidus was originally a gold coin of the Byzantine empire; in the Middle Ages the term was applied to several kinds of coins. Shilling is said to be derived from it. Cf. Black, II, 1565: *solidus legalis*.

1330. Quod si vero quispiam eciam Ciuis Ciuem... occiditur
Brucker, 371, quotes the law: "Wer einen tötet, dem sol man sin houbt abeslahen." The phrases *vim vi repellere* and *cum moderacione inculpate tutele* are legal terms, cf. Black, II, 1741: "Vim vi repellere licet, modo fiat moderamine inculpatae tutelae non ad sumendam vindicatam, sed ad propulsandam injuriam. It is lawful to repel force by force provided it be done with the moderation of blameless defense, not for purpose of taking revenge, but to ward off injury..." and *ibid.*, II, 1155: "Moderamen inculpatae tutelae. In Roman law, the regulation of justifiable defense. A term used to express that degree of force in defense which a person might safely use, although it should occasion the death of the aggressor..."

1331. Item Statuto cauetur: quod non potest testamento vel donacione causa mortis... pias causas.
In articles 3, 4, 5 of his "21 Artikel" Geiler demands that priests, other clergy and lay persons be allowed to dispose of their property in testament as they choose. As an example of the mishandling of wills, he cites in article 3 the breaking of Johann Simmler's* will. Cf. biographical note on Simmler;

P. 206   #187   N. 1331

cf. also biographical note on Ortwin for the litigation over Ortwin's will which left his property to the Dominican monastery in Strassburg.
    Donatio and *causa mortis* are legal terms, cf. Black, I, 278: "causa mortis. In contemplation of approaching death" and *ibid.*, I, 575: "Donatio mortis causa... The civil law defines it to be a gift under apprehension of death; as when anything is given upon condition that, if the donor dies, the donee shall possess it absolutely, or return it if the donor should survive or repent of having made the gift, or if the donee should die before the donor..."

1332. Item talias/ pedagia/ et teolonia exigunt a clericis... frumento.
Taxation of the clergy was a controversial issue of the times. The Council of Constance had forbidden lay authorities to tax the clergy (Horning, *Jung-St.-Peter*, 9ff.). In his questions put to Gabriel Biel,* Schott asks Biel's opinion about the legality of a number of practices, including taxation of clergy (#222, p. 250). Geiler's article 17 requests the city council to consider further the abolition of various levies on the income from benefices. Trithemius (*Ann. Hirs.*, II, 529) tells how in 1486 Innocent VIII's demand for a tenth part of all provender from lay and regular clergy throughout the empire roused such protest that the emperor wrote to Innocent and persuaded him to revoke the tax. A legitimate levy on the clergy was the *subsidium charitatis* which bishops by virtue of canon law exacted on all benefices, the incomes of which were more than necessary for livelihood.

1333. Item rusticanam quandam imaginem: in sublimi sub organis... perturbacionem.
The figure mentioned is the renowned *Rohraffe*, hallmark of Strassburg. Schott describes its location in the cathedral as "high above, under the organ" and Wimpheling (*Germania*, fol. f.2) describes it as "under the organ" (*sub organis*).
    As one enters the main portal of the cathedral and proceeds up the center aisle, one's eyes are drawn upward to the left of the aisle where – suspended between two pillars and facing the aisle – is the great organ. At the base of the organ case are three painted wooden figures of almost life size: on the left a trumpeter dressed as a medieval Strassburg herald; in the center Samson with the lion; on the right a bearded man with a pointed cap on his long, shaggy locks, whose garb is variously described as that of a peasant, an aged man, a Jew of the thirteenth century, a *Meistersinger*, and whose closed right hand is said to have once held a scroll or a baton for conducting music or a wooden stick (*Bretstel*) for punctuating his remarks. The three figures are provided with movable parts which can be manipulated by levers near the keyboard of the organ. In 1962 the entire machinery was repaired, and on very special occasions the figures are still set in motion.
    For centuries before the Reformation, on high feasts, especially Pentecost, when large processions of worshippers from the entire diocese moved into the cathedral, singing to the accompaniment of the great organ, the three figures began to move. The trumpeter raised his trumpet; Samson forced open the jaws of the lion; the bearded man gesticulated, moved his head, opened his mouth and grimaced while a glib rogue, hidden within the organ case near the figure, in stentorian voice sounding above the music and seeming to issue from the figure's gaping mouth, shouted bawdy jokes, bawled profane ditties and taunted the peasants. This buffoonery continued during divine services.
    All three figures were called *Rohraffen*. Geiler uses the word in both singular and plural: "Dass man das ror abtue"; "Do werden pfründen wol

verdient, So man dem roraffen zuo gient" (a quote from Brant's *Narrenschiff*, No. 91, 33f.); "Solche canonici schweigen und gienen im chor oder sehen den rohraffen zu." The most famous of the figures, or one might say *the Rohraffe*, was, however, the bearded man whose "voice" echoed through the cathedral nave and disrupted services. He it was whom Geiler so abhorred and whom he castigated in his article 16. Yet not even Geiler was strong enough to oust the *Rohraffe*, though he was doubtless able to curb excessive buffoonery during divine services. Only the radical changes of later times silenced the *Rohraffe*.

It must be noted that Geiler's pulpit (N. 80) stands between pillars to the left of the center aisle of the nave, near the transept, i. e., it is on the same side of the aisle as the organ, only farther down the aisle toward the altar. Thus while preaching Geiler could see the movements of the bearded man, the figure closest to him, and hear the voice clearly.

The meaning of the word *Rohraffe* has been a subject of dispute. The first part of the word, *Rohr-*, which some claim is derived from *Rohr*, i.e., hollow pipe, seems more correctly to derive from *röhren*, or *reren* (English roar), i.e., *schreien* (to shout) or *brüllen* (to bawl), hence also the name *Brüllaffe*. Wimpheling (*Germania*, folio f2) speaks of the bellowing or howling of the *Rohraffe:* "mugitum aut ululatum ex larva sub organis sanctissimo templo." The second part of the word, *-affe*, does not mean "monkey" or "ape," but rather "fool" in the Biblical sense, as *-affen* in *Schlaraffenland*. Thus the *Rohraffe* is the fool that roars; cf. the upper Swabian expression "schreien wie ein Roraffe."

A less common name for the figure of the bearded man, *Bretsteller* or *Brettstellermann*, seems to be a later appellation derived from the *Bretstel*, the wooden stick he is thought to have held in his right hand. In time, by folk etymology *Bretstel* became *Bretzel* or *Pretzel*.

The *Rohraffe* had been in its place at the foot of the organ case for several centuries before Geiler's time. The first organ of 1260 and the second organ of 1292 may already have had mechanical figures affixed to their cases. The third organ of 1327 is still in the cathedral today. Although the organ itself has been remodelled several times (N. 78), the organ case has remained the same since the restoration of 1385. That the *Rohraffe* pre-dates this restoration and was already in the cathedral before 1352-1354 when the great astronomical clock was installed is evident from the poem *Der Kampf des Roraffen under der Orgeln im Münster zu Strassburg mit dem Hanen daselbst auf dem Uhrwerk* – the fifteenth century version of which is said to differ only in language from the lost original of 1380 – for in the poem the *Rohraffe* scorns the much admired mechanical cock on the clock as a rank newcomer to the cathedral.

For decades scholars fought word battles over the *Rohraffe*, its meaning, identity, location and "voice." Some maintained it was the huge statue of St. Christopher which is said to have been 36 feet tall and which had to be dismembered before it could be removed from the cathedral in 1531. Some claimed it was a statue brought into the cathedral on special occasions; and some insisted that the old *Rohraffen* had disappeared at the time of the Reformation, hence nothing could be known of them. Others identified the bearded man at the foot of the organ case with the *Rohraffe*, because his location answered that described by Schott and Wimpheling, but opponents argued that the narrow, open space between the figure and the organ case was, as anyone could plainly see, much too small to conceal a person, whereas Schott definitely speaks of "a rogue hiding behind that statue." Still others believed that a speaking tube leading from the organ loft conducted the "voice" to the figure. It was left for Madame Vix-Benlay in 1935 to solve the problem: in the organ loft is a trap door by way of which a man can easily descend into the organ case, and at the bottom of the case within six feet of the bearded figure is a grill work through which he can project his voice.

The universal popularity enjoyed by the boisterous *Rohraffe* is apparent from frequent references in late medieval and sixteenth-century works, e.g., Thomas Murner, *Von dem grossen Lutherischen Narren*, 3665, and Sebastian Brant, *Narrenschiff*, No. 91, 33f. The *Rohraffe* appears as the main character in two satirical sixteenth-century poems: *Ein lustiges gespräch des Strassburgischen Rohraffens unnd Pfennig Thurns* and *Warnung des Rohraffens zu Strassburg an seinen Pasquillum* (1592); both poems are to be found in *Alsatia*, VII (1858-61), 52-97, 98-107.

The *Rohraffe* left his mark also on names of places and things. On the street *Am gebrannten End* stood an inn called *Zum Rohraffen* which is mentioned as late as 1580 when part of the street was known as *Roraffengasse*. A famous Strassburg cannon of the mid-fifteenth century bore the name Rohraffe; of this cannon Thomas Murner wrote: "Ob der Künig usz engelland ein lügener sey oder der Luther... ist er doch noch nit so starck als vnser Roraff/ der nar oder ketterlin von Einsen/ die stossen doch dicke muren vmb." Cf. Wolfgang Pfeiffer-Belli (ed.), *Thomas Murner, Kleine Schriften (Prosaschriften gegen die Reformation), Dritter Teil* (Berlin-Leipzig, 1928) = *Thomas Murners Deutsche Schriften mit den Holzschnitten der Erstdrucke*, VIII, 135, 181. It is the cannon which is meant in the couplet:

> Hett ich den Rohraffen schlaffen lohn,
> So wer mein Schloss gantz bliben stohn.
>
> (Stöber, *Sagen*, II, 216)

Cf. Dacheux, *Fragments*, IV, 121. *DW*, VIII, 1125. Gass, *Orgues*, 7-10. Hatt, *Vie*, 13. Haug, 133. Schmidt, *H. L.*, I, 174; *Namen*, 68. Schneegans, *Sagen*, 40. Stöber, *Sagen* II, 255, 315. Variot, 26f., 121. Vix-Benlay, *passim*. Wendling, "Der Kampf des Roraffen...;" has text of poem. Winckelmann, "Nachträge," 311, 321; "Rohraffen," *passim*. Zacher, 49. See also bibliographical references to N. 1326.

1334. Nebulo quispiam se post illam imaginem occultans
The rogue who gave voice to the *Rohraffe* was sometimes a lay employee in the cathedral (who was paid for his performance from cathedral funds) and sometimes a cleric or a choirboy. Variot (26f.) says that at Pentecost clerics and children of the choir had the right between church services to use the *Rohraffe* for making jokes, rude or otherwise. Apparently the right was carried too far. Indeed, the "voice" might say what it wished with impunity, because by virtue of old custom everyone participating in ceremonies of Pentecost week was free from arrest and legal prosecution (Winckelmann, "Rohraffen").

1335. Item Magister ciuium locum suum habet in ecclesia maiori... turbantur
The old practice allowing the mayor and *Stettmeister* to hold audience in the cathedral was recognized by a Strassburg statute of 1469: "Es söllent ouch alle ander lüte dhein tage, stunde oder gespreche in dem münster... haben noch halten... doch sol dis den stetmeister und den ammeister nit berüren; die mögent lüte verhören und usrichten als von alter harkommen ist" (Winckelmann, "Kulturgesch.," 280). In article 14 of his "21 Artikel" Geiler demanded that the practice be abolished.

1336. Item et alias irreuerencias locis sacris faciunt: ementes... ferentes
The din in the cathedral from the traffic mentioned by Schott was augmented by gossiping among those attending services or passing through and by hunters who came with falcons on their wrists and dogs at their sides. Cf. Brant, *Narrenschiff*, No. 43: "Wer vogel, hund inn Kirchen fuert;" and No. 44: "Gebracht in der Kirchen."

1337. Item specialiter a festo Sancti Nycholai vsque ad octauas Innocentum... perturbant.
At certain feasts in the year and especially during the Christmas season from 6 December, St. Nicholas Day, to 6 January, Epiphany, it was customary for school children, particularly choir boys, to celebrate with frolic and song. Originally these festivities were religious in character and the songs – led by the children's masters – were serious, as is attested by a song of 1404 to St. Nicholas; the first of its six verses runs as follows:

> Gaudet mater ecclesia,
> diem rependunt sidera,
> agit aetas qua tenera
> Nicolai sollempnia.

(Quoted from Mone, *Lateinische Hymnen des Mittelalters* (Freiburg, 1855), III, 465; cf. Engel, *Schulwesen*, 25, note 1).

Like other old customs, these festivities of the children deteriorated with time. Bawdy *cantilenae* displaced serious songs, and activities became rowdy to such a point that the Council of Basel had to reprove excesses. It was to correct such excesses that Schott composed poems to be sung by schoolboys (#246-#264) and chided the boys for desecrating holy places (#253 and #255, pp. 288f.; cf. N. 1626 and N. 1629).

In Advent poor scholars – "arme Schüler" (cf. N. 1002) – went around carolling and soliciting donations. During the Christmas season all school children sang from house to house and were given gifts of baked goods, eggs and wine. Masters accompanied the children to collect their pay and received what was left from the gifts to the children. After 1500 only poor scholars were allowed to beg before houses, on the streets, or in churches.

In Strassburg until 1570 a St. Nicholas market (*Klausenmarkt*) was held on the feast of the saint, 6 December; then it was forbidden as popish and in its stead the Christ Child market, *Christkindleinmarkt*, was inaugurated and gifts were given on 24 December rather than as previously on 6 December.

On St. Nicholas Day the children of the cathedral choir chose a boy bishop to represent St. Nicholas, then paraded about the streets and sang before houses.

During the chanting of the *Magnificat* in the vesper services on 27 December (the feast of St. John Evangelist, i.e., the eve of Innocents' Day) the choir boys, dressed as canons, installed their boy bishop, resplendent in full episcopal regalia, on the bishop's throne where he intoned the prayer, as they sat in the choir and sang psalms. At high mass on the following day, i.e., the feast of the Innocents, the boy bishop again occupied the episcopal throne; he chanted the prayers and gave benedictions, while the other boys, seated in the choir, sang and made the responses. This custom, says Grandidier (*Essais*, 72f.), began at Strassburg in 1135 when the choir boys celebrated the feast of the Innocents by participating in the mass which their master conducted. After high mass on Innocents' Day the choir boys donned masks and with song and dance conducted their bishop

P. 207   #187   N. 1337

in riotous pomp through the streets, chased noisily through churches and monasteries of the city and did much mischief.

On Epiphany certain dramas called *Königreichen* were performed. Details are unknown, but the dramas seem to have been a mixture of the classical year-end festivals and the story of the Magi. They involved chasing a king (or three kings) and street revelry, and had adults as well as children participating. Although adult participation was abolished by the Strassburg magistracy in 1437, the children's drama may well have continued, for Geiler preached several sermons on a quotation from this drama: "Herr der Kunig ich dienete gern."

The feast of St. Gregory on 12 March was celebrated by the choir boys with much the same revelry as the Christmas season; with their bishop they sang and romped in the streets. This practice was forbidden by the Strassburg magistracy in 1534.

Rowdiness similar to that mentioned in preceding paragraphs was by no means peculiar to Strassburg, as is indicated by the action taken against excesses by the Council of Basel. Kibre, *Privileges*, 219 (cf. also *Idem, Nations*, 47f.), relates that in 1468 the rector of the university of Paris authorized the provost to arrest scholars wearing masks and armed with sticks on the streets of Paris during the feasts of St. Catherine, St. Martin, and St. Nicholas; in the following year, because of difficulty in enforcing that authorization, all student celebrations on saints' days were forbidden.

Cf. Engel, *Schulwesen*, 24-26. Pfleger, "Christkindleinmarkt," *passim*. Stöber, *Neue Alsatia*, 278ff. Cf. also bibliography to #1326.

1338. Item diei Dominico vel abusu corrupto sic abrogatur... venalem habeant. From the fourteenth to the sixteenth century foreign bakers paid tax to the bishop for the right to sell bread on the streets of Strassburg and before the cathedral; this tax was called *Berenbrod* (*Inventaire*, III, 42). In article 10 of his "21 Artikel" Geiler asked that on Sunday foreign bakers be allowed to sell bread only after vespers.

#188. TO JOHANN KLITSCH [Strassburg, 1485-1490]

1339. Summary Schott is forwarding letters from Klitsch's* father. He urges Klitsch to apply himself diligently to the profession upon which he has embarked.

1340. Date There is no indication as to when this letter was written; its date could be anytime during the period: late 1485 when Klitsch first went to the Lowlands to study and mid-1490 when he was at the university of Paris (cf. #79 and #148).

1341. professioni cui coepisti operam et diligenciam probam impendas The "profession" may be music and organ playing, for Klitsch was later organist at the Strassburg cathedral.

#189. TO A FRIEND [LADISLAUS OF VESPRÉM] [Strassburg, after October 1481 and before May 1482]

1342. Summary Schott is glad that Ladislaus* likes the gift he sent; it is small return for Ladislaus' many kindnesses. He congratulates Ladislaus on his promotion, particularly since the next higher rank is that of bishop. He hopes Ladislaus will keep his promise to visit Strassburg and entreats him to watch carefully over Hassenstein whose mental outlook may have been affected by illness.

1343. Date There is no doubt that the friend to whom Schott is writing is Ladislaus. Schott had sent gifts to both Ladislaus and Hassenstein in September 1481 (#25, p. 34) and had heard from Ladislaus about Hassenstein's serious illness (#169, p. 189). The date of this letter must be somewhat after October 1481, when Schott wrote to Hassenstein, at that time not yet ill (#170 and N. 1204), and before 20 May 1482, when Hassenstein wrote about his recovery (#37). For chronology of the Hassenstein-Schott items, cf. Chronology III.

1344. Amico Nostro
Cf. N. 181.

1345. Ego accessioni tue plurimum sum gratulatus: praecipue... gradum Ladislaus' new post must have been that of *praepositus vespriminensis*, i.e., *praepositus* of the cathedral of the Veszprem diocese. Thus he was the highest ranking officer of the cathedral chapter and within the diocese second in rank, as Schott says, only to the bishop.

1346. Tu modo verba quibus te Argentinam inuisurum promisisti... velis
Cf. N. 101.

#190. TO A FRIEND [JOHANN WIDMANN?] [Strassburg, late December-early March 1483]

1347. Summary Although forbidden by Strassburg municipal law to accept game birds, Schott expresses thanks on behalf of his friends and himself for the gift of pheasants and hares, than which not even Apicius could have chosen finer to grace their feast. His books and other possessions – if desired – are at the friend's disposal. Because of the busy round of lunches and dinners, he begs to be forgiven for negligence in writing.

1348. Date This letter was written during the period of late December 1482 to early March 1483 when Schott was being feted as newly consecrated priest and as celebrant of his first mass (N. 340). He was still attending social functions in his honor on 1 March 1483 (#40, p. 47). It is quite possible that the friend to whom the letter is addressed is Johann Widmann* who was in Baden-Baden as physician to Christoph I* of Baden. Since Widmann did not come to Strassburg to live until later in 1483, although his parents may have moved to Strassburg some years previously (N. 290), he might not have been familiar with Strassburg municipal laws at this time. On another occasion he sent game birds to the Schotts at the baths (#67, p. 74).

P. 208   #190   N. 1349

1349. Amico Nostro
Cf. N. 181.

1350. nam si vel Apicius ipse coquinarius rei praefuisset edulio nostro
The Apicius alluded to here is almost surely Apicius Coelius, the third century author of a famous collection of recipes in 10 books entitled *De re coquinaria*. Several decades ago the collection was published by C. Giarrotano and F. Vollmer (Leipzig, 1922); recipes for *perdix, turdus* and *lepus* appear in books vi, 2 and 3; viii, 8; and *Excerpta* xxix (or pages 43f., 66f., 82, respectively of the edition).

The name Apicius has been connected with gourmet foods since the days of the early Roman epicure Apicius who lived during the republican period. It is from this epicure that both Marcus Gavius Apicius, a wealthy *bon vivant* of the time of Augustus and Tiberius, who also wrote a cook-book, and Apicius Coelius, the third century author mentioned above, took the appellation Apicius.

1351. Ait Marcialis in Xenijs suis. Inter aues Turdus... prima lepus.
Martial 13.92. The thirteenth book of Martial's epigrams is called "Xenia." Modern editions of Martial have slightly different readings in the two lines quoted by Schott: "si quid me iudice certum est" in the first line and "mattea prima lepus" in the second.

1352. quamquam municipali Argentinensium lege vetitus sim suscipere
According to Strassburg ordinances of 1381 and 1389, it was forbidden to buy or assist in buying game birds for persons not of one's own household, or to send birds to such persons, or to have birds brought by such persons to one's house or to any other place. Cf. Karl Schmidt, "Zwei Strassburger Ordnungen des Verkaufs von Vögeln und Wildpret, 1381 und 1399," *Alsatia*, VIII (1862-67), 301f.

1353. Tu si quid est in rebus meis vel libris... a paternis edibus (p. 209)
Widmann might have been planning a visit to Strassburg, and Schott wished to make him as comfortable as possible.

For the Schott house, cf. N. 1022. Schott had been living in Wolf, Sr.'s,* canonical house while Wolf was in Worms (N. 404), but during this period of festivity he seems to have stayed at home with his parents.

#191. TO A FRIEND [VITUS MAELER?] [Strassburg, 1481-1490]

1354. Summary Schott is sending an empty purse as a gift to Rome – empty, so that it may more safely slip through the midst of enemies. When in Rome, it will soon be filled by clients.

1355. Date There is no clue to the date of this note, but it may have been written soon after Schott returned home permanently from Italy, and it was probably written to Vitus Maeler.* The postscript to #29, written to Maeler 4 November 1481, employs the formal form of address as does the present item (cf. N. 330).

1356. Amico Nostro
Cf. N. 181.

#192. TO A FRIEND [JOHANN ROT] [Strassburg, early 1482]

1357. Summary Schott will do all in his power to help Rot* obtain the benefice at St. Thomas. Both *praepositus* and dean are very much in favor of Rot and the former is writing Rot particulars.

1358. Date Cf. N. 1278

1359. Amico Nostro
Cf. N. 181.

1360. si te vrbem nostram incolentem viderem
Rot was at this time in Dambach (cf. N. 239, also N. 1278).

1361. Preposito inquam et Decano sancti Thome
Cf. N. 1281.

#193. TO A FRIEND [Strassburg, 1481-1490]

1362. Summary In the name of his father Schott, Sr., young Schott has written a letter of recommendation for Johann Sifrid* who considered it advantageous to bear such a letter. Schott, Sr., would have gladly written the letter himself had he been at home, because he is deeply interested in the cause Sifrid represents, and he will be grateful for any help given Sifrid.

1363. Date If this letter was to be a recommendation from Schott, Sr., as mayor, its date would be either 1482 or 1488. If it was to be a recommendation from Schott, Sr., as director of the *fabrica*, its date would be 1481-1490. Cf. N. 113; biographical note on Schott, Sr.; also N. 76.

1364. Amico Nostro
Cf. N. 181. There is no clue as to the identity of the addressee, or to the cause Sifrid was representing.

#194. ORATION TO THE GENERAL OF THE DOMINICAN ORDER [SALVO CASSETTA] [Strassburg, late 1482]

1365. Summary As spokesman for the group of distinguished Strassburgers greeting the Dominican general, Schott speaks words of welcome in the name of the prioress and sisters of St. Nicholaus *in Undis* who are unable to be present themselves, their vows forbidding them to step more than seven paces beyond their convent walls, and who have therefore sent representatives.

P. 210   #194   N. 1365

Any benevolence the general may accord the sisters will be considered as a benevolence accorded to all Strassburg.

1366. Date In 1482 the general of the Dominican Order Salvo Cassetta* toured the German empire to reform Dominican institutions and was in Strassburg the latter part of that year (Barthelmé, 182). Judging from dates of letters he wrote in Strassburg, he was in Strassburg also from January to April 1483. One of these, a long letter of 21 February 1483, addressed to the prioress of "SS. Nicholai et Mathie Argentine in Undis," sets forth regulations concerning obedience to the provincial and to the rule (*Q. F. Domin.*, Heft 7, 72ff.). From the tenor of Schott's beginning remarks it is likely that Cassetta was being welcomed when he first arrived in Strassburg, i.e., in the latter part of 1482.

P. 211

1367. Priorissa atque sorores Conuentus sancti Nycholai in Vndis
The prioress has not been identified. The convent of St. Nicholaus and St. Mathias *in Undis* – also called *zu den Hunden* (the folk interpretation of the Latin phrase *in Undis*) an appellation which gave rise to the name *ad Canes* (the Latin translation of *zu den Hunden*) – was built and consecrated in 1252. Until the fifteenth century it stood outside the city walls. Originally Augustinian, the convent came under Dominican rule early in its history. It was levelled in the sixteenth century. Jacob Sprenger* was buried here (Barth, *Handbuch*, 1386ff. Borries, 64). For the paintings of Schott family members in the convent church, cf. biographical note on Schott, Sr.

#195. ORATION TO THE PREMONSTRATENSIANS [Hagenau?, mid-1481 to mid-1490]

1368. Summary The edition of *Breviarium horarum canonicarum* edited by Berchtold Dürr,* abbot of Adelberg, and printed at Strassburg is recommended to the Premonstratensians as an accurate and desirable edition prepared especially for them by one of their number.

1369. Date We have perused lists of fifteenth century printings at Strassburg without success to find an edition of the breviary edited by Dürr. Schmidt (*H. L.*, II, 22) says he also searched bibliographical material in vain for reference to it. One may conjecture that perhaps one of Schott's printer friends, Adolph Rusch* or Martin Flach, Sr.,* had published the breviary, and that being so excellent an edition, the copies were literally fingered away. The date of the speech cannot therefore be ascertained. It may have been delivered to the Premonstratensians in the monastery dedicated to the Virgin and Saints Paul and Nicholas at Hagenau. That Schott had connections with this monastery is evident from his elegiac of 1488 written in Hagenau (#262; cf. N. 1659); also in this speech Schott speaks of the Virgin's symbol displayed on the canons' robes; it is possible that in Hagenau the Premonstratensians wore such a symbol to honor the most exalted dedicatee of their monastery.

1370. Indicata vobis iam ab exordio fuerunt... Premonstratensium vobis inditum est nomen.
The Premonstratensians, known in English as White Canons from their habits, are an order of canons regular adhering to an austere version of the Augustinian rule. Although Schott, by way of tribute to his hearers, explains the name of Premonstratensian as derived from the integrity of life exemplified by members of the order and from the symbol of the Virgin displayed on their white habits, the more usual explanation is that the name derives from Prémontré in Aisne, the site of the first monastery of the order founded 1120 by St. Norbert (afterwards archbishop of Magdeburg).

1371. in Argentina inclita Elueciorum vrbe imprimi
The phrase "Strassburg, city of the Helvetians," was not uncommon in the fifteenth century, because the terms Helvetian and Alsatian were at that time considered synonymous. It is found, for example, in a poem by Rudolph Lang to Rusch,* and it is the designation Wimpheling urged all Strassburg printers to use in their colophons. The conclusion to the *Lucubraciunculae* Wimpheling addressed to "omnes Helueticos: id est Alsaticos" (#301, p. 322) and in its text he speaks to "gentiles meos Heluecios: hoc est Alsaticos" (p. 323). In a bitter quarrel with the Swiss over the use of Helvetian for Alsatian, Wimpheling even disputed the right of the Swiss to the name Helvetians (Schmidt, *H. L.*, I, 71ff.). The confusion of the terms Helvetian and Alsatian Schmidt (*Bibliotheken*, 82) traces to an erroneous statement by Aeneas Silvio Piccolomini; cf. also Weislinger, 681, n. (*).

#196. ORATION TO CERTAIN PRIESTS [Strassburg, 1488, late 1489 or early 1490]?

1372. Summary Gratitude is expressed to the priests who so continually on this day prayed for the soul of the noble patron and father.

1373. Date If this speech was delivered to priests officiating at the funeral of Gottfried von Adelsheim, Sr.,* (N. 1303), then the date of its delivery must have been late 1489 or early 1490; if the funeral concerned was that of Peter Müg, Sr.,* then the date of the speech must be sometime in 1488. Both Adelsheim and Müg were influential persons in Strassburg and both were related by marriage to the Schotts, so that Peter Schott would as a matter of course take a personal interest in their funeral ceremonies.

#197. EPITAPH [for Diether von Isenburg, Mainz?], 17 December 1483

1374. Summary Let no man become proud because of accumulated wealth or honors. Behold, the venerable man who held many a benefice is enclosed in so small a tomb.

1375. Date It is quite possible that Schott recited the epitaph in Mainz when the much-maligned archbishop of Mainz, Diether von Isenburg,* was laid in his tomb. The fact that the date of entombment (17 December 1483) is more than a year after the date of Diether's death is not surprising, for it took considerable time to fashion the elaborately ornamented, stone tombs of great personages.

1376. ecce vir venerabilis Archiepiscopus...
The incunabulum has "ecce vir venerabilis A.R." For the abbreviation "A.R.," Cappelli (22) gives "Anno Regni" and (435) "A rationibus, Anno resurrectionis," etc.; for the abbreviation "AR" Cappelli (434) gives "Ara, Arietes," etc. None of these readings fits the passage in the epitaph. Assuming then that here only part of a longer abbreviation is used, we find: 1) among various meanings of "A.R." in combination with other letters, where each letter represents the beginning of a word, the only reading which might fit our context is "anima requiescat," and 2) among single word abbreviations formed by "AR" in combination with other letters, the most likely reading is "archiepiscopus." This latter is the reading we have chosen, because in the sentence structure it balances the titles *Prepositus* and *Decanus*.

1377. Sanctorum Petri Fritçlariensis... Nostri Minstermeyfelt... Decanus
It is difficult to establish what specific benefices Archbishop Diether von Isenburg held, because he was once by papal command stripped of at least most, if not all, benefices; however, Würdtwein (544) has an entry verifying one of the benefices mentioned in the epitaph: "Ditherus de Isenburg comes in Büdingen... Prepositus ecelesie Sancti Petri Fritzlariensis moguntinensis diocesis... 1456."
Re: the phrase *N(ostri) Minstermeyfelt*, cf. N. 181; this is one instance where the *N.* of the incunabulum means "name unknown" or "X." The church referred to is very likely the *Monasterium Magnensiae* at Maifeld in the *Eifel* which in the tenth century was elevated to the status of a collegiate church and was dedicated to St. Severus of Valeria (cf. Josef Schramm, *Die Eifel* (Essen, 1963) =*Deutsche Landschaft*, XIII, 27f.).
Re: the phrase *huius tamen... Decanus*, the word *huius* here may mean either "of the latter" (i.e., Diether was dean of the church at Maifeld), or "of this" (i.e., Diether was dean of the cathedral at Mainz, in which he was being entombed).

#198. ORATION TO THOSE WHO ATTENDED PETER SCHOTT'S FIRST MASS [Strassburg, 2 February 1483]

1378. Summary Schott thanks the clerics and laymen who honored with their presence the celebration of his first mass; in this as in all things praise and honor is due the Lord, not man. (For correction in title, cf. *Errata*).

1379. Date Schott's first mass was celebrated 2 February 1483, cf. N. 340.

1380. amplissimi Patres et prestantissimi viri: qui inicialem... statueritis
For a notation about those present at Schott's first mass, cf. #40, p. 46, also N. 399 and N. 401.

P. 213 #199 N. 1381

#199. REQUEST FOR DONATIONS TO THE DOMINICAN PROVINCIAL ASSEMBLY [ADDRESSED TO GEILER?] [Strassburg, on or before 5 April 1488]

1381. Summary If his pleas be of any avail, Schott beseeches Geiler to urge the people to contribute liberally to the fund which the priest bearing this letter is collecting for the Dominican conference to be held at Pforzheim on *Cantate* Sunday. An unusually large crowd is expected because a new provincial is to be elected, and the town of Pforzheim cannot without help care for all the visitors. Aside from the fact that the bearer has close ties with Schott, as his spiritual father in Bologna for many years, and aside from the fact that Schott has already in Geiler's name so to speak promised him support, the cause itself is worthy; even good mendicants still have to beg. Believing them to be merely burdensome, Schott is not sending letters on hand from both the vicar and bishop of Strassburg which authorize collection of money for the conference, nor the letter from the Dominican provincial which declares those who contribute to be participants in the spiritual good issuing from the conference. Schott would himself come to Geiler, except for duty on the *nones*.

1382. Date The assembly of the Dominican *provincia Teutonica* mentioned in the item as about to be held at Pforzheim on *Cantate* Sunday is the assembly (documented by Loë, *Q.F. Domin.*, I, 42) at which Jacob Sprenger* was re-elected provincial: "A.D. 1488 in Phorzem, dominica cantate, sub reverendo patre et magistro in theologia, Jacobo Sprenger, priore Coloniensi, pro tunc vicario provincie propter absolucionem provincialis, et ibidem idem pater in provincialem electus." Sprenger's election received papal confirmation 18 June 1488.

In 1488 *Cantate* Sunday, the fourth Sunday after Easter, fell on 4 May. Obviously then the *nones* when Schott was having duty are not the *nones* of May (or 7 May) during the conference, but the *nones* of April or an earlier month; hence the date of the item cannot be later than the *nones* of April, or 5 April 1488.

1383. It should be noted that items #199-#207 are not listed separately in the *Registrum operis* of the *Lucubraciunculae* but are listed as *Promotoriales missive* (#303, p. 327); also that items #200-#207 have no Wimpheling headings (cf. N. 37).

P. 214

1384. si quid apud te preces mee valent... Hortari velis populum/ ut patri...
Dacheux (*Réf.*, 416) believes not only that this appeal was addressed to Geiler but also that the orders generally used Schott as an intermediary whenever they desired favors from Geiler. Certainly the tone of the appeal is very much like that of Schott's letters to Geiler, and just such cajoling from someone he loved was necessary to prevent the irascible Geiler, who had good cause to dislike the orders (N. 955, par. 6, and N. 1323) – the Dominicans in particular – from venting his spleen against the mendicants when announcing from his pulpit the collection of money for the Dominicans.

The priest who had been Schott's spiritual father in Bologna and who was being sent to collect the money has not been identified.

1385. mendicantes enim mendicant: et hi boni et... obseruantes
Geiler had close friends among the mendicant orders, e.g., Emerich Kemel,*

P. 214   #199   N. 1385

O.F.M., and Thomas Lampertheim,* O.P. For Dominicans of Observance, cf. N. 689.

1386. Litteras et Vicarij et Episcopi nostri... Item litteras prouincialis
I.e., letters of Andreas Hartmann,* episcopal vicar., of Bishop Albrecht* and of Jacob Sprenger,* "retiring" provincial of the Dominicans.

1387. Ipse venirem: sed oportet interesse nonis
A canon could not leave his post when he had special duties to perform (cf. N. 116, 2).

#200. REQUEST FOR DONATIONS TO AN IMPOVERISHED MOTHER [ADDRESSED TO GEILER?] [Strassburg, date unknown]

1388. Summary As requested by a lady of public charity, Schott asks the recipient of this note to commend to the people for alms at the church door a mother of many children, formerly a beggar, now after an illness insane to such a point that it is feared she may do bodily harm to the children. (Cf. N. 1383).

#201. REQUEST FOR PERSONAL INTERVIEW [Strassburg, 1482 or 1488?]

1389. Summary Schott, Sr., having read the letter brought to his son by a certain heir, advises a consultation on Strassburg laws. The addressee and the heir are therefore bidden to come to the Schott home for an interview on the morrow at the seventh hour. (Cf. N. 1383).

1390. Date It is possible that Schott, Sr., was being consulted as mayor of the city; if so, the date of this item could be either 1482 or 1488. For the Schott home, cf. N. 1022.

P. 215

#202. REQUEST FOR BOOK STATEMENT [Strassburg, 1482?-1490]

1391. Summary Martinus, the parish priest of St. Thomas, has asked that Schott and the addressee of this note render statements of books received on account with a certain Nürnberg printer and of the amount of money still in the account. These statements along with other business items are to be sent to Nürnberg. If the addressee will send his statement to Schott, it will be delivered to Martinus. (Cf. N. 1383).

1392. Date If the Martinus mentioned in this item is identical with Martinus Lauri de Vingen of #26, #27 and #29, who at the end of 1481 had no benefice, the date of the item can be no earlier than 1482.

P. 215 #202 N. 1393

1393. a Nurenbergensi Impressore
Which Nürnberg printer is concerned here is not known. According to Vouliéme (1922 edition, 122-132), there were ten printers active in Nürnberg during the period 1481-1490: Anton Koberger (1464-1491), Friedrich Creussner (1472-1499), Hans Folz, who printed *Schwänke* (1483-1488), the Augustinians (1479-1484), Konrad Zeninger of Mainz (1480-1483), Printer of the *Rochuslegende* (1480-1484), Max Ayrer (1483, 1487-1491), Peter Wagner of Nürnberg (*Currifex*, 1483-1500), Georg Stuchs (1484-1518), Peter Vischer (1487).

#203. QUESTION OF CORRECT USAGE [ADDRESSED TO GEILER?] [Strassburg, 1481-1490]

1394. Summary Geiler is asked to check two passages in his copy of St. John Chrysostom.* The proof reader questions the use of the accusative after the participle *exuti*, although Schott considers it correct. (Cf. N. 1383).

1395. Date There can be little doubt that this note was written during the period of Schott's activity in Strassburg. He would not have had time to edit works while studying in Italy. Nor can there be much doubt that Geiler is the recipient of the note, for he was a great admirer of Chrysostom and urged Schott to compose a poem of praise to him along with the two other Johns (#240 and #241); indeed, Geiler may well have instigated a Schott edition of Chrysostom; cf. N. 134.

1396. quando participium accusatiuum post se paciatur... perspicias oro...
Harpers' lists under *exuo* one example of the accusative after the past participle *exutum:* Vergil *Aen.* iv. 518.
Here is another example of the care with which editions were prepared (cf. #142, p. 157, and N. 1046. For Schott's activity as an editor, cf. p. xxx, N. 134-N. 139).

#204. REQUEST FOR LIST OF PLACES IN THE HOLY LAND [Strassburg early 1490]

1397. Summary Schott asks that names of places in the Holy Land about which first-hand information is desired be added to the list for Bohuslaus von Hassenstein. (Cf. N. 1383).

1398. Date This note must have been written sometime in the first months of 1490 in order to get the information to Hassenstein before he left Bohemia for his "grand tour"; by 16 May he was in Venice (#144, p. 159, and N. 1055).

#205. REQUEST NOT TO ATTEND CHOIR [Strassburg, early 1482-1490]

1399. Summary Johann Simmler* wishes the recipient of this note to refrain from attending choir; he will explain the reason at lunch.

1400. Date This note was no doubt written after Schott became canon (p. xxvii).

1401. ut visitacionem chori hoc mane deuites
Attendance at choir was obligatory for all members of a chapter (N. 116, 2); only permission from a chapter or higher officer could excuse one from attendance. Johann Simmler as an official of the bishop could excuse a member of any chapter, and as dean of St. Thomas could excuse a member of that chapter.

#206. REQUEST TO DELIVER LETTERS AND GREETINGS [ADDRESSED TO GEILER] [Strassburg, 1486-1490]

1402. Summary Schott asks Geiler to deliver a letter to Andreas and to extend greetings from his parents and himself to Friedrich von Zollern.*

1403. Date This note was written to Geiler when he was about to depart for one of his visits with Friedrich von Zollern, bishop of Augsburg, either at Dillingen or at the baths.

1404. domino Andree
The gentleman concerned may be Andreas Hartmann von Eppingen* who was accompanying Geiler or whom Geiler would see en route.

#207. REQUEST TO ANNOUNCE PAPAL INDULGENCES [Strassburg, 1486?]

1405. Summary For the salvation of souls and the benefit of the *fabrica* of New St. Peter, Schott asks that the people be informed about the great number of papal indulgences available at that *fabrica*. (Cf. N. 1383).

1406. Date It is possible that the papal indulgences for sale at the *fabrica* of New St. Peter were part of the indulgences brought to Strassburg in 1486 by the papal legate Raymund Peraudi* (cf. Specklin, 287). The request to announce the sale of indulgences at this *fabrica* was probably sent to all preachers, including Geiler.

1407. oro pro salute animarum et vtilitate fabrice ... denunciare velis populo
This passage is proof that Schott was not opposed to indulgences and that Specklin's account of how Schott viciously attacked the sale of such is incorrect (cf. N. 58). Very likely Schott had much the same attitude toward indulgences as Geiler who explained them as a remission of debt, a debt of temporal punishment. Dacheux (*Réf.*, 247) says Geiler was against only the abuse of indulgences; legitimate indulgences, Geiler felt, gave help to persons in distress and supported the defense of faith. Hieronymus de Zanctivis,* Schott's teacher at Bologna, wrote in his *De foro conscientiae* that indulgence does not remove guilt, because guilt is absolved by contrition and confession. Johann Burckard* probably expressed wide-spread contemporary belief when he stated that debt is not entirely cancelled when sin is forgiven; atonement, in which indulgences aid, is still necessary (cf. Thurston, 344f.).

1408. fabrice ecclesie sancti Petri iunioris
According to Horning ("Stift", no pagination), the *fabrica* of New St. Peter had so little income that it could not maintain the church. For this reason canons during their first three years in office paid annually 50 Rhenish florins to the *fabrica* fund.

#208. TO PETER SCHOTT FROM DANIEL FRIESENHEIMER [Strassburg, 1486?]

1409. Summary Daniel Friesenheimer,* provincial of the Augustinian Rhine-Swabian province asks Schott's opinion on the following case: A certain cleric had jotted down a list of his sins, and on the same slip of paper made a notation of the theft of a florin in Mülhausen. Another cleric found the memorandum in the first cleric's book and, recognizing the handwriting, not only kept the memorandum but used it to defame the writer among his fellows. The provincial wishes to know whether the writer can be accused of theft on the basis of the memorandum and whether the cleric who defamed the writer deserves punishment.

1410. Date This item and #209 form a unit; the present item states the case and #209 is Schott's opinion on the case. Friesenheimer states that the incidents related in the case took place while the indulgences of the year of jubilee were still in force. Such indulgences remained in force for a year, beginning 25 December and ending 25 December of the following year. The jubilee year referred to may have been either the regular Roman jubilee of 1475 (the first one to be held at the 25 year interval fixed by Paul II in 1470) or what is more likely the special jubilee year declared for the accession in 1484 of Innocent VIII. This year would have ended 25 December 1485; hence we may assume that the date of the present item is 1486.

1411. quare ad vos dominum meum/ et vtriusque Iuris redimitum...
Note that Friesenheimer, a provincial, addresses Schott with the formal form while Schott in his answer uses the familiar form; for Schott's views on the formal form of address, cf. #9, p. 15, and N. 184.

1412. Demum si lumen sciencie vestre non vellet ponere sub modio
Cf. Mt. 5:15.

1413. vellem vobis committere causam aduocacionis titulo... locuturus sum
Nothing is known of the case concerning a legal claim in Mainz against the city council of Freiburg im Breisgau. Schott declined the offer to act as attorney for the defense (#209, p. 218).

#209. TO DANIEL FRIESENHEIMER [Strassburg, 1486?]

1414. Summary The memorandum concerning the theft of a florin at Mülhausen proves absolutely nothing against the writer. In every criminal case suitable witnesses and evidence are necessary to prove guilt. The

P. 216   #209   N. 1414

memorandum concerning the theft is not an indisputable confession of theft on the part of the writer. He may have suspected someone of theft, or have been concealing the theft of another, or – if he were a priest – he may have heard of the theft in confession; there are many interpretations of the memorandum. The second cleric, however, who deliberately kept the memorandum for the purpose of defaming its writer has acted against law and brotherly love. He can be sued for libel by the writer. Canon law accords severe punishment to those who falsely vilify their brothers. (Cf. N. 1410).

P. 217

1415. Ita decidit Bartolus
Cf. N. 342.

P. 218

1416. Causam aduocacionis de qua scribis negocia alia... non paciuntur.
Cf. N. 1413.

#210. TO THE FACULTIES OF THEOLOGY AND LAW AT THE UNIVERSITY OF HEIDELBERG [Zabern, mid-1484]

1417. Summary Writing in the name of Bishop Albrecht* of Strassburg, Schott explains that in Strassburg it has long been customary to deny the Last Sacrament to those condemned to death. Some time ago there arose considerable dispute among the Strassburgers about the custom, some – principally Johann Geiler von Kaysersberg – urging its abolition as contrary to the Scriptures and harmful to the salvation of souls, others defending it as necessary for the public good. To settle the question, opinions of experts in religion and canon law were collected under the supervision of the episcopal vicar, but the opinions were so conflicting that no decision could be reached. It therefore seems fitting to solicit a verdict on the opinions of the Strassburgers from the faculties at the university of Heidelberg which has a higher reputation for faith and for zeal in defending the truth than any other institution of higher learning in the land.

1418. Date Items #210, #211 and #212 concern the question of administering the Last Sacrament to criminals condemned to death. For a discussion of the dates of these items, cf. N. 1319.

1419. ea consuetudine: que illic hactenus obtinuit... sacramentum denegetur
For details of the long battle over the administering of the Last Sacrament to criminals condemned to death, cf. N. 1325. It was an extremely bold move on Geiler's part to attack a custom so hallowed by tradition, and the hesitance of both the Strassburg city council and of Bishop Albrecht to assume full responsibility for its abolition is understandable, as is the length of time taken by the Heidelberg faculties to reach their unanimous decision.

P. 219 #210 N. 1420

P. 219

1420. Alijs quidem/ in primis autem... Magistro Iohanne de Keisersberg
In the long struggle to abolish the custom, the venerable doctor of theology Johann Freitag (called "von Düsseldorf," though by birth a Strassburger), prior of the Strassburg Carmelites, stood by Geiler. The chief opponents were the Franciscans and the Dominicans who had fought bitterly against the establishment of the cathedral chair and seized every opportunity to attack its incumbent, Geiler (cf. N. 955, par. 6).

1421. scandala suboriri... eos quos nobis peritos: per Vicarium fore consulendos
For *scandala*, cf. N. 978. Schott was one of the experts whose opinion (#212) was sought by the episcopal vicar Andreas Hartmann von Eppingen.*

1422. Verum cum eorum scripta dissonancia deprehenderimus
For a good example of the great difference between legal opinions, cf. Simmler's* and Schott's opinions on the grain loans (#214 and #215, also N. 1438 and N. 1442).

1423. Equidem pro ea confidencia: quam erga vos... praeelegimus.
Cf. N. 1325, par. 7.

#211. TO THE FACULTIES OF THEOLOGY AND LAW AT THE UNIVERSITY OF HEIDELBERG [Zabern, fall 1484]

1424. Summary In the name of Bishop Albrecht of Strassburg, Schott entreats the Heidelberg faculties to send their long awaited verdict as soon as possible. If they do not wish to give a verdict, would they so state, for the matter brooks no further delay (cf. N. 1417-N. 1419, also N. 1319, N. 1325).

P. 220

1425. Ante exactos menses aliquot: explanacionem veritatis... desiderauimus
Schott is referring to his letter in the name of the bishop, #210.

1426. tolerata falsitas insolenti peruicacie ansam ut aiunt suppeditet
Cf. N. 254

#212. OPINION OF PETER SCHOTT ON THE LAST SACRAMENT FOR THE CONDEMNED [Strassburg, early 1484]

1427. Summary By many references to both canon and civil law, to the glossators, to Duns Scotus and to the Scriptures Schott proves that the Eucharist cannot be denied criminals condemned to death. According to law, those guilty of capital crimes and even those guilty of heresy – the worst of all crimes – may not be denied the Last Sacrament. A custom contrary to law, though of long standing, cannot nullify law, nor can it render those entitled by law to receive the Last Sacrament legally unfit to receive it. Lay

P. 220   #212   N. 1427

authority metes out corporal punishment, but has no jurisdiction over the soul; such jurisdiction belongs to the province of divine law. (Cf. N. 1417-N. 1419, N. 1319, N. 1325.)

1428. utpote Euangelici. Luce xxij cum similibus tamen determinacio...
Cf. Lc. 22:19-20.

P. 224

1429. ut vult Bartolus in...
Cf. N. 342.

1430. Quod si dicatur aliam et diuersam esse racionem... non sic Eucharistia.
Geiler's opponents argued that it was enough to allow criminals condemned to death to repent, because repentance, not the Eucharist, is necessary for salvation.

P. 226

#213. CASE OF GRAIN LOANS, STATED BY JOHANN ROT [Strassburg, early 1483]

1431. Summary A certain man lent grain to four grain farmers, with the understanding that they return new grain after the coming harvest, whether or not the new grain were as good quality as the grain lent. At harvest time grain prices were low and his barns full, so the lender deferred return of the grain, although he would have accepted it. When, however, grain prices rose, because of shortages in the years 1481 and 1482, he demanded by court order that the grain be returned. Each of the four farmers – not having any grain to return – signed a personal notarized contract to pay for the grain on a stipulated day in 1482 at the current Strassburg market price; but on expiration of the contracts, none of the farmers was able to pay his debt and each signed a property mortgage at the accepted rate of 21% interest. Are these mortgages valid? According to law and the court of conscience is the lender guilty of usury?

1432. Date Items #213-#215 form a unit on the question of usury in lending grain, the present item being the statement of the case by Johann Rot,* the following two items being Simmler's* opinion and Schott's opinion. (Note how differently the two interpret the case).
    Since the latest date mentioned in the text is "sexta feria ante Lucie" 1482 (i.e., the sixth day before St. Lucia or 8 December 1482) after which date all three farmers had signed mortgages, Rot's statement of the case was very likely written in early 1483 and the two opinions (#214 and #215) shortly thereafter.

1433. Cum autem frumenta (caristia vrgente)... essent magni precij
According to Wencker's chronicle, 1478-1482 was a period of very hard times. Berler cites 1478 as a year of grasshoppers and plague. All Strassburg chroniclers give 1480 as an extremely bad year when summer floods, high

water and frost ruined crops, when people died of disease and famine, and when grains were very high priced. Trausch's note that in 1481 "was grosser und guter Herbst" must be an error in date or must have applied to only a small area, for Trithemius mentions the year of 1481 as one of high-priced grains and general scarcity of victuals in France, the Lowlands and the Rhineland. It was during the famine of 1481, Lauffer says, when Geiler demanded that grain for distribution to the poor be taken from the rich and paid for later.

Since the price of grain was low at the time of the grain loans and the lender did not insist upon return of grain at harvest time because his barns were full, the loans must have been made at the very beginning of the bad cycle 1478-1482, certainly before summer of the disastrous year 1480.

Cf. Dacheux, *Fragments*, II, 466; III, 58, 141; IV, 40, 41. Lauffer, 41. Strobel, 385. Reuss, "Meyer," 156. Trithemius, *Ann. Hirs.*, II, 512. *Luc.*, #248.

1434. in festo Assumpcionis Marie... feria sexta ante Lucie... lxxxij
The dates mentioned in the second and third paragraphs of the text are: *in festo Assumpcionis Marie*, 15 August; *ferie sexte ante festum Penthecostes*, 21 May (in 1482 Pentecost was on 26 May); *in festo natiuitatis beate Virginis*, 8 September; *ferie sexte ante festum beati Iohannis baptiste*, 19 June (the feast of St. John the Baptist is 24 June); *in feria sexta ante Lucie*, 8 December (St. Lucia is 13 December); *circa Hilarij*, around 13 January which is St. Hilary's day.

The borrowed grain was to be paid for at the market price obtaining on 21 May 1482, 19 June 1482 and 8 December 1482. Several of these days may have been quarter days; English quarter days were 25 March (Lady Day), 24 June (Midsummer's Day), 29 September (Michaelmas Day), 25 December (Christmas Day); in Scotland quarter days were 15 May (set as Whitsunday), 1 August (Lammas), 11 November (Martinmas), 2 February (Candlemas).

1435. quinque plaphardi... floreno... vel xij solidis
The relative value of Strassburg coins is difficult to assess, because there is little information about them, because their value varied from time to time and because terms for the coins differ from one source to another. So far as can be ascertained a florin was worth 10 *solidi* or 20 blapherts (cf. Appendix N, also N. 915 and p. xix). Therefore, when the personal contracts were signed by the farmers borrowing grain, the price of grain was about two to five times higher than when the grain was lent.

1436. foro consciencie
The *forum conscientiae* is an ecclesiastical court, also called *forum animae* and *forum poenitentiale* (cf. Du Cange, under *forum*). Oberman (470) defines *forus animae* as the courtroom of the soul, dealing with private sins, where the accuser and accused are the same person standing *coram Deo* (before God).

1437. A simile foecit cum colono... in preteritis gultis... par racio iuris...
The *colonus*, a small farmer or villager, was evidently not a Strassburg citizen. Rot was not sure whether the Strassburg statutes would apply to

such a person since the regulations concerning non-citizens differed from those concerning citizens (cf. #187, p. 206, and N. 1328). *Gulta, ae,* means harvest.

#214. OPINION OF JOHANN SIMMLER ON THE GRAIN LOANS
[Strassburg, early 1483]

1438. Summary The lender has transgressed the law of brotherly love and is guilty of usury. Had he lent his grain with the understanding that he would accept even old grain in return at whatever time his creditors could deliver it, he would not be guilty of usury, but he made the loans in order to profit by receiving new grain which is always considered better and of greater market value than old. If he had kept his grain, he would have had to suffer depreciation and to risk possible loss, as well as to pay hauling charges. In the written contracts he set the dates for the market prices at which the debtors were to pay, and for the first debtor he set the date in the week before Pentecost when grain prices are usually higher. He can be required to do penance and to give satisfaction to his neighbors, whom he has injured, by paying them the amount he demanded over and above what was actually due him. (Cf. N. 1432).

1439. Et verum in foro anime: non autem in foro iudiciali
For *forum animae,* cf. N. 1436. *Forum iudiciale* may be the same as *forus publicus in ecclesia* which is defined by Oberman (470) as the ecclesiastical court dealing with public sins.

1440. et procedit in foro contencioso
Cf. N. 738.

1441. sextam feriam ante festum Penthecostes... festum Assumpcionis
Cf. N. 1434.

#215. OPINION ON THE GRAIN LOANS [Strassburg, early 1483]

1442. Summary The loans cannot be called usury because the lender was willing to accept in return grain of equal or worse quality. Nor can the expectation of profit without detriment or fraud to the debtor be termed usury, else all loans, especially those dealing with weights and measures would be considered usury. It was not through the fault of the creditor but through the delay of the debtors that the grain was not returned before the years of scarcity. The harsh demand for the return of the grain, however, was contrary to brotherly love, but the lender cannot be held for restitution because he did not detain his debtors' goods. There should be a meeting of the parties concerned and the amounts of the debts should be diminished. (Cf. N. 1432).

1443. late ostendit Magister Iohannes consulens... ex mutuo consequi lucrum
The reference is to Johann Simmler.* Schott had read Simmler's opinion before he finished his own.

1444. in foro contencioso... in foro autem anime
Cf. N. 738 and N. 1436.

1445. Respondeo enim non haberi racionem
Cf. *Errata*.

#216. MORAL AND LEGAL QUESTIONS CONCERNING CLERICS [STATED BY JOHANN ROT?] [Strassburg, 1483-1490]

1446. Summary 1. Ought the holder of a benefice support his concubine and any children he has by her from goods of the Church, assuming she and the children are paupers? Ought he provide home, income and education for the children?
2. Ought the holder of a benefice help poor friends and relatives? Ought he maintain them at the standard of living commensurate with their social status; e.g., if he is of noble birth, does he support his father as a noble? In order to give proper aid ought he to accumulate benefices?
3. Do those attending chapter meetings while divine services are in progress commit mortal sin and are they liable for restitution of the goods distributed to chapter members?
4. Does the cleric who attends canonical hours, masses and wakes, but who, instead of participating in the songs or prayers, remains silent or occupies himself with other texts, commit mortal sin, and is he liable for restitution of goods distributed?
5. Is a notorious fornicator liable to restitution of the income from his benefice and of the goods distributed daily?

1447. Date These questions were very likely drafted, as was the case of grain loans, by Johann Rot* who in his capacity of *vicar in poenitentialibus* would have to do with problems in the forum of conscience. Since Rot did not arrive in Strassburg until mid-1482 to become lay preacher at the cathedral, his episcopal post must have been acquired sometime later. The date of these questions can then not be earlier than 1483. This item and #217 form a unit, #217 being Schott's opinion on the questions put in this item.

1448. Vtrum beneficiatus possit et debeat concubinam... negociorum aliorum
The support of concubines and children by holders of benefices with goods received from the Church was a formidable issue, because the highest church-

men were guilty of so doing. Innocent VIII had a recognized son and daughter and is said to have had many other children; Bishop Albrecht* of Strassburg had several children; Thomas Wolf, Sr.,* had a son whom he legitimatized and – because of his many illegitimate children – was the butt of biting epigrams (cf. his biographical note).

1449. Et ut hoc possit facere: debeat Beneficia congregare plura etc.
For Schott's views on the plurality of benefices, cf. p. xxx; N. 130, 5; N. 133.

1450. Vtrum celebrantes Capitula infra diuina officia... restitucionem...
One of the chief obligations of a chapter member was to attend choir during services and he might allow no other duties to interfere with this, except when excused. For duties of and distributions to benefice holders, cf. N. 116,2.
  One of the four *deputationes* of the Council of Basel (1431-1449) was devoted to reform, and – beginning in 1435 – decrees concerning church discipline, abuse of excommunication and interdicts, concubinage among the clergy, etc. were passed.

1451. Vtrum clericus presens in choro tempore horarum canonicarum...
Great emphasis was placed on attendance at canonical hours. Geiler mentions this in his *Monita* to Friedrich von Zollern* (Appendix H); Gallus'* poem (#298) treats the subject; one of the questions Schott put to Gabriel Biel* is about such attendance (#222, p. 250).

1452. sicut in Angelica dicitur
The reference is to the famous *Summa angelica* or *Summa casuum*, a dictionary or alphabetical guide for confessors, compiled by Angelus Carletus (†1495), O.F.M. *de Observantia*, who served as general vicar for the Italian Franciscan province and as *nuntius* to Sixtus IV. The guide went through 30 editions from 1476 to 1520.

#217. OPINION ON THE QUESTIONS CONCERNING CLERICS [Strassburg, 1483-1490]

1453. Summary 1. The holder of a benefice cannot support his concubine from goods of the Church. She who has transgressed against the Church ought not to receive its bounty. The children, however, must be supplied with food, shelter, clothing and education by their father according to his income from the goods of the Church.
  2. The holder of a benefice can help his poor relatives just as he would help the poor generally. The only difference is that he may help his relatives before he helps others.
  3. Those who call chapter meetings at the time of divine services, except in an emergency demanding immediate attention, do sin, but the subordinates summoned to the meeting and bound to obedience are not at fault. There is no question of restitution of goods distributed.
  4. Those who attend choir during canonical hours, masses, or wakes and neither sing nor pray but otherwise occupy themselves sin grievously, unless there is good reason for their silence. In many Gallic churches the

canons in the choir are supposed to keep silent, because a group of trained singers execute the songs and chants. There is no restitution.

5. (Schott does not answer the question about the fornicator.)

Schott notes that Simmler* who has tracts on these matters will state his opinion on the questions. He himself feels he requires more information and wishes to know Simmler's opinion before further committing himself. (Cf. N. 1447.)

1454. ut Bartolus... voluit Bartolus
Cf. N. 342.

1455. Immo eciam impense ad disciplinas mihi videntur... deberi.
As a humanist Schott would necessarily support the education of any children. For his interest in education, cf. xxviiif., N. 123, N. 125.

1456. formam Decreti Basiliensis
Cf. N. 1450.

1457. Magistrum Iohannem Symler... ad ecclesiam suam in Herlinsheim
It is not known what benefice Simmler held at the Herlinsheim church. Wuerdtwein (59) lists the benefices at Herlinsheim among those controlled by the Strassburg cathedral chapter.

#218. ADVICE ON A LITIGATION [Strassburg, *ca.* 1485-1490]

1458. Summary [Apparently a case of litigation brought by officials of a monastery against a papal commissioner, who had been authorized by the pope to reform their monastery, had been decided in favor of the commissioner and the officials had appealed the decision. The pope then had committed the case to a judge who asked Schott's advice.]

Schott explains that the case before the judge is not the original complaint but the appeal. He gives his opinion on the case and the appeal.

The pope had instructed the commissioner by letter to do what he, according to the dictates of his conscience, considered necessary to reform the monastery. The powers of the commissioner were thus not limited by specific instructions, nor were they limited by legal restrictions which do not apply to reform and correction of [monasterial] rules. He was to use his judgment in adjusting reforms to the conditions of the monastery, its location, its practices and so on. By this method all monasteries – lapsed from regular observance – have been reformed. How then did the commissioner sin, if he acted according to his instructions?

The appeal is unjust because it concerns first: the correction of a superior, i.e., the papal commissioner; and second: the action of a man guided by his conscience. Hence if the judge of the appeal finds that the commissioner proceeded as he felt he ought to proceed and did not offend

P. 239   #218   N. 1458

God's law, the judge will decide that neither the original complaint nor the appeal is just.

1459. Date There is no clue to the identity of the judge who asked Schott about the case, or of the papal commissioner, nor yet of the monastery. The only hint to a possible date for this item is Schott's comment at the beginning of the item that he has been hesitant about giving advice, because he has for a long time been out of touch with the legal profession. It is possible, therefore, that the date is some years after Schott's return to Strassburg in 1481, perhaps in the mid-1480's or later.

1460. Fateor etenim si expresse constaret de mente summi Pontificis
The pope mentioned is presumably Innocent VIII.

P. 240

1461. Deinde praesumitur in dubio Princeps
I. e., the pope.

1462. non video quomodo principalem querelam examinare iudicialiter possitis
Cf. *Errata.*

P. 242

#219. CASE ON THE VALIDITY OF AUTHORITY DELEGATED WITHOUT CONSENT OF BISHOP [STATED BY JACOB WIMPHELING?] [Spires, *ca.* 1485]

1463. Summary A parish priest of the Spires diocese sent a priest of the Constance diocese to the *vicar in spiritualibus* of the bishop of Spires to obtain license to celebrate mass in the Spires diocese and to act as assistant to him (the parish priest). The vicar, considering the assistant priest lacking in training, granted him authority to celebrate mass but not to hear confession or to preach publicly. The parish priest also obtained from the vicar for himself and for four competent priests – whom he was to select to help him hear confession in his parish during Lent – authority to give absolution in cases reserved for the bishop. The parish priest then named his assistant priest as one of the four competent priests and empowered him to hear confession, whereupon many parishioners confessed to him.

Since the authority delegated to the assistant priest by the parish priest exceeded the license given the assistant by the vicar, the questions are: Is the authority delegated by the parish priest valid? Is the absolution given by the assistant priest valid? Must those who confessed to him repeat their confessions? Can the bishop declare the absolution of the assistant priest valid?

1464. Date Items #219 and #220 form a unit; #219 is the statement of the case and #220 is Schott's advice. One clue to the date of these items is the possibility that Schott's advice in #220 may have been influenced by opinions on powers of absolution he solicited for another case from Johann

P. 242   #219   N. 1464

Rot,* Johann Simmler* and Johann Geiler (cf. items #223 and #224), which could have no earlier date than 1483 (N. 1447) but could well have a later one. Another clue is the likelihood that Wimpheling stated the present case which, as is noted above, occurred at Spires. So far as can be ascertained, Wimpheling could not have been in Spires before 1485; he may have arrived in that year and certainly by July 1486 he was nicely ensconced there (#89). An approximate date then for items #219 and #220 is *ca.* 1485.

1465. Spirensis Episcopi
The bishop of Spires at this time was Ludovicus von Helmstadt.*

1466. auctoritatem absoluendi in casibus Episcopo reseruatis
Items #223 and #224, as well as one of Schott's questions to Gabriel Biel* in #222 (p. 250), concern powers of absolution.

P. 243

#220. ADVICE ON THE CASE OF VALIDITY OF AUTHORITY DELEGATED
[Strassburg, *ca.* 1485]

1467. Summary There are two ways to solve the case so that the assistant priest might have jurisdiction over the parishioners of his parish priest.
1. By the way of delegation, which is the better way: A parish priest can delegate his jurisdiction to another, even to one not otherwise qualified to have jurisdiction, unless it is practice in the diocese to restrict delegation to those admitted by the bishop or by his vicar to the duties concerned. In this case the vicar delegated his office to the parish priest, because he assumed others were capable of jurisdiction. Hence those four priests chosen by the parish priest as helpers had episcopal jurisdiction, and although the parish priest appears to have transgressed the limits of the mandate by choosing as helper one not fully qualified and has thereby sinned, still the assistant priest was a priest in good standing who apparently performed his duties properly.
2. By the way of prorogation: Any priest has full authority to perform all priestly duties by virtue of ordination, as was the practice in the early church. To this way there is, however, opposition, because it is generally considered necessary that authority to hear confession be granted by the bishop or by his vicar. Hence in the minds of those who confessed there will be doubt about their absolutions being effective, and since absolution is effective because of the faith those confessing have in their priest, it will be safer for those who doubt the priest to repeat their confession.

As for the bishop's declaring the absolution valid: absolution can be given only to the one who has just confessed and is penitent, before he commits new mortal sins. (Cf. N. 1464).

1468. Prima est via delegacionis
Items #223 and #224 treat the question of delegation of authority.

1469. in sentencia fori poenitenciarij
Cf. N. 1436.

1470. Johannem Nider in Manuali confessorum in fine...
We have found no mention elsewhere of a manual for confessors by Johann Nider*; perhaps a passage of his writings was quoted in the manual Schott refers to.

#221. OPINION ON QUESTION CONCERNING CLERICS' HAIR (cf. *Errata*)
[Strassburg, late 1481- late 1487]

1471. Summary Eucharius Groshug* has asked Schott's opinion on two questions:
1. Is it sinful for a man, particularly a priest, to pray with his head covered?
2. Can regular clergy of a monastery with safe conscience conform to a monastery practice which allows the brothers to wear their hair with only part of the ears bared when canon law states that clerics must have their ears showing?

Schott answers: a practice which is not contrary to divine or natural law or to good morals should be preserved. The law of the New Testament, being the law of freedom and grace, does not stipulate any external observances, except the sacraments. Observances not affecting inner grace are left to human judgment, and any statement in the New Testament regarding external observances other than the sacraments need not be taken literally but can be adapted to environment, time and persons.

1. Covering or baring the head while praying is an external not an internal act. When the Apostle Paul recommended that all men should pray with their heads bared, he was adopting for the early church the practice of his time. Similarly St. Augustine urged that clerics pray with their heads bared and shaven, according to the practice of his time and area.

2. As for the tonsure: the regular clergy is supposed to be more closely shaven than the secular, and the practice of wearing the tonsure should be introduced where it does not obtain. Yet if a style of tonsure long customary in a reputable institution is suitable and can be a stumbling block to no one, it should not cause any pangs of conscience. The fact that not the whole but only part of the ears shows seems sufficient by synecdoche.

1472. Date A possible clue to the date of this item is Schott's use of the word *idolatras* (p. 248), a form he eschews as contrary to its Greek derivation when writing to Wimpheling (#113, p. 133) on 11 March 1488. It seems likely that this opinion must therefore predate the letter and have been written before Schott discovered the form *idolatra* to be incorrect.

1473. quandoquidem Apostolus prima ad Corinthios... Augustinus in libello de contemptu mundi
In 1 Cor. 11:4 and 7, St. Paul says a man should pray or prophesy with his head uncovered for he is the image and glory of God. In *Sermo de contemptu mundi*, cap. iii, St. Augustine says clerics' heads should be shaven and

P. 247 #221 N. 1473

clipped because the head is the seat of wisdom and any kind of covering – physical or mental – interferes with contemplation of God; hair, being an excrescence of the body and hence not belonging to the body, is to be considered as a covering. In cap. iv, St. Augustine says further that clerics participating in chanting psalms or in any spiritual activity are to remove hair, mitres and other coverings worn on the head.

1474. pro ea que ab ineunte etate inter nos conctracta est amicicia
Cf. N. 193. Groshug may have been also an alumnus of the Schlettstadt school, although his name does not appear in records.

1475. vbi Augustinus dicit. Quod enim neque contra fidem... seruandum est
This passage is from St. Augustine, *Ep.* CXVIII, cap. 1 and 2; it is quoted in the *Corpus iuris canonici, Decretales Gratiani prima pars*, Dist. xii. c. xi.

1476. Paulo dicanti. Omnis vir orans aut prophetans velato capite...
1 Cor. 11:4.

1477. si Scoto super tercio... et sancto Thome in prima... Doctor sanctus
The references are to Johannes Duns Scotus and St. Thomas Aquinas, known as *doctor sanctus*, (cf. N. 1537).

1478. Nolite possidere aurum neque pecunias in çonis vestris
The passage is from Mt. 10:9. Cf. also Lc. 9:3 and Mr. 6:8.

1479. quicquid in Euangelio vel in Apostolo videtur sonare in exteriorem...
I. e., in the Gospels or in the writings of St. Paul, called in earlier times "The Apostle."

P. 248

1480. Apostolus... velit omne genu debere flecti in nomine Iesu
Ph. 2:10.

1481. Non enim idolatras aut adulteros solum puniendos putamus...
Cf. #113, N. 896, N. 897.

P. 249

1482. neque scandalum proximo affert
Rm. 14:13. Cf. #222, p. 249.

1483. de tonendis capillis: in quo quidem Regulares secularibus clericis...
St. Paul had spoken against long hair for men (1 Cor. 11:14). Three styles of hair-cut or tonsure were used by clerics: the Roman, or that of St. Peter, which had the head shaven except for a circle of hair; the Eastern, or that of

P. 249   #221   N. 1483

St. Paul, which had the entire head shaven; the Celtic, or that of St. John, which had a shaven crescent on the front of the head.

1484. Quemadmodum Christus dixit se futurum tribus diebus et tribus... terre
Cf. Mt. 12:40.

#222. DIALOGUE BETWEEN PETER SCHOTT AND GABRIEL BIEL
[Strassburg, mid-1488]

1485. Summary Except in special cases, the laws of the court of conscience must be followed to the letter.

According to canon law, all those should be excommunicated who are guilty of the following: collecting taxes from clerics; legislating against ecclesiastical freedom; violating that freedom; absolving from excommunication such as have been *ipso facto* excommunicated. Practice, however, is to the contrary.

No other pressing duties, such as preaching, fasting, travelling, can excuse one from attending canonical hours.

One may complete the attendance on canonical hours in one session, in case of travelling, etc.

No one is obligated to give his life for his brother unless he is sure the brother is more useful to church or state.

If one has confessed a sin which one was not sure of having committed and discovers later that one has actually committed it, there is no need to repeat confession.

Geiler should remain in Strassburg and not yield to the subtle wiles of Satan which in the guise of good works are intent upon blighting the fruit of God's Word.

In practical matters Duns Scotus gives the best counsel, in theoretical matters William Occam.

In applying precepts concerning works, one should follow the regulations of the Church and of the general rule.

1486. Date That Gabriel Biel* was in Strassburg in the late summer or early fall of 1488 is known from Schott's letter of 25 October 1488 to Geiler (#124, p. 143). It is quite probable that the dialogue took place then, and that the *cartulam* mentioned in the letter as being sent to Geiler is this dialogue, especially since certain parts of it treat problems in which Geiler was interested. Indeed, Geiler himself may have instructed Schott to ask Biel about these problems.

Strictly speaking, this item is not a dialogue, for some of the questions and answers are in indirect discourse (cf. pp. 251f.).

P. 250

1487. de recipientibus talias etc. a clericis... absoluuntur in confessionibus
Collecting taxes from the clergy and legislation against willing property to the Church are listed among the abuses in #187, p. 206 (cf. N. 1331 and N. 1332). Items #223 and #224 discuss the question of who has authority to absolve from excommunication.

1488. Vtrum in horis Canonicis ad quas... quam continuatim simul.
Attendance at canonical hours figures in the questions put to Schott in #216. Cf. N. 1451. The *beatus Thomas* mentioned is St. Thomas Aquinas.

1489. Vtrum pro vita corporali fratris redimenda... vitam meam corporalem tradere... Gregorius
Cf. Jo. 15:13 and 1 Jo. 3-14. Bertrand Russell (*Autobiography* [Boston, 1967], I, 66) in adolescence pondered the problem whether – given the chance – he should try "saving a man who would be better out of this world." *Gregorius* apparently refers to the Decretals of Gregory IX in the *Corpus iuris canonici*.

P. 251

1490. Omnibus circumstancijs pensatis... fructum verbi dei satagit impedire.
For a translation of Biel's answer to Schott's question concerning Geiler, cf. N. 129.

1491. Quesiueram eciam ab eo... quando nam obligent?
Cf. *Errata*.

P. 252

#223. QUESTIONS ON POWERS OF ABSOLUTION PUT TO JOHANN ROT [Strassburg, ca. 1483-1485]

1492. Summary The brothers of a certain order (who claim that episcopal powers have been granted them) have asked Schott about powers of absolution. Before he gives his opinion, he wants information from Rot* who as vicar *in poenitentialibus* to the bishop has knowledge and experience in such matters.
Can Rot absolve from excommunication? If so, is his power to absolve based on his general authority or on a special authority?

1493. Date Cf. N. 1447, N. 1464. Items #223 and #224 form a unit, #223 contains Schott's questions to Rot, #224 is Rot's answer.

1494. Fratres certi ordinis habent ex indulto sedis Apostolicae... iniungere.
What order is concerned here is not known. Special privileges in matters of confession and absolution given by the Apostolic See to orders were apparently not uncommon. In 1477 Emerich Kemel* was granted by Sixtus IV the following privilege for his order: any brother of the Franciscan Order "ultramontane de Observantia" might select any suitable confessor and the the latter could absolve him from any sins except bigamy and homicide (*Anal. Francisc.*, II, 463f.).

1495. Vtrum absolutus per illos fratres... habendus sit pro absoluto?
For other questions on absolution, cf. #219 and #220, also N. 1466.

#224. REPLY TO ABOVE BY JOHANN ROT [Strassburg, ca. 1483-1485]

1496. Summary The brothers who have been allowed by apostolic permission to hear confession have no greater authority in matters of penitence than simple curates, and simple curates have not the power to absolve from public sins (because for these public penitence must be imposed), nor from sins punishable by excommunication, nor yet from those sins which the bishop reserves for absolution by his vicar general. Whatever the brothers have attempted beyond the authority of simple curates, without additional permission, is null and void. Absolution from excommunication pertains to the *forum iudiciale*; no one can be absolved from excommunication until he has first been absolved from his crime.

In the note appended to this item Schott observes that both Johann Simmler* and Johann Geiler have given similar opinions on the question of absolution.

1497. et illud pertinet ad forum animae... pertinet ad forum iudiciale
Cf. N. 1436 and N. 1439.

1498. Petrus Schottus
Schott apparently wrote his name here at the end of Rot's opinion to indicate that the sentence following was appended by him.

#225. ADVICE ON BURIALS AND SACRIFICES [Strassburg, mid-1481 to 1490]

1499. Summary Schott remarks that he has been asked to settle in a few words and in a very limited time a controversial matter which has embroiled almost the whole Christian world. He cites from canon law several of the many passages on burial regulations according to which Franciscans and Dominicans have the right to accept anyone for burial, provided the burial tax be paid by the survivors to the parish church; all sacrifices, i.e., offerings, which are made in chapels within any parish belong to the parish church.

1500. Date This short document could have been composed by Schott at any time after his settling in Strassburg on his return from Italy in mid-1481.

1501. Rem litigijs refertam: et quae fere totum Christiani nominis orbem plerumque turbauit
The reference is to the protracted quarrel between the secular and regular clergy over the *ultimum vale* (also known as *quarta funerum* and termed *quarta canonica* in the text below, in the passage cited by Schott), a tax levied by the secular clergy on the survivors of those buried by the regular clergy. This tax to be paid the parish priest was decreed by Boniface VIII in a bull of 18 February 1300. Benedict XI abrogated the bull, but Clement V reinstated it in 1312. For the effect of the quarrel on Strassburg, cf. N. 955, par. 3.

Barth, *Kreutzer*, 186. Barthelmé, 101. *Cath. Ency.*, VI, 283. Pfleger, "Predigtwesen," *passim*. Spach, *Histoire*, 147f.

#226. TO CONRAD BONDORF, ADVICE ON EATING FAT AND LARD [Strassburg, 1489 to mid-1490]

1502. Summary It was quite in keeping with the Attic spirit of their banquet, Schott observes, that the discussion turned to serious matters such as the use of meat, fat and lard. The references he could not cite on the spur of the moment he looked up immediately on returning home and submits herewith as promised.

One gloss states that fat may be eaten on days when eggs and cheese are allowed. Other glosses consider lard and meat as belonging to different categories. Hence the custom of using fat and lard on days when dairy products and eggs are eaten is confirmed by canon law, especially on Sunday when no law but only local custom forbids the use of meat.

1503. Date Since Conrad Bondorf,* addressed here as *lector* of the Strassburg Franciscans, is documented as having been appointed to that office in 1489, this letter must have been written after the appointment and before Schott's death in 1490.

1504. Per quem eciam Bartolus ibi notat
For "Bartolus," cf. N. 342.

1505. Per que videretur sustinenda consuetudo eorum: qui... sumerent.
Cf. Bishop Albrecht's dispensation for the use of butter and eggs during Lent, p. xxvi; #14, p. 22; and N. 224.

#227. OPINION ON A MARRIAGE CONTRACT [Strassburg, mid-1481 to 1490]

1506. Summary The case in question concerns the contract between an eleven year old girl and a mature man. Schott has been asked two questions. Is this contract legally a marriage contract or one of betrothal? If it is a betrothal contract, can the girl on reaching legal age withdraw?

To conclude a contract of marriage, the man must have completed his fourteenth year and the woman her twelfth. If both parties are minors or if one is a minor, the younger party must have attained the age of puberty. In the present case, if the girl had at the time of the contract undergone a physical examination, she would never have been judged mature enough for marriage. Therefore the contract is not one of marriage, but of betrothal [and according to the passage from canon law cited, the girl can withdraw on reaching legal age].

1507. Date This opinion could have been written at any time after Schott returned to Strassburg in 1481.

1508. Vtrum sit contractus Matrimonij iudicandus: vel... possit resilire?
Under Roman law the legal age for marriage was in case of a man fourteen,

in case of a woman twelve. Under canon law no one can be forced into marriage or betrothal; willingness of both parties to marry is necessary; a betrothal made before marriageable age can be dissolved. Cf. Plöchl, I, 402f., 405; II, 307, 317. *Corpus iuris canonici, Decretales Gregorii,* ix Lib. iv tit. de sponsatibus et matrimoniis c.2,13; tit. ii de desponsatione impuberium c. i, 8.

#228. TESTIMONIALS IN A SALE OF SEED Strassburg, 5 November 1490

1509. Summary Friedrich Bock* of the Strassburg magistracy certifies that the undersigned have singly and under oath given the following testimonials in his presence. Hans Trens, Hans Weldels, Hans Langen and Ruprecht Boner, members of the Strassburg gardeners' guild, have sworn that the 31 1/2 measures of onion seed sold to Strassburg citizen Florencius Müg* is good, new seed grown in the present year at Strassburg and that it is unmixed with old seed or any other kind of seed. Florencius Müg has sworn that he will not contaminate or mix the seed with any other kind of seed or allow such to be done and that he will deliver it in the prescribed condition to buyer or buyers.

1510. Date This item has the latest date of any item in the *Lucubraciunculae*, cf. N. 35.

1511. Nos Fridericus Bock eques auratus: Magistratus et consulatus Argent... Cf. N. 744 for the term *eques auratus*; cf. also N. 420.

1512. Nominatim Trenshans ortulanorum prosoneta dixit...
None of the four members of the Strassburg gardeners' guild mentioned has been identified. *Prosoneta=Proxoneta*, cf. p. xviii, under Spelling, 6.

1513. ad diem veneris post solennitatem omnium Sanctorum
All Saints Day, 1 November, fell on a Monday in 1490; the following Friday was therefore 5 November.

#229. OPINION ON THE PRODUCING OF WITNESS [Strassburg, mid-1481 to 1490]

1514. Summary Anyone fearing possible litigation may produce witnesses to make a permanent record of a case. Those involved must be cited to be present at the hearing of the witnesses. If the witnesses are not in the locality where the judgment is to be given, they may be heard by the judge in their own locality. This procedure is also proper when access to the judge of the case is not possible, as in the present case where the judge has not yet been selected. Statements of the witnesses may be made public if all statements can be produced at the same time.

1515. Date Cf. N. 1507.

1516. Testium productio
Cf. the section "Producere testes" of Anna H. Benna's article, "Iurisprudentia medii aevi: Eine Handschrift der deutschen Bearbeitung des Ordo 'Antequam'" [second half of the fifteenth century], *Festschrift zur Feier des 200-jährigen Bestandes des Haus-, Hof- und Staatsarchivs*, I (Wien, 1949), 534.

1517. ut est communis opinio Bartoli... Bartolus in auten...
Cf. N. 342.

#230. PETITION TO RESTORE AN OLD CHAPEL [Strassburg, 1487]

1518. Summary Almost 300 years ago the Strassburg knight Reimbold Stubenweg* built for himself and his descendants a family chapel, dedicated to St. Nicholas, by the stream called "Im Giessen" and established a benefice for a chaplain to care for the chapel. By inheritance the chapel has come into the possession of Johann Rudolf von Endingen,* knight of Strassburg, who wishes to restore the chapel, long neglected, to use. He petitions the pope to reactivate the post of chaplain, with the proviso that in perpetuity no one be appointed chaplain who has not first been approved by Endingen himself or his descendants.
    Philip von Endingen,* thirteen years of age, cleric and nobleman of Strassburg, petitions to be declared fit and able to hold this benefice.

1519. Date In the item the age of Philip von Endingen is given as thirteen. He was born in 1474, hence the date of the item must be 1487.

1520. Capellam quandam in honore sancti Nycholai: in torrente im giessen
Barth (*Handbuch*, 1411f.) lists the chapel "St. Nicolai im Metzgergiessen" (also called "Des Zollers Kapelle im Giessen") as having been built by Reimbold Stubenweg and consecrated 8 November 1198 by Bishop Konrad. Kindler von Knobloch (*Buch*, 363f.) describes how during the seventeenth century the chapel was converted into two dwellings. Hatt (*Ville*, 102) gives "Im Giessen" as the name of a street in Strassburg.

1521. per sanctitatem Domini Pape
Innocent VIII.

1522. Philippus de Endingen clericus Argentinensis
Philip von Endingen was probably at this time already a minor canon of New St. Peter, which would account for Schott's interest in the case. Evidently Innocent VIII granted the petition, for Ristelhuber lists the chaplaincy as one of Philip's benefices (cf. biographical note on Philip).

#231. QUESTION ON THE RIGHT OF A BISHOP TO DECLARE WAR [STATED BY JACOB WIMPHELING?] [Spires, 1486]

1523. Summary The following question has been put to Schott: to aid the

P. 258   #231   N. 1523

Pfalzgraf (Count Palatine) who is preparing to besiege the castle of Geroldseck, can the bishop of Spires rightfully declare war on Geroldseck?

Schott answers: Anyone to whom temporal jurisdiction is committed has also committed to him the powers necessary for preserving that jurisdiction. The jurisdiction of the bishop cannot be properly preserved without the protection of the *Pfalzgraf*, and this protection might cease if the bishop did not openly defy the *Pfalzgraf*'s enemy. Hence in order to preserve his jurisdiction the bishop may declare war and give aid which he cannot well refuse, especially in a just cause.

1524. Date In 1486 *Pfalzgraf* Philipp II* and his allies – among whom were Johann von Seckingen* and no doubt Ludovicus von Helmstadt,* bishop of Spires – destroyed the castles of Grossgeroldseck and Kleingeroldseck (above Zabern), because these were nests of robber knights. The present item must therefore have been composed in very late 1485 or in 1486 just before the siege of the castles began.

The several branches of the Geroldsecks held lands on both banks of the Rhine. In the late fifteenth century the once proud family became thorns in the flesh to all neighbors because of marauding and general lawlesnsess. Strassburg records repeatedly mention violation of the "Burgfrieden" and other misdeeds on the part of the Geroldsecks. In 1471 and 1472, for example, stock was stolen from villagers of Ottenheim. In 1474 several inhabitants of Lahr were taken prisoner. In 1473 a boat carrying passengers to the Frankfurt fair was attacked and its passengers not only robbed and mistreated but also held for ransom. In 1481 Strassburg was involved in a quarrel with the villainous *Graf* Dietrich (Thibault) of Hoh-Geroldseck in the Black Forest, because Dietrich had unlawfully seized grain from the abbot of Schüttern; the quarrel was arbitrated by *Pfalzgraf* Philipp.

Cf. Hertzog, II, 129. Inventaire III, 2,85,106, 117. Lehr, "Geroldseck," 85f. *NDB*, VI, 317. Wuerdtwein, 401.

1525. Sed iurisdicio Episcopi sine protectione Principis... teneri non potest
Lands belonging to the bishopric of Spires and the Alsatian holdings of the Palatinate were not only adjacent but intermingled (Plate 7) so that to reach territory belonging to the one it was necessary to cross territory belonging to the other. Therefore good relations between the two states were absolutely essential.

#232. EULOGY OF JEAN CHARLIER DE GERSON [Strassburg, mid-1488]

1526. Summary Jean [Charlier] de Gerson,* former chancellor of the university of Paris, has rightly been given the title of *doctor christianus* or *doctor christianissimus*, because he freed the Christians in his day from a confusing multiplicity of dogmas and showed the way of salvation to be smooth and secure. He selected the best from scholastic theology for his teachings and, by demonstrating that mysticism is not contrary to scholasticism, brought about harmony between the two.

From early childhood he was drawn to the love of God by his parents whose fervent piety is evident in the fact that almost all their children were dedicated to God. After completing the course in arts, Gerson became the most eminent theologian of his day at the university of Paris. He devoted his talents and zeal to the service of the king of France, the Gallic church and the university of Paris. At the council of Constance he contributed much toward ending the Great Schism.

This edition of Gerson's works in one volume of three parts contains as many of his writings as could be collected. The first part contains works on faith and the regimen of the Church and errors concerning these; the second part contains works on moral traditions; the third part contains works on mysticism. Writings attributed to Gerson are included, and at the end are appended works by known authors which treat related material, as for example, the little book *De contemptu mundi* by Thomas [à Kempis].

1527. Date This eulogy must have been composed about mid-1488 since it forms the introduction to Schott's edition of Gerson's works which came off the press 6 September 1488, cf. p. xxx, N. 135 and N. 136. It is possible that the eulogy was delivered as an address before a meeting of Strassburg savants.

1528. Iohannem de Gerson... si qui Doctorem christianissimum vocet
Gerson is referred to as "doctor resolutissimus et christianissimus" in Schott's edition of his works (Strassburg, 1488), folio a iv. For epithets applied to other outstanding doctors, cf. N. 1537.

1529. Si enim author christiani nominis Christus... luculentissime demonstraret
Here Schott draws an interesting parallel between Christ's work in freeing His followers from the old patriarchal law by giving them an easy yoke bound with only a few sacraments and Gerson's work in freeing the people of his age from dogmas accumulated over the centuries by stripping religious truth of all non-essentials.

1530. si leue et sacramentis paucis astrictum iugum posteris suis imposuit
Cf. Mt. 11:30.

1531. sed velut apis argumentosa singulorum depastus dulcorem... contexebat
This passage is a striking simile comparing Gerson's selection from scholastic writers for his works to the bee's selective sipping of nectar for the honeycomb.

1532. In mystica vero que ita est... ut autore Dionysio solis sit christianis concessa
The reference is to the Christian writer Dionysius, also called Areopagita for having been a member of the Areopagus at Athens, who was converted to Christianity by St. Paul's preaching and is said to have been appointed first bishop of Athens by Paul. A number of writings attributed to him in the Middle Ages are now deemed spurious; which work contains the statement alluded to, we do not know.

P. 260   #232   N. 1533

P. 260

1533. ab ineunte atate per Parentes ad dei amorem... deo dicati
Cf. N. 193, for references to the phrase *ab ineunte etate*. Cf. biographical note on Gerson for details about his life.

1534. Quis enim breuibus complecti posset... sue calamitose tempestati
Just as Gerson worked for unity and harmony in theological thought, so he championed unity and harmony in state and Church.
    In the struggle for control of the French throne between the two rival Valois factions he, as chancellor of the university of Paris, supported the cause of Charles VI (1380-1422) and Louis, duke of Orleans, against John the Fearless,* duke of Burgundy, who had allied himself with Henry V of England and who virtually ruled Paris from 1408 to 1413 – when he was expelled – and again from 1418 to 1419 – when he was assassinated. Because of John's occupation of Paris at the time when the council of Constance (1414-1418) disbanded, Gerson who had been a delegate from France at the council did not return to the university of Paris but went into exile (cf. his biographical note).
    At the council of Constance, Gerson used his considerable influence to heal the rifts in the Church caused by the Great Schism which had begun in 1378 and terminated when the council in 1417 deposed three popers reigning simultaneously – John XXIII at Rome, Benedict XIII at Avignon, Gregory XII at Rimini – and elected Martin V to govern the Church from Rome. It was this council which condemned John Hus and sentenced him to the stake for heresy; it was also this council which condemned the Forty-Five Wycliffite Propositions and ordered Wycliff's body to be exhumed and cast out of sacred ground. Gerson, opposed to heresies as disruptive forces within the Church, was instrumental in bringing about these condemnations.

1535. olim gloriosissimus Doctor Augustinus etati sue: Pelagianorum heresi
Pelagianism originated with Pelagius, a monk – perhaps British or Irish – of the early fifth century. Maintaining that human will is the determining factor in salvation, it denied the primitive state in paradise, original sin and Christian grace. It was branded as heresy by the council of Carthage in 418 and by the council of Ephesus in 431, as well as by St. Augustine.

P. 261

1536. Principis eciam potentissimi odium... velut alter Crysostomus aut Athanasius: ipsum tandem exilium...
As Gerson suffered exile because of John the Fearless (cf. N. 1534), so had Chrysostom* and Athanasius in earlier centuries suffered exile because of their convictions. For Chrysostom's (345/7-407) exiles, cf. N. 1586. Athanasius (ca. 296-373), bishop of Alexandria, was forced into exile five times because of his opposition to Arianism.

1537. Quamobrem honorentur Doctores alij: quisque epitheto suo... vocitetur.
The epithets mentioned in this passage were applied to the following outstanding doctors: *sanctus* – Thomas Aquinas; *seraphicus* – Bonaventura and St. Francis; *magnus* – Albertus Magnus, Alanus von Ryssel (both of whom were also called *magnus et universalis*) and Gilbert de Citeaux; *irrefragabilis* –

P. 261   #232   N. 1537

Alexander de Hales; *subtilis* – Duns Scotus, also the doctors of law in the fifteenth century Benedict Raymond and Filippo Corneo; *solemnis* – Heinrich Goethals von Gent; *illuminatus* – Johann Tauler (also known along with Aquinas as *illuminatus et sublimis*), François de Maykon de Digne en Provence (also known as *illuminatus et acutus*) and Raymond Lullus.

1538. quorum aliqua ex epistolis Archiepiscopi Lugdunensis: et fratri sui Prioris Celestinorum... ad finem huius operis
The letters of Amadeus de Talaru,* archbishop of Lyons, and of Gerson's brother, prior of the Celestines at Lyons, are to be found at the end of the third part of Schott's edition of Gerson's works (cf. N. 136).

1539. Huius itaque vtilissimi Doctoris tractatus et opera... non sine singulari labore
Cf. N. 135

1540. Hunc autem parcium ordinem non esse incongruum... Bonauenturam in libello de reductione arcium...
Works in the third part of the edition are arranged according to the scheme set up by Bonaventura in *De reductione artium ad theologiam:* "In omnibus enim...Scriptorum libris concipitur triplex sensus spiritualis, scilicet *allegoricus* quo docemur, quid sit credendum de Divinitate et humanitate; *moralis*, quo docemur, quomodo viuendum sit; et *anagogicus*, quo docemur quomodo est adhaerendum... Primum respicit *fidem*, secundum *mores*, tertium finem utriusque." Cf. Philotheus Boehner and M. Frances Laughlin, *Works of St. Bonaventure*, I *De reductione artium ad theologiam*, translation and commentary by Sister Emma Thérèse Healy (diss. St. Bonaventure College, 1939) p. 26, 5.

P. 262

1541. ut est libellus de Contemptu mundi... a quodam Thoma Canonico regulari
The reference is to Thomas à Kempis, *De contemptu Mundi*, later known as *Imitatio Christi*, cf. N. 137.

#233. APHORISMS FROM THE SERMONS OF GEILER [Strassburg, date unknown]

1542. Summary (Cf. p. xxvii, N. 114, N. 281.)
1) God makes us good by fear of punishment and promise of reward. To induce the cow to follow, one man coaxes her with spelt and salt, while another drives her with goads.
2) To conquer the flesh is not virtuous but necessary like building a fire before cooking or cutting trees before chopping wood.
3) Moderation is necessary in everything. The strings of the harp or of the bow, if too slack, are useless; if too taut, they break.
4) Contrition for sins must be immediate, for all works perish as useless when not earning eternal reward. Just so is it foolish to let money lie idle instead of putting it to gainful use.
5) As a coal near live coals begins to glow, so piety and love are inspired by fellowship with the devout.

6) The nose, if blown too hard, bleeds; errors erased too vigorously leave holes in the paper.
7) The pan placed on the anvil for mending, if struck too hard with the hammer, has ten holes for one. A belt too tightly bound breaks.
8) We must refrain not only from evil thoughts but even from day-dreaming which relaxes the mind and lets evil thoughts steal in, just as thieves enter a house when the doors are bolted but the windows left open.
9) God has given us precepts which we are to follow trustingly and unquestioningly, just as the architect gives tasks to workmen who perform them without having any conception of the plan.
10) Our pleasure in caring for our bodies should be like that of the lame in employing canes or of the sick in taking medicine, not out of preference but of necessity.
11) Since we cannot avoid involvement in worldly affairs, we must take care not to devote ourselves wholly to them.
12) Just as the eye looking through rose-colored glasses sees the same color in whatever it beholds, so the mind infected by passions judges everything according to them. So it is also true that love is blind.
13) An act not just in every respect cannot be termed just, even as a man unsound in one limb cannot be termed whole.
14) The word *sapientia*, wisdom, derives from the word *sapor*, taste, because all things taste as they really are. Just as gourmets know unerringly whether foods are seasoned or insipid, so the wise man knows or tastes that God is sweet and that created beings are bitter.
15) Things in themselves rich need not be larded. A savory *bon mot* needs no elaboration.
16) He is a fool who puts his treasure where thieves can steal it. Just so foolish are we to devote every effort in gaining riches, honor, or pleasure which, like the worldly gains of our ancestors, will perish. Rather we should strive for virtues, grace and glory which will endure eternally.
17) In training a dog to the leash it is at first often necessary to drag him struggling behind one. So he who in mastering his flesh does not conquer its reluctance and compel it to follow by force will never have quiet and subdued flesh.
18) It is dangerous for babes to cut bread for themselves. However useful and necessary bread is to them, it is better that adults cut it for them than that the babes injure themselves. So the Scriptures containing the food of God's Word must be read and explained only by those mature and trained in doctrine who can deduce the real meaning of the Word. The inexperienced in reading the Word are easily led astray and by interpreting it literally can bring disaster upon themselves.
19) Wild birds know none except their natural song, but if captured many can utter human sounds. So young people not yet degraded by vices, out of inborn integrity, spiritedly inveigh against vain pomp, avarice and passion; yet if they are taken captive by one such vice and have once sinned, they no longer fight the vice but even voice approval of it.
20) Repairing a house roof demands great caution because of the height and because tiles may break or fall and injure someone. Yet to neglect the roof is highly pernicious. The leak from a single eave can rot the wooden framework of the entire house. Similarly it is difficult and dangerous to correct prelates, but nonetheless necessary.
21) The ancients produced testimonials with a minumum of words and fortified them with a great seal; these were extremely efficacious. Now such records compiled of innumerable sections but confirmed with minute seals barely pass censure. Compare the ancients' testimonials with the doctrines of the "Preachers" (Dominicans) and compare the ancients' seals with the

works by which the "Preachers" bolster their preaching. You will see that with few doctrines and tremendous enthusiasm for works the apostles and others accomplished much in the primitive Church; moderns, on the other hand, with such numerous and such great doctrines accomplish little, because the seal of their works is exceedingly small. From St. Paul we learn that Christ and the Church are one body. Should anyone deem this thought foreign to elegant Latin, let him find similar thoughts expressed by Lucan and by Cicero who said, "If there is anything harmful in the body of the state – in order that the whole may be sound – let it be amputated."

22) If we were men, we could easily become Christians. That is: if reason ruled us, Christ's commandments would appeal to us, but because, like beasts, we are governed by feelings, His commandments have no appeal for us.

23) To leave our labors and responsibilities at times is advisable and salubrious, yet not for the purpose of seeking worldly consolations, or rather desolations.

24) Work with a fixed purpose is less tiring than undisciplined idleness.

25) Occupation with an inattentive mind differs little from idleness. Like idleness it provides opportunity for errant thoughts and suggestions of the devil.

26) Occupation without discipline is colored by vice and must be abandoned when tedium and lack of concentration or languid relaxation render one sluggish, for inattention differs little from idleness.

27) It is just as difficult to throw off carnal or evil thoughts as to throw off warm covers in the cold of the winter.

28) Psalms must be read with the same feeling as that with which they were composed.

29) A half-developed egg, when broken, is much more noisome than a fresh egg. So those having set forth on the way of the spirit, if they retrogress, are more abominable than those never having trodden it.

30) A pod full of dried peas makes no sound, but a pod with only three or four peas rattles. So those full of vile sins never hear the voice of conscience and consider themselves guiltless, but those who have committed one or two peccadillos are harassed by the din of conscience, as is a dog by a pod with a few peas tied to his tail. Similarly anyone full of garlic does not notice the odor, nor does one in a fog realize its density until he emerges from it.

31) A stick never makes a firm switch unless it is first dried by the fire. Iron cannot be forged or bent unless it is first heated red-hot in the furnace. Unless the soul has its rigidity of pride softened by the fire of chastisement and tribulation, it is unfit to bear the yoke of the Master.

32) The lead shot hurled by war machines penetrates even a coat of mail, because it is strengthened by an iron core. So all things moving us to anger and passion are rendered effective, because they are hardened by our pride.

1543. Perinde atque incaute agit: qui... pecuniam enim habet... sine lucro
Cf. Mt. 25:15-28.

1544. Quod rectum est: non videt omnis amans.
For *omnis amans*, cf. Ovid, *Ars Am.* i. 729. An eleventh century proverb reads: "Omnis amans cecus; non est amor arbiter equus" (*Die älteste deutsche Literatur*, ed. Paul Piper [Berlin, Stuttgart, 1884,] 285 = *Deutsche National Litteratur*, ed. J. Kirschner, I).

1545. Incaute immo stulte facit: qui thesaurum... mansura praeparemus.
Cf. Mt. 6:19.

P. 264   #233   N. 1546

P. 264

1546. Compara instrumenta doctrinis Praedicatorum: Sigilla... appendunt.
Geiler's barbs against the Dominicans may have been prompted by the Dominican Order's opposition to the doctrine of the virgin birth of Mary (cf. N. 1702, par. 3), also by the resistance of the Strassburg Dominicans to reform and their hostility toward the Observant faction (N. 689), as well as by his own troubles with the order (N. 955 par. 6).

P. 265

1547. Christum esse sponsum ecclesie: et vnum corpus... amputetur.
St. Paul's words concerning mystic union with Christ are in Eph. 5:23-32 and Col. 1:24-26. In modern editions the quotation from Lucan ii. 388 reads: "Urbi pater est..."; that from Lucan x.416f. reads: "...Dis placitum non in soceri generique"; that from Cicero *Phil.* viii 15 begins "Sic in reipublicae..."
  Geiler's point that ideas in the Scriptures are to be found also in elegant Latin works may have been directed against such sophisticated humanists as considered the Scriptures old-fashioned and scorned any idea not expressed by a classical author (cf. N. 228).

1548. Aphorisms 23-26 express ideas on work and leisure similar to those in the treatise on Christian life, section 7, p. 128, and in Geiler's *Monita*, LVI (Appendix H).

P. 266

1549. einer grieben
Cf. OHG *griubo, griupo, griebo* masc.; MHG *griube, griebe* masc. and *grife* fem.; Ger. *Griebe* masc. and *Griebe, Grieben* fem.; Eng. *graves, greaves*, a coarse sediment of animal fat that will not melt, a core, a crackling. The term was apparently quite common in proverbial expressions, cf., Cowie, *Proverbs*, 32f.

#234. FIRST POEM, elegiac verse [Schlettstadt, early 1470]

1550. Summary No one should invite into his home an old fool, a wild bear, a young priest.

1551. Date The phrase *nondum decennis* in Wimpheling's heading to this item indicates that Schott's Latin version of the Alsatian proverb was recited to Headmaster Dringenberg* in the Schlettstadt school (N. 88) before Schott's tenth birthday, 10 July 1470. Cf. p. xxivf.

1552. Prouerbium desuper Ludouici Ludimagistri Sletstatini... hus begeren
Wiskowatoff (26) notes that this proverb was a favorite of Dringenberg. Geiler quoted it in *Arbore humana*, folio XCI. Wander, I, 34, no. 14, gives the German version of the proverb and later, V, column 720, no. 14, quotes from Bebel Suringar, 87, a Latin prose version: "Non recipiendos in domum: iuniorem sacerdotem, vetulas simias et feras immansuetasque ursas."

P. 266   #235   N. 1553

#235. TO JOHANN GESLER Bologna, 26 December 1477

1553. Summary Delighted with Gesler's* letter and particularly with the poems accompanying it, Schott is prompted to send in return poems which he and Bohuslaus von Hassenstein have composed to one another, but he cannot do so now because the bearer is already impatient to be off.
    In the postscript, however, Schott explains that the bearer has delayed long enough to allow opportunity for sending the poems. On these Gesler is to pass judgment. (Cf. p. xv and N. 34; p. xxxf. and N. 140; N. 37).

1554. viro domino Iohanni Gesler amico sibi plurimum colendo
Potuček (vf.), having misread the name "Gesler," includes this item among the letters to Geiler.

1555. Plane que mihi misisti carmina: hortantur me... mutuis conscripsimus
For the custom of sending one's compositions to friends for criticism, cf. N. 309. The poems sent to Gesler were the four following the letter, #236- #239. These same poems may have been sent also to Sigmund Gossenbrot, cf. #171, p. 192 and N. 1218.

1556. Magistrum Iohannem Rot plurimum ex me saluere iube
Both Gesler and Rot* were studying at Paris. Rot must have left Paris to return to Strassburg soon after the date of this letter (cf. #9, p. 15, and N. 183).

1557. Data Bononia ad vij Kalendas Ianuarias
For the discussion of dates "before the kalends of January," cf. N. 218.

P. 267

#236. EPIGRAM TO BOHUSLAUS VON HASSENSTEIN in elegiac verse [Bologna, 1477]

1558. Summary O light of the Bohemians, so far outshining other mortals in nobility of birth and in learning, I fain would believe you the offspring of Clio and Jupiter himself!

1559. Date From internal evidence in the four poems (#236- #239) sent to Gesler at Paris from Bologna on 26 December 1477 it appears that the poems are chronologically arranged in the text and that the dates of their composition are sometime during the period: January to late December 1477; #238 (p. 269) alludes to the defeat of Charles the Bold at the Battle of Nancy which occurred 5 January 1477; the same poem also alludes to Hassenstein's recent laudatory verses to Schott, a reference no doubt to #237, which in turn is very likely an answer to the present item, while #239 is obviously an answer to #238.

1560. O lux Bohemorum
Cf. Vergil *Aen*.ii. 281 and #171, p. 192.

P. 267   #237   N. 1561

#237. POEM TO PETER SCHOTT BY BOHUSLAUS VON HASSENSTEIN in elegiac verse [Bologna, 1477]

1561. Summary The Thracian mount was not so astonished by Bacchus as we by your melodies. As Apollo outshines the stars, so you, Peter, born of barbaric blood, excel Homeric measures. Ye folk of Latium, celebrate your Vergil; our Rhine will be more famed than your Po. (Cf. N. 1559).

1562. Hismarius=Ismarius Thracian. *Iachum=Iacchum* Mystic name for Bacchus. *Sic te Barbarico natum de saguine... modos* Cf. similar passage in #238 (p. 268); for *saguine,* cf. p. xix, 12, b, and N. 39. *Alcreos=Alcaeos* Typographical error (cf. *Errata*). *Et niueas Tyria murice pingit oues* Cf. Ovid *Ars Am.* iii. 170; *Met.* xi. 166. *doctarum plectra Sororum... Medusee munera clara dee* Medusa's connection with the Muses stems from her being the mother of Pegasus whose hoof-print formed the Muses' fount of Hippocrene and who, according to some accounts, was the father of the Muses.

#238. POEM TO BOHUSLAUS VON HASSENSTEIN in elegiac verse [(Bologna, 1477]

1563. Summary Son of the Muses and Apollo, you, gifted like Orpheus, excel Homer, Vergil and Ovid as they excel Choerilus. In your recent verses you attribute to me praise which is your due. You are the one of Germanic blood who will drive the censure of barbarism from our realm.
    Did not Latium, once called the barbarous land by the Greeks, shed that name? Cannot the Germanic people do likewise? Germany has no barbaric rites, no more human sacrifices; it has morals equal to those of the ancients. Its fertile soil produces bountiful crops. Its many universities have outstanding scholars teaching the seven liberal arts, as well as medicine, law and theology. Nor is Germany lacking in military might; witness the tribes who were unconquered by Rome and the recent defeat of the Burgundian.
    You are distinguished in every way: as a Bohemian noble of high birth, a student of law, a poet, a husbandman. Happy the people who claim you as prince. You will banish heresy from Bohemia and bring back to the Christian fold your people, than whom none could be happier in fertility of the glebe or mightier in arms.
    Our bond of friendship is firmer than that of famous friends, such as Hercules and Philoctetes, Theseus and Pirithous, or Orestes and Pylades. One alma mater, one study, one fatherland and one faith join us. (Cf. N. 1559).

1564. Caballino... gurgite The Hippocrenean spring in the forest of Hippocrene, sacred to the Muses (cf. N. 1562), mentioned also in #242, p. 278, and in #287, p. 310. *Aufidus* A swift river in Apulia. *Te Vatem/ rapideque tygres...* Hassenstein is likened to Orpheus.

P. 268

1565. Eacide Achilles. *Meonides* Schott discusses this epithet of Homer in #264, p. 296. *Cherilus* Choerilus, an ineffectual Greek poet. *tuus* Probably a typographical error for *tui* or *tuos,* although the original has *tu* followed by the symobl for '*us. Vnum Barabarico natos quod... ab orbe notam* Schott is

P. 268   #238   N. 1565

referring to the assertion of the Italians (and of the French) that the Germans were barbarians. From this point the main theme of the poem is the accomplishments and resources of the German empire. For other writings of Schott with nationalistic flavor, cf. p. xviii and N. 124. *Hic nec Aricine sacra cruenta dee* Aricina, an appellation of Diana from Aricia, her sacred grove on Lake Nemi, where her priest the King of the Wood kept his grim vigil. *Nec Athlanciadem placamus saguins... Humano* Tacitus *Germania* 9.1f. speaks of human sacrifices to Mercury among the German tribes. *Palemonium* Remnius Palaemon, a Roman grammarian (†ca. 76 A.D.). *Tullo genitum* I.e., Romans. *Hermogenem* Hermogenes, a rhetorician of Tarsus.

P. 269

1566. Siracusij... viri The astronomer Pheidios of Syracuse, father of Archimedes. *Choi precoepta magistri: Peonis arte* Hippocrates of Cos, celebrated Greek physician said to have founded the art of medicine of which Paion (spelled *Peon–* in the text) was the god. *Aonides* The Muses. *Burgundio Gallis Inuictus* Charles the Bold, duke of Burgundy, defeated at Nancy on 6 January 1477, cf. N. 74. *Phoenissus... ipse Pater* Cadmus, inventor of the alphabet and first prose writer. *Rhodopeius heros* Orpheus.

P. 270

1567. Amphitryoniadem Hercules. *Peancius heros* Philoctetes. *Leli Scipiades* Laelius, friend of Scipio Africanus. *Feruentis gemme: rosei quoque collis* The university of Bologna. *sectam... infandam* The Hussites (cf. N. 379). *Pellei* Alexandrian; Pella in Macedonia was Alexander's birthplace.

#239. POEM TO PETER SCHOTT BY BOHUSLAUS VON HASSENSTEIN in elegiac verse [Bologna 1477]

1568. Summary Your eloquence surpasses that of Ulysses; and the waves of the sea when lashed by Boreas are never so many as the praises with which you adorn my verses. Not so sweetly did Tibullus sing of his Nemesis, or Ovid of his Corinna.

But what profits it to sow a sterile field? No son of Zeus or Apollo am I, neither am I favored by the Muses, nor deserving of such tributes from you who are learned in grammar and philosophy, who write with the acumen of Cicero and the sweetness of Homer, who encompass the lore of the constellations and ancient mythology. You liken us to Orestes and Pylades and to other friends famed in story with whom I, of German blood, may claim no kinship. You look to free my people from the error which has defied pope, king, council and war.

As Achilles cherished Patroclus, I cherish you. Let the ancients' poetry please others, I have been delighted by the songs of bard Peter. (Cf. N. 1559.)

1569. Dulichium Ulysses. *Nec tot in Ethnea... cum raperere Dee* A reference to the rape of Proserpine, daughter of Ceres, in the vale of Aetna.

P. 271   #239   N. 1570

P. 271

1570. Nemesis cantata Tibullo Nemesis, the mistress of the poet Tibullus. *Nasoni dicta Corinna suo* Cf. *Errata*; the lady Corinna figures prominently in Ovid's love poems: *Am.* ii.17.29, iii.1.49; *Tristia* iv.10.60; cf. also Martial viii.73.10. *supremi proles veneranda tonantis Alcides* Hercules, son of Zeus. *soboles non Citherea* I.e., "no son of Apollo." *Pegasides* Muses (cf. N. 1562 under *doctarum plectra Sororum*...). *Nostra nec Aonio labra liquore madent* Schott uses almost the same words in #244, p. 280, and in #279, p. 306. *Appollineum... ebur* the ivory lyre of Apollo. *Melethei... viri* Homer. *volucer Tegeaticus* Hermes. *Annei Vatis* The poet Lucan. *stellati lumina mundi* The following 15 lines treat various constellations. *Aries... qui detulit Hellen* The constellation Aries, the ram of the golden fleece which bore Phrixus and Helle. *Dentibus et Tirium qui spoliasse solum* Draco, the dragon slain by Cadmus at Thebes. *Agenoream... rapuisse puellam* Taurus, the bull of Poseidon which was sent by Zeus to abduct Europa, daughter of Agenor. *Oebalio natum... olore genus* Gemini. *Et tepidus cancer Iunonius numine lucens* Cancer, placed in the sky by Juno. *Herculeeque manens Sirius ore fere* Leo, considered by some to be the Nemean lion, overlaps with the constellation Canis to which belongs Sirius (*Canicula*) called by Ptolemy the bright star in the mouth of Canis; cf. Manilius' description in *Astronomicon* v.206f.

P. 272

1571. Virginis Astree radios Virgo. *Scorpius acer* Scorpio. *Centaurique trucis... grandesque sagittas* Sagittarius. *Quique nitet... Egoceros* Capricorn. *Ganimedeis vbi coelum claudditur vrnis* Aquarius, who is said to be the cupbearer Ganymede. *Dionea quo sit imago loco* Pisces; the fish were set by Dione (another name for Venus) into the heavens in gratitude for saving Venus and Cupid from the waters of the Euphrates; cf. Ovid *Fasti* ii.459ff. *geminas Arctos: toruumque Draconem* Ursa Major, Ursa Minor and Serpens. *Gnosiace liber queque dedit domine* Corona, the crown given to Ariadne by Bacchus. *Titan* The sun. *Aeoas=Eoas* From *Eos*, i.e., "eastern." *Cadmeo medicatum vellus aheno* Cf. Ovid *Rem. Am.* 707. *flaui diues arena Tagi* Cf. *Epithoma* III, 1.9, p. 333. *Te si dardanie vidisset* Cf. *Errata*. *Pilio... hero* Nestor. *Cecropio... seni* Socrates. *Peliaco... robore* The Argo, Jason's ship. *Cyanei grandia saxa freti* The *Cyaneae* or *Symplegades* were two rocky islands at the entrance to the Black Sea. *tumidum se iecit in equor... carbasa nigra ratis* Aegeus, father of Theseus, threw himself into the sea at the sight of the black sail on Theseus' ship. *Ipse ne fulmineum Rutuli clamantis... in ore Mucronem fixi* A reference to Aeneas' slaying of Turnus. *caecum errorem* The Hussite heresy (cf. N. 379). *Pontificum virtus immensa* From 1409 on, when Alexander V had condemned John Hus, all popes inveighed against the Hussites. *Ipsa Sigismundi cesserunt regna* Sigismund* as king of Bohemia and as emperor had fought against the Hussites. *sacri fulmina concilij* The council of Constance (N. 1534) and the council of Basel (which with the compact of Prague tried the way of compromise) had opposed the Hussites. *modo Pannonij certarunt pectore vasto* Hussite converts in Hungary had instigated dangerous uprisings, the worst of which were 1433-1436. Even before he became king of Hungary, Matthias Hunyadi* used his formidable troops against the Hussites and continued to suppress them after he ascended the throne.

1572. Eacides Achilles. *Bistonij* Orpheus. *fibrisque Amphiona notum* I.e., "Amphion, famous for his skill with strings," the king of Thebes whose magic music caused the stones for the city walls to come together.

#240. TO JOHANN GEILER [Bologna, summer 1480]

1573. Summary Geiler is at the baths, and since it is customary to send gifts to those undergoing the bath regimen, Schott thinks the time opportune for sending his poem "De tribus Iohannibus" which he has composed at Geiler's request. Geiler will have leisure to peruse the work and, relaxed by the baths, may not be too critical.

Schott offers as excuse for the ineffectual poetry his care for religiosity and the fact that the subject far exceeded his talent. Indeed, he would never have undertaken the task, had he not felt it ungrateful to refuse Geiler. Because he consciously avoided poetic devices foreign to the sacred theme, he believes the poem lacks polish. He awaits Geiler's judgment – one he hopes not too severe – and will consider himself amply compensated, should Geiler approve the work. (Cf. p. xxxi and N. 135, par. 3.)

1574. Date Both date and place of writing are missing in this letter. Internal evidence indicates that it was written in Italy: 1. There are no bits of news of Strassburg or the baths, no details about current family or business affairs or about things of common interest, no greetings to friends such as are found in letters to Geiler after Schott returned home in 1481 but are absent in letters to Geiler from Italy, 1479-1481 (#10, #13, #14, #18). 2. The style of the letter resembles Schott's early letters and its close, "Vale: doctrinae Religionisque columen" is almost identical with that of #14 from Bologna, 27 January 1480: "Iterum vale Sapiencie religionisque columen;" no similar phrases occur elsewhere in Schott's letters.

Internal evidence also indicates that the letter was written during the summer months, for it was sent to Geiler at the baths, and Geiler obviously preferred the time June through August for his bath regimen (cf. the dates of #20, #21, #34, #104, #119). Reviewing Schott's whereabouts during the summers of the period 1479-1481, we find that in the summer of 1479 he was at home about to return to Italy, that in the summer of 1480 he was in Bologna on the point of receiving his doctorate of laws, that in the summer of 1481 he came back permanently to Strassburg (cf. N. 96). It appears then that the present letter was written at Bologna, in the summer of 1480.

Our conclusion about the year when the letter was written (though not about its place of origin) was borne out by the "Wimpheling codex" (cf. Appendix D). This contains two copies of the letter (and of the poem "De tribus Iohannibus" which accompanied it). The copy on folio 170b lacks the salutation but is otherwise like the text in the *Lucubraciunculae*. The copy on folio 176b has the salutation as follows: "Egregio sacrarum litterarum doctori domino Iohanni Geyler de Keysersperg Petrus Schottus Junior S.P.D.," which one notes varies from that of our text in the order of Schott's name, in the spelling of Geiler's name and in the addition of Junior, an appellation Schott seems not to have used; at least it does not occur in the *Lucubraciunculae*. At the close of the letter in this same copy appear the words: "Ex Argentina Anno LXXX." (As already discussed above, the place of origin of the letter is Bologna, not Strassburg).

P. 273   #240   N. 1575

1575. eum apud nostros morem... balneantes donis... oblectent... Carminis tegmen
The long poem on the three Johns which Geiler had commissioned Schott to compose was, we are told here, sent to Geiler as a bath gift. For the popularity of baths and bath gifts, cf. N. 192. For the custom of sending one's compositions to friends for criticism, cf. N. 309.

P. 274

1576. Plane accurate studui... nonnihil Carminibus decorem ademit.
Schott avoided allusion to all things classical and the use of humanistic phrases such as *Deorum Rector* (#252, p. 286) or *Altitonans* (#266, p. 299) to denote God, or *ducem* (#252, p. 286) to denote Christ; cf. similar phrases in Hassenstein's poem, #37, and Cornova's criticism of these in N. 381. The one classical allusion in the entire poem "De tribus Iohannibus" is that to *Siculus iuvencus* (p. 278). To Gossenbrot (#242, p. 279) Schott describes the poem as "unsprinkled by waters of the Hippocrenean spring and the sweetness of the Muses."

#241. POEM TO THE THREE JOHNS: ST. JOHN THE BAPTIST, ST. JOHN THE EVANGELIST, ST. JOHN CHRYSOSTOM in elegiac verse [Bologna, early 1480]

1577. Summary of the general introduction On approaching the judgment seat of God, the suppliant Schott is so awe-struck that his tongue cleaves to his dry throat and his voice fails. He therefore needs a patron pleasing to God to plead for him. Doubtful at first about which of the many saints he should choose, he beholds three of like name who excel all others, and these three he elects as patrons, namely: John the voice, John the bird, John the golden-mouthed. (Cf. xii, p. xxxi, N. 12, N. 135 [par. 3], N. 141, Appendix D.)

1578. Date As noted (N. 1574), the letter with which this poem was sent was written in the summer of 1480 at Bologna. The poem, suggested by Geiler (probably while Schott was at home from Italy 1478-1479), may have been begun before Schott's return to Italy in the fall of 1479; certainly it must have been completed and have received its final polish at Bologna in early 1480.

1579. Hos ob saguineas circumdat... palmite turba nitet For the spelling of *saguineas*, cf. p. xix (Spelling, 12b) and N. 39. The wreaths and sprigs of plants carried by the saints have special significance in Christian symbolism: the laurel is symbolic of martyrdom, victory and righteousness; the olive, of chastity and peace; the ivy, of learning and faithfulness; the myrtle, of love, spiritual fruitfulness and conversion to the Christian faith.

P. 275

1580. Virginea redolent olea... fert sibi quisque iubas Note that each of the three Johns has wreaths of olive and ivy (cf. above N. 1579). *Est vox* I.e., St. John the Baptist, "the voice crying in the wilderness." *est volucer* I.e., St. John the Evangelist whose symbol was the eagle. *est aureus ore* I.e., St. John called "Chrysostom," "golden-mouthed." Geiler felt himself very much akin to Chrysostom, as he did to Gerson. Indeed, Geiler's life in many respects resembles that of Chrysostom and Gerson (cf. N. 1526, N. 1534 and N. 1586), and his thinking was influenced by their writings. Some of his sermons are based on theirs ,as for example his "Ein tröstliche predig Sant Johanns Chrisostomi" (cf. also N. 135). Schott compares Gerson in fearless attitude toward temporal power to Chrysostom (#232, p. 261).

1581. Summary of the section on St. John the Baptist The first John invoked to become Schott's patron is John the Baptist who yet unborn proclaimed the Saviour by leaping in Elizabeth's womb as she was greeted by Mary; who to escape worldly temptation fled to the wilderness; who surpassed the prophets by proclaiming Him to be alive whose coming they had only foretold; who baptised Him.

1582. Septus adhuc vtero... dum Virgo salutat Cf. Lc. 1:40. *maior ut omni Prole esses... foeminea* Cf. Mt. 11:11 and Lc. 7:28.

1583. Summary of the section on St. John the Evangelist The second John invoked is the Evangelist, Jesus' relative – though not of the same blood – and Jesus' beloved. Slumbering on Jesus' breast at the Last Supper, he murmured, "Who is a traitor?" To him Christ when dying entrusted His mother. To him He revealed the mystery that the "Word was made flesh." Greater than the other three evangelists, he, the eagle, soars above the earth and fathoms the secrets of the heavens.

1584. Quippe alio quam tu... alio sanguine prodieris Tradition claims that Salome, the mother of John, was a sister of the Virgin Mary; hence John was Jesus' cousin. John was also chosen by Jesus to be His brother when He committed His mother to John's care (cf. Jo. 19:26). *Dum caput in dominum... traditor ecquis? ais* Cf. Jo. 13:23-25. *Qui iamiam moriens: mulier... nate tua* Cf. Jo. 19:26. *Hinc te stelliferas Aquilam transscendere moles* The eagle is said to be the only creature capable of gazing at the sun without being dazzled. Hence by interpretation the eagle is supposed to be capable of contemplating the divine. This capacity is appropriated to St. John who is believed to have soared into heaven to gaze on the light of immutable truth. Medieval legend tells how the old eagle flies into the fiery region of the sun, how his feathers are burnt off and how he falls into a fountain where his youth is renewed. Thus, like the phoenix, the eagle is a symbol of physical and spiritual regeneration. Cf. Jobes, I, 482ff. *verbum caro factum est Principio quod erat* Cf. Jo. 1:14 and 1:1.

1585. bos leo sit vel homo The ox is the symbol of Luke, the lion of Mark, the man or angel of Matthew. *Tu super humanas caeca caligine nubes* and below *Insontesque mihi iuueniles innouet annos... adolere sinit* refer to qualities of the eagle discussed in N. 1584.

P. 277   #241   N. 1586

1586. Summary of the section on St. John Chrysostom The third John invoked is Chrysostom who as a young man was converted to Christianity, who became a priest and later bishop. He was noted for his great learning, his prolific writing and his zeal in preaching truth. Fearless and of unimpeachable integrity, he denounced the stupidity of the clergy and dared even to attack the base morals of the nobility, thereby creating powerful enemies. Twice he was deposed and driven into exile, the second time because he condemned the statue of the empress. Patiently he endured all persecutions until his death. (Cf. N. 1580).

1587. Tercius auriuomo... ore patronus Cf. *Errata. Cecropia teneram coluisti fruge iuuentam* I.e., Chrysostom of Antioch was educated in Greek philosophy.

P. 278

1588. Scilicet Auguste quod simulacra vetas Because the noisy revels accompanying the erection of a statue to the empress Eudoxia disturbed the divine services he was conducting in nearby St. Sophia(?), Chrysostom "not only protested but preached in unmeasured terms against the offenders, with allusions to Herodias and Jezebel which glanced at Eudoxia" (Previté-Orton, I, 118). *Siculus non ipse iuuencus* The brazen bull of Phalaris, tyrant of Agrigentum, in which those condemned were roasted; cf. N. 1576.

#242. TO SIGISMUND GOSSENBROT [Bologna, late summer 1480]

1589. Summary Since sending Geiler the poem "De tribus Iohannibus," Schott has received many requests for copies. Before answering these, however, he wishes to present Gossenbrot* with a copy and receive the latter's critical judgment. The verses are not classical in spirit but strictly religious. Because Gossenbrot belongs to the order of St. John, he will, Schott believes, particularly appreciate the sections on St. John the Baptist and St. John the Evangelist.

1590. Date From this letter which accompanied a copy of Schott's poem on the three Johns we learn that – after Geiler – Gossenbrot is the first person to receive a copy. Since we know from #240 (N. 1574) that Geiler's copy was sent from Bologna in the summer of 1480, this present letter must have been written at Bologna not too long thereafter, probably in late summer of 1480.

1591. te mei amantissimum/ dignum putaui: cui... dono darem
Schott evidently valued Gossenbrot's opinions on things literary very highly and had sent him works on an earlier occasion (#171, p. 191, and N. 1218). For the practice of sending compositions to friends, cf. N. 309.

1592. et si non Caballino fonte... gloria fulcitos
Cf. a similar remark to Geiler in #240, p. 274; cf. also N. 1576. For *Caballino fonte... Nympharum,* cf. N. 1564.

1593. templo consitus: eorum fratrum... degunt
For details on the Strassburg monastery of the Knights of St. John the Baptist of Jerusalem, cf. N. 1141.

#243. EPITHALAMIUM FOR MATTHIAS I OF HUNGARY AND BEATRICE OF NAPLES in elegiac verse [Bologna, 1477]

1594. Summary Sing the nuptial song and let the games in honor of the marriage proceed. Behold Matthias, who is second to none in military might and justice, and the royal bride from Naples, who would have outshone Venus at the judgment of Paris! May their son, like his father, be an invincible defender of the faith!

1595. Date This poem was very likely written in the early weeks of 1477. Histories cite the date of the marriage between Matthias I (Hunyadi)* of Hungary and Beatrice, daughter of Ferdinand of Aragon, king of Naples, as 15 December 1476. The date of 1477 given for the nuptials in the heading of the poem is either a typographical error for 1476 or refers to wedding festivities extending from mid-December 1476 into January 1477.

1596. Regi en Mathiae... viget Matthias Hunyadi, who combined political acumen, military genius and scholarship in such high degree that he is termed the greatest man of his age, won deep admiration from his contemporaries by his successful repulsion of the Turks, his ready defence of the faith against infidel or heretical Hussite, his learning and patronage of the arts. Perhaps this admiration was in part responsible for the feeble support Emperor Friedrich III was given by member states of the empire in his war with Matthias, even though Matthias not only overran Friedrich's eastern Austrian lands but also captured his capital Vienna (cf. N. 623). *Regia spondetur proles... Deam* Beatrice was Matthias' third wife. Cf. biographical note on Matthias. *Magnanimum... natum* The marriage was childless; in fact, Matthias left no legitimate heir.

#244. ELEGIAC TO JACOB WIMPHELING [Bologna, probably early 1477]

1597. Summary Everyone admires the verses which Wimpheling recently sent. Indeed, Schott considers him the most gifted poet of their country [Alsace?]. For just as Homer, Vergil, Lucan and Papinius have given to the ages heroic deeds of ancient warriors, so Wimpheling shall immortalize the deeds of those who vanquished Charles the Bold. Although deeming himself quite unworthy of the distinction, Schott is nonetheless proud to have been the subject of so eminent a poet's verses.

1598. Date The poem treats the decisive defeat of Charles the Bold at Nancy on 5 January 1477 (N. 74). It seems quite logical that Schott composed the poem very soon after the event while enthusiasm for the victory was still running high.

P. 280   #244   N. 1599

1599. Quos mihi dulciloquo numeros... Misisti nuper Schmidt (*H.L.*, I, 165) believes Wimpheling had sent Schott the poem on the defeat of Charles the Bold at Morat (1476) and the poem on Hagenbach's execution (N. 74). This may well be, but at least some of Wimpheling's verses sent to Schott were in praise of the latter, as is evident from the closing lines of this poem. *Fortibus Achiuum ceptis... concinnis foecit aperta modis* Cf. *Errata*; the spelling "Archiuum" appears also in the "Wimpheling Codex" (f. 170a). It is either a typographical error for "Achiuum" or is meant for "Argiuum". The epics alluded to in the eight lines indicated are: Homer, *Iliad*; Vergil, *Aeneid*; Lucan, *Pharsalia*; Papinius Statius, *Thebais*.

1600. Quippe canes rabido qui temneret omnia fastu... canens equabis
If Wimpheling composed a longer poem on the defeat of Charles the Bold at Nancy, it is not extant. He did compose an epitaph to Charles which is in the "Wimpheling Codex" (f. 6b):

            Epitaphium karli ducis Burgundorum

    Occubuit karolus regum festo nece strictus
    Karolus occubuit et campos corpore texit
    Habitatio eius deserta et episcopatum eius accipiat alter

In the left hand margin is the notation "Numerus anni P S," indicating that the epitaph contains quotes from the psalms: "Habitat eius deserta" is from Ps. 68:26a and "episcopatum ... alter" is from Ps. 108:8b, cf. also Ac. 1:20.
    Schott mentions the defeat of Charles the Bold at Nancy in #238 (p. 269) as one of the major military feats of the German peoples. For other patriotic writings of Schott, cf. p. xxviii and N. 124.

1601. Nam licet Aonio neque labra liquore madescam Cf. similar passages in #239, p. 271, and 279, p. 306. *Ipse licet scombris Phariam... quicquid aro* Cf. Catullus 95.7; Martial iii.50.9, iv.86.8, x.48.12; Ovid *Hol.* 94, 98.

P. 281

#245. ELEGIAC ON THE DEATH OF RUDOLPH AGRICOLA [Strassburg, early 1486]

1602. Translation
      Toying with happy verses, Ruscus, had been my intent; and
         Fitting my metres with care, I was obeying your wish.
      Woe me! Alas, as I wrote, not lightness but sadness resulted.
         Forced into measures of grief, slowly Calliope moved.
      Think you, I could have written dulsome songs at the moment
         When the radiant Muse flees in haste from our soil?
      What lament shall I pen? Or will words express all the anguish
         Nearly bursting our breasts, almost too much to endure?
      Oh, the honor was he, the brightest star of our country;
         Oh, the Germans' file, sole one to scrape and refine!
      He was the first to bring us the Grecian and Roman Minerva
         And from the Helicon mount bear the Aonian nine.

He had begun to rid our students' speech of its scabrous
    Hodge-podge, and also with skill smooth it to elegant sounds.
Lo, he is held by the tomb; but he seems to have hidden our very
    Flower of genius, too, down in the earth with himself!
After a time I perchance shall compose you laments for our Rudolph;
    Sorrowful songs will sing all too plaintively then.
So has the recent shock convulsed my viscera, that for
    Sobs and a broken heart I no longer can write.
                    first published in *Kunstmann Festschrift*, 148f.
(Cf. p. xxviii, N. 559, N. 651).

1603. Date Schott heard of Agricola's death on 30 December 1485, as he tells us in the postscript to #78. He must have composed this lament shortly thereafter.

1604. ad Adelphum Ruscum That Adolph Rusch was a friend of Agricola is attested by correspondence between the two (N. 646); it was thus quite fitting that he should commission Schott who so admired Agricola to compose a poem on Agricola's death. *pro lusu luctus* Note alliteration here and below (in *scabra sartagine, praecordia perculit, scribere singultus*). *Qui primus nobis Graiam... ex Helicone Deas* This statement is somewhat exaggerated, for there were before Agricola German humanists who studied in Italy and on their return home fostered the "humaniora." Notable among these was Albrecht von Eyb (1420-1475), canon at the cathedral of Bamberg, whose life and works have been the subject of various studies since 1890. Eyb, however, had no Greek; thus Agricola, some 10 years older than the great Greek and Hebrew scholar Johann Reuchlin,* may have been the first German to know Greek since the days of Hrabanus Maurus and his successors. Hartfelder (*Briefe*, 6) says of Agricola: "[Der Ruhm] gilt ihm zunächst als der erste Vertreter eines besseren Latein, als der Vater des humanistischen reineren Stils in Deutschland." *Coeperat et iuuenum scabra sartagine liguas... polire sonos* Schott had expressed the same idea in his first letter to Agricola (#65, p. 71). Contrast, in the lines indicated, the harsh sounding words *scabra... Radere*, representing the barbarisms Agricola was eradicating, with the smoothly flowing words *et in nitidos... sonos...*, representing the elegant language Agricola was teaching. That the Latin of many educated Germans needed polish is exemplified by an incident told about the chancellor of the university of Tübingen whose Latin was so unintelligible to the Italians of the papal delegation which came to Tübingen in 1482 that in his stead Reuchlin was called upon to deliver the welcoming address (Erhard, II, 161f.). *liguas* Cf. N. 39.

#246. ELEGIAC FOR THE SCHOOLBOYS OF SAINTS PETER AND MICHAEL [Strassburg], 1481

1605. Summary The architect seeks to surpass Daedalus; the sculptor to surpass Lysippus; the painter to surpass Apelles; every craftsman strives to emulate the best in his field. For shame then, lads, to read sensational trash when the finest Latin literature is readily available! Though Vergil may be sold for a penny and Cicero be bartered for fishes, youth seeks cheap adventures by cheap babblers and speaks uncouth jargon. What use to repeat innumerable paradigms, if you cannot put ten words together proper-

P. 281   #246   N. 1605

ly? Speaking and reading expedite the learning of language more quickly than mouthing rules.
   (Engel, *Schulwesen*, 26f., has a German verse translation of part of this poem, i.e., from *Quid pudor o pueri* to the end. Schmidt, "Notices... P.S.," 317, gives a French prose translation).

1606. Schott composed this and the thirteen poems following (#247-#263) for the Strassburg schoolmasters and their pupils. Four of the poems (#254, #257, #259, #263) have explanatory notes (#255, #258, #260, #264, N. 1630). It may well be that Schott wrote such notes to all fourteen of these poems, but that only those notes to the four poems mentioned have survived.
   As noted in the heading of #246 and in the first two lines of #247, these fourteen poems were intended to replace profane songs traditional in children's celebrations, particularly at Christmas time (cf. N. 1337; also N. 1626, N. 1629). It is possible that Schott composed the music (in tripartite harmony) for the poems, though there is no mention of his having done so.
   Hieronymus Gebweiler continued Schott's practice of composing such school poems. He composed, for example, "Panegyris carolina" to Saint Nicholas (cf. Schmidt, "Notices... P.S.," 318).

1607. Sanctorum Petri et Mihaelis Cf. N. 132. *Lysippum... Appelleum* These two artists Lysippus, a famous brass founder, and Apelles, a celebrated painter, lived at the time of Alexander the Great; cf. N. 1004.

P. 282

1608. ligue Cf. N. 39. *Et scombris Cicero det licet ipse togam* Cf. N. 1601. *Quid iuuat innumeros... latina lege* Schott does not mean that grammar is not to be thoroughly learned; no student without sound training in grammatical principles could have understood these poems and comments even with the instructor's aid. Schott was rather speaking to the schoolmasters about poor pedagogy which let students parrot rules and paradigms without applying them to writing, speaking and reading. *sapiencia... incipienda metu* Cf. Pro. 1:7. *Aliger e coelis... nocentes* St. Michael with his fiery sword. *Clauiger alme* St. Peter, the key-bearer.

#247. ELEGIAC TO SAINT NICHOLAS [Strassburg], 1483

1609. Summary We lads sing in three-part harmony our annual praises to Saint Nicholas through whom God restored children to life. (Cf. N. 1606).

1610. liguis Cf. N. 39. *Nanque ferunt calidi feruenti... Nycholae tuo* St. Nicholas is said to have restored to life three little boys (or three men) whom an inn-keeper having need for bacon had cut up and pickled in a tub. He also restored a child which had fallen into fire and been burnt. Cf. Baring-Gould, XV, 65ff. *Paeonijs actum: quis Virbius herbis...* Virbius, another name for Hippolytus who was healed with herbs by Aesculapius, son of Apollo; cf. N. 1678.

P. 283

#248. ELEGIAC ON THE HARSHNESS OF MAN'S LOT [Strassburg], 1483

1611. Summary Man suffers adversity because in prosperity he disobeys divine laws and is ungrateful to God. For three years we suffered misfortunes; floods devastated the fields and despoiled the cities; plague and famine bore off the wretched. Now our Heavenly Father, having warned with whips of fear, teaches with gentle hand; granaries groan with fruits of Ceres, and the abundance of Bacchus fills the wine bottles. With fear and trembling let us give thanks. (Cf. N. 1606).

1612. En dum signiferum Phoebus ter circuit orbem... peste fameque viros The period 1478-1482 was one of hard times, 1480-1482 being especially bad years (cf. N. 1433). *Pater ille flagellis Tunc monuit* The passage is reminiscent of 3 Rg. 12:11 and 14. *Vbere pressa gemunt Cereris... tanta cadis* The year 1483 brought bountiful harvests; prices of grain and wine were low (cf. Dacheux, *Fragments*, III, Part v, 141).

#249. PROPHETIC POEM in dactyllic hexameter [Strassburg], 1485

1613. Summary Earlier verses sung by children which called on men to be grateful to God for His gifts and to fear disobedience of divine laws have availed nothing, and men have heedlessly walked in the old ways. Now the heavens, plague, floods and heat witness God's wrath. May the Virgin, our patroness, plead for us! (Cf. N. 1606).

1614. Seria sub tenui quondam contexere versu... turpibus ausis Schott is referring to his poem #248, which warned man to be grateful for his blessings, and perhaps to other poems no longer extant which had the same theme.

P. 284

1615. Verum grandiloquo qui verba requirit hiatu... Inconstans series In 1485 there was an eclipse of the sun on 16 March; there were also outbreaks of the plague and a poor harvest. The price of wine was very high because grapes dropped from the vines "in der Nacht auf Laurenztag" (5 September); cf. Dacheux, *Fragments*, III, 58; IV, 41, 68; Specklin, 286. *rogat en genitrix tua magna... patrona* The Virgin was the patroness of Strassburg (cf. #254, p. 288; #255, p. 291; N. 1643).

#250. POEM TO SAINT NICHOLAS in dactyllic hexameter [Strassburg], 1485

1616. Summary The boys are now celebrating the joyous days in memory of St. Nicholas who in the cradle began his dedicated life by fasting. As a boy he distinguished himself in studies. After acquiring innumerable virtues he became a bishop and performed many a miracle. He saved many persons condemned to death. To him boys gathering the first seeds of knowledge vow their years. (Cf. N. 1606).

1617. Obtulit insolita primis ieiunia cunis Legend tells that on Wednesdays and Fridays the babe Nicholas refused to nurse until sundown. In #255, p. 288, Schott refers to Nicholas' showing evidence of sanctity as a child. *Pontificis meruit fastigia* Nicholas was bishop of Myra. *quem placentem... nauta* St. Nicholas' prayers are said to have saved the ship on which he was sailing to Jerusalem from being wrecked in a violent storm. For this reason the saint is invoked by sailors in distress. *Hic probro exemit natas... misso ere Parentem* By secretly throwing three bags of gold through the window of their home, St. Nicholas is claimed to have saved three maidens from being forced to become harlots, because their father was too poor to provide dowries for them. From these gifts is said to have originated the custom of gift-giving on the feast of St. Nicholas, later transferred to Christmas. Pawnbrokers have taken the three bags of gold as their symbol and consider St. Nicholas as their saint. *Quid referam tociens ab iniquo iudice... a morte rapit* St. Nicholas secured pardon for three men condemned to death and imprisoned in a tower. Cf. Baring-Gould, XV, 64-68, for the foregoing material on St. Nicholas. *Quid/ quos miseranda... fames* We have found no reference to this miracle of St. Nicholas. *aut quos calor vrne... enecuit* Cf. N. 1610 (*Nanque ferunt...*).

#251. ELEGIAC ON THE INCONSTANCY OF HUMAN AFFAIRS [Strassburg], 1485

1618. Summary Are our minds so befogged, our senses so dulled that we cannot perceive the dangers about us on this earth? What is the meaning of constant change? Why does the soil, which denied nourishment to the wretched and placed a premium on foods, suddenly cram storehouses with bounteous harvests and swell casks with wine? Let us, warned by the besetting inconstancy of our fortunes, beware lest we be deceived by the seductive sweetness of the world; let us rather set our minds on eternal tranquillity and peace. (Cf. N. 1606).

1619. de mutabilitate rerum humanarum The inconstancy of man's lot is a topic frequently treated by humanists and Renaissance persons; as in this poem, it is often linked with "the wheel of fortune"; cf. below "Que nos orbe rotant" (p. 285) and "Inconstans etenim... motibus orbis" (p. 286). Cf. also Wimpheling's phrase "fortune instabilitatem" in #301 (p. 323). *Quid sibi vult: quod quae... liquore tument* Cf. N. 1612, N. 1615.

#252. ELEGIAC TO FRIEDRICH VON ZOLLERN [Strassburg], 2 February 1485

1620. Summary You are dean because of high birth and recognized virtue, illustrious Count, but only your spiritual life fits you to perform these rites which transcend the world of man. The eucharist has power to cause sins to cease, virtues to multiply and glory to descend from on high. Mortal kind wearies itself with labor to gain heaven when it would be more efficacious to enter frequently into His presence. Be not, therefore, like the husbandman thirsting in the field, but pluck the fruit which gives strength for other tasks.

P. 286   #252   N. 1620

Thus you may accumulate days salubrious both for the people and for yourself and pleasing to God. (Cf. N. 1606.)

1621. Que superant hominem: Comes inclyte munia tentas... This poem was written for Friedrich von Zollern when he celebrated his first mass on 2 February 1485. Because Friedrich was at that time dean of the Strassburg cathedral, this event would be of general interest and a fitting subject for a school poem (cf. #256 and N. 1646). Neither the beginning nor the end lines of the poem give the feeling of incompleteness. One wonders, therefore, why Dreher (XVIII, 11) calls the poem a fragment. *Deorum Rector* and *ducem*, as applied to God and Christ, are terms characteristic of humanistic writing (cf. N. 1576).

P. 287

#253. ELEGIAC TO SAINT PETER [Strassburg], 1486

1622. Summary There is a time to be serious and a time to be gay. Labor is pleasanter after repose. The genial winter solstice is here and bids us be jolly. Come, let us loose voices, long silenced, in happy measures! Let us restore body and mind. Let the saddle ease the recent stings of switches. But away with buffoons, scurrilous ditties, impious masks which profane holy places! True pleasure is unmixed with irreverence. Saint Peter, grant your lads jollity! (Cf. N. 1606. Engel, *Schulwesen*, 27, has a German verse translation).

1623. Seria tempus habent... tempora risus For similar phrases, cf. Pliny *Ep.iv.*25.3; for similar parallelism with *tempus*, cf. Ecclesiastes 3:4. *Sed procul hinc scurre... larua sacras* At the beginning of his notes to #254 (#255, pp. 288f.) Schott discusses the profane practices referred to here. Cf. also N. 1337, N. 1626.

#254. ENCOMIUM TO STRASSBURG in dactyllic hexameter [Strassburg], 1486

1624. Translation
    Glorious city, which bears the famous name of Argentum,
    Mighty in noble gens, in wall and towering ramparts,
    'Mid the cities laved by Rhine's cerulean waters
    First of all in fruits of Ceres and wine of sweet Bacchus,
    Second to none in arms, in riches and competent leaders,
    Hear, dear Mother, our song, as we thy children salute thee,
    Voicing in joyous verse our deep and loyal devotion.
    Blessed, ah, thou'lt be! if with government prudent and just thou
    Rulest thy people; if thou sufferest not that the wicked
    Dare with impunity spurn thy God and thy venerable laws, or
    Wantonly waste their wealth in gaming and gluttonous banquets;
    If thou showest esteem and love by rewarding with honors
    Worthy sons of the state whose virtue and knowledge promote the
    Good of the country. Be warned by the perils menacing others!
    Heed the mournful example provided by this year's disaster!
    See thy illustrious sister! The noble Ratis they call her,

P. 287 #254 N. 1624

>Once the foundation and hallmark of sacred imperial power,
>Curbing the swift-flowing Danube with stony, obdurate shackles.
>Now, despoiling herself of the liberty held as her birthright,
>She, unfortunate one, must learn to be servile and bear the
>Yoke of another – indeed, because she has lived as a spendthrift.
>But to avert the chance that any misfortune befall thee,
>May thy patron saint, whose image emblazons thy banners,
>Whom thou rever'st in thy high and wholly marvelous temple,
>Mary – the Mother of God – defend, deliver, adorn thee!

Cf. N. 1606. Hammer's article on the encomium ("Peter Schott...") has a German prose translation; Schmidt ("Notices... P.S.," 343-344) has a French prose translation. At the very end of Schadäus' *Summum Templum* is an encomium of Strassburg by Nicodemus Frischlin. Schott's explanatory notes to his own encomium are in the following item (#255).

P. 288

1625. legesque ferendas [verendas] In his note to this passage (#255, p. 290) Schott has "verendas". *Marcia signa choruscant* Schott's note (#255, p. 291) has *bellica signa choruscant*. For our notes to the poem, see those to #255 below.

#255. EXPLANATORY NOTES TO THE ENCOMIUM [Strassburg], 1487

1626. Summary [of the first three paragraphs which serve as introduction to the notes]. As among the ancients children were wont to sing praises to Apollo and Diana at specified times, so in Strassburg it has been age-old custom for children to sing praises in harmony, particularly during the season of nativities: first at the feast of St. Nicholas who already as a babe was holy and learned; then at the birth of Christ who adorned childhood with His own divinity; lastly at the feast of the Innocents, the storied victory [of the first martyrs]. Being thus favored by God, children should express delight in their feasts with grateful praises and real joy, but not with wantonness, not with bawdiness, not in ways disruptive of divine services, such as racing through churches, or wearing masks, or mocking personages by impersonations. These desecrations are degenerate deviations from the original purpose of children's feasts and smack of the Devil's influence.

The argument of this song, which was sung by Strassburg children in 1486, is as follows: first the children salute their native land; then they indicate the way of future political felicity; lastly they invoke the protection of Heaven upon their land. (Cf. N. 1606).

1627. Date In the first paragraph of the item Schott observes that the encomium is a *carmen annale*, i.e., a song for the end of the year; in the third paragraph he speaks of the encomium as "having been sung" (*cantarunt*) in 1486, i.e., at the Christmas season 1486. The notes may, therefore, have been written sometime after the encomium was first performed.

1628. Seculari carmine impuberes mayorum liberi... apud Q. Horacium Cf. Horace *Car. saec.* 75f.; in the "carmen saeculare pro incolumitate imperii" choruses of boys and girls antiphonically and in unison invoke the gods to prosper Rome.

1629. Que cum omnia ad laudem: et preconium... conatur peruertere
From Schott's words here and in #253 (cf. N. 1622) it is obvious that in seeking to replace the bawdy cantilenae, which along with boisterous and sacrilegious behavior had in turn replaced more sedate customs, Schott (and Geiler, cf. p. xxviii) had no desire to spoil the youngsters' fun but wished rather to channel youthful enthusiasm and animal spirits into more worthwhile activities compatible with the original intent of children's feasts. These feasts and the practices connected with them are discussed in N. 1337.

1630. Cui dedit Argentum... nunc vocari
Schott's notes to the encomium begin here. It will be apparent that the first three words quoted above are from the opening line of the encomium. In the remainder of the item are quotations from successive lines of the poem – often individual words or phrases – followed by Schott's comments thereupon. In format Schott's notes to his poems resemble Servius' commentaries, on which generations of students were nurtured.

For various names by which Strassburg has been known, cf. N. 16. Ptolemy ii.9.9 calls the city "Argentoraton"; cf. Pauly-Wissowa, II, part 1. 713.

1631. Vrbs. Hic pro ciuitate... in exordio Valerij Maximi... et dicta
For the lines quoted from Valerius Maximus i, lines 1f., modern editions have the reading: "Urbis Romae... ac dicta."

1632. Valloque... triplici circumdata muro
The quotation from Vergil is in *Aen.* vi.549. O. Ribbeck, *P. Vergili Maronis Opera* (Leipzig, 1878), 206, has a different reading: "Moena lata videt, triplici circumdato Muro."

Strassburg's city walls had been rebuilt and extended in 1475-1476 to resist Charles the Bold (N. 83); the lofty cathedral spire which dominates the countryside for miles had been completed in 1439; with the many church spires and towers such as the *Pfennigturm*, Strassburg in Schott's day must have presented an imposing skyline, not too much different from that of the early sixteen hundreds (Plate 5).

1633. Cunctis ceruleo quas alluit... Rhenus
The quotations are from Persius i.94, Vergil *Aen.* vii.198 and *Aen.* ii. 781f.

1634. Dulcisque Lyei. Bacchum Lyeum dixerunt... in Eunucho Therencij
Cf. *Errata*. The lacuna of about 16 spaces may be for the Greek forms of Bacchus' name Λυαῖος (Lyaeus, "the Relaxer") and of the verb from which it derives λύω (Latin equivalent *solvo*). For the quotation from Terence *Eun.* iv.727-729, W. Ritchie, *The Plays of Terence translated into parallel English Metres* (London, 1927), 168, has the reading: "neque pes neque mens satis officium faciunt."

1635. Pietate. que ut Cicero tradidit erga Deum... debet
Cf. Cicero *De officiis* i. 160.

P. 290   #255   N. 1636

1636. Legesque verendas... sicut de non ludendo de non garriendo in ede sacra
Cf. N. 1625. For other examples of irreverence in churches, cf. N. 1326 and N. 1333-N. 1337.

1637. Et ludo sua etc. Hoc vicium quo... Patrimonia decoquant et prodigant
In his conclusion to the *Lucubraciunculae* (#301, p. 323) Wimpheling attacks the vices of gambling and prodigality.

1638. Ligurire. voluptuose et dulciter consumere... Donatus super... bona
Schott is quoting the meaning given by Donatus in commenting on Terence *Eun.* 235.

1639. Sicque bonos Ciues. Salus Reipublicae... bonos Ciues intellige
Hassenstein speaks of the efficacy of recognizing the worth of outstanding citizens (#297, p. 314). Schott's words concerning the emigration of worthy citizens from Strassburg to states where their abilities are appreciated refer to the increasing exodus of noble families during the 1480's because of growing antagonism, in the city government, of the powerful guilds toward the nobles. By 1482, when 100 noble families left Strassburg, the guilds held 2/3 of the seats in the city council (Spach, *Zunftwesen*, 4). The apt quotation from Juvenal is from x.141-142.

P. 291

1640. Aliena pericula etc. Nam ut Virgilius dixit... cautum
The proverbial expression erroneously attributed by Schott to Vergil derives from a sentence in a scene interpolated, supposedly by Hermolaus Barbarus, into Plautus' *Mercator* iv.7.40. Cf. Apperson, 698; *Oxford Dictionary of English Proverbs*, 592; Riley, 122; Stoett, no. 2119, 292.

1641. En tua etc. Ratisponam circumloquimur... mali regiminis
Ratispona (from the ancient Celtic name *Rathaspona*) was called by the Romans *Castra Regina* whence stems the modern name Regensburg.
    In 1486, as noted in the heading to #254, the historic city of Regensburg lost its status as a free city of the Holy Roman Empire and became a provincial town in the duchy of Bavaria. Some three hundred years earlier Regensburg had been the capital of Bavaria; then Barbarossa raised it to the status of a free imperial city. For several centuries thereafter Regensburg was a thriving center of commerce and culture, but in the latter part of the fifteenth century the city government by poor management incurred heavy debts, and Albrecht III (*der Weise*),* reigning duke of Bavaria, seized the opportunity – much against Emperor Friedrich's wishes – to regain the city for his duchy. Cf. Schell, Part ii, 204.
    The free imperial city of Worms suffered a similar fate in 1482 when it was forced to accept *Pfalzgraf* Philipp* as its ruler and become part of the Rhenish Palatinate; cf. Stenzel, "Politik," 65. Strassburg supported Worms and sent Schott, Sr., as representative to the negotiations, but was unable to give military aid. Emperor Friedrich III also supported Worms, yet was powerless to prevent Philipp from taking the city.

P. 291   #255   N. 1642

1642. Saxea Danubium etc. Inter ceteras Ratispone... vinxerat Enosygeum
The reference is to the mighty bridge built at Regensburg 1135-1146 by Heinrich X (*der Stolze*), duke of Bavaria, when Regensburg was the capital of Bavaria. This oldest bridge of Germany is still in use today; during World War II the two ends were badly damaged but have since been repaired.
The quotation from Juvenal is from x.182.

1643. Quae tibi tutela est. Tutelam nauibus... Miroque per omnia templo...
For the reference to Servius, cf. volume I, 324 of his commentary to Vergil. The quotation from Vergil is from *Aen.* v.116.

The Virgin was from apparently very early Christian times the patroness of Strassburg. Bishop Wilhelm (*Graf* von Diest) of Strassburg in an official communication of 1398 calls her "Dominam et Advocatam nostram." Until the Reformation the image of the Virgin appeared on the Strassburg coat-of-arms. This, as seen on the Strassburg banner of 1208, shows the Virgin enthroned, with the Child on her lap, her arms spread wide (Plate 6); on either side are helmets; the throne has four fleurs-de-lys; the Child holds a fifth. It may be noted that Strassburg is said to have had the fleur-de-lys in its coat-of-arms from the time of Chlodowig (reigned 481-511) who, having chosen the lily in a blue field as his own coat-of-arms, granted Strassburg the right to use it.

Not only all large Strassburg banners but also small flags of any type (*Ritter-* or *Rennfahnen*) carried the official coat-of-arms. The flags had on the one side the inscription: "Venite ad Puerum Christum Omnes qui onerati sunt," and on the other the inscription: "A solo Christo victoria." The small banner once suspended from the trumpet of the herald or trumpeter – one of the *Rohraffen* (N. 1333) – at the base of the cathedral organ bears the city coat-of-arms; it is now on display in the *Musée de l'Oeuvre de Notre Dame* (N. 76).

The Strassburg gold guilder showed the coat-of-arms encircled with the inscription: "Urbem Virgo Tuam Serva."

The great seal of Strassburg bore the coat-of-arms along with the motto: "Virgo roga prolem quod plebem servat et urbem." This motto was translated by Wimpheling into German:

O Jungfrau, bitte stets dein Allerliebstes Kind,
Damit das Volck und Statt allzeit Schutz bey Ihnen find.

Cf. Pfleger, *Kirchengeschichte, passim.* Seyboth, frontispiece. Schneegans, *Sagen*, 11. Weislinger, 312, 333.

The Strassburg cathedral (N. 77) was dedicated to the Virgin, and one of its beautiful stained glass windows represents her enthroned with the Child on her lap. This representation is as similar to the Virgin and Child on the Strassburg coat-of-arms as a representation of the same motif in two different art forms can be and may either have served as the model for the coat-of-arms or been taken from it.

The new and completely different coat-of-arms acquired by Strassburg during the early years of the Reformation shows lions rampant and couchant. This coat-of-arms with the inscription "insignia civitatis Argentinensis 1523" is pictured on a stained glass window from the defunct *Pfennigturm* and may be seen in the *Musée de l'Oeuvre de Notre Dame.*

#256. POEM TO FRIEDRICH VON ZOLLERN in dactyllic hexameter [Dillingen, July] 1486

1644. Summary If you as bishop wish to live for Christ and guide your people on the way of salvation, follow the lives and teachings of the Church fathers, for not along alluring, new by-paths but along ancient paths will they lead the blessed beyond the stars. (Cf. N. 1606).

1645. Date This poem accompanied a book on the lives of the Church fathers which Schott presented to Friedrich von Zollern in Dillingen at the time of the latter's coronation as bishop of Augsburg, 21 July 1486; cf. N. 674 and N. 811.

1646. ad donum vitas et Collacionum patrum: Heroicum... As in the case of #252, this poem may have been considered material for use in school because it concerned Friedrich von Zollern; cf. N. 1621. The book on the lives of the Church fathers was perhaps a copy of the edition of *Vitas Patrum* which Ritter (*Histoire*, 111) and Voulliéme (109) mention as having been published at Strassburg in 1483 by an unknown printer, although Dreher (XVIII, 50) believes that Schott wrote the book for Friedrich. *Si viuere christo* Cf. Ph. 1:21. *themonem flectere dextra* I.e., "temonem," (the tongue or pole of) a wagon. Dreher (XVIII, 51) sees in this passage allusions to 1 Cor. 9:24 and to Horace *Carm.* i.1.4.

#257. ELEGIAC FOR THE END OF THE YEAR 1487 [Strassburg], 1487

1647. Summary Every year a new bishop and a new troop succeed the old, only to yield in turn to the new; every few years a class of schoolboys reaches port; but the master at the helm stays on. Let him, grown hoarse with disciplining, enjoy well-earned rest! Spare his grey hair, and let him be succeeded by the new! (Cf. N. 1606. Engel, *Schulwesen*, 27, has a German verse translation of this poem. The item following, #258, contains Schott's explanatory notes to the present item. Note that #259 treats the same theme).

1648. Pontifici modulata nouo Schott means here the "boy bishop" chosen by the choir boys at the Christmas season (cf. N. 1337). *noua turma...Magister agit* For an explanation of the imagery in this passage, cf. N. 1649. *exponier* A rare form of the present passive infinitive; cf. #263, p. 295, "precarier." *Quos foueat placido... sinu* Cf. N. 1643.

#258. EXPLANATORY NOTES TO THE PRECEDING ELEGIAC [Strassburg], 1487

1649. Summary Schott explains that the analogy between troops, ships and school seemed apt in the poem because school terms such as class, exercise, gymnasium and school itself derive from military and naval vocabulary.

Expanding the theme of the poem, Schott remarks that the schoolmaster by his labors which are both mental and physical has merited his reward and should be replaced when old, because those who teach should be in the prime of life and physically vigorous, as well as equipped with knowledge of the highest type and morally above reproach. (Cf. N. 1606 and N. 1630.)

1650. Sicut apud Iuuenalem. Cum perimit... tyrannos Juvenal vii.151. *Virgilius in x. Interea... exponit* Vergil *Aen.* x.287-288. *Clauus autem fustis est... dicit Seruius* Servius' comment to Vergil *Aen.* v.177: "...clavumque ad litora torquet," is: "clauum fustem gubernaculi." *Cicero in Catone maiore. Ille autem... puppi* The quotation is from Cicero *Cato Maior de senectute* 17. *Cui tamen etc... Magister meruit ut sibi prouideatur* Schoolmasters received their pay during the Christmas season (cf. N. 1337). *Plautus in Aulularia. Vbi si quicquam... quicquam detur* A modern reading of the line from Plautus *Aul.* 336 is: "Ubi si quid poscam, usque ad rauim poscam prius quam quicquam detur."

#259. ELEGIAC FOR THE END OF THE YEAR 1488 [Strassburg], 1488

1651. Summary The sore toil of the farmer, the far travels of the merchant, the endless stalking of the hunter, the long service of the soldier are duly recompensed. Why then should not the arduous labor of the hard-working schoolmaster deserve just reward? Let him be granted the rest and the gratitude due him! (Cf. N. 1606. Engel, *Schulwesen*, 27f., has a German verse translation of this poem. Schott's explanatory notes, #260, follow below. Note that #257 has the same theme).

1652. Reddatur meritis gracia digna suis As noted above (N. 1650), schoolmasters received their pay at Christmas time. *Hoc faxit Genitrix... Deo* Cf. N. 1643.

#260. EXPLANATORY NOTES TO THE PRECEDING ELEGIAC [Strassburg], 1488

1653. Summary As in the year past, grateful pupils again ask in song that their master be given his rest. (Cf. N. 1606 and N. 1630).

1654. Improbus etc... Nullus enim est amator laboris. Seruius Servius, *Commentarii*, II, 194f. *Virgilij in primo Georgicorum... Improbus* Vergil *Geo.* i.145f. *Sic Terencius in Andria... decreuerunt tollere* Terence *And.* 219. *Tollere dulcem cogitat heredem* Juvenal 6.38f. *Sic apud Virgilium... metitur equorum* Vergil *Geo.* iv.388f. *Sic Virgilius in quinto... pariter sulcos* Vergil *Aen.* v.143. *Vnde eciam in tercio... arandum est* Vergil *Aen.* iii.495.

#261. ELEGIAC TO SAINT PETER [Strassburg], 1487

1655. Summary The ancients had different feasts from ours. At the time when they celebrated purification rites in February, we now honor the

P. 294   #261   N. 1655

Virgin. The first of the month *Sextilis* which they dedicated to Augustus is now sacred to St. Peter. The season when they held the feast of the Saturnalia we now devote to St. Nicholas, to the Innocents and to Christ. (Cf. N. 1606.)

1656. Date It will be noted that this item antedates #259 and #260. Either the date given is a typographical error for 1488 or items #259 and #260 were purposely placed immediately following #257 and #258 because these have the same theme; cf. N. 278, also N. 36.

P. 295

1657. fulgebat lustracio februa priscis... honore meat The Romans celebrated the Lupercalia on 5 February and the feast of purification on 15 February. The Christian feast of the Purification of the Blessed Virgin, the most ancient of all Mary festivals, (and that of the Presentation of Christ in the temple) are celebrated on 2 February. *Sextilis caput Augusto... esse sacrum* Augustus chose the sixth month (August) as the one to bear his name because he had won his greatest successes in that month. On 1 August is the feast of St. Peter (*in vinculis*). *Haud secus Aegoceros Saturni secula priscis... dedit* Capricorn is the sign of the zodiac for the winter solstice. On 17 December the Romans began celebrating the Saturnalia and on 23 December they celebrated the *Larentalia*, a feast which Ovid (*Fast.* iii.57f.) calls pleasing to the tutelar deities, *genii*.

#262. ELEGIAC WRITTEN IN HAGENAU   Hagenau, 1488

1658. Summary How well chosen for children are the patrons St. Paul and St. Nicholas! Both imbibed learning at a tender age and both were allotted a sainted end. They will be guardians of the boy who has now been drinking deeply of the arts in order that in old age he may proceed to the stars. (Cf. N. 1606).

1659. Quam bene patronos... Paule et te Nycholae In 1164 Friedrich I (Barbarossa) built outside the city of Hagenau for the poor and for travellers a hospital with an oratorium dedicated to the Virgin and to Sts. Paul and Nicholas. In 1189 he placed the foundation under the direction of Premonstratensians with four clerics and a *praepositus*. In 1208 the foundation became also the parish church. Cf. Barth, *Handbuch,* 499-503; Schöpflin, *Alsace,* V, 166; N. 1369. Schott may have been in Hagenau to attend special ceremonies, perhaps commencement exercises, at the school belonging to the church. *Ambo etenim tenera... pacta dies* Before his conversion which came at an early age St. Paul had been thoroughly grounded in Hebrew Law and is thought to have attended the university of Tarsus where he was schooled in Greek philosophy. St. Nicholas who, tradition says, came from a wealthy family would as a matter of course have enjoyed a sound education in Hellenic culture, as Schott indicates in #250, p. 285. Both St. Paul and St. Nicholas suffered persecution for their faith; and St. Paul died a martyr. Both became saints.

P. 295   #263   N. 1660

#263. ASCLEPIAD TO SAINT PETER ON THE CAPTIVITY OF MAXIMILIAN, 1488 [Strassburg], 1488

1660. Summary Others with the lyre of Homer and more favored by the Muse, who dare to treat in verse Achilles and the wandering Ulysses, will sing of the impious bonds, of Germany's hosts speeding at the aged father's plea to free the king, of fair Argentina unsurpassed in arts of war. For us it is enough to pray St. Peter that he may inspire the hearts of the princes to be just and wise toward the conquered. (Cf. N. 1606, also p. xxviii and N. 124. Schott's explanatory notes to this poem follow in the next item, #264.)

1661. Romanum procerem... non veritas For details on Maximilian's captivity at Bruges, cf. #118, p. 138, and N. 925. *Grandeuique patris* Emperor Friedrich III. *precarier* Cf. N. 1648 "exponier."

P. 296

#264. EXPLANATORY NOTES TO THE PRECEDING ASCLEPIAD [Strassburg], 1488

1662. Summary Schott explains in detail the different types of metric feet employed in asclepiadian verses. The purpose of the poem, Schott says, is to express the children's astonishment at the insolence of those who captured Maximilian, to laud the prompt action of imperial troops – particularly those of Strassburg – in freeing Maximilian, and to entreat the victors to show magnanimity, justice and wisdom toward the vanquished. (Cf. N. 1606, also N. 37 and N. 1630).

1663. Monocolon... Nam... solum... membrum est The two lacunae after *Nam* and *solum* are obviously for the Greek words from which *monocolon* is derived: Μόνος and κῶλον. *Nam cantanda sunt Carmina ut dicit Seruius... cano* Servius in his note to the well-known opening words of Vergil's *Aeneid* comments that "cano" in this context means "sing": "Nam proprie canto significat, quia cantanda sunt carmina." *Homerus: de quo dicit Horacius. Rex [Res]... Homerus* Cf. *Errata.* The quotation about Homer is from Horace *Ars poet.* 73-74. *ut Ouidius in tercio de sine titulo. Aspice... aquis* Ovid *Amores* iii. 9.25-26. Modern texts have for "Aspice" either "adice" or "adjice." *ut Horacius. Scriberis vario fortis... alite* Horace *Carm.* i.6.1-2. *Chely... Chelys testudo* The lacuna after "Chely" is for the Greek word χέλῡς. *Stacius libro primo thebaidos. Nunc tendo... Aonia* Statius i.33f. (The quotation continues to p. 297).

P. 297

1664. Proceres ait Varro capita trabium esse Varro *Fragment* 30b. *apud Iuuenalem lectum est Agnosco procerem* Juvenal 8.26. *Sic Virgilius in secundo Georgicorum... sua poma* Vergil *Geo.* ii.82. *apud Ennium Romulus in coelo... hominibus tribuitur* Ennius *Ann.* i.Fr. 48. *Sicut apud Virgilium in quinto... tendunt Custodes* Vergil *Aen.* v.256. *Sic Virgilius in sexto... Corpus in aeacide* Vergil *Aen.* vi.57f. *Virgilius Eneidos libro secundo... mercentur Atride* Vergil *Aen.* ii.104.

P. 298   #265   N. 1665

P. 298

#265. POEM TO BOHUSLAUS VON HASSENSTEIN in elegiac verse [Strassburg, summer 1481-spring 1482]

1665. Summary In obedience to your wishes I have recently sent you notes — scant but useful — on metrical position and syllable quantities. Rumor has it that you possess compositions unknown to me. Let me share them and then let me sing your praises to the skies.

1666. Date As observed in N. 47, this poem is rather conclusive proof that Schott wrote the *Epithoma* for Hassenstein, during the first months after his return in early summer 1481 from Italy.

1667. tibi misimus, nobis, nostra The first person plural forms here seem to be the editorial "we" (cf. N. 1036).

#266. POEM TO GEORG ERLEBACH in elegiac verse [Italy, before summer 1481]

1668. Summary Our friendship scarcely begun is now disrupted by your departure. No greater affection had Pylades for Orestes or Achates for Aeneas than I should have had for you, had there been longer time to know you. May you have a safe journey and find your loved ones well! May only auspicious stars and planets light your path! May no storms, no birds or animals of ill omen, no evil charms impede your way!

1669. Date This elegiac resembles in style and content the poems composed in Italy. There is little doubt that it was composed also in Italy (either at Bologna or Ferrara) to speed the departing fellow student Georg Erlebach on his way home to Regensburg. We have found no information about Erlebach.

1670. Nam ne vlla Alciden coluit... in Eurialum Cf. #238, p. 270. *Alciden* Hercules. *Peancius heros* Philoctetes.

P. 299

1671. Nec pluuium Orion exerat ense caput The constellation Orion was thought to bring rain and storms. *Alma sed eniteat... cum fugeret* The planet Venus (Dione) shone for Aeneas when he fled from Troy. *Luceat et clarum sydus Iouis* The planet Jupiter was considered beneficent. *ipseque Castor Pollucem redimens* Cf. Vergil *Aen.* vi.121. In his comment on this line of the *Aeneid* Servius says: "Castor Tyndarei filius fuit: cuius mortem suo intentu fraterna pietas redemit: quod ideo fingitur, quia horum stellae ita se habent, ut occidente una oriatur altera." According to one story about Castor and Pollux, when Castor who was mortal died, Pollux prayed to join him; then Zeus in reward for brotherly love placed the two brothers in the heavens so that as one rises the other sets. *Nulla tibi noceat... Thessala cantu* The Thessalonians were considered second only to the Persians in the art

P. 299   #266   N. 1671

of magic and sorcery. Their skill is mentioned by Pliny, Horace and Apuleius. The arch-sorceress Medea is said to have dropped a magic casket in Thessaly; cf. Joseph Ennemoser, *History of Magic*, translated by William Howitt, (London, 1854), I, 352. *Obscena haud Vulpes obuia rumpat iter* This is a reference to the belief that encountering a fox is unlucky; cf. Pauly-Wissowa, I, part 1, 71. Swabian forest and mountain spirits appear in the guise of a fox, as do witches; cf. *Handwörterbuch des deutschen Aberglaubens*, III, 178f. Apperson, 233, lists a proverb expressing the opposite belief: "good following the way where the old fox goes." *Sed precor Altitonans* Cf. N. 1576.

#267. POEM ON THE COLLAPSE OF THE TEMPLE OF SAINT ULRICH in elegiac verse [Strassburg, 1478-1482?]

1672. Summary In the reign of Emperor Friedrich, Peter shattered the house of Ulrich. The force of a mighty wind during vesper services for the dead disintegrated the church. Fallen blocks hindered flight and thirty-four persons perished. May these pious ones have received their rewards in heaven and may the anniversary of their tragedy be remembered!

1673. Date The church of St. Ulrich in the Benedictine monastery (within the walls of Augsburg) had been constructed from an ancient temple by St. Ulrich himself to celebrate the victory of Emperor Otto the Great over the Huns in 965. On the feast of Saints Peter and Paul (29 June) in 1477, during a fierce windstorm, the church collapsed, and thirty-four persons, including the priest and altar boy, were killed. The abbot Henricus Frisius (1447-1482) had the church rebuilt. Cf. Brusch, *Chronologia*, 503f.

Schott's elegiac may have been composed to celebrate the completion of the restored church on the anniversary of the ill-fated day.

1674. Sancti Vlrici Augustensis Cf. N. 961. *Caesar... Fridericus* Friedrich III.

P. 300

#268. SAPPHIC TO PETER SCHOTT BY HEINRICH [Bologna, 1477-1480]

1675. Summary Peter, the new sweetly singing Orpheus, breaks the hearts of the nymphs. Orpheus of old charmed the gods and brought all nature to a standstill, but averse to love, he incurred the wrath of Cupid, Venus and Juno and was rent asunder by the Thracian women. Chaste Hippolytus, having spurned his stepmother Phaedra, suffered dire punishment. Peter preserves the golden mean and is equally favored by all the gods.

1676. Date Heinrich, the composer of this sapphic, may well be Heinrich Moser,* one of Schott's close friends in Bologna. Since Moser came to Bologna in 1477 and Schott left in late 1480, this poem and Schott's reply (#269) may have been composed during the period 1477-1480.

1677. Rhodopeyus heros Orpheus. *Frater Aenee pharetratus* Cupid. *Editus Musa: fidicen superbus* According to some accounts, Orpheus was the son of Calliope.

P. 301   #268   N. 1678

P. 301

1678. Theseo quin ut genitus: nouercam... Delia cornu Hippolytus was falsely accused by his stepmother Phaedra, because he had spurned her advances. His father Theseus, believing him guilty, caused him to be slain by Poseidon. Thereupon Artemis had him restored to life by Aesculapius with healing herbs and transported him to Italy, where under the name of Virbius he was cherished by the nymph Egeria and was worshipped in the grove of Aricia. Cf. Servius' comments to Vergil *Aen.* vii.761; also #269, p. 303, and N. 1679.

#269. SAPPHIC IN RESPONSE TO THE PRECEDING [Bologna, 1477-1480]

1679. Summary You, like Orpheus, cause tigers to leap and pines to move to your measures. In artful verse you argue that love's sad arrows should pierce even unwilling breasts. Yet love did not profit unhappy lovers such as Pasyphae, Dido, or Paris. Orpheus, however, who resisted unwanted love, though torn by the Maenads, still plays in the glades for choruses of the devout; and chaste Hippolytus, though slain, was restored to life. Thus chastity is rewarding; the chaste, though they suffer a wretched death, live on. (Cf. N. 1676).

P. 302

1680. vxor aruis Cephali Procris. *inuise vico Lacene* Helen; cf. Vergil *Aen.* ii.601. *quippe que Princeps ... Pastors amore* Paris, Priam's son, because of ill-fated love, caused the fall of Troy. *Traci ... Vati* Orpheus.

P. 303

1681. Et licet poenas lacerus... Virbius herbis Cf. N. 1678.

#270. ELEGIAC AGAINST A GERMAN-ITALIAN [Bologna, 1474-1480]

1682. Summary Integrity is unharmed by your abuse, just as elephants are impervious to the stings of gnats. Do not pollute your lips with mean verses. Acknowledge your German heritage; leave vile language and ill intent to the Italians. (Cf. #272 which has the same theme).

1683. Date Poems #270-#275 and #285-#286 represent word battles against literary enemies; the first group was written by Schott, the second by Hassenstein in defense of Schott. All these poems were written in Italy – most likely at Bologna during the years 1474-1480.

1684. Asirei Carmina Vatis Is *Asirei* perchance a misprint for *Annei*? In #239 (p. 271) the phrase *Annei Vatis* is used to designate Lucan. We have been unable to identify an "Assyrian bard" whose poetry would have been known to fifteenth-century humanists. Is the thought in the lines *Esse bonos... destituere notas* reminiscent of Lucan v.298? *Sed tamen et barri... curant* Cf. the almost identical line in #286, p. 309.

#271. AN ABUSIVE ELEGIAC [Bologna, 1474-1480]

1685. Summary You have recently written to me halting verses, vile poet, which befit you. The adulteress often vilifies the virtuous matron, but the latter remains chaste. Stop your abuses or you shall feel the cudgel. (Cf. N. 1683).

#272. TETRASTICH AGAINST AN ITALIANIZED GERMAN in elegiac verse [Bologna, 1474-1480]

1686. Summary Why do you, a German, spurn the mores of your ancestors and delight in Italian deceits? By so doing you prove yourself unworthy of your heritage and ungrateful to your forbears. (Cf. N. 1683. Cf. #270 which has the same theme).

#273. TETRASTICH in elegiac verse [Bologna, 1474-1480]

1687. Summary Why do you, who threatened us, not reply? Are you fearful of being forced to admit that our verses speak the truth? (Cf. N. 1683).

1688. tela minatus Tincta Lycambeo sanguine Cf. Ovid *Ibis.* 53-54.

#274. DISTICH AGAINST THREATS in elegiac verse [Bologna, 1474-1480]

1689. Summary The flock does not always perish when the wolf attacks, nor do bold threats bring sudden disasters. (Cf. N. 1683).

#275. ELEGIAC AGAINST VICES OF THE GERMANS [Bologna, 1474-1480]

1690. Summary How the barbarous clan, inflamed by false Teutonic furor, keeps its own ways and knows nothing of Italy or of the Latin tongue! Behold, it even installs its own kind in office! How true the saying that like seeks like! (Cf. N. 1683).

1691. furore Theutonico Cf. Lucan i.255-256. Note that in this poem Schott criticizes the German student who associates only with his own kind and refuses to profit from his sojourn in a foreign land. In #270 and #272 Schott, on the other hand, scorns the German student who spurns his heritage and slavishly imitates the Italians. Schott obviously believed in the golden mean.

1692. ruber scriba est Laurenti The persons mentioned here have not been identified. *veterum sentencia Vatum... pares* The source of the proverb "Pares cum paribus facillime congregantur" is *Odyssey* xvii.218. It is quoted by Plato *Rep.* 329A and *Phaedrus* 240C, by Ptolemy *Tetrabiblos* i. 7.21, by Cicero *De Sen.* 3.7. Cf. Büchmann, 256; Stoett, I, no. 2104, 285; Wander, I, 1712-1715. For a similar proverb which probably arose from this, cf. M. A. Cowie, *Proverbs...*, 97.

#276. ELEGIAC TO A CERTAIN JOHANNES [Bologna, 1474-1480]

1693. Summary For Johannes the glory of the muses will never perish. I pray you grant me forgiveness. I am like the stupid sow when she vied with Athene and came forth a sow without triumph. I acknowledge that you have won. Such is your facility in speech, learned one, that it behooves me to hold my tongue. In the future I shall do homage to you in silence.

1694. Date. Like the poems preceding and following, this item was probably composed also at Bologna. Is it possible that the "Johannes" of the poem is Johann Müller?

1695. Sus cum Dia certauit Pallade Cf. N. 933.

#277. ELEGIAC TO BARTOLOMAEUS FAVENSIS [Italy, 1474-1481]

1696. Summary Let Vergil and Ovid yield their crowns to Bartolomaeus! In poems of battle, of gods, of death, or of humor he is preeminent.

1697. Date There was a Bartolomeus Favensis* who taught at Bologna and also a person of the same name at Ferrara. Schott might have met or studied with either.

#278. TETRASTICH AGAINST A SHAMEFUL EPIGRAM [Bologna, 1477]

1698. Summary The rash throng has dared to write and publicize a nefarious epigram slandering the absent professor whom, when present, it fears.

1699. Date Galeotus Marcius*, professor at Bologna, was imprisoned at Venice for heresy during the year 1477, and evidently at this time was attacked in an epigram by students.

#279. HEXASTICH ON JACOB WIMPHELING'S POEM TO THE VIRGIN in elegiac verse [Bologna, 1477-1480]

1700. Summary To your poem both the Virgin and our young folk owe a debt of gratitude. For her it is a pious tribute, for them an example. To them may the muse grant poetic talent and to you may the Virgin not deny rewards.

1701. Date As noted in the heading, Schott composed the hexastich in praise of Wimpheling's poem to the Virgin, a copy of which Wimpheling had evidently given him. Schmidt (*H. L.*, I, 20) places the date for the composition of Wimpheling's poem to the Virgin in the year 1492, and Pfleger ("Marienfeste," 55) quotes Schmidt. Yet in neither the 1493 edition nor the 1494 edition of Wimpheling's poem is there evidence to support 1492 as the date of composition. Obviously Schmidt is in error, for Schott – whose date of death is given by both Schmidt (*op. cit.*, II, 4) and Pfleger (*Kirchengeschichte*, 207) as 1490 – could not have written laudatory verses on a work composed in 1492.

There are indications that Wimpheling's poem and Schott's hexastich were composed during the period 1477-1480. 1) The hexastich is placed in the *Lucubraciunculae* among Schott's miscellaneous short poems written in Italy. Admittedly the order in the *Lucubraciunculae* is by no means infallible, but in this case where the editor Wimpheling was personally concerned one might expect the order to be correct. 2) The fifth line of the hexastich has the phrase "Musa Aonij ieiuna liquoris" which is very like line 22 in Hassenstein's poem of 1477 to Schott (#239) and line 33 in Schott's elegiac of 1477 to Wimpheling (#244). The only other similar passage in the *Lucubraciunculae* occurs in Schott's letter of 1480 to Gossenbrot (#242, p. 279). 3) That Wimpheling was composing on the subject of the Virgin (and the immaculate conception) during this period is clear from his lengthy disputation "Sermo de purificatione beatae virginis LXXX" ("Wimpheling Codex," folios 122a-127f.).

1702. Iacobi Vuimpfelingi... De Conceptu et triplici candore Diue Marie
Schott's hexastich along with other laudatory verses appeared in the first edition of Wimpheling's poem to the Virgin, a copy of which we have seen at the *Bibliothèque Nationale et Universitaire de Strasbourg*. The full title is: "De triplici Candore Mariae ad reuerendissimum D. Bertholdum Hennenbergensem Archiepiscopum Moguntinum et principem sacrosancti Romani imperij electorem." Although the date of printing is lacking, as well as the place and name of printer, the accepted date of the edition is 1493, because Wimpheling's letter (folio 1b of the edition), written from Spires to request the patronage of Berthold archbishop of Mainz, bears the date 1 May 1493. Contents of the incunabulum are in order: the above-mentioned letter; Wimpheling's introduction, a praise of the German people from the time of Caesar; a description of the three parts of the poem to the Virgin; the text of the poem in elegiac verse, covering 23 1/2 folios; poems by Wimpheling to well-wishing readers, to several canons of the cathedral chapter at Mainz and to Georg Gemmingen, *praepositus* of the cathedral at Spires; 12 poems in praise of Wimpheling's poem to the Virgin by the following: Georg Gemmingen (2 poems), Peter Schott, Jodocus Gallus,* Peter Boland Laudenburg (4 poems), Conrad Leontarius,* Adam Wernher,* Jacob Han, Johannes Bechenhub.

This edition is mentioned by Riegger, *Amoenitates*, 180; by Schmidt, *H. L.*, I, 20, and II (*Index Bibliographique*), 318; by Pfleger, "Marienfeste," 55. In 1494 a second edition of Wimpheling's poem with Sebastian Brant as editor was published at Basel by Johann Bergmann under the title: "De Conceptu et triplici Mariae Virginis... candore carmen" (Schmidt, *op. cit.*, II, 318, 357; Pfleger, *loc. cit.*). The latter title, it will be noted, is more like that in the heading to the item of the *Lucubraciunculae* than that in the first edition.

Wimpheling's poem to the Virgin supports the long contested doctrine that Mary, like Christ, was immaculately conceived, a doctrine voiced at least as early as the time of Charlemagne at a synod in Frankfurt. The real battle over the doctrine began in the thirteenth century when Duns Scotus, a staunch supporter of the doctrine, attacked Thomas Aquinas for the stand that Mary, though divine, was born in original sin. Following in the wake of Scotus, the Franciscans became the traditional leaders of the "Immaculist" faction, while the Dominicans, following Aquinas, became the traditional leaders of the "Maculist" faction. Pontiffs and councils generally supported the doctrine. The council of Basel, for example, passed a decree approving the doctrine, whereupon it is said an epidemic of plague raging in the city subsided.

The dispute between the two opposing factions waxed particularly hot during the second half of the fifteenth century after the Franciscan pope Sixtus IV in 1476 proclaimed 8 December as the day for celebrating the immaculate conception of Mary. Trithemius (*Ann. Hirs.*, II, 500) relates an incident which occurred at the 1478 Benedictine convention at Pforzheim: a certain brother, having delivered a diatribe against the doctrine of Mary's immaculate conception, died on the same day of an apoplectic stroke; this was no doubt considered punishment for his temerity. Johann Zierer, O.P. lector and confessor of the convent of St. Nicholas *in Undis*, spoke against the doctrine in 1479; Geiler preached a sermon supporting the doctrine in 1481.

To stop the dispute and perhaps to make public his reaction to the work of Bandello de Castelnuova, which declared the doctrine of the immaculate conception of the Virgin to be heretical, Sixtus IV in 1483 issued a decree condemning opponents of the doctrine and excommunicating those who claimed it heretical. The decree nonetheless did not prevent eruptions of the quarrel thereafter. A short work by Trithemius entitled *De purissima et immaculata conceptione virginis Marie. Et de festivitate sancte Anne matris eius* (Leipzig, no date, no printer) contains a letter on the subject written by Trithemius at Spanheim in 1494 and a statement of his on the subject made before the Benedictine convention at Paris in 1497. A Specklin entry of 1508 (299) mentions the opposing factions and their views.

The doctrine of the immaculate conception of Mary was finally defined and confirmed by the Roman Catholic Church through Pius IX on 8 December 1854.

Cf. Barthelmé, 146f. Landmann, "Empfängnis," *passim*. Oberman, 281ff. Schmidt, *H. L.*, I, 18ff. Ullanthorpe, 173-191. Cf. also: Raynaldus, 1477, par. 9; Trithemius, *Ann. Hirs.*, II, 518.

#280. TETRASTICH ON THE EIGHT FRUITS OF THE VIRTUOUS SOUL in dactyllic hexameter [Bologna, 1474-1480?]

1703. Summary The mind which is conscious of not sinning is pure, healthy, free from remorse and liberated from the yoke. It promotes talent, inspires good deeds, keeps the flesh under firm control and is in harmony with God.

1704. Date There is no evidence as to when this poem was composed. Only its placement with other poems composed by Schott in Italy indicates that it was perhaps also composed during his student days in Italy.

1705. de fructibus octo The number eight – significant perhaps because the eighth day is the day of rest, the *dies caelestis*, or because 1/8 of one's goods is to be paid to the master – seems to have figured in Christian literature. St. Bernard of Clairvaux, for example, preached a sermon on "Octo puncta perfectionis assequendae" (cf. *Sancti Bernardi abbatis primi Clarae-Vallensis* [Paris, 1719], II, 820ff.).

#281. POEM ON THE SIEGE OF RHODES (cf. *Errata*) in elegiac verse [Bologna, 1480]

1706. Summary The pagan speaks: flee unconquered Rhodes! Omens against us redden the sky. We, wretched and forsaken, are convinced that Rhodes is dedicated; it is sacred to Christ and therefore will remain inviolate.

1707. Date In 1480 Sultan Mohammed II sailed with a large Turkish force (according to Trithemius, 100,000 strong) to the island of Rhodes and on 22 June laid siege to it. After three months of constant fighting, Peter Dambusson, master of the Knights of St. John the Baptist in Jerusalem, with the aid of King Ferdinand of Spain and of Sixtus IV, both of whom sent two ships, routed the Turks in a decisive battle. Cf. Trithemius, *Ann. Hirs.*, II, 504, and "Chronicon Spon.," 392; Raynaldus, 1480, par. 2ff.

1708. Paganus The pagan may have been meant to be Sultan Mohammed II himself. Paganus (also Payens, Payns) was the name of several Mohammedan leaders who figure in the history of Jerusalem during the twelfth century.

P. 307

#282. TETRASTICH ON DEATH SPEAKING TO MAN in elegiac verse [Bologna, 1474-1480?]

1709. Summary Ho there! Haste! What madness delays you? Do good deeds and don't be loath. Tomorrow I shall be your finish. You laugh? Perchance this very evening I may hale you before the Judge.

1710. Date This and the two items following are on the theme of death. The placement of these three items among poems composed in Italy may indicate that they were products of Schott's student days at Bologna and Ferrara.

1711. Heus propera... This item was quoted by Geiler in one of his sermons and was translated into German by Johann Adelphus. The foregoing information stems from a handwritten note pasted in the margin beside the present item on folio CLXXVIb of the undamaged copy of the *Lucubraciunculae* in the *Bibliothèque Nationale...* at Strassburg (N. 3):

Hos versus, a Geilero in sermone aliquo citatos,
Joh. Adelphus sic germanice vertit.

> Heus yle und lauff, waz halt dich hie
> So falsche thorheit und vil mie?
> Thu guts, nit lass verdriessen dich!
> Morn wil ich's enden sicherlich.
> O lachestu, weist nit vilycht
> Das ich den Abent für gericht

P. 307   #282   N. 1711

>Dich stellen würd, mit starcker handt
>Usstruck die blinden pfyl gespant?
>
>Pater Noster, fo. 9a

#283. TETRASTICH ON DEATH in elegiac verse [Bologna, 1474-1480?]

1712. Summary I am a terror to the sinful, a desirable gain to the just. Therefore spend the days allotted you in doing only good lest I seize you unawares. (Cf. N. 1710).

#284. DISTICH ON DEATH in elegiac verse [Bologna, 1474-1480?]

1713. Summary Though grim Death is the ominous doom of all, for the pious he marks the beginning of life. (Cf. N. 1710).

#285. ELEGIAC OF BOHUSLAUS VON HASSENSTEIN TO A RIVAL OF PETER SCHOTT [Bologna, 1474-1480]

1714. Summary The heavenly bears will dip into the sea, and sun and moon will fail in their orbits ere a vile mind deserts its favorite vice. Your teeth have rent me, because I wished to diagnose your disease and because I warned you not to befoul your lips with outrage. Perchance your frail talent cannot express itself otherwise. Your ditties have no charm, not one whit of elegance. Because I protect the honor of gifted bard Peter, you menace me with dread imprecations. May they be turned on you! Repress your barbarisms or our muse shall reduce you to childish tears. (Cf. N. 1683).

1715. Ante Licaonius mergetur... clara vehi These are formulae for "never." For other such formulae, cf. #289, #300, N. 1729, N. 1780.

P. 308

1716. Cherilon et Bauum Choerilus was a Greek writer of very poor verses; Bavus was a stupid poet, an enemy of both Vergil and Horace. *liguae* Cf. N. 39.

#286. ELEGIAC OF BOHUSLAUS VON HASSENSTEIN IN DEFENSE OF PETER SCOTT [Bologna, 1474-1480]

1717. Summary Elephants do not feel the sting of gnats, nor do your poisonous verses injure the eminent bard. Would you shatter a marble tower with a club? As the locust fills the lonely summer countryside with senseless cacophony, so your strident verses shrill unheeded. Beware lest you suffer the punishment of Zoilus who slandered Homer. (Cf. N. 1683).

1718. in defensionem Petri Schotti contra quendam inuidum detractorem A later detractor of Schott, presumably Locher, is condemned by Wimpheling in *Diatriba...*, cap. 16; cf. Schmidt, *H. L.*, II, 34.

1719. Ista quidem culicum... spicula barri Cf. #270, p. 303, for a similar line. *cum bibulam Sirius vrit humum* Sirius rises with the sun as the latter enters the constellation of Leo 23 days after the summer solstice. This period is the hottest part of the year in Greece and was known to the Greeks as the "dog days." Pestilences, drought and other dread phenomena prevailed at that time, and offerings were made to placate the star of the "dies caniculares." The Romans and later peoples of different latitudes, where seasons would not correspond with those of Greece, adopted the Greek tradition about dog days. Manilius in his *Astronomicon* (v.17) says of the constellation Canis: "canis in totum portans incendia mundum," and in the same book (208ff.) he describes the heat, drought, storms, diseases and other ills brought by Canicula (Sirius). Cf. N. 1570 under "Herculeeque..." *Nictelij defers cornua fronte Dei* Nyctelius is an epithet of Bacchus referring to the nocturnal nature of his mysteries. As the giver of courage, Bacchus is represented with horns. *Meoniden fatuo lacerauit Zoilus ore* Zoilus, a rhetorician of the fourth century B. C., filled nine books with adverse criticism of Homer. He is said to have been cast from the Scironian rocks into the sea by indignant Greeks. His name has become proverbial for a carping critic. Cf. Harvey, 454.

#287. ELEGIAC OF BOHUSLAUS VON HASSENSTEIN, LAMENTING THE DEPARTURE OF PETER SCHOTT FOR ROME [Ferrara, March 1481]

1720. Summary Peter seeks Rome and the Tiber. Perchance I shall no more behold him. Lament with me, ye heavens! No such tears did I shed when my father died. Recently I was bereft of dear brothers and now I lose half of myself. Who will share my studies, or help me with verses? Who will explain to me the classics? All things are muted as when Orpheus sought the shades.

1721. Date Schott left Ferrara for Rome in Lent 1481. He was not to return to Ferrara except for a brief visit before setting out for Venice and Strassburg (N. 96). Hence Hassenstein's grief was not so much because Schott was going to Rome, but because their long association in Italy was virtually over.

1722. Cum Genitor stigias... delectis fratribus For the few details known of Hassenstein's family, cf. his biographical sketch. *Dimidia videor parte carere mei* See a similar description of a friend in Horace *Carm.* i.3.8. *Hic meus Alcides... fuit* "He was my Hercules, my Orestes, my Patroclus, my Nisus." Cf. #238, p. 270; #266, p. 298. *Nonne satis fuerat... imposuisse meis* Hassenstein had left Bohemia at the age of twelve or thirteen to go to Bologna (N. 59, par. 6).

1723. Quis mihi nunc dabitur... leget In the passage quoted (N. 144) from a letter to Johann Sslechta, Hassenstein describes how Schott helped him at Bologna. In his oration (#297, pp. 318f.) Hassenstein mentions the poems Schott composed to him and Schott's willingness to help his fellow students. *Caballini quem iuuet amnis aqua* Cf. N. 1564. *Strimonis* The river Strymon in Macedonia. *Dum peteret nigri Tracius antra Ducis* "When Orpheus sought the caverns of Hades." *Taliter Eaciden mortem fleuisse sodalis* "So Achilles mourned the death of Patroclus." *frigij... viri* Hector.

#288. ELEGIAC OF BOHUSLAUS VON HASSENSTEIN [ON PETER SCHOTT'S RETURN TO STRASSBURG [Ferrara, May 1481]

1724. Summary Peter now leaves his Italian haunts. May he be guided safely to his native land and be joyfully received by his family and friends. Grant that he may long be happy in this life and thereafter be blessed.

1725. Date When Schott hurriedly left plague-ridden Bologna in September 1478 to return to Strassburg, there was no time for leave-taking. This poem of farewell must have been composed for Schott's final departure from Ferrara in late May 1481, after he had been to Rome and was on his way home to Strassburg via Venice (N. 96).

1726. Ausoniam... gentem Ausonia refers to Lower Italy; here it indicates Ferrara. *Laciosque Penates* Latium was the original territory of Rome; here it indicates the city of Rome. *Phaetontei... arua Padi* I.e., the fields of the Po where Phaeton met his fate; here the phrase indicates Bologna. *Sancta Parens* The Virgin, patroness of Strassburg (cf. N. 1643). *Forsitan et Rhenus... agri* Hassenstein is expressing hope that the disastrous Rhine floods of the summer 1480 might not be repeated. Cf. N. 1433.

#289. ELEGIAC OF BOHUSLAUS VON HASSENSTEIN ON HIS LOVE FOR PETER SCHOTT [Italy, 1474-1481]

1727. Summary The sun will reverse its course, the waters of the ocean will overwhelm the sky, mountains will no more whiten with snow, fish will cease in the sea, rocks will produce honey, the oak will bear ears of grain, ere my love for Peter fails.

1728. Date There is no real clue as to the date of this poem. It was most likely composed during the years of Hassenstein's and Schott's close association as students in Italy.

1729. Ante reuertetur tepidos... producet aristas Note the five formulae for never. For similar formulae, cf. N. 1715. *Tethios vnda* Tethys was the wife of Oceanus. *Ripheus nimbus* A reference to the lofty Rhipaean range of mountains thought by the ancients to be in the far north, or in Scythia, or where the Danube rises; later geographers have identified the range with the western part of the Urals.

#290. POETIC INVITATION TO PETER SCHOTT BY JOHANN REUCHLIN [Strassburg? or Basel?, 1478?]

1730. Summary I pray you come to the inn of the Golden Lion. Dinner awaits and I cannot dine without you. Your charming presence will add the necessary spice. Do come! (Cf. p. xv, N. 32).

1731. Date Geiger, *Briefwechsel*, 38, quotes this poem by Reuchlin* and Schott's letter to Brant* (#10) in which Reuchlin is mentioned. In a note on the same page Geiger gives the date of Reuchlin's poem as 1477 or 1478. The year 1477 cannot be correct, because Schott was in Italy and Reuchlin did not set foot on Italian soil until 1482. The year 1478 is, however, quite a likely date for the poem, because (as already indicated in N. 196) Reuchlin must have been in Basel during the fall of 1478, while Schott was at home in Strassburg. The place of meeting could have been either Basel or Strassburg or the baths which Schott visited upon his return to Strassburg (#10 and N. 190). The Strassburg inn belonging to the Brant family bore the name "Golden Lion," and it is possible that Reuchlin invited Schott to dine with him there, but one can not be at all sure, because virtually every town has a "Golden Lion" inn.

1732. Hospes ad auratum diuerti Petre Leonem Cf. *Errata*.

#291. TO JACOB WIMPHELING FROM CONRAD LEONTARIUS [Maulbronn, after 12 September, 1490]

1733. Summary Leontarius* was distressed to hear of Schott's untimely death. He regrets that his friendship with Schott was of such short duration and feels that Wimpheling is fortunate to have known so intimately a gifted man whose equal is not to be found in Strassburg. In learning, in eloquence, in conduct Schott was an honor to the Muses and a unique example to the priests of the time.

1734. Date Leontarius' letter from which this item was excerpted appears to have been written not too long after Schott's death, perhaps in answer to a request for letters and other writings of Schott, at the time when Wimpheling and Geiler were beginning the task of collecting material for the *Lucubraciunculae* (cf. p. xiv).

1735. ego vero miserior qui incipientem medio... ad mutas litteras suas cogar The correspondence between Leontarius and Schott had begun in 1489 (cf. #126).

7136. Sed stat sua cuique dies... Omnibus est vite.
Vergil *Aen.* x.467-468.

#292. TO JOHANN GEILER VON KAYSERSBERG FROM BOHUSLAUS VON HASSENSTEIN [Bohemia, late summer 1491]

1737. Summay On arrival in Venice, Hassenstein had a letter ready to send to Strassburg when he received word of Schott's death. He was completely

P. 312   #292   N. 1737

shattered, not so much because of Schott whom he considered fortunate to have escaped this wretched world, as because of himself for he had lost a friend whose like he had possessed but this one time and never expected to possess again. He had contemplated writing to Schott's parents but feared he might only exacerbate their grief. He enjoins Geiler who had loved him for Schott's sake to continue loving him and to write. (Cf. N. 37).

1738. Date Hassenstein returned to Venice from his long voyage, in August 1491, as we learn from a letter written at Venice, 11 August 1491, to Stephan Piso (Potuček, 19). Informed on arrival that he was being considered as candidate for bishop of Olmütz, he hastened to Bohemia. His letter to Geiler was written probably in late August or early September – perhaps from Prague or Olmütz – after he had received a message from Strassburg in Bohemia, giving details of Schott's death.

1739. sed quod ipse eiusmodi amico orbatus sum... habiturus sum
The wording here is reminiscent of Cato Maior's statement at the death of Scipio (Cicero *De Am.* iii.10):
    Moveor enim tali amico orbatus qualis, ut arbitror, nemo umquam erit et confirmare possum, nemo certe fuit.

1740. Tu facito ut me ames... nunc sponte tua facias.
The affection between Geiler and Hassenstein is indicated in the Hassenstein-Schott correspondence, and in Hassenstein's other letters to Geiler (cf. N. 829). Even before Hassenstein visited Strassburg and met Geiler, Schott's glowing accounts of Hassenstein must have impressed Geiler, because he not only approved but even abetted the plan of the two students to spend a life of study together (cf. #25, p. 33, and N. 302).

#293. TO JOHANN GEILER VON KAYSERSBERG FROM BOHUSLAUS VON HASSENSTEIN [Hassenstein], 11 September 1492

1741. Summary Hassenstein sorrowfully reports the death of Friedrich Büchsner* who had been with him for years and had accompanied him on his travels. He is particularly disturbed at having failed Büchsner's mother who had entrusted her son to his care. Büchsner had suffered a light attack of fever, had recovered and then become seriously ill. On 8 September, after receiving the last rites, he had died peacefully with Hassenstein at his side. Hassenstein, still mourning the loss of Schott, is grief-stricken to have now lost Büchsner as well. (Cf. N. 37).

1742. Fridericus meus Busner... peregrinatus est: ipso die Natiuitatis...
Cf. Hassenstein's epitaph for Büchsner in the biographical sketch of Büchsner. The feast of the Virgin's Nativity is 8 September, which in 1492 fell on a Saturday. Hassenstein wrote to Geiler just three days thereafter, i.e., on the following Tuesday, 11 September.

1743. matri sue integerrime foemine: que se... putabat
We have not found information about Büchsner's mother. Hassenstein had met her on his visits to Alsace.

1744. Data die Martis post festum Natiuitatis beate Virginis
Cf. N. 1742.

#294. TO JACOB WIMPHELING FROM JOHANN SIMMLER [Strassburg, after 12 September 1490]

1745. Summary Peter Schott, the pearl of priests in the Strassburg diocese, has succumbed to fate. He was truly learned and talented, yet modest withal.

1746. Date Like #291, this item is an excerpt from a letter and was no doubt written under similar circumstances (cf. N. 1734).

#295. ELEGIAC BY JODOCUS GALLUS ON THE DEATH OF PETER SCHOTT [Heidelberg, after 12 September 1490]

1747. Summary While the plague rages in your city, keep serene. With equanimity endure your sorrow for Peter Schott. Though he was not the least in talent among your learned canons, nor the least in integrity among your upright, do not mourn him. You know how saintly was his life. He has shed his earthly shell and returned his purity to God. Let us rather rejoice and congratulate him.

1748. Date This poem, dedicated to Schott's colleagues at New St. Peter, must have been written very soon after his death, for Gallus* speaks of the epidemic of the plague as still raging in Strassburg. For details on the plague of 1490, cf. N. 59, 3.

#296. DISTICH BY JODOCUS GALLUS in elegiac verse [Heidelberg(?), 1490]

1749. Summary A good life is rewarded by a sweet sleep, and a beatific life follows a pious death.

1750. Date It is possible that Gallus wrote the distich to accompany his elegiac on Schott's death (#295).

#297. ORATION BY BOHUSLAUS VON HASSENSTEIN IN HONOR OF PETER SCHOTT [Strassburg, end 1482 or beginning 1483]

1751. Summary Nothing is more profitable to your republic, Strassburgers, than to reward with praise men who have from childhood devoted themselves to learning and virtue. Such praise inspires the upright to higher achievement, deters the base from misdeeds and stimulates others to desire glory. You need not search abroad for someone unknown to honor thus. You have in Peter Schott a man of learning and virtue to serve as an example for his contemporaries. He is a son of your own great city which excels its neighbors in beauty, in climate, in fertility of soil, in abundance of game, water and forests. Indeed, it is not just mere chance that great cities produce great men. Was not Plato born in Athens?

Peter's father – who is present – is known to you all as a man of rare wisdom and industry. Not one of you is unaware of his vigilance in preserving and increasing your prestige and safety, often with danger to himself. He took care not to pamper his son but to give him the best possible training. Unable because of pressure from state affairs to instruct the child himself and conscious of the lasting value in early discipline, he entrusted him to Johann Müller, that paragon of virtue, who loved the child as a son and used every opportunity to advance knowledge and mold character. Peter, whose respect and love for Müller increased with the years, responded eagerly to tutelage and even anticipated Müller's commands.

Having acquired the rudiments of education in his homeland, Peter, accompanied by Müller, went to the university of Paris, where there was no subject he did not master. Though he outstripped his fellow students, they did not resent him but loved him for his modesty and generous nature. The instructors, singularly fond of him, furthered him and considered his ability a promise of future greatness which would bring honor both to him and to them. Peter, wise beyond his years and never truculent or superficial, sought to imbue himself with disciplines useful not only in youth but also in old age. He avoided all excessive pleasures and preferred study in a foreign land to a life of ease at home. Thus not as a tyro, but as a veteran he acquitted himself in his examinations and not only won the degree of bachelor of arts but was also accorded the highest honor for learning by the members of his university nation.

You here heard of his successes at Paris, and when he returned home, you saw for yourselves that the reports had not been exaggerated. You encouraged your sons to follow his example; you congratulated his father and called him fortunate in having so talented a son to solace his old age. Although the father enjoyed having his son at home, he was foresighted enough to realize that the boy had to continue his studies, and after three months sent him to the university of Bologna.

At Bologna Peter not only mastered literature, oratory, Greek, canon and civil law, but also composed elegant poems – in all types of verse – and orations as well, the stylistic perfection of which is equalled by the subject matter. While others wasted time at dice, banquets, shows and other pleasures, he sat happily over his books and took advantage of every occasion – even social functions – to discuss problems of literature or law. His friends thronged to him for advice on orations, on disputations and on poetry. Surely his accomplishments prove the fallacy of the argument that it is impossible for one man to excel in all fields. Were not Plato, Aristotle, Cato and Cicero each preeminent in many fields?

In addition to learning and talent, Peter possesses high moral qualities: deep faith in God, abiding love for his parents and sisters (whom he has never offended in word or deed), integrity and purity. His moderation in all things, especially food and drink, kept him healthy and free from any illness in Italy, where even the native Italians find the climate trying. He does not retreat to his study but applies his abilities and energies to social problems and affairs of state.

Therefore, Strassburgers, if you honor a man of virtue and integrity who was born in a foreign land and whom you have never seen, what praises should you not heap upon such a man in your very midst whose person you see before you! (Cf. p. xxiii, N. 62 and N. 63).

1752. Date As already mentioned in N. 101, par. 3, Hassenstein's oration was doubtless delivered to the Strassburgers on the occasion of his first visit to Strassburg at the end of the year 1482 or the beginning of the year 1483.

1753. Nihil vtilius et comodius reipublicae... incitantur

P. 314   #297   N. 1753

A similar thought is expressed in Schott's encomium of Strassburg (#254, p. 288; cf. also Schott's note to the passage in #255, p. 290).

P. 315

1754. *hanc ciuitatem vestram Ducibus/ Militibus... fruges; vinum*
For details on the city-state of Strassburg, its government, its natural resources, etc., cf. N. 16, N. 69; for references to Schott's statements about his homeland, cf. N. 124, par. 3.

1755. *Platonem... eo quod nature gracias egit: quia Atheniensis esset*
Cf. Lactantius *Inst. Div.* iii.19.17, where Plato is claimed to have said he was grateful that he was born an Athenian and in the time of Socrates.

1756. *Pater Petri vir summi consilij... pro salute vestra obiecerit*
For the many services of Schott, Sr., to Strassburg, cf. pp. xxiiif. and his biographical sketch.

1757. *inquit vnus ex Poetis Genus et proavos... voco*
Ovid *Met.* xiii, 140f.

1758. *nullam capitaliorem pestem ipsa voluptate... impelleret*
This passage is a paraphrase of Cicero *De Sen.* 39f.

1759. *illa pertinacius herere: quibus tenera rudisque etas inficitur*
Cf. Quintillian *Inst. Or.* i.1.19. Hassenstein returns to this theme later in the oration (p. 316; N. 1763).

1760. *Iohanni Muller de Rastetten: quem ego vnicum... audeo appellare*
Hassenstein had known Müller very intimately in Italy. Cf. Brant's praise of Müller (biographical sketch of Brant).

P. 316

1761. *quo fiebat ut quotidie illius amorem in se magis... alliceret*
For Schott's devotion to Müller, cf. N. 527.

1762. *Postquam autem prima rudimenta... ex eo tempore carior fuerit*
Cf. Wimpheling's statements in #1 and #2. Cf. also p. xxivf.; #9, p. 16; Chronology I.

1763. *prouerbium Omnia illa que in puericia presumuntur... vtiles esse possent*
Cf. Quintillian *Inst. Or.* 1.1.19; Cicero *De Sen.* 9. Schott discusses this subject in #171, p. 192.

P. 317

1764. *Itaque non solum Baccalaurius factus: sed eciam... antelatus est*
When Schott received his baccalaurate degree at Paris in 1473, his fellow members of the *natio Alemanniae* made him *provisor* of the nation (N. 95),

P. 317   #297   N. 1764

an honor conferred by the nation on those of its members who were outstanding in learning. Johann Scriptor* had been an earlier recipient of this honor (cf. biographical note on him).

1765. et oraciones summo artificio edebat. Cuius rei testes... deuenerunt
None of the orations which Schott composed in Italy has survived (cf. N. 31; p. xiv). For a list of the few extant orations, cf. Special Index in this volume, p. XXV.

P. 318

1766. Et quanquam pro summa eius in me humanitate: innumera... celebraret
Schott's extant poems to Hassenstein are #236, #238, #265.

1767. Alij ocium sibi datum in fabulis/ alea... voluptatibus tempus trahebant
Mores of students have changed little through the centuries! In his *Modus studendi* Sebastian Brant not only gives sound advice on how to study law (careful attention during lectures, note-taking, reading notes out loud, repetition, memorization), but also with boisterous humour tells students what pitfalls are to be avoided: women, dice, drunkenness, gluttony, ornaments in dress, love of money, too much sleep, inane activity of games, useless consumption of time, etc.

1768. Audiebat alios libenter placideque illis respondebat... doctiores recederent
Hassenstein himself received considerable help from Schott (cf. #287 and N. 1723).

P. 319

1769. Que nam ars Helio hippio defuit... ope indigeret
Hippias of Elis, a versatile sophist and contemporary of Socrates, is the protagonist of Plato's *Hippias Major* and *Hippias Minor*. In the latter work (368b f.) is related the incident in which Hippias claimed on arrival at Olympia that he wore nothing he had not made with his own hands, even to coat, signet ring and sandals. Quintillian (*Inst. Or.* xii.11.21-24) retells the incident. It is from Quintillian that Hassenstein took the wording of the passage "qui non modo liberalium... indigeret." In the phrase "sed vestem/ annum/ crepidas" Quintillian has "annulum" (cf. *Errata*), as has Rybra (32) in his text of Hassenstein's oration.

1770. Gorgias quoque: querere auditores de... ad omnia responsurum
Gorgias of Leontini in Sicily, a great philosopher at the time of Socrates, is featured in Plato's *Gorgias*. Gorgias' claim that he could answer any question put by his hearers is made in *Gorgias* 447.

P. 320

1771. Quid enim de incredibili eius in Deum... de sua reliqua integerrima vita...
Schott's deep faith, his devotion to parents and sisters, his love for his friends, his integrity are evident in all his writing. (Devotion to parents and sisters is especially evident in #8; #73, p. 80; #136, p. 154; and in the

letter to Anna, p. 357, paragraph 2). The qualities mentioned by Hassenstein here are also stressed in his letter to Johann Sslechta, the pertinent section of which is quoted in N. 144. The same qualities are enumerated by Wimpheling in the introduction (#1) and conclusion (#301, p. 322) to the *Lucubraciunculae* and in the epitaph to Schott (#2). See also Jodocus Gallus' elegiac (#295).

1772. Qui ita se litteris abdunt: ut nihil offere... perdiscendas existimauit
This passage is a paraphrase of Cicero *Pro Arch.* vi.12. Hassenstein and Schott, like other fifteenth century humanists, were strongly influenced by the classical idea that a man steeped in philosophy (liberal arts) should devote himself to the public good. Writing to the elderly Sigismund Gossenbrot,* the student Schott cites Gossenbrot as a peerless example of such a man and declares his intention of following that example (#171, p. 192).

P. 321

1773. Quod si ob virtutem et probitatem eos sepe quos... diligere cogimini
Cf. Cicero *De Am.* 28.

#298. ELEGIAC BY ADAM WERNHER [Place and time of composition unknown]

1774. Summary If you seek to placate God, utter your [canonical] hours with fervor. Pay Him the time you owe Him. Never let work keep you away. Thus you will prosper in this life and in the hereafter. (Cf. N. 30).

1775. Horas septenas murmure funde pio
Cf. N. 1451.

1776. ast nullo fallitur asse Deus
Cf. *Errata*.

#299. AN OLD PROVERB

1777. Summary The one who injures writes in dust; the one who is injured writes in marble. (Cf. N. 30).

1778. Puluere qui ledit: scribit...
For other versions of this proverb, cf. Christie, I, 557, 11 and 558, 36; Tilley, I, 71; Wander, IV, 254.
  Schmidt (*H. L.*, II, 28) cites this proverb as appearing in several works of Wimpheling. Murner has a German translation in his *Schelmenzunft* (XIII, 19-20):
> Wen man schilt, der schribts in steyn,
> Der do schilt, in stoub hyneyn.

#300. DISTICH BY JACOB WIMPHELING

1779. Summary Happy the parish priest and happy the parish in which lives no leper, no Jew, no official, no monk. (Cf. N. 30).

P. 321   #300   N. 1780

1780. Foelix Plebanus... viuit Helias
That Naaman and Abraham should signify "leper" and "Jew," respectively, in the distich is understandable, but why does Elijah signify "monk?" Is it because he was a man of God, a hermit, the quintessence of a prophet? And why does Shem signify "the establishment?" Is it because he was the "father" of the Semites who have always been known for their shrewdness and business acumen?

Beside this distich on the left margin of the folio in the undamaged Strassburg copy of the *Lucubraciunculae* (N. 3) appears the notation: "Simile inuenies fol: 154"; that is to say, Schott's Latin rendition of Dringenberg's proverb (#234) has similar statements. Below the distich are entered two items – a Latin distich and its German equivalent – about the cleavage between lay persons and clerics (note the formulae for "never," examples of which have already been noted in #285 and #289, cf. N. 1715):

   1. Dum mare siccatur, dum daimon in astra levat,
      Tunc Laicus clerico fidus amicus erit.

   2. Wan das mehr in sich verseugt
      Wan der Thuffell gegen himmel fleugt
      Als dan wirt der lay gar fein
      Den christlichen gewogen sein.

P. 322

#301. CONCLUSION BY JACOB WIMPHELING [Soultz(?), July-September 1498]

1781. Summary Do not despise these few writings by Peter Schott. Many more issued from his pen but have disappeared. He wrote all these in his youth, at the age of not yet three and thirty. From the few you can conjecture what he would have produced had he lived to be sixty and been able to hear more of Geiler's teachings, as well as read more of the classics which would have been published in the meantime.

His letters are worthy of Cicero. The treatise on Christian life is admirable. If his works were inserted among those of Lactantius or St. Jerome or St. Augustine, no one would know but what one of these three had written them. You may learn for yourself from his letters what piety he observed toward his parents, with what fervor he cherished the Scriptures, how he urged many to fear the Lord, to lead a Christian life, to flee the Roman *Curia*, to beware of plurality of benefices.

Strassburg has been blessed through this son and would be more blessed if it had more sons of such calibre. Let Strassburg youth read Schott's works and follow his example.

1782. Date Wimpheling may have written this conclusion to the *Lucubraciunculae* at the same time when he wrote the introduction, that is in late July of 1498 at Soultz-les-Bains (#1; N. 152). In any case he had to have it ready before 2 October of that year when the printing was completed.

The material in paragraphs two and three of the conclusion is largely repetition of material in the introduction (#1). The "Opusculum de vita Christiana" mentioned is Schott's treatise on Christian life (#110; cf. also N. 103). For references to Schott's devotion to his parents and friends, his integrity, cf. N. 1771; for references to plurality of benefices, cf. N. 133, par. 3; of the many warnings to Vitus Maeler* against becoming too involved in the ways of the Roman *Curia*, that in #128 is the most explicit.

P. 322   #301   N. 1783

1783. ad omnes Heluecios: id est Alsaticos: praesertim Argentinenses...
The terms Helvetian and Alsatian were considered synonymous. Schott calls Strassburg "Argentina, the city of the Helvetians" (#195, p. 212). Cf. N. 1371.

P. 323

1784. mors sancta et in conspectu Domini preciosa sit
Cf. Ps. 115:15.

1785. Vidimus multos paterna nuper hereditate... (to end of paragraph)
Wasting of patrimony by gaming and riotous living is mentioned by Schott in #254, p. 288, and in #255, p. 290. This was one of the evils Geiler sought to eradicate; cf. N. 1326.

Note Wimpheling's use of the "unclassical" term *trutannos* (Baxter, *Medieval Wordlist:* "trutannus" = beggar). Did he feel that the usual Latin term "mendicus" was not strong enough here, because it had the connotation of "mendicant clergy?"

Note also the reference to the instability of human fortune in the phrase "fortune instabilitatem;" cf. N. 1619.

#302. COLOPHON OF MARTIN SCHOTT

1786. Summary Printed by Martin Schott, 2 October 1498. Whatever be lacking, supply; whatever be superfluous, delete; whatever be crude, polish; whatever be obscure, clarify; whatever be incorrect, emend. By such care the whole will be made flawless.

1787. Impressa a Martino Schotto...
The colophon with device as it appears in the *Lucubraciunculae* is reproduced in Plate 4, p. 324. For a description of Martin Schott's* device, cf. p. xiv and N. 22. The three lines of admonition to the reader which are above the device may have been composed at some time for Martin Schott by his cousin Peter Schott, for they appear in no other of Martin's colophons we have seen.

P. 325

#303. INDEX

1788. Cf. the *Table of Contents*, pp. 3-8, for translation of titles, for number of item and page in this edition.

P. 326-P. 327

1789. For comments on the *N[ostro]* on p. 326, column 2, lines 35f., and on p. 327, column 1, lines 15-19, cf. N. 181.

687

DE MENSURIS SYLLABARUM EPITHOMA

I. LETTER FROM JACOB WIMPHELING TO JOHANN ZWIG AND PHILIP FÜRSTENBERG Heidelberg, 27 November 1500

1790. Summary Wimpheling asks Zwig* and Fürstenberg* to compose for the edition of the *Epithoma* a few verses inviting youth to peruse the work. (Cf. p. xix-xxi, N. 42-N. 47, N. 50).

II. HENDECASYLLABICS BY JOHANN ZWIG [Heidelberg or Spires, end 1500]

1791. Summary If you would drink oft from the sacred font of the Muses and be crowned, like Hesiod, with laurel, then read, studious youth, this art of versification by learned Peter.

1792. Date This poem was composed in the weeks elapsing between 27 November 1500 (the date of Wimpheling's letter above) and 24 December 1500 – the date when the *Epithoma* came off the press.

1793. Culmen et Cyrre The phrase apparently means "Delphic mount"; "Cirrha" (Cirra) was a town which was devoted to Apollo and served as the harbor of Delphi. *Tempora ut cingat... Munere laudem* Hesiod is connected rather with Mt. Helicon than with Mt. Parnassus, as is inferred here. He is said to have been herding sheep at the foot of Mt. Helicon when the Muses appeared to him in a dream and consecrated him a poet by giving him a laurel staff and the gift of song (Pauly-Wissowa, VIII, part 1, 1170). He dedicated a prize tripod on Mt. Helicon to the Muses. *Et ferant Nymphae calathis anethum* Cf. Vergil *Ec.* ii.46-48.

III. ELEGIAC BY PHILIP FÜRSTENBERG [Heidelberg(?), end 1500]

1794. Summary The Parthian prizes the javelin; the Arabian prizes incense; some value garments dyed purple; others value gold-bearing rivers, Mentorean goblets and saffron. You who seek the reward of poets, study the work of this well-versed bard. (Cf. N. 1792.)

1795. Aonius... Vates I.e., Hesiod who was a Boeotian.

1796. Mentorei calices Famous embossed goblets of the artist Mentor. *Coriciumque crocum* Corycus in Cilicia was noted for its saffron.

IV. PREFACE [Heidelberg, 1500]

1797. Summary The following rules for judging syllable quantities, compiled from many examples in reading, will suffice for the beginner. He should remember that in Greek words and in words derived from the Greek, the Greek spelling indicating syllable quantity must be retained and that those forms which occur rather frequently in approved Greek and Latin poets are the ones to imitate. Further rules pertaining to niceties of poetic style may be learned from other sources.

1798. Date There can be no doubt that this preface issued from Wimpheling's pen and that it was written sometime during the year 1500 after Johann Schott undertook to publish the *Epithoma*. Schott had no reason to write a preface to his notes on syllable quantity; his poem (#265) adequately introduced these to Hassenstein. Furthermore, had Schott written a preface, he would most certainly – as in the case of the treatise on Christian life (#110) – have made personal reference to the recipient of the notes, Hassenstein, and he would not have used the term "beginner" of Hassenstein whom he considered a gifted poet.

V. GENERAL RULES FOR DISTINGUISHING QUANTITIES

1799. Prima A diphthong is long, as in *audax*, though it may sometimes be short when followed by a vowel, as in *praeire*.

1800. Secunda Position causes a syllable to be long. The term "position" signifies a syllable in which a vowel is followed by two consonants, as *carmen*, or by a double consonant, as *ille*, or by a consonant like *x* or *z* or *i* consonant between two vowels, as *aio*. If, however, a short vowel is followed by a mute and a liquid, the syllable may be either long or short, as *tenebre* (cf. Schott's letters #90 and #91 to Wimpheling on the subject of position).

1801. Tercia A vowel preceding a vowel is short. Exceptions are *fio*, genitives of nouns and pronouns in *-ius*, genitives and datives of the fifth declension. The rule does not apply to Greek words or Greek derivatives.

1802. Quarta Accent indicates the quantity of the penultimate, except in compounds of *facio*, as *califacis* and the like, and words which in oblique cases drop a syllable, as *Mercuri*.

1803. Quinta Derivatives regularly keep the quantity of the original, as *munero* from *munus*.

1804. Sexta In compounds, with few exceptions, syllables retain their original quantities.

P. 335   *Epithoma*   N. 1805

P. 335

1805. Septima Usually the first syllable of a verb in any tense will have the same quantity as in the first person singular present indicative.

P. 336

1806. Octava The surest way to ascertain syllable quantities is to follow examples in approved poets.

VI. SPECIAL RULES FOR DISTINGUISHING QUANTITIES

1807. In primis Syllabis
The outline form used throughout the remaining folios of the *Epithoma* is very like that used in the rules of quantity for hexameters which are given at the end of the edition of Alexander de Villa Dei's *Doctrinale* printed at Hagenau (no date) by Heinricus Grau. The method of presenting the examples is like that of Priscian's *De accentibus* (21-44).

P. 338

1808. E ante L
The quotation "Quod fieri ferro... electro" is from Vergil *Aen.* viii.402.

P. 340

1809. I ante P
In the examples "stipes is vulgo soldt" and "Stipes stipitis vulgo ein Stock" Schott gives the German meanings to avoid confusion of two similar words: *stipes*, meaning payment, and *stipes*, meaning stick.

P. 342

1810. O ante N... Praeter Donus apud Lucrecium
Neither the form *donus* nor any other form beginning with *don-*, in which the *o* is short, appears in modern editions of Lucretius. In fact, the form *donus* does not appear in any dictionaries we have consulted except in Du Cange (III, 182), where it is explained as a contraction of *domnus*, i.e., *dominus*. The passage "D ut donec. Praeter Donus apud Lucrecium" in the incunabulum is printed clearly and without abbreviations. Is it possible that *donus* or some such form was a reading in manuscripts or early editions of Lucretius?

1811. O ante P
The quotation "Opis ad ethereum pennis aufertur Olymphum" is from Vergil *Aen.* xi.867.

P. 343

1812. V ante L... Vligo apud Virgilium anceps reperitur
Cf. *uligine*, Vergil *Geo.* ii.184

1813. E ante M... Vindemiator Horacius corripuit
Horace *Sat.* i.7.30

1814. E ante R
"Hunc ego sopitum... Cythera" is from Vergil *Aen.* i.680.
"Est Paphos Idaliumque... Cythera" is from *Aen.* x.86.
"At Cytherea nouas arces etc." is from *Aen.* i.657.
"Orgia: nocturnusque... Cythaeron" is from *Aen.* iv.303

1815. I ante C
Below is reproduced from the incunabulum the arrangement of the passage "Genitiuus in icis a nominibus... Fredericus":
1.   In ex corripitur ut verticis.   Praeter Lodicis.
2. Gtis I icis   In masculinis corripi-   Bombicis.
3. a noïbus   In   tur ut Calicis   Praeter Phoenicis.
4.   ix   Adde Salicis & Silicis.   Masticis.
5.   In alijs producitur ut felicis radicis pernicia.
6. Propria in icis aliqua corripiunt ut Alaricus Cimicis.
7. Producunt alia ut Caicus. Fredericus

It will be noted that the arrangement in the first four lines is somewhat confusing. To add to the confusion, a misprint in the present edition has shifted *Cimicis* in line 6 to line 5; *Cimex, cimicis*, however, is a common noun ending in *-ex* and illustrates the short *i* before *c* in oblique cases; it belongs rightly, therefore, in the first line which should read: "In ex corripitur ut verticis. Cimicis. Praeter Lodicis."

Judging from the proper nouns given as examples – *Alaricus* in line 6 and *Caicus. Fredericus* in line 7, the ending *-icis* in line 6 must a be misprint for *-icus*. Furthermore *Alaricus* in line 6 has a long *i* (cf. *Harpers'* and Claudian *Bell. Get.* 492 and 623) and is thus not an example for the statement in line 6 that some proper nouns in *-icus* have a short *i*, but rather an example for the statement in line 7 that some proper nouns in *-icus* have a long *i*. Line 7 should then read: "Producunt alia ut Caicus. Fredericus. Alaricus."

It appears as if the printer of the incunabulum omitted in line 6 the original example(s) of proper nouns in *-icus* having a short *i*; possible examples would be *Alemmanicus, Dominicus, Firmicus, Germanicus, Urbicus.*

1816. I ante N
In the section "Deriuata et possessiua longa sunt... perendie," the word *perendie* is obviously not an illustration of short *i* before *n*. Probably the word in Schott's original manuscript was *perendinus*.

The quotation "Et clamdestinis surgencia fraudibus arma" is not from Lucretius but from Manilius *Astronomicon* i.897, as we discovered quite by accident when searching for material on constellations and planets

P. 348   *Epithoma*   N. 1816

in that work. Lucretius does, however, use the word *clandestinus* in i.779 and ii.128 and in both instances the *i* before *n* is long; these may have been the passages Schott had in mind.

For the two words ("bombycinus" and "sanguineus") questioned in the passage "Graeca eciam a lapillis..." the incunabulum has *bōb. san.*; these are the only abbreviated words in the lists of examples in the *Epithoma*.

P. 349

1817. I ante T... anachorita
Cf. *Errata*.

1818. O ante B
The quotation "Ne laceres versus dux Iacobe meos" is from Claudian *Car. min.* 50.

P. 350

1819. O ante N... Sydonius indifferenter a Virgilio ponitur
Vergil employs the *o* in *Sidonius* as short in the following lines: *Aen.*i.678; iv.75, 137, 545, 683; v.571; *Ci.* 387. He employs it as long in the following lines: *Aen.* i.446, 613; ix.266; xi.74.

1820. O ante R... Decor decoris... et indecorus
There is confusion here among the derivatives of *decor* and *decus*. The printer may have repeated some words and put others into the wrong line. Perhaps the two lines should read: "Decor decoris. Inde decorus a um et indecorus. Decus decoris. Inde decoro as indecoris."

P. 351

1821. V ante G... Sanguisuga
Since *sanguisuga* has a long *u* before *g*, it illustrates the rule, not an exception to the rule, and hence belongs in the line above, which should read "producitur ut Ferrugo Sanguisugo."

P. 352

1822. C finita... Hoc eciam naturaliter breuem esse ex verbis Prisciani
This is perhaps a reference to Priscian's statement (*De accentibus* 10f.) that short vowels in monosyllables must be pronounced with an acute accent, because – though naturally short – they are long by position. The old grammarians usually give *hic* and *hoc* as either short or long, depending upon position; cf. Keil, VI, 29, 30, 31, 36, 230, 242, 587.

1823. E finalis
In the Greek words given as examples in the paragraph "Greca que ad nos..." (cf. *Errata*) the correct accents for the Greek form of Helen should be ἑλένη and for the Greek vocative of Anchises should be ὤ 'Ανχίση.

P. 352   *Epithoma*   N. 1823

The form *tabe* is used by Lucretius i.806; iii.553. The form *tabes* also occurs in Lucretius vi.1202.
The phrase "Insulae Ionio in magno" is from Vergil *Aen.* iii.211.

1824. L finita... Barbara in el ut Daniel Michael
Cf. *Errata*

P. 353

1825. R finita
The quotation "Lucidus umbroso miscebitur aer auerno" is from Claudian *Rapt. Pros.* i.116.

P. 354

1826. Vs finita... Sed Horacius licenciose palus corripit
Cf. Horace *Ars poet.* 65.

VII. COLOPHON

1827. Impressum per Iohannem Schottum... nono Kalendas Ianuarias...
The printing of the *Epithoma* was finished 24 December 1500. For a discussion of dates before the kalends of January, cf. N. 218.

P. 357 *Letter to Anna* N. 1828

LETTER IN GERMAN FROM PETER SCHOTT TO HIS SISTER ANNA SCHOTT
Bologna, 28 February 1476

P. 357

1828. Summary Schott was very happy to receive Anna's letter with its expressions of sisterly affection and concern for his welfare. There would be in its pages enough instruction to keep him on the right path even if he had no other guidance at all. She need have no fear that he might resent any of her admonitions, because he knows these are prompted by her deep interest in his salvation.

As for Anna's request that he commend her to St. Dominic, he wishes her to know that he remembers his parting promise to her to be mindful of her whenever he visits St. Dominic's tomb. Indeed, he has in her name often kissed the tomb.

He disagrees with her contention that knowledge of law is senseless knowledge. She has, he believes, misinterpreted St. Paul's words concerning the senselessness of all human knowledge, and he cites passages from the Scriptures which express high regard for law and lawgivers.

He bids her commend him to her prioress and sister nuns and thank them in his name for their prayers. He asks for prayers on behalf of their native city in its perilous hours of war and on behalf of their father Schott, Sr., and all their friends.

Anna must write to him whenever she can and tell particulars about her studies; such information will be a source of great interest to him. Even though she is now in another convent, God grant her happiness and health. (Cf. p. xi, p. xxif., N. 3, N. 5, N. 51-N. 55, Appendix A).

1829. Date In 1476 Ash Wednesday, the first day of Lent, fell on 28 February and Easter Sunday on 14 April. Schott dated the letter as "the first day of Lent."

1830. Selikeit der selen vnd libes winsch ich dier in brüderlichen trüwen...
For variant spellings and punctuation, see Charles Schmidt's handwritten copy of this letter in Appendix A. In the notes following, reference is made to Schmidt's copy only when his version makes for better understanding of the text.

1831. Wen ob mich gantz kein andere lere uff dein rechten weg wisse
Schmidt's copy also has *dein,* but in a marginal note Schmidt suggests *den* which is a more sensible reading.

1832. mocht ich doch genugsamklich uss diner geschrifft... sag ich dir gar grossen Danck
This passage illustrates Schott's "pietas in Sorores" mentioned in Hassenstein's oration (#297, p. 320).

P. 357   *Letter to Anna*   N. 1833

1833. vnd auch mine wercke in sinen lob vnd ere...
Schmidt's copy has *all mine wercke.*

1834. wolmögen vnd gesuntheit mines Ersammen Meister hansen
The reference is to Johann Müller,* Schott's tutor at Bologna. Weislinger (680, note m) mistakenly identifies the "master" as Geiler.

1835. van diner Erwirdigen muter Priorin
The prioress of the combined convents of Sts. Margaret and Agnes was Anna Zorn.* Cf. N. 83.

1836. das ich dich entphelen sol dinem Vatter Sancto Dominico
St. Dominic (1170-1220) – founder of the Dominican Order – had died in Bologna and was buried there in the San Dominico chapel of the San Dominico church. He had been canonized in 1234. Just three years prior to the date of this letter, in 1473, the Bolognese had given a sarcophagus for his remains (Heimbucher, I, 478). Bologna was thus, so to speak, a holy city to the Dominicans, and Anna, being a devout Dominican nun, would naturally wish her brother to pay respects to the saint in her name.

1837. Justi autem in perpetuum viuent... et ostendit illi regnum
The Latin passages in this paragraph are in part paraphrases and in part quotations from the Vulgate:
  Justi autem in perpetuum... Cf. Ps. 36:29-30.
  Justorum animi in manu dei sunt... Cf. Ps. 36:33.
  Justus ut palma florebit... Ps. 91:13.
  Os justi meditabitur sapientiam Ps. 36:30.
  Justum deduxit Dominus per vias rectas et ostendit illi regnum Dei Cf. Ps. 22.

P. 358

1838. Paulus... sprichet ein jegliche mönschliche kunst sie ein dorheit gegen göttlicher wiszheit
It is interesting to compare Schott's rendition of I Cor. 3:19 ("ein jegliche mönschliche kunst sie ein dorheit gegen göttlicher wiszheit") with the rendition in early printed German Bibles. Mentel's Bible (Strassburg, 1466), the earliest printed German Bible translation, has

>   Wann   (51)
> die weysheit dirr werlte ist ein tumpheit bey gott. (52)

Zainer's Bible (Augsburg, 1475) has in place of "tumpheit" the word "torheyt," as do all subsequent German Bibles to Luther. Cf. W. Kurrelmeyer, *Die erste deutsche gedruckte Bibel*, V = *Bibliothek des litterarischen Vereins in Stuttgart*, CCXXXVIII (Tübingen, 1905), 68.
  Luther has:

> Denn dieser Welt Weisheit ist Torheit bei Gott.

One may say then that – except for word order and spelling – German Bibles from 1475 on agree in the translation of this passage.
  It will be noted that Schott uses the word "dorheit," although he is writing in February 1476 from Italy where he would not be likely to have access to Zainer's Augsburg edition of 1475. It will also be noted that Schott's

P. 358   *Letter to Anna*   N. 1838

entire phrasing of the passage is different from that in the printed Bible translations. Was he giving his own translation, was he quoting a translation current in Alsace (Geiler's?), or was he repeating Anna's translation (paraphrase) of the passage?

1839. Dan min liebe swester ist nitt zwifel kunst
Instead of "Dan," Schmidt's copy has "Nun."

1840. vnd bitte auch den almechtigen gotte für unsere statt... lieben vatter
In 1476 Strassburg with its allies was fighting against Charles the Bold (cf. N. 72 and N. 74), and Schott, Sr., was serving as mayor of Strassburg.

1841. viel fierd wurd entston
The word "fierd" is probably an error on Weislinger's part. Cf. "freid" above on p. 357, paragraph 4, and "freiden" two lines below on p. 358. Schmidt's copy has "freid."

1842. Und ob du nun zu mol in einem andern kloster bist
Anna's convent of St. Agnes had been merged, about two months previous to this letter, with the convent of St. Margaret (cf. N. 83).

BIOGRAPHICAL SECTION

The numbers immediately following the name and dates of a person refer to items and pages in volume I where the person is mentioned. Further information may be found in volume II in the notes to the items and pages concerned.

For the arrangement of entries in this section, see p. XI.

For the form of bibliographical references, see p. 813.

BERNHARD ADELMANN (1457/1459-1523) #108, p. 118
Born of a noble Swabian family, Bernhard Adelmann von Adelmannsfelden studied in Heidelberg, in Basel – where he was a pupil of Reuchlin, with whom both he and his younger brother Conrad later corresponded – and in Ferrara, where he and Conrad were friendly with Hassenstein. He became canon at Eichstätt in 1472, at Ellwangen in 1486, at Augsburg in 1498 (*scholasticus*, 1505), and in 1498 *praepositus* at St. Gertrudis. He was instrumental in obtaining books for Hassenstein and was the recipient of thirty-three letters from Hassenstein – the largest number written by Hassenstein to a single individual. In the letter of 9 June 1505 Hassenstein mentions the rumour current in Bohemia that Adelmann had refused the episcopal seat of Augsburg (on the death of Friedrich von Zollern). Adelmann travelled extensively: to France in 1486, to England in 1492 – when he brought relics to Henry VIII, to Rome in 1497 and to Holland in 1506. He was a member of the humanistic society in Augsburg and friendly with Peutinger and Pirckheimer. He edited works of older writers but was himself not a creative writer.

ADB, I, 79; XIII, 792. *NDB*, I, 60f. Carro, 16. Cornova, 96-97. Geiger, *Briefwechsel*, 9, VIII; 27, XXIV; 28, XXVI (Conrad Adelmann to Reuchlin). Fabricius, *Bohuslai*, folios 60-62, 68, 78, *passim*. Hämmerle, 1f. Khamm, 611. H. Lier, "Der Augsburger Humanistenkreis mit besonderer Berücksichtigung Bernhard Adelmanns," *Zeitschrift des historischen Vereins für Schwaben und Neuburg*, VII (1880), 68-108. Potuček, VI, IX, XII(n. 20). Santifaller, 606. Toepke, 338. Zoepfl, 536f., 562, 586.

ADELSHEIM FAMILY
The Adelsheims came to Alsace from the little town of Adelsheim in Baden. This town which lies north and east of Wimpfen (modern Bad Wimpfen) is said to have been built by Poppo von Düren *ca*. 1298. Apparently members of the family arrived in Alsace in the mid-fifteenth century. According to Schott (#184), the family in Alsace at his time consisted of the brothers Gottfried (Götz), Sr., and Zeisolf, Sr., who married Schott's sister Ottilia, Gotz' wife (unidentified) and Gotz' children, two of whom are named: Zeisolf, Jr., who inherited Götz' property and Götz, Jr., who entered the Church. Schöpflin names two other sons of Götz: Georgius and Stephanus.

Kindler von Knobloch, *Buch*, 10. Schöpflin, *Alsatia*, 209. Wuerdtwein, 123.

1. GOTTFRIED VON ADELSHEIM, SR. #184, #196(?)
The elder Gottfried (Götz) von Adelsheim, *eques auratus*, is documented in Alsatian records to 1489. No date of death is given, but an approximate date of death in late 1489 or early 1490 can be set, because Schott's letter of condolence to Adelsheim's son on his father's recent death was written during that period (#184).

Adelsheim was *Landvogt* of Alsace from 1458 until the year 1480. He also served as *Hofmeister* and councillor to *Pfalzgraf* Philip and fought in the siege of Geroldseck in 1486. In 1481 at the tourney in Heidelberg he received in fief the castle and villages at Wasselonne (Wasselnheim), situated in the Vosges foothills about mid-way between Strassburg and Zabern, and in 1483 he received in fief the castle of Klein-Arnsberg. Strassburg records contain many notations about quarrels, contracts, etc. concerning Wasselonne. In 1496 it was sold by Götz' sons to the city of Strassburg.

Castle Stettenfels in Untergruppenbach near Heilbronn was acquired by Adelsheim *ca*. 1480, and as owner of this castle he did service for *Graf*

Eberhard of Württemberg. The family remained in possession of Stettenfels after the war of succession between Bavaria and the Palatinate in 1509, although for a time they had to share it with Conrad Thumb von Neuberg (the hereditary marshall of Duke Ulrich of Bavaria), Thumb and Zeisolf (Götz' son) ruling jointly. After Zeisolf's death, Thumb's son Hans, who had married Zeisolf's niece, became sole owner 1525-1527. Then the Hürnheim family owned Stettenfels until 1551 when they sold it to the Fuggers of Augsburg. Today lofty Stettenfels, in excellent repair, is still inhabited.
      Bouchholtz, 43. J. R. Frank, "Aus alten Tagen," *Heimattage Untergruppenbach 1963* (hrsg. vom Bürgermeisteramt, Untergruppenbach, 1963), 79-80. *Inventaire*, VI, 96, 215. Schmidt, H. L., II, 32.

2. GOTTFRIED VON ADELSHEIM, JR. #184, #185
From Schott we learn that Gottfried, Jr., a younger son of Gottfried, Sr., was doctor of civil and canon law and held the post of *praepositus* in Wimpfen. He was one of the claimants of Schott's benefice.
      Meister, 151. Santifaller, 623. Dacheux, *Réf.*, 352.

3. ZEISOLF VON ADELSHEIM, SR. (†1503) #111, p. 131; #184, p. 203.
Zeisolf, Sr., was the brother (presumably younger) of Gottfried, Sr. Since he and his nephew Zeisolf, Jr., are often confused in records, it is difficult to differentiate between references to the one and to the other. He may be the Zeisolf von Adelsheim who is mentioned as bailiff of Ortenberg. As we know from Schott's letters, he is the Zeisolf who married Ottilia, the third daughter of Peter Schott, Sr., and Susanna von Cöllen, after the death of Ottilia's first husband Peter von Cöllen. In 1477 he became through his wife a citizen of Strassburg. After giving up this citizenship in 1479, he bought it again in 1484. In 1493 he had a plaque to himself and his wife erected in the church of St. André.
      Grandidier, *Mélanges*, 400. *Inventaire*, IV, 12, 37. Straub, 83, 85; *Geschichtskalender*, 285. Wittmer-Meyer, I, 338, 363.

4. ZEISOLF VON ADELSHEIM, JR. #184
Zeisolf, Jr., was the elder (or eldest) son of Gottfried, Sr., and the heir to his father's estates. Cf. under Gottfried, Sr.
      Frank, *op. cit.*, 80-81. *Inventaire*, IV, 12, 36, 37; VI, 86, 96, 102. Wuerdtwein, 265.

RUDOLF AGRICOLA (1442/43/44-1485) pp. xiii, xx, xxviii; #65, #78, #245.
Agricola was born near Laflo, near Gröningen. He received his A.M. degree in Louvain and studied in Paris. In the seventies he was in Italy. He spent several years in Ferrara and in 1476 was treated there for dysentery by his friend and compatriot Adolf Occo. By the end of 1480 he had returned to Germany, and it is possible that shortly thereafter he went to Heidelberg for a time (cf. N. 566). In 1482 he was in Antwerp. His letter congratulating Alexander Hegius on becoming rector of the Latin school at Deventer ("ut felix faustumque tibi eveniat") was written in 1483 – incorrectly dated as 1473 by ter Kuile (11); indeed, his correspondence with Hegius may be responsible for Hegius' introducing Greek at Deventer. Agricola was called to Heidelberg in 1484 by Johann Dalberg who had become bishop of Worms in 1482 and who had met Agricola at Pavia in 1479. (Adam Wernher* also

arrived in Heidelberg in 1484). Here Agricola belonged to the circle of humanists around Dietrich von Pleningen, taught such persons as Celtis and studied Greek with Reuchlin. In 1485, with a delegation headed by Dalberg he went to Rome to greet the newly elected Pope Innocent VIII in the name of Pfalzgraf Philip (Agricola wrote the oration which Dalberg delivered). On the return journey he became ill and arriving at Heidelberg would not be treated by the local physicians but sent for Occo who unfortunately came too late. Others besides Schott wrote eulogies to Agricola, e.g. Occo, Hegius, Erasmus. The epitaph by the Venetian orator and patriarch of Aquileja Hermolaus Barbarus is quoted below:

> Invida clauserunt hoc marmore fata Rodolphum
> Agricolam Phrysij spemque decusque soli
> Scilicet hoc uivo meruit Germania laudis
> Quicquid habet Latium, Graecia quicquid habet.
> (Pantaleon, 449f.)

ADB, I, 151-156, 781. *NDB*, I, 103f. *Acta bonon.*, 234. Allen, 313ff. Borsetti, I, 57; II, 68. Eysengrein, 172f. Erhard, I, 374-415. Geiger, *Briefwechsel*, 6, V; 9, VII. Hartfelder *Briefe*, 31f. Hasse, I, 102-113. *GGr*², 6-8. Kisky, 124. ter Kuile, 11. Pantaleon, 449f. Pardi, *Studio*, 143; *Titoli*, 65, 69, 71. Röhrich, I, 80. Schmidt, "Notices... P. S.," 339f. L. Spitz, "The *Theologia Platonica*...," *Kunstmann Festschrift*, 122f. Trithemius, *Liber*, fol. 125b; *Cathalogus*, fol. 53b. Velden, *passim*. W. Vilmar, *Dietrich von Pleningen*, diss. Marburg, 1896, *passim*.

ALBERTUS MAGNUS, O.P. (*ca.* 1200-1280) #1
Albertus de Laugingen was born in Lauingen on the Danube, of a knightly family. He is called by Wimpheling "Suevus" from his native principality of Swabia; to his contemporaries he was known by the epithets "Teutonicus," "Alemmanus," "Coloniensis" and "doctor universalis." The epithet "magnus" occurs from the middle of the fourteenth century. Because of his knowledge of sciences, Greek and Arabic, Albertus (like his pupil Thomas Aquinas) became in folk saga a magician, miracle worker and master of natural forces. A member of the Dominican Order, he was professor of theology at Paris and Cologne and became bishop of Ratisbon (Regensburg). He was frequently in Strassburg.
ADB, I, 186ff. *NDB*, 144ff. Gesner, 18b. *Die Grossen Deutschen*. (45 vols., Berlin, ²1956-57), I, 201-216. Pfleger, "Albert der Grosse...," *passim*.

BISHOP ALBRECHT OF STRASSBURG († 1506) p. xxvi; #14, p. 22; #85, p. 92; #151, p. 165; #170, p. 190; #210, p. 218; #211, p. 219; #212, p. 220
Albrecht, duke of Bavaria, *Pfalzgraf bei Rhein, Landgraf* of Alsace, was the son of Duke Otto of Bavaria. He held canonicates at Augsburg (1452-68), Bamberg (1474-78) and Cologne. In 1464 he was in Rome. In 1478 he became *praepositus* of the Strassburg cathedral chapter and soon thereafter was elected the seventy-eighth bishop of Strassburg, receiving the episcopal mitre in 1479. To raise money for repairing the episcopal palace at Zabern, badly damaged in the Burgundian wars, he obtained permission from Sixtus IV to allow the use of butter, eggs and fats during Lent to such persons as would pay taxes directly to him for the privilege. That he was interested in reform is shown by his calling in 1482 the first synod of the diocese since that of 1335 – Geiler opened the meeting – and by his sending Geiler, Johann Simmler, Christoph von Uttenheim and Melchior Kungsbach to tour the diocese to investigate the morals of the priests. Albrecht had sons "out of

human frailty," as Wimpheling puts it, but detested the public display of clerical concubines. Although he expelled the Jews from his diocese, he later allowed them to return. Contemporary accounts describe him as a gentle, patient man.

    NDB, I, 175. Dacheux, *Réf.*, 33, 38f. Dacheux, *Fragments*, II, 464; IV, 41, 67. Eubel, II, 94. Grandidier, *Oeuvr. hist.*, IV, 365-369. Hertzog, 114f. Laguille, I, livre xxxii, *passim*. *Liber Confrat.*, 22. Schmidt, *Chapitre*, 192. Specklin, 297, 298, 300. Wimpheling, *Cat. ep.*, 113-119.

JOHANN AMERBACH (*ca.* 1440-1513)   p. xiv

Johann von Amerbach (Hans von Amorbach), whose real name seems to have been Johann Welker, studied under Johann Heynlin in Paris, where he received his A.B. in 1461 and his A.M. in 1462. He worked in Venice as a printer, whence his other names Johannes de Venetus and Hans von Venedig von Emrebach. He also worked in Nürnberg under the printer Anton Koburger. In 1477 he came to Basel. He married Barbara Ortenberg, widowed daughter of a Basel councilor, in 1483, and in 1484 became a citizen of Basel. His sons (Bruno, Basilius and Bonifacius) studied at the Latin school in Schlettstadt. He was friendly with Reuchlin, Wimpheling, Leontarius and Pellican. Johann Heynlin who retired to the Carthusian monastery at Basel in 1484 corrected books for him. Amerbach was one of the first printers to use Latin type. His first printing is an almanac for the year 1478; his greatest piece of work is Reuchlin's *Vocabularius breviloquens*. He edited Augustine and Jerome.

    ADB. I, 398. *NDB*, I, 247. Hartmann, xixff. Voulliéme, 25-28.

JOANNES DE ARAGONIA (†1485)   #162, p. 176

Joannes was created cardinal of Aragonia by Sixtus IV on 10 December 1477. He died on 17 October 1485.

    Eubel, II, 18.

HOUSE OF BADEN

Englert, 24; 60, n. 151. Schell, part II. *Code hist.*, II, 215.

1. BERNARD II (III), "THE BLESSED BERNARD" (1428/30-1458) #122, p. 141; #124, p. 143

Bernard was the son of Jacob I (one of the first scientifically educated Baden princes, praised by Piccolomini for his sense of justice and wisdom) and of Katherine, daughter of Charles I, duke of Lorraine. Sources disagree as to whether he was the second or third ruling *Markgraf* by the name of Bernard. In order to enter the Church and devote himself to religious pursuits, he abdicated in favor of his brother Karl I. Emperor Friedrich III called him to preach the crusade against the Turks at various courts. He died on the way to Rome in 1458. Pope Sixtus IV beatified him in 1481 and Clement XIV re-beatified him in 1769. Apparently there have been and still are moves to have him declared a saint.

    ADB, II, 416. *NDB*, II, 109. Stadler, I, 462f.

2. CHRISTOPH I (1453-1508) #20, p. 29; #41, p. 47; #46, p. 51; #56, p.

62; #60, p. 65f.; #62, p. 68; #73, p. 80; #87, p. 95; #101, p. 112; #118, p. 138; #152, p. 165; #175, p. 195f.

Christoph was the son of Karl I († 1475) and Catherine, daughter of Ernst von Hapsburg and sister of Emperor Friedrich III. Until 1488 Christoph and his brother Albrecht (cf. below) ruled jointly. For his services in the rescue of Maximilian from captivity in Bruges, Christoph was made governor of Luxemburg. He married Ottilie of Katzenellenbogen with whom he had 15 children. His name appears among those of the princes attending the coronations of the Strassburg bishops Albrecht (1479) and Wilhelm von Honstein (1506). He was one of the delegation which escorted Maria Sforza from Mals to Innsbruck for her marriage to Maximilian I in 1494. His brother Karl (third son of Karl I) became bishop of Utrecht in 1496, and his brother Friedrich was archbishop of Trier, a position later held by his son Jacob (see below). He is described by Pantaleon as a man of rare piety and humanity and as being most kind to his subjects. At his death he left his principality to be divided among three sons (Bernard, Philipp, Ernst), an unfortunate move which plagued Baden with internal strife until 1515 when the law of primogeniture was passed.

ADB, XV, 228-233. Englert, 24, n. 51. Geiger, *Reuchlin*, 8. Hämmerle, 14f. Hertzog, 115. *Inventaire (Spach)*, III, 414; IV, 88. Pantaleon, III, 15-21. Saladin, 284. Schell, part II, *passim*. Schmidt, *H. L.*, II, 16. Straub, *Geschichtskalender*, 67. Trithemius, *Ann. Hirs.*, II, 517. *Universal=Lexikon*, V, 2257f. Wimpheling, *Cat. ep.*, 122. Zoepfl, 496.

3. ALBRECHT (†1488) #118, p. 138; #121, p. 140
Albrecht and his brother Christoph I had ruled Baden jointly since 1475, when in 1488 they were commanders of the imperial camp during the siege of Bruges to free Maximilian. In August of that year, at the siege of Damm in Flanders, Albrecht was killed.
Code hist., II, 215.

4. JACOB (1471-1511) #46, p. 51; #54, p. 60; #55, p. 61; #56, p. 62; #60, p. 65f.; #62, p. 68; #63, p. 69; #73, p. 80; #87, p. 95; #92, p. 104; #101, pp. 111f.; #103, p. 113; #175, p. 196.

Jacob, the eldest son of Christoph I, was early placed under the tutelage of Johann Müller. At the age of twelve, he travelled in 1483 with Müller to Paris, where – with the exception of a possible stay at Orléans – he studied until the summer of 1486, when he returned to Baden. Late in 1486 he and Müller left for Ferrara and Padua. After a trip home and a sojourn at Paris in 1488, they again went to Italy. From late October 1489 to February 1490 at least, they were in Rome, where Jacob had an audience with Innocent VIII. They returned to Baden in the summer of 1490. By Eastertide 1491 they were back in Rome. After Müller's death there in August of that year, Jacob remained in Rome and became quite a favorite in *Curia* circles. His visit to Rome (1489-1490) was chronicled by Müller. Johann Burchard's famous *Diarium* also mentions Jacob's activity in Rome.

When he returned to Baden in 1493, Jacob held benefices at Mainz, Trier, Salzburg and Augsburg. In that year he became coadjutor to the archbishop of Trier (his uncle Johann) and in 1496 he was made imperial chamberlain to Maximilian I. Because Maximilian felt that Jacob's excellent training would be more useful as archbishop-elector than as ruling *Markgraf*, he persuaded Jacob to renounce his claim to Baden and accept the post of archbishop of Trier in 1500. Jacob was extremely well versed not only in liberal arts (he held the degree of A.M.) but also in jurisprudence, music, business and military affairs. Pantaleon reports how Jacob confounded his audience at the imperial diet in Cologne (1505), as he welcomed delegations in the name of the emperor, by addressing the French legates in French, the pontifical legates in Latin, the Venetian legates in Italian, and the German legates in German.

  Auct., III, 679. Dacheux, *Réf.*, Appendix VII. Eubel, II, 255. *Gallia Christiana*, XIII (1785), 476f. Hämmerle, 14. Kisky, 116. Khamm, 610. Pantaleon, III, 21. Sachs, III, 150. Weech, 223-231. Pardi, *Titoli*, 80 (mentioned as witness for Johann Müller when Müller received his doctorate in law).

5. KARL (†1510) #152, p. 165
Karl, third son of Christoph I, was canon at the Strassburg cathedral chapter and became its grand *custos* in 1486. He also held the honorable post of archpriest in Strassburg and benefices in Trier. He is recorded as having been in Rome 21 November 1496.

  Glöckler II, 344. Dacheux, *Eccl. arg.*, 10. Grandidier, *Oeuvr.*, *hist.* IV, 371. Meister, 145. Straub, *Geschichtskalender*, 221.

MARCUS BARBUS (BARBO) (†1491) #85, p. 92; probably "Cardinal N." of #160, p. 174
  Barbus, Patriarch of Aquileja, was created cardinal of St. Mark in 1467 by Paul II. When in 1471 Sixtus IV chose five cardinals to travel the various parts of Christendom for the purpose of calling Christians to fight against the Turks, Marcus Barbus was chosen to go to the German empire and to Hungary. He is recorded as being at Augsburg in 1474.

  Dreher, XX, 39. Eubel, II, 15, 41.

HOUSE OF BAVARIA

1. ALBRECHT III (THE WISE) (†1508) #254, p. 287; #255, p. 291
Albrecht was the third son of Duke Albrecht II (†1460) of the Bavaria-Munich line and grandson to Duke Ernst of Agnes Bernauer fame. Upon the death of Albrecht II, the two elder sons, Johann and Sigismund ruled jointly. Johann died in 1463 and Albrecht who had been educated for the Church – he resigned as canon of Augsburg in 1468 – joined Sigismund in the rule. When Sigismund abdicated in 1467, Albrecht reigned alone over the objections of his younger brothers Wolfgang and Christoph who apparently were to share in ruling upon coming of age. Albrecht set about enlarging his domain. He regained the city of Regensburg which had been for centuries a free imperial city within Bavarian territory; in so doing, he aroused the anger of his father-in-law Emperor Friedrich III who wished to retain Regensburg as a separate entity in direct fealty to him. By winning the war of succession to the Bavaria-Landshut line in 1504, Albrecht reunited the whole duchy which had been repeatedly segmented since 1253. In 1506 he introduced the law of primogeniture, and on his death his eldest son Wilhelm IV succeeded him without opposition. Albrecht was well educated (proficient in Latin) and proved himself an able ruler.

  ADB, I, 233ff. *NDB*, I, 157f. Aventinus, II, 601-60. Hämmerle,

15, 18, 154. *Mon. Boica*, II, 94; VII, 319, 321; VIII, 293; X, 212, 219, 364; XI, 481; XIV, 294; XV, 513; XIX, 323; and *passim*. Schell, II, 204.

2. WOLFGANG AND CHRISTOPH #118, p. 138
These were younger brothers of Albrecht III. Like Albrecht, they were under age and unable to share in the rule at the time their father died, Wolfgang being but nine years old and Christoph apparently even younger. In 1464 the three brothers were taken to Italy. Wolfgang became a minor canon at Augsburg in 1458, but resigned in 1463. In the siege of Bruges to free Maximilian (1488), Wolfgang and Christoph (along with the Baden princes Albrecht and Christoph) were commanders of the imperial camp. Christoph died in 1493 on the island of Rhodes while on a pilgrimage to Jerusalem.
For bibliography, cf. under Albrecht III above.

3. JOHANN (†1486) #44, p. 49
Johann, brother of Bishop Albrecht of Strassburg, succeeded the latter as *praepositus* of the Strassburg cathedral chapter in 1478 on Albrecht's election as bishop. He is listed as Johann VI of the grand chapter.
Meister, 144.

HIERONYMUS BERLIN #10, p. 18
Matriculation records of the university of Basel list in 1475 a *Magister* Hieronymus Berlin as "Regent in der Hieronymus Bursa" – the "bursa" being evidently one of the university colleges. This person may be identical with Hieronymus Perler/Berlem of Dinckelsbühl, who is recorded as being at the university of Bologna in 1473 and as receiving a doctorate there in 1475, and with Jeronimus Berler of Dinckelsbühl, who is recorded as being at Basel 1477-1478. If all these notations refer to the same person, it would appear that Schott met Berlin as a fellow student at Bologna and that Berlin, on finishing his study in Italy, came to the university of Basel.
Acta bonon., 218, 220. Knod, *Studenten*, no. 282. Schmidt, *H. L.*, I, 193. Wackernagel, I, 136, 150.

PHILIPP BEROALD (BEROALDUS) (1453-1505) p. xxv
Philipp Beroald, the Elder, a native of Bologna, was considered one of the most eminent and learned humanists. He taught rhetoric and poetry at Pavia, Milan, Paris and Bologna, where he was from 1477 until his death. Most of his published works were dedicated to his German students, some of whom lived in his home.
Acta bonon., xxxi. Ellinger, 107ff. Mazzetti, 51. Meuschenius, II, 171; III, 92.

GABRIEL BIEL (*ca.* 1418-1495) p. xxix; #124, p. 143; #136, p. 153; #138, p. 155; #222, pp. 249ff.
Having received his early schooling at St. Peter in his native Spires, Gabriel Biel matriculated at Heidelberg (1432), where he became master of arts, and then attended Erfurt, where he earned his licentiate in theology. Orator,

poet, writer, preacher and philosopher, he is often called the last exponent of scholasticism. He developed the ideas of Occam and made a concise presentation of scholastic thought from the nominalist point of view; this scholastic writing had considerable influence upon Luther. After preaching for a time in Spires, he went to Mainz and appears to have been preaching there by 1462. At Mainz he held the post of cathedral preacher (established in 1465 by Archbishop Adolf I of Nassau), but it is not certain whether he was the first incumbent. While still at Mainz, he joined the Brethren of the Common Life and lived for a time in the house of the Brethren at Marienthal in the Rheingau. In 1468 he moved to Butzbach, where he became *praepositus* of the Brethren's new house of St. Mark and also reorganized the local school. At the request of *Graf* Eberhard of Württemberg, Biel founded the first house of the Brethren in that principality at Urach in 1477 and became its *praepositus* in 1479. In 1482 he was invited (along with Reuchlin *et al.*) to accompany *Graf* Eberhard to Rome. In 1484 he was appointed the first professor of theology in the theological faculty at Tübingen and served twice as university rector (1485/86 and 1489). After 1489 he seems to have retired from academic life, and from 1492 he devoted his entire attention to the Brethren's new house of St. Peter at Einsiedel in the Schönbuch (near Tübingen), where he is buried.

ADB, II, 622f.; X, 767. *NDB*, II, 225f. Erhard, I, 190-194. Eysengrein, 166. Falk, 65. Geiger, *Reuchlin*, 23. Hermelink, *Register*, xxvif.; *Matrikeln*, 54, 75. Oberman, 10-21. Pantaleon, part ii, 456. Trithemius, *Cathologus*, folio 57b; *Liber*, folio 130b. Wolf, I, 308, 706.

BLASIUS, ABBOT OF HIRSAU, O.S.B. #131
In his detailed history of the ancient Benedictine abbey of Hirsau (founded 830) in Württemberg, Trithemius gives the following information: in 1484 Blasius, a Swabian from Oettingen, was elected forty-first abbot of Hirsau and held that office 18 years; he succeeded Georgius who resigned after two years because of unrest among the brothers. Brusch, however, in his account of monasteries, which is later than Trithemius' work, claims that Georgius Sperlin was abbot from 1467 to 1489 and was succeeded by Paulus Spreu who ruled 1489-1505. It would seem that Trithemius – himself a Benedictine abbot and a contemporary of Blasius – gives the more reliable information. This conclusion is supported by references in other contemporary material to Blasius, abbot of Hirsau, as one of the presiding abbots at a provincial meeting in Nürnberg (1489) and as active in the reform of the monastery at Schüttern and in the attempt to reform the abbey at Gengenbach.

Brusch, *Chronologia*, 227. *Gallia Christiana*, V (1731), 773, 885. Trithemius, *Ann. Hirs.*, II, 441, 515, 520f., 534. Volk, 173f.

FRIEDRICH BOCK #228, p. 255
Friedrich Bock, also called Sturmfelder, was a knight – *eques auratus* – and magistrate of Strassburg. He had given up his Strassburg citizenship in 1462 but bought it again in 1463. With Peter Schott, Sr., he headed the Strassburg troops fighting against Charles the Bold. At the request of the city council of Strassburg he arbitrated a dispute involving *Pfalzgraf* Philip and the rights to the town of Türckheim in 1485. In the same year and also in 1486, Bock and Schott. Sr., were delegates from Strassburg to the imperial diet at Frankfurt. Bock, his cousin Ulrich Bock, and Dr. Jacob Merswin fought in the Strassburg contingent before Ghent in 1488, where Ulrich

was drowned. Bock held various properties in and around Strassburg, and is frequently mentioned in Strassburg records.

Grandidier, *Mélanges*, 401. Hatt, *Ville*, 48. Hertzog, 228. *Inventaire*, III, 71; IV, 62, 154; VI, 102. *Inventaire* (*Brucker*), I, 80, 95, 108, 110f. *Inventaire* (*Spach*), IV, 88. Ritter, *Histoire*, 1471. Saladin, 283. Sitzmann, I, 177. Wencker, *Juris*, III, 30-41. Wittmer-Meyer, I, 188, 193.

KING OF BOHEMIA (Cf. Emperor Sigismund)

1. VLADISLAUS, KING OF BOHEMIA (LADISLAUS, VRATISLAUS, WLADISLAUS) (†1516) #110, p. 122; #171, p. 192

Vladislaus, son of Casimir king of Poland, was elected by the Bohemian nobles of the national party as king of Bohemia in 1471, defeating Matthias of Hungary who had already been proclaimed king of Bohemia by the nobles of the party adhering to Rome. Desultory warfare between Vladislaus and Matthias ended with the treaty of Olmütz in 1478. Under Vladislaus' rule the power of the nobles grew at the expense of the royal prerogative and of the rights both of townspeople and free peasants who for the first time were reduced to serfdom.

At the death of Matthias in 1490, Vladislaus was elected King Vladislaus II of Hungary. Vladislaus was even less successful as a ruler of Hungary than of Bohemia. "The personification of helpless inertia," he was a mere puppet of the Magyar oligarchs and was dubbed "King All Right." During his reign, Matthias' structure, which had made Hungary the most powerful central European state, crumbled and the country retrogressed several hundreds of years.

EB, IV, 127f.; XIII, 908ff. Trithemius, *Ann. Hirs.*, II, 535.

CONRAD VON BONDORF (BONDORFFER), O.F.M. (†1510) #54, p. 59; #143, p. 158; #226, p. 254.

A famous and learned preacher of the Franciscan Order, Bondorf came from a noble family in Villingen in the Black Forest. He received his A.M. at Padua in 1482 and before 1484 became doctor of theology (place unknown). The Franciscan school at Strassburg, in which he taught, had a high reputation and Bondorf was one of its finest teachers. Murner, one of his pupils, praises his enthusiasm and his solicitude for his pupils. Bondorf held various posts in his order in Strassburg: *baccalaureus*, 1479; *discretus discretorum*, 1482; vicar, 1483; *lector*, 1489. He served as the twenty-seventh provincial of the Alsace Franciscans 1498-1510. On chapter business he visited Rome in 1479, Brescia in 1482 and Assissi in 1491. At the Strassburg chapter meeting of 1484, he was chairman of the "sollemnis et publica cathedralis disputatio" and preached at a disputation in the university of Freiburg 1484. He is mentioned as "Ehrenrat" of that university in 1492. He left many manuscripts and books to the church library of his native Villingen. Jacob Sprenger, provincial of the Dominicans, reputed to have been the most learned (if misguided) man of his age, had the courage to say about the provincial of the Dominicans' traditional enemies that he had seen "neminem Conrado de Bondorf doctiorem et subtiliorem."

Bauer, 36, n. 153. Engel, *Schulwesen*, 39. Eubel, *Minoriten*, 166; 167; 345, n. 721; 346, n. 722, n. 723, n. 724, n. 725; 349, n. 727; 350, n. 728; 351, n. 729. Grandidier, *Chevaliers*, 33. Ignace-Marie, 284-296. Knepper, *Schulwesen*. Schmidt, *Chapitre*, 163; *H. L.*, I, xli, 345, and II, 12; "Notices... P.S.," 254.

HEINRICH BOYCK (HEINRICUS BOYK) (*fl.* 1360) #1, p. 9
Heinrich Boyck, a Carmelite, was professor of the Carmelite province in the Lowlands, and became bishop of Croatia *ca.* 1360. Extremely learned and versatile, he wrote on the celebration of the mass. So far as can be ascertained he was not a specialist in law and therefore may not have been the person Wimpheling had in mind when citing great exponents of law who were of German birth. See Henricus Boyk below.
Jöcher, I, 1317. Maximilian, 276.

HENRICUS BOYK (BOYCK, BOHIT, BOYC) (*fl. ca.* 1375) #1, p. 9
Henricus Boyk, a learned lawyer from Lion in Armagnac (Brittany), wrote commentaries on the decretals. He lived towards the end of the fourteenth century. Although not a German, he was a legal expert and may be the person whom Wimpheling was citing as an outstanding lawyer. The Heinricus Boit mentioned as a legal authority in #214, p. 229 is presumably identical with this Henricus Boyk.
Gesner, 303b. Jöcher, I, 1189. Trithemius, *Cathalogus*, folio 95a.

JOHANN VON BRANDIS (†1512) #167, pp. 187f.
In 1488 the chapter of the Strassburg cathedral elected Baron Johann von Brandis, one of their own number, to the post of dean which had been vacated by Friedrich von Zollern two years previously. The pope (Innocent VIII) refused to confirm the appointment and insisted that the chapter put aside Brandis in favor of his own candidate Hieronymus (Hoyer) von Barby-Mulingen. The ensuing legal battle between the chapter and the pope ended in the chapter's capitulation 1491 and the installation of Barby. Brandis was a fellow student of Peter Schott at Bologna. In 1482 he became canon and *praepositus* of the cathedral of Chur. His name appears on the lists of "Anima" members who participated in papal processions.
Acta bonon., 222. Dacheux, *Eccl. Arg.*, 7 (gives erroneous information that Brandis was *praepositus* of the Strassburg cathedral 1486-1491). Dacheux, *Réf.*, 413. Glöckler, I, 345. Grandidier, *Essais*, 136. Hertzog, 114f. Piton, 322. Ristelhuber, 117ff. Schadäus, 73. Schmidlin, 105. Stenzel, 83 (82-95 details of legal battle). Straub, *Geschichtskalender*, 223. Wimpheling, *Cat.ep.*, 120.

SEBASTIAN BRANT (1458-1521) pp. xiii, xv, xxiv; #10
Sebastian Brant, also called Sebastian Tito, was the son of the Strassburg innkeeper Diebolt Brant who owned "zum goldenen Löwen." His grandfather Diebolt Brant was eight times elected by the wine merchants' guild to the city council. An ancestor Diebolt Brant, whom Kindler von Knobloch mentions as knight and founder of the family, gave up his mill at Spires to answer Emperor Sigismund's call to arms against the Turks (1398); from him stem the epithet "Spirer" ("Brand genannt Spirer") and the mill-wheel in the Brant coat-of-arms. Brant's brother Matthias was a printer in Strassburg (Voulliéme, 114f.).
Brant's name does not occur on the list of famous alumni of the Schlettstadt school; nor, for that matter, does Reuchlin's, although GGr^2 (I, 413) mentions Reuchlin as having studied under Dringenberg at Schlettstadt. Perhaps neither Brant nor Reuchlin completed the course of study at Schlettstadt and were therefore not considered bonafide alumni. Whatever the reasons for such omission, there are strong indications that Brant did attend the school and that he was there at the same time as Peter Schott, who was about two years younger.
Replying in December 1478 to a letter from Brant, Schott (#10, p. 17) quotes Brant's admonishment to him that he preserve the friendship

they began at an early age ("abineunte aetate"). Since Schott from about age six to eleven was at Schlettstadt and then went to Paris and Bologna, he spent scarcely enough time in Strassburg to develop a friendship which could continue through adolescence into young manhood. And since Brant did not go to Paris or Bologna, one must conclude that the only place where the two lads could have associated for a considerable length of time was Schlettstadt.

In his poem to the chapter members of the principal church at Baden-Baden (*Varia carmina*, published 1498, folio h. 7), Brant expresses deep affection for one of the chapter's deans, whom he calls his *doctor*, his "teacher" and his "first nourisher." We know that the dean was Johann Müller, and that he became Schott's tutor when Schott was a small child and accompanied Schott to Schlettstadt, to Paris and to Bologna. The one place where Brant during his formative years could have had close contact with Müller over a longer period was Schlettstadt. In fact, Müller may have become tutor to both lads in Strassburg and gone with them to Schlettstadt.

Schmidt also believes that Brant attended the school at Schlettstadt, but his assumption that Brant went to school to Müller at Baden-Baden has no basis in fact, because Müller did not become dean of Baden-Baden until very late 1478 or early 1479, and by that time Brant had been at the university of Basel for almost four years.

From the entry in the university of Basel matriculation records that Brant paid no fees because he was a servitor ("Sebastian Brant de Argentina nichil quia servitor. Solvit 1475/76") and from the length of time he spent acquiring his education, it is apparent that he – like Müller and Reuchlin – was an impecunious student who could attend university only in the employ of his wealthier fellows and therefore progressed more slowly, often having to interrupt his studies when his employer left. Wackernagel (I, 137) suggests that Brant was employed by Jacob Hugonis.

As indicated in the quotation from Basel matriculation records above, Brant was studying at Basel by 1475. Here he met Geiler and in 1477 received his A.B. degree. He was at Padua in 1480; then he returned to Basel to take his licentiate in law (1483) and his doctorate in civil and canon law (1489). He was professor of law and poetry at Basel and in 1492 served as dean of the law faculty. In 1494 – at Geiler's request – he moved to his native Strassburg. He was *syndicus* to the city of Strassburg 1499-1501 and 1503-1521 secretary to the city council. In 1502 he became imperial councillor to Maximilian I. He had married Elizabeth Burg while still in Basel and had several children. His eldest son Onophrius studied at Basel, Paris and Freiburg and was in service to the city of Strassburg (Wackernagel, I, 221); he also wrote German poetry in the style of his father but never became a poet of note.

Brant's famous *Narrenschiff*, on which Geiler preached a series of sermons, appeared at Strassburg in 1494. His many other writings include poems, epigrams, odes to the Virgin, the *Annales* of Strassburg (in Dacheux, *Fragments*, IV, part x) and a legal work *Titulorum omnium juris tam civilis quam canonici expositiones* which was obviously written for his students, as was the *Modus studendi*. One of the epitaphs to Geiler in the Strassburg cathedral is by Brant. Besides all his other activities, Brant had time for a tremendous amount of editing; Schmidt's bibliographical index devotes 33 pages to Brant's editions of other writers' works (*H.L.*, II, 340-373).

ADB, III, 256-259. *NDB*, II, 534ff. *Athen. Raur.*, 103f. Ellinger, 374-379. Erhard, III, 350. Eysengrein, 182. Freudgen, 163. Glöckler, I, 341. *GGr*^{2}, I, 381-392. Grandidier, *Nouvv. oeuv.* II, 67-78. Hasse, I, 330ff. Kindler von Knobloch, *Buch*, 46. Pantaleon, part ii, 472. Ristelhuber, 109. Schmidt, "Brant"; *H. L.*, I, 189-333; *H. L.*, II, 340-373; "Notice...

Brant," *passim*. Specklin, 301. Strobel, *Beiträge*, 11, n. 1. Trithemius, *Cathalogus*, fol. 68b; *Liber*, fol. 134b. Wackernagel, I, 138, 1371. Wencker, *Apparatus*, 15-26ff. *passim*; *Arch.*, 139-143. Zacher, 47.

JOHANN VON BROCKINGEN (†1539) #148, p. 162
Johann von Brockingen, whose real name was Sutor, was also called Calceatoris but is better known as Brisgoicus, because he came from the small town of Brockingen (now Broggingen near Keuzingen) in Breisgau. He was a pupil – and perhaps *famulus* – of Johann Rot and is mentioned in the *Lucubraciunculae* as studying at Paris in 1490. He lectured on the Bible at Paris in 1494 and served as *receptor* of his nation in 1500. In 1499 he left Paris for a short stay in Freiburg, where he is registered as "master of arts." He must have made a good impression in Freiburg, for he was called there to teach in the faculty of arts in 1502 and by 1504 he was professor and dean of theology. He remained at Freiburg until his death; some of the university *Acta* are from his pen.
Bauer, 22, 28, 53, 162ff, 174.

HIERONYMUS BRUNSCHWIG (BRUNSCHWEIG) (*ca.* 1450-1512) #119, p. 139, #155, p. 170.
Brunschwig, whose real name was Jerome Saler, a physician and apothecary of Strassburg, is considered to be the most experienced herbologist of his age. He published works on surgery (1497), bubonic plague (1500), syphillis and distilling (1500).
ADB, III, 453. *NDB*, II, 688. Grandidier, *Nouv. Oeuvr.*, II, 441. Hatt, *Ville*, 379. Knepper, *Schulwesen*, 286, n.6. A. Pfleger, "Die elsässischen Kräuterweihen," AEK XI (1936), 232.

SIGISMUND BRUSCHENCKNER (PRUSCHENK, BUSCHENCK, PRUESCHINK) (†1502) #105, p. 115.
Chamberlain and court marshall of Emperor Friedrich III and Maximilian, King of the Romans, Bruschenckner belonged to an old Austrian family which in 1495 became counts of Hardegg. He fought in the Burgundian war of 1474. When in 1482 the city of Strassburg was asked to send military aid to Friedrich III against Matthias I of Hungary, negotiations were carried on between a Strassburg delegation and Bruschenckner.
ADB, III 455. Chmel, 710. Dreher, XIX, 63f.; XX, 12f. Reuss, *Meyer*, 70. Saladin, 299.

FRIEDRICH BÜCHSNER (BUSSENER, BUSNER, BÜCHSENER) (†1492) p. xxv; p. xxvi; #15, p. 23; #95, p. 107; #107, p. 117; #108, p. 120; #109, p. 120 and p. 121; #293, pp. 312f.
Friedrich Büchsner came of an old Strassburg family which is documented from the beginning of the fourteenth century; the several branches of the family held fiefs from the bishops of Strassburg and the lords of Rappoltstein and shared in the ownership of the castle at Dambach. A Friedrich Büchsner is recorded as repeatedly buying and relinquishing his Strassburg citizenship from 1463 to 1469; he may be the father of our Büchsner.
Büchsner accompanied Schott on the second trip to Bologna in 1479 and was living with Schott when he suddenly left for a visit to Rome in March of 1480. He and Hassenstein became great friends. When Hassenstein, on finishing his studies at Ferrara in 1482, returned to Bohemia via

Strassburg, Büchsner seems to have gone with him. At least by 1485 he was in Bohemia and remained there except for visits to Strassburg and the months spent travelling with Hassenstein on the "grand tour" to the Near East. One of his chief interests was birds. He died of a fever in 1492. Hassenstein, deeply grieved, composed the following epitaph to him:

> Qui mecum Syriam, Lybiaeque calentis arenas
> Vidisti, et Nilum, palmiferasque Arabas,
> Hic te, care comes, miserando funere raptum,
> Hic, Friderice, brevi condidimus tumulo.

Acta bonon., 227. Carro, 15. Cornova, 31, 51. Erhard, II, 209. Kindler von Knobloch, *Buch*, 51f. Knod, *Studenten*, #515. Ristelhuber, 119-121. Schmidt, *H. L.*, II,7. Wittmer-Meyer, I, 195, 225, 245. (Except for the material given in the *Acta bonon.*, the epitaph from Carro, and the information about the Büchsner family in Kindler, all data about Büchsner stem from the *Lucubraciunculae*).

JOHANN BURCKARD (BURCHARD) (*ca.* 1450-1506) #26, pp. 34f.; #27, p. 35; #29, pp. 36f.; #30, p. 38; #55, p. 61; #74, pp. 81f; #86, p. 94; #172, p. 193.

A native of Haslach in Alsace, Johann Burckard was educated at St. Florentius at Haslach and became clerk in Strassburg to Johann Wegerauft, canon of St. Thomas and vicar general *in spiritualibus*. Because of a scandal about his falsifying documents and stealing, Burckard left Strassburg and went to Rome in 1467. Here he soon became a familiar of Cardinals Marcus Barbus (Barbo) and Johannes Arcimboldi. For a time he was in the service of Thomas Vincenzi, general treasurer of the Holy See. He studied law and theology, presumably at the university of Rome, and seems to have acquired the degree of doctor of decretals and to have entered the priesthood. In 1475 he became a favorite of Sixtus IV (to whom he confessed his early sins) and the way to his rapid advancement at the *Curia* was open: papal acolyte and chaplain; abbreviator of apostolic letters (1478); apostolic protonotary (1481); master of ceremonies to the pope (1483), for which post he paid 450 gold ducats; member of the pope's immediate family, i.e., taking meals with the papal servants, etc. (1484). Three weeks before his death he paid 2040 ducats to become papal *referendar* and *abbreviator de parco minori*.

During these years Burckard was busily piling up benefices. In 1478 he was already drawing a small pension from a canonicate and prebend at St. Thomas in Strassburg although he did not hold a canonicate and prebend there until 1479. In 1477 he acquired a prebend at Piacenza; in 1479 he became canon of St. Thomas, as well as canon, provost and dean of St. Florentius at Haslach. In 1482 he received benefices in Basel, Strassburg and Metz. From 1482 to 1489 he was involved in a contest for the deanship of St. Thomas (Strassburg) which he finally acquired with the help of the pope and the resignation of Johann Simmler. In 1484 he received a canonicate and prebend at Old St. Peter (Strassburg) and resigned a similar benefice at St. Thomas (Strassburg). In the same year Innocent VIII gave him a benefice at Bamberg. In 1485 he acquired the office of *scholasticus* at St. Thomas. In 1490 he gained various posts at the Strassburg cathedral and began his fight for the canonicate at New St. Peter (left vacant by Schott's death); this benefice he won only after six years. In 1503 he was made bishop of Orta and Civita Castellana (i.e., a suffragan bishop).

Burckard became a member of Santa Maria de Anima in 1489 and was made master of ceremonies there in 1494; later he was instrumental in promoting the rebuilding of the "Anima" church. He was often in Strassburg: in 1477, when he bought Strassburg citizenship; in 1481, when Schott sent money by him to Maeler; in 1489; in 1490, when he represented St. Thomas in a lawsuit vs. Johann von Sickingen of the diocese of Worms. As procurator and lawyer at the *Curia* he was involved in the establishment of the chair at the Strassburg cathedral and represented Thomas Wolf, Jr., in the case vs. Engelhard Funck.

Burckard was also a writer. He carried on correspondence with German humanists, such as Mutianus Rufus; he wrote the ritual of the mass (1502) and helped correct the *Liber Pontificalis* (1485-97). His most famous – or infamous – work is his *Diarium* in which he kept a detailed record of all events at the Holy See from 1483 to 1506. For several centuries the contents of the *Diarium* were considered too scandalous to be published in full and only excerpts were made. An almost complete edition by Thuasne appeared in Paris 1883-1885. Burckard died in 1506, having faithfully served five popes: Sixtus IV, Innocent VIII, Alexander VI, Pius III, and Julius II.

ADB, XLVII, 377. *NDB*, III, 34. Dacheux, *Réf.*, 116, 124. Grandidier, *Nouv. oeuvr.*, II, 104-110. Jöcher, I, 1489. *Liber confrat.*, 85. Nagl, 21, 23. Oliger, 199-232. Schmidlin, 125f. Schmidt, *Chapitre*, 93; "Notices... Wolf," 449. Sitzmann, I, 262. Burchard, I, i; III, ii-LXVIII. Wittmer-Meyer, 339.

HOUSE OF BURGUNDY

For a modern account of the dukes of Burgundy, see Joseph Calmette, *The Golden Age of Burgundy*.

1. JOHN THE FEARLESS (reigned 1404-1419) #232, p. 261
John was the son of Philip the Bold, the first great duke of Burgundy. In the fifteen years of his meteoric reign – cut short by his assassination in 1419 – the Orléans-Burgundian rivalry for control of France came to a head. In 1407 John had Louis, duke of Orléans, murdered; the city of Paris was in turn terrorized by Armagnacs (Orléans' faction) and Burgundians; the English under Henry V, aided and abetted by John, conquered large portions of French territory; and the principality of Liége came under the protection of Burgundy.

2. CHARLES THE BOLD (reigned 1467-1477) p. xxiii; p. xxviii; #238, p. 269; #244.
Grandson of John the Fearless and son of Philip the Good and Isabella of Portugal, Charles was the last of the dukes of Burgundy. Well-educated and willing to work hard to realize his ambitions, he was nonetheless impatient and impulsive and lacking in every restraint. His epithet "the Bold" might better be "the Rash," as he is sometimes called. His career is discussed in relation with the Burgundian wars (cf. N. 74).

LUDOVICUS DE BURSES DE NEAPOLI (†1486) #162, p. 176
Ludovicus de Burses, a doctor of decretals, was created bishop of Aquila by Sixtus IV in 1477.
Eubel, II, 91.

OLIVIER CARAFFA, O.P. (†1511) #162-#163, pp. 176-181.
Olivier Caraffa, son of a powerful knight, studied at several universities and received a doctorate in civil law at Ferrara in 1458. He was created cardinal *Neapolitanus* by Paul II on 18 September 1467. Sixtus IV (1471) chose him

as one of the five cardinals to call Christians to fight against the Turks and gave Caraffa the region "apud regem Ferdinandem [of Naples] et per mare." Accordingly Caraffa was admiral of the papal fleet which fought against the Turks off Rhodes and Smyrna. In 1489 he became protector general of the Dominican Order. A theologian, jurist, politician, and a man of great wealth, he was a patron of scholars and himself studied Roman antiquities.
Dacheux, *Réf.*, 413. Eubel, II, 14, 41, 44. Pastor, II, 288. Pardi, *Titoli*, 34, 35. A. Vorberg, "Das Dominikanerkloster zu Röbel," *Q. F. Domin.*, Heft 9 (1913), 36.

SALVO CASSETTA, O.P. #194, p. 210
Salvo Cassetta of Parma succeeded Jacob Stubach as general of the Dominican Order (1481-1483) and was the general who came to Strassburg 1482/83.
Barthelmé, 182. Dacheux, *Réf.*, 318. R. P. Mortier, *Histoire des Maîtres-généraux de l'ordre des Frères Prêcheurs*, IV (Paris, 1901), 542-569. *Q. F. Domin.*, Heft 7, 72ff.

GABRIEL CHABOTUS #10, p. 18
Gabriel Chabotus from the town of Cambrai on the Scheldt received his doctorate in civil and canon law at the university of Tübingen in 1482. Since Schott mentions him as "Doctori Gabrieli de Chambriaco" in 1478 and as being at Basel, it is possible that – like Müller – Chabotus had a doctorate in philosophy before the doctorate in law.
Hermelink, *Matrikeln*, 39.

CLINGENTHAL SISTERS, O.P. p. xxix; #49- #53, pp. 52-59; #85, pp. 92f. (Notes to these items contain considerable information).
Originally an Alsatian foundation begun in 1233, the Dominican convent of St. Leonard was moved in 1273 to Klingenthal near Basel and changed its name to Clingenthal. It became one of the richest convents, with holdings in Alsace and in the Breisgau; and it counted among its benefactors nobles, dukes of Austria, kings, emperors and popes. Its inmates were noble ladies of wealth who had not found in the world a place befitting their rank. During the fourteenth century the convent flourished, but in the fifteenth century decadence set in. Attempts to bring Clingenthal to a stricter way of life began before 1429 when Johann Nider of Nürnberg was sent by the master of the Dominican Order, Bartholomeus Texery, to ask the aid of the Basel city council in reforming the convent. Although Pope Martin V wrote to the city council, to the bishops of Basel, Constance and Strassburg, as well as to the *Markgraf* von Rateln, urging the reform, resistance from the city council and the convent was so strong that the attempt was abandoned. An attempt in 1462 by Johann Kreutzer, at the request of Pius II and the Basel city council, also failed.
In 1480 Sixtus IV sent Jacob Stubach, the Dominican Provincial to reform Clingenthal. To aid him in his work, Stubach brought to the convent with him thirteen nuns from the reformed convent of Engelspforten at Gebweiler, whom he placed in charge. Only two of the Clingenthal ladies accepted the new order; the other 39 protested, fought and schemed until finally in 1482 they won for their cause (with money) Archduke Sigismund of Austria, despite the plea of Nicolaus von Flüe (q.v.). At a conference attended by Oswald von Dyrstein (representing Sigismund), the *Bürgermeister* of Zürich and other notables, it was decided that the newcomers had to go, that the convent should be detached from the Dominican Order, and

that the Order be recompensed with a payment of 12,500 crowns. The sisters from Engelspforten and their converts were thus after nearly three years of labor forcibly expelled; for a long time they wandered about homeless, living from alms and forgotten by those who had brought them to such straits.

In 1485 Christoph von Uttenheim bought a retreat, Santa Maria in Obersteigen near Wasselonne, for the ejected nuns. This gift was authorized in 1487 by Innocent VIII who also restored all privileges to the nuns. In 1507, however, as the nuns could not make a living at Obersteigen, they gave the retreat to Bishop Wilhelm von Honstein of Strassburg and went to the convent at Gnadental in the bishopric of Constance.

The Clingenthal ladies who would not reform became Augustinians. During the years 1525-1555 many became Lutherans; fourteen of them threw away their habits and married apostate priests or men of the lower classes.

Barthelmé, 114f. Barth, *Handbuch*, 611f. Bernoulli, VI, 286, 301. Dacheux, *Réf.*, 305-328. Glöckler, II, 492-497. *Q.F. Domin.*, Heft 1, 41; Heft 3, 51, 70ff., 115f., 117ff., 126, 140; Heft 7, 35, 52, 77, 82f. Schmidt, "Notices... P.S.," 320f. Schoepflin, *Alsace*, IV, 22. Wuerdtwein, 109.

FERRICUS DE CLUNIACO (†1483) #158, p. 173
Sixtus IV in 1480 created de Cluniaco, already bishop of Tornacensis, Cardinal of St. Vitalis. Eubel, II, 19, 65.

CÖLLEN FAMILY (Coellen, Collen, Coln, Coeln, Cölle, Kölle)
Of the Strassburg Cöllen family there are few existing records. The first Cöllen mentioned is the founder of the family Rudolfus Coloniensis who came apparently from Cologne and settled in Strassburg in 1202. In the church of St. Thomas there was at one time a plaque with the inscription "Katharina Kölle, uxor Jacobi Mug [the elder] †1470," and in the church of the convent St. Nicholas in *Undis* there was a painting (cf. biography of Peter Schott, Sr.), under two figures of which appeared the names "Susanna von Cöln" and "Margrede von Cöln." The third daughter of the Schotts, Ottilia, married a Cöllen, whose first name Straub gives as Peter and Kindler von Knobloch gives in one account as Peter and in another as Jacob; the daughter of this marriage, Ottilia Cöllen, is the last Cöllen mentioned in documents.

Grandidier, *Mélanges*, 381. Kindler von Knobloch, *Buch*, 10, 55. Straub, 83, 86. Schneegans, *Église*, 229f.

1. SUSANNA VON CÖLLEN (†1498) p. xxiv; #1; #6-#193, *passim*; #297, p. 320
Little is said of Susanna von Cöllen, but one may imagine that as the mother of five children, as the wife of Strassburg's foremost citizen and mistress of the Schott home, she led a busy and varied life. To the Schott home came visiting dignitaries like Emerich Kemel, family friends like Johann Widmann and friends of young Peter like Bohuslaus von Hassenstein and Walter Halewin. Even after young Peter became canon, he lived at home and his protégés were part of the family. Susanna von Cöllen was evidently fond of these lads and remembered them after they were sent off to school. The Schott daughters and grandchildren were in and out of the house; some of them seem to have stayed for long periods. To have had time and energy left from the demands of her household for worthwhile contributions to affairs in the church, for herbology and for other interests Susanna von Cöllen must have been indeed an intelligent and capable woman.

Dacheux, *Réf.*, 23, 285f. Dacheux, *Fragments*, IV, 173. Grandidier, *Mélanges*, 381. Kindler von Knobloch, *Buch*, 55. Schmidt, *H. L.*, II, 13. Straub, 83, 86. Wencker, *Arch.*, 428.

2. OTTILIA CÖLLEN p. xxiv; #54, p. 60; #88; #107, p. 118; #108, p. 120.
Daughter of Ottilia Schott and Peter (Jacob?) Cöllen, this Ottilia married
Martin Sturm and was the mother of Jacob Sturm.

JACOB DEDINGER (de Dinger, Deninger, Tedinger, Tädinger) #6, p. 12,
#173, p. 194
A native of Offenburg, Dedinger held a post in the parish church there.
Until 1461 he had a benefice at St. Agnes in Strassburg. He acquired the
post of perpetual chaplain at St. Georg in Ruprechtsau in 1462. Two years
later he became a citizen of Strassburg and in 1465 he secured a chaplaincy
at St. Thomas. During 1476 he was active in the unification of the convents
Sts. Agnes and Margaret, *et al*. He was *praepositus* of Surburg when in 1478
he visited Rome as a member of a Strassburg delegation to the *Curia*.

Barth, *Handbuch*, 1558. Kindler von Knobloch, *Buch*, 58. Meister,
111, 120f., 142f. Straub, *Geschichtskalender*, 43. Wittmer-Meyer, I, 203.

FLORIANUS DE DOLPHOLIS (Floriano, Febriano; Dulfus, Dolfo, Dolfi)
(†1506) #71, p. 77
Born in Bologna, Florianus de Dolpholis took degrees there in canon law
(1466) and in theology (1485). He taught canon law at Bologna 1475-1506
and was one of Schott's professors. In 1494 he corresponded with Isabella
d'Este. His pupil Nicolaus Burtius writes of him: "Sic Florianus Dulfus,
triplici scientiarum gradu jugatus, nec laboribus nec vigiliis parcens, me suis
limitationibus consiliisque jura interpretando non desinit illustrare, quinimo
et aedificiorum superbia decorare."

Cosenza, II, 1240 (date of death appears erroneously as 1656). "Rotoli"
(1471-72, 1475-79). "Liber Secretus *iuris pontificii*," f. 148 and *passim*.
Mazzetti (1847), 113. Meuschenius, II, 169; III, 91.

LUDWIG DRINGENBERG (ca. 1415-1490) p. xxiv; #1, p. 9; #154, pp. 168f.;
#234, p. 266.
Dringenberg was born in the town of Dringenberg, near Paderborn in
Westphalia. He studied under Thomas à Kempis at the school of the
Brethren of the Common Life at Zwolle (also at Deventer?); then he apparently went to Cologne and Paris before matriculating at Heidelberg in 1430,
where he received his A.B. degree in 1432. It may be true that students
from Schlettstadt who were studying with Dringenberg at Heidelberg were
instrumental in bringing him to the school at Schlettstadt as rector. Certainly it cannot be true, as Hammelmann claims, that Rudolf Agricola was
responsible for Dringenberg's coming to Schlettstadt, for – as Röhrich
points out – Agricola was not born until 1442 (and this is the earliest possible
date for his birth). There can be no question that Dringenberg began his
work at Schlettstadt in 1441; according to Hieronymus Gebweiler, himself
a later rector at the school, Dringenberg had served 36 years ("so alda Schul
gehalten und mit grossem Lob regiert") when in 1477 he was succeeded by
Crato Hoffmann. He died in 1490, probably in the late summer, for on 6
September Peter Schott promised Hoffmann he would write an epitaph for
his former master.

ADB, V, 411-412. Dacheux, *Réf.*, 443. Dorlan, *Notices*, part ii,
101ff.; "Nouv. études," 338f., and *passim*. Freundgen, 110. Gény, 20.
Gény-Knod, I, 18-20. Glöckler, I, 338. Grandidier, *Nouv. oeuvr.*, II, 153f.
Herrmann, 119. Hertzog, 32. Knepper, *Schulwesen*, 237, 240, 327, 402;
Wimpheling, 6. Knod, "Schlettstadt," 431-439. Röhrich, I, 78-94 *passim*.
Strüver, 7-23. Toepke, I, 186; II, 382. Voigt, II, 308.

CONRAD DUNZENHEIM (Dünzenheim) (†1486) #162, p. 176; #163, pp.
178, 180

Conrad Dunzenheim belonged to a family – later ennobled – which originated from the village of Dünzenheim. Heinz Dunzenheim served in the Strassburg city council 1331. Conrad was mayor of Strassburg in 1484. He had made two visits to the Holy Land and was on his way for a third visit when he died at Venice in 1486. This is the Conrad whom Procurator Rot defamed.

A younger Conrad, perhaps son of the above Conrad, attended the university of Heidelberg in 1483, wrote a chronicle to 1495 and served three times as mayor of Strassburg (1505-1529); he also died in Venice.

Barth, "Pilger", 176. Kindler von Knobloch, *Buch*, 66f. Reuss, Meyer, 36. Saladin, 300. Schmidt, *H. L.*, I, 345. Schöpflin, *Vind. Typ.*, 113 (younger Conrad). *Strassburg Chronik*, VIII, 64 (younger Conrad). Toepke, 373 (younger). Wuerdtwein, 122, n. g.

BERCHTOLD DÜRR (†1501) #195, p. 212
Dürr was abbott of the Premonstratensian abbey of Adelberg 1461-1490. Adelberg, founded as a priory in 1173 and made an abbey in 1440, was the last Swabian double convent (that is, its inmates were both monks and nuns) in Württemberg, and it was during Dürr's term of office that the nuns were sent in 1475 to the convent at Lauffen (on the Neckar), at the insistence of *Graf* Ulrich "der vielgeliebte" of the Württemberg-Stuttgart line, an ardent reformer. Dürr collected and edited the liturgical books of the Premonstratensians and had them printed at Strassburg; they were used for years in Swabian monasteries. The breviary mentioned by Schott was without doubt one of these liturgical books. A contemporary Premonstratensian calls Dürr: "abbatem boni communis promovendi studiosissimum et ordinis sui zelo plane exaestuentem."

Backmund, I, 62-63. *Gallia Christiana*, V (1731), 1109f. Schmidt, *H.L.*, II, 22. Joseph Zeller, "Das Prämonstratenserstift Adelsberg, das letzte schwäbische Doppelkloster in Württemberg," *Vierteljahreshefte*, XXV (N.F. 1916), 108-162.

OSWALD VON DYRSTEIN (Dierstein, Thierstein) #76, p. 83
Graf Oswald was one of the councillors of Archduke Sigismund of Austria. He is mentioned as acting for Sigismund at a conference in Basel 1475 and in the case of the Clingenthal sisters in 1480. In 1479 Emperor Friedrich III gave Hohkönigsburg (in Alsace) to the Dyrstein family as a fief.

Bernoulli, VI, 301. Bouchholtz, 109. Horning, *Jung-St.-Peter*, 48f. *Inventaire*, IV, 75. Pantaleon, part iii, 10. Riegger, *Anal.*, 133.

LEONARD VON EGLOFFSTEIN (†1531) #72, p. 79; #75, p. 82; #76, p. 83; #86, p. 95.
Egloffstein studied at Ingolstat and Leipzig, where he received the A.M. degree in 1477. In 1478 he is inscribed in the *Acta bonon.* as doctor of arts and doctor of both laws, but we have been unable to discover at what university he won these degrees. He is mentioned in Pardi, *Titoli*, as a witness for others receiving doctorates at Ferrara in 1481 and 1482. He became canon (later *scholasticus*) at the Bamberg cathedral in 1484. From references to him in Schott's letters we know that he was in Rome during the years 1485-1486. His name appears in the lists of visitors at the "Anima" for 1485 (?). In 1492 he went to Bologna and spent several years there.

Amrhein mentions another Leonard Egloffstein, canon at the cathedral in Würzburg, who was a cousin or nephew of our Egloffstein and who died in 1514. *NDB* mentions a Leonard Egloffstein, canon of Bamberg, in the genealogical list of the Egloffstein family, but gives his date of death as

1514; it would appear that the writer of the *NDB* article has confused the two Leonard Egloffsteins.
NDB, IV, 340. *Acta bonon.*, 225. Amrhein, XXXIII, 57. Knod, *Studenten*, #720. *Liber confrat.*, 84. Pardi, *Titoli*, 73. Santifaller, 648 (probably the Würzburg Egloffstein). Simon, 16.

ENDINGEN FAMILY
The nobles of Endingen are documented from the middle of the thirteenth century. They came originally from the small village of Endingen at the foot of the Kaiserstuhl.
Kindler von Knobloch, *Buch*, 72f. Anon.,"Das Stift Andlauschen Fronhöfe im Breisgau," ZGORh, XXXIV (1882), 122ff.

1. JOHANN RUDOLF VON ENDINGEN (†1494) #230, p. 257
Johann Rudolf von Endingen became a citizen of Strassburg in 1467 and was active in the public life of the city, serving on the city council and for sixteen years on the *fabrica* of the cathedral. He is mentioned as a delegate to various conferences, as a leader of Strassburg troops against Charles the Bold and as an emissary to Emperor Friedrich III in 1473 and to King Louis XI of France in 1475. In 1473 he was appointed one of the secular protectors (*tutores*) of the Order of St. John of Jerusalem, a position open only to the nobility of Strassburg. He was an "Auss-Bürger" in 1484, i.e., he maintained his citizenship of Strassburg although living outside the city limits.
Dacheux, "Münsterchronik," 16. Grandidier, *Chevaliers*, 66. *Inventaire* (*Brucker*), I, 88, 90, 92, 96. *Inventaire*, II, 53, 68. *Inventaire*, IV, 35, 75. Ristelhuber, 122f. Schadäus, 106. Stenzel, "Gerichte," 220ff. Wittmer-Meyer, I, 232.

2. PHILIPP VON ENDINGEN (1474-1505) #230, p. 257
Son of Johann Rudolf von Endingen, Philipp was no doubt a minor canon at New St. Peter when in 1487 Schott wrote to Innocent VIII to petition in the name of Johann Rudolf that the defunct chaplaincy in the old family chapel be reinstituted and that the post of chaplain be granted to the thirteen year old Philipp. Philipp was matriculated at Bologna in 1492 and some time later became doctor of arts. He was a fellow student and close friend of Thomas Wolf, Jr., who dedicated his first three dialogues to him. He died at the age of thirty-one of dropsy. His tombstone on which is carved the figure of a young canon holding a scroll may still be seen in the Zorn chapel of New St. Peter.
Acta bonon., 244. *Cambridge Med. Hist.*, VIII, 790f. Horning, *Jung-St.-Peter*, 54. Kindler von Knobloch, *loc. cit.* Knod, *Studenten*, #783. Ristelhuber, 121ff. Saladin, 281. Schmidt, "Notices... Wolf," 451ff.

BARTOLOMAEUS FAVENSIS #277, p. 305
The more likely of the two possible candidates for Schott's Bartolomaeus of Faenza is "Bartholomeus de Faventia" whom Pardi lists as receiving a doctorate in civil law 16 July 1470 and mentions in 1487 as a witness for a doctorand at Ferrara. Schott could have met him or even have taken courses from him at Ferrara.
The less likely candidate – because he may no longer have been teaching at Bologna during Schott's time there – is the professor of "Latinitá" in Corradi's lists for 1452-54 and 1458-59, "Bartolomeo da Faenza."
Corradi, 416, 417. Pardi, *Titoli*, 50, 83.

MARTIN FLACH, SR. p. xxx; #142, p. 157
According to Ritter's recent history of Alsatian printing, Martin Flach, Sr., was born at Kuttolsheim near Strassburg and became a citizen of Strassburg in 1472 by marriage to Catherine Dammerer; like all printers, he became a member of the Strassburg goldsmith's guild. He may have been apprenticed to Mentelin and to Rusch, but he did not occupy Mentelin's press at the death of Rusch in 1489, because by that time he had had his own press for two years. He was active as a printer 1487-1500. His widow married Johann Knoblouch who carried on the Flach press for some months until the son Martin Flach, Jr. (active 1501-1539) took over. Martin Flach, Sr., is not to be confused with the printer Martin Flach of Basel who was a native of that city and began printing in 1477; *ADB* (VII, 87) has erred in identifying the one with the other.
    ADB, VII, 87. *NDB*, V, 219f. Grandidier, *Nouv. oeuvr.*, II, 180f. Ritter, *Histoire*, 75-79. Schmidt, *Bibliotheken*, 106-108; *H. L.*, II, 30. Schoepflin, *Vind. typ.*, 103. Voulliéme, 112 (second edition, 1922, p. 157).

NICOLAUS VON FLÜE (1417-1487) #107, pp. 116, 117f.
Nicolaus, also known as "Bruder Clauss," was the son of a simple Swiss peasant. He spent his early years in the country, then became a townsman and did military service. At the age of 50 he left his wife and children to become a hermit in Obwalden, near his birthplace. The community built him a cell and chapel. He lived a very strict life, made monthly confessions, went on annual pilgrimages to Einsiedeln and Engelberg and himself received pilgrims. Geiler visited him often (the years 1473-1475 and 1486 appear in records), and Schott with his father visited him in 1482. According to tradition, he is supposed to have lived for 20 years without human food or drink, and Trithemius writes that the personal physician of Archduke Sigismund of Austria – Dr. Burkard von Hornack – examined him and said there was no trace of food in him. His greatest service to Switzerland was his causing the Swiss cantons which had quarreled among themselves for four years to make peace in 1481; so great was the people's rejoicing that the bells pealed everywhere. At the request of the Basel Dominicans, he tried to intercede (16 January 1482) with Archduke Sigismund so that reform might be brought to the Clingenthal convent, but his efforts were vain. He is the national saint of the Swiss and was beatified in 1947.
    ADB, VII, 135-139. *NDB*, V, 260. Baring-Gould, III, 421-434. Barth, "Pilger," 183. Bernoulli, VI, 305. *Cambridge Med. Hist.*, VII, 210. Dacheux, *Réf.*, 277. Pantaleon, pars ii, 459. Raynaldus, 1480. Specklin, 287. Trithemius, *Ann. Hirs.*, II, 504ff., 527f. Wittmer, "Flüe," 157-174. Cf. also John Chr. Schaad, *Nicolas of the Flue. The Saviour of the Swiss Republic*, a dramatic poem in five acts (Washington, 1866).

KINGS OF FRANCE

1. CHARLES VI (1368-1422) #232, p. 260
At the age of twelve Charles VI, son of Charles V the Wise, ascended the throne. Royal authority was divided among his paternal uncles until he should come of age, and it was this arrangement along with the feeble mindedness of Charles which led to the struggle for the control of France between the dukes of Orlèans and Burgundy.

2. LOUIS XI (1423-1483) p. xix; #48, p. 53; #50, pp. 54f.; #51, pp. 55f.
When Louis XI came to the throne in 1461, France was on the verge of dismemberment by English, Burgundians and rebellious nobles. When he died in 1483, France was united and strong, with all fear of dismemberment a thing of the past. In addition to building France into a leading power, Louis supported the bourgeoisie (hence his appellation "the bourgeois king") and out of genuine religiosity lavished money upon the Church.

DANIEL FRIESENHEIMER, O.S.A. #208-#209, pp. 216-218
The Augustinian Daniel Friesenheimer studied in Bologna 1438. He was prior of the Strassburg Augustinians 1468, 1481, 1483, and in 1488 he was principal teacher and director of the monastery school. He served two terms as provincial of the Augustinian Rhine-Swabia Province 1474-77 and 1480-83.
Grandidier, *Augustins*, 61-78 *passim*. Höhn, 113ff. Knepper, *Schulwesen*, 88.

ULRICH VON FRONSPERGER (ULRICUS, UDALRICUS: FRAINTSPERG, FRUNTSBERG, FRUNDSBERG, FREUNDSBERG) (†1493) #25, p. 34
The Fronspergers belonged to the family of the *Grafen* von Liechtenstein and lived originally in Liechtenwerth in the lower Inn valley; an Ulricus von Freundsberg is documented at a tourney in Merseburg in 968. Ulrich, Sr., (1425-1501), father of our Ulrich, a councillor of Archduke Sigismund of Austria, came to Swabia in 1467/68 and bought the town of Mingelheim (Mindelheim); in 1488 he became the leader of the Danube circle of the "Foedus Clypei S. Georgij," an organization of knights working against evildoers. Georg (1473-1528), brother of our Ulrich, was a famous military man under Charles V. Ulrich studied at Bologna, where he is listed in 1468, and at Ferrara, where he is named as a witness for a doctorand in 1481 and where he met Schott, Hassenstein and the Adelmann brothers. He held canonicates at Brixen, Freising and Augsburg. He was called to preach at Trent – according to Khamm in 1473, an obvious misprint, because he would not have been finished with his education at that time. In 1485 he is documented as visiting the "Anima" in Rome. In 1486 he was one of the two Augsburg canons sent from Augsburg to obtain from Innocent VIII confirmation of Friedrich von Zollern's election as bishop of Augsburg. In the same year he was elected bishop of Trent, but did not take immediate possession of his episcopate, as Friedrich III had selected another candidate for the post and the ensuing strife was not settled until 1488 when Innocent VIII confirmed Ulrich's election (although Ulrich seems to have carried on the administration of the diocese from 1487). Hassenstein wrote Ulrich a letter of congratulation on his election, and Ulrich in 1490 strongly supported Hassenstein as candidate for the bishop's seat of Olmütz. Ulrich made a competent bishop: he enriched the episcopal library, had a stone bridge built across the Avisio, revised old city statutes and issued new ones, and rebuilt the episcopal palace.
NDB, V, 670. *Acta bonon.*, 213. Cornova, 53. Eubel, II, 256. *Liber confrat.*, 83. Khamm, 299, 604. Kreuter, II, 178. *Mon. Boica*, XXXIV, vii, 195; XXXV, viii, 81. *Mon. Eccles. Trident.* 161ff. Pardi, *Titoli*, 73. Potuček, vi, vii, xii, 7. Riegger, *Anal.*, 236f., 237f. I. Schöntag, *Untersuchungen über die persönliche Zusammensetzung des Augsburger Domkapitels im Mittelalter* (diss. Breslau, 1938), 34. Steichele, *Beiträge*, I, 118. *Universal = Lexikon*, IX, 2188. Zoepfl, 456, 488, 494, 510, 557.

THEOBALD FUCHS (†1484?) #30, p. 38; #35, p. 42; #57, p. 62
Theobald (Diebolt) Fuchs became canon of St. Thomas in 1465 and *scholasticus* there in 1475. In 1480 he bought Strassburg citizenship. He acquired a canonicate and in 1482 the post of *scholasticus* at New St. Peter, where he helped educate Thomas Wolf, Jr. Schmidt gives for Fuchs the death date of 1475; this is erroneous, for Schott makes references to him as living in 1482; Schott's comment in July 1484 about the house "formerly that of Theobald Fuchs" may indicate that Fuchs had died earlier in the year of 1484.
  Knepper, *Schulwesen*, 137. Schmidt, *Chapitre*, 274; "Notices... Wolf," 449. Wittmer-Meyer, I, 368.

ENGELHARD FUNCK (FUNK) (*ca.* 1450-1515) #30, p. 38; #55, p. 61; #75, p. 82; #86, p. 94; #93, p. 104.
Funck, also known as "Scintilla," was born in Schwabach near Nürnberg. He matriculated at Erfurt in 1468, where he met Wimpheling, and after receiving his A.B. degree in 1470, studied at various German and Italian universities. From about 1480 to 1500 he was a much sought after procurator at the *Curia* in Rome; he is listed in the membership of Santa Maria de Anima as "procurator causorum famosus." In 1500 he obtained the fat benefice of dean at Neumünster in Würzburg and seems to have spent the remainder of his life in that city, active as poet, epigrammatist, editor and member of a literary society. He was a close friend of Trithemius. Well-educated and a student of Greek, he helped to spread Italian humanism. He was also critical of conditions at the *Curia*.
  NDB, V, 732. Bauch, 52, 84-86. Jöcher, II, 809. *Liber confrat.*, 107. Meister, 136f. *Mon. Boica*, XXIII, 637. Schmidt, "Notices... Wolf," 448f. Trithemius, *Liber*, f. 135a; *Cathalogus*, f. 70a. Weissenborn, I, 328, 47. Welzenbach, 49.

PHILIPP FÜRSTENBERG p. 332
Philipp Fürstenberg from Mittelhain near Wiesbaden was a pupil of Wimpheling and studied at the university of Tübingen in 1496. He later became a senator of Frankfurt. Besides the poem he wrote for Wimpheling to be included in Schott's *Epithoma*, he is known to have written a tetrastich for Wimpheling, "De hymnorum et sequentiarum auctoribus..."
  Hermelink, *Matrikeln*, 110. Schmidt, *H. L.*, I, 5. Riegger, *Amoen.*, 197.

JODOCUS GALLUS (JOST HAN, GALTZ) (*ca.* 1459-1517) #295-#296, pp. 313f.
Orphaned by the plague of 1472, Jodocus Gallus, also known as Rubeacensis from his birthplace Ruffach, was educated by the Franciscans in Ruffach and sent by them to Dringenberg's school in Schlettstadt, where he was a fellow pupil with Schott. He studied at Basel, where he served as prefect of the "Nova Bursa," and then went to Heidelberg in 1476. Here he was befriended by the procurator of the Franciscans and studied under Agricola. He received his baccalaureate and licentiate in theology and served often as rector of the university to 1493. Years later he obtained his doctor of arts degree. At Heidelberg he taught philosophy and logic and is said to have given more speeches in Latin than anyone else. He was friendly with the circle around Johann Dalberg and Pleningen. He became curate at Steinach and councilllor to *Pfalzgraf* Philipp II and acted as mediator for the bishop

of Spires in 1511. Succeeding Wimpheling, he was appointed canon and preacher of the cathedral at Spires. He published a great deal in favour of church reform and attacked the faults of his age. One of his *Scherzreden* (edited by Wimpheling and published 1487/1488), "Monopolium et societas vulgo des liechtschiffs" may have given Brant the first idea for his *Narrenschiff*. Gallus was the uncle of Conrad Pelican.
 ADB, VIII, 348; IX, 826. *NDB*, VI, 55. Eysengrein, 187. Freundgen, 110. *GGr²*, 435. Grandidier, *Nouv. oeuvr.*, II, 188ff. Knepper, *Schulwesen*, 78, 324. Pantaleon, pars ii, 35. Ritter, *Histoire*, 504. Röhrich, I, 92. Sitzmann, I, 692f. Trithemius, *Cathalogus*, f. 72b. Weislinger, 505.

JOHANN GEILER VON KAYSERSBERG (1445-1510) *Luc., passim.* Cf. Special Index and General Index.
The Geilers are documented from about 1400 as citizens of the small Alsatian town of Kaysersberg, nestled in the foothills of the Vosges. Johann Geiler, father of our Geiler, moved with his bride Anna Zuber to Schaffhausen to take a post in the town clerk's office. In Schaffhausen were born a daughter and a son. Shortly after the latter's birth, Johann Geiler, Sr., accepted the position of notary in Ammersweiler (Ammerschwier), a town in the valley below Kaysersberg, and the young family returned "home." In the winter of 1448 Johann, Sr., – on a hunt with the men of Ammersweiler for a bear which was devastating the vineyards – was attacked by the cornered beast and so badly lacerated that he died several days later. The widow with her two children then went to live in the home of her father-in-law Burchard (?) Geiler at Kaysersberg, and here the young Geiler spent his childhood, hence his appellation "von Kaysersberg."
 In June 1460 Geiler enrolled as one of the first students in the arts faculty of the new university of Freiburg which had opened its doors on 27 April of that year. In 1462 he became bachelor of arts, in 1463 licentiate and in 1464 master of arts. He taught in the faculty of arts and 1469-1470 served as its dean. In 1471 he went to the university of Basel to study theology; here he lectured in arts and in 1474 served as dean of the arts faculty. On receiving his doctorate in theology in 1475, he was made professor of theology. In 1476 he was called to his first alma mater, the university of Freiburg, as professor of theology and during the winter semester of 1476/77 served as rector of the university. In the same winter he was offered the chair of cathedral preacher at Würzburg.
 According to Rathgeber (*Gottesmänner*, 9), the Würzburg offer came about thus: Geiler's health failed in 1476 and he went – presumably during the summer months – to the baths at Baden-Baden to recuperate. While there he preached to the crowds frequenting the fashionable spa and was heard by influential Würzburgers who were greatly impressed by him and had him called to Würzburg. Geiler went to Würzburg to preach a trial sermon which Falk (91) claims was such a success that he was then and there offered the post permanently.
 On the way from Würzburg to Freiburg to resign his professorship and to Basel to collect his books, Geiler stopped in Strassburg, where Schott, Sr., a director of the cathedral *fabrica*, persuaded him to decline the Würzburg chair and to inaugurate the newly conceived cathedral chair at Strassburg (N. 955).
 Despite Rathgeber's claim (*loc. cit.*) that Geiler stopped in Strassburg to tell his "good friend Schott" of the Würzburg offer, and Wuttke's claim (*NDB*, VI, 150f.) that in coming to Strassburg Geiler yielded to the persuasion of "his pupil Peter Schott" to accept a new chair financed by Schott, there is no evidence whatsoever of any personal ties between the Schotts

and Geiler before Geiler came to Strassburg. Furthermore neither Schott, Sr., nor Schott, Jr., could have studied under Geiler, the elder Schott being about 18 years Geiler's senior and the younger Schott not having attended either university where Geiler taught; in fact, at the time Geiler accepted the Strassburg offer, young Schott – then seventeen years old – was in Italy. To be sure, the Schotts and Geiler must have known one another by reputation, because they were all noteworthy residents of the southwestern Rhine area. If Rathgeber is correct about Geiler's sojourn at Baden-Baden in 1476, it is very possible that Schott, Sr., and Susanna von Cöllen heard and perhaps even met Geiler there. Indeed, both Dacheux and Schmidt credit Susanna with securing Geiler for Strassburg, for it was she who urged her husband and the *fabrica* members to approach him.

For 33 years Geiler was cathedral preacher in Strassburg despite opposition to his moves for reform, despite tempting offers from Augsburg and Basel, despite his longing to retire into a life of study and contemplation (plans to retreat to the Black Forest with friends such as Christoph von Uttenheim, Johann Laudenburg and Wimpheling came to naught in 1497, 1498 and 1501). His powerful sermons, spiced with wit and vivid *exempla*, attracted people from all classes in such flocks as had never been seen at Strassburg. No one escaped his scathing satire – be he bishop, king, pope or emperor. Yet Maximilian I made him imperial chaplain in 1503.

Unfortunately – according to Frenken (*Die Exempla*, 68) – we do not have Geiler's sermons in the exact form in which he delivered them. We have only notes taken down by his hearers, his own Latin sketches or German translations of his sketches. The *Monita* written for Friedrich von Zollern (Appendix H) exemplify Geiler's completely practical, direct, concise and lucid manner of expression. Schott's "Imitaciunculae" also give us some idea of Geiler's picturesque language.

In addition to the onerous duties as cathedral preacher (N. 955, par. 5), Geiler preached in Strassburg monasteries and convents. He preached weekly to the Magdalenes whom he had reformed. He also preached outside the city of Strassburg for anniversaries of church consecrations, particularly in his homeland of Upper Alsace. He led pilgrimages to holy places, as for instance when he escorted 100 pilgrims to Einsiedeln in 1484. He also wrote, published and participated in disputations. Not only did he help in acquiring materials for the cathedral library, but he also assembled an excellent library of his own which he willed to the cathedral chair with the stipulation that the books remain in the preacher's home and be moved only if the office were discontinued. The library was used by his successors and by the first Lutheran preachers of the cathedral; then it vanished; perhaps it was sold along with the cathedral library (N. 56).

During his holidays Geiler often travelled to Upper Alsace, to Baden and to Switzerland. He repeatedly visited the hermits Sebastian and Nicolaus von Flüe, both of whom he greatly admired. One year – possibly 1484, as Schmidt (*H. L.*, I, 352) believes – he made an extensive tour through France to places of pilgrimage, one of these being the cave at La Sainte Baume near Marseilles, where Mary Magdalene is supposed to have done penance for 30 years. Here Geiler acquired (or himself made) a copy of Petrarch's 36 Latin hexameters composed at Sainte Baume in 1338 to the saint ("Epistulae Seniles," XIV, 17, in Petrarch, *Opera omnia*, Basel, 1581). This poem appeared in the 1506 edition of Schott's *Epithoma* and is in the "Wimpheling Codex" (folio 50b f.). On the tour through France, Geiler also visited the grave of Gerson in the monastery church of the Celestines at Lyons. To this monastery and to that of the Carthusians at Avignon Gerson had willed his works. At both these monasteries Geiler had copies of Gerson's works made for himself.

With all his zeal and application to work, Geiler was extremely human.

He felt for the needy, the hungry, the leper, the poor in wretched hospitals, the stranger. He tells how he once found succor for a sick stranger whom no one in the Strassburg hospitals would help and who was finally deposited at the church door. He enjoyed a good joke and he was not above a bit of vanity. For example, at Freiburg – like many another – he refused to conform to the university rule obliging masters and students to wear ecclesiastical attire. He had enough money to permit himself little extravagances and wore chains, bracelets and ornate shoes. In punishment for his behavior, he was disciplined before his examination for the licentiate by being made to take an oath that he would not wear such attire.

Geiler outlived most of those whom he held dear: Peter Schott and his parents, Friedrich von Zollern, Johann Rot, Andreas Hartmann and Johann Simmler; and during his later years Wimpheling and Christoph von Uttenheim were no longer in Strassburg. A touching anecdote is told by Beatus Rhenanus of Geiler's last days. He received a letter from a young woman in Augsburg who had heard him preach. Having had strange dreams about him for some weeks, she believed he was soon to die; "Set your house in order" ("Bestelle dein Haus!"), she wrote, and Geiler followed her advice. He preached his final sermon on the first day of the year 1510, a Sunday. On 10 March, as he was resting after lunch, he slipped quietly away.

He was buried at the foot of the lovely Gothic chancel which Schott, Sr., had put into the cathedral for him; later his body was transferred to the chapel of St. Catherine. Shortly after his death, the Knights of St. John in Strassburg had the first four lines of the 24 line epitaph composed by Brant for Geiler incised on the first pillar of the choir (opposite the great clock) in the cathedral. In their own church the knights placed a second epitaph which was moved in 1633 to the cathedral and put on the same pillar with the first; there both may still be seen today.

Many honors have been paid Geiler through the centuries. One such honor belongs to the early years of our own century when Ammersweiler named a street for Geiler and dedicated a plaque in his memory. On the plaque are quoted Schiller's words:

> Wer den besten seiner Zeit genug getan,
> Der hat gelebt für alle Zeiten.

ADB, VIII, 509-518. *NDB*, VI, 150f. Adam *Theolog.*, 6-11. *Athen. Raur.*, 3. Barth, "Pilger," 183. Bauer, 15, 46, 67. Brant, *Narrenschiff*, 154. Braun, 3, 92-98, 114. Cave, *Appendix*, 122. *Code hist.*, I, part ii, 91, 110-119. Dacheux, *Fragments*, I, part ii, 65; III, part v, 145. Dacheux, *Réf.*, *passim*. Dreher, *passim*. Erhard, III, 359-372. Falk, 84f., 88, 91. Frenken, 68-70. Freyer, 836. Geiger, *Reuchlin*, 38. Gesner, 419b-420. Glöckler, I, 334-336, 342, 344; II, 496, 497, 520. *GGr.*², I, 396-404. Grandidier, *Chevaliers*, 58; *Essais*, 63-71, 274-280, 361; *Mélanges*, 383; *Nouv. oeuvr.*, II, 198-205; *Oeuvr. hist.*, IV, 369. Graesse, 586. Hasse, I, 330ff. Hatt, *Vie*, 13; *Ville*, 425, n. 7. Hertzog, iv, 113; vi, 203. Illyricus, II, 895. *Inventaire*, IV, 137. Kempis, 14. Knepper, *Sprüche*, 160. Languille, 366. Landmann, "Empfängnis," 192, 194. Lauffer, *passim*. Mayer, I, 63. Meister, 143. Pantaleon, II, 474. Pfleger, "Predigt," 698; "Kult," *passim*; "Aest," *passim*; *Menschen*, 9-22; *Kirchengeschichte*, 164-223, *passim*; "Kunst," *passim*; *Pfarrei*, 250ff, 265; "Predigtwesen," 543 and *passim*. Piton, I, 333. Potuček, #21, #24, #119. Rathgeber, *Gottesmänner*, 1-21; *Strassburg*, 16-21. Reuss, "Männer," 42f. Rhenanus. Riegger, *Amoen.*, 3, 56ff., 67, 68, 100-26. Roeder, *passim*. Schadäus, 82-92. Scherlen, 198, 257-264. Schmidt, *Chapitre*, 192, 193; *H.L.*, I, 337-461 and II, 373-390; "Notices... P.S.," 250, 252, 309f.; *Bibliotheken*, 9. Schneegans, *Sagen*, 36f., 41; "Pfingstfest," *passim*. Schöpflin, *Alsace*, 344, n. t. Specklin, 283, 285, 287, 288-291, 292, 297, 300, 301, 312f.

Steichele, 149, 152f., 154, 158ff., 164, 166. Stenzel, 77. Strobel (1843), 427.
Thurston, 345. Trithemius, *Cathalogus*, f. 60a; *Liber*, f. 133b. Wackernagel,
I, 90. Wencker, *Arch.*, 427, 428-429, 433. Wetzer-Welte, V, 188-195.
Wimpheling, *cat. ep.*, 110, 111, 117, 123; *De integritate*, folio Ei. Winckelmann, "Roraffen," *passim*; "Kulturgesch.", 263-285 *passim*. Wittmer,
"Flüe," 170, 172. Wiskowatoff, 16, 27, 73. Wolf, I, 337. Zacher, *passim*. For
a fairly complete bibliography on Geiler, cf. Clauss "Geiler;" this includes
editions of his works. Geiler's sermons delivered in Augsburg are in a
manuscript of 1509 in Kemnat: Kreis- und Studienbibliothek *Hs. 31*.

GEORGIUS UNGARUS #15, p. 24; #173, p. 194
This fellow student of Schott and Maeler is without doubt the Georgius
Heess (Theess, Thess, Thetze "de Agaria"), "plebanus ecclesie Wermesch in
Ungaria," listed as attending Bologna during the years 1477, 1479, 1480,
who served as *procurator* of his nation 1479-1480. He may be identical
with the Dominican Georgius von Ungarn, whose manuscript book *De ritibus
Turcarum* in "St. Maria super Minerva" at Rome is mentioned by Jöcher,
and just possibly with the Georgius of an undated entry (before 1450?) in
the "Anima" register: "Georgius Ungeren. canon Tarbatensis."
    Acta bonon., 224, 227, 228. Jöcher, II, 934. *Liber confrat.*, 71.

JOHANN CHARLIER DE GERSON (JARSONNO, YARSONNO) (1363-1429)
p. xxx; #5, p. 11; #60, p. 65; #176, p. 196; #232, pp. 258ff.
Gerson, the eldest of 12 children, was born in the village of Gerson (now
disappeared), near Barby in the Ardennes, of very pious parents. At age
14 he entered the college *le Navarre* at Paris and by 1394 was doctor of
theology. He became chancellor of Notre Dame and of the university of
Paris in 1395. Other posts he acquired were: 1397-1401 dean of St. Donatien
at Bruges, 1403 curé of St. Jean-en-Grève at Paris. Sent to the council of
Constance in 1414, he became one its leading spirits. After the council, he
did not return to his post in Paris because of his opposition to Duke John
the Fearless of Burgundy; instead he went to Melk and Vienna. Even when
John was assassinated in 1419, Gerson did not go back to Paris, but retired
to the monastery of the Celestines in Lyons, where his brother was prior, to
spend the remainder of his life in writing and teaching.
    Two *contrafaçons* of Gerson's works printed in 1489 (N. 136, par. 7)
have the following quatrain to Gerson:

> Fortis in ecclesia bellator, maxime Gerson,
> Armatus gladio/ cingis ouile dei;
> Viuunt scripta tua... quamuis sint ossa sepulta,
> Omnibus exemplar se dant imitabile doctis.
>   – Kessler edition of Gerson, *Opera* (Basel, 1489),
>   folio Ia 5; and Stuchs edition (Nürnberg, 1489), folio fa2.

Auct., III, 452, 454, 501, 515, 582, 595, 616, 625; IV, *passim*. *Cath. Ency.*,
IV, 288ff.; VI, 530ff. Dacheux, *Réf.*, 337, 568. *Dictionnaire de théol. cath.*,
VI (1920). 1313-30. Erhard, I, 459. Eysengrein, 159. Jöcher, I, 1843.
Riegger, *Amoen.*, 74. Schmidt, *H. L.*, I, 129; II, 13, 325, 332, 374. Trithemius, *De script. eccl.*, folio 160a.

JOHANN GESLER (GESSLER, GÄSSLER) p. xv; #235, pp. 266f.
Schott's former literary schoolmate at Paris, Johann Gesler, may be identical
with the Johann Gesler from Ravensburg who studied at Tübingen in 1481
and became the twenty-seventh abbot of the Premonstratensian abbey of
Minderau (near Ravensburg in Württemberg) in 1483 and after 12 rewarding

years in office resigned in 1495. Minderau (now listed as Weissenau SS Peter and Paul), founded as a priory in 1141, became an abbey in 1257. This same Gesler may very well be the Johann Gosseler, "Pfarrherr und doctor zu sant Jost zu Raffenspurg," who wrote a poem on St. Ursula's ship, which was printed with music by Bartolomeus Kistler at Strassburg 1497.

A Johann Gessler from Ulm was matriculated at Erfurt in 1482, and a Johann Gessler was active as a lawyer in Strassburg during the latter part of the fifteenth century; he published precedents and rhetorical writings in German.

Backmund, I, 88f. Brusch, 17. *Gallia Christiana*, V (1731), 1106. Jöcher, II, 1433. Ritter, *Hist.*, 138. *Universal=Lexikon*, X, 1296. Weissenborn, I, 392.

JOHANN GOETZ (GOETZONIS, GOSZE, GOCZS) p. xv; p. xxxi; #120, p. 139; #157, p. 172

The Johann Goetz of Augsburg for whom Schott requested Wimpheling to write letters of recommendation to Heidelberg and whom Schott informed about the vacant post of parish priest at New. St. Peter, because he had learned from Geiler that Goetz was interested in coming to Strassburg, is listed in Heidelberg matriculation records for 12 July 1488: "Johannes Goczs ex Augusta (bacc. in art. Libicensis)." Ca. 1501 he wrote a letter to Johann Amerbach, in which he identifies himself as "Johann Goetzonis Augustensis, plebanus Argentinensis." According to Schmidt, he was a priest at the cathedral in Augsburg before becoming a priest in Strassburg, a friend of Brant and a member of the Strassburg humanistic society.

Hartmann identifies this Johann Goetz with the Goetz who had studied at Ingolstadt and Paris before matriculating at Leipzig in 1482, received a licentiate in the "via moderna" in 1489, matriculated at Basel 1494/95 as "Joh. Goetzonis arcium mag. ex Augusta, pedagogus Melchioris baronis Limperg," and may have been teaching as "lector biblicus" at Basel in 1497.

Hartmann, I, 132. Schmidt, *H. L.*, 197. Toepke, I, 391

SIGISMUND GOSSENBROT (GOSSEMBROT, COSMIPROT) (1417-1493) #171, pp. 191ff.; #242, pp. 278f.

After studying arts and law at Vienna from 1433 on (A.B. in 1436), Gossenbrot, scion of an old Augsburg family, devoted himself to trade. He also served his city of Augsburg in various capacities and was mayor in 1458. In 1461 he gave his possessions to his sons and retired to the monastery of the Knights of St. John of Jerusalem at Strassburg. In 1468 he bought Strassburg citizenship. A staunch supporter of Piccolomini and the new learning, he reveals his interest in humanism in the letters he wrote to his Viennese professor Konrad Säldner with whom he carried on a long literary debate. In Strassburg he collected a considerable library and was friendly with Johann Rot, Geiler, Dringenberg, Schott, Bohuslaus von Hassenstein, Hartmann Schedel, *et al.* He encouraged the Benedictine monk Sigismund Meisterlin to write the *Augsburg Chronik* and was himself urged by Meisterlin to write one of his earliest works, *Chronographia Augustana*, which has been called "the first humanistic historical work in Germany" (*ADB*). From Schott's comment about the cross fashioned for the Schotts, it is apparent that Gossenbrot was a skilled craftsman in wood or metal. Two sons he sent to study at Ferrara; one of these became a priest (†1465), the other (†1502) was an official of Archduke Sigismund of Austria and later in the service of Maximilian I. The third son, Sigismund the Younger, *miles auratus*, was in the government of Augsburg and served as mayor every even numbered year from 1484 to the year of his death, 1500.

ADB, XLIX, 475-477. *NDB*, VI, 648f. Dreher, XVIII, 39. Schmidt,

Chapitre, 243; *H.L.*, II, 30. Voigt, II, 291f., 303. Wittmer-Meyer, I, 244. Wattenbach, 36-69.

EUCHARIUS GROSHUG #181, pp. 201f.; #182, p. 202; #221, pp. 246ff.
Groshug, a friend of Schott from childhood, is mentioned as being prior of the Knights of St. John of Jerusalem at Strassburg in 1505.
    Grandidier, *Chevaliers*, 20.

JACOB HAGEN (†1489) #38, p. 45; #45, p. 50
A native of Strassburg, Hagen attended Erfurt in 1453 and Heidelberg in 1464. He was canon of New St. Peter by 1459 and was involved in the quarrel between the churches and the bishop who claimed that the churches were receiving money rightly belonging to the cathedral. The pope, to whom the churches appealed, referred the matter to Dr. Rudolph von Rudesheim, dean in Worms. From Rudesheim, Hagen obtained permission for a new screen in New St. Peter; whereupon the bishop sought to excommunicate all canons, but was prevented from doing so when the churches again appealed to the pope. Having served as *cantor* and *scholasticus*, Hagen became also dean of New St. Peter in 1482 and took possession of the office on 3 November (#38). In that year he resigned, in favor of Thomas Wolf, Jr., the canonicate he had acquired at St. Thomas on the death of Johann Hell, dean of St. Thomas, in 1481.
    Horning, *Jung-St.-Peter*, 51-52. *Inventaire (Spach)*, IV, 87. Schmidt, *Chapitre*, 278; *H.L.*, II, 59; "Notices... Wolf," 448. Toepke, 310. Weissenborn, I, 239.

WALTER VAN HALEWIN (GUALTERUS, GAUTHIER; HALEWYN) p. XXV; #17, p. 26; #94, p. 105
The Halewins were an old noble family from the neighborhood of Menin in the French part of Flanders. During the fourteenth and fifteenth centuries the family supplied many bailiffs and other officials to the service of the counts of Flanders. From Schott's letters we know that Walter Halewin studied at Bologna, possibly also at Ferrara, and received a doctorate of law. Since he is not listed by Pardi among those obtaining doctorates from Ferrara, he probably took his doctorate at Bologna; his name does not appear in the *Acta bonon.*, because Flemish students were ejected from the German nation at Bologna in 1475 and were not reinstated until 1543 (*Acta bonon.*, xxx). From Schott we also know that Halewin was an *eques auratus* and that sometime before October 1486 he was married and appointed to the bailiff's office in Bruges.
    Matriculation records of Louvain list a "Walterus Haelwiin, Tornacensis" 18 November 1471 who may be identical with our Halewin; and Gaillard has information about a "Gauthier van Halewyn, pensionnaire du Franc en 1484", son of Jean van Halewyn, "chevalier, président de la Hollande, de la Zélande," etc. († 1478) and of Béatrice van den Ryne, "dame de Swevezeele" (†1507). This Gauthier, who could be our Walter, died 31 October 1487. Bruges archives, sparse for the period, do not mention Walter but note that on 11 December 1487 "Charles van Halewyn, chevalier, bailli de Bruges, est nommé hoofman de la gilde de vieux serment; . . . et Corneille van Halewyn est nommé lieutenant bailli." Might one of these two have succeeded Walter in office?
    Biographie nationale . . . de Belgique, VIII (1884), 727. J. Gaillard, *Bruges et le Franc ou leur magistrature et leur noblesse, avec des données historiques et généalogiques sur chaque famille* (Bruges, 1857), I, 228. *Inventaire des Chartes*, Section I, volume VI, 1e Série, 13e au 16e siècle, of *Inventaire des Archives de la Ville de Bruges* (1776), 293. H. Nowé, *Les baillis comtaux de*

Flandre. ₁Des Origines à la fin du xive siècle (Bruxelles, 1929). Wils, II, 259.

CONRAD HAMMELBURGER #34, p. 41
Hammelburger served as procurator of the Strassburg cathedral *fabrica* 13 years and is last mentioned in 1494. He was a vicar of the cathedral chapter and served as one of the executors of Jacob Reiffsteck's will, to set up a prebend at New St. Peter. He was also responsible for the renovation of the cathedral organ in 1489.
Dacheux, "Münsterchronik," 16. Dacheux, *Réf.*, 359, n. 1. Schadäus, 110.

HOUSE OF HAPSBURG

1. FRIEDRICH III (1415-1493) Roman Emperor 1452-1493 #5, p. 11; #73, pp. 79f.; #80, p. 87; #83, p. 90; #118, p. 138; #121, pp. 139f.; #170, pp. 189f.; #263, p. 295; #264, pp. 296f.; #267, p. 299.
Friedrich III was born at Innsbruck, the son of Ernst von Hapsburg, duke of Styria and Carinthia. In 1440 he was chosen King of the Germans and crowned 1442. Under the influence of Aeneas Silvio Piccolomini (later Pope Pius II), Friedrich negotiated the Concordat of Vienna in 1448 with Pope Nicholas V, in which he pledged the allegiance of the German people to Rome in return for the promise of the imperial crown. His marriage to Leonora, daughter of Edward King of Portugal, took place in Rome, as did his coronation as emperor in 1452. On the death of his brother Albrecht in 1463, Friedrich united the Hapsburg dominions of upper and lower Austria, but his claim to those territories was disputed by Matthias Hunyadi of Hungary who drove Friedrich from Vienna. After the election of his son Maximilian as King of the Romans in 1486, Friedrich spent much of his time in retirement at Linz.
ADB, VII, 448-452. *NDB*, V, 484-487. *EB*, XI, 49f.

2. MAXIMILIAN I (1459-1519) Roman Emperor (1493-1519) p. xxiv; #83, p. 90; #118, pp. 137ff.; #121, pp. 139f.; #128, p. 148; #153, pp. 167f.; #155, pp. 169f.; #263, pp. 295ff; #264, pp. 296f.
Born in Wiener Neustadt, son of Emperor Friedrich III, Maximilian – through his marriage with Mary of Burgundy in 1477 – brought the Lowlands under Hapsburg dominion. In 1486 he was elected King of the Romans at the diet in Frankfurt and crowned at Aachen a few weeks later. From this time on he virtually led the empire. Captured at Bruges in 1488 by the Flemish who resented his being regent for his young son Philipp the Fair, he was freed by an imperial army under Friedrich III. He became emperor in 1493 but was not crowned until 1508 at Trent. Maximilian was a good ruler and established the supremacy of Roman law throughout the empire. Well-educated and himself a writer of romances, he fostered education and the arts, and is often termed "the last knight."
EB, XVII, 922f.

3. SIGISMUND, ARCHDUKE OF AUSTRIA (†1496) #76, p. 83; #101, p. 112; #170, p. 190.
Son of Friedrich of Hapsburg and Anna of Brunswick, Sigismund ruled as count – later as duke – of Tyrol from 1440 to 1490. He was also landgrave of Alsace. Until 1474 he was often at war with the Swiss and at one time allied himself with Charles the Bold to get money for campaigning against them. He was apparently originator of the plan that Maximilian should marry Mary of Burgundy. In 1490 he adopted Maximilian as his heir and retired from public life.
Bernoulli, VI, 301. Glöckler, II, 120ff. Kreuter, II, 178. Laguille,

II, part i, 368. Pantaleon, II, 488f. Rapp, 37. Riegger, *Anal.*, 203, n.; 213, n.; 236f. Trithemius, *Ann. Hirs.*, II, 491, 503, 529.

ANDREAS HARTMANN VON EPPINGEN (GEPPINGEN) (†1507) #87, p. 95; #157, p. 172; #199, p. 214; #206, p. 215; #210, p. 219
Hartmann, from the village of Eppingen, studied at Heidelberg, where he served seven times as rector 1463-1492 and received a licentiate in civil and canon law. He held the posts of canon at New Saint Peter, of almoner and of vicar at the Strassburg cathedral and became vicar general of Bishop Albrecht by 1479; in that capacity he represented the bishop on a commission to settle the law suit between Nicolaus Jörger and Hans von Sickingen in 1491; in 1491 he was one of the spokesmen for the lay clerics versus the mendicants. He corrected the *Apparatus* of Innocent IV on the *Decretals* which was published by Heinrich Eggestan on the press in the monastery of the Strassburg Carthusians in the year 1478. Hartmann belonged to the Hermits of St. William. His seal (of 19 March 1493) is in the archives of the chapter at St. Thomas. A relief of him showing him in a doctor's robe and holding a book in his hand is in the Zorn chapel at New St. Peter. Straub calls him "vir mirae gravitatis, justitiae, simul et miseri cordiae cultoris."

Barth, "Florentius," 121. Dacheux, *Réf.*, 176f. Glöckler, I, 340. Horning, *Festschrift*, 52f. *Inventaire... St. Thomas*, 37. Ritter, *Histoire*, 40. Schadäus, 49. Schmidt, *Chapitre*, 163; "Notices... P. S.," 249. Stenzel, "Gerichte," 235, 245. Straub, *Geschichtskalender*, 16, 36. Strobel, (1843), 449. Toepke, I, 343 and *passim*. Truttmann-Burg, 185.

BOHUSLAUS VON HASSENSTEIN (BOHUSLAUS VON LUBKOVITZ UND ZU HASSENSTEIN) (1461-1510) *Luc., passim.* Cf. special index, general index and chronology III.
Baron Bohuslaus von Lubkovitz and zu Hassenstein, one of the most interesting men of his age, came from a noble Bohemian family which is documented as early as 861. Emperor Sigismund had bestowed the castle of Hassenstein upon the family and Emperor Friedrich III had conferred the rank of baron upon Hassenstein's father Nicolaus (†1462). Perhaps because his family fortunes were so closely tied to the empire, Hassenstein often speaks of himself as a German. His mother Sophia von Zierotin seems to have died when he was quite young, for there is no mention of her in his writings. He was the youngest of four sons, the three elder being: Johannes (1450-1517), Nicolaus († *ca.* 1499) and Jaroslaus who died as a child. Hassenstein's date of birth is – so far as we can ascertain – not recorded, but from what he himself writes of his age and from his association with Schott (N. 59, par. 5) the year 1461 appears to be the most probable date.

Hassenstein apparently received his early education under the auspices of the Calixtine fathers; by 1475 he was in Bologna. Like Schott, he may have matriculated at the university of Bologna in 1474 even though the first entry for him in the *Acta bonon.* is 1475 (N. 95, 3). His companion (and probably his tutor) was the Hungarian priest Ladislaus (von Veterebuda?) of the Veszprém diocese. With Schott he studied classics, Greek and law. In 1478 during the epidemic of the plague which drove Schott and Müller from Bologna and home to Strassburg, Hassenstein may have returned to Bohemia or – what is more likely – may have gone to another Italian university, such as Ferrara. By 1479 he was back in Bologna. When student friction in September 1480 caused many members of the German nation to leave Bologna (N. 609), there is no doubt that Hassenstein and Schott went to Ferrara. At Ferrara Hassenstein became friendly with the Adelmann brothers and with Ulrich von Fronsperger. Some months after Schott had finished his study and left, Hassenstein in the winter 81/82 suffered a severe illness which must have delayed his work considerably. On 26 November 1482 he received his doctorate of canon law at Ferrara. Before returning to Bohemia in the company of Ladislaus and perhaps also of Friedrich Büchsner, he evidently made his first of three visits to Strassburg (N. 101).

In 1483 or 1484 King Vladislaus named Hassenstein *praepositus Wyssegradensis*, i.e., archchancellor of Bohemia, a post Hassenstein held at least until October 1486 when Schott reports him as still being archchancellor (#95, p. 107). By 1487 he had resigned, however, and was supervising the family estates. In that year strife over their inheritance broke out among the Hassenstein brothers and also in that year Hassenstein accepted the post of royal secretary. It was for this post that he requested Schott to compose guiding rules (treatise on Christian life, #110), and he seems to have gone to court at Prague early in 1488. He may have served in the Silesian campaign during the year 1487. Soon tiring of life at court, especially as he received no remuneration – in fact, he received none for either public office until 1507, which was a constant grievance in his letters – Hassenstein resigned and returned to the estates. In April 1490, after the brothers' quarrel over inheritance was settled – all retaining common possession of castle Hassenstein, and Hassenstein receiving two villages with the land belonging to them – Hassenstein with Büchsner set out on the odyssey to Greece and the Near East.

Returning from the voyage to Venice in August 1491, Hassenstein learned that he was being proposed as candidate for the bishop's seat at Olmütz and hastened home. Yet despite the support of King Vladislaus (now also king of Hungary) and other influential people, including Bishop Ulrich Fronsperger of Trent who wrote to Innocent VIII on Hassenstein's behalf, Alexander VI finally confirmed someone of his own choice in 1496. Hassenstein was also disappointed in his try first for the post of coadjutant to the bishop and then for the bishop's seat at Pressburg in 1500; even though the former bishop had asked that Hassenstein succeed him and even though the king with other powerful persons supported him, Alexander again appointed his own candidate in 1502. The move a year later to secure the post for Hassenstein by transferring the incumbent also failed. Nonetheless Hassenstein remained a staunch defender of the papacy and the popes.

In 1499 Hassenstein spent some time visiting friends in the chancellery at Buda and comrades of the *Sodalitas Litterariae Danubiana*. He was also in Vienna, where he became reconciled with Conrad Celtis who had repaid Hassenstein's kindness some years previously by publishing as his own several of Hassenstein's poems (Potuček, #5, #6, #56, #73), a stupid bit of plagiary for which Hassenstein had only contempt.

In 1502 he took a post in the chancellery at Buda, but the next year he retired definitely from public life to his estates and occupied himself with his literary work and his correspondence. He served as president of the *Sodalitas Leucopolitana* at Wittenberg. He collected one of the most famous libraries of the age and one of the two most important in the empire. With the Fuggers in Augsburg, an agent in Venice and Bernard Adelmann helping him, he spared neither effort nor expense in procuring rare books and is said to have paid 2000 florins for a Greek edition of Plato. After his death, 700 of his books were lent to Wittenberg, where they were used by Luther and Melanchthon. On the return journey some were destroyed by fire. The rest of the library, eventually given to a Jesuit college, was destroyed in a popular uprising during the year 1595.

In addition to poems, Hassenstein wrote on morality and history. His *Annales Bohemiae* have been lost. Eight epigrams to a certain Carlotta

(Charlita) have intrigued investigators; perhaps the young lady was a daughter of the "domina Margarita" mentioned by Schott in a letter of 29 June 1480 (#17, p. 26). An interesting bibliographical item is the de Carro edition of Hassenstein's "Ode to Carlsbad" with two verse translations in each of the following languages: French, German, Hungarian, Bohemian, English, Greek, Hebrew, Italian, Swedish, Dutch, Russian, Polish, Gaelic, Spanish, Portugese – a fitting monument to a humanist!
        ADB, XIX, 47-50. *Acta bonon.*, 219, 222, 228. Carro, 13, 15, 18. Colerus, 37f., 46. Cornova, *passim*. Dacheux, *Réf.*, 422f., 423, n. 1. Ellinger, I, 411-415. Erhard, III, 200-220. Fabricius, *Bohuslai, passim*. Hasse, I, 137ff. Knod, *Studenten*, #2131. Pantaleon, II, 474. Pardi, *Titoli*, 60, 61. Potuček, v, vi, xi, xii. Prochaska, 231, 239, 265ff. Ristelhuber, 114f. Ryba, iii. Schmidt, "Notices... P.S.," 255. Schröder, 168-177. Trithemius, *Cathalogus*, folio 69b; *Liber*, folio 138a. Weislinger, 678. Wolkan, 110-121.

HELL FAMILY

The Hells were a very wealthy and influential family in religious and social circles of Strassburg during the last decades of the fifteenth century. To clarify relationships and references elsewhere, it is expedient to mention Johann Hell (†1481), although he does not figure in Schott's works. He was dean of St. Thomas and set up regulations for helping poor but apt students receive an education and left a definite sum in his will to be used for that purpose. He also initiated a *prebendum sacerdotale* to be exercised after his death successively by his brother Nicolaus, by his nephews Thomas Wolf, Sr., and Laurentius Hell, by his grandnephew Thomas Wolf, Jr., and by male descendants in perpetuity. His sister Anna married Andreas Wolf of Erckbolsheim; the children of this marriage were Thomas Wolf, Sr., Johann Wolf and an unnamed son who was a layman and father of young Thomas. His brother Nicolaus was the father of Laurentius Hell. When Johann Hell died, his canonicate at St. Thomas was acquired by Jacob Hagen, who, however, resigned this benefice a year later (1482) in favor of Thomas Wolf, Jr.
        Grandidier, *Mélanges*, 358, 402. Knepper, *Schulwesen*, 128. Schmidt, *Chapitre*, 140f., 144, 194, 272, 274; "Notices... Wolf," 447f.

1. JOHANN HELL (ONHEIM) #30, p. 38

This Johann Hell, called Onheim to distinguish him from the Johann Hell above, seems to have belonged to the same family; some form of relationship to the Hell family is the only logical explanation for the fact that the young Thomas Wolf, Jr., was removed from the care of the *scholasticus* Theobald Fuchs and placed in the hands of Johann Hell (Onheim) and "his Otilia" (sister or housekeeper). Johann Hell (Onheim) studied at Erfurt in 1470 and at Heidelberg in 1471, where he received his A.B. degree. He held the benefices of vicar at St. Thomas and vicar at New St. Peter. The archives at St. Thomas have a copy of a letter written to him in 1506 by Pope Julius II.
        Gallia Christiana, V, 841. *Inventaire... St. Thomas*, 43. *Inventaire (Spach)*, IV, 224. Meister, 137. Schmidt, *H. L.*, II, 60; "Notices... Wolf," 449. Toepke, 335. Weissenborn, I, 337.

2. LAURENTIUS HELL #40, p. 47

Laurentius Hell was the son of Nicolaus Hell and the nephew of Johann Hell. He was a lawyer and held a canonicate at New St. Peter, a vicarate at

St. Thomas and a vicarate at New St. Peter. In 1512 he became dean of New St. Peter and in 1516 he was apostolic commissioner.
Schmidt, *Chapitre*, 52; *H.L.*, II, 60; "Notices... Wolf," 448.

LUDWIG VON HELMSTADT (†1504) #231, p. 258
Ludwig von Helmstadt matriculated at Heidelberg in 1457. He held canonicates in the cathedral chapters at Mainz and Spires and in 1478 was elected bishop of Spires. He supported *Pfalzgraf* Philipp at the siege of Geroldseck in 1486. Dacheux calls him one of the better bishops of his age. He was zealous for reform of the clergy, both secular and regular.
Dacheux, *Réf.*, 428. Eubel, II, 241. *Gallia Christiana*, V, 735. *Liber confrat.*, 26. Toepke, 287. Trithemius, *Ann. Hirs.*, II, 498.

HEINRICH VON HENNENBERG (HENNEBERG) (†1526) #114, p. 135; #124, p. 142; #130, p. 150
Graf Heinrich was the elder brother of *Graf* Berthold von Hennenberg who became archbishop-elector of Mainz (1484-1504). Both brothers matriculated at Erfurt in 1455. From 1451 Heinrich was canon, *scholasticus* (1470), vice-dean and 1486-91 acting dean of the Strassburg cathedral chapter. He was *concubinarius* and during the chapter's contest with Innocent VIII over the deanship supported Hoyer von Barby-Mulingen.
Dacheux, *Eccl. Arg.*, 11; *Réf.*, Appendix LXXV. Dreher, XIX, 55. Glöckler, 344. Knepper, *Schulwesen*, 115. Pfleger, *Pfarrei*, 250f. Schadäus, 69f. 70, 72. Stenzel, 89; "Gerichte," 95. Straub, *Geschichtskalender*, 116. Trithemius, *Ann. Hirs.*, II, 518, 522. Weissenborn, I, 247. Wimpheling, *Cat. ep.*, 119.

HEINRICH VON HEWEN (HÖWEN) (†1530) #95, p. 106
Graf Heinrich was canon and *custos* of the Strassburg cathedral chapter and dean at Constance. In 1491 he became bishop of Chur. To arbitrate a quarrel between him and Emperor Maximilian I, in 1498, Lodovic Maria Sforza, duke of Milan, appointed Friedrich von Zollern (then bishop of Augsburg). He attended the coronation of Bishop Wilhelm von Honstein of Strassburg in 1506.
Dacheux, *Eccl. Arg.*, 10; *Réf.*, 486. Dreher, XIX, 30. Eubel, II, 141. Glöckler, 345. Stenzel, 91; "Gerichte," 95. Straub, *Geschichtskalender*, 176. Wimpheling, *Cat. ep.*, 120. Zoepfl, 499.

JOHANN HEYNLIN A LAPIDE (VON STEIN) (1425/30-1496) p. xxv; #63, p. 69
A native of Stein near Schaffhausen (or Spires?), Heynlin matriculated at Leipzig in 1452 and at Freiburg possibly by 1461, where he received his A.M. in 1463, before going to Paris; 1464 he came to teach at Basel; 1466 he was back in Paris where he served as rector in 1467 and received the degree of doctor of theology. As professor of theology there he called the first printers to Paris (the printer Johann Amerbach was his pupil at Paris). In 1474 he returned to Basel, where in 1476 he was preaching at the church of St. Leonhard. In 1478 he became professor and in 1479 rector at the university of Tübingen. In 1480 he was at Bern. Perhaps it was thereafter that he accepted the post of canon and preacher at Baden-Baden, a post which he resigned, as we know from Schott, in 1484 to become cathedral preacher at Basel, succeeding Wilhelm Textor whom he had replaced while Textor visited the Holy Land March 1477 to March 1478. He resigned the chair at

the Basel cathedral in 1487 to enter the Carthusian monastery at Basel. His library of 283 volumes he willed to the Carthusians. His writings were published in five volumes by Jakob Lauber in 1498.
ADB, XII, 379. *Auct.*, III, 196; columns 49, 52, 67-84 and *passim*. Geiger, *Briefwechsel*, 39f.; *Reuchlin*, 10, 12. Gesner, 430. Landmann, "Predigt," 205-234. Pantaleon, part ii, 461. Schmidt, *H. L.*, II, 5; "Notices... P.S.," 310. Trithemius, *Cathalogus*, folio 58a; *Liber*, folios 129a f.

CRATO HOFFMANN VON UDENHEIM (CRAFT HOFMANN VON UTENHEIM, UTTENHEIM (*ca.* 1450-1501) #154, p. 168
Hoffmann, also known as "Osiander," matriculated as pauper at Heidelberg in 1468 and received his A.B. degree in 1470. His A.M. degree he obtained at Freiburg in 1472(?). He succeeded Dringenberg as rector of the school at Schlettstadt in 1477 and is said to have instilled into his pupils such a love of classics that "children of uncouth stutterers became Latin orators." Two of his former pupils at Maximilian's court, Jacob Villinger and Jacob Spiegel, placed an epitaph to his memory in the church of St. Georg at Schlettstadt, and twenty years after his death the literary society of Schlettstadt honored his memory.
ADB, IV, 568. Dorlan, "Nouv. études," 385-391; *Notices*, part ii, 104. Gény, 28. Grandidier, *Nouv. oeuvr.*, II, 262f. *Inventaire*... *St. Thomas*, 266. Knepper, *Schulwesen*, 240, 327, 410. Röhrich, 28. Ritter, *Histoire*, 511. Sitzmann, I, 329. Toepke, 323.

KINGS OF HUNGARY (Cf. Emperor Sigismund)

1. MATTHIAS HUNYADI (CORVINUS) (1440-1490) #73, p. 80; #170, p. 190; #243, p. 279
Matthias, son of general János Hunyadi, is often called "Corvinus" from the raven in his escutcheon. He was elected king of Hungary (Matthias I) in 1458 and ruled 33 years. Taught by János Panonius, he was highly educated: he mastered German, Latin and Slavic languages; studied mathematics, physics and astrology; painted. He founded a library and a university at Buda. Many Italian humanists dedicated their works to him. A master of military strategy, he conquered much of Upper and Lower Austria, including the city of Vienna (all of which was regained by Maximilian at his death), and for his victories over the Turks was known as "malleus Turcorum." Such was his fame for military prowess that after the murder of Girolamo Riario in 1488 the Italian city of Ancona hoisted the Hungarian flag and placed itself under Matthias' protection. In 1476 he married Beatrice of Aragon, daughter of Ferdinand I of Naples, a precocious girl who at the age of ten read Cicero and spoke Latin fluently. She was a strong personality and added many books to the library at Buda. For the fate of Hungary under Vladislaus II, cf. under Bohemia.
Cosenza, II, 1124ff. Dreher, XIX, 74. *EB*, XIII, 907ff; XVII, 900f. Freher, 729ff. Previté-Orton, 1009, 1013f, 1047ff, 1050, 1110. Raynaldus, 1478, par. 35ff. Reuss, *Meyer*, 69f. Saladin, 299. Schmidt, *Bibliotheken*, 146f. Strobel, III, 306. Trithemius, *Ann. Hirs.*, II, 535.

2. VLADISLAUS II (cf. Bohemia, king of)

MATHIAS HUPFUFF p. xix
A native of Württemberg, Hupfuff was active as a printer at Strassburg

from 1498 to 1520; 140 books are attributed to him. Little is known of his life.
Grandidier, *Nouv. oeuvr.*, II, 284. Ritter, *Histoire*, 145-157.

HIERONYMUS DE IM(M)OLA (HIERONYMUS FOROCORUELIENSIS, FOROLIUIENSIS; GIROLAMO RIARIO (†1488) #121, p. 140; #159, p. 174
Hieronymus de Imola or Girolamo Riario was the favorite nephew of Sixtus IV and is often called "the archpope," because Sixtus submitted to his tyranny. He is doubtless responsible for much of the calumny charged to the memory of Sixtus, who not only made him captain general of the papal troops but the richest man in Rome. His wife Catharine Sforza, an able and fundamentally upright woman, aided him in some of his intrigues. In 1477, abetted by King Ferdinand of Naples, he led a plot to assassinate the Medici brothers, his aim being the control of Florence. Sixtus knew of the plot and tacitly supported it. Julian de Medici was slain, but Lorenzo escaped with a wound. In retaliation the Florentines imprisoned Raphael Riario, cardinal of St. George, grandnephew of Sixtus, one of the co-conspirators. In 1482 Riario was involved in a league with Venice against Ercole d'Este, duke of Ferrara, which came to naught. In 1484, coveting the possessions of the wealthy Colonna family in Rome, he had Lorenzo Colonna basely tortured to death. After the death of Sixtus he retired to his towns of Forli and Imola, which he had acquired *ca.* 1477 and 1480, and enriched them with beautiful buildings. Unable to keep out of politics, however, he intrigued against Innocent VIII and was assassinated in 1488.
Burckard, III, 304. Cosenza, II, 1631, 1762. Michaud, XXXI, 534f. Vincenzo Pacifici (ed.), *Un carme biografico di Sisto iv del 1477* (Tivoli, 1921), 51, 54. Rodocanachi, 16-67. Trithemius, *Ann. Hirs.*, II, 498. Young, 166ff., 179ff., 516.

DIETHER VON ISENBURG (*ca.* 1412-1482) #197, p. 213
Diether von Isenburg, *Graf* in Büdingen, received his A.B. degree at Erfurt and in 1434 served as rector of that university. In addition to benefices in a number of churches and to canonicates at the cathedrals of Trier, Cologne and Mainz, he held the post of *custos* at Mainz. In 1459, by a majority vote of the Mainz cathedral chapter, he was elected archbishop of Mainz, and his election was confirmed by Pius II. The minority candidate Adolf von Nassau and his followers, however, would not accept defeat and began political maneuvers to unseat Diether. Their action is understandable, for the office of archbishop of Mainz was a coveted political plum, its incumbent being not only primate of Germany but also archchancellor and elector of the empire. Whether won over by intrigues of Adolf and his followers or angered by Diether, Pius II on 8 January 1461 issued a bull deposing Diether and recognizing Adolf as archbishop. When Diether, supported by the people of Mainz, would not abdicate, Adolf marched on Mainz and in 1462 captured and sacked it. After ruling as archbishop for thirteen years, Adolf died, and the chapter again elected Diether. Sixtus IV confirmed the election. During the five years of his second period of rule as archbishop, Diether was almost solely responsible for the founding of the university of Mainz under a charter granted in 1477 by Sixtus IV.
The affair of Diether's deposition is somewhat of an enigma. It was certainly not common practice to depose an archbishop, especially one who was also primate of Germany and a prince of the empire. Church sources naturally state the papal side of the case, while other sources laconically state the bare facts without comment. Yet one may suspect that the whole empire was shocked. Pius' bull of 1461 contains extremely strong language:

it not only excommunicates Diether and strips him of all benefices, but on pain of excommunication warns the archbishops of Cologne and Trier and the bishops of Strassburg and Spires against either associating with Diether themselves or allowing their subordinates to associate with him; it terms Diether among other things a fraud, a traitor and a Judas Iscariot, but it does not give one concrete example of Diether's sins. Records do not mention any sin of Diether's, but they do show that Diether paid more than 20,000 gold florins to Rome for the archbishopric – moneys never acknowledged by Pius; they also show that Diether wanted a council of German churches – a move which would have been highly unpopular in Rome. Perhaps, as one historian puts it, Diether's cause was the cause of Germany.

At least some of the clerics in the empire aligned themselves either with Adolf von Nassau and the pope or with Diether and the people of Mainz. Gabriel Biel sided with Adolf, and Jacob Wimpheling seemingly with Diether. On folio 7a of the "Wimpheling Codex," Wimpheling entered the following item, the four-line text of which is from Ps. 2-4 and 5:

> Maguntia ab Adulpho de Nassare archipiscopo Maguntino capta ac direpta 1462
>
> > Qui habitat in caelis irridebit eos
> > > ac domninus subsannabit eos
> > Tunc loquetur ad eos in ira
> > > sua et furore suo conturbabit eos.

Wimpheling also wrote a life of Diether for his projected biographical dictionnary of the archbishops of Mainz. One may judge that Geiler was in sympathy with Diether. Certainly Schott, though too young to have been involved in the cause, must have felt Diether had fought against the same ills in the *Curia* as he himself was facing, else he need not have written the epitaph for Diether (which he may have spoken on the occasion of Diether's entombment).

ADB, V, 164ff. Eubel, II, 184. Falk, 6. Gabel, 25, 123f., 180f., 196ff., 198n., 300. Kisky, 143. K. Menzel, *Diether von Isenburg. Erzbischof von Mainz 1459-1463* (Erlangen, 1868). Pastor, II, 128-132, 135-138, 146, 150-162. Sattler, 170-174 (174, Latin text of bull). Simon, 16. Trithemius, *Ann. Hirs.*, II, 512, 514, 518. Wuerdtwein, *Diocesis*, 544.

JOHANN JÖRGER #54, p. 60

A Johann Jörger of Zürich is inscribed in the *Acta bonon.* for the year 1479. He would therefore have known Schott and Müller at Bologna. In 1476 he was already canon at the cathedral of Zürich.

Acta bonon., 226. Knod, *Studenten*, #1617.

Another Johann Jörger of Strassburg is mentioned in Strassburg records from 1481 to 1505. In 1481 he gave up his Strassburg citizenship and was admitted to the protection of *Pfalzgraf* Philipp on payment of four gilders a year for 10 years, but he bought his Strassburg citizenship back again in 1482, and in 1484 is recorded as being an "Auss-Bürger" (a citizen not resident in the city).

Inventaire (Brucker), I, 86. *Inventaire*, III, 40, 117; IV, 154. Wencker, *Juris*, 111, 113. Wittmer-Meyer, I, 381, 383.

NICOLAUS KAGEN (†1485?)   #180, p. 201.

Kagen or Kage is listed in the records of Santa Maria de Anima at Rome as being prior of the Hermits of St. William at Marienthal (Strassburg diocese).

The date of the entry is probably 1485 because entries preceding are of that year. He died on his way home from Rome.
Liber confrat., 84.

JACOB KELLER #60, p. 66; #103, p. 113
Jacob Keller, chaplain of Christoph I of Baden, matriculated at the university of Basel 1465/66. He was a native of Ettlingen in Baden.
Wackernagel, 87.

EMERICH KEMEL, O.F.M. p. xiii; p. xxvii; #32, pp. 39f.; #69, p. 76; #186, p. 204; #187, pp. 205ff.
Emerich Kemel is surely the "Emericus de Kaniel de Alemanea, art. D. ord. Minor." listed by Pardi as receiving a doctorate in canon law at Ferrara in 1468. Franciscan documents mention Kemel as vicar of Saxony in 1469, as "commissarius Romanus" in 1473, as recipient of certain dispensations from Sixtus IV for the Franciscan Order in 1477 (N. 1494) and as having been appointed "nuntius apostolicus" by Sixtus in 1478. In 1480 Sixtus gave Kemel authority to preach the crusade against the Turks and to collect money for it by selling indulgences; this authority was renewed 1482 and 1483 and reaffirmed 1484; money collected from these sales was sent to Rome to the head church of the Franciscan Order, Ara Coeli. During the early months of 1482, Kemel was in Strassburg, helping to draft statutes for the Order of the Knights of St. John of Jerusalem at Strassburg. In the spring of the same year Sixtus commissioned Kemel to go to Basel for the trial of Archbishop Andreas Zamometił of Carniola, to see that Andreas was jailed secretly and put on bread and water (N. 351). Also in 1482 Kemel is reported as having preached at Lübeck. He was again at Strassburg in April 1483 and in that year, too, he visited the Metz diocese.
Anal. Francisc., II, 440, 457, 463f., 480-484. *Bullarium*, III, 1415, 1467, 1504, 1574f., 1582f., 1588, 1617, 1621, 1624ff., 1628, 1632, 1681-83, 1715, 1736, 1768, 1832. Grandidier, *Chevaliers*, 58. *Inventaire... St. Thomas*, 46. Pardi, *Titoli*, 48. Dacheux, *Réf.*, 46f., and Stöber, *Neue Alsatia*, 281, n. 2, give only information from the *Lucubraciunculae*.

THOMAS À KEMPIS (HÄMMERLIN, MALLEOLUS) (1380-1471) p. xxx; #232, p. 262
Thomas Hämmerlin, better known as Thomas à Kempis, from his birthplace Kempen on the upper Yssel river, studied at Deventer in the school of the Brethren of the Common Life (1393). He preached at Zwolle and founded the school of the Brethren at the monastery of St. Agnes, where he was canon (1499) and later prior. His authorship of the *Imitiato Christi* (*De contemptu mundi*) was disputed for centuries (N. 137).
Dorlan, "Nouv. études," 338. *Dictionnaire de théol. cath.*, VI (1920), 1313-1330. Jöcher, IV, 1150. Trithemius, *Liber*, folio 100a.

JOHANN KERER (1430-1507) #20, p. 29; #21, p. 30; #86, p. 95; #104, p. 114; #125, p. 146
The son of a weaver, Kerer was born in Wertheim an der Tauber. As a cleric of the Würzburg diocese, he entered the university of Heidelberg in 1451 and received his A.B. in 1453, his A.M. in 1456. In 1457 he became rector of the Latin school in Freiburg and in 1461 professor of philosophy at the university there. In 1474 he was appointed sub-deacon at the cathedral

of Freiburg and rector of *Beata Maria Virgo* (succeeding Kilian Wolf) and, on confirmation of this appointment by Sixtus IV, he was installed in 1475. In the same year he became imperial notary. After obtaining his doctorate of decretals in 1481, Kerer joined the law faculty at Freiburg and was rector of the university in that year, and in the years 1490 and 1492 dean of the law faculty. He was named court chaplain to Archduke Sigismund in 1485 and to Maximilian I in 1490. Bishop Albrecht of Strassburg gave him a chaplaincy in 1486 and in the same year Innocent VIII gave him a canonicate at St. Thomas. In 1493 he was consecrated titular bishop of Adrimentum (Adrymitum, now Susa, in Tunis) and served as suffragan bishop in the Augsburg and Constance dioceses. He established a college at Freiburg and drafted statutes for its administration, for instituting bursaries and fellowships, including promissory notes to be signed by recipients. On his death he left to the college stipends and two houses with furnishings to be used as dormitories.

Bauer, 14, n. 36; 175. Beckmann, 5-10. Dacheux, *Réf.*, 394, n. 3. Dreher, XX, 28ff. Eubel, II, 80, 277f. Mayer, II, 7. Paulsen, "Organization," 415. Riegger, *Amoen.*, 3f.; *Anal.*, 15, 59, 60, 65, 68, 111. Santifaller, 591. Schmidt, *H. L.*, II, 32. Werk, *passim*.

JOHANN KLEIN #47, p. 51; #62, p. 68; #68, p. 75; #69, p. 76; #72, p. 79. The Johann Klein of "Plienswiler," priest of the Strassburg diocese, who, Schott tells us, procured a curacy in the diocese in 1485, may be identical with the Magister Johann Klein mentioned as curate of Zellweiler in 1511 – Bliensweiler is the chief town of the district in which Zellweiler is situated. He may also be identical with the Johann Klein from Constance who received his A.B. degree at Paris in 1473 (at the same time as Schott) and his licentiate in 1474.

Auct., III, 225 (24), 271 (28). Barth, "Pfarreien," 162f.

JOHANN KLITSCH VON RIXINGEN (†1519?) #70, p. 77 (?); #79, p. 85; #96, p. 107; #102, p. 112; #146, p. 160; #148, p. 162; #188, p. 207. Klitsch, a native of Rixingen (about mid-way between Strassburg and Nancy), was a *famulus* and protégé of Schott. In 1485 he was sent off to study – probably to Deventer or Zwolle – in the Lowlands. By 1490 he was at the university of Paris, where he received his A.M. degree in 1492. He may be identical with the "Johannes Nicolavi de Rixingen" who was recommended for an A.B. degree at Paris on 9 February 1491, and he is quite surely the Johann Klitsch, organist at the Strassburg cathedral, whose death in 1519 is mentioned by Gass.

Auct., III, 793, 804. Gass, *Orgues*, 31.

MATTHIAS KOLB (KOLBE, COLBE, COLABY, COLLEBI, KOLBRE) #54, p. 60; #60, p. 66; #103, p. 113; #63, p. 69; #177, p. 198
From Schott's letters we learn that Kolb was in Paris during the period 1484-1487 and that on his way home from Paris with his students in 1487 he stopped in Strassburg. A native of Posen ("de Srvebissin, d. Posnanien ex ducatu incliti ducis et domini Henrici de Slesia"), he was at the university of Paris at the same time as Schott and Müller. He received his A.B. degree in 1471, his licentiate in 1472 and is listed in 1473 as "procurator mag. M. Kolbe" and in 1476 as "receptor" (i.e., he was procurator and "receptor" of his nation). He served as rector of the university and is recorded as being "socius Sorbonicus." In 1495 he was in Rome and is listed among the

"Anima" members as canon of the Pressburg cathedral. In that year he received a benefice and in the following year a perpetual benefice at the parish church of St. Elisabeth in Pressburg. In 1496 he became archdeacon at the Pressburg cathedral and in 1498 was granted a pension as "familiaris papae."
 Auct., III, 169-617, *passim*; 631, n. 1; 871. *Liber confrat.*, 110.

MELCHIOR KUNGSBACH (KÖNINGSBACH, KÜNIGSBACH) (†1508) #102, p. 112(?); #156, p. 171; #157, p. 173
The learned theologian Kungsbach was at one time parish priest at New St. Peter in Strassburg and became canon of St. Thomas in 1483. He was one of the committee sent by Bishop Albrecht to investigate the morals of priests in the Strassburg diocese. Resigning his canonicate in 1495, he entered the Carthusian monastery at Strassburg and served as its twenty-eighth prior 1505-1508.
 Dacheux, *Réf.*, 473. *Inventaire (Spach)*, IV, 229. Passmann, 94. Schmidt, *H.L.*, I, 349.

LADISLAUS OF VESZPRÉM (LAUDISLAUS DE VETEREBUDA?) #19, p. 28; #25, p. 34; #169, p. 189; #170, p. 191; #189, pp. 207f.
Ladislaus, priest in the diocese of Veszprém (at the cathedral?) in Hungary, accompanied Bohuslaus von Hassenstein to Italy and seems to have been Hassenstein's tutor; at least he supervised the boy's activity. In 1481/1482 he became *praepositus* of the cathedral of Veszprém (N. 1345) and is probably identical with the "Ladislaus de Veterebuda" mentioned as *praepositus* in the Veszprém diocese in 1484. It is very likely that he visited Strassburg with Hassenstein in 1482.
 Fabricius, *Bohuslai*, x, 3. *Monumenta Romana Episcopatus Vesprimiensis*, 289. Potuçek, v; xii, n. 15.

THOMAS LAMPERTHEIM (LAMPARTER, LAMPERTIUS, LAMPERTHEN, LAMPACHER; ALSO THOMAS DE ARGENTINA OR STRASSBURG), O.P. #52, pp. 56f.; #125, p. 146; #79, p. 85?
A native of Zabern, Lampertheim entered the university of Heidelberg in 1450 and received the degree of *baccalaureus* in 1452. He served as secular priest and *plebanus* of St. Thomas (Strassburg) and as parish priest of St. Andreas at Andlau before entering the Dominican Order. In 1475 he was prior of the monastery at Chur. In 1482 he was appointed *visitator* of the convent of Engelspforten and in 1483 confessor and vicar of the ejected Clingenthal sisters, with full authority to place them in convents of the order; in this capacity he accepted Obersteigen as a refuge for the sisters and served as *vicarius in temporalibus et spiritualibus* at Obersteigen in 1488. He was *lector* of the convent at Gebweiler and was empowered by the general of the order Salvo Cassetta to accept the convent at Schwarzau which the *Graf* of Rappolstein had constructed for the nuns of Engelspforten. In 1501 the sisters of Reutlingen and of St. Nicolaus (Strassburg) were placed under his authority. Because of his learning, Lampertheim was considered to be an exception among members of the mendicant orders.
 Anal. Francisc., II, 485. Dacheux, *Réf.*, 320, 429f. Glassberger, 485. Glöckler, II, 496. Grandidier, *Nouv. oeuvr.*, II, 556. Knepper, *Schulwesen*, 49f., 87f. *Q.F. Domin.*, VI, 83; VII, 52, 77, 82, 83; X, 23, 130. Riegger, *Amoen.*, 101. Schmidt, *Chapitre*, 163; *H. L.*, I, 23, 259; *Notice... Couvent*,

64. Schöpflin, *Histoire*, 56. Toepke, 265. Trithemius, *Cathalogus*, folio 72a; *Liber*, folio 90a.

JOHANN VON LAUDENBURG, O.F.M. #6, p. 12(?); #32, p. 40; #143, pp. 158f.
From the *Lucubraciunculae* we know that Johann von Laudenburg was an intimate friend of Johann Rot, a friend of Emerich Kemel, a Franciscan and in 1490 a resident of Mainz. He may be identical with Johann Sartoris (Certoris) of Laudenburg in the diocese of Worms who matriculated at Heidelberg in 1472 and received in 1473 an A.B. degree.
   Toepke, 338, 341, 343.

CONRAD LEONTARIUS (LEONTORIUS) (*ca.* 1465-1511) p. xiv; #126, pp. 146f.; #291, p. 311.
Conrad Leontarius, so-called from his birthplace Löwenberg, studied in Italy and France. He entered the Cistercian order and became abbot of the monastery at Maulbronn in Württemberg. He was well-versed in the Scriptures and knew Hebrew, as well as Greek and Latin. His chief activity was teaching but he also worked with Basel printers on editions, wrote poetry and carried on correspondence with Reuchlin, Occo, Gresemund, Wimpheling *et al.* His best known pupil was Bonifatius Amerbach. In 1505 he went to the Begine monastery in Engelthal, where he remained until his death.
   ADB, XVIII, 315. Geiger, *Briefwechsel*, 22, 361. Schmidt, H. L., II, 30. Trithemius, *Cathalogus*, folio 70a; *Liber*, folio 134a. Weislinger, 678. Wiskowatoff, 216.

HOUSE OF LORRAINE

I. REINHARDT, DUKE OF LORRAINE (RENÉ, RENATUS OF LOTHARINGIA) (†1508) #170, p. 190
Reinhardt, son of Frederick of Vaudemont, succeeded Nicholas duke of Calabria as duke of Lorraine; however, Charles the Bold of Burgundy disputed the inheritance and abducted the young Reinhardt with his mother, but was forced by Louis XI to release them. After the death of Charles, Reinhardt claimed his dukedom.
   EB, XVII, 10f. Horning, *Festschrift*, 48f. Raynaldus, 1483. Trithemius, *Ann. Hirs.*, II, 535.

LYNINGEN FAMILY (LYNINGEN-RHENTINGEN, LINANGE-RÉCHICOURT)
The family of the counts of Lyningen is documented from the fourteenth to the eighteenth century. Bishop Wilhelm of Strassburg (1394-1439) had trouble with *Graf* Johann von Lyningen who was guilty of breaking the peace and of seizing property by force. *Graf* Friedrich (1423-1470) was *scholasticus* at the Strassburg cathedral. Another *Graf* Friedrich is listed as canon of St. Thomas in 1699.

1. and 2. GRAF WECKER AND GRAF HANNEMANN (HANNAN) p. xxix, #49, p. 53, #50, pp. 54f.; #51, pp. 55f.; #52, p. 57.
Bishop Ruprecht of Strassburg had such difficulties with these two counts of Lyningen that he obtained from Emperor Friedrich III a mandate to the

Strassburg magistracy to give aid in freeing the lord of Ramstein whom Wecker had imprisoned and in stopping aggression on the highways. Hannemann is mentioned as being an "Auss-Bürger" of Strassburg and as being involved in a quarrel with Hans Jörger to whom he owed money. Both Wecker and Hannemann rode in the retinue of Bishop Albrecht when he entered Strassburg for his coronation in 1479. During the years 1483 to 1485 the two counts provided shelter at Rhentingen for the ejected Clingenthal nuns.

Dacheux, *Eccl. Arg.*, 11; *Réf.*, 320, n. 2. *Inventaire*, I, II, III, *passim*. *Inventaire* (*Brucker*), I, 76; III, 58f., 74. Saladin, 281. Schmidt, *Chapitre*, 278. Schneegans, "Pfingstfest," 204f. Wencker, *Juris*, 111.

VITUS MAELER VON MEMMINGEN (VEIT MÄLER, MELER, MELLER) (*ca.* 1445-1517) *Luc.*, *passim*; cf. special index and general index.

Maeler may be the "Vitus de Alamana" listed as studying at Siena in 1471. The first entry for Maeler in the *Acta bonon.* is 1473, where he is described as "arcium doctor canonicus August."; the second entry in 1478 describes him as "arcium doctor utriusque iuris scholaris" and procurator of the nation. Often entries in the *Acta*... list degrees and benefices acquired later. In the case of Maeler it seems that he received his doctorate in arts between 1473 and 1478; when he became canon of Augsburg is not known, but from the note "Sic" added to the 1473 entry after "August.," one assumes that he was not at that time canon. In December 1478 he resigned as procurator of the German nation and left Bologna, perhaps to return home or to attend another university (Rome?). Writing to Maeler at Rome on 12 March 1480 (#15), Schott addresses him as "Canonum doctor," and writing to Maeler at Pavia on 29 June 1480, Schott addresses him as "Pontificij Iuris et Arcium Doctor" (#17); it appears then that between 1478 and early 1480 Maeler received the degree of doctor of canon law, possibly at Rome. Sometime later he apparently became doctor of both canon and civil law, for Khamm in 1495 lists him as "I.U.D."

By 1480 Maeler was more or less permanently in Rome, first as solicitor in the *Curia*, then as procurator and solicitor of apostolic letters (1482). He acted as procurator for Archduke Sigismund of Austria (from 1481 on), for Bishop Friedrich of Augsburg, for the university of Freiburg (1482) and for Johann Kerer (1494); he became "orator" for Maximilian I in 1501. In 1485 he joined the "Anima" and was made its prior (*Oberprior*) in 1489.

Maeler accumulated many benefices: priest of St. Moritz at Augsburg and a benefice in the Trent diocese (which he resigned almost immediately) in 1483; dean of Jungingen in 1483 or 1484 (#39, #55); *praepositus* of St. Veit at Freising in 1484 (#59, p. 64); priest at Petersthal in 1485; *Praepositus* of Bischofszell in 1489; canon at the Spires cathedral in 1489; canon and archdeacon at the Augsburg cathedral by 1495.

In 1484 Maeler was influential in reforming the Franciscan monastery at Ulm (#55). He established a bursary of 80 florins annually for students from his birthplace Memmingen and gave funds for an "anniversarium" at St. Martin's church in Memmingen.

Acta bonon., 218, 225, 226. Dacheux, *Réf.*, 113. Hämmerle, 115f. Hofmann, II, 297. Khamm, 610. Knod, *Studenten*, #2263. *Liber Confrat.*, 83. Riegger, *Anal.*, 68, 203, 213, 214, 216. Schmidlin, 105, 125, 135, 193. Schmidt, "Notices... P.S.," 309; "Notices... Wolf," 449. Zoepfl, 533.

PAUL MALLEOLUS (HÄMMERLIN) #146, pp. 160f.; #148, pp. 161f.
Malleolus, a native of Andlau, studied and taught at the university of Paris

and was procurator of the German nation there in 1488. He was called home from Paris in 1490 at the death of his good friend Johann Meyger (whose protégé he seems to have been), as we learn from Schott's letter (#148). Apparently he received a benefice thereafter in Andlau, for he is listed as priest of Andlau in 1516. He and Peter Mars collaborated on a commentary to Terence's comedies, which was published at Strassburg in 1503 and in 1506.

Dacheux, *Réf.*, 343. Gesner, 538b. Grandidier, *Oeuvr. hist.*, V, 205-231; *Nouv. oeuvr.*, II, 254f. Jöcher, *Fortsetzung*, IV, 503.

GALEOTTI MANFREDI (†1488)   #121, p. 140
Galeotti was a member of the Manfredi family who became masters of Faenza in the early fourteenth century and remained in power until 1501 when the city was captured by Cesar Borgia and the last legitimate members of the family were thrown into the Tiber. In May 1488 Galeotti Manfredi was assassinated by his jealous wife Francesca Bentivoglio. His brother Frederico was bishop of Faenza; apparently both Galeotti and Frederico were interested in humanistic studies.

Cosenza, III, 2117. *EB*, X, 123.

ANTHONIUS MANLIUS BRITONORIENSIS (BRITENORIENSIS BERTINO-RO) p. xxv; #73, pp. 79f.; #76, p. 83; #86, p. 95.
Anthonius Manlius seems to be identical with the professor of canon law at Bologna whom Mazzetti lists as Giovanni Antonio Bottoni (†1489), canon of San Petronia (1464), teaching 1461-1489, and whom Dallari lists as Io. Ant. de Botonibus and as Ioannesanntonius Botorus, teaching during the same period. Though Schott speaks of Manlius as his Greek teacher, it must be remembered that professors of law taught also literature.

He may also be identical with Antonius de Betonto (Bitonto), O.F.M. of Observance, who taught theology at Ferrara, Bologna and Mantua "after 1440" and wrote among other works a *Summa theologica* and a *Tractatus de causis*...; Betonto is listed by both Jöcher and Fabricius, as well as in the recent supplement to Cosenza's dictionary. One wonders, however, whether Betonto would have lived until 1486 when Schott last mentions Manlius; the phrase "after 1440" above is indefinite.

Cosenza, VI, 20. Dallari, I, 94-115 *passim*. Fabricius, *Biblio. Lat.*, I, 115, 227f. Jöcher, I, 454. Mazzetti (1847), 69, #621.

GALEOTTUS MARCIUS (MARTIUS, MARZI, MARZIO) (ca. 1427-ca. 1490) #278, p. 306
Marcius, a native of Narni, studied at Bologna and did a turn of soldiering before going to Ferrara (1447-1449). While teaching humanities at Padua (1449), he studied medicine. From 1465 to 1468 or 1470 he was director of the royal library at Buda and served as secretary to Matthias I and as tutor to Matthias' natural son János Corvinus. During the periods 1463-65 and 1473-77 he taught poetry and rhetoric at Bologna. Accussed of heresy, he was imprisoned at Venice in 1477, but was soon freed by Sixtus IV who had apparently been his pupil. He is thought to have helped edit Ptolemy's Geography; he compiled a book about the sayings and deeds of Matthias I of Hungary and wrote medical works.

Carlo Calcaterra, *Alma Mater Studiorum l'universitá di Bologna nella storia della cultura e delle civiltà* (Bologna, 1948), 157, 164f. Cosenza, III, 2313f. Mazzetti, 203. "Rotoli," 1475, 1476.

JOHANN MEYGER #7, p. 12
The Johann Meyger, who in 1478 delivered money from Schott, Sr., to young Peter at Bologna, may be identical with Johann Meiger, who at that time was secretary of the city of Strassburg and could have been en route to Rome on official business. Or this Johann Meyger may be identical with the priest Johann Meyger discussed below.
Inventaire, II, 53; IV, 153. *Inventaire (Spach)*, IV, 230.

JOHANN MEYGER (Meiger) (†1490) #87, p. 95; #148, p. 162
A highly educated *magister*, Meyger is mentioned among the learned men of the late fifteenth century. He was parish priest at Blienswiler and, as we learn from Schott, canon at New St. Peter; in 1490 he became *archpresbyter*. He may have been a native of Andlau, because Schott asked him in 1486 to use his influence in securing for Müller a vicarate in Andlau and because his protégé Paul Malleolus came from there. He died at Baden-Baden where he may have gone for a course of treatment at the baths.
Barth, *Handbuch*, 172. Hatt, *Ville*, 457. Strobel, III, 554.

HEINRICH MOSER p. xxv; #95, pp. 106f.; #268 and #269, pp. 300ff.(?)
A native of Zürich, Moser was a fellow student of Schott at Bologna, where he was studying by 1477 and received his doctorate of decretals in 1481. From Schott's letter to him, we learn that in 1486 he was married and both practising and teaching canon law at Constance. He was active there until at least 1496 when he was one of the speakers greeting Hugo, the newly elected bishop of Constance.
Acta bonon., 224. Knod, *Studenten*, #2447.

MÜG FAMILY (MUG, MIEG)
The Mügs – a populous, old patrician Strassburg family of many branches – are mentioned in documents from 1320 to the present; in the late nineteenth century there were many Mügs in upper Alsace, especially at Mülhausen. Peter Müg, Sr., (†1488) served on the city council in 1472 and was knighted in 1482. His two sons Jakob Müg, Sr., of Boofzheim and Matthäus Müg of Mülhausen were founders of the two lines of later Mügs.
Hertzog, 266. Kindler von Knobloch, *Buch*, 206. J. Rathgeber, "Stammbaum der Familie Mug von Boofzheim und Mieg von Mülhausen im Oberelsass," JbGElsLotr, IV (1888), 69. Schadäus, 110. Schneegans, *Église*, 229f., n. 256. Sitzmann, II, 298f. Toepke, 287 (1457).

1. JAKOB (JACOBUS) MÜG, SR., VON BOOFZHEIM (†1498) #156, p. 171
Jakob was the elder son of Peter Müg, Sr., His son Jakob, Jr., married Columba Bettscholt, the daughter of Peter Schott's sister Margred and Wilhelm Bettscholt. Jakob, Jr., is mentioned in 1504 as one of the Strassburg government officials responsible for censoring books published against pope, emperor, etc.
Schöpflin, *Vind. typ.*, 113. Cf. also bibliography above.

2. FLORENCIUS MÜG (†1511) #79, p. 85; #94, p. 105; #168, p. 188; #228, pp. 255f.
Florentius was the son of Matthäus Müg von Mülhausen (†1483) and in 1488 served on the Strassburg city council. He married Merga (Maria) Schott,

Peter Schott's sister. He and Ludovicus (Ludwig) were Strassburg merchants (with a depot in Antwerp, as we learn from Schott); they are probably the brothers ("hos fratres probatissimos viros") who took Schott's letter to Halewin in Bruges (#94, p. 105).

Schmidt, "Notices... P.S.," 312. Straub, 86 (cf. Appendix L). Cf. also bibliography above.

3. LUDOVICUS (LUDWIG) MÜG #79, p. 85; #94, p. 105; #168 p. 188(?)
Ludovicus Müg is not mentioned in the Müg genealogy as described by Rathgeber, but he was apparently a son of Matthäus Müg von Mülhausen. As noted under Florencius above, he and Florencius were in business together. He may be the "alterum affinem" of #168. His name appears in records as giving up his Strassburg citizenship in 1479 and buying it again in 1490, as being involved in litigation 1494-99 and as receiving letters of safe conduct from Maximilian I during those same years. He seems to have kept a calendar or diary of family events, for it is from this that the date of death for Susanna von Cöllen is quoted in Straub, 86 (cf. Appendix L).

Inventaire (*Spach*), I, 108, 109. Wittmer-Meyer, I, 363, #3222; II, 442, #4078.

4. PETER MÜG, JR. (†1507) #156, p. 171
Peter Müg, Jr., may have been a younger son of Matthäus Müg von Mülhausen. He became canon of St. Thomas in 1484 and may be identical with the "Peter Mage," who is recorded in that year as having resigned a canonicate at Old St. Peter and having received a canonicate at St. Thomas.

Kindler von Knobloch, *Buch*, 206. Meister, 128, 137. Schmidt, *Chapitre*, 278. Schneegans, *Église*, 229f., n. 256.

JOHANN MÜLLER (MOLITORIS, MOLATORIS, MULTOR) (†1491) *Luc.*, *passim*. Cf. Special Index and General Index.
Johann Müller of Rastatt in the principality of Baden was a brilliant but impoverished scholar who gained his education by acting as tutor. There is no record of his date of birth, nor do we know when he studied under Dringenberg at the Schlettstadt school; there can be no doubt that he received his early training there, because he is listed among the alumni of the school.

In 1463 he matriculated at the university of Erfurt and obtained his A.B. degree there (probably by 1465). Even though universities accepted students at about age twelve, it is extremely doubtful that Müller was that young when he went to Erfurt. Being poor, he could have attended only as tutor or servitor to a more affluent student and would almost necessarily have had to be somewhat older than twelve. One may assume that at the time he left Erfurt he was in his late teens and mature enough to accept responsibility, else the Schotts would certainly not have entrusted to him their little son.

With young Schott, Müller spent the years *ca.* 1465 to *ca.* fall 1470 at Schlettstadt, where he may have had other pupils to tutor – perhaps young Brant – and may have taught some of the classes. By 4 January 1471 Müller with Schott was at Paris (N. 92). Here in April 1472 he received his licentiate and was master of arts by 21 October when he was elected procurator of the "Alemmania" nation.

In early 1474 (N. 95) he and Schott arrived at Bologna. The first entry (1475) for Müller in the *Acta bonon.* terms him "doctor of arts," while the second entry (1476, when he was serving as procurator of the German nation) and the third entry (1477, when he and his fellow procurator surrendered the nation's effects to the incoming procurators) term him "master of arts from Paris and scholar in canon law." Since the *Acta* entries often list degrees and honors earned subsequently and since Schott first refers to Müller as "Doctor" in late 1478 (#178, p. 199), it would appear that Müller received his doctorate in arts at Bologna sometime during the period January 1477 (when he finished his year as procurator, cf. N. 93, par. 7) and September 1478 (when the plague caused him and Schott to leave, cf. N. 190).

From late 1479, i.e., from the time Schott returned to Bologna without Müller, to 6 September 1490, the last dated letters of Schott, Müller's career can be closely followed in Schott's correspondence, not only in that with Müller but also in that with others, where references to Müller are exceeded in number only by those to Schott's parents. By April 1479 Müller was canon and dean at Baden-Baden (#12, p. 20, also N. 211) and by 2 February 1480 he resigned in favor of Johann Rot the perpetual vicarate at Dambach (#16, p. 24) which he had held since 1470. In June 1483 he was being considered for the post of canon and dean at Pforzheim (#43, p. 49), but he does not seem ever to have received it, for it is never again mentioned (N. 423). In the autumn of that year he went as tutor to Jacob, heir apparent of the principality of Baden, who had been under his care since early 1479, to Paris (#46, p. 51), where Jacob studied until 1486, except for a possible stay of some months in Orléans during 1484 for special courses in imperial law (#55, p. 61). During these years Müller was professor of arts (#84, p. 92; also N. 477) and devoted himself to theology (#74, p. 82). In March 1486 Schott writes that Müller is rector of the university of Paris (#77, p. 84); this passage answers the question in a note to the records of the "Alemmania" nation (*Auct.*, II, 593, n. 3) as to whether it was Johann Müller or Johann Stanton who was elected rector on 16 December 1485 (for presumably the rector then elected would still be serving in March).

Müller and Jacob returned to Baden-Baden in the summer of 1486 (#92, p. 104; #174, p. 195) and had a brief respite before proceeding to Italy. They went first to the university of Padua, but were apparently forced to leave because of the war between Austria and Venice (#101) and go to Ferrara, where on 17 May 1487 Müller received his doctorate in both civil and canon law. By 31 May 1488 they were back in Baden-Baden (#118, p. 138), but not for long. Sometime after 19 June, when Müller is reported as having been at the baths (#119, p. 139), they left again. On 8 August they were in Paris (*Auct.*, III, 679) and from there seem to have travelled to Italy. From late October 1489 to February 1490 (#141, p. 157) they are known to have been in Rome. They came home to Baden-Baden by late August of that year (#151, p. 165). In early September 1490 Müller became canon of Old St. Peter in Strassburg, a post long desired and one Schott had expended much energy to secure (N. 527). Unfortunately, Müller did not enjoy the fruits of his benefice many months and seems to have spent little, if any, time at Old St. Peter, for by Palm Sunday 1491 (27 March) he with Jacob was again in Rome, and there on 29 August of that year he died. He was buried in the "hospital" of Santa Maria de Anima.

From Schott's almost filial love, Hassenstein's admiration, Brant's deep affection and Christoph I of Baden's high regard for Müller, it is evident that he must have had not only a winning personality but a fine, disciplined mind and considerable teaching ability. He was also a scholar and doubtless would have written much had he not been bound by constant obligation to teach and tutor. In 1479 he painted in red the initial letters of a copy of *Summa de casibus conscientiae* which he presented to Martin

Egerstein of Schlettstadt. His diary of his and Jacob's trip to Rome (1489-1490) which included letters of state *et al.* was published along with the *Germania* of Aeneas Silvio Piccolomini in a book of miscellanies (for which Wimpheling wrote an introduction) by Renatus Beck at Strassburg in 1515. The incunabulum in the Strassburg collection entitled: Johannes Molotoris, *Tabula summae theologicae Antonini Florentini* printed by J. Grüninger at Strassburg in 1490, may be his work.

Acta bonon., 220, 222, 403. *Auct.*, III, 161f., 201.f, 217-222 *passim*, 224, 593 (n. 3), 679. Barth, *Handbuch*, 247f., 251. Dacheux, *Réf.*, 353-361, 286f. Freundgen, 110. Geiger, *Briefwechsel*, 22 (XIX). Knod, *Studenten*, #2471. *Liber confrat.*, 247. Pardi, *Titoli*, 80. Riegger, *Amoen.*, 454f. Ristelhuber, 109ff. Sachs, 147. Santifaller, 263. Weech, 223ff. Weissenborn, 299. Wiskowatoff, 25.

THEOBALD VON MÜLNHEIM (Milheym, Mülenheim, Mulnheym, Müllenheim) #113, p. 133
The Theobald Mülnheim whom Schott wished to have continue his studies may be the son of the knight Theobald (Diebolt) Müllenheim who is so often mentioned in Strassburg records of the 1470's and 1480's. He is listed as having matriculated at Heidelberg in 1476 and may be identical either with the canon of New St. Peter whose tomb in that church is described by Grandidier or with the canon of Old St. Peter whose tomb in that church is described by Nanton.

Grandidier, *Mélanges*, 338. Nanton, 10. Toepke, I, 251.

CONRAD MUNTHART (1437-1509) #42, p. 48; #44, p. 49
The Munthart family had come to Strassburg from Offenburg. During the last half of the fifteenth century three Munthart brothers held high positions in the two major collegiate churches of Strassburg. Paul Munthart (†1481), a licentiate in canon law and a learned jurist, was canon of St. Thomas and *praepositus* of New St. Peter; the latter post he resigned in 1480, a year before his death. He held various legal offices in the state and diocese of Strassburg and assembled an excellent legal library which he willed to St. Thomas. His *anniversarium* was celebrated on the date of his death, 19 March, by the choirs of St. Thomas and New St. Peter. Jacob Munthart (†1504) was canon and vice-dean of St. Thomas.

Conrad Munthart succeeded his brother Paul as *praepositus* of New Saint Peter in 1480. He had held a canonicate at St. Thomas since 1465, according to Meister, but according to Schmidt, since 1440. Conrad's year of death is given by Schneegans, who quotes the tomb inscription (now lost) in New St. Peter, as 1509, at age 72; Schmidt gives it as 1500.

Grandidier, *Nouv. oeuvr.*, II, 367f. Horning, *Festschrift*, 49, n. 4. Meister, 131, 135, 143. Schmidt, *Chapitre*, 278; "Notices... P.S.," 249. Schneegans, *Église*, 227, 269. Stein, 128.

JOHANN NEGUILER #64, pp. 69f.
Neguiler, a member of the Carthusian Order at Strassburg, matriculated at the university of Erfurt in 1444.

Weissenborn, I, 199 (4).

JOHANN NIDER (NIEDER, NYDER), O.P. (1380/90-1438) #220, p. 246
Johann Nider, from Isny in Württemberg, was a member of the Dominican

monastery at Colmar by 1400. He studied at Vienna and Cologne and for several years was a travelling preacher. In 1425 he received his doctorate at Vienna and taught there during the periods 1425-1427 and 1436-1438. In 1427 he became prior of the Dominican monastery at Nürnberg and was active in the reform of monasteries. In 1431 he was transferred to Basel and as prior of the Dominicans there took an active part in the Council of Basel. He was sent as a *legatus* to Bohemia. Not only did he preach against the Hussites but he showed excessive rigor as an inquisitor. His most important work is *De formicis moraliter (Formicanus)*.

ADB, XXIII, 641ff.; mentioned XXIV, 743. Barthelmé, 52-530 *passim*. Freher, (under *N*.). K. Schieler, *Magister Johannes Nider aus dem Orden der Prediger = Brüder. Ein Beitrag zur Kirchengeschichte des 15. Jahrhunderts* (Mainz, 1885), 139-171 and *passim*.

JOHANN NIGRI, O.P. #25, p. 33; #36, p. 44; #106, p. 116
Hassenstein gives Nigri the title of *magister* (p. 116), but we have been unable to ascertain where Nigri obtained his degrees; Toepke lists 2 persons by the name of Johann Nigri and Weissenborn lists one. In 1475 Nigri was transferred from Nürnberg to Regensburg to be prior of the Dominicans there. In that year he was also in Rome. His name appears in documents as having served as vicar to the Dominican conventions of 1482 (at Basel) and of 1487. Nigri was already a good friend of Hassenstein when he met Schott at Wildbad in the summer of 1481. He met Schott again in Strassburg in November 1482, probably as he was on his way home to Regensburg from the convention in October at Basel.

Q.F. Domin., VI (1911), 78; VII (1912), 32; X (1914), 3.

ADOLPH OCCO (1447-1503) p. xxviii; #139, p. 155; #150, pp. 163f.
Occo came from a wealthy family in Osterhausen in Friesland. He studied Greek with Reuchlin and was friendly with Johann von Dalberg. His contemporaries thought highly of him both as a physician and as a humanist. Celtis praised his poetry; Geiler and Schott tried to persuade him to write a history of Germany. His patients included Agricola whom he treated in 1476 at Ferrara; bishop of Augsburg, Johann von Werdenberg, to whom he was personal physician in 1486; *Pfalzgraf* Philipp by whom he was named personal physician in 1488; and Archduke Sigismund of Tyrol and Austria whom he treated at Innsbruck in 1491. He may also have been personal physician to the new bishop of Augsburg, Friedrich von Zollern, who succeeded Johann von Werdenberg in 1486, cf. #139, p. 155, which places him in Augsburg by 1489, five years earlier than the date given in *ADB*. For his patients when they died Occo composed epitaphs in Greek and Latin. For Agricola he wrote a eulogy in both languages.

ADB, XXIV, 126f. Allen, 313. Dreher, XIX, 15. Hartfelder, *Briefe*, 9. Schmidt, *H. L.*, II, 30. Velden, 92, 130ff., 255.

JOHANN ORTWIN, O.P. (†1514) #164- #166, pp. 181-186.
Ortwin from Vendenheim is first mentioned in 1465 as one of the preachers opposed to reform who was in the convent of St. Agnes at Strassburg when an attempt to reform the convent was foiled by the prior of the Strassburg Dominicans, Johann Wolfhart, by barring the street to the reforming sisters. Ortwin also carried to the general of the Dominican order, Marcialis Auribelli, at Paris a letter from Wolfhart attacking the Provincial Peter Wellen. To settle the dispute Auribelli came to Strassburg. In 1470 and 1471 Ortwin is

registered at the university of Freiburg, where he probably received his doctorate in theology and where he taught as professor of theology. He served as prior of the Dominican monastery at Freiburg. In 1477 he was appointed suffragan to the bishop of Strassburg and was given the title of bishop of Mathone (N. 1167). In 1490 he is mentioned as being prior of the Dominican monastery at Strassburg and as buying his citizenship.

That Ortwin was an avid Thomist is apparent from his letters to Schott. Indeed, these are the only extant examples of writings which made his contemporaries consider him unusually well-educated for a mendicant. His will leaving his property to the Dominican monastery at Strassburg was contested by his family, but the outcome of the case is not known. He was buried in the monastery church, now part of the wall of the Temple Neuf.

Bauer, 186. Dacheux, *Eccl. arg.*, 15f. Dacheux, *Fragments*, VI, 220. Eubel, II, 277. Knepper, *Schulwesen*, 49f. Meister, 127. Schmidt, *Chapitre*, 163; *H.L.*, II, 13; *Notice... couvent*, 59f., 64. *Q.F. Domin.*, III, 126, 140; VI, 90. Sitzmann, II, 408. Wimpheling, *Cat. ep.*, 121. Wittmer-Meyer, II, 444.

JOHANN OTMAR (OTHMAR, OTTMAR) pp. xix, xx
Otmar from Reutlingen is listed as a master of arts in the matriculation records of Tübingen, but it is not known where he received that degree. He began work as a printer in Reutlingen in 1482; in 1497 he went to Tübingen and began publishing there in 1498. In 1502 (or 1501) he went to Augsburg and was active there until 1513.

ADB, XXI, 548ff. Voulliéme (1922), 136f.

ANDREAS OUDORP (ONDORP, ANDORP) (†ca. 1501) #115, p. 135; #116, p. 136
Oudorp, a native of Alkmaar in Holland, studied at the university of Basel in 1483, receiving the degrees of doctor of arts and doctor of medicine. In 1484 and 1491 he served as rector of the university, and in 1485 he was second in the list of professors of medicine. During 1488 he was for a time in Strassburg and went from there to Basel, where between the years 1488-1492 he acquired the degree of bachelor of theology (1491) and was city physician. Either in Bologna or in Rome he obtained his doctorate in theology and in 1498 was recorded in Rome as doctor of theology, arts and medicine. He held the office of *poenitentiarius* at St. Peter in Rome and was canon of Liége.

Athen. Raur., 168, 460. Wickersheimer, 25.

PAULUS IURISCONSULTUS #181, p. 201
According to Jöcher, *Fortsetzung*, V, 1961, the name Paulus Iurisconsultus was applied to Paulus Julius, a philosopher and jurist of the second century, who was active in Padua and Rome and served as councillor to Septimus Severus and Antoninus Caracalla. He wrote many works on Roman law, some of which are still extant. (Jöcher, III, 1329, for Paulus Julius).

It is possible that Schott was referring to Paulus de Castro or Cachensis (†ca. 1420/37), a famous law teacher for over 50 years in Florence, Siena, Bologna and Padua, who wrote legal commentaries (Jöcher, III, 1325).

RAYMUND PERAUDI (RAIMOND BERAUDI; RAYMUND GURCENSIS, RAYMUND VON GURK) #146, p. 160; #148, pp. 161f.
By birth a Frenchman, Peraudi went to Rome where he worked as *protonotar*

and *orator* in the *Curia*. He held the benefice of archdeacon at Xanten. In 1488 he became procurator and *orator* at the *Curia* for Emperor Friedrich III; in 1493 he was created cardinal by Pope Alexander VI; and in 1501 he was elected bishop of Gurk (Klagenfurt). His contemporaries esteemed him highly as a man of pure morals and virtuous living. He is perhaps best remembered for his activity in selling indulgences about which he wrote *Resolution betr. den Ablass des goldenen Jahres (en bas allemand)*: [*H*]*yr volget nae eyn seker Resolutzye*, which was published by Johann Prüss at Strassburg in 1500.

Having been appointed commissioner of indulgences by Pope Innocent VIII, Peraudi crossed the Alps to collect money for fighting the Turks by the sale of indulgences; in 1486 and 1490 he was at Strassburg, in 1488 in France, in 1489 at the diet in Frankfurt. So successful was he that his supply of indulgences was exhausted by 1488. Specklin notes that at Strassburg in 1486 he collected large sums of money and that to obtain an indulgence for daily sins one paid five *blapperts* ("[für] taegliche sünd gab einer 5 blappert"). Nicolaus von Siegen (1488) speaks of the efficacy of the indulgences: "Iam dicunt seculares et clerici concubinarii: 'iam volumus audacter et libere peccare, quia de facile absolvi possumus'."

In the year of jubilee 1500 Alexander VI again sent Peraudi north to collect money by selling indulgences. Emperor Maximilian I attempted to prevent his entering German lands, but without success. These indulgences – apparently even more liberal than before – were interpreted by the well-known preacher of indulgences Johann von Pfalz as not only forgiving sins already committed but also any committed in the future. With each indulgence the buyer was given a letter saying that he would not go to purgatory no matter where or when he died. The scope of Peraudi's undertaking may be realized from the salutation of his letter sent from Strassburg in 1502: "ad omnem Germaniam, Daciam, Sueciam, Norwegiam, Frisiam, Prussiam, omnesque et singulas illarum Provincias, civitates, terras et loca eciam sacro Romano Imperio in ipsa Germania subiecta." (The 4-page text of the letter is in Riegger, *Anal.*, 311ff.).

ADB, XIV, 471 (article on Johann von Pfalz). Chmel, 758. *Chronicon Ecclesiasticum Nicolae de Siegen O.S.B.*, edited by Franz X. Wegerle (Jena, 1855) = *Thüringische Geschichtsquellen*, II, 479. Eubel, II, 23, 64, 76, 156. Gass, *Blätter*, 20. Geiger, *Briefwechsel*, 77 (letter of Peraudi to Reuchlin). Hofmann, II, 134. Khamm, 303. Nagl, 21. Pastor, II, 555, 611; III, i, 258f., 378. Saladin, 300. Santifaller, 588. Specklin, 46. Trithemius, *Ann. Hirs.*, II, 536. Zoepfl, 495, 501.

PHILIPP II, COUNT PALATINE (PFALZGRAF) (†1509) #231, p. 258
Philipp, who had been adopted as heir by his paternal uncle Friedrich I (*der Siegreiche*), became *Pfalzgraf* in 1481. During his reign, humanism, already given impetus by Friedrich and nurtured by Johann Dalberg, bishop of Worms, flourished at the university of Heidelberg. Philipp's endeavor to gain Bavaria-Landshut which had been bequeathed to his son Rupert (†1504) came to naught when he lost the war of succession to Albrecht III of the Bavaria-Munich line.

E.B., XX, 595. Raynaldus, 1481.

STEPHAN PISO #107, p. 118; #108, p. 120
Piso came from Siebenbürgen in Hungary. A close friend of Hassenstein, he is doubtless the "alium Pannonium studiosissimum virum" mentioned by Schott (#173, p. 194) as a fellow student at Bologna. He must also have been at Ferrara, for he was a witness when Hassenstein obtained his doctorate

there. From a letter to him written by Hassenstein on 16 April 1491, on board ship off the Peloponnesus, we know that he was left in charge of Hassenstein's library during the latter's absence on his trip. Piso was a poet laureate and a member of the learned society of Siebenbürgen. He died at an early age, as we learn from the epitaph composed for him by Hassenstein.

Cornova, 31. Jöcher, *Fortsetzung*, VI, 288. Fabricius, *Bohuslai*, fol. 65f., 66f. Pardi, *Titoli*, 61. Potuček, vi, xiii (n. 28), 17f., 18f.

POPES

1. Innocent VI (reigned 1352-1362) #165, p. 183

2. Pius II (reigned 1458-1464) #36, p. 43

3. Sixtus IV (reigned 1471-1484) p. xxix; #32, pp. 39f.; #52, pp. 56f.; #53, pp. 58f.; #80, p. 86; #158, p. 173; #159, p. 174; #160, p. 175; #161, pp. 175f.

4. Innocent VIII (reigned 1484-1492) #5, p. 11; #80-#82, pp. 86-90; #162, p. 176; #163, p. 177; #167, pp. 186ff.; #208, p. 216 (?); #230, p. 257

GOTTFRIED QUINCKENER (GEOFFREY QWINCKER) #151, p. 165; #152, p. 165
Quinckener of Saarburg is mentioned as episcopal chancellor of the Strassburg diocese from 1475 to 1491.

Inventaire, IV, 34, 58. Stenzel, "Gerichte," 235.

RABANUS #1, p. 9
The "Rhabanus" whom Wimpheling cites as an example of the learned men allotted in former times to Germany may be Hrabanus Maurus (776-856), the abbot of Fulda and archbishop of Mainz (847-856) whom the humanists greatly admired. Reuchlin edited a work of his: *Magnentii Rabani Mauri de laudibus sancte crucis opus* (Pforzheim, 1503), and inserted into the edition a poem he wrote to Hrabanus.

ADB, XXVII, 66ff., Geiger, *Briefwechsel*, 83. Trithemius, *Cathalogus*, folio 5b; *Liber*, folio 43b.

Another Rabanus of whom Wimpheling might have been thinking is Rabanus bishop of Spires (1396-1438) and archbishop of Trier (1430-1439). He was educated at Heidelberg and served as court chancellor to *Pfalzgraf* Ruprecht. He is mentioned by Schott (#80) as having obtained papal authority to allow non-noble scholars to become canons. He is noted in the

Inventaire (1397) as asking the city of Strassburg for free passage of his wine along the Rhine.
   ADB, XXVII, 74ff. *Inventaire*, III, 101; IV, 44.

PHILIPP VON RAVENSTEIN #118, p. 138
Philipp von Ravenstein is mentioned in a letter of state written by Friedrich Bock from Ghent in 1488 to the city of Strassburg. Ravenstein was a small county east of Cleves on the River Maas; counts of Ravenstein and St. Pol in 1465 were in command of a detachment of Burgundian troops fighting against Louis XI.
   Calmette, 174. Wencker, *Juris*, 37.

JACOB REIFFSTECK (†1490) #145, p. 160; #149, p. 163; #151, p. 165; #152, p. 166; #153, p. 168; #154, p. 170.
Jacob Reiffsteck was canon and *custos* of St. Thomas and canon of Old St. Peter. As we learn from Schott, Reiffsteck died either in the night of 24 August 1490 or very soon thereafter (Schmidt errs in giving the year as 1489), and his funeral was held on 29 August. It was his canonicate at Old St. Peter to which Müller succeeded. In his will Reiffsteck set up a prebend for a *summissarius* at Old St. Peter; provisions of the will were carried out 9 May 1491 by the executors among whom were his brother Peter, Conrad Hammelburger (procurator of the cathedral *fabrica*), Bishop Albrecht and Thomas Wolf, Sr.
   Dacheux, *Réf.*, 359, n. 1. Schmidt, *Chapitre*, 273.

PETER REIFFSTECK #145, p. 160; #147, p. 161
Peter Reiffsteck, brother of Jacob Reiffsteck, was canon of Old St. Peter. From Schott we learn that he was very ill in May 1490 but recovered under the care of Johann Widmann. He is quite certainly the "brother of Jacob" mentioned in #149, p. 163. He was one of the executors of Jacob's will.
   Dacheux, *Réf.*, 359, n. 1.

CASPAR DE REIN (GASPAR DE RENO, ZU RHEIN) #170, p. 190
Caspar de Rein matriculated at the university of Heidelberg in 1452 and at the university of Basel in 1460. In 1479 he was elected bishop of Basel and served in that office until 1502. His successor was Christoph von Uttenheim.
   Eubel, II, 102. Toepke, I, 269. Wackernagel, 6.

JOHANN REUCHLIN (RÖCHLIN, JOHANNES CAPNION) (1450/1455-1522)
p. xiii; p. xv; #10, pp. 17, 18; #290, p. 311.
Reuchlin, Melanchthon's great-uncle, was born at Pforzheim. Having received his early training at Schlettstadt under Dringenberg, he matriculated at Freiburg in May 1470 and in 1473 accompanied to Paris the third son of Karl I of Baden whose name was Karl and who in 1496 became bishop of Utrecht. In Paris Reuchlin studied under Johann Heynlin and met Agricola; he must also have met Schott and Müller there, for he was in Paris by 1 March 1473, months before Schott and Müller left. In 1474 he went to Basel (as did Johann Heynlin); here in 1475 he received his A.B. degree, in 1474 his A.M. and studied Greek. He was still at Basel in late 1478, as we know from Schott's letter of 12 December 1478, although Geiger claims that he went to

Orléans in early 1478. He became *baccalaureus* in law 1479 at Orléans, studied at Poitiers, where in 1481 he received his licentiate, and then returned to Germany. He went to Tübingen to teach but was employed by *Graf* Eberhard of Württemberg as translator and accompanied him to Italy and Rome in early 1482. On their return from Italy, Reuchlin was appointed to Eberhard's privy council and settled as a lawyer in Stuttgart. He became a doctor of laws and married. In 1486 he was sent as envoy by Eberhard to the diet at Frankfurt, when Maximilian was elected King of the Romans, and went to Aachen for the coronation. In 1490 he accompanied Eberhard to Italy a second time. At Eberhard's death, he left Württemberg for Heidelberg, where he was councillor to *Pfalzgraf* Philipp and supervisor of education for Philipp's sons. *Ca.* 1498 he was sent to Rome. When Maximilian deposed the duke of Württemberg Eberhard the Younger, and made Ulrich ruling duke, Reuchlin returned to Stuttgart, but left for Ingolstadt in 1519 where he taught Hebrew. In 1521 he went to Tübingen.

Reuchlin was not only among the first German humanists to teach Greek, but he was the first German humanist of Christian faith to know Hebrew. Because he published a Hebrew grammar, he was attacked by the reactionary Pfefferkorn, who wanted to destroy all Hebrew books. In the battle of words that ensued Reuchlin was excommunicated. His supporters with their letters (*Clarorum virorum epistulae*) caused the sentence of excommunication to be rescinded, but Reuchlin did not live to hear himself cleared.

ADB, XXVIII, 785-799. Cave, 122. Dacheux, *Fragments*, IV, part ix, 70. *Epistulae illustrium virorum ad Reuchlinem* (Tübingen, 1514), folio e. Erhard, II, 147, 460. Geiger, *Briefwechsel*, 6, 9, 22, 27; *Reuchlin*, 9f., 18ff., 23, *passim*. Gesner, 390. GGr^2, I, 413. Hermelink, *Matrikeln*, 39. Pantaleon, part iii, 23. Schmidt, "Notices... P.S.," 339. Trithemius, *Cathalogus*, folio 61a; *Liber*, folios 133b f.

BEATUS RHENANUS (BEATUS BILD) (1485-1547) p. xxix
Beatus, the only son of Anthonius Rhenanus from Rheinau in Alsace (hence the appellation Rhenanus), attended the Schlettstadt school under Crato Hoffmann von Udenheim and Hieronymus Gebweiler. From 1503 to 1507 he studied at the university of Paris. He learned Greek at Basel and applied himself to the art of printing which he studied for a time with Lazarus Schürer in Strassburg. He was a friend of Erasmus and Peutinger. As a critical historian he had connections with Celtis because of the latter's work on the prehistory of the Germans. He planned a history of great scope, beginning with the classical period. Among his contributions to the historical field are editions of the Roman historians and his own works: *Vita Geileri*, *Rerum Germanicarum Libri III*, and a commentary to Tacitus' *Germania*. From 1527 on he seems to have lived in Schlettstadt, studying and collecting books. He was ennobled in 1523 by Emperor Charles V.

ADB, XXVIII. *NDB*, I, 682f. Grandidier, *Nouv. oeuvr.*, II, 46-51. Hertzog, vii, 34f.

THEODORICH RIBYSEN (RIBISEN, RIBYSE) (†ca. 1503) #70, p. 77; #154, p. 169
Ribysen, as we learn from Schott, held one of six benefices reserved for non-noble scholars at the cathedral of Spires and was skilled in herbology. He also held a canonicate at New St. Peter in Strassburg.

Dacheux, *Réf.*, 342. Meister, 132. Santifaller, 645.

JOHANN RIEDNER (RIDNER) #56, p. 62
A native of Ludersheim near Altdorf (near Nürnberg) and a peripatetic humanist-poet, Riedner attended the university of Bologna, where he is entered in the *Acta bonon.* for 1473 and 1477, where he received his doctor's degree in canon law and where he met Schott and Hassenstein. In 1479/80 he was at the university of Krakow, in 1480 at Rostock, where he is entered as "poeta honoratus," and in 1482 at Erfurt, where he matriculated "gratis ob reverenciam universitatis huius et rectoris studii Maguntini." In March 1484 he became professor of rhetoric and poetry at Ingolstadt, a position he held at least until 1494. In 1495 Hassenstein wrote him a somewhat jocular letter to congratulate him on his marriage "at the age of a grandfather." Because he prevented Celtis from securing a position at Ingolstadt, Celtis called him "vetulus poeta."

Acta bonon., 218, 225. Bauch, 56ff. Ellinger, "Humanisten," II, 7:2. Fabricius, *Bohuslai*, folios 55b, 56, 57b f. Jöcher, *Fortsetzung*, VI, 2124. Knod, *Studenten*, #3054. Potuček, 126f. Weissenborn, I, 394 (27).

GUILLAUME DE ROCHEFORT (GUILLERMUS DE RUPEFORT) (1433-1492) p. xxix; #49, pp. 52ff.; #50, p. 54; #51, p. 56
Rochefort, a doctor of laws, served under the dukes John the Good and Charles the Bold of Burgundy and is said to have originated the geographical unit Franche Comté. In 1474 he prevented the Swiss and Germans from attacking Burgundy by giving them money. After the death of Charles the Bold in 1477, he became councillor to Louis XI and in 1483 was made chancellor of France.

Dacheux, *Réf.*, 321ff. *Nouvelle Biographie Générale*, ed. M. Hoeffer, 46 vols. (Paris 1857-1866), XLII, 457. *Universal=Lexikon*, XXXII (1742), 137.

NICOLAUS ROESLIN, O.S.B. (†1492) #43, p. 48; #46, p. 51; #59, p. 65; #62, p. 68
Roeslin, from Elchingen, is given the title "professor." He served as abbot of the Benedictine abbey of Ottobeuren in Bavaria 1479-1492. After his election some of the dissident brothers elected a rival abbot, Wilhelm Steudlin, but he was never confirmed in office.

Lindner, 91.

JOHANN ROT, THE CLERIC (†ca. 1493) *Luc., passim*; cf. special index and general index.
Johann Rot, a native of Strassburg, studied at Paris at the same time as Schott and received his A.B. degree there in 1473. In 1474 he became *licentiatus* and by August 1475, when he was elected procurator of the "Alemmania" nation, is addressed as *magister*. Apparently he left Paris in late 1477 or early 1478 to return to Strassburg (#9, p. 15). In 1480 he succeeded Johann Müller in the post of perpetual vicar at Dambach (#16, p. 24), a post which he resigned in 1482 after he became parish priest at the altar of St. Laurentius in the Strassburg cathedral. He was a close friend of Geiler and Friedrich von Zollern, whose enthronement as bishop of Augsburg in 1486 he attended with Geiler and Schott. Considered an authority on church ceremony and ritual, he revised the books of ceremonies and rituals for the Strassburg cathedral. As *vicarius in poenitencialibus* for Bishop Albrecht (#223, p. 252), he stated the case of the grain loans (#168, p. 188; #213, p. 226) to ascertain whether usury was involved. He was responsible for ordering the mural painted in the St. Laurentius chapel

which aroused the ire of the mendicant orders, particularly the Franciscans (#143, pp. 158f.). In 1490 Rot resigned his secular position as parish priest of St. Laurentius in the cathedral to enter the Carthusian Order (#148, p. 162). His death – not earlier than sometime in 1493 – is mentioned by Geiler in *Emeis.*

Auct., III, 225, 271f., 307-317. Barth, *Handbuch*, 274f., 1421, 1450. Braun, III, 101. Dacheux, *Réf.*, 411. Dreher, XVIII, 10f., 27f.; XX, 4. Hartmann, #27. *Inventaire*, IV, 155. Knepper, *Schulwesen*, 115f. Pfleger, *Pfarrei*, 250f. Schmidt, *H. L.*, I, 345; II, 5; "Notices... P.S.," 312. Sitzmann, II, 614. Steichele, 148, 167f. Stenzel, 68.

JOHANN ROT, THE PROCURATOR #162, pp. 176f.; #163, pp. 177ff.
This Johann Rot (confused by Schmidt, *H. L.*, I, 345, n. 23 with the cleric Johann Rot above) was not a native of Strassburg. He received his citizenship in 1479 but was not required to pay the usual fee, presumably because of his position as procurator of the Strassburg ecclesiastical tribunal. He was married and had several children. In his capacity as procurator, he is cited in 1478 as harassing a certain Peter Löbel whose friends requested the Strassburg magistracy to give him a safe conduct; in 1484-1485 he was involved in a libel case with the Dunzenheims.

Dacheux, *Réf.*, 413f. *Inventaire*, IV, 55. Wittmer-Meyer, I, 363. Cf. also N. 1157.

ADOLF RUSCH (RAUSCH, RUSCUS) (*ca.* 1435-1489) p. xiii; p. xxx; #16, p. 25; #63, p. 69; #65, p. 71; #78, pp. 84f; #117, pp. 136f.; #122, pp. 140f.; #130, pp. 149ff.; #135, p. 153; #183, p. 202; #245, p. 281
Adolf Rusch of Ingweiler, probably the same Adolf Rusch who was clerk to the nobles of Lichtenberg and bought Strassburg citizenship in 1479, was a humanist, an important Strassburg printer and a book and paper dealer. He is claimed to have been the first to use Roman type and has been identified with the "R" printer of Strassburg. He may have attended the university of Paris and seems to have learned the printing trade under Mentelin and not in Basel, as Schmidt assumes on the basis of his gifts to the Basel Carthusians, for – as Voulliéme points out – Basel had no printing at that time. He began printing between the years 1464 and 1467 and was active until his death.

Both Rusch and Martin Schott married daughters of Johann Mentelin; Rusch's wife Salome must have been the elder daughter, because she and Rusch inherited Mentelin's press in 1477. After Rusch's death Salome married Philip Sturm who, though not it seems a printer, managed the press until his death, presumably in 1516, when Salome's nephew Johann Schott (q.v.) took it over.

Rusch was active in publishing manuscripts. In 1470 he himself stated that he had published editions of Terence and Valerius Maximus. Among the editions ascribed to him are an *Imitatio Christi* and a large Bible of *ca.* 1480, *Biblia latina cum glossa ordinaria Walfridi Strabonis...*, said to have been a "chef d'oeuvre" of the time. He was preparing an illustrated edition of Vergil when he died on 26 May 1489. His friends included Brant, Geiler, Wimpheling, Agricola, the Basel printer Johann Amerbach, Schott, *et al.*

ADB, LIII, 646-650. Allen, 314f. Bogeng, 281. Grandidier, *Nouv. oeuvr.*, II, 427. Hartfelder, *Briefe*, 31f. Hartmann, if., 3, 8, 13f., 15f., 16f., 18f. Hawkins, 15f. Ritter, *Histoire*, 45-50. Schmidt, *H. L.*, I, 72, 181; II, 23, 31; "Notices... P.S.," 250; *Bibliotheken...*, 100-104. Schöpflin,

Vind. typ., 100. Sitzmann, II, 627. Straub, *Geschichtskalender*, 286. Voulliéme, 104. Wittmer-Meyer, I, 363.

JOHANN GASPAR SALA (GIOVANNI GASPARO DELLA SALA) (†1511) #71, p. 77; #173, p. 194
Sala, son of the famous doctor Bornio of Bologna and pupil of Guarinus, received his A.B. in 1460. He was professor of civil law (1460-1463) and canon law (1464-1511) at Bologna and wrote legal commentaries.
Cosenza, IV, 3143f. Mazetti, 276.

WOLFGANG SCHENCKER (SCHENCK) p. xix
Schencker began printing at Erfurt in 1499 and printed 15 works to 1500. Nothing is known of his life except that he was a native of Leipzig and matriculated at Erfurt in 1502. He is important in the development of printing, because he was the first German printer to use Greek type to any extent.
Voulliéme (1922), 63f.

HEINRICH SCHONLEBEN (SCHÖNLEBEN) #74, p. 81
Schonleben was already active as a procurator at the *Curia* in Rome by 1477 when he is listed as a member of Santa Maria de Anima. He appears to have been a canon at Eichstätt in 1478 or 1479. He sponsored Conrad Munthart as *praepositus* of New St. Peter and succeeded to the canonicate left vacant at St. Thomas by the death of Paul Munthart in 1481. He is given the title *magister*, but where he received his training we do not know.
Liber confrat., 105. Meister, 118, 123, 131, 136, 137. Schmidt, *Chapitre*, 278; *Notices... Wolf*, 448f. Schneegans, *Église*, 227. Stenzel, 71.

SCHOTT FAMILY p. xxiii
Hertzog lists two branches of the Schott family, one at Hagenau ("genannt Waldel") and one at Strassburg. These two branches were related but had different coats-of-arms. Kindler von Knobloch lists, in addition to these Schotts: 1) a Schott family of two branches, one at Arnoltzheim and one at Schafftolsheim, with a coat-of-arms different from those above; 2) an upper Alsatian noble family of two branches, the Geer (Gyre, Gyrelin, Geyer) branch and the Giersberg branch, with a coat-of arms unlike those of any Schotts already mentioned. This family which flourished in the fourteenth century used Schott as a secondary name, e.g., "Johannes Schott gyr, Ottemann von Giersberg genannt Schötin." Whether the three different Schott families were interrelated is not documented.
    As indicated above, the Schotts of Strassburg belonged to one original family, but just what degree of relationship existed between the two heads of Schott families in the late fifteenth century, namely Peter Schott, Sr.' and Friedrich Schott, is not known.
    Dacheux, *Réf.*, 285. Friese, II, 105. Hertzog, vi, 2, 203; ix, 163. Horning, *Festschrift*, 36. Kindler von Knobloch, *Der alte Adel im Oberelsass*, 27; *Buch*, 330f. Schmidt, *H. L.*, II, 2ff.; "Notices... P.S.," 241ff. Schöpflin, *Alsatia*, 356. Straub, 80-88 (cf. Appendix L). Weislinger, 681, 685, 687.

1. ANNA SCHOTT pp. xi, xxif., xxiv, xxvii, 357f.
Anna was the youngest daughter of Peter Schott. Sr., and Susanna von Cöllen. The exact dates of her life are not given in records; Sitzmann's

modern biographical dictionary of Alsace has the date of her birth as "*ca.* 1450," but a date in the late 1450's is much more likely, for doubtless her three elder sisters were born during the period: very late 1440's, or early 1450's to mid 1450's. She may have been younger than her brother, who was born in July 1460, but since she seems to have entered the convent of St. Agnes in 1471 (N. 83, last paragraph), the probability is that she was older. When her brother wrote to her from Bologna in February 1476, she had been in the convent some time. Her last known work was dated *ca.* 1500.

According to accounts, Anna was very learned and not only wrote but spoke excellent Latin. One questions Schmidt's assertion (*H. L.*, II, 29) that her brother completed her education and taught her Latin, because from *ca.* 1466 to 1481, i.e., from about age six to twenty-one, Peter was in Strassburg for only short periods of time, except for the break in his study at Bologna from fall 1478 to fall 1479; at that time, however, Anna was already in the convent. Weislinger speaks very highly of her learning and apparently considers her equal in importance to Heradis von Landsperg, the twelfth-century abbess of the Alsatian convent Hohenburg, author of the *Hortus deliciarum*.

On one occasion Anna wrote to Maximilian about the humble vestments of the convent sisters; on another she delivered before him a Latin address on behalf of the convent, which thereupon was granted special privileges.

In Weislinger's library was a book of verse prayers compiled in 1480 by Anna. At the beginning of the book (since lost) was the poem below, of which some interested person made a copy and which Straub took down from that or a later copy thereof. If the poem was composed by Anna, it is the only extant piece of her writing.

> Loss den eigen willikeit,
> Blibe veste in Widerwertigkeit,
> Durchbrich die Ungestorbenheit,
> So wirt dir fliehen lieb und leit,
> Nit such zu vil ergetzlichkeit,
> So ist din Hertz wol bereit
> In göttlicher Heimlichkeit.
> Des helf uns Jesus in euuigkeit.   (Straub, 87)

Also in Weislinger's library was Anna's little book (since lost) composed 1480 on the Passion of Christ, a series of meditations on the texts John 12:24 and John 15:1. This work Weislinger describes as "sehr sauber... sehr geistreich und schriftmässig geschrieben."

Among the manuscripts in the Strassburg city library before 1870 was Anna's work of at least 175 folios on the lives of the saints.

Dacheux, *Réf.*, 285, 286, 425 (n. 1), 426f. Grandidier, *Nouv. oeuvr.*, II, 483. Hatt, *Ville*, 48, 425f. Knepper, *Schulwesen*, 99. Piton, I, 32. Schmidt, *H. L.*, II, 3, 29. Sitzmann, II, 723. Straub, 80, 83, 84, 86, 87. Weislinger, 679, 680, 681, 685, 687, 780. Wencker, *Arch.*, 428.

2. CLAUS SCHOTT #20, p. 29
Claus (Nicolaus) Schott, probably the "Vetterclaus" mentioned in #20, is named in an entry of Reichard's genealogy as having served in the Strassburg city council as a representative of the grain guild in 1500.

Dacheux, *Réf.*, 297. Straub, 83.

3. JOHANN SCHOTT (1477-*ca.* 1550) p. xixf.; p. 354
Johann, son of the Strassburg printer Martin Schott, received humanistic

training at the universities of Freiburg, Heidelberg (where he obtained his bachelor of arts degree in 1493) and Basel. At the end of 1499, on the death of his father, he came home to take over the Schott press. After two years he left and set up shop in Freiburg but returned to Strassburg in 1504. From information in Straub, it appears that in 1516 he took over the management of his grandfather Mentelin's press for his aunt Salome Mentelin on the death of her second husband Philipp Sturm (cf. Straub, 84, in Appendix L). Perhaps he inherited the press after Salome died.

Johann continued the Schott tradition of illustrating books with woodcuts and is credited with printing the first physiological pictures of the human body and skeleton, as well as with the first scientific illustrations of plants. During his career as printer 1500-1548, 150 books are known to have issued from his press. He never deviated from his firm conviction that his grandfather Johann Mentelin had invented the art of printing.

ADB, XXXII, 402-404. Grandidier, *Nouv. oeuvr.*, II, 483f. Hatt, *Ville*, 48. Hertz-Barach, 4 and "Tafel" II. Ritter, *Histoire*, 170-186. Schmidt, *H. L.*, II, 2 (n. 2), 3; "Notices... P.S.," 242; *Bibliotheken*, 121. Schöpflin, *Vind. typ.*, 101f. Sitzmann, II, 719f. Straub, 84. Toepke, I, 403. Voulliéme, 114. Wackernagel, I, 248.

4. MARGRED SCHOTT p. xxiv
Margred, the eldest child of Peter Schott, Sr., and Susanna von Cöllen, was first married to Wilhelm Bettschold who once served as mayor of Strassburg. The Bettscholds, an old Strassburg family later ennobled, numbered among their members mayors, as well as canons and deans of the collegiate churches. Margred and Wilhelm Bettschold had two children, a son Eucharius and a daughter Columba, whose first husband was Jacob Müg, Jr., and whose second husband was Caspar Zorn von Bulach, *eques auratus*. After Bettschold's death, Margred married a man named Dolden, of whom we have found no other mention in records.

Dacheux, *Réf.*, 285ff. Kindler von Knobloch, *Buch*, 33. Schmidt, *H. L.*, 3. Straub, 86. Wencker, *Arch.*, 428. Weislinger, 681.

5. MARIA (MERGA) SCHOTT (†1524) p. xxiv
Maria, the second child of Peter Schott, Sr., and Susanna von Cöllen, married Florentius Müg. Their children were:
1. Peter Müg who married Margred Dedinger
2. Florentius who died in infancy
3. Daniel who was mayor and a member of the *Dreizehner*; he first married Clara Prechter, then Margretha Dolden.
4. Maria who died in infancy
5. Veronica who married Jacob Ingold.

Dacheux, *Réf.*, 285ff. Schmidt, *H. L.*, II, 3; "Notices... P.S.," 241f. Straub, 84, 86. Weislinger, 681. Wencker, *Arch.*, 428.

6. MARTIN SCHOTT (†1499) pp. xiiif., xx, xxiii; #303, pp. 323f.
Martin was the son of Friedrich Schott, a wood engraver and sculptor. Friedrich gave up his profession as sculptor in 1491, according to Ritter, not in 1451 as Sitzmann and Schmidt claim. At first Martin followed his father's trade, then learned printing, probably under Mentelin. He married one of Mentelin's daughters and thus became brother-in-law to Adolf Rusch. His first dated printing is 1481, his last 1498. The books from his press, 21 to 25 of which are known, are not only artistically printed and bound

but among the first in Strassburg to be ornamented with wood cuts. He is called a cousin of the "learned" Peter Schott.
ADB, XXXII, 405. Grandidier, Nouv. oeuvr., II, 484. Hatt, Ville, 55. Hertz-Barach, 4 and "Tafel" II. Ritter, Histoire, 69-74, 494, n. 1. Schöpflin, Vind. typ., 101. Schmidt, Bibliotheken, 111; H. L., II, 2 (n. 2), 3; "Notices... P.S.," 242. Sitzmann, II, 719. Straub, 83. Voulliéme 108f. Weislinger, 679. Stammler, 58 (errs in terming the two Schott printers "die Brüder Schott").

7. OTTILIA SCHOTT (†1519) p. xxiv; #54, p. 60; #88, p. 96; #107, p. 118; #108, p. 120; #111, p. 131; #115, p. 135; #184, p. 203.
Ottilia, the third child of Peter Schott, Sr., and Susanna von Cöllen, was first married to Peter (?) von Cöllen, possibly a distant relative on her mother's side. Their daughter was Ottilia Cöllen. After the death of Peter von Cöllen, Ottilia Schott married Zeisolf von Adelsheim, Sr. Their son Lucas died in 1505.
Dacheux, Réf., 285ff. Grandidier, Mélanges, 400. Kindler von Knob-. loch, Buch, 10. Straub, 84, 86. Weislinger, 681. Wencker, Arch, 428. Wittmer, "Église rouge," I, 338.

8. PETER SCHOTT, SR. (1427/34-1504) Luc., passim. Cf. Special Index and General Index.
Peter Schott, Sr., the most distinguished public figure of his day in Strassburg and the father of our Peter Schott, was the only child of Jacob Schott and Ottilia (family name unknown). The date of his birth is given in an old record, cited by Straub and by later sources, as 1434, but Brant's *Annales* (Dacheux, *Fragments*, IV, 124) has the comment that the bell of 1427 was cast on the day Schott, Sr., was born. Since Brant, a native Strassburger, had not only known the Schotts from childhood but was a good friend of Peter, Jr., and had returned to Strassburg to enter a public office while Schott, Sr., was still active in the government, his word may be considered more reliable than that of a later genealogist. Indeed, the date 1427 seems more likely, considering that Schott, Sr., had already begun his public career by 1465 and by that time had a wife and five children, the youngest of whom was five years old; also that by 1477 his third child Ottilia had been widowed and remarried and by 1484 her daughter was married. Furthermore it is probable that one was not eligible for an office in the Strassburg government until age 33; this is the age limit given by Borries for those elected to the *Fünfzehner*.

Schott, Sr., was a man of considerable wealth, most of which he may have inherited. One supposes that some of his income came from grain farms, mills and furs, because he was a member of both the furriers' guild ("Kürschner") and the grain guild ("Kornleute," later "Luzern") which included grain dealers, millers (not only of mill ground flour but also of fine flour – "Amelung" – not prepared in mills), flour dealers and chirurgeons.

From 1465 to 1500, Schott, Sr., is documented as being constantly in office. His name appears in records almost annually as member of the city council or of the permanent magistracy, as mayor (1470, 1476, 1482, 1488). The Strassburg *Inventaires* mention him repeatedly as delegate to foreign conferences, e.g.: 1469-72 to Weissenburg and Germarsheim, 1473 to Trier, 1475 to Neuberg and Bern, 1477 to Basel and Zürich, 1478 and 1480-82 to Zürich, 1482 to Worms, 1485-1486 to the diet at Frankfurt, 1490 to Oppenheim.

In 1474 he was one of the judges at the assembly ("Malesitz") in Breisach when the tyrannical governor of Charles the Bold, Peter von

Hagenbach, was condemned to death. In 1475 he with Friedrich Bock commanded Strassburg troops against Charles the Bold. From 1475-1476 he served on the committee of eight Strassburgers whose responsibility it was to strengthen the city defenses.

During the 22 years of Schott, Sr.'s, service as director of the cathedral *fabrica*, considerable improvements were made: the organ and choir ambulatory were renovated, the choir ceiling was adorned with frescoes, the chapel of St. Laurentius was completed, the baptismal font of the sculptor Hans Hammer and the carved pulpit for Geiler were installed. Schott, Sr., is listed as one of the chief contributors of books to the cathedral library. He not only gave 200 gold florins for founding the chair of cathedral preacher but for years paid 30 gold guilders annually toward Geiler's salary.

Among his many gifts to churches were two lovely paintings to the church of St. Nicholas *in Undis*. These Grandidier, writing before the French Revolution when much was destroyed, describes as hanging by the windows near the capitulary. On one painting were the figures of two men and the words:

> O Sant Peter, du heiliger zwölfbott,
> Bitt für uns den barmherzigen Gott.
> Doctor Peter Schott, Peter Schott altammeister.

On the other painting were the figures of two women and the words:

> O sant Clor, du eine dienerin Gotts und Marien bist,
> Bitt für uns zu aller Frist.
> Margrede von Cöln. Suzanna von Cöln.

Adam, 7. Büheler, 65. *Code hist.*, I, ii, 112-113, 119, 133, 196, 209ff., *passim*. Dacheux, *Fragments*, I, i, 64f.; ii, 65; III, iv, 18; v, 143, vi, 220; IV, ix, 124, 173. Dacheux, *Réf.*, 29f., 285f., 300. Eheberg, 229, 304, 309, 495. Erhard, III, 361. Friese, II, 105. Grandidier, *Essais*, 63, 69, 273, 362; *Mélanges*, 381. Hatt, *Ville*, 47, 48, *passim*. Hertzog, iv, 82, 86, 88, 113; vi, 203; viii, 140. *Inventaire*, II, 48, 68, 139; III, 110; IV, 35, 75, 153. *Inventaire (Brucker)*, Part I, 80, 92, 93f., 96, 102, 107. *Inventaire... St. Thomas*, 346. Kindler von Knobloch, *Buch*, 331. "Die kleine Münsterchronik," 16f. Laguille, 366. Lehr, *Mélanges*, 153. Pastorius, 186. Reuss, *Meyer*, 36. Rathgeber, *Schätze*, 177; *Gottesmänner*, 9, 11. Schadäus, preface (no pagination), 32f., 79, 83-86, 109. Schmidt, *H. L.*, II, 3; "Livres," V, 441; "Notices... P.S.," 242. Schöpflin, *Alsatia*, 668. Seyboth, 177f. Sitzmann, II, 720f. Stenzel, 69f., 72; "Politik," 65; "Gerichte," 220ff. Straub, 80, 81-83, 84, 86. Weislinger, 333, 334, 681 (n. bb). Wencker, *Arch.*, 428. Wimpheling, *Cat. ep.*, 110, 118. Winckelmann, "Kulturgesch.," 253, 275.

JOHANN SCRIPTOR (SCRIPTORIS, SCHREIBER) (†1493) p. xxv; #58, pp. 63f.; #60, p. 66; #178, pp. 198f.

Johann Scriptor, a native of Kaysersberg in Alsace, is confused by Falk (12) with a Johannes Scriptoris from Ulm. The latter may be identical with the Johannes Scriptoris "de Buyren" whose A.B. degree at Basel in 1464 is attributed by Gabriel (92, n. V.4) to our Scriptor.

Johann Scriptor of Kaysersberg was a fellow student of Geiler at Freiburg and the two received the A.B. degree there in 1462. Scriptor went to Paris in 1464 and during the period 1464-1480 he received further academic degrees (Schott in 1484 addresses him as doctor of theology, cf. #58, p. 63) and was active as professor of arts and theology. He served the university in various capacities, e.g., as rector and as prior (1478) of the Sorbonne; he also served the "Alemmania" nation as procurator (1467). Gabriel (92f., n.

V.7 and V.11) remarks that the editors of the *Auctarium* (records of the "Alemmania" nation at Paris) erred in stating that Scriptor and Petrus Voleau held the office of *provisor*, because although each was prior of the Sorbonne, neither ever held the highest office of the college, that of *provisor*. It appears rather that Scriptor and Voleau, like Peter Schott, were named *provisor* of the "Alemmania" - "provisor provintiae" (*Auct.* III, 224), an honorary title bestowed by the nation upon its outstanding scholars (#297, p. 317; cf. also N. 95, paragraph 4, and N. 1764).

In 1473 Scriptor participated in the meeting at which Nominalism (unpopular with Louis XI) was condemned and its study at the university of Paris forbidden. In 1482 he became cathedral preacher at the archepiscopal cathedral of Mainz and was still the incumbent of the post in late August 1484 when Schott wrote to request from him letters of recommendation to the Sorbonne and to inquire about the possibility of occupying the house which was reserved for Scriptor at the Sorbonne (#58, pp. 63f.). At some time later he seems to have returned to Paris. He was in Strassburg in 1483 and would have been pleased to receive a benefice in that city, but Schott was unable to secure one, there being no vacancies at the time.

Auct., III, *passim*. Bulaeus, V, 706ff. Dacheux, *Réf.*, 26, 286f., 352. Falk, 12. Gabriel, 87. Schmidt, *H. L.*, II, 5, 12. Sitzmann, II, 760f.

FRATER SEBASTIAN #99, p. 110
Sebastian, a venerable and saintly hermit, was the custodian of an old chapel to St. Bernard in the Rohrtal, a valley near Ammersweiler in upper Alsace. Since early childhood, when with his grandfather he used to visit Rohrtal, Geiler had known Sebastian and was deeply impressed by his austerity and consecrated life. In later years Geiler often returned to see Sebastian and several times on the feast of St. Bernard (August 20) he preached in the chapel. The chapel, mentioned in documents in the fourteenth century, was burned in 1739, rebuilt in 1749 and demolished in 1788; its ruins were still to be seen in 1918.

Dacheux, *Réf.*, 406, 518. Levy, 201. Schmidt, *H. L.*, I, 338.

JOHANN VON SECKINGEN (HANS VON SICKINGEN) #96, p. 106
Johann von Seckingen, *eques auratus*, belonged to an old merchant family originally from the town of Säckingen. He served on the Strassburg city council 1470-1477. After the battle of Nancy in 1477 he was knighted and became a landowner. In 1479 he was in the party which greeted Bishop Albrecht on his arrival in Strassburg; in 1486 he fought in the siege of Geroldseck on the side of *Pfalzgraf* Philipp; in 1491 he was involved in litigation with Hans Jörger. From 1480 he served as a noble in the government of Strassburg; he was *Stettmeister* in 1488, 1489, 1491, 1494, 1495.

Hertzog, ii, 129. Kindler von Knobloch, *Buch*, 343. Saladin, 283. Stenzel, "Gerichte," 245; "Politik," 5.

JOHANN SIFRID (SYFRIDUS) #88, p. 96; #193, p. 210
From Schott we learn that Sifrid was an older man of whom the Schotts were very fond, that he held an A.M. degree and was parish priest of St. Martin in Strassburg. In 1486 he was apparently in Tübingen, perhaps at the university, since the Schotts sent him greetings via Widmann who was professor of medicine there. Strassburg records list him as receiving his citizenship in 1480; he was a native of Überlingen.

Wittmer-Meyer, I, 365.

EMPEROR SIGISMUND (1368-1437) #239, p. 272.
Sigismund, the last of the Luxemburg line, Elector of Brandenburg

(1376-1415), King of Hungary (1387-1437), King of Bohemia (1420-1437), King of the Germans (1410-1437), was elected emperor in 1414, but not crowned until 1433. He was instrumental in having the Council of Constance convened. Though his role in the condemnation of Hus is rather ambiguous, there is no doubt of his militant antagonism against the Hussites.
EB, XXV, 66f.

JOHANN SIMMLER (Simler, SYMLER) (1429-1492) p. xxxi; #30, p. 38; #114, p. 134; #124, p. 143; #151, p. 165; #152, p. 165; #153, p. 166; #155, p. 170 and p. 171; #157, p. 172; #168, p. 188; #179, p. 200; #192, pp. 209f.; #205, p. 215; #214, pp. 227ff.; #215, p. 233 and p. 235; #217, p. 236 and p. 238; #224, p. 253; #294, p. 313

Johann Simmler, a licentiate in law and one of the best legal minds of his day in Strassburg, was the son of Walter Simmler, a prosperous merchant of Strassburg, and Wibelina Olerin from Zabern. He is an example of the holder of many benefices (cf. N. 130, 5, par. 2) who used his influence and wealth for good. He was dean of St. Thomas, an official of the bishop and *visitator* to the convent of the Magdalenes. In 1482 he helped formulate new statutes for the Order of St. John of Jerusalem in Strassburg. At St. Thomas he was instrumental in making regulations favoring and providing stipends for gifted students who were poor but diligent. He was exceedingly generous with his money and, with the consent of the bishop, he disposed of much of his fortune to the poor and to the church during his lifetime. In 1486 when the cathedral library was enlarged, he was one of the chief donors of books. In his will – after making bequests to his sisters and domestics – he left vestments and books to Geiler; the bulk of his library went to the cathedral. He died of the plague in 1492. There were two epitaphs to him in the church of the Magdalenes and one in the cathedral.

Simmler is often confused with his nephew, also named Johann Simmler, who was canon and cantor at Old St. Peter and who in some sources is called the uncle rather than the nephew. We have been unable to find dates when he lived or when he held his benefice at Old St. Peter, but we are quite sure he does not figure in the *Lucubraciunculae*. Hartfelder errs when he comments (*ADB*, XXXV, 350ff.) that Georg Simmler (†1535) of Wimpfen is often mentioned in the *Lucubraciunculae*; there is no reference to Georg. Simmler. He may be the "Magister Georius mentioned pp. 139, 156, 163.

Geiler was one of the executors of Johann Simmler's will and vigorously opposed two heirs who claimed a silver vase which Simmler had willed to someone else. The heirs had four priests who had witnessed the will haled into court on a Sunday before the city council, which acted as judge, and accused the priests of keeping the vase. The council ruled in favor of the claimants and ordered the priests to produce the vase on pain of death. Geiler was incensed and cited both civil and canon law to prove that the council had no jurisdiction in the case, that no priest was subject to lay judgments, and that being haled into court on Sunday was illegal. He quoted this case in his "21 Artikel" as an example of gross mishandling of wills.

Dacheux, *Réf.*, Appendix XIIff., 52ff., 124, 146. Glöckler, I, 341. Grandidier, *Chevaliers*, 58; *Essais*, 362; *Mélanges*, 398f.; *Nouv. oeuvr.*, 504-507. Meister, 123. Nanton, 9. Schadäus, 49, 79. Schmidt, *Chapitre*, 144, 192, 272; "Notices... P.S.," 249f. Sitzmann, II, 854f. Stein, 128. Trithemius, *Cathalogus* (in "Addenda" by Wimpheling). Wencker, *Arch.*, 428-430.

PALLAS SPANGEL (PALLANTIUS) (†1512) #142, pp. 157
Spangel, a native of Neustadt *an der Hardt* (in the Palatinate), matriculated

at Heidelberg in 1460, received his A.M. degree in 1466 and his licentiate in theology in 1477. He served as dean of arts in 1473, vice-chancellor in 1477-78 and rector in 1477 and 1484. He is said to have studied Latin under Agricola. As professor of theology at Heidelberg he taught Wimpheling and Melanchthon; the latter lived in Spangel's home 1509-1512. In 1483 he presented in the name of the university a gift to Johann von Dalberg, the new bishop of Worms, and in 1489 he welcomed Maximilian with Latin speeches; in 1501 he delivered a funeral oration in Latin for Margaretha, wife of *Pfalzgraf* Philipp.

ADB, XXXV, 32f. Holstein, *Gelehrten*, 12-16. Ritter, *Histoire*, 78. Ritter, *Heidelberg*, 502.

JACOB SPRENGER, O.P. (†1496) #199, p. 214
Sprenger, a master of theology, was a native of Basel. He was prior of the Dominicans at Cologne when in 1473 he was elected vicar of the "Brabantia" province. In 1483 he was made vicar of St. Gertrud in Cologne and in the same year introduced the *confraternitas* of the rosary into the Dominican monastery at Cologne. In 1485 he was named vicar and in 1486 he was elected provincial of the "Teutonica" province (N. 1382); the latter position he held until his death. He composed the infamous *Hexenhammer (Malleus Maleficarum)*, which was responsible for condemning hosts of innocent victims to be burned as witches, and was himself an unrelenting inquisitor; in 1488 he sent a copy of the *Hexenhammer* to Reuchlin. To him and Alanus de Rupe (Alain de la Roche) is credited the founding of the *confraternitas* of the rosary in 1457; he was influential in spreading the organization along the Rhine (N. 1039, par. 3). He was buried in the church of St. Nicholaus *in Undis* at Strassburg.

Barth, *Handbuch*, 1386-1388. Barthelmé, 90, 108, 151, 183. Eubel, *Minoriten*, 346, n. 723. Geiger, *Briefwechsel*, 20. *Q.F. Domin.*, I, 4 (in the passage "...1475 Jacob Sprenger zum Provinzial gewählt wurde," read for "Sprenger," "Stubach," who was Sprenger's predecessor), 42; VII, 63; X, 17.

GANGOLF STEINMETZ VON LÜTZELSTEIN (LAPICIDA DE LUTZELSTEIN; GANGOLYPHUS LUCELSTEINUS) p. xxvii; p. xxix; #60, p. 65, p. 66; #63, p. 69; #146, p. 160; #148, p. 162; #174, p. 195; #176, p. 196; #177, pp. 197f.
When Schott was prevented from going to Paris for further study in 1484, his *famulus* Gangolf Steinmetz, who had been sent ahead, stayed in Paris to study and work under the supervision of Müller. Gangolf received his A.B. in 1488 and his A.M. in 1490. Thereafter he entered the priesthood and became Geiler's secretary. According to Clauss, Rhenanus' biography of Geiler is chiefly oral information from Gangolf and data from Geiler's entries in his diary. Rhenanus himself acknowledges Gangolf's help near the end of the biography; "Adiuvit nos in hec re partim Gangolyphus Lucelsteinus religiosus sacerdos, qui viro huic multis annis fideliter ministravit."

Auct., III, 693, 732. Clauss, "Geiler," 487. Dacheux, *Réf.*, 331; 344, n.1; Appendix LXXII. Knod, "Bibliographie," 472. Schmidt, *H. L.*, I, 371ff.; "Notices... P.S.," 253, n. 1. Zacher, 26f.

UDALRICH STROMEIGER (ULRICH STROHMAYR)
1. STROMEIGER, SR. #163, p. 178(?)
"Ulricus Stromair notarius," possibly identical with the Udalricus Stromeyer from Spires who matriculated at Heidelberg in 1475, obtained his Strassburg citizenship in 1485 and is recorded as being court notary 1490-1499. He may be the *protonotarius* mentioned by Schott in the Dunzenheim case (p. 178).

Stenzel, "Gerichte," 202, 203 (n. 2); Toepke, 348. Wittmer-Meyer, II, 414.

2. STROMEIGER, JR. #48, p. 52
Young Stromeyer whom the boy canon Thomas Wolf, Jr., injured was very likely the son of the notary above. As suggested in N. 442, he may have been a choir boy in the cathedral.

REIMBOLD STUBENWEG #230, p. 257
The knight Reimbold Stubenweg, of an ancient noble family of Strassburg, founded the family chapel to St. Nicholas behind the church of St. Nicholas in 1198 (N. 1520); most members of the family were buried there. Reimbold served on the city council 1230-1260 and was *Stettmeister* in 1240, 1245, 1246 and 1250. The male descendants of the family died out in the second half of the fourteenth century. The family held many fiefs (from the bishopric of Strassburg, the landgraves of Alsace, the lords of Lichtenberg, Rappoltstein and Henneberg) and was known for its generous donations to the Church.
Kindler von Knobloch, *Buch*, 363f.

GREGORIUS STUCKMANN (†1485) #63, p. 69 ("decrepitus"); #72, p. 78
Stuckmann who lived to be extremely old may be identical with the Gregorius Stuckmann listed as matriculating at Erfurt in 1460. He held perpetual vicarates at the Strassburg cathedral and at St. Thomas (N. 529 and N. 612).
Dacheux, *Réf.*, 111. Ristelhuber, 109. Weissenborn, I, 284 (1).

STURM FAMILY
The Sturms were an old noble family of Strassburg. The first member of the family to be mentioned in records is Heinrich "civis arg. 1240."
Hertzog, vi, 277ff. Kindler von Knobloch, *Buch*, 365ff.

1. JACOB STURM VON STURMECK (1489-1553) p. xiii; p. xxiv
Jacob, son of Martin Sturm and Ottilia Cöllen (daughter of Schott's sister Ottilia), received a thorough education in the humanities under the supervision of his tutor Wimpheling. In 1501 he went with Wimpheling to Heidelberg, where he received his A.B. in 1503, and in 1504 to Freiburg, where he received his A.M. in 1505. He remained at Freiburg for several years more to study theology and law, and during these years preached his one and only sermon. In 1509 he studied at Paris and Liége. It may have been at this time that he obtained his degree of doctor of philosophy. In 1510 he was at Heidelberg, helping to reorganize the university, and here he became a staunch supporter of the Reformation. In 1524 he taught at Heidelberg. Then his public career in Strassburg seems to have begun; during the years 1527-1550 he served 10 times on the city council. Along with Bucer, Melanchthon *et al.*, he went on a mission to London (1536) to persuade Henry VIII to join the *Schmalkalden* league. It was due largely to his efforts that the gymnasium of Strassburg was founded (N. 18). His fine library which he had willed to the gymnasium was destroyed in 1870.

Jacob Sturm was strongly influenced by Geiler, with whom he as a youngster was a favorite, by Wimpheling and through them by his great-uncle Peter Schott, whose example Wimpheling urged him to follow and whose treatise on Christian life Wimpheling recommended to him for perusal. It was for Jacob that Wimpheling prepared the collection of miscellaneous items which we know as the "Wimpheling Codex" (cf. Appendix D). On one occasion, upon being chided by Wimpheling for having espoused the cause

of the Reformation, Jacob is supposed to have replied, "If I am a heretic, you [i.e., Wimpheling and Geiler] have made me one."
ADB, XXXVII, 5-20. Dacheux, *Réf.*, 434, n. 4. Dacheux, *Fragments*, IV, ix, 69, 70. Grandidier, *Nouv. oeuvr.*, II, 528-533. Hatt, *Ville*, 41. Hertzog, vi, 278f. Holstein, "Codex," 213. *Inventaire*, IV, 59. Kindler von Knobloch, *Buch*, 365ff. Lehr, *Mélanges*, 147-288. Pfleger, *Menschen Gottes*, 9-22. Schmidt, *H. L.*, I, 26, 48, 75, 76; II, 80. Specklin, XIII, 301, 351. Sitzmann, II, 849f. Straub, 86. Toepke, I, 442. Wimpheling, *De integritate*, iv, xiii, xxix.

2. MARTIN STURM VON STURMECK p. xxiv; #54, p. 60
Martin, the father of Jacob Sturm, is mentioned in records as being a Strassburg magistrate, as one of the nobles contributing horses to the city in 1479, and as serving on the city council in 1502. In 1484 he received through sale the rights of his brother Ludwig to the village and castle of Breuschwickersheim and became sole proprietor of the estate. During a visit of Wimpheling, Matthias Ringmann, Johann Gallinarius, Thomas Wolf, Jr., and his son Jacob to his home, a statue of Juno or Minerva or Venus was found while digging a moat; this statue Martin presented to young Wolf.
Hatt, *Ville*, 41. Lehr, *Mélanges*, 152. Schmidt, *H. L.*, I, 26, 48, 74, 75f.; II, 80. Straub, 86.

3. OTTO STURM (OTHON) #129, p. 149
Otto was knighted in 1476 during the Burgundian War. In the period 1484-1512 he served 20 terms on the city council, and during this time was sent as delegate to the diet at Cologne 1505-1506, to the diet at Trier 1512 and attended conferences in Spires, Ulm and Augsburg 1501-1504.
Dacheux, *Réf.*, 487. *Inventaire (Brucker)*, I, 110, 113, 115, 117. Kindler von Knobloch, *Buch*, 365ff.

GEORG SUMMER, O.F.M. (†1498), #55, p. 61
Dr. Georg Summer was elected provincial of the Alsatian (Upper German) Franciscans in 1483. This position he held until his death in 1498 and was succeeded by Conrad Bondorf. Summer had previously held various offices in his province: vicar, *lector* (1475), *custos* of Alsace. In 1479 he went with Bondorf to Rome and in 1482 he attended a convention at Brescia.
Eubel, *Minoriten*, 166, 345, n. 721.

AMADEUS DE TALARU (†1444) #232, p. 261
Amadeus de Talaru became archbishop of Lyons in 1417. He was one of the pseudo-cardinals created in 1440 by Felix V, the antipope.
Eubel, I, 316; II, 9, 182.

JOHANN TEUTONICUS #1, p. 9
Johann Teutonicus is the name applied to three clerics who lived during the first half of the thirteenth century.

1. JOHANN TEUTONICUS (ZEMECKE, SEMECA) (†1245)
Johann Zemecke was born in Halberstadt, studied canon law at Bologna, where he may have received the degree of *magister*, and held benefices at the cathedral of Halberstadt, being *praepositus* there when he died.
ADB, XIV, 476. Jöcher, IV, 496.

2. JOHANN TEUTONICUS (DE STRASSBURG, PONSA), O.P. (*ca.* 1180-1253/54)
This Johann Teutonicus, an able jurist (doctor of law) and preacher com-

manding many languages, including Hungarian and Roumanian, was born in Wildersheim (diocese of Osnabrück); Grandidier, apparently confusing him with the Teutonicus above, attributes to him the name Semeca. He became chaplain and confessor to Honorius III and undertook diplomatic missions for Honorius; he was sent out, for example, to preach the fifth crusade. *Ca.* 1220 he entered the Dominican Order (at Strassburg?) and after serving as Dominican provincial in Hungary (1228), he was made bishop of Bosnia (Lindemann says bishop of Pressburg), i. e., suffragan to the archbishop of Kalocsa, in 1232. He resigned this office to become a hermit, but was called from retirement to be provincial of the Lombardy Dominicans and then was elected fourth general of his order in 1242. He died at Strassburg and was buried in one of the cathedral chapels. Grandidier claims that miracles followed his death.

Grandidier, *Nouv. oeuvr.*, 295-298. Lindemann, 2f. Sitzmann, I, 853f.

3. JOHANN TEUTONICUS (FRIBURGENSIS), O.P. (†1250)
Johann Friburgensis, born in Freiburg (Breisgau), hence his appellation "Friburgensis," was a scholastic philosopher and wrote various works, including notes to the decretals. Trithemius and Gesner (who took material form Trithemius) confuse this Dominican monk with the general of the order above by assigning to him the office of bishop of Bosnia.

Gesner, 457b. Jöcher, II, 1921. Trithemius, *Liber*, fo. 65.

THOMAS VON STRASSBURG (THOMAS ARGENTINENSIS, THOMAS DE ARGENTINA), O.S.A. (ca. 1300-1357) p. xxx; #1, p. 9; #142, p. 157
A native of Hagenau (older sources say of Strassburg), Thomas is known to have studied at Padua in 1315. He taught theology at Strassburg and at Paris, where in 1340 he became doctor of theology. In the same year he was elected Augustinian provincial, and in 1345 he was made general of his order, the first German to hold that position. In 1348/1349 he obtained from Clement VI a bull exempting his order from episcopal jurisdiction. He died at Vienna. His commentaries on the four books of the *Sentences* by Peter Lombard were edited by Schott and published by Martin Flach in 1490.

Dacheux, *Réf.*, 389, n. 1. Eysengrein, 254, 255. Jöcher, IV, 1145. Grandidier, *Nouv. oeuvr.*, II, 553-556. Nikolaus Paulus, "Der Augustinergeneral Thomas von Strassburg," AEK, I (1926), 49ff.; "Die Doktorpromotion des Thomas von Strassburg," AEK, II (1927), 44ff. Sitzmann, II, 869. Trithemius *De script. eccl.*, fol. 135b. Weislinger, 548.

Thomas Lampertheim or Lamparter is often called Thomas de Argentina or Thomas von Strassburg (cf. Trithemius, *Liber*, fol. 90.; Grandidier, *Nouv. oeuvr.*, 556.; Knepper, *Schulwesen*, 87f.).

JOHANN TORTELLIUS ARRETINUS (ARETINUS) (*ca.* 1400-1466) #183, p. 202
Johann Tortellius of Arezzo was the first librarian of the Vatican (under Nicholas V). He studied Greek in Constantinople 1435-1438 and was at Bologna *ca.* 1442. Among his many writings is a work on orthography *Commentaria gramatica de orthographia* (1449).

Cosenza, IV, 3436ff. Gény-Knod, i, 27. Gesner, 458. Trithemius, *Liber*, fol. 106a.

JOHANN TRITHEMIUS (JOHANN VON HEIDENBERG), O.S.B. (1462-1516) p. xxiii; #5, p. 11
Johann von Heidenberg, of whom we learn through autobiographical pas-

sages in his works, was the son of Johann von Heidenberg and Helisabet von Longovico and was born in Trittenheim on the Moselle. Though the family was in comfortable circumstances, he ran away – when on the death of his father his mother remarried – to escape his stepfather. He went to Trier and then to Heidelberg, where he formed a lifelong friendship with Wimpheling under whom he may have studied. In 1482 he entered the Benedictine monastery at Spanheim and sixteen months later became its twenty-fifth abbot. He spent the year 1489 taking courses from Celtis and Reuchlin at Heidelberg. During his 24 years as abbot, he reformed the monastery and enlarged its library. In 1506 he became abbot of St. Jacob in Würzburg.

Among his many works, the most valuable today are the biographical dictionaries *Liber de scriptoribus ecclesiasticis* and *Cathalogus illustrium virorum*, both of which have gone through many editions, and in both of which he included himself. His chronicles of Spanheim and Hirsau contain – besides data on the monasteries – considerable miscellaneous information on history and other subjects of interest at the time; the miscellaneous information in the two chronicles is much the same.

ADB, XXXVIII, 626. Erhard, III, 379-394. Eysengrein, 184. Hasse, 118ff. Trithemius, *Cathalogus*, fol. 75a; *Liber*, folios 139bf.; *Ann. Hirs.*, I, 517; *Polygraphiae libri sex*... (Oppenheim, 1518), folios aii ff.

UDALRICUS ARGENTINENSIS (UDALRICUS VON STRASSBURG), O.P.
#1, p. 9
Udalricus of Strassburg lived in the latter part of the thirteenth century (*fl. ca.* 1280). He wrote many theological works, including a commentary on Peter Lombard's *Sentences*.

Jöcher, IV, 1483. Trithemius, *De script. eccl.*, fol. 106b.

ANTONIUS CODRUS URCEUS (ANTONIO URCEO) (1446-*ca*. 1500) p. xxv
Urceus (called "Codrus"), a native of Modena, was a noted professor of oratory and poetry at Bologna in the late fifteenth century. Ristelhuber (124) mentions two biographical studies of him.

Ellinger, 98-102. Gesner, 55. Mazzetti, 512.

CHRISTOPH VON UTTENHEIM (CHRISTOPHORUS VON UTENHEIM, UDENHEIM) (†1527) #30, p. 38; #179, p. 200; #192, p. 209
Uttenheim, a doctor of canon law, became *praepositus* of St. Thomas at Strassburg in 1473. In the same year he attended the university of Basel and served as rector of the university. In 1494 he left Strassburg to be *custos* of the Basel cathedral, where he already held a canonicate, and in 1503 he was elected bishop of Basel to succeed Caspar de Rein. His election put an end to the cherished plan of the circle of friends – Geiler, Lampertheim, Wimpheling and Uttenheim – to retire from active life and become hermits. In 1497 Wimpheling had gone so far as to interview a certain hermit to obtain information. In a letter to Geiler's nephews, Wimpheling writes of the friendship between Geiler and Uttenheim: "Fuit praeterea Christophoro Basiliensi antistiti carus, Friderico Augustensi carior."

ADB, VIII, 510 (article on Geiler). *ADB*, XXXIX, 409. Dacheux, *Réf.*, 429f., 473. Eubel, II, 102. Glöckler, II, 493. Grandidier, *Nouv. oeuvr.*, II, 560f. Hertzog, vi, 285. Riegger, *Amoen.*, 116, 122. Schmidt, *Chapitre*, 192; "Notices... P.S.," 249. Volk, 173. Wimpheling, *Cat. ep.*, 118. Wiskowatoff, 77, 96.

EUCHARIUS VOELTSCH (VOILTSCH, VEILTSCH, VOELSCH, FELSCH, VOLTZ) (†1510) #156, p. 171
The Voeltsch family, first mentioned in records in 1225, was an old Strassburg family of knights, holding fiefs from the empire, the Strassburg bishopric and Alsatian abbeys and landowners. It contributed members to the city government and to the collegiate churches, as well as to monasteries and convents. A number of Voetschs appear in documents of the late fifteenth century; in 1475 one Voeltsch had five daughters in the convent of St. Mark.

Eucharius, son of Reimboltz, is recorded as relinquishing his Strassburg citizenship in 1478 and purchasing it again in 1482, as serving in the Strassburg government in 1500 and as taking oaths for imperial fiefs 1494-1499. From Schott we learn that Eucharius was the son-in-law of Jacob Müg, Sr.

Barthelmé, 143. Horning, *Festschrift*, 47. *Inventaire (Brucker)*, I, 108. Kindler von Knobloch, *Buch*, 388. Schmidt, *H. L.*, I, 45. Wencker, *Arch.*, 433. Wittmer-Meyer, I, 353, 392.

ADAM WERNHER (WERNER, WERNHERUS, WERHNER) (*ca.* 1470-1537) #298, p. 321
Adam Wernher, from Themar on the Werra in Thüringen (hence his appellation "Temarensis"), studied at Heidelberg, where he received his A.B. degree in 1485. He taught at the Latin school in Neustadt on the Hardt, then became tutor to the sons of *Pfalzgraf* Philipp – particularly to the eldest son Ludwig, the later elector. Wernher lectured at Heidelberg on classics 1489-1492 and, after taking a degree in law, he lectured on law 1506-1522 and at other times until his death. He served as rector of the university in 1497, 1504 and 1510. In 1519 he was assessor of the law court at Worms. An active humanist, he was associated with Agricola, Wimpheling, Dalberg, Reuchlin, Celtis, *et. al.* Among his works were poems in Latin and translations from the Latin (Vergil, Horace, Hrotsvitha).

ADB, XLII, 39-41. GGr^2, 445. Karl Hartfelder, *Werner von Themar, ein Heidelberger Humanist* (Karlsruhe, 1880). Pantaleon, part 11, 477. Trithemius, *Cathalogus*, fol. 71b; *Liber*, fol. 139b. Velden, 234.

JOHANN WESCHBACH (WESPACH, WESTPACH) #12, p. 21; #17, p. 26; #47, p. 52; #55, p. 61; #59, p. 65; #68, p. 76; #69, p. 76; #72, p. 79; #75, p. 82; #76, p. 83.
Weschbach, a fellow townsman of Maeler from Memmingen (Knod says from Nürnberg), matriculated at Ingolstadt in 1473 and was at Bologna by 1477. During the plague at Bologna in 1478, he seems to have gone to Ferrara, where he completed his studies for the doctorate in canon and civil law in 1482 (Bernard Adelmann was one of his witnesses); Schott visited him in Ferrara in the spring of 1480 (#17, p. 26). Until 1485 he was mainly in Rome, apparently at the *Curia*, and in November of that year he accompanied Oswald von Dyrstein to Strassburg. In 1488 he was teaching civil and canon law when he received a fief at Ulm, and in 1499 he was a judge in Ulm. The last record of him is dated 1507.

Acta bonon., 225. Chmel, 761. Knod, *Studenten*, #4160. Pardi, *Titoli*, 73 (witness for a doctorand), 74.

JOHANN WIDMANN (WIDEMAN, WIEDMAN, ALSO SALICETUS, MÖCHINGER, MECHINGER, MEUCHINGER) (*ca.* 1440-1504) #22, pp. 30f.; #33, pp. 40f.; #41, p. 47; #42, p. 47; #44, p. 49; #66, pp. 72ff.; #67, pp. 74f.;

#88, p. 96; #111, p. 131; #112, pp. 131ff.; #115, p. 135; #116, p. 136; #129, p. 149; #131, p. 151; #132, pp. 151f.; #135, p. 153; #138, pp. 154f.; #140, pp. 155f.; #145, p. 160; #147, p. 161; #149, pp. 162f.; #154, p. 169; #190, p. 208(?)

Johann Widmann, from Maichingen (hence the appellation "Möchinger," etc.), southwest of Stuttgart in Württemberg, matriculated at Heidelberg 1459, receiving his A.B. degree in 1461 and his A.M. in 1463. He was at Pavia in 1466, at Padua in 1469 and from there went to Ferrara, where he obtained his degree of doctor of medicine. For a while he worked as physician in Ulm and wrote his *Pestregimen* there. In 1474 he was physician at the university of Ingolstadt and in 1476 he became personal physician to Christoph I of Baden. In 1477 he was city physician at Basel, then became again personal physician to Christoph of Baden. In 1483 he came to Strassburg and was city physician; in that year he became a Strassburg citizen. It may have been in the next year that he addressed a memorandum to the Strassburg government on the urgent need for reform of sanitation.

During this period he married; his wife was apparently a Strassburg girl of whom the Schotts, especially Susanna von Cöllen, were very fond, as is evident from the frequent references to her and the many messages sent her by Susanna in Schott's letters to Widmann from 1485 on; unfortunately, nowhere is there mention of her by name. Following are the references to her: #66, p. 74; #88, p. 96; #111, p. 131; #112, p. 132 and p. 133; #115, p. 135; #116, p. 136; #129, p. 149; #131, p. 151; #132, p. 151; #138, p. 155; #140, p. 156, #147, p. 161, #149, p. 163.

By 1 March 1485 (#66), Widmann was professor of medicine at Tübingen and personal physician to *Graf* Eberhard V (later Duke Eberhard I) of Württemberg. In 1497 he was dean of the Tübingen faculty of medicine; at this time he organized the midwives and the pharmacy at Stuttgart. In 1506 he went to Ulm, but continued to be physician to Duke Ulrich I of Württemberg until 1511. Some time thereafter he moved to Pforzheim. His works include *Tractatus de pustuis et morbo qui vulgato nomine mal de Franzos appellatur*, which is one of the first scientific studies of syphilis and the first study by a German; in this Widmann proves that from the year 1457 the disease had spread over Europe. His work on the plague mentioned above was published in both German and Latin, as was his monograph on the baths at Wildbad.

ADB, XLII, 355-357. *Biograph. Lexikon... Ärtzte*, V, 925. Dacheux, *Réf.*, 348. Gordon, 536, 665. Hartmann, #402. Hatt, *Ville*, 379, 380. Pardi, *Titoli*, 50. Schmidt, H. L., II, 31. Toepke, 299. Wickersheimer, II, 503. Wittmer-Meyer, II, 400. Zeiller, 240f.

JACOB WIMPHELING (WIMPFELING) (1450-1528) pp. xiii-xxxi *passim*; #1-#4, pp. 9-11; #82, pp. 88ff.; #89-#91, pp. 96-103; #113, p. 133; #120, p. 139; #122, pp. 140f.; #244, p. 280; #279, p. 306; #291, p. 311; #294, p. 313; #300, pp. 321f.; #301, pp. 322f.

Wimpheling, one of the most widely known German humanists, was born in Schlettstadt and studied under Dringenberg at the Schlettstadt school. After the death of his father in 1463, he went to live with an uncle, Ulrich Wimpheling, who was parish priest at Soultz. In 1464 he matriculated at Freiburg, where he lived for that year in the home of Kilian Wolf, heard lectures from Geiler and in 1466 received his A.B. degree. Because of an outbreak of the plague in 1469 at Freiburg he went to Erfurt (but was not entered in the matriculation records), then to Spires and Heidelberg by 1470. There in 1471 he took a bachelor of arts degree in the *via moderna*. During the year 1479-80 he served as vice-chancellor and dean at Heidelberg. In

1483 because of the plague at Heidelberg, he spent some months at Schlettstadt, then returned to Heidelberg, where possibly in that year or in 1484 he obtained his licentiate of theology. From his correspondence with Schott, we know he was in Spires by 1486 and held a vicarate at the cathedral there (#82); in 1488 Schott addresses him as *prebendarius* of the Spires cathedral (#113). At about this time he was appointed cathedral preacher at Spires, a post he held until 1491. For some years thereafter he seems to have remained at Spires, perhaps until he became tutor to Jacob Sturm. In 1498 when he was writing the introduction to the *Lucubraciunculae* he was at Soultz. In 1500 while editing the *Epithoma*, he was in Heidelberg and in 1501 while editing the fourth volume of Gerson's works, he was in Strassburg. In that same year he went with Jacob Sturm to Heidelberg and from then on for several years his movements paralleled Jacob's.

Though a rather superficial scholar, Wimpheling wrote so much and was active in so many fields that he won among his contemporaries the reputation of having great learning and has retained this reputation through the centuries. Thomas Wolf, Jr., writes of him: "Siquis nostra aetate philosophi nomen meretur: dispeream si is non est Vuimphelingus"; and Weislinger (680) in the mid-eighteenth century speaks of him as our "nie genug gepriesenen Jacob Wimpheling." Literary histories devote lengthy sections to him and in the last hundred years there have been many articles about him and at least two biographies.

ADB, XLVI, 524ff. Bauch, 86f. Cave, *Appendix*, 123. Dacheux, *Fragments*, IV, ix, 69, 70. Dacheux, *Réf.*, 428-441, 451-454. Dorlan, *Notices*, i, 334-343; ii, 103. Ellinger, 379-382. Erhard, I, 428-467. Eysengrein, 184f. Falk, 83. Gény, 28. Gény-Knod, 21f. *GGr²*, I, 406-413. Grandidier, *Nouv. oeuvr.*, II, 580-595. Hasse, I, 122-130. Hertzog, vii, 32-34. Holstein, "Codex," *passim*; "Beilage," *passim*; "Mitteilungen," *passim*; "Biographie," *passim*. *Illustrierte Zeitung*, #1496 (Leipzig, 1872), 155. Knepper, *Wimpheling*, 132. Knod, "Bibliographie," 463-481. Pantaleon, iii, 20. Riegger, *Amoen.*, 161-581. Röhrich, I, 90, 91, and *passim*. Santifaller, 639. Schmidt, *Chapitre*, 52, 144; *H. L.*, I, 1-185; II, 317-340; "Notices ... Wolf," 455-468 and *passim*. Sitzmann, II, 1000ff. Specklin, 301-304. Stöber, *Neue Alsatia*, 281, n. 3. Trithemius, *Cathalogus*, fol. 65b; *Liber*, fol. 134f. Truttmann-Burg, 198. Weislinger, 677-681 and *passim*. Wiskowatoff, *passim*.

LEONHARD WIRT (LEONHARDUS, LIENHART, LEOHARD) #66, p. 73, #112, p. 132 and p. 133.
Wirt, known as *Magister* or *Meister* Leonhardus, was a physician in Strassburg. In 1483 he became a citizen of the city.
Baas, 87ff. Hatt, *Ville*, 379. Wittmer-Meyer, I, 398.

WOLF FAMILY
The several Wolfs who held prominent positions in the three collegiate churches of Strassburg during the last decades of the fifteenth and the first decade of the sixteenth century belonged to the wealthy Wolf family of Eckbolsheim and were closely related to the elder Hells who had for some time been incumbents in influential positions of those churches and supported their nephews in obtaining benefices.

1. JOHANN WOLF #48, p. 52; #145, p. 160; #147, p. 161
Johann Wolf, canon and dean of Old St. Peter, was, according to Grandidier, the brother of Thomas Wolf, Sr., and the father of Thomas Wolf, Jr.; at the

death of his wife he resigned as sheriff of Eckbolsheim, became a cleric and
received the benefices mentioned above. Schmidt, however, says Johann
was not the father of young Thomas (cf. below).
    Grandidier, *Nouv. oeuvr.*, II, 596. Knod, *Studenten*, #4278. Schmidt,
H. L., II, 58f.; "Notices... Wolf," 448.

2. THOMAS WOLF, SR. (*ca.* 1450-1511) #30, pp. 37ff.; #35, p. 42; #38, p.
45; #40, pp. 46f.; #42, pp. 47f.; #45, p. 50; #55, p. 61; #57, pp. 62f.;
#62, p. 68; #65, p. 71; #74, p. 81; #78, p. 84; #86, p. 94; #93, pp. 104f.;
#100, pp. 110f.; #172, p. 193

Thomas Wolf, Sr., was the son of Anna Hell and Andreas Wolf and nephew
of Johann and Nicolaus Hell. As a child he became canon of St. Thomas.
In 1461 he matriculated at Erfurt and by 1470 he was at the university of
Bologna, where he received the degree of doctor of decretals. In addition
to his many benefices (cf. N. 130, 5, par. 2), he was *praepositus* of Old St.
Peter and *conservator* of the bishop of Strassburg. He was not only extremely
able in legal matters but a man of culture who had the means to indulge his
tastes. He acquired a fine library and had his canonical house painted with
moral inscriptions and classical quotations. In honor of his parents and his
uncle Johann Hell, he had the choir ambulatory of Old St. Peter painted
with scenes from the life of St. Amand. He also had the cloister of New St.
Peter rebuilt and ornamented with frescoes.

    He had his natural son Johann educated at Bologna and legitimized
so that Johann might become a priest. His lack of chastity and the number
of his illegitimate children were satirized by his detractors, one of whom –
Engelhard Funck – composed the following epigram:

> Ad Thomam Wolfium seniorem
>
> Si thermae in Venerem stimulant, quibus arrigis undis?
>   Ex quo tot vernae sunt tibi fonte Lupi?
> Argentina tibi tales tibi, furcifer, undas
>   Sufficit et nutrit, proh sua damna lupas.

ADB, XLIV, 51. *Acta bonon.*, 214. Bauch, 51f. Dacheux, *Réf.*, 359, n. 1.
Grandidier, *Nouv. oeuvr.*, II, 596ff. Hartfelder, *Briefe*, 32. Hell, 377.
Inventaire, VI, 178. *Inventaire* (Spach), IV, 84. Knod, *Studenten*, #4277.
Meister, 113, 136. Schadäus, 50. Schmidt, "Notices... P. S.," 245, 447ff.;
Chapitre, 163, 193, 274; "Notices... Wolf," 448. Schöpflin, *Alsatia*, 344.
Sitzmann, II, 1012f. (completely confuses Thomas Wolf, Sr., and Thomas
Wolf, Jr.). Stein, 130f. Velden, 224. Wittmer-Meyer, II, 416.

3. THOMAS WOLF, JR. (1475-1509) #30, p. 38; #35, p. 42; #55, p. 61;
#57, p. 62; #74, p. 81; #75, p. 82; #86, p. 94; #93, p. 104; #100, p. 111

Thomas Wolf, Jr., was the eldest son of a brother of Thomas Wolf, Sr.,
who according to Grandidier was Johann Wolf, but according to Schmidt
was named Andreas and was sheriff of Eckbolsheim. For some reason
the boy was placed under the guardianship of his uncle Thomas, Sr.,
and at the age of seven became canon of St. Thomas. The story of the lengthy
lawsuit with Engelhard Funck over the canonicate is told in the Schott's
letters (cf. N. 334). In 1488 Thomas, Jr., matriculated at Erfurt, received
his A.B. in 1491 and in 1492 went to Bologna, where he spent ten years
studying law and classical literature and in 1501 obtained his degree of doctor
of laws.

    He became interested in antiquities, collected inscriptions in Rome and
left behind two volumes of manuscript on antiquities. He was the first Alsa-

tian archeologist, as well as a poet, an historian and an editor. Wimpheling and Geiler expected him to continue the biographical work on the bishops of Strassburg begun by Wimpheling. In addition to his canonicate at St. Thomas, young Wolf was canon of New St. Peter (1487) and *praepositus* of St. Martin in Colmar (1503). Like his godfather Schott, he helped educate promising students; one of these was Maternus Pistor of Ingweiler, later prominent at Erfurt. His last year of life was embittered by a quarrel with Thomas, Sr., over a benefice; Thomas, Sr., had procured an edict against Thomas, Jr., and the latter was in Rome to appeal the edict when he died. Epitaphs to him were composed by Reuchlin, Rhenanus, Wimpheling and Boniface Amerbach. Wimpheling's is quoted below:

Argentina tibi vitam dederat, dat Roma sepulchrum.
Vix potius nasci clarius atque mori.

ADB, XLIV, 52. *Acta bonon.*, 244. Bauch, 128-131. Burchard, v. Grandidier, *Nouv. oeuvr.*, II, 599-611. *GGr²*, 433. Knepper, *Schulwesen*, 157, 185, 278, 348. Knod, *Studenten*, #4278. Meister, 131. Ristelhuber, 124. Schmidt, *H. L.*, II, 58-86; *Chapitre*, 140f., 193, 278; "Notices... Wolf," 447-469, 481-485; "Recueil... Wolf," 157, 160. Schöpflin, *Alsatia*, 344. Sitzmann, II, 1013f. Stein, 133f. Wimpheling, *Cat. ep.*, 123.

HOUSE OF WÜRTTEMBERG

1. EBERHARD V, GRAF (LATER EBERHARD I, HERZOG) OF WÜRTTEMBERG (1445-1496) #112, p. 132
Eberhard "der Bärtige," or "im Bart," is called by historians the ablest ruler of Württemberg, not only because during his reign the principality of Württemberg was united and declared forever indivisible, but also because the arts flourished, economic conditions were good and changes were progressive not retrogressive. Eberhard began ruling at the age of fifteen in 1460. In 1468 he visited the Holy Land and in 1471 entered the Cistercian Order for a time. In 1474 he founded the university of Tübingen. He brought outstanding people in different fields to Württemberg, such as: Reuchlin, the scholar in classics, Hebrew and law; Biel, the theologian and schoolman; Widmann, the physician. Accompanied by Reuchlin, Biel *et al.*, he went to Italy and Rome in 1482 and again in 1490. At the diet in Worms in 1495 Maximilian I raised Württemburg to a duchy and declared it indivisible. The following year Eberhard died without issue and was succeeded by his cousin Eberhard II (the Younger) who was deposed after two years of misrule, by Maximilian, and Ulrich I, son of Eberhard I's brother Heinrich, became duke. Unfortunately after the first decade of the sixteenth century Ulrich became intolerably tyrannical and cruel and undid much of the good done by the first Duke Eberhard. Many an outstanding person who could left the duchy, i. e., Widmann and Reuchlin.

Geiger, *Reuchlin*, 21-56 *passim*. Sattler, 2ff. Trithemius, *Ann. Hirs.*, II, 503, 509, 512. Wickersheimer, 503.

HIERONYMUS DE ZANCTIVIS (GIROLAMO ZANETINIS, ZANETTINI, ZANETINUS, ZANETIVIS; JEROME DE ZANETTIS) (†1493) #71, p. 77
Zanctivis (whose name with its varied spellings is a good example of the confusion between c and e and between n and v) was the son of the knight and count Tommaso Zanctivis of Bologna. He received his baccalaureate in law in 1457 at Bologna. He taught canon and civil law at Bologna 1469-1473,

was in Pisa for about five years and returned to Bologna where he again was professor of civil and canon law 1478-1493. Burtius in his *Bononia Illustrata* (published 1494) has an epitaph to Zanctivis:

> Hic Zanetinus adest, Felsina quam tulerat,
> Unius hic tumulus non est, spes, fama, decusque
> Justitiae, probitas contumulata jacent.
> Hic patriae lumen, splendorque, jubarque suorum
> Jam fuit, et vivet gloria parta diu.

Dallari, I, 106. "Liber secretus iuris caesaris," folios 171-176ff., and *passim*. "Liber secretus iuris pontificii," fol. 147b (mentioned as *prioratus*, 1480). Mazzetti, 328. Meuschenius, II, 163 (for Burtius). "Rotoli," 1470-1480, and *passim*. Thurston, 344.

FRIEDRICH VON ZOLLERN (ZOLRE, HOHENZOLLERN) (1450-1505) p. xii; p. xxx; #48, p. 52; #60, p. 66; #61, p. 67; #83, pp. 90f.; #99, p. 110; #105, pp. 114ff.; #114, p. 134; #123, pp. 141f.; #124, pp. 142f.; #127, p. 147; #137, p. 154; #174, p. 195; #175, p. 196; #206, p. 215; #252, p. 286; #256, p. 292; Appendix B; Appendix H.

Friedrich von Zollern, of the family later called Hohenzollern from its ancestral castle, was the son of *Graf* Jost (Jodocus) Niklas von Zollern and *Gräfin* Agnes von Werdenberg. Emperor Friedrich III was his godfather; a paternal uncle Friedrich von Zollern and a maternal uncle Heinrich von Werdenberg were canons at the Strassburg cathedral; a second maternal uncle Hugo von Werdenberg served in the emperor's privy council; a third Johann von Werdenberg was Friedrich's predecessor as bishop of Augsburg.

Friedrich studied at Erfurt and by 1468 was at the university of Freiburg. Here he met Geiler as fellow student, perhaps also as teacher, and the two began a friendship which lasted until Friedrich's death. Friedrich served as university rector in 1468 and again in 1477 following Geiler's term. He held canonicates at Augsburg, Constance and Strassburg (from at least 1467); apparently he was already *camerarius* at Strassburg before he came there to take up residence *ca.* 1479 (he is listed as one of those escorting Bishop Albrecht into Strassburg for his coronation – sometime after 18 January 1479) and he seems to have become dean of the cathedral on his arrival in Strassburg to succeed Johann von Helfenstein who is named as dean to 1478. He entered the priesthood and celebrated his first mass on 2 February 1485. In 1486 he was elected fifty-third bishop of Augsburg (N. 674 and N. 679) and was crowned 21 July of that year.

Just before his formal installation as bishop, Friedrich represented his relative Albrecht, *Markgraf* and elector of Brandenburg (†11 March 1486) – who in 1481 had offered him a bishopric in Brandenburg – at Maximilian's coronation as King of the Romans at Aachen on 5 April 1486. Bernard Hertzog (ii, 141) describes the colorful procession from the historic cathedral: after the various ranks of nobles and the trumpeters, came "die Churfürsten des Reichs/ gekleidet/ als sich gebürt/ rott mit Hermelin gefüttert/ unnd rotte hohe Hūttlein auf mit Hermelin. Zuerst der Erzbishoff von Trier, darnach Herzog Ernst von Sachsen/ trug das Schwerdt bloss vor dem König... Philips Pfaltzgraff bei Rhein truge... den Apffel for... Friderich Graff von Zollern erwâlet zu Augsburg bey ihme einer truge den Scepter/ von wegen des Marggraffen von Brandenburg/ Churfürsten. Auf diese gieng der Römische König... Neben ihm zur rechten handt der Ertzbischoff zu Cöllen: auff der linken handt der Ertzbischoff von Meintz. Der Römische Keyser gieng nach." Then came the banquet: "Da nun der Keyser und König zu tisch giengent/ da kam Friderich/ Graff zu Zollern/ erwälter zu

Augsburg/ an statt des Churfürsten zu Brandenburg mit ellichen Herren und bracht handtzweheln und Wasser in silbern Becken."

Friedrich labored to serve his bishopric well and was truly a model bishop (N. 988). He convoked a diocesan synod, affirmed the disciplinary rules of his predecessor, made ordinations, consecrated churches, visited his diocese, reestablished discipline in monasteries and convents and restored them. One of his main contributions was the establishment of the chair of cathedral preacher which was confirmed in 1505. He willed 25,000 florins cash and 20,000 florins of grain to the cathedral. As a person he remained uncorrupted by luxury and vice. Wimpheling says of him, "Novi ego viros elegantissimos nulla unquam libidinis macula notatos: in primis unum ex generoso comitum sanguine cuiusdam suevice diocesis reverendissimum episcopum cui Frederico nomen." Friedrich was buried in a tomb of Salzburg marble still to be seen in the Augsburg cathedral; a painting of him hangs among the paintings of his predecessors and successors on the wall of the cathedral.

Braun, 87-151. Dacheux, *Réf.*, 362-395. Dreher, XVIII, 3ff., 8f., 11, 13, 15f., 27f., 31ff., 50, 51ff.; XIX, 18ff., 30, 50, 75; XXI, 52f.; in all three issues, *passim*. Eubel, II, 98. Falk, 88f. Hämmerle, 199. Hertzog, ii, 141, 142, 155; iv, 114f. Hofmann, I, 279. Riegger, *Amoen.*, 3. Saladin, 284. Schmidt, *H. L.*, I, 353; "Notices... P.S.," 249. Steichele, *Beiträge*, I, 115-144; "Friedrich Graf von Zollern," 143-172. Stenzel, *passim*. Trithemius, *Ann. Hirs.*, II, 524. Wimpheling, *De integritate*, iv. Zoepl, 482f., 484f., 488, (first line should read *Peter Schott* instead of *Johann Schott*), 499, 533.

ANNA VON ZORN (†1511) pp. 357f.

Anna von Zorn was prioress of the convent of St. Agnes in Strassburg and when the convent was razed in 1475, she and her nuns were transferred to the convent of St. Margaret (N. 83); she then became prioress of the united convent, called Sts. Margaret and Agnes; the union of the convents was approved in 1476 by Sixtus IV. Anna was apparently quite a scholar, for she is said to have given a long address in Latin before Maximilian I in 1511 (has she been confused with Anna Schott?).

Barthelmé, 147, 189f. Bussierre, 21-28, 31. Gass, *Dominikanerinnen*, 14; *Blätter*, 19f.

ANNA ZUBER #34, p. 41; #61, p. 67; #114, p. 134; #124, p. 143

Geiler's mother Anna Zuber seems to have been a native of Kaysersberg. Apparently she came to live with Geiler at Strassburg soon after his move there, for in Schott's letters of 22 July and 7 August 1481 (#20, #21) her presence with Geiler at the baths is inferred by second person plural forms of verbs, possessive pronouns and adjectives. Schott's last mention of her is in October 1488 (#124, p. 143). According to Schmidt, she remarried. While with Geiler, she accompanied him often on his holidays to the baths and to Upper Alsace.

Riegger, *Amoen.*, 107. Schmidt, *H. L.*, I, 372.

JOHANN ZWIG (ZWICK) p. 332

The Johann Zwig "Nemetensis," i.e., of Spires, is doubtless identical with the "Joannes Zwick de Spira," cleric of the Spires diocese who matriculated at Heidelberg 5 October 1490 and received his baccalaureate in arts *via antiqua* in 1492. He was most probably a pupil of Wimpheling at Heidelberg.

Toepke, 397.

APPENDICES

A. Charles Schmidt's manuscript copy of Peter Schott's German letter to his sister Anna.
B. Manuscript letter from Peter Schott to Friedrich von Zollern, with English summary and notes.
C. Copy of *Lucubraciunculae* item #83 from the Strassburg Archives.
D. Description of the "Wimpheling Codex."
E. Letter from the Sforzas to Zürich and Schott's German translation.
F. Letter from Duke Giovanni Galeazzo Maria Sforza to Strassburg and Schott's German translation
G. Letter from Duke Giovanni Sforza to Peter Schott, Sr.
H. Precepts composed by Geiler von Kaysersberg for Friedrich von Zollern.
I. Texts of two items from the *Lucubraciunculae* as they appeared in Goldast, *Centuria*.
J. Letter from Bohuslaus von Hassenstein to Geiler von Kaysersberg.
K. Documents concerning the chair of cathedral preacher and the Last Sacrament for criminals condemned to death.
L. Genealogical material on the Schott family.
M. Quotable passages from Peter Schott's *Lucubraciunculae*.
N. Strassburg money and its relative value.

APPENDIX A

Five leaves containing facsimile of a Schott coat-of-arms and Charles Schmidt's manuscript copy of Peter Schott's letter to his sister Anna Schott. (These leaves are pasted onto a rear blank folio in the undamaged copy of the Lucubraciunculae at the Bibliothèque nationale et universitaire de Strassbourg, cf. N. 3.)

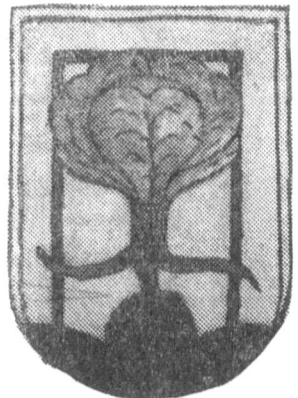

Fig. 1.

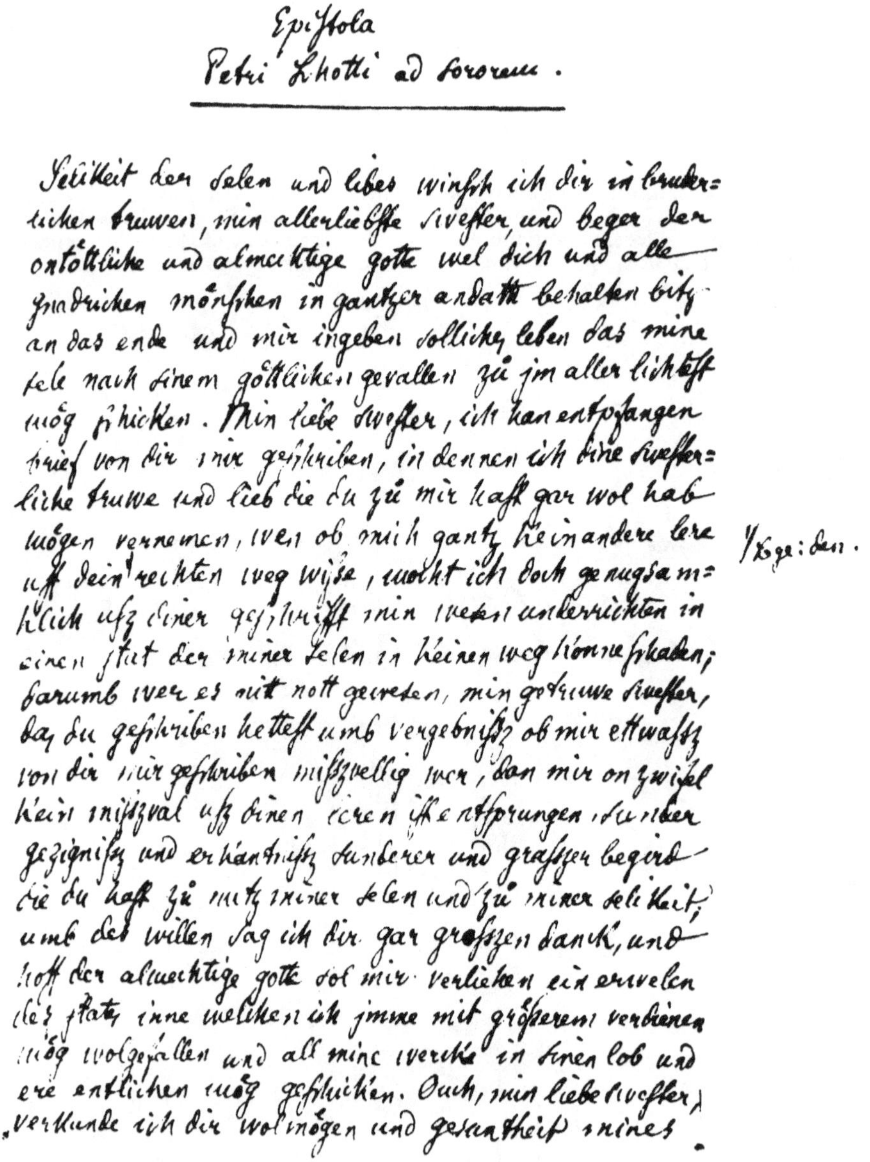

Epistola
Petri Lhotti ad sororem.

Selikeit der selen und libes wünsch ich dir in bruder=
lichen truwen, min allerliebste swester, und beger der
ontödtliche und almechtige gotte wel dich und alle
zuodrücken mönschen in gantzer andatt behalten biss
an das ende und mir ingeben sollich leben das mine
sele nach sinem göttlichen gevallen zu jm aller lichteft
mög schicken. Min liebe swester, ich han entpfangen
brief von dir mir geschriben, in dennen ich dine swester=
liche truwe und lieb die du zu mir hast gar wol hab
mögen vernemen, wen ob mich gantz kein andere lere / sogeiben.
uff dem rechten weg wise, wohte ich doch genugsam=
lich uss diner geschrifft min wesen unterrichten in
einen stat der miner selen in keinen weg könne schaden;
darumb wer es nit nott gewesen, min gotruwe swester,
das du geschriben hettest umb vergebniss ob mir ettwas
von dir mir geschriben misswellig wer, den mir on zwifel
kein misszval uss dinen ieren ist entsprungen, sunder
gezignuss und erkantnuss sunderer und grosser begird
die du hast zu nutz miner selen und zu miner selikeit;
umb des willen sag ich dir gar grossen danck, und
hoff der almechtige gotte sol mir verlichen ein ervelen
des stats inne welichen ich jmme mit grösserem verdienen
mög wolgefallen und all mine werck in sinen lob und
ere entlichen mög geschicken. Ouch, min liebe swester,
verkünde ich dir wol mögen und gesuntheit mines

Fig. 2.

ersammen meister Hansen und mine unss von gnaden
des milten gottes verliehend. Des glichen und gar vil me
gütes wer mir ein sundere freid von diner erwirdigen
muter priorin, dir und allen dinen mittswestern alezyt
vernemen. Alz du mich gebetten hast, min liebe swester,
das ich dich entpfelhen sol dinem vater sancto Dominico,
wiss das ich noch in gedehtnys hab verstrechnisse die ich
dir in minem abscheid dete, wan ich glich mich das uch
dine nimmer vergiss wan ich zu sinem grab kumme,
das ich zu manichem mal in dinem nammen hab
gekusset; wolt gott das es imme geneme wer. Das du
aber, min liebe swester, kunst der rechten dorechte kunst
nennest, kan ich dir nitt wol recht geben, dan geistliche
rechte alle genummen sint uss dem heiligen evangelien,
und der heiligen lerer bucher und besstetiget von dem
heiligen bebsten die man nitt minner ist schuldig zu halten
dan das heilige evangelien; und die weltlichen rechte
alle for orden haben gerechtikeit durch die man
einem jeglichen das imme zuhöret sol verliehen, von
welchen gestriben ist: justi autem in perpetuum
vivent etc, et rursus: justorum anime in manu dei
sunt etc, et iterum: justus ut palma florebit etc, et darco:
os justi meditabitur sapientiam etc, de sigte: justum
deducit dominus per vias rectas et ostendit illi regnum
dei; und in gar vil andern enden in denen gestriben
sint verdienst und lon der die gerechtikeit den mönschen
erzeigen; ouch sanctus paulus, in dem er spricht: ein
jegliche mönschliche kunst die ein dorheit gegen göttlicher wissheit, hat nit zuwelt sphrechen darnach
alz du es vernimmest, sunder sine meinung ist gewesen

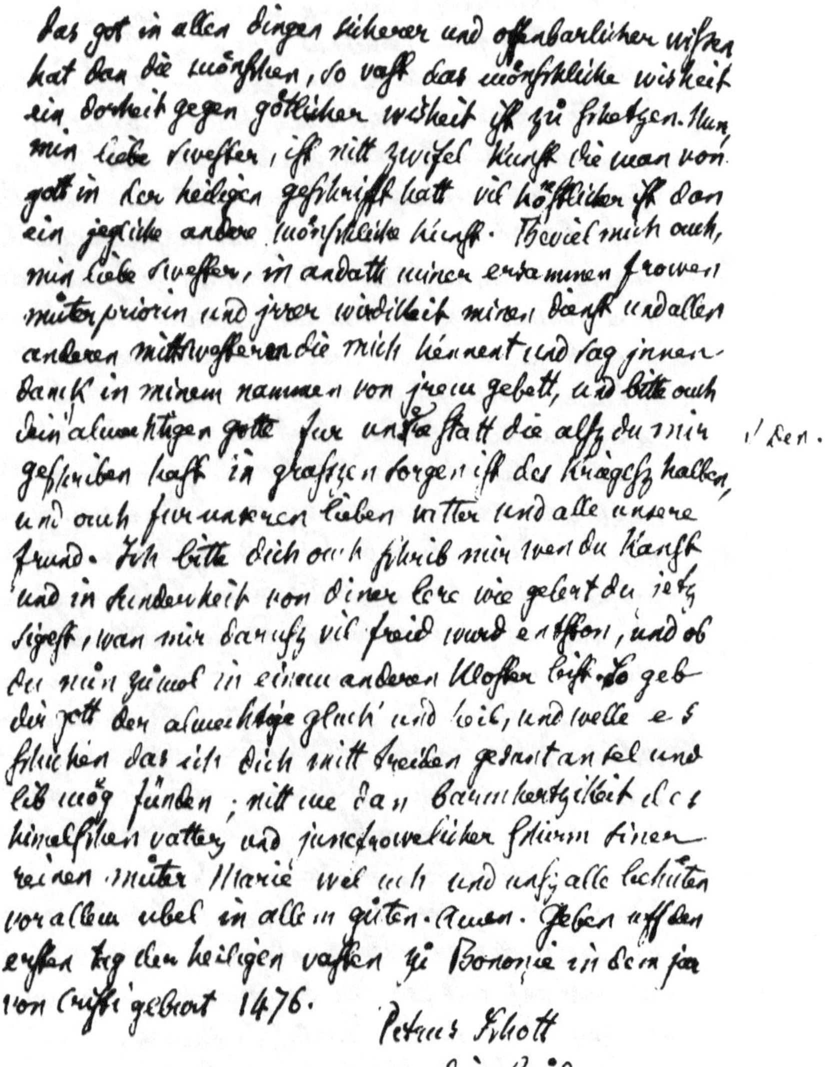

das got in allen dingen sikerer und offenbarlicher wissen hat dan die mönschen, so vast das mönschliche wisheit ein dorheit gegen götlicher wisheit ist zu schetzen. Nun, min liebe swester, ist nit zwifel kunst die man von got in der heiligen geschrifft hat vil höfflicher ist dan ein jegliche andere mönschliche kunst. Thevil mich ouch, min liebe swester, in andacht miner erdamnen frowen muter priorin und irer windikeit minen danck und allen anderen mitswesteren die mich kennent und sag innen danck in minem nammen von irem gebett, und bitte ouch den almechtigen gotte fur un stat die alz du mir geschriben hast in grossen sorgen ist des krieges halber, und ouch fur unseren lieben vater und alle unsere frund. Ich bitte dich ouch schrib mir wen du kanst und in sunderheit von diner lere wie gelert du jetz sigest, wan mir darusz vil froid wurd entston, und ob du nun zumol in einem anderen kloster bist. So geb dir gott der almechtige gluck und heil, und welle es schicken das ich dich mitt freiden gesunt an sel und lib mög funden; nit me dan barmhertzigkeit des himelschen vatter, und junckfrowelicher schirm einer reinen muter Marie wel uch und uns alle behüten vor allem ubel in allem guten. Amen. Geben uff den ersten tag den heiligen vasten zu Bononie in dem jar von Cristi geburt 1476.

Petrus Schott
Ein bruder.

Disen brief hat mir min allerliebster bruder petrus

Fig. 4.

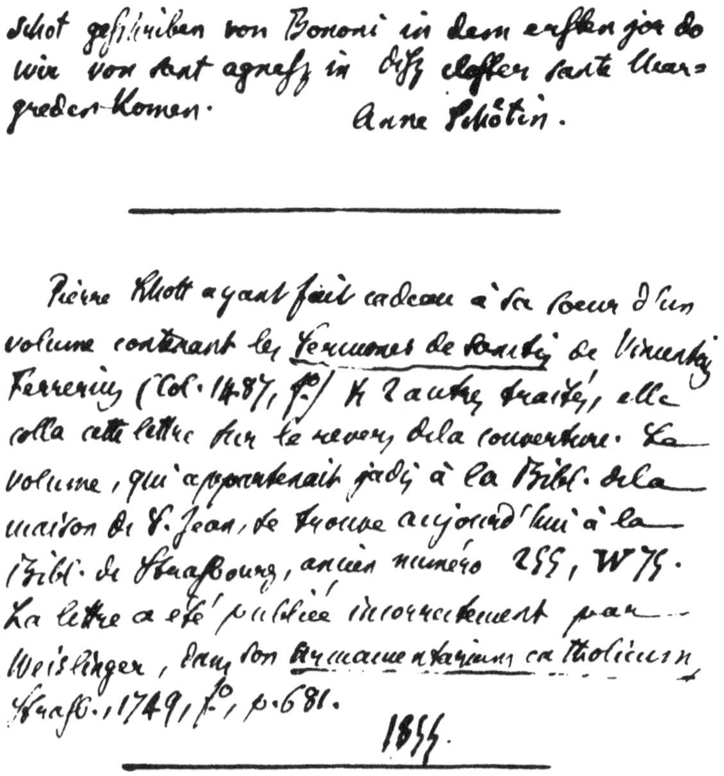

Schot geschriben von Bononi in dem ersten jor do
wir von sant agnesz in diss closter sant Mar-
greden komen. Anne Schötin.

Pierre Schott ayant fait cadeau à sa soeur d'un
volume contenant les Sermones de Sanctis de Vincentij
Ferrerius (Col. 1487, f°.) st 2 autres traités, elle
colla cette lettre sur le revers de la couverture. Le
volume, qui appartenait jadis à la Bibl. de la
maison de S. Jean, se trouve aujourd'hui à la
Bibl. de Strasbourg, ancien numéro 255, W 75.
La lettre a été publiée incorrectement par
Weislinger, dans son Armamentarium catholicum
Strassb. 1749, f°, p. 681. 1855.

Fig. 5.

APPENDIX B

Letter of Peter Schott to Friedrich von Zollern from the Strassburg Archives (Inventaire des Archives de la Ville de Strasbourg, Série IV, 156: IV, 105.B)

Post submissam et humilem obseruantiā prosperitatis et salutis plurimum dicit. Quum viderem comes generosissime: profecturū ad te reuerendissimū praesulē nostrū. non abs re iudicaui fore si animi mei promissimā erga te obsequentiā: perseue ratē atq̃ perpetuam esse: vel his literis meis paucissimis attestarer. Poterat enim forsan tanta temporis intercapedo / quo dignatione tua nobis omniū desideratissima / carere cogimur / languidioris cordis suspicionem afferre. Verū tanta sunt clarissime magnifice tuae ī me merita: tam profusa in me et meos benignitas: vt ea nec plagarū et lori distantia nec temporis quantulibet longi discrimina abolere atq̃ obliterare possint Itaq̃ tibi persuade nobilissime comes: virtutibus tuis / quas hic enarrare nec carta nec tempus patit ī me tantopere deuinctū esse: vt quoad vixero seruulū obsequentissimū sis in me possessurus. Vtinam deus clementissimus ita paret et componat omnia quae acturus es / vt si nos minus digni sumus qui te principe gubernemur, apud alios: qd mussari audio, ea felicitate ac salute vitam hanc mortalē exigas: vt et tibi et populo tuo: gratiam et gloriam aeternā illā diro nō terrenā sis consecuturus. Attamen quū in loco fueris vt mej et magistri mej solis quem tua clementia nuper benigne inuisse nisi ego nimiū cōfisus aliis circumuentus p eos fuissem) nostrū ingꝛ vt in gratia et fauor memineris: te iterū atq̃ iterū maximopere oro et obsecro Comendant se tibi et spontaneam seruitutem pollicentur pater et genitrix mej. Dn̄s omīpotens tecū sit preclarissime atq̃ nobilissime domīe Ex argentina pdie kal͑ Martij Anno a natali christiano ⅿccclxxxvj

1486.

28. feb.

Petrus · Schott ·
Argentinensis

APPENDIX B

Transcription of the foregoing letter of Peter Schott to Friedrich von Zollern
Strassburg, 28 February 1486

Post submissam et humilem obseruantiam prosperitatis et salutis plurimum dicit.
    Quum viderem: comes generosissime: profecturum ad te reuerendissimum praesulum [praesulem] nostrum. non abre iudicaui fore. si animi mei promissimam erga te obsequentiam: perseuerantem atque perpetuam esse: vel his litteris meis paucissimis attestarer. Poterat enim fortassis tanta temporis intercapedo/ quo dignatione tua nobis omnium desideratissima/ carere rogimur/ languidioris cordis suspitionem afferre. Verum tanta sunt clarissime magnificentie tuae in me merita: tam profusa in me et meos benignitas: vt ea nec plagarum et loci distantia: nec temporis quantumlibet longi discrimina: abolere atque obliterare possint. Itaque tibi persuade: nobilissime comes: virtutibus tuis/ quas hic enarrari nec carta nec tempus patitur/ me tantopere deuinctum esse: ut quoad vixero seruulum obsequentissimum sis in me possessurus.
    Vtinam deus clementissimus ita paret et componat omnia quae acturus es/ vt si nos minus digni sumus qui te principe gubernemur/ apud alios: quod mussari audio/ ea felicitate ac salute vitam hanc mortalem exigas: vt et tibi et populo tuo: gratiam et gloriam aeternam illam dico non terrenam/ sis consecuturus.
    Attamen quocumque in loco fueris vt mej: et magistri mej Ioannis [(]quem tua clementia nuper benigne iuuisset nisi ego nimium confisus aliis circumuentus per eos fuissem) nostrum inquam vt in gratia et fauore memineris: te iterum atque iterum maximopere oro et obsecro[.]
    Commendant se tibi et spontaneam seruitutem pollicentur pater et genitrix mej. Dominus omnipotens tecum sit preclarissime atque nobilissime domine. Ex argentina pridie kalendas Marcij Anno a natali christiano Mccclxxxvj[.]

Notes to letter

Summary
In this letter which the bishop of Strassburg is delivering, Schott affirms his continuing respect and affection for Friedrich von Zollern. It is rumored that Friedrich may assume another position and leave the Strassburgers. Whatever the course, Schott asks that God may guide Friedrich in pursuing for himself and his people grace and eternal glory rather than earthly glory. Schott bids Friedrich to be mindful of Johann Müller's interests and sends greetings from his parents.

Date
This letter chronologically precedes Schott's letter of 30 March 1486 to Friedrich von Zollern (#83). Both letters were written at the time when Friedrich was being elected bishop of Augsburg (N. 674).

profecturum ad te reuerendissimum praesulem nostrum... carere rogimur
Bishop Albrecht* of Strassburg was leaving Strassburg to attend Maximilian's coronation as King of the Romans in Aachen on 9 April 1486. He may have been going first to Frankfurt to join Maximilian's retinue and proceed with it to Aachen. Friedrich von Zollern, dean of the Strassburg cathedral, had been in Frankfurt for some time, and was present at Maximilian's election as King of the Romans on 16 February. For his part in the coronation at Aachen, cf. biographical note on Zollern.

quod mussari audio/ ea felicitate... sis consecuturus
On 23 February 1486 – just five days previous to Schott's letter – the bishop of Augsburg Johann von Werdenberg, an uncle of Friedrich von Zollern, had died. Friedrich was being considered as candidate for the vacant benefice. Cf. N. 674.

magistri mej Iohannis... maximopere oro et obsecro
Schott is hinting that Friedrich von Zollern should obtain from Maximilian *preces primae* (N. 130, 2) for Johann Müller. In the letter of 30 March 1486, written after the Augsburg cathedral chapter had elected Friedrich as bishop, Schott asks outright for the *preces* (#83, cf. also N. 680). The allusion to the help Friedrich would have given Müller and to Schott's betrayal by those he trusted probably refers to the abortive attempts to procure for Müller the benefice of perpetual vicar at the Strassburg cathedral in September 1485 (cf. N. 529).

APPENDIX C

Copy of Lucubraciunculae *item #83 from the Strassburg Archives* (Iventaire des Archives de la Ville de Strasbourg, Série IV, 156: IV, 105B)

APPENDIX D

The "Wimpheling Codex" (*University of Uppsala Codex No. 687*)

"Habent sua fata libelli!" How the "Wimpheling Codex," now in the *Carolina Rediviva* – the library of the university of Uppsala – came from Alsace to Sweden no one knows, but the supposition is that, like the "Codex Argenteus," it was brought home by the Swedes during the Thirty Years' War. Swedish troops may have touched Alsace in early 1632 when Gustavus Adolphus was in the Rhine area; they were actually in Alsace during the 1640's. We today should be grateful that the "Wimpheling Codex" has been preserved in Uppsala. Had it remained in Strassburg, it would very probably – like so much valuable material – have long since disappeared. Its most recent journey was apparently to a Reuchlin exhibit in 1957.

Little interest was shown in the "Wimpheling Codex" until Hugo Holstein during the last decades of the nineteenth century briefly described the contents in two short articles of the same title ("Ein Wimpheling Codex" in ZvLR and "Ein Wimpheling Codex," *Beilage zur Allgemeinen Zeitung*) and published six selections from the codex in "Neue Mitteilungen. Alsatica" (cf. bibliography for exact data).

The codex of 300 large vellum folios contains miscellaneous material collected by Wimpheling and is probably typical of collections made by literary men of the age. Wimpheling presented his collection to his pupil Jacob Sturm,* as is indicated by the inscription on the inside cover of the codex: "Jacobi Sturm Ex dono Jacobi Wympfelingii, Sacrae paginae Licentiati." Except for the folios which have been left blank on one or both sides and those folios which have had items – either handwritten or printed – pasted on them, the folios are covered with handwritten items. Letters, poems, orations and other compositions by Wimpheling form the major part of the collection. The second largest bulk of material consists of compositions by important people of the age, such as Reuchlin* (who is represented by letters, poems and the humanistic drama *Henno*), Brant,* Scintilla, (Funck*) Ludwig von Helmstadt,* Celtis, Schott, *et al.* There are also historical accounts, papal edicts, quotations from the classics, Latin and Italian epitaphs, Petrarch's poem to Mary Magdalene (cf. biographical note on Geiler) and so on. Cf. N. 1600 and N. 1701, par. 2.

In 1964 at Uppsala we checked the contents of the *Wimpheling Codex* to ascertain whether it contains any unpublished writings of Peter Schott. We found none. The Schott items in the codex are:

f. 169a	Letter to Geiler	*Luc.* #18
ff. 170a-170b	Elegiac to Jacob Wimpheling	*Luc.* #244
f. 170b	Letter to Geiler	*Luc.* #240
ff. 171b-173a	Poem *De tribus Iohannibus*	*Luc.* #241
ff. 176b	Letter to Geiler (second copy, cf. N. 1574)	*Luc.* #240
ff. 177a-179a	Poem *De tribus Iohannibus* (second copy)	*Luc.* #241
ff. 179b-180a	Excerpt from treatise on Christian life "De fide in affectionem trahenda"	*Luc.* #110, 3

f. 255b	German translation of the Sforza letter to Strassburg (cf. N. 2); year erroneously given as 1486	Appendix E
f. 258a	German translation of the Sforza letter to Zürich (f. 257a has the original Latin text)	Appendix F

At the top of folio 181a of the codex is the notation: "Petrus Schottus filius Argentinensis." Under this was once pasted an item either by or about Schott, but unfortunately there remains only a glue spot to mark its place. One may conjecture that perhaps a few other glue spots or empty parts of folios were originally covered with items by or about Schott.

APPENDIX E

Letter in Latin of 27 November 1478 from Bona and Giovanni Galeazzo Maria Sforza to the city of Zürich
(Text from Holstein's transcription of "Wimpheling Codex," folio 257a, in "Mitteilungen," 76f.; copy of letter also in Zürich archives)

Bona et Joannes Galeacius Maria Sfortiae Vicecomites, duces Mediolani etc. Papie Anglerieque Comites ac Janue et Cremone domini gubernatori et populo opidi Thuricensis.

Per litteras vestras datas die Jouis post sanctum Othmarum indixistis nobis bellum, utpote requisiti ab Vraniensibus sociis vestris, mortes hominum, depredaciones, incendia, diruptiones castellorum, agrorum et villarum depopulaciones et omne malum quod poteritis comminantes. Profecto ut motus bellorum, quos Vranienses in nos moliti sunt, sine ulla racione siue iusticia, quin pocius contra federa nostra, ius iurandum ac diuina et humana iura, processerunt, ita et hec vestra denunciacio belli admiracionem nobis attulit, quippe quod putauimus vos qui urbem non Alpes incolitis racione viuere et ut cultu ita et moribus his prestare qui ab humanitate absunt. Sed hec nostra opinio nos admodum fefellit, quod videmus vos eodem appetitu duci quo Vranienses. Quid est quod de nobis merito conqueri ualeatis aut que iniuria a nobis subditis uel mercatoribus vestris illata est, nisi fortasse quod nimium arbitrium nimiasque amplas immunitates et quas nequaquam debuissemus, etiam cum iactura maxima vectigalium et intratarum nostrarum et nostrorum subditorum vobis indulsimus?

Nihil est profecto, nihil nisi ceca quedam et auara cupiditas desideriumque et fames rerum alienarum. Quod speramus vos fallet, primum enim iusticia pro nobis militat quam fouere immortalis et optimus deus iuuareque semper consueuit viduasque et pupillos protegere. Habemus deinde vires non vestris et Vraniensium inferiores, immo vero gentibus et neruis belli multo maiores, nec timemus quod ligas iactetis, cum et ligas et societates amiciciasque potentissimas habeamus, que nobis quandocunque opus foret presidio essent. Scitote igitur nos constanti animo ad utrum malueritis, pacem vel bellum paratissimos esse, nec est quod amplius vestris aut commercium aut immunitates in dominio nostro esse velimus quibus vos sine honestate, sine iusticia renunciastis. Si nobiscum manus conserere decreveritis, excipiemus vos quidem his dapibus quas gentes nostre hostibus suis dare consueverunt, experieminique tandem, quid arma nostra ualeant. Habetis itaque ad vestram belli denunciacionem responsum nostrum per hunc vestrum tabellarium, in quem humanius egimus quam illi veri et recti violatores Vranienses, qui nostrum tabellarium maximis uerberibus affectum remiserunt; que res apud infideles et ipsos denique inferos indignissima videtur.

Datum Mediolani die XXVII Nouembris anno etc. LXXVIII.

Peter Schott's German translation of the Sforza letter to the city of Zürich (Text from Holstein's transcription of "Wimpheling Codex," folio 258a, in "Mitteilungen," 76f.)

Bona Galeacz Forcia vicecomites und herzogen zů Meylon etc. grafen zů

Pafye vnd zů Anglerien herren zů Jenuowe vnd zů Cremone dem gubernator vnd dem volk zů Zurich. Durch vwere briefe geben zů Zurich vff donrstag nach Othmari habent ir vns verkundet ein strit, als erfordert von den von Vre vwren gesellen, vnd trowent vns doslege der menschen, beroubunge, brant, zersterunge der stette, verherunge der åcker vnd dorffer vnd alles böse das iz vermögent. Fur wor als vns die bewegunge der strite, so di von Vre wider vns vnderstanden hant, one alle vrsach oder gerechtikeit, sunder wider vnsere bunde, gesworen eyde, gotlich vnd menschlich recht, widerfuren, also hat vns dise vwere verkundunge des strites verwundern broht, vnd wir wondent, nach dem ir in einer stat vnd nit vff den Alben wonent, ir soltent leben nach vernunft vnd als ir sint in der wonunge, als soltent ir ouch in den sytten anders syn den dye von den luten sint. Aber disse vnser meynunge hat vns betrogen, dan wir sehent, das ir in glicher begirde gefurt werdent als die von Vre. Was ist es das ir von vns clagen mögent, oder was vnrechts ist von vns vwren vndertonen oder kouffluten zůgefuget, es sie dan das wir villiht uch zů vil uwren willen vnd zů vil vorteils oder friheit, vnd die wir uch nit schuldig gewesen sint ouch mit grossem schaden der furunge vnd vnserer ingenge vnd vnser vndertonen zůgelossen vnd vergunstiget habent.

Es ist sicher nit anders dan ein blinde vnd gritige begirde, ein begirlicheit vnd hunger noch fremden gůt, do wir hoffent es sol uch velen, dan des ersten so vihtet die gerechtikeit fur vns, die do der vntötlich vnd öberste got gewonet hat alwegent zů stercken vnd zů helffen, wittwen vnd weysen zů schyrmen, darzů habent wir macht, die do nit mynner sint dan vwer vnd der von Vre macht vnd joch mer sint von luten vnd anderen dingen zům state geherende; wir vorchtent ouch nit, das ir vch vff vwer buntgenossen verlossent, nach dem wir ouch habent buntgenossen geselschafften vnd fruntschafften, die vast mechtiger sint, die do vns, so uerre es vns not were, zů hulffe kement, vnd ir sollent wissen, das wir eins steten gemuts vnd bereit sint zů wellichin ir wellent, es sy fride oder strit, vnd darumb so wellent wir nit, das die vwren furbass eynichen handel vorteyl oder fryheit in vnserer herschafft habent, deren ir uch one gerechtikeit vnd one ersammekeit verzigen habent. Ist es, das ir mit vns hande anlegen wellent, das nemmen wir uff vnd satigen uch mit den spisen, die vnsere lute iren vigenden gewonet habent zů geben, vnd ir werdent leste befinden, was vnser wofen vermogent, vnd also habent ir uff vsskundung vwres strites vnser antwort durch disen vwern botten, gegen dem wir vns gutlicher gehalten habent dan die von Vre, die do sint verbrecher der gerechten vnd ersammen dinge, die do vnseren botten widergesant hant als si ine vbel geslagen habent, welliche dinge by den vngloubigen vnd ioch by denen in der hellen vnbillich werent.

Geben zů Meyelon am XXVII. tag des monats nouembris anno etc. LXXVIII.

APPENDIX F

Letter in Italian of 27 June 1481 from Duke Giovanni Galeazzo Maria Sforza to the city of Strassburg
(Text from Holstein, "Mitteilungen," 81; text also in Schadäus', preface)

Lettera ducale ai magistrati e governatori di Strasburga.
Addì 27 giugno.
Magnifici insignesque cives amici nostri carissimi. Questi fabricieri del celeberrimo templo de questa nostra inclyta città stano in suspensione de non fare furnire el tuburio, se prima non consultano bene con optimi ingegneri, utrum le columne maestre, sopra le quale va fabricato, serano forte e sufficiente a sostenir tanta machina e peso incredibile, quanto haverà esser dicto tuburio, che sarà cosa stupendissima; unde saria eterno vilipendio, se dopo fornito ce occorresse alcuno manchamento. Però essendone per diverse vie fatto intendere del optima sufficientia de lo ingegnero del famoso templo de quella vestra città, pregamovi ce vogliati compiacere in mandarnelo fin qua, o luy o altro più sufficiente che si trovasse in quella patria. Joanne Antonio de Gesa nostro citadino, quale si manda li ad questo effecto, gli farà bona compagnia per camino. Qua sarà bene ricevuto e meglio tractato, e faremo per modo ch'el ritornerà ben contento.
    Non vi ricrescha ad pigliare questo carico per amor nostro in persuadergli ch'el vegni, che ne fareti cosa grata, e sempre ne trovareti paratissimi a li vestri piaceri.
    Mediolani, in arce nostra portae Jovis, die 27 junii 1481.
    Johannes Galeaz Maria Sfortia Vicecomes dux Mediolani etc.

Peter Schott's German translation of the Sforza letter to the city of Strassburg
(Text from Holstein's transcription of "Wimpheling Codex," folio 255b, in "Mitteilungen," 81f.)

Den grosstügigen vnd wolgeadelten mannen der gemein vnd den burgern zu Strassburg.
    Grosztugige vnd wolgeadelte burger, vnser liebsten fründ, Die buwmeister des witgerümpten tempels disser vnser hochgelobten statt stont in zwifel nitt zu vollenden den vbergebuw. sy siggen denn vor wol zu rot worden mitt den besten sinnrichen werckmeistern, ob die furnemen sülen, vff denen es gebuwen sol werden, siggen starck vnd gnusam zu enthalten ein so grosszen gebuw vnd ein vnglouplichs gewicht, als dann sin soll der gemeldt vbergebuw: wenn es wurt sin ein ding sich uber die mosz zu erstutzen vnd deshalben wer es ein ewiger schad: ob noch dem es volendet wurd widerfür etlicher gebrust, Dorvmb als wir durch manigerley weg vnderricht sint worden von der besten genugsamme des synnrichen werckmeisters des gerümpten tempels in der selbigen vwren statt: bitten wir vch das Ir vns wellen zu willen werden iñ zu schicken biszhar: antweders iñ oder ein andern den genugsamsten so man vinde in dem selben land. Hans Anthoñ von Gesa vnser burger, der zu vch geschickt wurt der sachen halb, wurt im thun

gûte gesellschaft uff dem weg. Hie wurt er wol vor ougen gehaben vnd wert gehalten werden vnd wir wellen also handlen das er wurt widerkeren wol begnügt.

Nitt lon vch vertriesszen uffzunemen semliche bürd vmb vnsren willen in zu uberreden das er kumm, denn ir vns bewisen werden ein angenâme sach vnd werden vns vinden alle zit bereit zu vwrn wolgefallen Zü Meylan in vnser vôste der porten Jouis an dem XXVII tag Junii 1481.

Johans galeatz maria sfortia ein stathaltender groff Hertzog zu Meylan etc.

APPENDIX G

Letter in Latin of 19 April 1482 from Duke Giovanni Galeazzo Maria Sforza to Peter Schott, Sr.
(Text from Holstein, "Mitteilungen", 82f.; manuscript copy also in the Strassburg archives: *Inventaire... St. Thomas*, 345)

Magnifico amico nostro carissimo domino Petro Schotto, gubernatori civium et consiliario civitatis Argentinae, praefectoque fabricae templi maioris ibidem.
Magnifice amice noster carissime. Rogavimus per litteras superioribus mensibus magnificentiam vestram, ut cum in hac urbe nostra templum ad honorem beatae Mariae Virginis mirae magnitudinis et pulchritudinis struatur, nec deesse velimus quominus omnia rectissime fiant et tanto operi nihil imputari queat, ad nos mittere vellet quendam architectum seu ingeniarium, quem isthic praestantissimum esse intelligebamus, ut templum ipsum videre et omnia recte metiri valeret ac suum super agendis iudicium edocere; et quia idem architectus non venit et ut veniat eodem tenemur desiderio, rogamus rursum magnificentiam vestram, ut nos huiuscemodi voti compotes efficiat, et ipsum architectum mittat; id enim gratissimum habebimus, parati in similibus et maioribus vobis gratificari, et hac de causa mittitur isthuc praesentium lator cum facultate praebendi modum ipsi architecto veniendi.
  Mediolani 18 aprilis 1482. Johannes Galeaz Maria Sfortia Vicecomes dux Mediolani etc.

APPENDIX H

Precepts composed by Geiler von Kaisersberg for Friedrich von Zollern
(Text from Dacheux, *Réf.*, Appendix LIV-LVIII)

III.

(V. pag. 36a et suiv.)

MONITA JOANNIS GEILERI AD FRIDERICUM, COMITEM DE ZOLLERN, 1478 [1](?)

Animo et sanguine generoso comiti domino *Friderico* de *Zolr*, Jo. de *Keisersperg*, mandatorum Dei solicitam scrutationem! Quod a me requiris, alterius, qui pro consuetudine exercitatos haberet sensus ad discretionem boni ac mali, munus foret, non ejus qui crebris affectuum concutitur procellis. Quomodo enim ego, in quo sanguis fervet, passiones ebulliunt, extersos oculos haberem quo tibi ejusdem fere etatis homini remedia prestarem? hoc enim ipsum, quod tu desideras, ego mendico. Sed non est qui consoletur me. Nec quia non sunt, mihi consolationi esse poterit, sicque in spe pendens salutem meam cum timore, adjutore Deo, operari conabor. Tu autem quia non semel plusculis id ipsum postulasti vicibus, non quod efficax sed quod saltem rectum et Deo placitum est, ne tibi contraveniam annotabo, cum te sincero corde hec affectare scire non dubitem. Indolem tibi a domino insitam ad bonum cave ne negligas, sed donis a domino tibi datis ad ejus utere gloriam, sic (crede mihi) hic generosior ceteris (quod tamen neutiquam eo intuitu facere cogites), nedum in eterna gloria reputaberis. Nolo autem ante omnia ut in mentem tibi veniat te huic seculo, puta tibi sanguine similibus, conformari oportere. Scis quid Paulus contra talem dyabolicum singulorum secularium saltum in suarum libertatum defensionem objectum exclamet: Nolite confor-

---

1. Nous avons réussi à nous procurer le texte de cet écrit si intéressant de Geiler, et nous sommes sûr de faire plaisir au lecteur en le publiant intégralement.

mari huic seculo. Profecto timeo et ego mihi judicium a Domino imminere, si meorum actuum regulam plerosque in eo quo ego, etsi immerito, gradu constitutos, statuero. Volo igitur ut te Cristianum primum, postea autem Comitem consideres. In omnibus igitur, primo ut christianus et pro regno eterno hic viriliter agonizans pugnare oportet; postea comitatum te abnegare non precipitur. Quod si quidpiam te agere ob tue et tuorum generositati similium conscientiam duxeris, si id tale fuerit quod majori professioni tue, quam supremo regno fecisti, non contraierit, placet quod agis. Sin autem, cave, quia hoc non tue congruet generositati quam Christo dedicasti, sed aliorum sub vexillo dyabolico pugnancium. Te igitur que subnotata sunt decebunt.

Consorcia juvenum et maxime illorum, qui imberbes sunt, devita quanto conveniencius poteris; quos autem apud te habere cogeris, retine in freno. Maturum, non dico gravem, te eis ostende. Nunquam patiaris ut te videant nisi honesta veste circumamictum. Neque in conspectu tuo audeant nisi sicut coram comite utcunque astare, eciam si solus fueris, nec aliquid scurrilitatis vel dicere vel moribus gerere, sed ut singuli ad tui excreationem (?) ab eciam jam inceptis obticescant. Paucis sis familiaris, tamen omnibus communis. In conspectu tuo non paciaris ut quispiam alteri detrahat. Cum loqui volueris quid, prius ad limam quam ad linguam fac ut perveniat. Honestatem morum et vestitus quam in te diligis, et in famulis tuis fac relucere; ex familia dominus qualis sit conjicitur. Thesaurum, quem habes Domini dono, appreciare, et tute pro Dei gloria conserva, ne alius tuam coronam accipiat. Cave ne primum postquam amiseris ipsum, quam carus fuerit habendus sero consideres. Fuge omnem quarumcumque feminarum confabulationem. Crede mihi, alias non tutus eris; momentum affert quod totus denegat annus. Non solum juvenes, sed et viros sub hac peste corruisse vidimus, de quorum casu mihi minor fuerat suspicio quam de Hyeronymi et Ambrosii. Etsi enim nihil aliquando in te commotionis sentias cum apud ipsas conversaris, non tamen caute huic baculo inniteris ; arundineus est. Hec dyaboli est astucia ut tibi quandam inducat securitatem ipsis cohabitandi, ut tandem opportunitate capta te precipitet. Poterunt tibi alia esse solacia quam cum scorpionibus. Non poteris servire mundo et domino. Amor Domini liber est, solus in corde hominis vult dominari. Fateor, pacieris fatuas muliercularum et aliorum nobilium oblocutiones. Dicent : Et unde istec religio ? et profecto itidem te ex tibi subditis exprobrabitur, etsi non in faciem, tamen in terga ; sed hoc vince. Tandem enim cum viceris, lumen tuum clarius sole effulget omnibusque exemplar eris virtutum et in omnium admirationem statueris.

Preterea nunquam ocieris, sed diem divide et cuilibet tempori opera aceomoda. Quid mali ocium afferat, edici sufficienter non poterit; ipsum est efficacissimum ad castitatem expugnandam, noverca omnium virtutum. Igitur semper aliquid facito, ut dyabolus te occupatum inveniat. Cum evigilaveris, nullo pacto in lecto vigilans maneas, sed surge ne in cogitationes turpes incidas et Deum offendas. Cumque surrexeris, humilia te Deo, quia dignus est, flexis genibus et protensis palmis versus celum ad creatorem tuum et profitere sibi sicut tuo regi. Dic *Credo in Deum Patrem*, etc., *Pater noster, Ave Maria*, et cruce te signa *in nom. P. et F. et Sp. S.*, et surge. Deinde te ad dicendas canonicas horas dispone, in silentio te super brachiis appodiando vel alio modo te aliqualiter recolligendo, et Deum interius deprecando ut det graciam, vel aliud cogitando de Deo, sicut dominus inspiraverit. *Et tunc incipiendo cum ea honestate morum sicut si omnis populus adesset, non autem in transvolatu assuesce dicere, sed mature et ita diligenter ac si adeptio vite eterne in hoc solo consisteret. Neque festines absolvi cicius ut ad studium literarum te recipias, sed hoc perfice. Eo perfecto, aliorsum te transferas. Sit tibi hec generalis regula : in omnibus majoribus et minoribus faciendis operibus omnem diligentiam adhibeas, ut quomodocunque melius poteris facias, quasi tota salus tua et omnis laus Dei et universitatis utilitas ex hoc uno opere dependeat, quasi nunquam ad id opus reversurus neque opus aliud postmodum incepturus. Scis enim quod, quotiens opus aliquod facimus ad aliud opus ferventer properantes, ex solo desiderio alterius operis statim lassus fit animus in opere in quo sumus : v. g. cum sumus in oratione vel alio opere, et proponimus scribere vel studere vel aliud opus facere, statim contra orationem minuitur noster affectus et cicius absolvimur ab incepto, et sic nulla nostra perfecta sunt opera, neque a quo absolvi festinamus, neque ad quod incipiendum properamus, quia etiam illo inchoato ad alia attediati conamur. Istiusmodi igitur opere puta te pro tunc nil melius agere posse et quiesce.*

Diem sine misse auditione non transeas ibique cum devotione, si quas peculiares orationes habueris, attente dicas, cogitando hic esse redemptorem et salvatorem nostrum, et similia. Cum ad manducandum accesseris, retine mentem : cogitando hic esse locum refectionis pro necessitate, non pro voluptate. In risus incompositos non erumpas vociferando chachinnis, pocius silenter subridendo ; sed ad impudica aut detractoria cave ne rideas, sed faciem ostende tristem que tales pocius linguas dissipet sicut ventus aquilo pluvias, vel eciam, si congruat, verbo repugna. Pauca loquere in mensa et cum maturitate. Non approbo diuturnam moram post comestionem in mensa, quia plerumque lingue in ludicra, scurrilia et detractoria verba solvuntur, sed utilius est aliquo deambulare. Nonas post prandium dicere congruum est et non nisi diebus jejuniorum ; vesperas hora congrua, completorium post cenam statim. Cumque dormitum ire volueris, iterum, sicut surgendo, *Credo, pater noster, ave,* etc., flexis genibus dicas. Et talis sit tibi honestas jacendo qualem a te videri non verecundareris. Lassatus venias ad stratum, te morigerate componens, non resupinus jacens nec genua elevando calcaneos jungas ad nates et tibias. Non nudus jacere sed vestitus honestissimum esset, et homo ad surgendum expeditior; saltem ne camisia exueretur. De hiis tamen rebus quid tibi prodesse possit, tu ipse consule. Scio quia utile est homini benevolenti se in talibus modice exercitare, et illis neglectis raro ad majora perveniri. De confitendo et communicando nescio quid tibi moris sit neque de hoc scribo, cum te statim sacerdotium accepturum existimem. Quantum autem bonum sit crebra cum communione confessio nemo scit quam qui experitur; et quid periculi ex talium omissione patiatur, nemo scit quam qui periculum cum sui jactura fecit. Contine cor tuum et evagari non permittas. Cave ne alterius dicta vel facta jocose vel seriose eo absente sive presente deprehendas : sed si non vis commendare, sile, nisi putes te posse proficere. Habe semper oculum ad tua facta et dicta et statera rationis trutina, facile deprehendes quid bonum aut malum. *Hoc unum serva : fac ea que scis, et indubie dominus intelligere tibi dabit quod nescis. Nam qui negligit facere bonum quod novit faciendum, non meretur accipere notitiam faciendi id quod nondum novit; qui vero in talento intellectus, quod jam accepit, fideliter negociatur, dignus est ut talento ejus addatur.*

Hoc tibi, generose Comes, et si non dedignari volueris sicut neque debes, in Domino carissime frater, sicut calamus accepit tibi assignare statui : malim enim tibi in consilio meo simplex et indoctus videri quam non esse morigerus. Si placet quod concepi, approbare poteris ; est et tibi facultas ut eis lectis igni tradas. Vale et Dominum pro me exora. Ignosce quod non tibi quemadmodum tua posceret dignitas scripsi, quoniam hoc quod tibi literis loquor, non in aperto, sed in aure dictum esse velim. Singula que ac si nihil dicta sint, habere si volueris, duo tamen, manibus signata, cave ne spernas.

A. Steichele. *Archiv fur die Geschichte des Bisthums Augsburg*, I. Bd. pag. 154, sqq.

APPENDIX I

Texts of two letters from the Lucubraciunculae *as they appeared in* Goldast, Centuria.

1. Epist. XIIX [XVIII], 54-58 = *Luc.*, #65, pp. 70-72 (Schott to Agricola)
2. Epist. XIX, 58-65 = *Luc.*, #91, pp. 99-103 (Schott to Wimpheling)

EPIST. XIIX.
Heidelbergam.

Petrus Schottus Rodolpho Agricolæ Oratori priscarum elegantiarum.
S. P. D.

SI epistolarum genus illud est præcipuum, vt Ciceroni videtur, quo certiores facimus absentes, si quid sit quod eos scire aut nostra

CENTVRIA VNA.   55

nostra aut ipsorum intersit, veniam mihi dabis, vir doctissime, qui te mihi nondum plane cognitum his meis ineptiis adoriri non erubescam. Nam tametsi faciem tuam nunquam viderim, nec dextera dextram (vt aiunt) contigerim, tamen posteaquam honestissimarum artium tuarum quam plures & eos grauissimos testes audiui: quin & Italos ipsos alioquin gloriam propriam exaggerare, alienam attenuare solitos, te tamen & eruditionem tuam incredibili quodam peritissimorum assensu mirari & extollere, dum Ferrariæ tertium ante annum agerem præsens intellexi: continuo coepi & amare te quamuis ignotum (id quod virtus efficere consueuit) & in commune gratulari Germaniæ nostræ, quam sperarem tanto politiorum literarum principe a squalida illa & penitus radicata barbarie aliquando auferendam liberandamque fore. Itaque & tunc libellos, qui in manus meas venire poterant, quos tu è Græcis Latinos fecisti, exscribere curaui, & vbivbi occasio præberetur familiaritatem tuam, quo eruditior euaderem, inquirendam mihi constitui. Tandem Argentinam reuersus cum à Domino Thoma Vuolfio Iure consulto, & Adelpho Rusco, viris mihi singulari amicitia iunctis, intellexissem te Heidelbergæ iam coepisse

D 4

Fig. 1.

pisse purgare & linguas iuuenum & aures, vt ille nil scelerosum balbuciant, hæ vero tuis tam peritis & dulcibus elegantiis delibatæ omnes illas sciolorum insulsas & verbosas ineptias quasi magicas incantationes declinent: tum ego vehementer sum gauisus, & ilico meditatus familiaritatem litteris inchoare, si forte (quod Deus, ex re tua tamen, faxit) & præsens conuictus accederet. Idque eo audentior egi, quo plurimum ad me ore vno perferebatur, te non tam humanitatis artes profiteri quam ipsum ōmnium esse humanissimum. Quia igitur argumentum quærebam, quo te ad scribendum prouocarem, visum fuit super his tuum requirere iudicium, quæ & tu promptissime doces & ego studio singulari desidero. Ea licet minutissima sint, nec digna quibus doctrina tua solicitetur, tamen quo videntur abiectiora eo me vehementius pudet ipsa negligere, qui sim memor eius quod Horatius monet.

Vilibus in sepis, in mappis, in scopę quantus
Consistit sumptus, neglectis flagitium ingens?

Primum igitur te obsecro, vir literatissime, ne te pigeat certiorem me facere, quum in hymno quopiam Ambrosii canimus:

Os lingua mens sensus vigor
Confessionem personent,
Flammascat igne charitas.

Et quæ sequuntur: *Flammascat* an *flammescat* legendum sit. Inuenio siquidem *labasco* & *ingrauesco*. Deinde si eam dictionem, quam litteræ sacræ toties frequentant, *charitatem* dico, Græcam arbitreris an Latinam. Et si Græcam, qua deductione ἀπὸ τοῦ χαρίτος deriuetur. Sin Latinam duntaxat, cur ab his qui eruditiores haberi volunt aspiretur. *Auctor* per *c.* scribendum sit semper. *Lachrima* & *pulcher*, in quo Apuleius & Seruius dissentiunt, aspirationem patiantur, *Euxenia* vel, vt quidam contendunt, *Enxenia* idonea sint vocabula pro strenis & xeniis. Et si quid de *morticinis* habes, quo accentu proferantur, & quam apud priscos significationem obtinuerint. Plura sunt alia, sed vereor obtundere. Tuum igitur erit, vir doctissime, ignoscere impudentiæ meæ. Equidem cum te propter doctrinam maximi faciam, atq; ideo mirifice desiderem à te doceri, inductus sum ex meo animum tuum expectare, & proinde persuadere mihi ipsi, non passurum te pro liberali ingenio tuo hanc me spem frustrari. Sic enim habeto, si meum in hac re studium non aspernatus fueris, fore vt tibi tanta sim debiturus quanta ei, qui me beneficio supra quam dici possit grato affecerit. Vale. Datæ Argentinæ ad duodecimum Kalend.

Flammascat & Flammescat.
Auctor.
Lachrima.
Pulcher.
Euxenia vel Enxenia.
Morticina.

lend. Martii. Anno à natiuitate Saluatoris
M. CCCC. LXXXV.

EPIST. XIX. Spiram.

Petrus Schottus Iacobo VVimpfelingio Schlet-
statenſ. S.D.

Poſitionē
ex muta
& liqui-
da torripi
in proſa.
Tenebræ,
latebræ
quo acci-
in proſe-
rantur.

Quoniam priori epistola tua me oraueras, vt in ligato campo oſtenderem medias syllabas dictionum eius generis, qualis ſunt *tenebræ, latebræ,* breues incedere poſſe. Ego tibi carmina probatiſſimorum non pauca congreſſi, quibus id luce meredianâ clarius appareret, nihil tum de ſoluto ſtylo, super quo non inquiſieras: nihil de accentu dubitari poſſe ſuſpicatus. Quippe cum perſpectum eſſet tempus penultimæ ſyllabæ, quam penes Latini pleriq; omnes accentum in triſyllabis metiuntur. Sane perſpectum eſſe dixi, quamuis in poſterioribus literis tuis ſignifices illius probationes alias deſiderari. Nam quid, obsecro, apud ſtudioſum præclariſſimorum ingeniorum sectatorem indubitatius atq; fidelius erit pro dignoſcendis ſyllabarum quantitatibus, quam ſi exempla & celebres obſeruationes receptorum Poetarum intueantur? Ex eorum ſiquidem auctoritate quum omnes Latinæ vocales dichronæ ſint, omnes ferme quantitatum illæ regulæ prodierunt. Nec eſt quod dicunt aliqui, Poetica quadam licentia committi vt vel poſitio corripiatur: id vero in
ſolu

Fig. 3.

ſoluto campo nequaquam licere. Nam non iam licentiæ ſed vicio merito dabitur (quanquam etiam licentia vitium ſonat) ſi tam frequenti & crebra exorbitantia Poetæ numeros ſuos, quib. vel ſoli vel cæteris peculiarius ſtudent, aſſerantur neglexiſſe. Quod profecto de hiſce viris quiſquis ſenſerit, is non modo ipſos ſed & omnem priſcorum ætatem, quæ eos vt certiſſimos & exactiſſimos venerata eſt, videbitur iuſticiæ notâ contaminare. An non callidiſſimi eorum Critici, qui non ſolum inemendate ſed etiam figurate dicta calumniati ſunt? Nunquid Grammatici plurimi, qui vix pauca aliqua in Poetis, quæ producenda erant correpta per ſyſtolem deprehenderunt, hunc quoq; manifeſtarunt, & celeberrimum vſum ſi ſyllabarum tempori præiudicaſſet, non vidiſſent, notaſſent, caſtigaſſent? Num faciliora opera excuſaſſet Priſcianus illud Virgilii:

Ponite ſpes ſibi quiſque ———

Et hinc quam plura ſimilia, ſi aſſeueraſſet ille poetica licentia poſitionem correptam eſſe, quam quod ad id recurrit S. literam vim ſuam dimittere. Mirum ſane eſt Poetas, qui alioqui rariſſime longarum ſyllabarum naturam accurtaſſe reperiuntur, in hoc genere non ſolum longas natura (vt illi aiunt) ſed etiam poſitione arctatas tam crebro & paſsim corripere. Mirandum vero magis ſi Poetis, qui ligatiſſimi ſunt, diſſolutio tanta
con-

concedatur, eos qui solutam orationem effundunt ligatos magis esse debere, præcipue cum licentia illa Poetarum non ad numeros, in quibus astrictiores sunt oratoribus, vt M. Cicero dixit, sed ad verborum libertatem spectet. Quid ergo? inquiunt. Num in his, de quibus est quæstio, positionem esse negas? Equidem fateor positionem esse. Nam duæ consonantes contiguæ vocalem in vno etiam sequuntur vocabulo. Verum in hoc distare dico positionem, quæ ex muta & liquida resultat, ab ea quam mutæ duæ constituunt, quod quum hæc vocalem præcuntem vtcunque breuem longam perpetuo reddat, duriori nimirum enunciatione fluxum cohercente, illa quod salebrositate quadam moretur præcipitationem, non adeousque tamen vt lapsum prorsus exasperet. Hoc efficit vt in carmine, si ex vsu Poetæ sit, longa constituere possit præcuntem vocalem breuem. In oratione vero soluta si nonnunquam longe prolatam excuset, frequentius tamen breuem efferre & vsus & doctrina tradit. Ecce sententiam nostram, quam si qui minus recipiant, nihil mirum profecto in Grammatica, quæ inter artes cæteras professoribus est opulentior, sectas inueniri, quum etiam Astronomi quamuis paucissimi non sint semper vnanimes. Verum vt responsum nostrum, quantum ad id quod de Oratione soluta diximus, astruamus.

(Nam

Fig. 4.

(Nam quod ad carmen attinet cum aduersariis conuenit.) Allegare primo possem celeberrimorum omnium, quos equidem in Italia & extra noui plurimos, consuetudinem & vsum, *Quem penes* (vt Horatius ait) *arbitrium est & vis & norma loquendi.* Sed ne calumniæ locus aliquis detur, audiantur tres testes meo iudicio omni exceptione maiores, quibus si non credatur, nescio quid in Grammatica solidum præcipi possit. Loquatur igitur Diomedes ille antiquus inter Grammaticos nominis, qui in traditione de accentibus: *In trissyllabis,* inquit, *& tetrassyllabis & deinceps secunda ab vltima semper obseruanda sit. Hæc si positione longa fuerit, acuetur: vt, Catullus, Metellus, Marcellus. Ita tamen si positione longa non ex muta & liquida fuerit, nam mutabit accentum: vt Latebræ, Tenebræ.* Hæc ibi: Et paulo post: *Si penultima positione longa ita fuerit vt excipiat tam ex muta quā ex liquida, accentus transfertur ad tertiam ab vltima: vt, Tenebra, latebra.* Et postea apertius: *Et tenebras,* inquit, *& latebras acuto accentu prima syllaba effertur.* Tantum à Diomede. Accedat & Priscianus diligentissimus in re Grammatica, qui in tractatu, quem de accentibus reliquit, his verbis testimonium nobis perhibet: *Trissyllaba vero, & tetrassyllaba, & deinceps si penultimam correptam habuerint, antepenultima acuto accentu profertur, vt, Tullius, Hostilius. Nam si pura positione longa fuerit acuetur, antepenultima* *ma vero grauabitur: vt, Catullus, Metellus. Si verò ex muta & liquida longa in versu constat, in oratione mutat accentum: vt, Latebræ, Tenebræ.* Sic Priscianus. Num hæc clara satis · Numquid apertè & sine vlla circuitione, quod asseuerauimus, illi sunt testati? Forsitan adhuc videri poterunt alicui iustum auctoritatis pondus in Grammatica Grammaticorum Principes non habere, qui in re tanta sublimiorem quempiam tractatorem desiderabit. Sed vt huius quoq; insolentiæ morem geramus, adducatur Rhetor longe amplioris nominis, quam vt in tam friuolis ei fides non habeatur. Audiatur itaq; Quintilianus, qui in primo Institutionum Oratoriarum libro sic ait: *Euenit vt metri quoq, conditio mutet accentum: vt —— pecudes pictæq, volucres. Nam volucres media acuta legam, quia etsi natura breuis, tamen positione longa est ne faciat Iambum quem non recipit versus Heroicus.* Ecce quam dilucide declarat positionem quæ ex muta & liquida constat syllabam breuem prolongare posse, si id versus conditio requirit. Verum extra carmen accentu proprio debere proferri, qui nimirum alius est ab eo quem versus exigit. Aliter enim non diceret Quintilianus *metri conditione accentum mutari.* Hæc sunt, vir amicissime, quæ super his ad te scribenda putaui. Quibus si quid pro veritatis tuitione esse effectum putabis, nihil mihi fuerit gratius: sin minus, solabor ego me

Fig. 5.

me saltem testificatione grati erga te animi, qui videas me ineptias effundere malle quam impositam per te mihi scribendi prouinciam omnino declinare. Vale. Datæ Argentinæ ad Nonum Kalend. Octobres: Anno à natiuitate Domini M. CCCC. LXXXVI.

En tibi exempla, quibus præscripta in priore epistola approbauimus.

Virgilius Georgicor. tertio:
Nocte premunt, quod iam tenebris & Sole cadente.
Idem Æneid. tertio:
Noctem hyememque ferens & inhorruit vnda tenebris.
Idem in eodem:
Rursum ex diuerso cœli cæcisq, latebris.
In eodem idem:
————*Et regna recludat*
Pallida Diisq, inuisa superq, immane baratrum cernatur————
Horatius:
Pernicies & tempestas baratrumq, macelli
Iuuenalis:
————*Menius vt rebus*
Quæq, reportandis posita est Orchestra cathedris
Idem in eadem.
————*Et spes & oratio*
Pœnituit multos vana sterilisq, cathedræ.
Idem in eadem:
Respexit cum iam celebres notisq, Poetæ.

Qui-

Ouidius Metamorphos. primo.
Menala transieram latebris horrenda ferarum.
Idem in eodem:
Interea repetit cæcis obscura latebris.
Idem in eodem:
Quod si sola times latebras intrare ferarum.
Idem in XIII.
Funeribus ferri celebriq, in parte cremari.
Idem in quindecimo:
Quid Styga? quid tenebras & nomina vana timetis?
Idem secundo de Arte:
Vt ne te capiat latebris sibi fœmina notis.
Idem tertio de Arte:
Etsi non tenebras & quiddam lucis opacæ,
Quærimus, est aliquid luce patente minus.
Lucanus in primo Pharsaliæ:
Inuoluitq, orbem tenebris gentesq, coegit
Disperare diem———
Idem in tertio:
Attonitus mortisq, illas putat esse tenebras:
Nox subit atque oculos vastæ obduxere tenebræ.
Idem in quarto:
Venturi discrimen habent perire latebræ.
Idem in septimo:
licet *latebras* produxerit quod iuste potuit, sicut & *tenebræ* sæpe loquuntur:
Inq, vicem vultus tenebris mirantur opertos.
Hanc fuge mens partem belli tenebrisque relinque.
Mar-

Fig. 6.

Martialis in Xeniis:
Pascitur & dulci facilis gallina farina,
Pascitur & tenebris: ingeniosa gula est.
Claudianus in Stillicone:
Interius fuscata genas & amicta dolosis
Illecebris totos auro circumlinit hydros.

APPENDIX J

Letter of 16 March [1507] from Bohuslaus von Hassenstein to Geiler von Kaysersberg

(Text from Potuček, 97-98)

119.
Ad Ioannem de Keysersberg.
16. Mart. [1507.], Hassensteyna.

Clarissimo viro domino Ioanni de Keysersberg. etc. s. p. d. Literae, quas ad me dedisti, etsi perbreves fuerunt, mirifice tamen me delectarunt. Intellexi enim ex his nihil te ex veteri affectu erga me remisisse neque tantam locorum temporumque intercapedinem efficere potuisse, ut mei obliviscereris. Id mihi perinde, ut debet, gratum acceptumque est: subiit etiam simul memoria Petri mei Schotti, cuius dulcissima consuetudo atque familiaritas semper haeret haerebitque animo meo, atque adeo, ut vel in adversis eius meminisse mihi solatium sit. Te autem precor, ut perseveres in hoc de me iudicio meque dignum existimes, quem in numero tuorum habeas: si enim id impetravero, fortunatum me arbitrabor et amicitiam tuam omnibus Croesi Sardanapalique divitiis anteponam. Spero enim futurum, ut Dominus immortalis tuis santissimis precibus vincula peccatorum meorum dissolvat et inter regulos scorpionesque degentem sua dextera protegat et tueatur. Peius enim, quam quisquam credere possit, res huius provinciae se habent: non solum quod domesticis seditionibus laborantes externum quoque bellum, ubi vicinae nationes paululum quieverint, timemus, sed etiam, quod tot haereses quotidie pullulant, ut tempora illa Ioannis Hus et Wiklefi, quae avi nostri tantopere detestati sunt, nostris comparata, aurea fuisse videantur: neque tamen his malis ullum adhibetur remedium. Nam et pastores, quos pro grege Domini excubare oporteret, impares se tantae invidiae iudicant, et principes praesenti rerum statu contenti atque oc o voluptatibusque marcentes, non modo perniciosissimum hunc ignem extinguere negligunt, sed etiam luporum, adversus quos more generosi canis certare aequius foret, pellem saepenumero induunt. Vehementer haec me angunt, et cum patriae calamitatibus tum Christianae religionis periculo non ingemescere non possum. Iuvencus, quem mihi misisti, etsi iampridem alius ad me ex Italia perlatus est, gratus fuit, neque etiam est, cur de Alchorano solicitus sis: quoniam is mihi dudum opera Bernardi Adelmanni mei exscriptus est. Vale, mi optime atque dignissime pater. Commendo autem me tuis pientissimis orationibus, commendo item adolescentem, qui has literas ad te defert, si saltem se dignum exhibuerit amore tuo: est enim meae ditionis. Datae Hassens'eynae XVI. Martii.

APPENDIX K

From Wencker, Arch., 430-434, texts of:
1. *Charter for chair of cathedral preacher in Strassburg,* 1 April 1478 (cf. N. 955, par. 5)
2. *Letter of 1483 from Geiler von Kaysersberg to Maternus Trachenfels,* concerning the Last Sacrament for criminals condemned to death (cf. N. 1325)
3. *Entries in minutes of Strassburg city council,* concerning the Last Sacrament (cf. N. 1325)
4. *Decree of 1485* concerning the Last Sacrament (cf. N. 1325)

II.

Stifftung Bifchoff Ruprechts, daß zu evvigen Zeiten ein Prediger beym Stifft Strafsb. foll gehalten vverden, Actum 4. Pafcha. A.1478.

ndatio
·edicatura.

IN dem Namen des Herren Amen. Wann under anderm, das do gehört zu heyl des Chriftl. Volkes, dafs fürter des wort Gottes aller gröft notdurfftig ift, und darumb fo hat fel. gedechtnifs Bobeft Innocentius der dirte in gemeiner Satzunge geordent, daz Bifchöfe follent uffnemen Manne die tögelich fient zu dem Ampt der H. Predigen das heilfamklich zu volbringen, die mechtig

IMPERIALIBUS.

tig fiend in Wercken und Predigen, die do die Völcker die Inen bevolhen fint an Irer ſtatt, fliſslich beſehent, und fie beſſerent mit worten und biſpeln, denen ſie ſo ſie des notdurfftig ſint hantreichen ſollent notdurfft eines zymlichen lebens, das ſie nit umb breitens willen irer notdurfft getrungen werdent abezuſtande von irem anfange. Darumb wir Ruprecht &c. mit rat und gehelle unſer brüder Dechans und Cappittels unſer würdigen Stifft Straſsb. So wöllent, ſetzent und ordnen wir, daſs nu fürbaſs in unſer Stifft ſy und ewiglich ſin ſol, ein Ampt des Predigers, zu demſelben Ampt wir ſorgfeltig ſin ſollent, und wöllent daſs uffgenomen werde, ein Man der nit allein an guten ſitten und bewertem Wandel, ſunder auch fürtreffen ſy an kunſt und lere &c. Darumb ſollent wir Ime ein zymlichen lone zu uff habunge ſiner notdurfft billich hantreichen und zu beſcheiden, als wir auch ordenent und beſcheident in diſe nochgeſchriben wiſe.

Erſtl. wöllent und gebietent wir, daſs der tittel der Pfrunden die nun zumol Herr Schimpfele Ole im Chore unſer Stifft Strasb. hett und beſitzet, genannt die Cappellanie des Biſchofes ufsgelöſchet, und die fruchte Zinſe nutze und gevelle &c. fürbaſs und zu künfftigen ziten eim yeglichen Prediger und dem Ampt des Predigens zugehören, geben und gehantreichet werdent. &c.

It. Die tagelichen teylungen die do gewönlich im Chore allein den gegenwertigen geben werdent, ſoll er gantz er ſy gegenwertig oder abewaſig empfohen &c.

It. Die ufsteilungen die der Celler tun ſol. It. das teil das der Portner von den lehen ſchuldig iſt zu geben &c.

It. Es ſol demſelben Prediger gelehent werden ein erſam Huſs, das nit verre von der egen. unſer Kirchen zu Strasb. gelegen iſt, darinne er komelich wonen möge, und ſo lange mit ſinem gehelle alle Jore one entgeltniſs oder ſchaden des Predigers gnug getan werde, bitz das dem Ampt des Predigers ein wonunge die ſchicklich für ein Prediger ſy ewiglich zu bliben, beſcheiden und zugeordnet wurt.

It. Dechan und Cappittel unſer Stifft Strasb. ſollen ſorgfaltig ſin, daſs ſie ſo dick das egen. Ampt ledig wirt, den Erſammeſten gelerteſten, den ſie finden oder erfaren mögent, lidiglich uffnement zu dem Ampt des Predigens one alle beſwerunge, der

do

DE CANCELLARIIS, & VICE-CANCELLARIIS

do fy Doctor oder Licencyat der H. gefchrifft, und denfelben follent fie vorhin zwen monat hören predigen und verfuchen, und ift es dafs derfelbe Doctor oder Licencyat durch diefelben unfer brüder Dechan und Cappittel beftattiget wurt, fo fol er one verfagunge und one alle widerrede durch uns und unfer nochkomen confirmiret werden, luterlich umb Gottes willen fry und one alle befwerunge.

It. Er foll alle Jore friheit haben dafs er möge ufs der Stat Strasb. fin wo er wil, vier wochen und nit lenger, oder zu andern zyten, dan mit erloubunge des Dechans, und doch zu den zyten des Jores fo es nit ift dem predigen obe zu ligen, als es dan notdurfftig ift in der Vaften. Nit deftmyner fol das zyt fins ufswefens das predigen an Sontagen und Hochzytl. tagen, durch einen andern erfollet werden, der do fy von der zale weltl. Priefterfchafft, und nit ein Profefs einichs Ordens.

It. Wer es dafs Er mit ettwas kranckeit fchwacheit oder fiechtagen begriffen würde, fo fol er einen andern weltl. Priefter der nit Profefs oder Münch ift einichs ordens, beftellen, fonften aber nit one des Dechans oder fins Stathalters funder erlaubunge, fich nit entfchuldigen perfönlich zu predigen.

It. Er foll verbunden fyn zu predigen in unfer Stifft alle tage in der Vaften; item alle Hochgezyt, nemlich den Wynachttag, der 3. Künige tag, den Oftertag, den Nonetag, Pfingefttag, am Hochzyt der Kirwihe am obent und am tage noch Imbifs. Item, Allerheiligen tag. It. alle unfer Frowen Obent des obends und an Iren tagen noch Imbfs. It. uff den achten tag zu Wynachten. It. uff der zwolff botten tag S. Peter und Paulus, S. Jacobs, S. Mattheus, S. Andres, noch Imbfs. It. uff unfers Herren Fronlichnams tag und den Sungiht tag. It. uff S. Annen tag. It. alle Sontage noch Imbfs. Und ouch uff ander Hochzyt nemlich Verfamelunge groffer und erlicher Procefs, es were wider die Peftilentye, Ungewitter, widerwertig Wetter, Kriege oder Widerwertikeit, oder umb Friden und eynikeit uffgefetzet. &c. Und dafs zu allen predigen obgen. gelutet werde. Er foll zum Chorgange nit fchuldig fyn. It. Er foll nit underfton die Pfarre zu S. Laurentyen zu hindern. &c.

It. Er foll kein Bullen oder Procefs verkünden offenen
oder

Cf. p. 808

IMPERIALIBUS.

oder exequiren one befunder wiffen des Dechans oder fins Stathalters und des Cappittels, denen er auch fonften zu gehorfamen.

It. Wir ordnen, dafs alle und ygliche vorgefchr. dinge den gefwornen Statuten unfer Stifft follent zugefetzt und one alle mynnunge ewiglich gehalten werden. Item der Eyt den er tun foll. &c.

III.
De communicandis his qui ultimo fupplicio plectuntur.

I. Cedula Dr. Johannis Keiferfpergij ad Confulem Maternum Trachenfels, Anno 1483.

Gar fürfichtiger wyfer lieber Herr. Ich bitt uch mit ernftlichem flyfs, wellend anbringen der armen lüth halb fo zu dem tod verurteilt werden, daz Inen zugelaffen werd Entpfohung des H. Sacraments und Chriftenlich Begrebde. Ift Gott ein befunder Glory, den fo gar elenden in iren gröften nöten befunders troft und hilff, uch gegen Gott grofser verdienft, und in der welt rum mit lob. Wellend uch difes anlygen lofsen umb Gotts willen, will ich gegen uch wo ich vermag, williklich verdienen. Darzu Ir auch zu ewigen ziten hinfür Lon entpfohen werden von Gott von dem lobl. werck, des ir ein anfeher feyn werden. Uwer williger Johannes von Keiferfperg.

Dem gar fürfichtigen Herren Herr Maternen Trachenfels Ammeifter, meinem befundern lieben Herren.

II. *Annales Argent.*

An. 1482. 5. poft Catharinæ.
    Item, den verurteilten Lüten das Sacrament zu geben.
    Erkant, man foll es betrachten, Völtfch und Trachenfels.
An. 1483. 2. poft Luciæ.
    Item, der armen verurteilten Lüt halb, Inen das Sacrament zu geben und die geiftl. begrebde zuzulofsen.

Eod.

434 DE CANCELLARIIS, & VICE-CANCELLARIIS

Eod. Sabbato Vigil. Thomæ Apli.

Erkant, Lot es bliben wie harkommen, alſo das Sacrament zeigen, * und obe ertrencken zu St. Martin zeigen &c. der begrebde halb lot bliben wie erkant.

* Monſtrabatur autem in Capella Stæ. Crucis Exulum, *zum elenden Creutz im grünen Bruch gelegen.*

III. *Decretum de Anno* 1485.

DEmnach alten Harkommens in der Statt Strafsburg gehalten iſt wann übeltätige Perſonen eingezogen worden ſint, die das leben verwürcket haben, daſs ſie die gewönlich an Donrſtag verurteilt und an Fritag gerichtet worden ſint; und obe jemans vor Rat verrechtiget und Im ſin leben abe erkant wart, daz der ſlechts ganges von der Pfaltzen hinweg gefürt und hingerichtet wart, und aber unſer gnediger Herre von Strazburg durch ſiner gnaden Rete an Meiſter und Rat der Statt Strazburg hat loſsen bringen, wie daz ſin gnade ſich an den Gelerten in den Hohen Schulen erfaren habe und erfunden, daz die chriſtenliche ordnung derſelben deheim der das H. Sacrament begert, und dozu geſchickt iſt, ſollichs zu verſagen ſy; So habent ſie erkant ſo ferre unſer gnediger Herr von Strazburg durch ſiner gnaden Vicarien oder wem ſin gnade das befilhet, verfüget zu ordnen zwen oder drye Prieſter in der Statt Strafsburg, die dazu tougelich und geſchickt ſint, der armen Lüte die alſo verrichtet werdent, bichte zu hören; Alſo welcher unter Inen denſelben Prieſtern, ſo ein menſch alſo verurteilt, beruffet wirt, daz der des gehorſam ſy, und eins ſolchen armen menſchen bicht höre, wann dann der arme menſch verhört, bedunket Ine dann daz derſelbe menſch ſchicklich dazu ſy, daz man Ime dann das H. Sacrament geben ſol, dem ſol man es loſsen werden, und darauff derſelbe menſch an Zinſtag verurteilt, und ſin bicht gehört: Item an Mitwoch mit dem H. Sacrament verſehen, und donoch an Fritag gerichet werden ſol. Und habent ſemlichs verwilliget mit ſolicher gedinge obe ſie hinfürter yemer beduchte ſemmlichs zu andern &c. Actum ſecunda poſt Invocavit Anno 1485.

Add: Item, der Lütprieſter zum Münſter, item zu St. Thoman und zum alten St. Peter.

Cos-

APPENDIX L

Genealogical material on the Schott family from Straub, 84-86

— 84 —

Fol. 69ᵇ. A° 1505. OTTILIA SCHOTTIN relicta vidua ..... Zevssolff von Adoltzheim. Lucas Zeyssolff von Adoltzheim eorum filius.

A° 1519. Obiit OTTILIA SCHOTTIN. relicta vidua dni'.... Zeyssolfs de Adoltzheim[1]

A° 1524. 30 Xᵇʳⁱˢ. Obijt MERGA CHOTTIN.

NOTA. In dem Closter St. Margred vndt Agnes in' Straszburg. auff der Borkirchen, da die Closterfrawen Ihren Gottesdienst pflegen zu verrichten, ahne dem fron Althar stehen hier bey gesetzte 3 Wapen vndt Soll Hr. Peter Schott Altammeister eben diesen Althar seiner tochter, welche eine Closter Frauw, in diesem Gotteshausz geweszen dahien zu Ehren haben machen lassen, Anna Schöttin genandt, welche eine grosse lieb hat gehabt zu dem Prediger Orden v. zu diesem Closter v. hat kost 200 K Actum A° 1494.

Schott   Cöllen

---

1. «In der Kirche zu Sᵗ. Andreas befindet sich in der Mauer ein Stein, Gedächtniss des vesten Zeysolf v. Adelzheim und Ottilie Schottin, seiner hausfrau 1493.» (Manuscr. Heitz.)
D'après le même ouvrage il faudrait placer ici:
« 1516. Joh. Schott impressor librorum, curator Salome Mentlerin, relictæ quondam Philippi Sturm, armigeri.
 «Lorentz, 1523, 1524, 1525, 1526, 1527.
« 1538. Brigitta S. uxor Johannis Lindenfelser, Mag. Scab.
« 1554. Sebastian S. Dreier auf dem Pfenningthurm.
   «Laurentius Schott 1523. Seine 2ᵗᵉ Gattin : Elisabeth Storckin : Kinder erster Ehe:
     1) Brigitta verm. an *a*) Johann Lindenfelser *b*) Jacob Hessmann.
     2) Ansel . Gem : Daniel Vogler.
     3) Margareth. Gem ; Christopf Stædlin.
     4) Gertrud . Gem : Sebastian Jung.
     5) Einbetha . Gem : Georg Leimer.

Fol. 70ª. Dieszes gleichnachfolgende Epitaphium ist im Jungen St. Peter alhier in Straszburg in der Zornen Capell in der kirchen zu befünden. Ist ein vbergulter stein

PETRO · SCHOTTO · ARGEN · DIVI · IVNIORIS
PETRI ÆDIS CANONICO PRESBYTERO
INNOCENTISSIMO IVRISCONSVLTO ET
ORATORI POETÆQVE · DOCTO · PETRI SCHOT
TI SENATORIS SVSSANNÆQVE FILIO PIEN
TISSIMO · AMICI MESTI POSVERE ·
MOR · ANNO · CHRI M·CCCC·LXXXX ·
II YD · SEPTEB

Gedächtnus des vesten Beyszolffs von= Adelsheim vnnd Otily Schottin: sinn huszfrow 1493.

NOTA. In der Kirchen zum alten St. Peter in Straszburg ligt ein gaar· alter groszer grabstein, gegen dem steinernen Lettner vor dem Chor, doch dieser Zeith gegen der Thüren wo von dem + gang ausz der Straszen hinen gehet, mitt 2 Schilten unter einander, hat der oberste Schild einen

Adler, der unterst ist der Schotten Schilt mit dem Kölkopff vnndt dem Berglein. hæc pro memoria.

Anno 14... Jacobus Schott et Ottilia eius vxor.	Petrus Schott Altammeister zu Straszburg zeugt mit Susanna. v. Colle oder Cöllen seiner hauszfrau: 5 Kinder wie folgt. Er starb A° 1504 8 Aug: Sie starb A° 1498 18 Februarij Vermög Ludowici Mügen Calendres.	1. Petrus Schott J. v. D. Canonicus S^{ti} Petri junioris Argentinæ ☉ 1490. 2 Idus 7^{bris}.	1. Columba Bettscholdt vxor 1) Jacobi Muegij 2) Caspari Zornen von Bulach Equitis aurati.
		2. Margred Schottin vxor fuit 1) Wilhelmi Bettscholdts olim Mag. Scabinorum. 2).... Dolden.	2. Eucharius Bettscholdt.
		3. Merga od. Maria Schottin vxor Dni Florentzii muegij Obiit Illa 1524. 30 X^{bris} ☉ ille 1511. 19 februarii zeugten	1. Petrum Muegen. eius vxor Margred Dedingerin. 2. Florentzium Muegen †. 3. Danielem Muegen. Consul. et XIII vir. Argent. eius vxor 1) Clara Prechterin 2) Margretha Dolpin. ☉ ille peste A° 1541 27 8^{bris}. 4. Maria Muegen †. 5. Veronica Muegin vxor Dni Jacobi Ingold.
		4. Ottilia Schottin 1) vxor Petri von Cöllen, 2) Zeyssolphi von Altzheim oder Adeltzheim ☉ illa A° 1519.	1. Ottiliam v. Cöllen vxor. Dni Martini Sturmij de Sturmeck. genuerunt filium Jacobum Sturmen. eius vxor fuit... Joh. Bocken Prætoris Argent. et Equitis filia.
		5. Anna Schöttin die wahr ein Closterfrauw zu St. Margred in Straszburg A° 1494.	

Schœpflin, Hermann et alii litterati Alsatiæ. T. II.

Fol. 91ª., Anna Schotta.

Anna hæc Petri Schotti, Consulis Argent. Filia monialis S. Margarethe ordinis S. Dominici, circa A° 1480, perdocta fuit; soror Petri Schotti, J. U. D. atque Canonici S. Petri Junioris, ex antiqua nobili familia.

NB. Die Schotten waren Patrizier, nicht Adeliche.

Hæc Anna Maximilianum Cæsarem nomine totius conventus S. Margarethe allocuta est lingua latina atque plura cœnobio privilegia aquisivit.

APPENDIX M

Quotable passages from Peter Schott's Lucubraciunculae

#14, p. 22	Ut laborem tute exigas: ne ab eo te exigi paciaris.
#18, p. 27	Non enim sciencie vitam accomodare decreui: sed vite scienciam.
#46, p. 51	Scilicet ne apostolice littere te vetent: apostolicis monitis obtemperare.
#73, p. 80	Apud nostros... ubi amplior est epulis atque armis locus quam litteris.
" "	Sed prebendas tibi apud nos/ facilius tu in vrbe conflabis: vbi officina est: in qua hae cuduntur.
#76, p. 83	Memini... nequaquam velle te amplioribus prouentibus beneficiatum lucupletare: quam quadraginta aureis Renensibus annuis. O quanta rerum immutacio? Iam tu quadraginta Beneficia malles: quam quadraginta aureos annuos.
#86, p. 95	Inter tela Martis et Apollinis hoc est bellorum et estus.
#109, p. 121	Haud bene conueniunt: nec in vna sede morantur Mars et Calliope. (Is this a quotation from another's work?)
" "	O si te armatum contueri mihi liceret: quam tu mihi ut studijs et bonis artibus aptissimus: ita militaribus insanijs ineptus videreris. (said of Hassenstein)
#110, p. 129	An ignoras miliciam esse vitam hominis super terram?
#118, p. 137	Beneficij vacantis anhelam venacionem
#125, p. 145	Pro incredibili facundia tua (said of Geiler)
#128, p. 148	Non sit verisimile: te tot annis in Vrbe sancta versatum: non vel vnciam sanctitatis: hoc praesertim tam sancto tempore contraxisse.
" "	Nam quam fluxa: quam caduca sit omnis mundi potencia. (Is this a quotation from another's work?)
#221, p. 247	Cum lex Christiana sit lex libertatis et gracie.

APPENDIX N

Strassburg Money and its relative Value

1 Schilling (solidus)	= 12 Pfennig (denarii)
	= 2 Blapparts
	= 1 Groschen
	= 6 Kreutzer (Zweyling)
	= 24 Liard
	= 48 Oertlein

1 Strassburg Florin	= 2 Livres
	= 10 Shilling
	= 15 Batz
	= 30 Demi-Batz
	= 2 Dicker Pfennig
	= 20 Blapparts
	= 60 Kreuzer
	= 10 Groschen
	= 120 Pfennig

20 Schilling = 1 oz. silver

1 Eçu = 17 Batz
There were also ½ Eçu and ¼ Eçu
1 Groschen = 2 Blapparts
1 Blappart = 6 Pfennig
1 Pfennig = 2 Liard
1 Liard = 2 Oertlein
1 Dicker Pfennig = ½ Strassburg Florin

1 Rhenish Florin = 1 Strassburg Florin
1 ordinary Florin = 6 Schilling
1 Gulden (in 1424) = 124 Pfennig
1 Strassburg Ducat = 1 Florin and 6 Pfennig

To the time of Maximilian I only the bishops of Strassburg had the right to coin gold money; the state of Strassburg could coin only silver money. All coins bore the fleur-de-lis. Kreutzer or Zweyling were first struck in 1482; these bore the inscriptions "gloria in excelsis Deo" and "Moneta Argentinensis." (Cf. N. 1197).

    Cf. Dacheux, *Réf.*, 418; Hatt, *Ville*, 478; Knepper, *Schulwesen*, 289; Levrault, 323, 326; Piton, I, 149, 182, 186; Specklin, 286, 298.

BIBLIOGRAPHY

1. Bibliographical references are cited as follows:
   a. By abbreviation of frequently cited references and periodicals.
   b. By the last name of the author(s).
   c. Where several works of the same author are listed or in case of several authors with identical last names, by the last name of the author and the first word(s) of the title, unless a shortened form of reference is indicated.
   d. Where there is no author, by the first word(s) of the title.

2. Abbreviations for periodicals appear on p. 814.
   Abbreviations for other works appear at the left of the respective entries. See also p. X.

3. *S* before entries and the numbers in parentheses following those entries indicate references to Peter Schott.

4. For scope of the bibliography, see p. XI, final paragraph.

PERIODICALS

(Only those periodicals, for which abbreviations are used, appear in this list.)

AEA	*Archives de l'Église d'Alsace.*
AEK	*Archiv für Elsässische Kirchengeschichte.*
AGBA	*Archiv für die Geschichte des Bistums Augsburg.*
BSCMH	*Bulletin de la société pour la conservation des monuments historiques d'Alsace.* German title: *Mitteilungen der Gesellschaft für die Erhaltung der geschichtlichen Denkmäler im Elsass.*
CBL	*Centralblatt für Bibliothekswesen.*
ElsMGV	*Elsässische Monatsschrift für Geschichte und Volkskunde.*
FKE	*Forschungen zur Kirchengeschichte des Elsass.*
FDA	*Freiburger Diöcesan-Archiv. Organ des kirchlich historischen Vereins der Erzdiöcese Freiburg für Geschichte, Altertumskunde und christliche Kunst, mit Berücksichtigung der angrenzenden Bisthümer.*
Hist.-Pol. Blätter	*Historisch-Politische Blätter für das katholische Deutschland.*
HZ	*Historische Zeitschrift.*
JbGElsLotr	*Jahrbuch für Geschichte, Sprache und Litteratur Elsass-Lothringens.*
JbL	*Jahresberichte für neuere deutsche Literaturgeschichte.*
QFPh	*Quellen und Forschungen zur lateinischen Philologie des Mittelalters.*
RA	*Revue d'Alsace.*
SP	*Studies in Philology.*
StbSt	*Strassburger Studien für Geschichte, Sprache und Litteratur des Elsasses.* (Same as ZGSEls.)
StzvLg	*Studien zur vergleichenden Literaturgeschichte.*
VfKLRen	*Vierteljahrsschrift für Kultur und Litteratur der Renaissance.*
ZEK	*Zeitschrift für elsässische Kirchengeschichte.*
ZfdPh	*Zeitschrift für deutsche Philologie.*
ZfSL	*Zeitschrift für französische Sprache und Literatur.*
ZGORh	*Zeitschrift für die Geschichte des Oberrheins.*
ZGSEls	*Zeitschrift für Geschichte, Sprache und Litteratur des Elsasses.* (Same as StbSt.)
ZfvLg	*Zeitschrift für vergleichende Literaturgeschichte.*
ZvLR	*Zeitschrift für vergleichende Literaturgeschichte und Renaissance Literatur.*

OTHER BIBLIOGRAPHICAL MATERIALS

		Acta, Akten, matriculation and other university records, cf. *Matrikel*
Acta bonon.	S	*Acta nationis germanicae universitatis Bononiensis ex archetypis tabularii malvezziani.* Ediderunt Ernestus Friedländer et Carolus Malagola. Berolini, 1887. (220, 228, 403)

Adam	S	Adam, Melchior. *Vitae germanorum philosophorum qui seculo superiori... floruerunt.* Heidelberg, 1715. (24f.)
Adam, *Theolog.*		Adam, Melchior. *Vitae germanorum theologorum.* Frankfurt, 1653.
		Ady, Cecilia M. *The Bentivoglio of Bologna.* London, 1937.
		Alfonsus Rex Aragonum. *Margarita facetiarum* (together with *Scomata Ioannis Keiserbergii*). Strassburg (Argentina), 1508.
ADB	S	*Allgemeine Deutsche Biographie.* Leipzig, 1875-1912. (XIX, 48, 49 article on Hassenstein; XXXII, 406f.)
	S	Allen, P.S. "The Letters of Rudolph Agricola," *English Historical Review,* XXI (1906), 302ff. (315)
Alsatia		*Alsatia, Jahrbuch für elsässische Geschichte, Sage, Alterthumskunde, Sitte, Sprache und Kunst.* Cf. Stöber, *Alsatia.*
		Amrhein, August. "Reihenfolge der Mitglieder des adeligen Domstiftes zu Würzburg, St. Kilians-Brüder genannt, von seiner Gründung bis zur Säkularisation 742-1803," *Archiv des historischen Vereines von Unterfranken und Aschaffenburg,* XXXII (1889), 1-315; XXXIII (1890), 1-380.
Anal. Francisc.		*Analecta Franciscana sive Chronica aliaque varia documenta ad historiam Fratrum Minorum.* Ed. a patribus collegii S. Bonaventurae. Tomus II. Quaracchi prope Florentiam, 1887.
		Andreas, Willy. *Deutschland vor der Reformation.* Stuttgart-Berlin, ²1934.
		Anthon, Charles. *Classical Dictionary.* New York, 1862.
		Apperson, G. L. *English Proverbs and Proverbial Phrases. A Historical Dictionary.* London, 1929.
		Armellini, Mariano. *La chiesi di Roma dal secolo iv al xix.* Roma, 1962.
Athen. Raur.		*Athenae Rauricae, sive catalogus professorum academiae Basiliensis ab MCCCLX ad a. MDCCLXXVIII cum brevi singulorum biographia. Adiecta est recensio omnium eiusdem academiae rectorum.* Basel, 1778.
Auct.	S	*Auctarium chartularii universitatis parisiensis sub auspiciis ejusdem studii generalis ab Henrico Denifle et Aemilio Chatelain inceptum.* Produxerunt Carolus Samoran, Aemilius A. van Moë auxiliante Susanna Vitte. Tomus III: *Liber procuratorum nationis Alemanniae in universitate parisiense ab anno 1466-1492.* Paris, 1935. (224)
	S	"Aus dem neuen deutschen Reichsland: Schlettstadt," *Illustrierte Zeitung.* No. 1496. Leipzig, 1872. (155)
		Aventinus (Johannes Turmair). *Bayerische Chronik,* II. Sämmtliche Werke, V. Hrsg. von der König-

lichen Akademie der Wissenschaften (Munich, 1886).

Baas, R. "Gesundheitspflege im mittelalterlichen Strassburg," *Archiv für Kulturgeschichte*, IX, 1 (1911), 87f.

Backmund, Norbert. *Monosticon Praemonstratense*. 3 vols. Straubing, 1949-56.

Barge, Hermann. *Geschichte der Buchdruckerkunst von ihren Anfängen bis zur Gegenwart*. Leipzig, 1940.

Baring-Gould, S. *The Lives of the Saints*. 16 vols. Edinburgh, 1914.

Barth, *Kreutzer* Barth, Médard. *Dr. Joh. Kreutzer (gest. 1468) und die Wiederherstellung des Dominikanerinnenklosters Engelporten in Gebwiler*. Sonder-Abdruck aus dem AEK, 8. Jahrgang (Strassburg, 1933).

Barth, "Pilger" Barth, Médard. "Elsässer Pilger an den berühmten Wallfahrten des Mittelalters," FDA, LXXX (1960); (Dritte Folge, XII).

Barth, *Handbuch* S Barth, Médard. *Handbuch der Elsässischen Kirchen im Mittelalter*. Strassburg, 1960-63. AEA, XI. Études générales (Forschungen zur Kirchengeschichte des Elsass), publiée sous les auspices de la Société d'histoire de l'Église d'Alsace, Nouvelle Série, Tome IV. (251, 1421, 1450)

Barth, "Florentius" Barth, Médard. "Der heilige Florentius," AEA, IV (1951-52), 121.

Barth, *Odilie* Barth, Médard. *Die heilige Odilie, Schutzherrin des Elsass; ihr Kult in Volk und Kirche*. 2 vols. Hrsg. von der Gesellschaft für Elsässische Kirchengeschichte. Strassburg, 1938 = FKE, IV-V.

Barth, "Kult" Barth, Médard. "Der Kult der drei heiligen Strassburger Jungfrauen Einbeth, Worbeth und Vilbeth," AEK, XI (1936), 57-106.

Barth, "Pfarreien" Barth, Médard. "Zur Geschichte der Elsässischen Pfarreien," AEA, II (1947-48), 63-172.

Barthelmé, Annette. *La Réforme Dominicaine au xve siècle en Alsace et dans l'ensemble de la province de Teutonie*. Collection d'Études sur l'histoire du droit et des institutions de l'Alsace, VII (Strasbourg, 1931).

S Bauch, Gustav. *Die Universität Erfurt im Zeitalter des Frühhumanismus*. Breslau, 1904. (52, 56, 129)

Bauer, Joh. Joseph, SCJ. *Zur Frühgeschichte der theologischen Fakultät der Universität Freiburg i. Br.* (1460-1620). Diss. Freiburg i. Br., 1957.

Bäumer, E. "Die Geschichte des Badewesens," *Abhandlungen zur Geschichte der Medicin*, VII (Breslau, 1903).

Baxter, James H. *Medieval Latin Wordlist*. London, 1934.

Beck, Balthassar. *Das kreüter buoch oder herbarius*. Strassburg, 1528.

Beckmann, Joseph Hermann (ed.). *Johannes Kerer,*

Statuta Collegii Sapientiae: Satzungen des Collegium Sapientiae zu Freiburg i. Br. 1497. Facsimile Ausgabe. Mit einer Einführung hrsg. von Joseph Hermann Beckmann. Lateinischer Text besorgt und ins Deutsche übersetzt von Robert Feger. 2 vols. Lindau & Constance, 1957.

Beckmann, Joseph Hermann. *Johannes Kerer, Statuta Collegii Sapientiae: The Statutes of the Collegii Sapientiae in Freiburg University.* Freiburg, Breisgau, 1497. 2 vols. Lindau & Constance, 1957. [cf. also: Werk, Franz Xaver]

Beissel, Stephan. *Geschichte der Verehrung Marias im 16. und 17. Jahrhundert.* Freiburg i. B., 1910.

S Berler, Maternus. *Chronik.* Code hist. [q.v.], I, ii. (114). [Same text in Dacheux, *Fragments*, IV, viii.]

Bernegger, Casper. *Forma reipublicae argentoratensis delineata olim a Matthia Berneggero.* Strassburg, 1667.

Bernoulli, August. *Basler Chroniken.* Hrsg. von der historischen und antiquarischen Gesellschaft in Basel. Bearbeitet von August Bernoulli. 7 vols. Leipzig, 1872-1915.

Biograph. Lexikon... *Biographisches Lexikon hervorragender Ärzte aller*
Ärzte *Zeiten und Völker.* Ed. W. Haberling, F. Hübotter & H. Vierordt. 6 vols. Berlin-Wien, ²1929-1935.

Bishop, John. *The Marrow of Astrology.* Cf. R. Kirby.

Black, H. C. *Black's Law Dictionary.* 2 vols. St. Paul, ⁴1951.

Bock, Hieronymus. *Kreuter buch.* Strassburg, 1560.

Bogeng, G. A. E. *Geschichte der Buchdruckerkunst. I: Der Frühdruck.* Dresden, 1930.

Bömer, A. *Die lateinischen Schülergespräche der Humanisten. Auszüge mit Einleitungen, Anmerkungen und Namen- und Sachregister. Quellen für die Schul- und Universitätsgeschichte des 15. und 16. Jahrhunderts.* Texte und Forschungen zur Geschichte der Erziehung und des Unterrichts in den Ländern deutscher Zunge. Hrsg. von Karl Kehrbach. I (Berlin, 1897).

Bonatti, Guido. *De astronomia tractatus.* Basel, 1550.

Bonaventure, Saint. *De reductione artium ad theologiam.* A commentary with an introduction and translation by Sister Emma Thérèse Healy. The Franciscan Institute, Saint Bonaventure University, Saint Bonaventure, N.Y., ²1955.

Borries, Emil von. *Geschichte der Stadt Strassburg.* Strassburg, 1909.

Borsetti, Ferranti. *Historia almi Ferrariae gymnasii.* Ferrara, 1735.

Bouchholtz, Fritz. *Burgen und Schlösser im Elsass nach alten Vorlagen.* Frankfurt, 1962.
Brant, Sebastian. *Das Narrenschiff,* Ed. F. Zarncke. Leipzig, 1854.
Brant, Sebastian. *Titulorum omnium iuris tam civilis quam canonici expositiones.* London, 1610.
Braun, Placidus. *Geschichte der Bischöfe von Augsburg.* III. Augsburg, 1814.
Braunschweig (Brunschwig), Hieronymus [Jerome Saler]. *Das ist das buch der Cirurgia. Hantwirkung der wund artzney von Hyeronimo brunschwig.* Strassburg, 1497.
Brown, Horatio F. *The Venetian Printing Press.* London, 1891.
Brucker, J. *Zunft- und Polizei Verordnungen des 14. und 15. Jahrhunderts.* Strassburg, 1889.
Brusch, Caspar. *Chronologia monasteriorum Germaniae praecipuorum ac maxime illustrium in qua origenes, annales ac celeberiora cujusque monumenta bona fide recensentur.* Sulzbach, 1682. [later edition of Brusch, *Monasteriorum,* I].
Brusch, Caspar. *Monasteriorum Germaniae praecipuorum ac maxime illustrium centuria.* I. Ingolstadt, 1551.
Büchmann, Georg. *Geflügelte Worte. Der Zitatenschatz des deutschen Volkes.* Ed. Bogdan Krieger. Berlin, ²⁴1910.
Büheler, Sebald. *Strassburgische Chronik.* BSCMH IIe Série, XIII (1887-1888), 41-150.
Bulaeus, Caesar E. *Historia universitatis Parisiensis.* Paris, 1670.
Bullarium Franciscanum continens constitutiones epistolas diplomata Romani Pontifices. Collegit et edidit Fr. Joseph M. Pou Y Marti, O.F.M. Nova Series III. Quaracchi, 1949.

S Burckard, Johann. *Johannes Burchardi argentinensis capelle pontifice sacrorum ritum magistri Diarium sive rerum urbanarum commentarii (1483-1506).* Ed. L. Thuasne. 3 vols. Paris, 1883-85. (III, iii, iv, v)
Burtius, Nicolas. *Bononia illustrata (1494)* [Cf. Meuschenius, Johann Gerhard].
Bussierre, Th. de. *Histoire des religieuses dominicaines du couvent de Ste. Marguerite et Ste. Agnes à Strasbourg.* Paris, 1862.
Butler, Alban. *Lives of the Saints.* 4 vols. Ed. H. Thurston and D. Attwater. New York, 1956.
Butler, H. E. *The "Institutio Oratoria" of Quintilian with an English translation.* London, 1921.
Calmette, Joseph. *The Golden Age of Burgundy. The Magnificent Dukes and their Courts.* Translated from the French by Doreen Weightman. New York, 1963.

Cambridge Med. Hist. *Cambridge Medieval History.* VII and VIII. Cambridge, 1936.
Campbell, Thomas. *The Sonnets, Triumphs and*

                     other Poems of Petrarch. London, 1890.
Capelli, Adriano. *Dizionario di Abbreviature.* Milan, [5]1954.
Cardano, Girolamo. *Libelli quinque.* Nürnberg, 1547.
Carro, Le Chevalier Jean de, M. D. *Ode Latine sur Carlsbad, composée vers la fin du quinzième siècle par le baron Bohuslas Hassenstein de Lobkowitz, avec une traduction polyglotte,...* Prague, 1829.

Cath. Ency.   *The Catholic Encyclopedia.* New York, 1907-1913.
                     S Cave, William. *Scriptorum ecclesiasticorum historia literaria.* Geneva, 1694. *Appendix.* Geneva, 1693. (*Appendix*, 118)
Cencetti, Giorgio. *Gli Archivi dello Studii Bolognese.* Bologna, 1938.
Chmel, Joseph. *Regesta chronologico-diplomatica Fridericii III Romanorum imperatoris (Regis IV).* Vienna, 1859.
Christy, R. *Proverbs, Maxims and Phrases of all Ages.* Two vols. in one. New York, 1888.

Strassburg Chronik   *Chroniken der deutschen Städte.* VIII & IX: *Strassburg.* I & II. Hrsg. von C. Hegel. Leipzig, 1870 (Neudruck, Leipzig, Göttingen, 1961). [Same text as *Chroniken der oberrheinischen Städte vom 14.-16. Jahrhundert.* VIII: *Strassburg.* Leipzig, 1871 (Neudruck, Stuttgart, 1961)].
Chronique d'Alsace [Cf. *Code hist.*].
Clauss, J. M. B. *Historisches-Topographisches Wörterbuch des Elsass.* Zabern, 1895-97.

Clauss, "Geiler"   S Clauss, J. M. B. "Kritische Übersicht der Schriften über Geiler von Kaysersberg," *Historisches Jahrbuch*, XXXI, 3 (1910) 485ff. (512)

Code hist.   *Code historique et diplomatique de la ville de Strasbourg.* Strasbourg, 1843. I,i: *Chronique d'Alsace.* I, ii: *Maternus Berler, Chronik.* II: *Strassburgische Archiv-Chronik.*
                     S Colerus, Johann Christoff. *De Vita summisque in rem literariam meritis Bohuslai Hassensteini lib. bar. Lobcovici.* Wittemberg, 1719. (37f.)
Colerus, Johann Christoff. *Commentatio historica de Bohuslai Hassensteini lib. bar. Lobcowicii vita et summis in rem literariam meritis.* Wittemberg, 1721 [Same text as *De Vita...* above].
                     S Cornova, Ignanz. *Der grosse Böhme Bohuslaw von Lobkowicz und zu Hassenstein nach seinen eigenen Schriften geschildert.* Prague, 1808. (13-28 *passim*, 79, 201, 247, 250, 258, 267, 289)
Corpus Chronicorum Flandriae sub auspiciis Leopoldi Primi. Ed. J. J. Desmet. Vol. IV: *Histoire des guerres et troubles de Flandres. Mutinations et rébellions des Flamens contre Maximilian, Roy des Romains,* pp. 508-586. Bruxelles, 1865.
Corpus iuris canonici. Ed. Aemilius Friedberg. 2 vols. Graz, 1959 [Reprint of edition by A. L. Richter, Leipzig, 1879].
Corradi, Augusto. *Notizie sui professori di Latinità*

nella studio di Bologna. Documenti e Studj... per le Provincie di Romagna (Bologna, 1887), 453ff.

Cosenza, Mario Emilio. *Biographical and Bibliographical Dictionary of the Italian Humanists and of the World of Classical Scholarship in Italy, 1300-1800.* 5 vols. Boston, ²1962. Vol. VI: *Supplement.* Boston, 1967.

Cottineau, L. H., O.S.B. *Répertoire Topo-Bibliographique des Abbayes et Prieurés.* Macon, 1935-39.

Cowie, Murray A. *Proverbs and Proverbial Phrases in the German Works of Albrecht von Eyb.* Diss. University of Chicago (1942).

S Cowie, M. A. and M. L. "Geiler von Kaysersberg and Abuses in Fifteenth Century Strassburg," SP, LVIII (1961), 483-495.

S Cowie, M. A. and M. L. "Rudolph Agricola and Peter Schott," *Kunstmann Festschrift* [q.v.], 141-155.

Dacheux, Leo. *Die ältesten Schriften Geilers von Kaysersberg.* Freiburg i. B., 1882.

Dacheux, Leo. *Auszüge aus dem nicht gedruckten 4. Buche.* Strassburg, 1889 [Same text as: Grandidier, *Nouv. oeuvr.*, II. Colmar, 1897-1900].

Dacheux, "Münsterchronik"   Dacheux, Leo. "Die kleine Münsterchronik," BSCMH. II. Série, XIII (1887-1888), 5-20 [Same text in: Dacheux, *Fragments*, I, i: "La petite chronique de la cathédrale"].

Dacheux, *Réf.*   S   Dacheux, Leo. *Un réformateur catholique à la fin du XV. siècle.* Paris, Strassburg, 1876. (284-427, and *passim*)

Dacheux, *Eccl. Arg.*   Dacheux, Leo. "Revue de Grandidier, *Essais*," *Ecclesiasticum Argentinense*, I (1889), 15f.

Dacheux, *Fragments*   Dacheux, Louis. *Fragments des anciennes chroniques d'Alsace.* 5 vols. Strassburg, 1887-1906.
   I. i La petite chronique de la cathédrale (Die kl. Münsterchr.).
      ii La chronique de Sebald Büheler (Sebald Bühelers Strassburg Chronick).
  II. iii Les collectanées de Daniel (Daniel Specklins Collectanea).
  III. iv La chronique de Jacques Trausch (Jacob Trausch jur. lic. strassburgische Chronick).
      v La chronique de Jean Wencker (Summarische Chronik und Zeitregister der Stadt Strassburg).
      vi Annales de Sébastien Brant (Sebastian Brants Annalen).
  IV. vii Koenigshoven. Fragments de la chronique latine.
      viii Fragments de la chronique de Berler (Maternus Berler, *Chronik*).
      ix Fragments de diverses vieilles chroniques, 1. Geschichtliches; 2. Von Kirchen, Kapellen und Klöstern.

x Annales de Sébastien Brant, suite et fin.
Dallari, Umberto. *Rotuli dei lettori legiste e artiste delli studii Bolognese dal 1384 al 1799.* Vol. I. Bologna, 1888.
Decretum D. Gratiani. Universi iuris canonici pontificias constitutiones et canonicas brevi compendio complectens. Unacum Glossis, Epitomis et Thematibus, ac multorum Iurisprudentum tam ad textum quam ad glossas adnotationibus illustratum... Venice, 1572.
Denifle, Henricus. *Chartularium universitatis Parisiensis* [cf. *Auct.*].
A Dictionary of Latin and Greek Quotations [Also called: *A Dictionary of Classical Quotations*] Ed. H. T. Riley. London, 1891.
Dictionnaire de l'histoire universelle de l'église. Ed. Guérin. Paris, 1854-73.

Dictionnaire de théol. cath.   S *Dictionnaire de théologie catholique.* Ed. A. Vacant and E. Mangenot. 15 vols. Paris, 1908. Paris, ²1939. (XIV², 1575f.)

Dollinger, Philippe. *Strasbourg du passé au présent.* Strassburg, 1962.

Dorlan, *Notices*   S Dorlan, Alexandre. *Notices historiques sur l'Alsace et principalement sur la ville de Schléstadt.* Colmar, 1843. (ii, 103, 107)

Dorlan, "Nouv. études"   Dorlan, Alexandre. "Nouvelles études historiques sur l'école et la société littéraires de Schléstadt aux 15e et 16e siècles," RA, VI (1855), 337-349, 385-391.

Dreher   S Dreher, Theodor. "Das Tagebuch über Friedrich von Hohenzollern, Bischof von Augsburg (1486-1505), historisch erläutert und zum Lebensbilde erweitert," *Mitteilungen des Vereins für Geschichte und Alterthumskunde in Hohenzollern,* XVIII-XXI (1884-1888). (*passim*)

Dreher, Theodor. [Same title as above, without the 4 page introduction]. Sigmaringen, 1888.
Du Cange, Charles Du Fresne. *Glossarium mediae et infimae Latinitatis.* Niort, 1886.
DW [cf. Grimm].
Eheberg, Karl Theodor. *Verfassungs-, Verwaltungs- und Wirtschaftsgeschichte der Stadt Strassburg bis 1861.* Strassburg, 1899.

S Ellinger, Georg. "Humanismus," Merker-Stammler, *Reallexikon* [q.v.]. (I, 535, 538)
S Ellinger, Georg. "Humanisten und Neulateiner," JBL, III (1892). (ii, 8:71)

Ellinger   S Ellinger, Georg. *Italien und der deutsche Humanismus in der neulateinischen Lyrik.* Geschichte der neulateinischen Literatur Deutschlands im 16. Jahrhundert, I (Berlin, Leipzig, 1929). (411)

EB   *The Encyclopedia Britannica.* Cambridge,¹¹ 1910-1911.
Enders. "Der Roraffe zu Strassburg im Münster," *Hist.-Pol. Blätter,* CXL (1908), 656-674.
Engel, Charles Frédéric. *Les commencements de l'instruction primaire à Strasbourg au moyen*

	âge et dans la première moitié du 16ème siècle. Paris, 1889.
Engel, *Schulwesen*	Engel, Carl. *Das Schulwesen in Strassburg von der Gründung des protestantischen Gymnasiums 1538.* Strassburg, 1886.
	Englert, Georg. *Alma Juliae Maximilianae Herbipolensi... commentatio de catalogo archiepiscoporum Moguntinensium Wimphelingians.* Aschaffenburg, 1882.
	S *Epistolae illustrium virorum ad Reuchlinum.* Tübingen, 1514. (fol. E3)
	S Erhard, H. A. *Geschichte des Wiederauflebens wissenschaftlicher Bildung, vornehmlich in Teutschland bis zum Anfange der Reformation.* 3 vols. Magdeburg, 1827-1832. (I, 457; III, 202ff., 207, 209, 220, 278f.)
Eubel, *Minoriten*	Eubel, Conrad. *Geschichte der oberdeutschen (Strassburger) Minoriten-Provinz.* Würzburg, 1886.
Eubel	Eubel, Conrad. *Hierarchia catholica medii aevi sive summorum pontificorum, S. R. E. cardinalium ecclesiarum antistitum series.* 6 vols. Münster, ²1914.
	S Eysengrein, Wilhelm. *Catalogus testium veritatis locupletissimus, omnium orthodoxae matris ecclesiae doctorum...* Dilingae, 1565. (176)
Fabricius, *Bohuslai*	S Fabricius, Georgius. *Bohuslai Hassensteynii, Lucubrationes oratoriae. His addita sunt collecta per Thomam Mitem diversorum elogia D. Bohulai vitam concernentia.* Chemnitz, Prague, 1563. (*passim*)
Fabricius, *Biblio. eccles.*	S Fabricius, Johann Albert. *Bibliotheca ecclesiastica...* Hamburg, 1722. (92)
Fabricius, *Biblio. Lat.*	Fabricius, Johann Albert. *Bibliotheca Latina mediae et infimae aetatis.* 3 vols. Florence, ²1858.
	Falk. "Dompredigerstellen am Ausgang des Mittelalters," *Hist.-Pol. Blätter*, LXXXVIII (1881), 1-15; 81-92; 178-187.
	Forcellini, Egidio. *Totius Latinitatis Lexicon.* Prati, 1858-1875.
	Freher, Paul. *Theatrum virorum eruditione clarorum. In quo vitae et scripta theologorum, jurisconsultorum, medicorum et philosophorum...* Nürnberg, 1688.
	Frenken, Goswin. "Die Exempla des Jacob von Vitry. Ein Beitrag zur Geschichte der Erzählungsliteratur des Mittelalters." QFPh, V, Heft 1 (1914), 1-92.
	S Freundgen, Joseph. *Jakob Wimphelings pädagogische Schriften.* Paderborn, 1892. (110, 153, 163, 533)
	Freyer, Hieronymus. *Universalhistorie.* Halle, Magdeburg, 1742.
	Fricker, Bartholomaeus. *Geschichte der Stadt und Bäder zu Baden.* Aarau, 1880.
Friese, *Merkwürdigkeiten*	Friese, Johannes. *Historische Merkwürdigkeiten des ehemaligen Elsasses aus den Silbermannischen Schriften.* Strassburg, 1804.

Friese	S	Friese, Johannes. *Neue Vaterländische Geschichte der Stadt Strassburg, von den ältesten Zeiten bis auf das Jahr 1791.* 4 vols. Strassburg, 1791. (II,105)
		Fuchs, Leonhard. *New Kreuterbůch.* Basel, 1543.
		Gabel, Leona C. (ed.) and Gragg, Florence A. (translator). *Memoirs of a Renaissance Pope. The Commentaries of Pius II. An Abridgment.* New York, 1959.
		Gabriel, Astrik L. "The Foundation of Johann Hueven de Arnheim for the College of Sorbonne (1452)," *Kunstmann Festschrift* [q.v.], 83-94.
		Gallia Christiana. Ed. Denis de Sainte Marthe, O.S.B., et al. V (Paris, 1731); XIII (Paris, 1785).
Gass, *Orgues*		Gass, Joseph. *Les orgues de la Cathédrale de Strasbourg à travers les siècles.* Strasbourg, 1935.
Gass, *Dominikanerinnen*		Gass, Joseph. *Strassburger Dominikanerinnen. Ein Beitrag zur Geschichte von St. Margaretha.* Strassburg, 1907.
Gass, *Blätter*		Gass, Joseph. *Vergilbte Blätter. Notizen und Excerpte aus alten Büchern und Handschriften.* Strassburg, 1918.
Geiger, *Reuchlin*		Geiger, Ludwig. *Johann Reuchlin. Sein Leben und seine Werke.* Leipzig, 1871.
Geiger, *Briefwechsel*	S	Geiger, Ludwig. *Johann Reuchlins Briefwechsel.* Bibliothek des litterarischen Vereins in Stuttgart, CXXVI. (Tübingen, 1875). (22, 38)
Geiger, *Ren.*	S	Geiger, Ludwig. *Renaissance und Humanismus in Italien und Deutschland.* Berlin, 1882. (387)
		Geiler von Kaysersberg, Johann. *Das buoch Arbore humana von dem menschliche baum/ Gepredigt von dem hoch gelehrte Doctor Johannes Keysersperg.* Strassburg (J. Grieninger), 1521.
		Geiler von Kaysersberg, Johann. *Ein tröstliche predig Sant Johanns Chrisostomi.* Strassburg (Grüninger), 1514.
		Geiler von Kaysersberg, Johann. *Passio domini nostri Jesu Christi.* Argentina (Joannes Knoblouchus), 1517.
		Geiler von Kaysersberg, Johann. *Predigen über das Narrenschiff.* Strassburg, 1520.
		Geiler von Kaysersberg, Johann. *Sermones et varii tractatus.* Strassburg (Grüninger), 1521.
		Geiler von Kaysersberg, Johann. *Trostspiegel.* Basel (Berckman von Olpe), sine dato [150?].
Gény		Gény, Joseph. *Schlettstadter Chronik des Schulmeisters Hieronymus Gebwiler.* Schlettstadt, 1890.
Gény-Knod		Gény, Joseph and Knod, Gustav. *Die Stadtbibliothek zu Schlettstadt. Festschrift zur Einweihung des neuen Bibliotheksgebäudes am 6. Juni 1889.* Part i: *Die Stadtbibliothek zu Schlettstadt.* Part ii: *Aus der Bibliothek des Beatus Rhenanus.* Schauberg, 1889.
	S	Gerson, Johann Charlier de. *Opera.* 3 parts. Ed. Peter Schott. Strassburg (Johann Prüss), 1488.
	S	Gerson, Johann Charlier de. *Opera.* 4 parts [first three same as above edition; part IV ed. Jacob

	Wimpheling]. Strassburg (Martin Flach, Jr., and Mathias Schürer), 1501.
	S Gesner, Konrad. *Bibliotheca instituta et collecta...* Zürich, 1574. (566)
Gesner	S Gesner, Konrad. *Bibliotheca universalis...* Zürich, 1545. (552)
	Gillis, J. H. *A Latin Manual.* (Classical Grammar; Ecclesiastical Vocabulary). Antigonish, N. S., 1948.
	Glassberger, Nikolaus. *Chronica Minorum observantium.* Anal. Francisc. [q.v.].
	S Glöckler, Ludwig Gabriel. *Geschichte des Bisthums Strassburg.* Part i: *Geschichte der Bischöfe.* Part ii: *Eine geschichtliche Skizze der Klöster.* Strassburg, 1879. (Part ii, 495)
GGr[2]	S Goedeke, Karl. *Grundriss zur Geschichte der deutschen Dichtung aus den Quellen.* I: *Das Mittelalter.* Dresden, ²1882. (I, 419)
	S Goldast, Melchior. *Philogoricarum epistolarum centuria una.* Frankfurt, 1610. (56-65)
	Gordon, Benjamin L. *Medieval and Renaissance Medicine.* New York, 1959.
	S Graesse, Johann G. T. *Lehrbuch einer allgemeinen Literärgeschichte aller bekannten Völker der Welt.* II. Dresden, 1840. (Part i, 390).
	Grandidier, Philippe André. *Augustins, chanoines réguliers et Ermites d'Alsace.* Paris, Colmar, 1903.
	Grandidier, Philippe André. *Chevaliers de St. Jean, templiers, chevaliers, teutoniques, Béghards et Béguines d'Alsace.* (Extrait de *L'Alsatia Sacra*). Paris, Colmar, 1903.
	Grandidier, Philippe André. *Essais historiques et topographiques sur l'église cathédrale de Strasbourg.* Strasbourg, 1782.
	Grandidier, Philippe André. *État ecclésiastique du diocèse de Strasbourg en 1454.* Strasbourg, 1897.
	Grandidier, Philippe André. *Fragments d'une Alsatia Litterata, ou dictionnaire biographique des littérateurs et artistes alsaciens.* Colmar, 1898 [First published as Vol. II of *Nouv. oeuvr.*].
	S Grandidier, Philippe André. *Mélanges historiques sur Strasbourg...* Paris et Colmar, 1903. (352, 381) [First published in vol. V of *Nouv. oeuvr.*].
Grandidier, Nouv. oeuvr.	S Grandidier, Philippe André. *Nouvelles oeuvres inédites.* 5 vols. Colmar, 1897-1900. (II, 485-492) I. [Biographical material on Grandidier]. II. *Fragments d'une Alsatia Litterata ou Dictionnaire biographique des Littérateurs et artistes alsaciens.* III. IV. *Alsatia Sacra ou statistique ecclésiastiques et religieuse de l'Alsace avant de Révolution.* V. *Ordres militaires et mélanges historiques.*
Grandidier, Oeuvr. hist.	S Grandidier, Philippe André. *Oeuvres historiques inédites.* 5 vols. Colmar, 1867. (V, 208)
	Grandidier, Philippe André. *Über die Entstehung*

des Frei Maurer Ordens. Ein Brief von Herrn Abt Grandidier. (Beitrag: die Strassburger Münsterbauhütte). Kehl, 1782.

Grandidier, Philippe André. Vues pittoresques de l'Alsace, dessinées, gravées, terminées en bistre par Walter, accompagnées d'une texte historique par Grandidier. Strasbourg, 1785.

DW   Grimm, Jacob and Wilhelm. Deutsches Wörterbuch. Leipzig, 1893-.

Hain, L. Repertorium bibliographicum. Stuttgart, 1831.

S Hammer, Wilhelm. "Peter Schott und sein Gedicht auf Strassburg (1486)," ZfdP, LXXVII (October, 1958), 361-371.

Hämmerle, Albert. Die Canoniker des hohen Domstifts zu Augsburg bis zur Säkularisation. Zürich, 1935.

Handwörterbuch des deutschen Aberglaubens. Hrsg. E. Hoffmann Krayer. Berlin and Leipzig, 1927-1942.

Harpers'   Harpers' Latin Dictionary. Ed. Charlton T. Lewis and Charles Short. New York, 1907.

Harpers' Dictionary of Classical Literature and Antiquities. Ed. Harry Thurston Peck. New York, 1897.

Hartfelder, Karl. "Analekten zur Geschichte des Humanismus in Süddeutschland," VfKLRen., I (1886), 121-128, 494-503.

Hartfelder,   S Hartfelder, Karl. Unedierte Briefe Agricolas.
Briefe   Karlsruhe, 1886. (31f.)

S Hartmann, Alfred. Die Amerbach-Korrespondenz. I: 1481-1513. Basel, 1942. (42, n. 3)

Harvey, Paul. The Oxford Companion to Classical Literature. Oxford, 1940.

Hasse, Karl P. Die deutsche Renaissance. I: Ihre Begründung durch den Humanismus. Meran, 1920.

Hassenstein, Bohuslaus von. [Cf. G. Fabricius, Potuček, Ryba]

Hatt, Vie   S Hatt, Jaques. La vie Strasbourgeoise. Il y a trois cent ans. Strasbourg, 1947. (13)

Hatt, Ville   S Hatt, Jaques. Une ville de xve siècle: Strasbourg. Strasbourg, 1929. (48; 81, n. 2; 348; 424; 425, n. 2; 435, n. 4)

Hauck [cf. Realencyklopädie].

Haug   Haug, Hans; Will, Robert; Riegler, Theodore; Beyer, Victor; Ahnne, Paul. La cathédrale de Strasbourg. Strasbourg, 1957.

Hawkins, R. C. Catalogue of Books mostly from the Presses of the First Printers, showing the Progress of Printing with Movable Types through the Second Half of the Fifteenth Century. London, 1910.

Heimbucher, Max. Die Orden und Kongregationen der katholischen Kirche. 2 vols. Paderborn, 1934.

Hell, Lucien. "Zur Baugeschichte der Alt-St.-

	Peterkirche in Strassburg im Mittelalter," AEK, XIII (1938), 355-384.
	Hermelink, Heinrich. *Die Matrikeln der Universität Tübingen.* Stuttgart, 1906.
	Hermelink, Heinrich. *Register zu den Matrikeln der Universität Tübingen 1477-1600.* Stuttgart, 1931.
	Herrmann, Max. "Ludwig Dringenberg in Heidelberg," ZGORh, Neue Folge, IV (1889), 119.
Hertz-Barack	Hertz, Paul and Barack, K. A. *Elsässische Büchermarken...* Strassburg, 1892.
	Hertz, W. *Deutsche Sage im Elsass.* Stuttgart, 1872.
	Hertzog, Bernhart. *Chronicon Alsatiae.* Strassburg, 1592.
	Hofmann, W. v. *Forschungen zur Geschichte der kurialen Behörden vom Schisma bis zur Reformation.* Bibliothek des Königlichen Preussischen Historischen Instituts in Rom, XII, XIII (Rome, 1914).
	Höhn, Antonin. *Chronologia Provinciae Rheno-Suevicae ordinis FF. Eremitarum S. P. Augustini.* sine loco, 1744.
Holstein, "Beilage" S	Holstein, Hugo. "Ein Wimpheling Codex," *Beilage zur Allgemeinen Zeitung,* 18 April, 1888.
Holstein, "Codex" S	Holstein, Hugo. "Ein Wimpheling Codex," ZvLR, II (1889), 3, 213-215. (213)
Holstein, "Mitteilungen" S	Holstein, Hugo. "Neue Mitteilungen. Alsatica," ZfvLg, Neue Folge, XIII (1899), 75-87. (78-82)
Holstein, "Biographie"	Holstein, Hugo. "Zur Biographie Jakob Wimphelings," ZvLR, Neue Folge, IV (1891), 227-252.
Holstein, Gelehrten	Holstein, Hugo. *Zur Gelehrtengeschichte Heidelbergs beim Ausgang des Mittelalters.* Elfter Jahres-Bericht über das königliche Gymnasium zu Wilhelmshaven (Wilhelmshaven, 1893).
	Horning, Wilhelm. *Guide de l'église collégiale (Protestante) de Saint-Pierre-le-Jeune.* Strassburg, 1902.
Horning, *Festschrift* S	Horning, Wilhelm. *Die Jung St. Peterkirche und ihre Kapellen. Festschrift zur 600jährigen Feier der Grundsteinlegung der Kirche (1290).* Strassburg, 1890. (35-39)
Horning, *Kirche* S	Horning, Wilhelm. *Die Kirche und das Stift Jung-Sanct Peter in Wort und Bild.* Strassburg, 1889. (5)
Horning, "Stift" S	Horning, Wilhelm. "Das Stift Jung-St. Peter. Beiträge zu seiner Geschichte," JbGElsLotr, VI (1890), 11-61. (42, 44f.)
Horning, *Jung-St.-Peter*	Horning, Wilhelm. *Das Stift von Jung-Sankt-Peter in Strassburg. Urkundliche Beiträge zur Geschichte desselben aus sechs Jahrhunderten (1200-1700).* Strassburg, 1891.
	Ignace-Marie, P. "Liste des Provinciaux franciscains d'Alsace," *Revue d'Histoire franciscaine,* VII (1930), 284-296.
	Illyricus, Flacius. *Catalogus testium veritatis qui*

Inventaire		*ante nostram aetatem Pontifici Romano atque Papismo erroribus reclamarant.* Strassburg, 1562. *Inventaire des Archives de la Ville de Bruges.* Vol. VI, 1e Série: *13e au 16e siècle; Inventaire des Chartes,* Section 1. 1878. *Inventaire des Archives de la ville de Strasbourg antérieures à 1790.* Strasbourg, 1949-60. Série I, and supplément de la série AA, edited by J. Fuchs. 1954. Série II, edited by J. Fuchs. 1953. Série III, edited by E. Raeuber. 1950.
	S	Série IV, edited by E. Raeuber. 1949 (156, no. 105B) Série V, edited by J. Fuchs. 1952. Série VI, edited by J. Fuchs. 1960.
Inventaire... St. Thomas		*Inventaire des Archives du Chapitre de St. Thomas de Strasbourg.* Strasbourg, 1937.
Inventaire (Brucker)		*Inventaire-Sommaire des Archives Communales de la ville de Strasbourg antérieures à 1790.* Série AA: *Actes constitutifs et politiques de la commune.* 4 vols. Ed. J. Brucker. Strasbourg, 1878-86.
Inventaire (Spach)		*Inventaire-Sommaire des Archives Départementales antérieures à 1790. Bas Rhin.* 4 vols. Ed. L. Spach. Strasbourg, 1863-1872. James, Edith E. C. *Bologna: Its History, Antiquities and Art.* London, 1909. James, Percival R. *The Baths of Bath in the Sixteenth and Seventeenth Centuries.* London, 1938. Jente, R. *Proverbia communa.* Indiana University Publications, Folklore Series, IV (1947).
	S	Joachimsen, Paul. "Der Humanismus und die Entwicklung des deutschen Geistes," *Deutsche Vierteljahrsschrift für Literaturwissenschaft und Geistesgeschichte,* VIII (1930), 3, 419-448. (441) Jobes, Gertrude. *Dictionary of Mythology, Folklore and Symbols.* 2 vols. New York, 1961.
Jöcher	S	Jöcher, Christian Gottlieb. *Allgemeines Gelehrten-Lexikon.* Leipzig, 1751. (IV, 341)
Jöcher, Fortsetzung		Jöcher, Christian Gottlieb. *Fortsetzung und Ergänzungen zu Jöchers allgemeinem Gelehrten-Lexikon, angefangen von Johann Christof Adelung und vom Buchstaben K fortgesetzt von Heinrich Wilhelm Rotermund.* I & II (Leipzig 1784-87), III (Delmenhorst, 1810), IV, V & VI (Bremen, 1813-1819), VII (Leipzig, 1897). Joyce, G. H. *Die christliche Ehe, eine geschichtliche und dogmatische Studie.* Leipzig, 1934. Keil, Heinrich. *Grammatici latini.* 6 vols. Leipzig, 1857-80. Kempis [cf. Thomas à Kempis]. Kerer, Johannes. *Statuta Collegii...* [Cf. Beckmann; Werk]. Khamm, Corbinianus, O.S.B. *Hierarchia Augustana, chronologica tripartita...* Augsburg, 1709.

Kibre, *Privileges*		Kibre, Pearl. *The Nations in the Mediaeval Universities.* Cambridge, Mass., 1948. Kibre, Pearl. *Scholarly Privileges in the Middle Ages.* London, 1961. Kindler von Knobloch, Julius. *Der alte Adel im Oberelsass.* Berlin, 1882. Kindler von Knobloch, Julius. *Beiträge zur Geschichte des elsässischen Adels* [Auszug aus BSCMH, X]. Strassburg, 1878. Kindler von Knobloch, Julius. *Die Burggrafen und Vitzthumgeschlechter im Elsass.* Berlin, 1881.
Kindler von Knobloch, *Buch*	S	Kindler von Knobloch, Julius. *Das goldene Buch von Strassburg.* 2 parts in 1 vol. Wien, 1885. (ii, 331) Kirby, Richard and Bishop, John. *The Marrow of Astrology.* London, 1688. *Kirchen-Lexicon* [Cf. Wetzer-Welte]. Kisky, Wilhelm. *Die Domkapitel der geistlichen Kurfürsten im 14. und 15. Jahrhundert.* Quellen und Studien zur Verfassungsgeschichte des Deutschen Reiches in Mittelalter und Neuzeit. Hrsg. Karl Zeumer. Vol. I, 3 (Weimar, 1906). "Die kleine Münsterkronik," [cf. Leo Dacheux].
Knepper, *Wimpheling*	S	Knepper, Joseph. *Jakob Wimpfeling (1450-1528). Sein Leben und seine Werke nach den Quellen dargestellt.* Freiburg i. B., 1902. (95f.) Knepper, Joseph. "Kleine Funde zum elsässischen Humanismus," ZGORh, Neue Folge, XXI (1906), 40-49.
Knepper, *Schulwesen*	S	Knepper, Joseph. *Das Schul- und Unterrichtswesen im Elsass von den Anfängen bis gegen das Jahr 1550.* Strassburg, 1905. (68, 69, 99, 171, 185, 278, 305, 320, 326 and *passim*)
	S	Knepper, Joseph. *Sprüche und Anekdoten aus dem elsässischen Humanismus.* Berlin, 1903 [Sonderabdruck aus StzvLg, III (1903), 156ff.]. (160, 167, 176)
Knod, *Studenten*	S	Knod, Gustav C. *Deutsche Studenten in Bologna (1288-1562). Biographischer Index zu den Acta Nationis Germanicae universitatis Bononiensis.* Berlin, 1899. (#3397)
Knod, "Wimpheling"		Knod, Gustav C. "Neun Briefe von und an Jacob Wimpheling," VfKLRen, I (1886).
Knod, "Bibliographie"	S	Knod, Gustav C. "Zur Bibliographie Wimphelings", CBL, V (1888), 463-481. (472)
Knod, "Schlettstadt"	S	Knod, Gustav C. "Zur Schlettstatter Schulgeschichte," StbSt, II (1884), 431-439. (435) Könnecke, G. *Deutscher Literaturatlas.* Marburg, 1909. *Das kreüter buoch oder herbarius* [Cf. Balthassar Beck]. Kreuter (Kreutter), Franz. *Geschichte der K. K. Vorderösterreichischen Staaten...* Hrsg. von einem Kapitular des Fürstlichen Reichsstiftes St. Blasii im Schwarzwalde, 1790. Krieger, Joseph. *Beiträge zur Geschichte der Volks-*

seuchen zur medicinischen Statistik und Topographie von Strassburg im Elsass, 1. Heft: Beiträge zur Geschichte der Volksseuchen = Statistische Mittheilungen über Elsass-Lothringen, 10. Heft. Strassburg, 1879.

ter Kuile, G. T. "De Latijnse School te Deventer 1311-1811," *Stedelijk Gymnasium te Deventer 1848-1948. Gedenkboek.* Sine dato, sine loco [Deventer, 1948?], 5-16.

Kunstmann Festschrift. [cf. *Middle Ages-Reformation-Volkskunde*...]

Laguille, Louis. *Histoire de la Province D'Alsace depuis Jules César jusqu'au mariage de Louis XV.* Strasbourg, 1727.

Landmann, "Empfängnis"   Landmann, Florenz. "Die unbefleckte Empfängnis in Strassburger Predigten," AEK, VI (1931), 189-194.

Landmann, "Predigt"   Landmann, Florenz. "Zur Geschichte der oberelsässischen Predigt in der Jugendzeit Geilers von Kaysersberg: Der Zyklus der Adventpredigten des Wilhelm Textoris vom Jahr 1476 nach den Aufzeichnungen seines Basler Berufsgenossen Heynlin von Stein," AEA, II (1947-48), 205-234.

Lauffer, O. "Geiler von Kaisersberg und das Deutschtum des Elsass im Ausgange des Mittelalters," *Archiv für Kulturgeschichte*, XVII, 1 (1926), 38-49.

Lee, Frederick George. *A Glossary of Liturgical and Ecclesiastical Terms.* London, 1877.

S   Lefftz, Joseph. *Die gelehrten und literarischen Gesellschaften im Elsass vor 1870.* Schriften der Elsass-Lothringischen Wissenschaftlichen Gesellschaft. Reihe A: *Alsatica und Lotharingica.* Buch VI (Colmar, 1931). (8, 2)

S   Lehr, Ernest. *Mélanges de littérature et d'histoire alsatiques.* Strasbourg, 1870. (153)

Lehr, "Geroldseck"   Lehr, Ernest. "La Seigneurie de Hohengeroldseck et ses possesseurs successifs," BSCMH, 2e Série, XVI (1869), 62-93.

Levrault, Louis. *Essai sur l'ancienne monai de Strasbourg et sur ses rapports avec l'histoire d'Alsace.* Strasbourg, ²1874.

Levy, Joseph. "Die Einsiedeleien im Elsass," BSCMH, 2e Série, XXV (1918), 199-211.

Liber confrat.   *Liber confraternitatis Beatae Marie de Anima Teutonicorum de Urbe/ quem rerum Germanicarum cultoribus offerunt sacerdotes aedis teutonicae B. M. de anima Urbis.* Rome, 1875.

S   "Liber secretus iuris caesarii," Vol. I: 1378-1512. Ms. 137, *Archivio di Stato* in Bologna. Listed in Cencetti as #137-#149: "Liber segreti del coll. civ. vol. I." (folio 170b).

Il "Liber secretus iuris caesarii" dell Università di Bologna. I (1378-1420) and II (1421-1450). Ed. Albani Sorbelli. Bologna 1938, 1942.

S "Liber secretus iuris pontificii." Vol. I: "Ab anno 1377 ad annum 1528." Ms. #126, *Archivo di Stato* in Bologna. Listed by Cencetti as #126-#136: "Libri segreti dell coll. canon." (folio 148a)
Liber Usualis. Edited by the Benedictines of Solesmes. Tournai, 1953.
Liddell and Schott. *Greek-English Lexicon.* Oxford, 1925.
Linckenheld, E. "Essai sur les débuts de la typographie greque en Alsace," BSCMH, II. Série, XXVI (1926), 167-174.

Lincy — Lincy, Le Roux de and Tisserand, L. M. *Paris et ses historiens aux xive et xve siècles.* Paris, 1867.
Lindemann, W. *Johann Geiler von Kaisersberg nach dem Französischen des Abbé Dacheux bearbeitet von W. Lindemann.* Sammlung historischer Bildnisse. 4. Série, II (Freiburg i. B., 1877). [Cf. Dacheux].
Lindner, Pirmin. *Monasticon Episcopatus Augustani antiqui. Verzeichnisse der Äbte, Pröpste und Äbtissinnen der Klöster der alten Diözese Augsburg.* Bregenz, 1913.
Lion, Albertus H. *Commentarii in Virgilium Serviani; sive Mauro Servio Honorato tribuunter.* 2 vols. Göttingen, 1826.
Lipsius, Iustus. *Epistularum selectarum centuria prima miscellanea.* Antwerp, 1603.
Lipsius, Iustus. *Manductionis ad stoicam philosophorum libri tres.* Antwerp, 1604.
Loë, Paulus von, O.P. *Statistisches über die Ordensprovinz Teutonia* [cf. Q. F. Domin.].
Lübker, Friedrich. *Reallexikon des klassischen Altertums für Gymnasien.* Leipzig, ^{7}1891.

S Lurwig, Marian T. *Studies in the Lucubratiunculae by Peter Schott.* Diss. University of Chicago, 1946.
Lycosthenes (Wolfhart), Conradus. *Elenchus scriptorum omnium veterum...* Basel, 1551. [2d ed. of Conrad Gesner, *Elenchus...*].
Maigne D'Arnis, W. H. *Lexicon manuale ad scriptores mediae et infimae latinitatis.* Paris, 1866.
Manilius, M. *Astronomicon.* Ed. A. E. Houseman. Cambridge, ²1937.

Martin, *Badewesen* — Martin, Alfred. *Deutsches Badewesen in vergangenen Tagen.* Jena, 1906.
Martin, E. E. and Lienhart, H. *Wörterbuch der elsässischen Mundarten.* Strassburg, 1907.
Marzell, Heinrich. *Wörterbuch der deutschen Pflanzennamen.* Heidelberg, 1913.
Mas Latrie, L. de. *Trésor de chronologie d'histoire et de géographie.* Paris, 1889.
Matrikel, Acta and other records of universities:
   For Basel, cf. Wackernagel
      Bologna, *Acta bonon.*
      Erfurt, Weissenborn

Freiburg, Mayer
Heidelberg, Toepke
Louvain, Wils
Paris, *Auct.*
Tübingen, Hermelink.
Maximilian, P. F. *Johann Trithemius. Vermehrter Catalogus oder Register...* [translation and expansion of Trithemius' biographies]. München, 1746.
Mayer, Hermann. *Matrikel der Universität Freiburg i. B. 1460-1656.* 2 vols. I: *Einleitung und Text.* II: *Tabellen, Personen- und Ortsregister.* Freiburg i. B., 1907-1910.
Mazzetti, Serafino. *Repertorio di tutti i professori antichi e moderni della famosa università Bologna.* Bologna, 1847; ²1848.

S Meister, Aloys. "Auszüge aus der Camera apostolica," ZGORh. Neue Folge, VII (1892), 104ff. (131)
Menge, H. *Lateinisch-deutsches Schulwörterbuch.* Berlin, ³1911.

Merker-Stammler   Merker, P. and Stammler, W. *Reallexikon der deutschen Literaturgeschichte.* Berlin, 1925-26.
Meuschenius, Johann Gerhard. *Vitae summorum dignitate et eruditione Virorum.* 3 vols. in 1. Coburg, 1736. [Vol. II contains: "Bononia illustrata Nicolai Burtii" (printed at Bologna, 1494)].
Meyer, Jean Jacques. *La chronique strasbourgoise* [cf. Reuss].

Meyer, Reformacio   Meyer, Johannes. *Buch der Reformacio Prediger-Ordens* [cf. *Q.F. Domin.*].
Meyers Konversations-Lexikon. 15 vols. Leipzig und Wien, 1895.
Michaud, Louis Gabriel. *Biographie universelle ancienne et moderne.* 85 vols. Paris, 1811-62.

Kunstmann   *Middle Ages-Reformation-Volkskunde. Festschrift*
Festschrift   *for John G. Kunstmann.* University of North Carolina Studies in the Germanic Languages and Literatures, XXVI (Chapel Hill, 1959).
Middleton, John. *Practical Astrology.* London, 1679.
Migne, J. P. *Patrologiae cursus complectus, seu bibliotheca universalis omnium SS patrum doctorum scriptorumque ecclesiasticorum. Series latina.* Paris, 1844-1900.
Mitis, Thomas. *Bohuslai Hassensteynii Lucerbrationes...* [Cf. G. Fabricius].

Mon. Boica   *Monumenta Boica.* Edidit Academia Scientiarum Boica. Munich, 1784.
Mon. Eccles. Trident.   *Monumenta Ecclesiae Tridentinae.* Vol. III, Pars Altera: *Tridentinorum Antistitum series universa.* Ed. B. Bonelli. Tridenti, 1765, 161ff. = *Notizie istorico-critiche della Chiesa di Trento,* vol. IV.
Monumenta Romana Episcopatus Vesprimiensis. Budapest, 1902.

S Moréri, Louis. *Le Grand Dictionnaire historique ou*

  le mélange curieux de l'histoire sacrée et profane. Basel, 1740. (VI, 373)

Müller, Gunther. *Deutsche Dichtung der Renaissance und des Barocks.* Wildpark, Potsdam, 1927.

S Müller, J. G. "Johann Geiler von Kaysersberg," Wetzer-Welte [q.v.], V, 188-195. (191)

Murner, Thomas. *Die Badenfahrt.* Hrsg. Victor Michels. Berlin, Leipzig, 1927.

Muzzi, Salvatore. *Annali della cittá di Bologna dalla sua origine al 1796.* Bologna, 1845.

Nagl, Franz. *Urkundliches zur Geschichte der Anima in Rom.* Römische Quartalschrift für christliche Alterthumskunde und für Kirchengeschichte. 12. Supplement: *Mitteilungen aus dem Archiv des Nationalhospizes S. Maria dell Anima in Rom,* 1. Teil (Rome, 1899).

Nanton, Sabourin de. "Les tombes de Saint-Pierre-le-Vieux à Strasbourg," BSCMH, II. Série VII (1870), 8-12.

NDB *Neue deutsche Biographie.* Berlin, 1953-.

Nork, F. *Der Festkalender.* Das Kloster, vol. VII. Ed. J. Scheible. Stuttgart, 1847.

S Oberman, Heiko Augustinus. *The Harvest of Medieval Theology: Gabriel Biel and Late Medieval Nominalism.* Cambridge, Mass., 1963. (55)

Oliger, Pater Livarius. "Der päpstliche Zeremonienmeister Johannes Burckard von Strassburg 1450-1506," AEK, IX (1934), 199-232.

The Oxford Companion to Classical Literature. Ed. Paul Harvey. Oxford, 1940.

The Oxford Dictionary of English Proverbs. Ed. W. G. Smith. Oxford, 1936.

The Oxford Dictionary of Quotations. Ed. A. M. Smyth *et. al.* London, New York, Toronto, 1943.

S Pantaleon, Heinrich. *Prosopographiae heroum atque illustrium virorum totius Germaniae.* Basel, 1565. (458)

Pardi, *Studio* Pardi, Guiseppe. *Lo Studio di Ferrara nei secoli* xv⁰ *e* xvi⁰. Ferrara, 1903.

Pardi, Guiseppe. *Titoli Dottorali conferti dallo Studio di Ferrara nei secoli xv e xvi.* Lucca, 1901.

Pareus, Philippus (Ursinus Zacharias?). *Historia bavarico-palatina.* Frankfurt, 1717.

Pareus, Philippus (Ursinus Zacharias?). *Electa Symmachiana.* Frankfurt, 1642.

Passmann, Pater Antonin. "Die Kartause zu Strassburg," AEA, IX (1958), 81-97.

Pastor Pastor, Ludwig. *Geschichte der Päpste im Zeitalter der Renaissance.* II³⁻⁴ (Freiburg, 1904), III 1. 2. ⁵⁻⁷ (Freiburg, 1924).

Pastor, Ludwig. *The History of the Popes from the close of the Middle Ages.* Ed. Frederick Ignatius Antrobus. 40 vols. London, 1938-1953.

Pastorius, Johann Martin. *Kurze Abhandlung von*

	den Ammeistern der Stadt Strassburg. Strassburg, 1761.
	Paulsen, Friedrich. "Gründung der deutschen Universitäten im Mittelalter," HZ, XXXXV (1881), 251ff.
	Paulsen, Friedrich. "Organisation und Lebensordungen der deutschen Universitäten im Mittelalter," HZ, XXXXV (1881), 385ff.
	S Paulus, Nikolaus. "Der Augustiner-General Thomas von Strassburg," AEK, I (1926), 49-66. (60)
Pauly-Wissowa	Paulys Realencyclopädie der Classischen Altertumswissenschaft. Neue Bearbeitung, hrsg. von Georg Wissowa. Stuttgart, 1893-1962.
	Pfleger, Lucien. "Albert der Grosse und das Elsass," AEK, V (1930), 1-18.
Pfleger, "Kult"	Pfleger, Lucien. "Das Auftreten der Syphilis in Strassburg, Geiler von Kaysersberg und der Kult des heiligen Fiakrius," ZGORh, Neue Folge XXX, 2 (1915), 153-173.
Pfleger, "Predigt"	Pfleger, Lucien. "Beiträge zur Geschichte der Predigt und des religiösen Volksunterrichts im Elsass während des Mittelalters," JbGElsLotr., XXXVIII. 4 (1922).
Pfleger, Pfarrei	Pfleger, Lucien. Die elsässische Pfarrei. Ihre Entstehung und Entwicklung. Strassburg, 1936.
Pfleger, "Kunst"	Pfleger, Lucien. "Geiler von Kaysersberg und die Kunst seiner Zeit," ElsMGV, I (1910), 428-434.
Pfleger, "Marienfeste"	S Pfleger, Lucien. "Die geschichtliche Entwicklung der Marienfeste in der Diözese Strassburg," AEK, II (1927), 1-88. (55)
	S Pfleger, Lucien. Kirchengeschichte der Stadt Strassburg im Mittelalter, nach den Quellen dargestellt. Alsatia-Forschungen zur Kirchengeschichte des Elsass, VI (Colmar, 1941). (207)
Pfleger, "Gottesdienste"	Pfleger, Lucien. "Die Stadt- und Rats- Gottesdienste im Strassburger Münster," AEK, XII (1937), 1-55.
	Pfleger, Lucien. Menschen Gottes. Gesammelte biographische Essays. Regensburg, 1924.
Pfleger, "Wallfahrten"	Pfleger, Lucien. "Sühne Wallfahrten und öffentliche Kirchenbusse im Elsass," AEK," VIII (1933), 130.
Pfleger, "Predigtwesen"	Pfleger, Lucien. "Über das elsässische Predigtwesen im Mittelalter," ElsMGV, IV (1913), 529-538.
Pfleger, "Christkindelmarkt"	Pfleger, Lucien. "Vom Strassburger Christkindelmarkt," ElsMGV, I (1910), 513-521.
Pfleger, "Aest"	Pfleger, Lucien. "'Von dem xv Aest'. Eine unbekannte Predigt Geilers von Kaysersberg. Erstmalig herausgegeben von L. Pfleger," AEK, X (1935), 139-151.
Pfleger, "Münsterkanzel"	Pfleger, Lucien. "Wo stand die Münsterkanzel vor Geiler von Kaysersberg?" AEK, II (1928), 377.
Pfleger, Gesch. d. Predigtwesens	Pfleger, Lucien. Zur Geschichte des Predigtwesens in Strassburg vor Geiler von Kaysersberg... Strassburg, 1907.

Pfleger, "Predigttexte"	Pfleger, Lucien. "Zur handschriftlichen Überlieferung Geilerscher Predigttexte," ZEK, VI (1931), 195ff.
	Piton, Frédéric. *Strasbourg illustré... ou Panorama... de Strasbourg et de ses environs.* 2 vols. Strasbourg, 1855.
	Plöchl, Willibald M. *Geschichte des Kirchenrechts.* München, 1960.
	S Potuček, Augustinus. *Bohuslaus Hassensteinius Baro a Lobkowicz. Epistolae.* Bibliotheca scriptorum medii recentisque aevorum saecula xv-xvi, XIV (Budapest, 1946). (v-xix *passim*, 1f., 8f., 16, 19, 20, 55, 97f., 137-143)
	Previté-Orton, C. W. *The Shorter Cambridge Medieval History.* 2 vols. Cambridge, 1952.
	Prochaska, Faustinus. *De saecularibus liberalium artium in Bohemia et Moravia fatis commentarius.* Pragae, 1782.
	Proctor, Robert. *An Index to the Early Printed Books in the British Museum.* London 1898.
Q.F. Domin.	*Quellen und Forschungen zur Geschichte des Dominkanerordens in Deutschland.* Hrsg. von Paulus von Loë und Benedictus Maria Reichert. Leipzig, 1907-14.
	Heft 1: Loë. *Statistisches über die Ordensprovinz Teutonia.* 1907.
	Heft 3: Reichert. *[Johannes] Meyer, Buch der Reformacio des Predigerordens.* 1908.
	Heft 6: Reichert. *Registrum litterarum... Leonardi de Mansuetis 1474-1480.* 1911.
	Heft 7: Reichert. *Registrum... Salvi Cassettae 1481-1483.* 1912.
	Heft 10: Reichert. *Registrum litterarum Joachimi Turriani 1487-1500.* 1914.
	Radermacher, L. *M. Fabii Quintiliani institutiones oratoriae.* Leipzig, 1907.
	Rapp, Alfred. *Reichstadt am Oberrhein. Strassburg in der altdeutschen Geschichte* [Published by *Strassburger Neueste Nachrichten* between 1940-45].
	Rathgeber, Julius. *Beiträge zur Geschichte des Elsasses.* Göttingen, 1875.
Rathgeber, *Sprichwörter*	Rathgeber, Julius. *Elsässischer Sprichwörterschatz...* Strassburg, 1883.
	Rathgeber, Julius. *Die Geschichte des Elsass.* Strassburg, 1879.
Rathgeber, *Schätze*	Rathgeber, Julius. *Die handschriftlichen Schätze der früheren Strassburger Stadtbibliothek. Ein Beitrag zur elsässischen Geschichte.* Gütersloh, 1876.
	Rathgeber, Julius. *Strassburg im XVI. Jahrhundert. Reformationsgeschichte der Stadt Strassburg.* Stuttgart, 1871.
Rathgeber, *Humaniste*	Rathgeber, Julius. *Un Humaniste de l'école de Schlestadt.* Colmar, 1870.
Rathgeber,	Rathgeber, Julius. *Zwei Gottesmänner aus Kaysers-*

Gottesmänner		burg. Mülhausen, 1865.
		Raynaldus, Odoricus. *Annales Ecclesiastici ab anno MCXCVIII ubi Card. Baronius desinit.* Tomus XIX (1458-1503). Rome, 1663 [No pagination].
Hauck		*Realencyklopädie für protestantische Theologie und Kirche.* 24 vols. Ed. A. Hauck. Leipzig, ³1896-1913.
Reichert, *Meyer*		Reichert, Benedictus Maria. [*Johannes*] *Meyer, Buch der Reformacio des Predigerordens* [cf. *Q.F. Domin.*, Heft 3].
		Reichert, Benedictus Maria. *Registrum litterarum... Leonardi di Mansuetis 1474-1480.* [cf. *Q.F. Domin.*, Heft 6].
		Reichert, Benedictus Maria. *Registrum... Salvi Cassettae* [cf. *Q.F. Domin.*, Heft 7].
		Reichert, Benedictus Maria. *Registrum litterarum Joachimi Turriani 1487-1500* [cf. *Q.F. Domin.*, Heft 10].
		Reuchlin, Johann. *Vocabularius breuiloquens.* Strassburg, 1488.
Reuss, *Meyer*		Reuss, Rodolphe Ernest. *La Chronique Strasbourgeoise de Jean-Jaques Meyer.* Strasbourg, 1873.
		Reuss, Rodolphe Ernest. *Kleine Strassburger Chronik.* Strassburg, 1889.
Reuss, "Männer"		Reuss, Rodolphe Ernest. "Sieben elsässische Männer," *Elsass-Lothringischer Familienkalender*, IV (1896), 40-47.
		Rhenanus, Beatus. "Vita Geileri" [To be found in 1. J. Geiler von Kaysersberg, *Navicula sive speculum*. Strassburg, 1513 (at end). 2. *Idem, Sermones et varii tractatus.* Strassburg, 1521, folios CLIf. 3. Riegger, *Amoen.*, 56ff.].
Riegger, *Amoen.*	S	Riegger, Joseph Anton Stephan. *Amoenitates literariae friburgenses.* Freiburg i. B., 1779. (180, 187, 189)
Riegger, *Anal.*		Riegger, Joseph Anton Stephan. *Analecta Academiae Friburgensis...* Ulm, 1774.
		Riehm, Eduard. *Handwörterbuch des Biblischen Altertums.* 2 vols. Bielefeld and Leipzig, ²1893-1894.
		Rieple, Max. *Malerisches Elsass.* Bern, 1964.
		Riley, H. T. *A Dictionary of Latin and Greek Quotations.* London, 1891.
	S	Ristelhuber, Paul. *Strasbourg et Bologne.* Paris, 1891. (112-117, 121)
Ritter, *Histoire*	S	Ritter, François. *Histoire de l'Imprimerie alsacienne aux xve et xvie siècles.* Publications de l'Institut des hautes Études Alsaciennes, Tome XIV (Strasbourg, Paris, 1955). (50, 69, 494)
Ritter, *Heidelberg*	S	Ritter, Gerhard. *Die Heidelberger Universität: ein Stück deutscher Geschichte. Im Auftrag der Heidelberger Akademie der Wissenschaften.* I: *Das Mittelalter 1386-1508.* Heidelberg, 1936. (531)
Ritter, "Geiler"	S	Ritter, O. "Geiler von Kaysersberg und die Reformation in Strassburg," *16. Jahresbericht des*

Königlichen Real-gymnasiums und der Landwirtschaftsschule zu Döbeln, Programm Nr. 553 (1895), II-XXXVII. (XXXIV)

Rodocanachi, E. *Histoire de Rome. Une cour princière au vatican pendant la Renaissance (Sixte IV – Innocent VIII – Alexandre VI Borgia) 1471-1503.* Paris, 1925.

Roeder von Diersburg, Elvire Freiin. *Komik und Humor bei Geiler von Kaisersberg.* Berlin, 1921.

Röhrich, Timotheus Wilhelm. *Mitteilungen aus der Geschichte des Elsasses.* 3 vols. Paris, Strassburg, 1855.

"Rotoli nel archivio de toti legisti dal 1432 al 1599." Ms. #412, *Archivio di Stato* in Bologna. Listed by Cencetti as #412 Elenchi dei lettori.

S Rupprich, Hans. *Humanismus in den deutschen Städten und an den Universitäten.* Deutsche Literatur. Reihe Humanismus und Renaissance, VII. (Leipzig, 1935). (76-78, 316)

S Ryba, Bohumil. *Bohuslaus Hassensteinius, Baro a Lobkowicz. Scripta Moralia, Oratio ad Argentinenses, Memoria Alexandri de Imolo.* Edidit B. Ryba. Bibliotheca scriptorum medii recentisque aevorum saecula xv-xvi. Rediget Ladislaus Juhasz Szeged (Hungaria). VIII (Leipzig, 1937). (ii, v, 28-33)

Sachs, Johann Christian. *Badische Geschichte.* Carlsruhe, 1769.

Sachse [no given name]. "Glossarium des XIV. oder XV. Jahrhunderts." *Archiv für das Studium der neuern Sprachen und Literaturen*, XLVII (1871), 403-448.

Saint Bonaventure. [cf. Bonaventure, St.].

Saladin, Johann Georg. *Die Strassburger Chronik* [cf. "Die Strassburger Chronik des J. G. Saladin"].

Sancti Bernardi Abbatis primi Clarae-Vallensis genuina sancti doctoris opera. Ed. Johann Mabellon. 2 vols. Paris, 1719.

Santifaller, Leo. *Urkunden und Forschungen zur Geschichte des Trientner Domkapitels im Mittelalter.* I. Band: 1147-1500. = Veröffentlichungen des Instituts für Österreichische Geschichtsforschung, hrsg. von Leo Santifaller, Band VI (Wien, 1948).

Santifaller, Leo. "Die preces primariae Maximilians I." *Festschrift zur Feier des 200-jährigen Bestandes des Haus-, Hof- und Staatsarchivs.* I (Wien, 1949), 578-661.

Sattler, Christian Friderich. *Geschichte des Herzogtums Würtemberg.* Tübingen, 1775.

Schadäus, Oseas (Oscar Schad). *Summum Argentoratensium Templum.* Strassburg, 1617.

Schell, Johann Wilhelm. *Boicae gentis annales.* Pars II. München, 1663.

Scherlen, August. "Beziehungen der Familie

		Geiler zu Kaysersberg und Umgebung," ElsMGV, IV (1913), 193-200, 251-264.
		Schmidlin, Joseph. *Geschichte der deutschen Nationalkirche in Rom S. Maria dell' Anima*. Freiburg i. B. und Wien, 1906.
Schmidt, "Brant"		Schmidt, Charles Guillaume Adolphe (Karl). "Einige deutsche Gedichte von Sebastian Brant," *Alsatia*, X (1873-74), 43.
Schmidt, *Chapitre*		Schmidt, Charles Guillaume Adolphe (Karl). *Histoire de la chapitre de Saint Thomas de Strasbourg pendant le moyen âge*. Strasbourg, 1860.
Schmidt, *H. L.*	S	Schmidt, Charles Guillaume Adolphe (Karl). *Histoire Littéraire de l'Alsace à la fin du xve et au commencement du xvie siècle*. 2 vols. [vol. I has livres 1-3; vol. II has livres 4-5 and *Index Bibliographique*]. Paris 1879. (I, *passim*; II, 2-34).
Schmidt, *Wörterbuch*		Schmidt, Charles Guillaume Adolphe (Karl). *Historisches Wörterbuch der elsässischen Mundart*. Strassburg, 1901.
	S	Schmidt, Charles Guillaume Adolphe (Karl). "Livres et bibliothèques à Strasbourg au moyen-âge," RA, V (1876), 433-454; VI (1877) 59-85. (67f.)
Schmidt, "Recueil... Wolf"		Schmidt, Charles Guillaume Adolphe (Karl). "Note sur un recueil d'inscriptions fait par Thomas Wolf de Strasbourg, au commencement du seizième siècle," BSCMH, 2e série, IX, ii (1876), 156-160.
Schmidt, *Notice... Couvent*		Schmidt, Charles Guillaume Adolphe (Karl). *Notice sur le couvent et l'église des dominicains de Strasbourg. Suivre d'une notice sur l'ancien Temple-Neuf et l'ancien Gymnase de Strasbourg par E. Salomon*. Strasbourg, 1876.
Schmidt, "Notice... Brant"	S	Schmidt, Charles Guillaume Adolphe (Karl). "Notice sur Sébastien Brant," RA, III (1874), 3-56. (4f., 7, 8, 42)
Schmidt, "Notices... P.S."	S	Schmidt, Charles Guillaume Adolphe (Karl). "Notices sur les humanistes strasbourgeois, II Pierre Schott," RA, VIII (1857), 241-256; 308-321; 337-352.
Schmidt, "Notices... Wolf"	S	Schmidt, Charles Guillaume Adolphe (Karl). "Notices sur les humanistes strasbourgeois. Thomas Wolf," RA, VI (1855), 447-469, 481-485. (449, 455)
Schmidt, *Repert. biblio.*		Schmidt, Charles Guillaume Adolphe (Karl). *Repertoire bibliographique jusque vers 1530*. Strasbourg, 1893-96.
Schmidt, "Beginen"		Schmidt, Charles Guillaume Adolphe (Karl). "Die Strassburger Beginenhäuser im Mittelalter," *Alsatia*, VIII (1862-67), 149-210.
Schmidt, *Namen*		Schmidt, Charles Guillaume Adolphe (Karl). *Strassburger Gassen- und Häusernamen im Mittelalter*. Strassburg, ²1888.
Schmidt, *Bibliotheken*		Schmidt, Charles Guillaume Adolphe (Karl). *Zur Geschichte der ältesten Bibliotheken und der ersten Buchdrucker zu Strassburg*. Strassburg,

| | | 1882. |
| | | Schmoller, Gustav. *Strassburg zur Zeit der Zunftkämpfe und die Reform seiner Verfassung und Verwaltung im 15. Jahrhundert.* Strassburg, 1875. |

Schneegans, Église   Schneegans, Louis (Ludwig). *L'Église de St. Thomas à Strasbourg et ses monuments.* Strasbourg, 1842.

Schneegans, "Pfingstfest"   S   Schneegans, Louis (Ludwig). "Das Pfingstfest und der Roraffe im Münster zu Strassburg," *Alsatia*, III (1852), 189-242. (227-228, n. 1)

Schneegans, *Sagen*   Schneegans, Louis (Ludwig). *Strassburger Münster-Sagen.* St. Gallen, 1852.

Schneider, Eugen. "Johann Reuchlins Berichte über die Krönung Maximilians I. im Jahre 1486," ZGORh, Neue Folge, XIII (1898), 547-559.

   S   Schöpflin, Johann Daniel. *Alsatia illustrata Germanica Gallica.* Colmar, 1761. (341, 344)

Schöpflin, *Alsace*   Schöpflin, Johann Daniel. *L'Alsace illustrée ou son histoire sous les empereurs d'Allemagne et depuis son réunion à la France.* 5 vols. Mulhouse, 1851.

Schöpflin, Johann Daniel. *Histoire des dix villes jadis libres et impériales de la prefecture de Hagenau.* Colmar, 1825.

Schöpflin, Vind. typ.   S   Schöpflin, Johann Daniel. *Vindiciae typographicae...* Strassburg, 1760. (101)

Schorbach, Karl and Spirates, Max. *Bibliographische Studien zur Buchdruckergeschichte Deutschlands.* Strassburg, 1808.

   S   Schröder, Johann Fr. *Das Wiederaufblühen der klassischen Studien in Deutschland im 15. und zu Anfang des 16. Jahrhunderts.* Halle, 1864. (169-171)

Scomata Joannis Keisebergii concionatoris ecclesiae Argentinensis. Argentinae, 1508 [in same volume with Alfonsus Rex Aragonum..., q.v.].

Seckel, Emil *Beiträge zur Geschichte beider Rechte im Mittelalter.* Band I: *Zur Geschichte der populären Literatur des Römisch-Canonischen Rechts.* Tübingen, 1898.

Servius Honoratus, Maurus. *Commentarii in Virgilium.* [cf. Lion].

Servius Honoratus, Maurus. *Servii grammatici qui feruntur in Vergilii carmina commentarii.* Ed. Georgius Thilo and Hermannus Hagen. Hildesheim, 1961 [Photographic reproduction of edition at Leipzig, 1881].

Seyboth, Adolph. *Das alte Strassburg vom 13. Jahrhundert bis zum Jahre 1870. Geschichtliche Topographie nach den Urkunden und Chroniken.* Strassburg, 1890.

Seyboth   S   Seyboth, Adolph. *Strasbourg historique et pictoresque.* Strasbourg, 1894. (77-79)

Simler, Josias. *Regiment gemeiner loblicher Eyd-*

	genossenschafft... Zürich, 1576.
	Simon, Johannes. *Stand und Herkunft der Bischöfe der Mainzer Kirchenprovinz im Mittelalter.* Weimar, 1908.
	S Sitzmann, Fr. Edouard. *Dictionnaire de biographie des hommes célèbres de l'Alsace depuis le temps les plus reculés jusqu'à nos jours.* 2 vols. Rixheim (Alsace), 1909-1910. (II, 721f.)
	Sleumer, Albert. *Kirchenlateinisches Wörterbuch.* Limburg a.d. Lahn, ²1926; Bonn, ³1962.
	Souter, Alexander, *A Glossary of Later Latin to 600 A.D.* Oxford, 1949.
	Spach, Louis (Ludwig). *Histoire de la Basse Alsace et de la ville de Strasbourg.* Strasbourg, 1858.
Spach, *Zunftwesen*	Spach, Louis (Ludwig). *Das Zunftwesen in Strassburg.* Strassburg, 1856.
	Spalding, Georg L. *M. Fabii Quintiliani de institutione oratoria libri duodecim.* Leipzig, 1798.
	Spano, Nicola. *L'università di Roma.* Roma, 1935.
	S Specklin, Daniel. "Collectanea (Fortsetzung)," BSCMH, II. Série XIV (1889), 1-178 (ca. 1330-1402), 201-404 (1403-1589) (287) [Text also in Dacheux, *Fragments,* q.v.].
	Stadler, Johann Evangelist. *Vollständiges Heiligen-Lexikon oder Lebensgeschichten.* Augsburg, 1858-82.
	S Stammler, Wolfgang. *Von der Mystik zum Barock 1400-1600.* Stuttgart, 1927. (56, 58). 1950. (65)
	Steichele, Anton. *Beiträge zur Geschichte des Bisthums Augsburg.* 2 vols. Augsburg, 1850.
Steichele	S Steichele, Anton. "Friedrich Graf von Zollern, Bischof zu Augsburg und Johann Geiler von Kaysersberg. Mit Briefen," *Archiv für die Geschichte des Bistums Augsburg,* I (1856), 143-172. (149, 162, 167)
	S Stein, Edmund Ludwig. *Geschichte des Kollegiatstifts Jung St. Peter zu Strassburg von seiner Gründung bis zum Ausbruch der Reformation.* Freiburg i. B., 1920. (131 ff.)
Stenzel	S Stenzel, Karl. "Geiler von Kaysersberg und Friedrich von Zollern. Ein Beitrag zur Geschichte des Strassburger Domkapitels am Ausgang des 15. Jahrhunderts," ZGORh, Neue Folge, XL, Heft 1 (1926). (69-80 *passim*)
Stenzel, "Gerichte"	Stenzel, Karl. "Die geistlichen Gerichte zu Strassburg im 15. Jahrhundert," ZGORh, Neue Folge, XXX (1915).
Stenzel, "Politik"	Stenzel, Karl. "Die Politik der Stadt Strassburg am Ausgange des Mittelalters in ihren Hauptzügen dargestellt," *Beiträge zur Landes- und Volkskunde von Elsass-Lothringen und den angrenzenden Gebieten,* XLIX (1915).
Stenzel, *Chronik*	Stenzel, Karl. *Die Strassburger Chronik des elsässischen Humanisten Hieronymus Gebwiler.* Schriften des Wissenschaftlichen Instituts der Elsass-

Lothringer... (Berlin und Leipzig, 1926).
Stevenson, Burton. *The Home Book of Proverbs, Maxims and Familiar Phrases.* New York, 1948.
Stöber, August. *Alsatia, Jahrbuch für elsässische Geschichte, Sage, Alterthumskunde, Sitte, Sprache und Kunst.* Hrsg. von August Stöber. 12 vols. Mülhausen, 1852-1885. [Cf. next entry for title of vol. XII].
S Stöber, August. *Neue Alsatia, Beiträge zur Landeskunde, Geschichte, Sitten- und Rechtskunde.* Mülhausen, 1885. [Schlussband der *Alsatia*=*Alsatia,* XII]. (281, n. 2, n. 3)
Stöber, August. "Note sur lieu de naissance de Jean Geiler von Kaysersberg," RA, XVII (1866), 59-61.

Stöber, *Sagen* Stöber, August. *Die Sagen des Elsasses.* Strassburg, 1892.

Stöber, "Sprichwörter" Stöber, August. "496 Sprichwörter aus den Schriften Geilers von Kaysersberg, "*Alsatia,* VIII (1867), 131-163.

Stöber, August. *Zur Geschichte des Volksglaubens im Anfange des XVI. Jahrhunderts. Aus der Emeis von Dr. Johann Geiler von Kaisersberg.* Basel, ²1875.
Stoett, F. A. *Nederlandsche Spreekworden, Spreekwijzen, Uitdrukkingen en Gezegden.* 2 vols. Zutphen, ⁵1943.
Stoffel, Georges. *Topographisches Wörterbuch des Oberelsasses.* Mülhausen, 1876.
Strassburg Chronik [cf. *Chroniken*].

Saladin "Die Strassburger Chronik des J. G. Saladin." Ed. A. Meister and A. Rappel. BSCMH, IIe Série, XXIII (1911).

Strassburgische Archiv-Chronik [cf. *Code hist.*, vol. II].

Straub, "St. Pierre" S Straub, A. "L'église de Saint Pierre-le-Jeune à Strasbourg," BSCMH, IIe Série, IX (1876), 88-94. (88).

Straub, A. *Geschichtskalender des Hochstifts und des Münsters von Strassburg.* Rixheim (Alsace), 1891.

Straub S Straub, A. "Notes généalogiques sur une ancienne famille patricienne de Strasbourg," BSCMH, IIe série, IX (1876), 80-88. (80, 81, 83, 85, 86)

S Strobel, Adam Walther. *Beiträge zur deutschen Literatur und Literaturgeschichte.* Strassburg, 1827, (11, n. 1)

Strobel S Strobel, Adam Walther. *Vaterländische Geschichte des Elsasses von der frühesten Zeit bis zur Revolution 1789.* Hrsg. v. H. Engelhardt. Vol. III. Strassburg, ²1851. (III, 454) [The few references to vol. III (Strassburg, 1843) are cited as: Strobel (1843)].

S Strüver, Wilhelm. *Die Schule zu Schlettstadt von 1450-1560.* Leipzig, 1880. (7, 19, 22f.)

Suringar, W. H. D. *Erasmus over Nederlandsche Spreekwoorden... Adagia...* Utrecht, 1873.
S Taylor, Archer. *Problems in German Literary History of the Fifteenth and Sixteenth Centuries.* London, 1939. (48)
Taylor, Archer. *The Proverb.* Cambridge, 1931.
Taylor, Archer. *English Riddles from Oral Tradition.* Berkeley and Los Angeles, 1951.
Thesaurus Linguae Latinae. Leipzig, 1906-1912.
S Thomas de Argentina. *Scripta super quattuor libros sententiarum.* Ed. Peter Schott. Argentorate: Martin Flach (Sr.), 1490 [Not in Hain].

Kempis
S Thomas à Kempis. *Imitatio Christi.* Antwerp, 1664. (14)
S? Thomas à Kempis. *Tractatio de imitatione Christi. Cum tractatulo de meditatione cordis.* Ed. Peter Schott[?] Argentina: Martin Flach (Sr.), 1487.
Thorndike, Lynn. *A History of Magic and Experimental Science.* Vol. I. New York, 1923.
Thurston, Herbert. *The Holy Year of Jubilee.* London, 1900.
Tilley, Morris Palmer. *A Dictionary of the Proverbs in England in the sixteenth and seventeenth Centuries.* Ann Arbor, 1950.
Toepke, Gustav. *Die Matrikel der Universität Heidelberg.* Vol. I: 1380-1563. Heidelberg, 1884.
Traube, Ludwig. *Nomina sacra. Versuch einer Geschichte der christlichen Kürzung.* Quellen und Untersuchungen zur lateinischen Philologie des Mittelalters, II (München, 1907).
S Trausch, Jacob. "Strassburg Chronick" [Cf. Dacheux, *Fragments*, III], (29)

Trithemius, *Ann. Hirs.*
Trithemius, Johann (Johann von Heidenberg). *Annales Hirsaugensium, opus... complectens historiam Franciae et Germaniae, gesta imperatorum, regum, principum, episcoporum, abbatum et illustrium virorum.* St. Gall, 1690.
S Trithemius, Johann (Johann von Heidenberg). *Cathalogus illustrium virorum germaniae suis ingenijs et lucubrationibus omnifariam exornantium.* Mainz: Peter v. Friedberg, 1495. (folio 55b)

Trithemius, "Chronicon Spon."
Trithemius, Johann (Johann von Heidenberg). "Chronicon huius monasterii Sponheimensis, ab exordio fundationis suae complectens successiones omnium abbatum breviter." *Opera*, II. Frankfurt, 1601, 236-435.

Trithemius, *De script. eccl.*
S Trithemius, Johann (Johann von Heidenberg). *De scriptoribus ecclesiasticis collectanea...* Paris, 1512 [new edition of *Liber*]. (folio cxc f. 1)
S Trithemius, Johann (Johann von Heidenberg). *Liber de scriptoribus ecclesiasticis.* Basel: Amerbach, 1494. (folio 126b)
Trithemius, Johann (Johann von Heidenberg). *Opera.* 2 vols. Frankfurt, 1601.

Truttmann-Burg   Truttmann, Joseph and Burg, A. M. "L'Ordre des
                  Guillemites en Alsace," AEA, II (1947-1948),
                  173-204.
                  Ullanthorpe, W. B. *The Immaculate Conception of
                  the Mother of God.* Westminster, 1904.
              S   *Universal=Lexikon. Grosses vollständiges Universal
                  =Lexikon aller Wissenschaften und Künste.*
                  [Often called *Zedler's Lexikon*]. 64 vols. Hrsg.
                  von Johann Peter von Ludewig *et al.*, Leipzig,
                  Halle, 1732-1750. (XXXV, 1038)
Variot   Variot, Jean. *Chroniques et légendes des villes
                  alsaciennes, Strasbourg. Collection de la vie en
                  Alsace.* Strasbourg, 1927. [Cf. next entry].
                  Variot, Jean. *L'Alsace éternelle.* Paris, 1929. [Same
                  text, same index, same notes as entry above,
                  but different pagination].
                  Varrentropp, C. "Nicolaus Gerbel, ein Beitrag zur
                  Geschichte des wissenschaftlichen Lebens in
                  Strassburg im sechzehnten Jahrhundert,"
                  *Strassburger Festschrift zur XLVI. Versamm-
                  lung deutscher Philologen und Schulmänner.*
                  Strassburg, 1901.
              S   Velden, Hendrik E. J. van de. *Rodolfus Agricola.*
                  Leiden, 1911. (240)
                  *Verfassungs-, Verwaltungs- und Wirtschaftsgeschichte
                  der Stadt Strassburg bis 1681.* Strassburg, 1899.
              S   Vix-Benlay, A. M. "L'Enigme du Roraffe," *Revue
                  de L'Alsace Française,* XX (1935), 7-59. (40)
                  Voigt, G. *Die Wiederbelebung des klassischen
                  Altertums, oder das 1. Jahrhundert des Humanis-
                  mus.* 2 vols. Berlin, ³1893.
                  Volk, Paulus, O. S. B. "Die Strassburger Benedik-
                  tiner-Abteien im Bursfelder Kongregations-
                  verband 1481-1624," AEK, X (1935), 153-293.
                  Vollert, Konrad. *Zur Geschichte der lateinischen
                  Facetiensammlungen des 15. und 16. Jahr-
                  hunderts.* Berlin, 1911.
                  Voulliéme, E. *Die deutschen Drucker des 15.
                  Jahrhunderts.* Berlin, 1916. Berlin, ²1922.
              S   Vulpinus, Thomas. "Sechzehn Briefe Peter Schotts
                  an Geiler von Kaysersberg. Deutsch,"
                  JbGElsLotr, X (1894), 37-61.
                  Wackernagel, Hans Georg. *Die Matrikel der
                  Universität Basel.* 3 vols. Vol. I: 1460-1529.
                  Basel, 1951.
                  Waddell, Helen. *The Wandering Scholars.* London,
                  1944.
                  Walde-Hofmann. *Lateinisches etymologisches Wör-
                  terbuch.* Heidelberg, ³1938.
                  Wander, Karl F. W. *Deutsches Sprichwörter-
                  Lexikon.* 5 vols. Leipzig, 1867-1880.
                  Wattenbach, W. "Sigismund Gossembrot als
                  Vorkämpfer der Humanisten und seine Gegner,"
                  ZGORh, XXV (1873), 36-69.
                  Weech, Friedrich von. "Besuche Badischer Fürsten
                  und Fürstinnen in Rom," ZGORh, Neue Forge,

	IX (1894), 221-239.
	S Weislinger, Johann Nicolaus. *Armamentarium catholicum perantiquae rarissimae ac pretiosissimae bibliothecae...* Argentina, 1749. (677-682, 780)
	Weissenborn, Hermann. *Akten der Erfurter Universität.* Geschichtsquellen der Provinz Sachsen, Nr. 8, T. 1-3, (Halle, 1881-1899).
	Welzenbach, Thomas. *Geschichte der Buchdruckerkunst im ehemaligen Herzogthum Franken und in benachbarten fränkischen Städten.* Würzburg, 1858.
Wencker, *Arch.*	S Wencker, Jacques. *Collecta archivi et cancellariae jura...* Argentorate, 1715. (428, 632)
Wencker, *Juris*	Wencker, Jacques. *Collectanea juris publici quibus res germanicae per aliquot secula illustrantur...* Argentorate, 1702.
	Wencker, Jacques. *Apparatus et instructus archivorum ex usu nostri temporis vulgo...* Strassburg, 1713.
	Wendling, E. "Der Kampf des Roraffen under der Orgeln im Münster zu Strassburg...," *Alsatia,* X (1873/74), 111-122.
	Werk, Franz Xaver. *Stiftungsurkunden akademischer stipendien und andrer milden Gaben an der Hochschule zu Freiburg im Breisgau von 1497-1842...* Freiburg i. B., 1842 [Cf. recent edition by Beckmann of *Johannes Kerer, Statuta...*].
Wetzer-Welte	Wetzer and Welte. *Kirchen-Lexicon.* 12 vols. Freiburg, i. B., 1886-1901.
	Wickersheimer, Ernest. *Dictionnaire biographique des médecins en France au moyen âge.* 2 vols. in one. Paris, 1936.
	Wils, J. *Matricule de l'Université de Louvain.* Vol. II. Bruxelles, 1926.
Wimpheling, *Cat. ep.*	Wimpheling, Jacob. *Iacobi Wimphelingis Catalogus episcopum Argentinensium.* Ed. J. M. Moscherosch. Strassburg, 1651.
	Wimpheling, Jacob. *Argentinensium episcoporum catalogus: cum eorundem vita atque certis historijs rebusque gestis: et illustratione totius fere episcopatus Argentinensis.* Argentina, 1508.
	S Wimpheling, Jacob. *De integritate Libellus cum epistolis prestantissimorum virorum hunc libellum approbantium et confirmantium.* Argentina, 1506. (folios Aiii, Civ, Caxiii, Caxix, Gii)
	S Wimpheling, Jacob. *Germania. Übersetzt und erläutert von Ernst Martin mit ungedruckten Briefen von Geiler und Wimpheling.* Strassburg, 1885. (Capitula 52, 56, 57)
	S Wimpheling, Jacob. *De triplici candore Mariae.* Sine loco et dato; no name of printer. [1493]. (folio 31)
"Wimpheling Codex"	S Wimpheling, Jacob. "Wimpheling Codex." University of Uppsala Codex no. 687, in the Carolina Rediviva. (folios 169a-181a *passim*, 255b, 258a)

Winckelmann, "Roraffen"	Winckelmann, Otto. "Die Roraffen im Strassburger Münster," *Strassburger Post* (20. Mai 1906).
Winckelmann, "Kulturgesch."	S Winckelmann, Otto. "Zur Kulturgeschichte des Strassburger Münsters im 15. Jahrhundert," ZGORh, Neue Folge, XXII (1907), 247-290. (262, 263, 271)
	Winckelmann, Otto. "Nachträge zur Kulturgeschichte des Strassburger Münsters im 15. Jahrhundert," ZGORh, Neue Folge, XXIV, Heft 2 (1909).
	S Wiskowatoff, Paul von. *Jacob Wimpheling, sein Leben und seine Schriften. Ein Beitrag zur Geschichte der deutschen Humanisten.* Berlin, 1867. (16, 26, 58, 69 [n. 2], 73)
	Witte, Heinrich. "Zur Geschichte der Burgunderkriege. Das Kriegsjahr 1475," ZGORh, Neue Folge, VII (1892), 414-477.
Wittmer, "Église rouge"	Wittmer, Charles. "L'Obituaire de l'Église Rouge de Strasbourg" AEA, nouv. Série I (1946), 87-131.
Wittmer, *Obituaire*	Wittmer, Charles. *L'Obituaire des Dominicains de Colmar.* Diss., University of Friburg – Suisse. Mulhouse, 1934.
Wittmer, *Reform.*	Wittmer, Charles. *Reformversuche im Dominikanerinnenkloster zu Strassburg 1492-93.* Strassburg, 1943.
Wittmer, "Flüe"	S Wittmer, Charles. "Zur Mystik des seligen Nikolaus von Flüe, seine Beziehungen zum Elsass," AEK, XI (1936), 157-174. (171)
Wittmer-Meyer	Wittmer, Charles and Meyer, J. Charles. *Livre de la bourgeoisie de Strasbourg 1440-1530.* 3 vols. Strassburg, 1948-1961.
	Wolf, Gustav. *Quellenkunde der deutschen Reformationsgeschichte.* 3 vols. Gotha, 1915-23.
	S Wolkan, Rudolf. *Böhmens Antheil an der deutschen Litteratur des sechzehnten Jahrhunderts.* Prag, 1890-94. (111f., 115)
	Wuerdtwein, Stephan Alexis. *Diocesis moguntina in archdiaconatus distincta... III.* Mannheim, 1777.
Wuerdtwein	Wuerdtwein, Stephan Alexis. *Nova subsidia diplomatica ad selecta juris Ecclesiastica Germaniae...* Vol. VIII. Heidelberg, 1786. [14 vols. Heidelberg, 1781-1792].
	Young, G. F. *The Medici.* New York, 1930.
	S Zacher, Franz. *Geiler von Kaysersberg als Pädagog.* I. Burghausen, 1913, (18f., 22, 27, 29)
	Zedler, Johann Heinrich (publisher). *Universal= Lexikon* [Cf. under *Universal=Lexikon*].
	Zeiller, Martin. *Chronicon Parvum Sueviae oder kleines Schwäbisches Zeitbuch...* Ulm, 1653.
	S Zoepfl, Friedrich. *Das Bistum Augsburg und seine Bischöfe im Mittelalter.* München, 1955. (487)

GENERAL INDEX

Aachen (city), 425, 502f., 538, 727, 750, 770, 782; see *Aquisgranum*
Aar (river), 368
Abbas (glossator), 234, 237, 243, 244, 246, 253, 254, 255, 256
Abbas Siculus (Nicolas de Tudeschi, glossator), 194, 588
abbot of Hirsau (Blasius), 151
abbreviations, xvf., X, 504, 813
Abraham, 321, 686
Absolution, delegated powers of, 252f., 633f.
Abuses, xxvii, 145, 188, 205ff., 287, 288f., 406, 581f., 599-608, 660f.
Achates, 298, 668
Achilles, 297, 646, 647, 649, 667, 678
Acta bononiensis, xxvi, 367, 397, 400, 491, 716, 726, 728, 734, 739, 743
ad Lunam (inn), 149
Adalbert (brother of St. Odile), 449
adaquacio, 50, 464
address, use of formal and informal, 423 (N. 184)
Adelberg, abbey of, 212, 716
Adelmann, Bernhard, 118, 399, 699, 719, 728f., 765, 802
Adelmann, Conrad, 699, 719, 728f.
Adelphus, Johann, 375, 484, 675
Adelsheim (town in Baden), 699
Adelsheim family, 699
Adelsheim, Georgius von, 699
Adelsheim, Gottfried, Jr., von, 202f., 203f., 411, 567, 568, 597ff., 699, 700
Adelsheim, Gottfried, Sr., von, 202f., 597, 612, 699f.
  funeral of, 212 (viri huius)?
  wife of, 203, 699
Adelsheim, Lucas von, 450, 756, 808
Adelsheim, Stephanus von, 699
Adelsheim, Zeisolf, Jr., von, 203, 366, 598, 699, 700

Adelsheim, Zeisolf, Sr., von, 118 (*coniuges*), 120 (*Genero*), 366, 371, 525, 531, 597, 699, 700, 756, 808, 809, 810
  wife of, 96, 131, 203
Adolf von Nassau, archbishop of Mainz, 706, 733, 734
Adrimentum, titular bishop of, 736
advice on appeal in case of a monastery vs. papal commissioner, 239-242, 627f.
advice on burials, 253f., 634
advice on eating fat and lard, 254, 635
Aeacides (Achilles), 295, 297
Aegean Sea, 159
Aegeus, 648
Aegidam (Theseus), 270
Aegoceros (Capricorn, constellation), 295
Aeneas, 191, 280, 298, 300, 648, 668
  frater Aenee pharetratus (Cupid), 300
Aeoas (Eous), 272
  Aeoos, 308, 648
Aesculapius, 656, 670
Aesop, 600
Aetna, 647
Africa, 248, 312
Agamennone natus (Orestes), 309, 677
Agenor, 648
  Agenoream puellam (Europa), 271, 648
Agricola, John, 497
Agricola, Rudolph, xii, xiii, xx, xxviii, 70, 84, 281, 370, 376, 392, 406, 431, 482ff., 496ff., 654f., 700f., 715, 720, 745, 749, 752, 760, 765, 796ff.
  translations from Greek to Latin by, 483
agriculture, *see* economic conditions
Albert of Bavaria, son of Ludwig von Mainz, 107, 514f.

845

Albertus Magnus (Alemannus, Coloniensis, Suevus, Teutonicus), 9, 417, 701
Albrecht, duke of Bavaria, bishop of Strassburg, xxvi, xxviii, 22 (*principis*), 92, 165, 190, 214, 218, 219, 220, 400, 406, 408, 433f., 516, 522, 544, 565, 601f., 616, 620f., 626, 635, 701f., 703, 705, 728, 736, 737, 739, 749, 751, 758, 770, 780, 782, 807 (*unser Herre von Strassburg*)
Albrecht II, duke of Bavaria, 704
Albrecht III (*der Weise*), duke of Bavaria, 138, 287, 291, 502, 538, 662, 704, 705, 747
Albrecht, *Markgraf* of Baden, 138, 140, 538, 540, 703, 705
Albrecht, *Markgraf* and Elector of Brandenburg, 502, 770
Albrecht Ernst of Saxony, archbishop of Mainz, 420
Alcaeus, 267
Alcibiades, 22
Alcides (Hercules), 271, 298, 309
Alcoran, 802
Alemanni, 368, 654
Alemannia nation (student association at Paris), 396, 683, 742, 751, 757f.
procurator of, 736, 740, 742, 751, 757
provisor of 396, 683f., 758
receptor of, 736
Alexander the Great, 150, 270, 551, 647, 656
Alexander V (pope), 648
Alexander VI (pope), 712, 729, 747
Alexander de Villa Dei, *Doctrinale*, 393, 690
Alexandria, 559, 640
Alkmaar (town in Holland), 746
Alsace, plate 7, xxv, 218, 367, 368, 376, 377f., 385, 386, 387, 393, 403, 435, 445, 484, 496, 514, 538, 653, 680, 696, 699, 711, 713, 716, 722, 728, 741, 750, 757, 758, 761, 762, 771, 784
Alsatian, synonymous with Helvetian, 613, 687
Alsatian wine, 368
Alsatians, xii, xxv, 9, 434
Altammeister, definition of, 384
Altdorf (town near Nürnberg), 751
Altitonans (Jupiter), 299
Alujs (Loys), Jehan, 562

am gebrannten End (Strassburg street), 606
Amadeus de Talaru, *see* Talaru
Amalia, abbess of St. Stephan, 449
Amerbach, Basilius, 393, 702
Amerbach, Bonifatius, 702, 738, 769
Amerbach, Bruno, 393, 702
Amerbach, Johann (printer), xiv, 373, 393, 541, 561, 702, 725, 731, 752
Ammeister, definition of, 384
Ammersweiler (Ammerschwier, town in Alsace), 721, 723, 758
Amorbach, Johann, *see* Amerbach, J.
Amphiona, 273, 649
Amphitryoniadem (Hercules), 270, 649
anceptemve canem (Cerberus), 282
Ancona (town in Italy), 732
Andelacensis (Andlau, adj.), 162
Andeloensis (Andlau, adj.), 160
Andelahe (Andlau), 160, 161
Andelum (Andlau), 95
Andlau (Alsatian town), 51, 68, 75, 95, 160, 161, 162, 507, 561f., 737, 739, 740, 741
Andorp, *see* Oudorp
Andreas, 85, 107, 498
Andreas, *Dominus* (Hartmann?), 215, 618
Andreas, Iohannes (glossator), 217, 218, 221, 228, 229, 232, 245
Andreas Phisicus, *see* Oudorp
angel, good or bad, perceiving human thought, 182ff., 577ff.
Angelica, 236, 242, 626
Angleria, 786, 787
Anglicos (English), 188
Anima (church), *see* Santa Maria de Anima
animissarius, duties of, 404
Annei Vatis (Lucan), 271, 648
anniversarium, -ia, 402, 416, 739, 744
Anthonius (glossator), 233, 245, 246; *see* Buttrio, A. de
Anthonius, *Dominus*, licentiate, 139, 540
Antigonus Doson, 92, 505
Antioch, 652
Antwerp (city), 85, 498, 514, 700, 742
Aonia, 297
Aonias Deas (Muses), 281, 654f.

Aonij liquoris, 306, 673
Aonio, 271, 279, 280
Aonius Vates (Hesiod), 332, 688
Aonides (Muses), 269, 647
Apelles, 150, 281, 551, 655f.
aphorisms from Geiler's sermons, see *Lucubraciunculae*
Apicius, 208, 609f.
Apicius, Marcus Gavius, 610
Apicius Coelius, 610
Apollineus, 271, 305, 319, 648
Apollo, 95, 271, 288, 304, 646, 647, 656, 660
Apollonius Rhodius, 588
Apostolus (St. Paul), 121, 130, 247, 248
Apuleius, 669, 721
Apulia, 439, 646
aqua endiuie, 132, 532
aqua hysopi, 132, 532
Aquarius (constellation), 648
Aquila, bishop of, 176, 712
Aquileja, patriarch of, 92, 704
Aquinas, St. Thomas, 181-185, 247, 250, 577ff., 631, 633, 640, 647, 701
Aquisgranum (Aachen), 138
Ar (river), 368
Ara coeli, 76; see Santa Maria de Araceli
Arabia, 159, 559
Arabas, 711
Arabic, 701
Aragon, Beatrice of, see Beatrice
Aragon, Ferdinand of, see Ferdinand
Aragonia, Joannes de, 176, 574f., 702
archbishop of Lyons, 261; see Talaru
archbishop of Mainz, 213; see Isenburg
Archidiaconus (glossator), 229, 245, 246
Archivi (*Argivi*), 280, 654
Arcimboldi, Johannes, 711
Arctos, geminas (Ursa Major and Ursa Minor), 272, 648
Ardennes, 724
Areopagita, 639
areopagus, 639
Arezzo (Italian town), 763
Argenta and Argentilla (Strassburg), 368
Argentos, 368
Argentum, 287, 659

Argentina (Strassburg), 10, 212, 289, 295, 322, 323, 368, 613, 661, 667, 687
Argentinensis (adj.), 9, 10, 11, *passim*
Argentina, Thomas de, see Thomas von Strassburg, *also* Lampertheim
Argentoracum and Argentoratum (Strassburg), 289, 368, 661
Argo, 648
Argonauticon, 194, 588
Arianism, 640
Aricia (grove in Latium), 670
Aricina dea (Diana), 268, 647
Aries (constellation), 271, 533, 648
Aristides, 147, 548
Aristotle, 181, 191 (*philosophorum Principis*), 271, 319, 577, 585, 588, 594, 596, 647, 682
Armagnacs, 712
Arretinus, Johann Tortellius, 202; see Tortellius
Artemis, 442, 670
Asclepiades (Asclepiadic verse), 296
Asia, 192, 312
Asia Minor, 296, 302
Asirei Vatis (*Annei...*, Lucan?), 303, 648
aspirating, 485
Assirius, 271, 332
Assissi, 707
Astree, Virginis (Virgo, constellation), 272, 648
astrologers, 442, 591
astrology, 29, 133, 197, 198, 299, 425, 442f., 531, 533, 592, 677
Athanasius, 261, 640
Athene, 672
Athenian, 315, 683
Athens, 639
Athlanciadem (Mercury), 268
Atrides... heros (Agamemnon), 272, 273, 297
Atropos (a Fate), 44
Attila, 481
Aufidus (river in Apulia), 267
Augsburg, xix, xxix, 153, 407, 522, 534f., 541, 542, 545, 546, 548, 554, 580, 586, 588, 618, 695, 704, 722, 725, 745, 746, 762;
bishop of, xxx, 90, 91, 110, 114, 115, 134, 141, 143, 147, 745, 770
see Werdenberg, Johann von, and Zollern, Friedrich von
cathedral, 142, 147, 522, 534,

725, 771
  canon of, 699, 701, 703, 704, 705, 719,739, 770
  chapter of, 90, 502, 782
  preaching chair of, 534f., 543, 544, 771
  diocese, 471, 502, 545, 701
Augusta (Augsburg), 153
Augustensis (Augsburg, adj.), 20, *passim*
Augustenses (Augsburgers), 115, 134, 142, 163
Augustinians, Order of, 93, 714
  general of, 763
  printers at Nürnberg, 617
  provincial of, 763
  Rhine-Swabian province of, 216, 619, 719
  at Strassburg, 719
Augustus (Roman emperor), 295, 368, 610, 666
Aurelianensem Academiam, 61; see university of Orléans
Auribelli, Marcialis (Dominican general), 390, 745
Ausoni-, 268, 271, 281, 289, 310
Auss-Bürger, 717, 734
Austria, 727, 732, 743; duke of, *see* Sigismund, archduke of
Austrum, 299
autor Summe pisane (Pisana, glossator), 233, 246
Avernus, 307
Avignon, 640
Avisio (river), 719
Ayrer, Max (Nürnberg printer), 617

Bacchus, 283, 302, 339, 346, 602, 646, 657, 659, 677; see *Liber*, *Lyaeus*
bacularius, duties of, 404
Baden, house of, 702ff.
      Markgrafen of, *see* Albrecht, Bernard II, Bernard (*praepositus*), Christoph I, Ernst, Friedrich, Hermann V, Jacob I, Jacob (archbishop of Trier), Karl I, Karl, Philipp
Baden (principality), 138, 410, 429, 478, 521, 537, 565, 582, 590, 699, 702f., 722, 742, 743
Baden-Baden, 31, 41, 69, 79, 104, 137, 138, 151, 152, 153, 162, 165, 193, 195, 424, 425, 426, 429f., 441, 446, 455, 460, 464, 472, 475, 476f., 512, 521, 539f., 550f., 552, 562, 564, 588, 590, 609, 721, 722, 741
  collegiate church of, 140, 165, 169, 429f., 436, 449, 478, 479f., 491, 550, 589f., 709, 731, 743
Badensis, -es (Baden, adj.), 20, 29, *passim*
Baden-Württemberg, 448
Bamberg, 711
  bishop of, 502
  cathedral of, 655
  canon of, 701, 716
Barbarossa (Emperor Friedrich I), 396, 566, 662, 666
Barbatia (Barbazza), Andreas (glossator), 24 (*barbacianis*), 194, 245, 434, 453, 588
Barbarus, Hermolaus, 662, 701
Barbitonsor, Nicholaus, 26, 435, 436, 438
Barbus, Marcus, 92, 174 (*Cardinal N.*)?, 505, 574, 704, 711
Barby-Mulingen, Hieronymus (Hoyer), 187 (*aliqui*), 188 (*qui prius prouidisset*), 504, 580f., 708, 731
Bargellini, Giacomo, 549
Barr (village), Franciscan monastery at, 169, 552, 569
Bartholomaeus Brixiensis (glossator), 246
Bartolomaeus Favensis, 305, 672, 717
Bartolus de Saso (glossator), 39, 217, 224, 237, 254, 256, 452
Basel, xiv, 53, 54, 56, 57, 58, 69, 144, 190, 372f., 385, 386, 410, 413, 425, 428, 454, 480, 481, 505, 518, 534, 593, 673, 679, 702, 711, 713, 716, 722, 735, 738, 752, 756, 760, 766
  bishop of, 190, 385, 749, 764
    see Caspar de Rein, Christoph von Uttenheim, Johannes
  cathedral, 764 (*custos* of)
    chapter of, 518, 547, 548
    preaching chair of, 143, 145, 479f., 543, 544, 545ff., 731
  city council of, 713
  diocese of, 469
  university of, 17, 145, 480, 501, 547, 699, 705, 709, 713, 720, 721, 725, 731, 735, 746, 749, 750, 755, 757, 764
Basilea (Basel), 144, 145

Basiliensis, -es, (adj.), 144, 145, passim
Basse Ligue, 385
Baths, 425f. (426, N. 192, list of references in Vol. I), 441ff., 445, 455, 463f., 488, 518, 521, 523, 550ff., 564f., 570, 609, 618, 649, 679, 741, 743, 771; see Baden-Baden, Hub, Tamina, Wiltbad, Zellerbad
  dangers of, 425
  gifts to patients at, 425, 426 (N. 192, list of references in Vol. I), 441, 444, 464, 488, 537, 538, 550f., 570, 650
  medical supervision of, 425
  months for, 425
  regimen of, 425
Bavaria, 138, 218, 287, 291, 502, 538, 662f., 700, 701, 704f., 751
  house of, 704
    dukes of, see Albrecht II, Albrecht III, Christoph, Ernst, Georg *der Reiche*, Heinrich X, Johann (son of Albrecht II), Johann (son of Otto), Otto von Neumarkt, Sigismund, Wilhelm IV, Wolfgang
Bauarij (adj.), 107
Bavus (poet), 308, 676
Beata Maria Virgo (church in Freiburg i. B.), 736
Beatrice of Aragon, daughter of Ferdinand, king of Naples, 279, 406, 653, 732
beatus Bernardus, 143; see Bernardus II, *Markgraf* of Baden
beatus Thomas (St. Thomas Aquinas), 183
Bebel, Heinrich, 484
Bechenhub, Johannes, 673
Beck, Renatus (Strassburg printer), 744
bees, symbol of vices, 18, 428
Beghards, 447
Beginalem doctorem, 33, 447
Begines, 447; monastery of, 738
Benedict, *Dominus*, 115, 522
Benedict XI (pope), 634
Benedict XIII (pope), 640
Benedictines, Order of
  abbey at Hirsau, 706
  at Gengenbach, 706
  at Ottobeuren, 751
  convention, 674
  monastery at Schüttern, 706
  at Spanheim, 764
  St. Jacob at Würzburg, 764
benefices, xxvii, xxixf., 9, 32, 35, 38, 39, 40, 50, 61, 65, 66, 76, 79, 80, 83, 86, 94, 95, 96, 104, 110, 112, 114, 137, 169, 170, 172, 174, 195, 198, 199, 200, 203, 204, 257, 401ff., 404, 405, 407ff. (N. 130, detailed discussion of), 430, 436, 446, 448f., 450, 451f., 455f., 459f., 461, 463, 464f., 474f., 476ff., 479, 489, 491f., 492ff., 500, 505, 520, 564-568, 569-592, 589f., 590, 591, 592, 593ff., 598f., 604, 611, 613f., 625, 637, 703, 704, 733f., 737
  absenteeism from, 200, 410, 595, 759
  cathedral benefices restricted to nobles, 86ff., 499ff.
  conflict with emperor over, 408, 409f.
  conflict with pope over, 185ff., 409f., 580f.
  income from, 83, 172, 495f., 507, 572
  litigation over, 407f., 410f., 451 (N. 334), 494, 571
  plurality of, 59, 64f., 76, 82, 83, 115, 201, 322, 410f., 417, 472, 475, 477, 489, 495f., 506, 516, 522, 540, 599, 625, 686, 711, 739
  warning against plurality of, 411 (N. 133)
  see *menses ordinariorum, menses papales, preces primae*
Bentivoglio family, plot against, 549
Bentivoglio, Francesca, 740
Berenbrod, 608
Bergmann, Johann (printer), 673
Berlem *or* Berler, Hieronymus, 705
Berlin, Hieronymus, 18, 705
Berman, Jacob, 539
Bern (city), 455, 732, 756 (library of), 377
Bernard II (III), *Markgraf* of Baden, 141 (?), 143, 430, 441, 702
Bernard, *Markgraf* of Baden (*praepositus* of church in Baden-Baden), 430
Bernard, *Markgraf* of Baden (son of Christoph I), 703

849

Bernardus (glossator), 453
Bernauer, Agnes, 704
Beroald, Philipp, xxv, 705
Betonto, Antonius de, 740
Bettscholt, Columba, 742, 755, 810
Bettscholt, Eucharius, 755, 810
Bettscholt, Wilhelm, 742, 755, 810
Beuri, Dominus de, 138; *see* Albrecht III, duke of Bavaria
Biblical references, *see* Vulgate references
Bibliopola, Friedrich, 162, 163, 563
Bibliothèque nationale et universitaire de Strasbourg, 364f., 375, 378, 673, 675
Biel, Gabriel, xxix, 143, 153f., 155, 249ff., 366, 392f., 407, 508, 542, 543, 545, 554, 604, 626, 629, 632f., 705f., 734. 770
  brother of, 154, 554f. (same as *Gualterus*, 155?)
  Schott-Biel dialogue, 249ff., 632f.
Biethen von Reichenweyer, Jakob, 401
Bild, Beatus, *see* Rhenanus, Beatus
birth charms, *see* folklore
Bischofszell, church at, 739
Bistonij, 273 (Orpheus)
Black Forest, 368, 542, 638, 707, 722
Black Sea, 648
Blasius, 151 (abbot of Hirsau), 552, 706
Blienswiler (Bliensweiler, *also* Plien –), 51, 68, 75, 95, 507, 736, 741
Bock, Friedrich, 255, 390, 514, 636, 706f., 749, 757
Bock, Hans Conrad, 455
Bock, Johann, 810
Bock, Sophie, 455, 603
Bock, Ulrich, 514, 706f.
Bockel, Caspar, 455
Bohemia, xxv, xxvi, 43, 270, 399, 457, 458, 526, 559 (*Patria*), 617, 646, 648, 677, 680, 699, 707, 710, 711, 729, 745
  king of, 122, 192; *see* Vladislaus *and* Sigismund, emperor
Bohemian(s), xxv, 42, 107, 267, 268, 269, 645, 646, 707
  Bohemian Ulysses, xxv, xxvi; *see* Bohuslaus von Hassenstein
Bohit, Henricus, *see* Boyck
Boit, Henricus, 229; *see* Boyk
Bologna, xxii, xxx, 12, 13, 17, 18, 20, 23, 24, 25, 26, 34, 44, 77, 105, 148, 191, 193, 194, 199, 214, 266, 358, 363, 391, 405, 414, 415, 420, 421, 422, 423, 424, 428, 430, 433, 435, 436f., 438, 440, 448, 482, 491, 549, 577, 585, 587, 596, 615, 618, 645, 649, 650, 652, 669, 670, 677, 678, 685, 695, 705, 710, 715, 739, 754, 763, 766, 770
  university of, xxv, xxvi, 13, 77, 80, 105, 106, 199, 270, 317, 367, 382, 383, 395ff., 417, 420, 422, 423, 429, 430, 437f., 472, 473, 481, 490f., 492f., 513, 514, 588, 593, 647, 672, 675, 682, 705, 708, 709, 715, 716, 717, 719, 724, 726, 728, 734, 740, 741, 742, 743, 744, 746, 747, 753, 762, 763, 764, 765, 768, 769, 770, 778, 779
Bolzheim, Johann, 493
Bonaventura, St., 261, 640f.
Bondorf (Bondorffer), Conrad, 59, 158, 254, 369, 401, 470, 474, 558, 635, 707, 762
Boner, Ruprecht, 256, 636
Boniface VIII (pope), 634
Boniface IX (pope), 398
Bononia, see Bologna
books, xxvi, 24, 82f., 139, 141, 142, 155, 156, 164, 190, 193f., 201, 202, 208, 215, 292, 298, 365, 370f., 375, 400, 425, 435, 440, 446, 458, 481, 483, 495, 523, 524, 525, 534f., 539, 541, 542, 555, 557, 563f., 583f., 587f., 596, 609, 616, 617, 618, 664, 668, 707, 716, 721, 722, 724, 725, 728, 729, 730, 732, 733, 735, 740, 741, 743f., 747, 748, 750, 752, 754, 757, 759, 760, 761, 763, 764, 766
Boreas, 270, 299, 647
Borgia, Cesar, 740
Bornio, Doctor, 753
Bosnia, bishop of, 763
Bottoni, Giovanni Antonio, 740
Boulogne, Jeanne de, 470
boy bishop, 207, 292f., 607f., 664
Boyc, Henricus, *see* Boyck
Boyck, Heinrich, 9, 417, 708
Boyk, Henricus, 9, 229, 417, 708
Brabant, 386
Brandenburg, Elector of, 502, 758, 771

Brandis, Johann von, 187, 188, 516, 580f., 708
Brant family, 679
Brant, Diebolt, 708
Brant, Matthias (Strassburg printer), 708
Brant, Onophrius, 709
Brant, Sebastian, xiii, xv, xxiv, 17f., 366, 369, 372, 373, 394, 410, 425, 426, 427, 427, 453, 593, 673, 684, 708ff., 721, 723, 725, 742, 743, 744, 752, 756, 784
bread prebend, 403
Breisach, 386, 756
Breisgau, 386, 710, 713
Brescia (Italian city), 707, 762
Brethren of the Common Life, 370, 392f., 448, 490, 498, 520, 706, 715
  foundations of, 392f., 706, 735
Breusch (river), 368
Breuschwickersheim estate and castle, 762
Brisgoicus, see Brockingen
Britain, 396, 481
British Museum, 372, 375
Britonoriensis, Antonius Manlius, xxv, 79, 83, 95; see Manlius
Brittany, duke of, 538
Brixen, cathedral canon of, 719
Brockingen (Broggingen, Breisgang, town), 710
Brockingen, Johann von, 162, 561, 562, 710
Bruder Clauss, see Flüe, Nicolaus von
Bruges, xxv, 105, 402, 513, 514, 537f., 540, 667, 703, 705, 727, 742
  bailiff of, 105, 726
  people of (*Brugenses*), 137, 138, 139, 140
Brunschwig, Hieronymus, 139, 170, 538f., 570, 710
Brunswick, Anna of, 727
Bruschenckner, Sigismund, 115, 522, 710
Brutum, 192
Bucer, Martin, 761
Büchsner, Friedrich, xxv, xxvi, 23, 107, 117, 118, 120, 121, 312f., 435, 456, 514, 524, 525, 526, 527, 680, 710f., 729
  mother of, 312, 680
Buck, Udalricus, 107, 514
Buda (city), 729, 732, 740

Büdingen (town), 614, 733
Burckard, Johann, 34, 35, 36, 37, 38, 61, 81, 82, 94 (*procurator Thome*), 193, 409, 410, 448, 449, 451, 515, 586f., 618, 703, 711f.
Diarium, 703, 712
Burg, Elizabeth, 709
Burgundian(s), 712, 719
Burgundian Wars, see hostilities
Burgundio (Charles the Bold), 269
Burgundy college at Paris, see *collegium Burgundie*
Burgundy, duchy of, 386f., 712, 718, 751
  house of, 712
  duchess of, see Mary
  dukes of, see Charles the Bold, John the Fearless, Philip the Bold, Philip the Fair, Philip the Good, Philip the Long
Burials, advice on, see advice
Burses de Neapoli, Ludovicus de, 176, 575, 712
Burtius, Nicolas, 715, 770
Buschenck, Sigismund, see Bruschenckner
Buttrio, Anthonius de (glossator), 241, 242; see Anthonius
Butzbach, foundation of Brethren of the Common Life at, 393, 706
Bysancion (Byzantium), 159, 559

Caballini amnis (Hypocrenean spring), 310, 646
  Caballino fonte, 278, 652
  Caballino gurgite, 267, 646
Cadmeo vellus aheno, 272, 648
Cadmus, 647, 648
Caesar, 673
Caesarorius, Doctor, see Geiler
Calaber, Crassus, see Alujs
Calceatoris, see Brockingen
Calixtines, 525, 728
Calliope, 121, 280, 281, 310, 669
Calvin, Johann, 461
Calvinist, 544
Calydne (island group), 332
Cambrai (city on Scheldt), 713
camera apostolica, 104, 512
camerarius, duties of 404
  Camerarius of Peraudi, 161, 562
Cancellarius, 65, see Gerson; 165,

851

see Quinckener
Cancer (constellation), 271, 648
Canicula (dog-star, Sirius), 442, 648, 677
Canis (constellation), 648, 677
canon, duties and privileges of, 402f.
  installation of, at Old St. Peter, 571
canon and civil law, items on, *see* advice, case, opinion, question, testimonials; *see also* abuses, canonical hours, clergy, confession, excommunication, fasting, Lenten foods, Strassburg laws
canonical hours, 236, 237f., 250, 402, 561, 625ff.
canonical houses, 23, 237f., 250, 402, 461, 473f., 561, 625f.
canonicates, restricted in cathedrals to nobles, 86-90, 498ff.
Canonicos Regulares, 112; *see* Brethren of the Common Life
cantor, duties of, 404
Capella Sanctae Crucis Exulum, *see* zum elenden Kreuz
Capnion, Johannes, *see* Reuchlin
Capricorn (constellation), 648, 666
Capua, Raymond de, 505
Caracalla, Antoninus, 746
Caraffa, Olivier, 176, 177, 489, 574ff., 712f.
Cardinal de Arragonia, 176; *see* Aragonia, Ioannes de
Cardinal N., 174 (Marcus Barbus?), 574
Cardinal Neapolitanus, 176, 177; *see* Caraffa
Cardinal Sancti Vitalis, 173, 573; *see* Cluniaco, Ferricus de
Cardinalis (glossator), 241, 243, 253
Carletus, Angelus, *Summa angelica (Summa casuum)*, 626
Carlotta (Charlita), Hassenstein's unknown lady, 437, 729f.
Carmelites, Order of; in Strassburg, 621
  province in Lowlands, 707
Carneades, 16, 424, 735
Carniola (Austrian province), archbishop of, 454, 735
Carthusians, Order of, 57, 69f., 161, 162, 481, 548, 561, 562, 752
  at Avignon, 412
  monastery at Basel, 702, 732, 752
  monastery at Strassburg ("St. Ursula Schifflein"), 481, 728
  (printing press), 737, 744
Case of abbot of Ottobeuren, *see* Ottobeuren, abbot of
Case of Clingenthal sisters, *see* Clingenthal sisters
Case of grain loans, xxvii, 226-235, 622-625, 752
Case of Last Sacrament for criminals condemned to death, xxvii, 145, 205, 218-255, 406, 599-602, 620-622, 806f.
  decree of 1485, 807
Case of libel, Dünzenheim vs. Rot, 176ff., 574ff., 752, 760
Case of litigation, Funck vs. Wolf, 451 (N. 334), 768
Case of marriage dispensation, 34, 35, 36, 37, 49, 448, 449, 450, 463
Case of marriage dispensation for consanguinity, 103f., 104, 108, 111, 512f., 519
Case of a matron, 133, 534
Case of restricting cathedral canonicates to nobles, 86-99, 498-501
Case of stolen confession, xxix, 215ff., 619f., 406
Case of validity of delegated authority, 242ff., 628ff.
Casimir, king of Poland, 707
Caspar (organist), 52, 466
Caspar, *Magister*, 132, 133, 532
Cassetta, Salvo (Dominican general), 210, 391, 611f., 713, 737
Castalie... dee (Muses), 268, 271
Castor and Pollux (Gemini), 299, 668
Castra Regina (Regensburg), 662
cathedra, syllable quantity of, 96f., 99, 508f.
cathedral chairs for lay preachers, 542f.
cathedrals, *see* Strassburg et al.
Catholics, 381, 404, 411
Cato the Elder, 24, 119, 265, 269, 319, 424, 525, 680, 682
Cato Uticensis, 436
Catullus, 155, 485, 555, 654
Cautes Marpesia, 20, 429
Cecropia fruge, 277, 652
Cecropia seni (Socrates), 272, 648
Celestines at Lyons, 412, 641, 722, 724
  prior of, 261
cellarius, duties of, 404

Cellense balneum (Zellerbad), 169
Celtis, Conrad, 369, 701, 729, 745, 750, 751, 764, 765, 784
Celts, 368
Centaurique trucis (Centaur, constellation), 272
Cephali, uxor (Procris), 302
Ceres, 283, 287, 442, 647, 657, 659
Ceresio, Jacob de, 412
Cesena, Antonius de, 493
Chabotus, Gabriel, 713
Chambriaco, Gabriel de, 18; see Chabotus
Charlemagne, 368, 425, 673
Charles V, emperor, 370, 750
Charles V, king of France, 718
Charles VI, king of France, 260 (Francorum Rege), 638, 640, 718
Charles VIII, king of France, 467, 538
Charles I, duke of Lorraine, 702
Charles the Bold, duke of Burgundy, xxiii, xxviii, 269, 280 (Burgundio), 385, 386f., 390, 406, 432, 471, 645, 646, 647, 653f., 661, 696, 706, 712, 717, 727, 738, 751, 756
Chartres cathedral, "butter" towers of, 434
Chartreuse (city), 561
Cherilus, 308; see Choerilus
Chicago university library, X
Childeric II, 449
children, festivities of, 207, 599, 607f.
Chlodowig, 663
Choerilus (Choerilos), 268, 308, 646, 676
Choi magistri (Hippocrates), 269, 647
Christian, Dominus, 134, 135, 143, 154, 535
Christian symbolism: in animals, 276, 277, 651
 in plants, 274, 650
Christoph, duke of Bavaria, 138, 538, 704, 705
Christoph I, Markgraf of Baden, 29 (eo duce), 40, 47, 51, 62, 65, 68, 80, 95, 112, 138, 152, 195, 196, 403, 424, 429f., 441, 445, 463, 471, 472, 476ff., 480, 486, 491, 521, 538, 540, 589f., 702f., 703, 735, 743, 766
Chrysostom, St. John, see St. John

Chrysostom
Chur (town), 737
 bishop of, see Hewen
 cathedral canon of, 708
 Dominican monastery of, 737
Cicero, xxx, 10, 17, 31, 71, 90, 100, 121, 150, 194, 203, 265, 268, 271, 282, 290, 293, 319, 320, 321, 322, 393, 417, 427, 438, 439, 441, 445, 482, 485, 503, 510, 514, 524, 526, 535, 539, 584, 586, 588, 594, 595, 597, 644, 647, 655f., 661, 665, 671, 680, 682, 683, 685, 686, 732, 783
Cilicia (country), 688
Cinthius (Cynthius, Apollo), 267
Cistercians, Order of, 738, 769
Citeaux, Gilbert de, 640
Citherei (Apollo), 267, 271, 279
Citramontani (sector of students at Bologna), 395f., 490f.
Claudian, 103, 334, 349, 353, 511, 691, 692
Clement V (pope), 472, 634
Clement VI (pope), 763
Clement XIV (pope), 702
clergy: concubines of, 236f., 238, 580, 625f.
 legal and moral questions concerning behavior, 236ff., 625ff.
 loss of inheritance on entering an order, 205, 603
 quarrel between regular and lay members over
 (1) fresco in the St. Laurentius chapel of the Strassburg cathedral, 158f., 558
 (2) the Strassburg cathedral preaching chair, 543f.
 (3) ultimum vale, 543, 634,
 taxation 205, 206, 250, 604, 632
 tonsures, 246, 626
 see canonical hours, canon and civil law
Cleves (town), 749
Clingenthal convent, 53, 54, 57, 58, 466ff., 713f., 716, 718
 sisters, xxix, 52-59, 92f., 407, 466ff., 713, 737, 739
Clio (Muse), 267, 310, 645
Clotho (a Fate), 44
Clovis, 388
Cluniaco, Ferricus de, 173, 573, 714
Coblenz (Confluentes), 589

853

Codicillum de vita Christiana, see
    Luc., treatise on Christian life
Codicillum... nomina instrumentorum, xi, 33, 447
Codrus, see Urceus, Antonius
coinage *and* coins, adulteration of, xxvii, 163, 188f., 406, 581f.
    relative value, 623, 812
    weight regulation of gold coins 163, 563
Colaby (*also* Colbe, Collebi), Matthias, see Kolb, Matthias
collegiate chapter, officers of, 403f.
collegium Burgundie (*Collège de Bourgoinge*), 59, 160, 161, 470, 560
Cöllen family, 714
    coat-of-arms, 391
Cöllen, Margrede von, 714, 757
Cöllen, Ottilia von, xxiv, 60 (*filia*), 96 (*filiam*), 118 (*filia*), 120 (*nepte*), 471, 495, 507f., 525, 715, 756, 761
Cöllen, Peter (Jacob?) von, 700, 715, 756, 810
Cöllen, Susanna von, xxiv 12, 13, 14, 30, 31, 33, 36, 41, 48, 50, 75, 85, 131, 132, 135, 141, 156, 161, 163, 169, 190, 193, 198, 310, 320, 379, 416, 423, 443, 444, 462, 486f., 498, 531, 541, 543, 556, 561, 563, 566, 569, 583, 586, 591, 700, 714, 722, 743, 753, 755, 756, 766, 809, 810
Colmar (town), 180, 190, 385, 529, 576, 769
    Dominican monastery at, 557
    prior of Dominican monastery at, 156f.
Cologne, 77, 107, 392, 413, 481, 483, 489, 499f., 515, 556, 704, 714, 762
    archbishop-elector of, 449, 770
    archdiocese of, 434
    cathedral canon of, 701, 733
    cathedral chapter of, 499f.
    university of, 475, 501, 701, 715, 745
Colonia, see Cologne
Coloniensis, Rudolfus, 714
Colonna family, 733
Colonna, Lorenzo, 733
colonus (farmer, villager), 227, 623f.
colophon, of Martin Flach, Jr., 413
    of Martin Flach, Sr., 414
    of Johann Schott, 354
    of Martin Schott, plate 4, 323ff.
Columbaria, see Colmar
    Columbariensis (Colmar, adj.), 156
Columbus, Christopher, 553
commater mea, 41, 456
commentary on John 13, xi, 365
compendiosa laus Gersonis, see *Luc.*, eulogy of Gerson
confederation of Rhine cities, xxiii, 385, 386, 393, 471, 485
confession, 242ff., 251, 628ff., 632; see case of stolen c...
Confluentia, 203, see Wimpfen
Confoederati, xxiii, 41, 60; see league of 1474
Conrad, 169, 569
Conrad von Rotenburg, 387
Conrad von Zabern, 390
consanguinity, 103, 512
conservatore Episcopo Argentinae, 61; see Wolf, Thomas, Sr.
Constance, xxv, 106, 448, 741
    bishop of, 434, 713, 741; see Hermann, Hugo
    cathedral, canon of, 770
    dean of, 106, 731
    diocese of, 34, 212, 242, 448, 628, 714
Constantine, 420
Constantinople, 764
consulatus (city council), 255
consules, 48; *consulibus*, 176; *consulum*, 178; see 463 (N. 420)
contrafaçons, 375, 413
Coriciumque crocum (crocus of Corycus), 333
Coridones (Corydon), 119, 525
Corinna, 271, 647, 648
Corneo, Filippo, 641
Corvinus, János, 741
Corvinus, Matthias, see Hunyadi, Matthias
Corona (constellation), 648
Council of Basel, 236, 238, 272, 408, 499, 539, 542, 581, 605, 608, 626, 648, 674, 745
Council of Carthage, 640
Council of Constance, 260, 261, 409, 499, 604, 639, 640, 648, 724, 759
Council of Ephesus, 640
Cretensibus, 332
Creussner, Friedrich (Nürnberg printer), 617

Creyznach (Creuznach), Johann von, 195, 589
Christianus, Dominus, see Christian
Christoferus Augustensis, 20, 429
criticism, works sent for, 448 (N. 309)
Croatia, bishop of, 707
Croesus, 802
Cupid, 300 (*frater Aenee*), 648, 669
Cusa, Nicolas de, 392
Cyanei... saxa (Cyaneae islands), 272, 648
Cymbros (Danes), 188
Cynthia (Diana), 307, 676
Cyrre (Cirrha, Cirra, town), 332, 688
Cythaeron, 346
　Cythera, 346
　Cytherea, 279, 346
　Cytheron, 332
Cytharedus (*citharoedus*), 300
Dacia (Roumania), 747
Daedalus, 655
Dagobert, 388
Dalberg, Johann, 497, 700, 701, 720, 745, 747, 760, 765
Dambach (Alsatian town), 423, 436, 450, 477, 594, 611, 743, 751
　castle of, 710
Dambusson, Peter, 675
Damm (town in Flanders), 703
Dammerer, Catherine, 718
Danais, 268
Danes (*Cymbros*), 188
Daniel, 44, 459
Daniel, *Frater*, 216ff.; see Friesenheimer
Danube (river), 288, 522, 660, 663, 701
　bridge at Regensburg, 288, 663
dapifer, duties of, 404
Dardani-, 192, 272, 297, 308
Dates, before the kalends of January, 431f. (N. 218)
　errors in, 438, 532
　reckoned by fixed feasts, 466 (N. 445), 486 (N. 582)
　reckoned by movable feasts, 374 (N. 36, 2 and 3)
De contemptu mundi, see *Imitatio Christi*
De tribus Iohannibus, see *Luc.*, poems
De vita Christiana, see, *Luc.*, treatise on Christian life
decanatus, 45, 460

decanus, duties of, 403
　qualifications of for Strassburg cathedral, 187
Decanus noster, 45; see Jacob Hagen
　Decani Argentinensis, 52;
　Domino Decano, 196; see Friedrich von Zollern
　Decanus sancti Thome, 38, 200, 210; see Johann Simmler
　decanus Sancti Petri senioris, 160, 161; see N. 1063 (560)
dedalea arte (Daedalean...), 192, 585
Dedala, 302
dedalijs vijs, 281
Dedinger, Jacob, 12, 194 (*praepositus Surburgensis*), 420, 588, 715
Dedinger, Margred, 755, 810
Delia (Diana), 301
Delphi, 688
Delphin, Jacob, 394
Demosthenes, 202, 596
desecration, see abuses
D'Este family, 398
D'Este, Ercole, duke, 439, 482, 733
D'Este, Isabella, 715
Deventer (Dutch town), 392f., 700, 715, 735, 736
　Alexander Hegius gymnasium of, 393
　Latin school of, 392f., 490, 498, 700, 735
Dia Pallade (Minerva), 305
dialogue between Biel and Schott, see *Luc.*
Dianam, 288, 647, 660
Dido, 302, 670
Dierstein, Oswald, see Dyrstein
Diest, Wilhelm von, 663, 738
Dillingen (Bavarian town), 115, 292, 483, 503, 522, 588, 618, 664
　castle of, 522
Dillingen, *Graf* Hartmann V von, 522
Dinckelsbühl, 705
Diocletian, 420
Diogenes, 424
Diomedes, 100, 508, 509ff.
Dionea imago (Venus), 272
　Dione, 299, 648
Dionysius (Christian writer), 259, 639
dispensation, marriage, see case of marriage dispensation
Ditis (Pluto), 300, 305

855

diva parens (Virgin), 44
doctor, angelicus, 578
   Christianissimus, 258, 638
   Christianus, 261, 638
   illuminatus, 261, 641
   illuminatus et acutus, 641
   illuminatus et sublimis, 578, 641
   irrefragibilis, 640f.
   magnus, 261, 640
   magnus et universalis, 640
   resolutissimus et Christianissimus, 639
   sanctus, 182, 249, 261, 578, 631, 640
   seraphicus, 261, 640;
   solemnis, 261, 641
   sublimis, 578
   subtilis, 63, 261, 474, 641
   universalis, 578, 701
Doctrinale, see Alexander de Villa Dei
Dolden, (given name unknown, second husband of Margred Schott), 755, 810
Dolden, Margretha, 755, 810
Dolpholis (Dolfus, Dolfo, Dolfi, Dulfus), Florianus (Febriano) de, 77, 490, 715
Domina (moon) *insanit*, 29, 442
Dominicans, Order of, 253, 369, 505f., 634, 642f., 644, 695, 701, 707, 713, 737
   at Basel, 718, 754
   at Chur, 737
   at Colmar, 506, 557, 745
   at Cologne, 760
   at Freiburg, 746
   at Nürnberg, 745
   at Regensberg, 745
   at Spires, 558
   at Strassburg, 543, 577, 604, 621, 644, 745f., 763
   convention, 213, 615, 747
   Observants, 93, 156, 214, 644, 724
   provincia Brabantia, 760
   provincia Teutonica, 213, 760
Dominicus (university beadle), 26, 437
donations, to mendicant orders, 57, 213f.
   for impoverished mother, 214
Donatus, 194, 290, 588, 662
double convent, 716
Dozinger, Jodok (Jost), 364

Draconem (constellation), 272, 648
Dreizehner, 384, 755
Dringenberg (Westphalian town), 715
Dringenberg, Ludwig, xxiv, 9, 168, 169, 266, 370, 392, 393, 394, 417, 568f., 644, 686, 708, 715, 725, 732, 742, 749, 766
   proverb of, 266, 644
Dulichium (Ulysses), 270
Duns, Johannes, *see* Scotus, Johannes Duns
Dunzenheim (village), 716
Dunzenheim, Conrad, 176, 178, 180, 556, 574ff., 715f.
Dunzenheim, Conrad, the Younger, 716
Dunzenheim, Elizabeth, 176, 178, 180, 574ff.
Dunzenheim, Heinz, 716
Dunzenheim, Ursula, 156, 168, 556, 568
Dunzenheims, 463, 752, 760
Durandus, Guillemus, 588
Düren, Poppo von, 699
Dürr, Berchtold, 212, 612, 716
Dyrstein, Oswald von, 83, 496, 716, 765

Eacide (Achilles), 268, 273, 310, 646
Eberhard V, *Graf* (Eberhard I, duke) of Württemberg, 132 (*Comitis tui*), 471, 502, 508, 531f., 597, 700, 706, 750, 766, 769
Eberhard II, duke of Württemberg, 750, 769
Eckbolsheim (Alsatian village), 767f.
economic conditions, book prices, 194, 587f.
   clothes cheaper in Paris than in Strassburg, 195, 589
   conservation of wildlife, 208, 610
   contract for sale of seed, 255f., 636
   effect of Reformation, 388
   farming on a Bohemian estate, 119
   fertility of Strassburg lands, 199
   floods, famine and poor harvests 1480-82, 190, 283, 584, 622f., 657; 1485, 284, 657
   good harvest in 1483, 283, 657
   grain loans and mortgages, 226ff. 622ff.

poor, care of, 214, 602, 607
prosperity of Bohemia, 270, 641
prosperity of Strassburg, 387
regulation of weights, coins, 563
support of illegimate children, 236, 625f.
education, xxviif., xxxi, 13f., 16, 63f., 66, 80, 85, 95, 107, 112, 139, 195, 198, 199, 207, 236, 260, 268f., 281f., 315ff., 369f., 370, 392ff., 401, 403, 406f., 551, 625ff., 730
see schools, universities
Edward, king of Portugal, 727
Egerie (nymph), 303, 670
Egerstein, Martin, 744
Eggestan, Heinrich (Strassburg printer), 728
Egloffstein, Leonard von, 79, 82, 83, 95, 492, 496, 506, 516, 716f.
Egloffstein, Leonard von (cousin of aforementioned) 716f.
Egoceros (Capricorn, constellation), 272, 648
Egypt, 159, 559; papyrus of, 136, 536
Eichstätt (town), 457, 525
  bishop of, 502
  cathedral canon of, 699, 753
Einsiedeln (Swiss pilgrimage center), 455f., 718, 722
Einundzwanziger, 384f.
Elchingen (Bavarian town), 751
elementi Samij ramum, 20; see Samian letter
Elhart, Udalrich, 473
Elijah, 321, 686
Elisabeth, 29, 67 (*ministra tua?*), 442
Elisios campos (Elysian fields), 24
Elizabeth (mother of John the Baptist), 275, 651
Elizabeth (wife of Johannes), 103, 512
Ellwangen (town), cathedral canon of, 699
Elsass, 368
Elveciorum urbe, 212; see Helvetians
Elysio, 311
emperor, 11, 79, 80, 87, 90, 138, 139, 140, 532, 537f., 704, 770
  see Barbarossa, Charles V, Friedrich III, Karl III, Maximilian I, Otto the Great, Rudolf von Habsburg, Sigismund

empire, xxv, 368, 396, 437, 476, 538, 542, 549, 574, 604, 612, 647, 662, 673, 727, 728, 730, 737, 765
Emser, Hieronymus, 562
encomium to Strassburg, see *Luc.*, poems for Strassburg schoolboys
Endingen (village), 717; family, 717
Endingen, Johann Rudolf von, 257, 390, 637, 717
Endingen, Philipp von, 257, 369, 637, 717
Engelberg (pilgrimage center), 718
Engelbrecht, Ulrich, 389
Engelpforten *or* Engelspforten (Augustinian convent at Gebweiler), 58, 469, 713, 737
Engelthal, Begine monastery at, 738
England, 368, 386, 699
English, 712, 719
Ennius, 297, 667
Enosygeum (Neptune), 291
Entz (river), 426
Eolus (Aeolus), 299
Eous (Eos), 272, 332, 648
Epicureas tradiciones, 137
epitaph to Schott, xii, xxxi, 10, 366, 371, 378ff., 415 (new epitaph in Zorn chapel)
epithalamium for Matthias I of Hungary and Beatrice of Naples, 279, 653
Epithoma, xi, xixff., xxix, 372, 375ff., 407, 432, 720, 767
  date of composition, 376
  notes, 688-693
  poems, xi, xixff., 332f., 688f.
  rules, see prosody
  text, 331-354
Eppingen (village), 728
eques (*miles*) *auratus*, 105, 106, 202, 255, 513, 699, 706, 725, 726, 755, 758, 810
Erasmus, 368, 369, 370, 372, 392, 461, 483, 701, 750
Erfurt, xix
  university of, 65, 475, 480, 501, 705, 720, 725, 726, 730, 731, 733, 742, 744, 751, 753, 761, 766, 768, 769, 770
Eridano, 267
Erinnys, 442
Erithreis (*Erythraeis*, Boeotian), 267
Erlebach, Georg, 298, 398, 668

857

Ernst von Hapsburg, 703, 727
Ernst, duke of Bavaria, 704
Ernst, *Markgraf* of Baden, 703
Ernst, duke of Saxony, 770
escorts, 62, 69, 204, 473, 599
Eselbergum Nurenbergensem, 117, 524
Eselsberg, Elbin von, 524
Ethnea (Aetnaea), 270
Ettlingen (town in Baden), 735
euacatio, 114, 521
Eudoxia, empress, 278 (*Auguste*), 652
Eulogy of Gerson, xxx, 11, 261, 412f.
Eumenides, 282
Euphrates, 648
Europa, 648
Euryalus, 270, 298
Eusebius, canons of, 117
excommunication, 250, 252f., 409, 632, 750
Eyb, Albrecht von, 655

fabrica, of Milan cathedral, 364
   of New St. Peter, 215, 618f.
   of Santa Maria de Anima, 515
   of Strassburg cathedral, see Strassburg cathedral
Faenza (town), 140, 540, 717, 740
Faenza, Bartolmeo de, 717
fairs, 33, 113, 440, 446, 571, 638
Falckner, Johann, 69, 473, 480
famulus, xxvii, xxviiif., 26, 28, 30, 75, 77, 134, 139, 143, 151, 153, 154, 400, 406f., 427, 437, 443, 470, 475, 476, 490, 498, 535, 542, 554, 590ff., 710, 736, 760
Fanckel, Mathias, 557
fasting, 250, 433f.; *see* Lenten foods, fat and lard
fat and lard on fast days, 254, 635
Favencia (Faenza), 140
   Favensis (adj.)
Favensis, Bartholomaeus, 305, 672, 717
Faventia, Bartholomeus de, 717
feast days: Advent, 607
    All Saints, 155, 255, 555, 636, 805
    Ash Wednesday, 358, 602, 694, 778
    Ascension, 138, 153, 538, 551, 554
    Annunciation, 57
    Assumption, 30, 41, 226, 231, 623, 624
    Cantate, 149, 151, 214, 550, 551, 615
    Candlemas, 623
    Christmas, 43, 226, 288, 599, 607f., 623, 656, 665, 658, 660, 666, 805
    Corpus Christi, 112, 519, 805
    Easter, 12, 132, 551, 561, 694, 703, 805
    Epiphany, 534, 607, 608, 805
    Exaudi, 75, 110, 488, 518
    Holy Sacrament, 402
    Innocents, xxviii, 207, 281, 288, 534, 605f., 655, 660, 666
    Invocavit, 73, 486, 602, 807
    Lady Day, 623
    Lammas, 623
    Letare, 132, 532
    Martinmas, 623
    Michaelmas, 534, 623
    Oculi, 109, 516
    Palm Sunday, 743
    Pascha, 12; *see* Easter
    Pentecost, 160, 206, 226, 232, 402, 560, 561, 562, 602, 604, 606, 623, 624, 805
    Presentation of Christ, 666
    Rogation, 151, 551f.
    Sabbath, 12, 138, 519, 538, 601; *also diei Dominico*, 207
    St. Adelphus (dedication of Strassburg cathedral), 602, 805
    St. Andrew, 805
    St. Anna, 805
    St. Apollonia, 52, 466
    St. Bartholomew, 62, 165, 565
    St. Catherine, 608, 806
    St. Gregory, 608
    St. Hilary, 226, 623
    St. Jacob, 805
    St. John the Baptist, 226, 623
    St. John Evangelist, 607
    St. Laurentius, 657
    St. Lucia, 226, 601, 622f., 806
    St. Martin, 45, 459, 608
    St. Matthew, 73, 487, 805
    St. Nicholas, xxviii, 207, 281, 288, 607, 608, 655, 658, 660, 666
    St. Othmar, 786, 787
    St. Peter *in vinculis*, 666
    St. Peter's Chair at Antioch, 73, 486
    St. Thomas, 601, 807

St. Ulrich, 41, 454
St. Ursula and her 11,000 Virgins, 481f., 545
Sts. Peter and Paul, 669, 806
Trinity, 161, 162, 561, 562
Virgin, Nativity of, 107, 226, 312, 313, 515, 623, 680
  Presentation of, 135, 536
  Purification of, 295, 666
  Visitation, 111, 519
  Whitsunday, 623
Felix V (antipope), 762
Felsch, *see* Voeltsch
Ferdinand of Aragon, king of Naples, 279, 653, 712, 732, 733
Ferdinand, king of Spain, 675
Ferrara, xxv, xxvi, 21, 26, 27, 28, 34, 71, 138, 398, 399, 430f., 436ff., 440, 448, 458, 459, 482, 483, 519, 538, 677, 678, 700, 716, 726, 733, 745
  cathedral of, 398
  university of, 398, 399, 417, 430, 437f., 457, 459, 490, 519, 520, 525, 668, 672, 675, 699, 703, 710, 712, 717, 719, 725, 729, 735, 740, 743, 747, 765
  Ferrariensis scholari, 189
Fischart, Johann, 385
Flaccus (Horace), 17
Flaccus, Valerius, 588
Flach, Martin, of Basel, 718
Flach, Martin, Jr., 413, 718
Flach, Martin, Sr., xxx, 157, 411, 413, 414, 557, 612, 718
Flanders, 386, 538, 550, 703
  duke of, *see* Philip the Fair;
  counts of, 513, 728
  Flandrenses, 138
  Flemish, 538, 727
Flegetonta (Phlegethon), 44, 271, 310
Florence, 424, 436, 733, 747
Flüe, Nicolaus von, 116, 117f., 365, 523f., 713, 718, 722
Foederati, 36; *see* league of 1474
Foedus Clypei S. Georgij, 719
folklore: birth charms,
  Agnus Dei and pregnant Virgin, 74, 131, 486, 487f., 531, 556
  folk etymology, 605, 612
  formulae for never, 678 (N. 1729)
  golden apple, 162, 563
  phases of moon affecting health, 131, 531

prayer beads, 156, 161, 163, 556, 561, 563
propitious stars, 299, 668
unlucky animals, 299, 669
walnut having curative properties, 141, 541f.
see astrology, proverbs, riddles
Folz, Hans, 617
Forli (Italian town), 733
Formiani, 155
forum (forus) animae, 228, 229, 230, 231, 253, 623, 634
forum conscientiae, 226, 236, 249, 618, 623, 625
forum contentiosum, 104, 230, 233, 512
forum iudicale, 228, 230, 253, 624, 634
forum poenitentiale (poenitencie, poenitentiarij), 246, 252, 623
forum salutis, 230
forus publicus in ecclesia, 624
Franc (province of Belgium), 726
France, 10 (*Gallia*), 162 (*Galliam*), 386, 387, 403, 412, 413, 417, 418, 424, 466, 623, 640, 699, 718, 719, 722, 747, 751
  king of, xxix, 53, 54, 55, 56, 260;
  see Charles V, Charles VI, Charles VIII, Louis XI, Louis XIV
Franche Comté, 351, 386
Franciscans, Order of, 61, 135, 158, 169, 254, 369, 401, 471, 472, 536, 539, 558, 621, 635, 674, 707, 720, 735, 738, 739, 752, 762
  church at Rome, *see* Santa Maria de Araceli
  Observants, 39, 205, 453, 489, 633
Franco-Prussian War, *see* hostilities
Frankfurt, 493, 502, 504, 673, 706, 720, 727, 747, 750, 756, 782
  fair, 33, 440, 446, 571, 638
Fratres Minores, see Franciscans
Fratres Praedicatorum, see Dominicans
Frau Holle, 442
Frederick of Vaudemont, 738
Free Masons, Order of, 363, 388
Freia, 442
Freiburg i. B., 216, 619, 755, 763
  cathedral of, 735
  college at, 736
  Latin school at, 735
  university of, 394, 501, 503, 707, 709, 710, 721, 731, 732, 735f.,

859

739, 746, 749, 755, 757, 671,
  766, 770
Freising, 64, 76
  canon of, 719
Freitag von Düsseldorf, Johann,
  621
French, 9 (*Gallijs*), 54 (*Gallorum*),
  55, 56, 188 (*Gallos*), 491, 647,
  747
  churches, 238
  language, 704
  Revolution, see hostilities
Freundsberg, Ulricus von, see
  Fronsperger
Fridericus de Senis (glossator), 232,
  242
Friedrich III, emperor, 11; (*imperator*) 79, 80, 87, 138, 190;
  (*Cesar*) 139, 140; (*Grandevi patris*) 295; (*Imperatorio ductu* 296, 297, 299, 383, 385, 386, 408, 419, 449, 492ff., 500, 502, 553. 583f., 604, 662, 667, 669, 702, 703, 704, 710, 716, 717, 719, 727, 728, 739, 747, 770,
Friedrich, *Markgraf* of Baden, 703
Friedrich I, *Pfalzgraf*, 455, 515, 747
Friedrich Bibliopola, see Bibliopola
Friesenheimer, Daniel, 216ff., 423, 508, 619, 719
Friesland (Frisia), 745, 747
frigij viri (Phrygians), 310
Frischlin, Nicodemus, 660
Frisingensis (Freising, adj.)
Frixo, 271, 648
Fronsperger, Georg, 719
Fronsperger (Freundsberg, Fruntsberg), Ulricus, 34, 398, 516, 719, 729
Fronsperger, Ulricus (Ulrich), Sr., 719
Fuchs, Theobald, 38, 42, 62, 431, 452, 456, 474, 720, 730
Fuggers of Augsburg, 700, 729
Fulda, abbot of, 748
Funck, Engelhard (Scintilla), 38, 61, 81, 82, 94, 104, 408, 451, 472, 494f., 506, 513, 586, 712, 720, 768, 784
Fünfzehner, 384, 756
furor Theutonicus, 304, 671
Fürstenberg, Philipp, 332, 688, 720

Galen, 568f.
Galilee, 159, 559

Gallia, see France; *Gallij, Gallos*, see
  French
Gallinarius, Johann, 406, 762
Gallus, Jodocus, 313f., 383, 394, 416, 484, 500, 673, 681, 720f.
gambling, 29, 288, 290, 323, 441f., 602, 662, 687
Ganimedeis urnis (Aquarius, constellation), 272, 648
Gaul, 368, 542
Gebweiler (Alsatian town), 469, 713, 737
Gebweiler, Hieronymus, 369, 393f., 406, 656, 715, 750
Gebwiller, Protois, 544
Geiler, (Burchard?), 518, 721
Geiler von Kaysersberg, Johann,
  xii, xiii, xiv, xv, xxiii, xxiv,
  xxvi, xxvii, xxviii, xxix, xxx,
  xxxi, 18f., 21, 22, 26, 28, 30, 33,
  41, 52, 67, 76, 90, 91, 97, 109,
  113, 114, 115, 118, 120, 121,
  134, 138, 141, 142, 143, 144,
  145, 146, 147, 152, 153, 154
  (*doctorem nostrum*), 159, 164
  (*Doctor Caesarovius*), 172, 188,
  195, 205, 219, 251, 253, 262,
  273, 274, 278, 312, 322, 365,
  366, 369, 370, 372, 373, 374,
  377, 389f., 391, 392, 400, 401,
  405f., 407, 410, 411ff., 415, 419,
  421, 428ff., 430, 431, 433ff.,
  438f., 441ff., 447, 448, 455f.,
  460, 465, 475, 478, 489, 503,
  508, 516ff., 521, 522, 525, 527,
  529, 534ff., 538ff., 541, 542-
  549, 550, 553, 554f., 559, 563,
  572, 575, 580ff., 588ff., 599-
  608, 615, 616f., 618, 620f., 623,
  626, 629, 632f., 634, 641-644,
  645, 649ff., 661, 675, 679f.,
  686, 695, 701, 709, 718, 721ff.,
  725, 734, 745, 751, 752, 753,
  757, 758, 759, 760, 761, 762,
  764, 766, 769, 770, 771, 783,
  791-795, 802, 803, 806
  appointment as cathedral
    preacher at Strassburg, xxiii,
    xxix, 142f., 407, 421, 430, 439,
    441, 543f.
  ascetism, 443f.
  house and furniture, 134, 534,
    535 (bed), 804
  ideal bishop and ideal priest of,
    549
  library, 377, 722

860

mother of, *see* Zuber, Anna
offers elsewhere, 546
precepts for Schott, 18, 428
precepts for Zollern, 503, *see Monita*
reforms, xxviif., 145, 188, 205ff., 599-608
Rhenanus' description of, 433
secretary, xxix, 760
successors, 544
travels, 722
wit, 30, 143, 443f., 546
works, 401, 412, 428, 433, 527, 529, 530, 602, 608, 626, 644, 722, 752, 791-795
Geiler, Johann, Sr., 721
Gellius, 485
Gemagen, Georg von, 411
Gemini (constellation), 648
Gemmingen, Georg von, 500, 673
Generalis ordinis Predicatorum, 210, *see* Salvo Casseta
Geneva (city), 368
Gengenbach, abbey of, 706
Genius, 295, 666
Genoa (city), 368, 786, 787
Georg *der Reiche*, duke of Bavaria, 502
Georius, *Magister* (+1487), 112, 519f.
Georius, *Magister*, 139, 156, 163, 540
Georius (a *famulus?*), 197, 591
Georgius Ungarus, 24, 194, 436, 588, 724
Gerhardt, archbishop of Mainz, 403
German: Bible translations, 695f.
churches, 88, 515f.
language, xi, xx, xxif., 84, 107 (*barbare*), 357f.
words and phrases in Latin texts, xix, 29, 114, 165, 266, 321, 340
German nation (student association at the university of Bologna), 396f., 430, 490, 726, 736, 740, 743; *see Alemannia*
Germanic peoples, 646, 647, 654
soldiers, 295
Germans, xxviii, 164, 647, 655, 671, 673, 727, 751
king of, *see* Sigismund, emperor *and* Friedrich III, emperor,
Germany, xxviii, 9, 34, 71, 85, 87, 202, 296, 387, 417, 427, 440, 445, 481, 483, 492, 500, 587, 597, 598, 646, 663, 700, 701, 725, 733, 734, 745, 747, 750
universities of, 87, 501, 646
Germarsheim (town), 756
Geroldseck(*also* Geroldzeck), castle of, 258, 638, 699, 731, 758
family, 638; Walter von, 387; *see* Hoh-Geroldseck, Dietrich von
Gerson (village near Barby, Ardennes), 724
Gerson, Jean Charlier de, xxx, 11, 65 *and* 196 (*cancellarius*), 258ff., 392, 411ff., 414, 419, 475, 590, 636-640, 651, 724, 767
edition of xxx, 411ff.
grave of, 722
Gerson, Johann (Jean) de (prior of Celestines at Lyons, brother of above), 261, 412f., 641, 724
Gesa, Joannes Antonio de, 788
Gesler, Johann, xv, 266, 373f., 423, 432, 448, 481, 645, 724f.
Gessler (governor in *Wilhelm Tell*), 387
Gessler, Johann, 725
Getulo murice (Gaetulian dye), 333
Ghent, 363, 514, 538, 706, 749; duke of, 538
gifts, xxiv, 34, 44, 74, 116, 118, 136, 141, 147, 192, 206, 207, 389f., 391, 486, 487f., 506, 523, 525, 536, 541, 548f., 556, 563, 585, 603f., 608, 609, 610
to patients at baths, 425, 426 (N. 192)
glossators of civil and canon law, *see* Abbas; Abbas Siculus; Archidiaconus; Bartholomaeus Brixiensis; Bartolus de Saso; Bernardus; Buttrio, Anthonius de; Cardinalis; Fridericus de Senis; Goffredus; Hostiensis; Imola, Alexander de; Innocent III; Ligia, Paulus de; Ludovicus de Roma; Paludi, Petrus de; Panormitanus; Pisana; Raymundus; Richardus; Speculator; Tudeschi, Nicolas (Abbas Siculus), Vicentius.
Gnadental convent, 714
Gnosiace domine (Ariadne), 272, 648
Goethals von Gent, Heinrich, 641
Goetz, Johann, xv, xxxi, 139, 172, 374, 415, 540, 572, 725
Goffredus (glossator), 229
Gorgias of Leontini, 319, 684

861

Gorgoneum caput, 271
Gosseler, Johann, 481, 725
Gossenbrot, Sigismund, 191, 278, 374, 415, 448, 585f., 645, 650, 673, 685, 725
Gossenbrot, Sigismund the Younger, 725
Gracianus (Gratian), 223
 decretals of, 588
Graiam, 281
 Graiis, 308
 Graio, 268
Grain loans and mortgages, *see* case of
Grammar, question of, 215
Granser, Georg, 152, 552
 wife of, 152, 552
 sister-in-law of, 152, 552
gratia (papal), 401, 410, 411, 491, 494, 571, 573, 591f., 594
 gratia apostolica, 408f. (defined), 451
 gratia expectativa, 34, 35, 36, 46, 51, 68, 69, 75, 76, 78, 79, 409 (defined), 448, 450, 459f., 465, 478, 479, 488, 489, 491f., 598
Grau, Heinricus (Hagenau printer), 690
Grave, Laurencius, 12, 24, 37 (*altero L.*), 46, 49, 420, 421 (N. 170), 435, 450, 460, 463
Grecian Isles, 559
Greece, 559, 577, 677, 701, 729
Greek language, xiv, xv, xix, xx, xxi, xxv, xxvii, 9, 10, 17, 18, 62, 71, 72, 80, 83, 99, 117, 133, 158, 191, 192, 194, 248, 333, 371f., 374, 376, 393, 400, 417, 418, 427, 472 (Greek psalter), 483, 484, 485, 492f., 509, 523f., 559, 589, 588, 630, 655, 661, 667, 681, 682, 689, 700, 701, 720, 729, 738, 740, 745, 749, 750, 763
Greek typography, xiv, 352, 372, 375, 692, 753
 lacunae for, plates 2 and 3, xiv, xx, 98, 371 (N. 23), 372, 376 (N. 45), 509, 524, 584, 661, 667
Greeks, 646, 677
Gregory IX (pope), 251, 633
Gregory XII (pope), 640
Greifswald, university of, 501
Grenoble (town), 561

Gresemund, Theodoricus, 738
Gretzer, Johann, 457
Gröningen (Dutch town), 483f., 700
Groot, Gerhard de, 392
Groshug, Eucharius, 201, 202, 246ff., 448, 596, 630ff., 726
grosser Rat, 384
Grossgeroldseck castle, 638
Grummel (Grymmel), Nicolaus, 59, 198, 470, 592
Grünenworth (Strassburg island), 572
grüner Bruch (Strassburg marsh), 807
Grüninger, Johann (Strassburg printer), 372, 481, 744
Gualterus (Biel?), *Magister*, 155, 554, 555
Guarinus, 753
guilds, *see* Strassburg
gulta, ae (harvest), 227, 624
Gunzelin von Frankfurt, 389
Gurk (Klagenfurt), bishop of, 747
Gurk, Raymund von, *see* Peraudi
Gustavus Adolphus, 784

Hagen, Jacob, 45 (*decanus noster*), 50, 451, 459, 464, 726, 730
Hagenau (Alsatian town), 295, 385, 612, 666, 690, 753, 763
Hagenbach (town), 385
Hagenbach, Peter von, 386f., 654, 757
Halberstadt cathedral, 762
Hales, Alexander de, 641
Halewin, Walter de (van), xxv, 26, 105, 437, 513, 714, 726f., 742
Halewyn, Charles van, 726
Halewyn, Corneille van, 726
Halewyn, Jean van, 726
Hammelburger, Conrad, 455, 727, 749
Hammer, Hans, 390, 757
Hämmerlin, Thomas, *see* Kempis, Thomas à
Hämmerlin, Paul, *see* Malleolus, Paul
Han, Jacob, 673
Hannibal, 117, 524
Hapsburg, faction, 502
 house of, 727, *see* Friedrich III, Maximilian I, Sigismund (archduke of Austria)
Hapsburg, Albrecht von, duke of Austria, 727
Hapsburg, Catherine von, 703

862

Hapsburg, Ernst von, duke of Styria and Carinthia, 703, 727
Hapsburg, Friedrich von, 728
Hardegg, counts of, 710
Hartmann von Eppingen, Andreas, 95, 172, 214 (*vicar noster*), 215 (*domino Andree*)?, 219 (*vicar noster*), 369, 507, 572, 616, 618, 621, 723, 728
Haslach (Alsatian town), 711
Hassenstein, Bohuslaus von Lubkovitz, xi, xii, xiv, xxiii, xxv, xxvi, xxviii, xxxi, 28, 32, 42, 44, 62, 79, 107, 116, 118, 120, 121, 130, 159, 189, 192, 208, 215, 266, 267, 270, 298, 307, 308, 309, 310, 312f., 314-321, 365, 366, 369, 373, 374, 376, 382, 383, 391, 396, 398f., 401, 405f., 415f.,'417, 419, 422, 423, 424, 430, 431, 432, 437, 439, 440, 441, 446ff., 457ff., 461, 472f., 490, 491, 492, 514, 523-528, 530, 559, 577, 582ff., 585f., 607, 617, 645ff., 662, 668, 670, 673, 676ff., 679f., 681-685, 689, 699, 710, 714, 719, 725, 728ff., 737, 744, 745, 747, 751
  castle and estate of, 43, 116, 523, 525f., 728, 729
  epitaph for Büchsner, 711
  Hassenstein-Schott items in *Luc.*, XXf., 399; see *Luc.* letters, poems
  letter(s) to Sslechta, 415f. (tribute to Schott)
    to Geiler, 312f., 679ff.
  ode to Carlsbad, 730
  odyssey, xxv, xxvi, 159, 215, 399, 559, 577, 617
  trips to Strassburg, xxv, 79, 107, 398f.
Hassenstein, Jaroslaus von, 728
Hassenstein, Johannes von, 728
Hassenstein, Nicolaus von, 728
Hassenstein, Nicolaus, Jr., von, 728
Haut Barr (Hoh-Barr), 566
head of man covered or uncovered during prayer, 246ff., 630ff.
Hebrew (language), xx, 738, 750
Hecate, 442
Hector, 191, 192, 678
Hedion, Caspar, 544
Hees, Georg, see Georgius Ungarus
Hegius, Alexander, 392f., 484, 700, 701
Heidelberg (city), 497, 699, 750
  university of, xxviii, 71, 139, 157, 205, 218, 219, 332, 382, 390, 482, 483f., 501, 540, 545, 599f., 601f., 620f., 699, 700, 701, 705, 715, 720, 725, 726, 728, 730, 731, 732, 735, 737, 738, 744, 747, 749, 755, 760, 761, 764, 765, 766, 767, 771,
Heidenberg, Johann von, Sr., 764
Heidenberg, Johann, see Trithemius
Heinrich X, duke of Bavaria, 663
Heinrich, *Graf* of Württemberg, 769
Heinricus (*tabernarius* at Bologna), 191, 585
Heinricus (Erlebach? Moser?), 300, 301, 514
Heinricus Frisius, 669
Helen, 670
Helfenstein, *Graf* Johann von, 543, 771
Helias (Elijah), 321, 686
Helicon, Mt., 654, 688
Helicone, 281
Helycon. 269
Helio Hippias, 319; see Hippias of Elis
Hell, Anna, 730, 768
Hell, Johann, 451, 520, 726, 730, 768
Hell (Onheim), Johann, 38, 431, 451, 730
Hell, Laurencius, 47, 79?, 461, 492, 730f.
Hell, Nicolaus, 730, 768
Hellen, 271, 648
Helmstadt, Ludwig von, bishop of Spires, 242 and 258 (*Episcopus Spirensis*), 629, 638, 731, 784
Helvetian, 60, 116, 212 (*Eluecioruм*), 323, 687; synonymous with Alsatian, 613, 687
Hemonie (Thessaly), 280
Henne(n)berg, lords of, 761
Hennenberg, Berthold von, 500, 516, 673, 731
Hennenberg, Heinrich von, 135 (*dominus de H.*), 142, 150, 410, 500, 536, 544, 551, 580, 731
Henry V, king of England, 640, 712
Henry VIII, king of England, 699, 761
Henry, duke of Silesia, 737
Herbipolensis (Würzburg, adj.), 20

863

herbology, xxiv, 117, 132, 154f., 169, 198, 390, 523, 532, 538, 539, 552, 553, 556, 568f., 710, 750
   acorus, 169, 568
   aqua endivie, 132, 532
   aqua ysopi, 132, 532
   cardo, 169, 569
   herba fullonum, 169, 569
   mesa (cannabis), 132, 532
   syrupus acetosus, 132, 532
Hercules, 62 (*erumnis Herculeis*), 271 (*herculee fere*, Leo, constellation), 388, 646, 647, 648, 668, 677
heresy, 221, 223, 260 (*Pelagianorum*); see Hussites
Herlinsheim, church at, 238, 627
Hermann, bishop of Constance, 434
Hermann V, *Markgraf* of Baden, 430
Hermann of Swabia, 403
Hermes, 648
Hermits of St. William of Maleval, Order of the, 79, 105, 369, 413, 491, 492, 513, 728, 734
   monastery at Marienthal, 734
   at Strassburg, 492
Hermogenes, 268, 647
Hermus (river), 333
Herodias, 652
Hertzog, Laurentius, 12, 32, 33, 34, 37, 420, 421 (N. 172), 435, 446, 448, 450, 460, 463
Hesiod, 18, 44, 194, 332, 418, 427, 588, 688
Hess, Georg, see Georgius Ungarus
Hessmann, Jacob, 808
Hewen (Höwen), Heinrich von, 106, 514, 731
Heynlin a Lapide, Johann, xxv, 69, 366, 424, 479f., 518, 548, 731f., 749
Hibleo (*Hyblaeo*), 271
Hieronymo Doctori Medico, 139; also *doctorem Hieronymum*, 170; see Brunschwig, Hieronymus
Hieronymus, Count, 174; see Imola, Hieronymus de
Hieronymus Forocorueliensis (Foroliuiensis), see Imola, Hieronymus de
Hieronymus de Zanctivis, 77; see Zanctivis
Hiperion (Hyperion), 310
Hippias of Elis, 319, 684

Hippocrates, 166, 647
Hippocrenean spring, 646, 650
Hippolytus, 656, 669, 670
Hirsacensis (Hirsau, adj.), 151
Hirsau monastery, abbot of, 151, 552, 706
Hirtacides (Nisus), 309, 677
Hismarius (Orpheus), 267, 646
Historiae Vates (Livy), 10, 418
Hoffmann von Udenheim, Crato, 168f., 393, 568, 715, 732, 750
Hofmann, Craft, see Hoffmann, Crato
Hoh-Barr, 566
Hoh-Geroldseck, Dietrich von, 446, 638
Hohenburg, convent of, 754
Hohenzollern, castle of, 770
Hohkönigsburg, castle, 716
Holland, 386, 699, 746
Holy Land, 215, 617, 716, 731, 769
holy Roman emperor *or* empire, see emperor, empire
Holy Sepulchre, 513
Homer, 268, 271, 280, 295, 296, 297, 309, 646, 647, 653f., 667, 677
Honorius III (pope), 763
Honstein, Wilhelm von, bishop of Strassburg, 703, 714, 731
Horace, 17, 70, 71, 98, 100, 102, 160, 192, 194, 288, 296, 346, 354, 427, 439, 482, 484, 560, 585, 588, 660, 664, 667, 669, 676, 677, 691, 765
Horesti (Orestes), 270; *Horeste*, 272; *Horestem*, 298
Hornack, Burkard von, 718
Hörwart, Susanna, 401
Hostiensis (glossator), 217 (*Ostiensem*), 228, 229, 244 (*Ostiensem*), 245, 246, 249, 253
hostilities, 25, 27, 41, 44, 80, 95, 140, 148, 190f.
   assassination of Galeotti Manfredi, 540, 740
   assassination of Hieronymous Imola, 540, 732, 733
   French Revolution, xxii, 377, 378, 385, 404, 415
   Malvezzi conspiracy against Bentivoglios, 549
   Pazzi conspiracy against Medicis, 424
   Peasant War, 389
   Quarrel between Strassburg and

Zürich, *see* Püller von Hohenburg, Richard
sack of Mainz 1462, 733, 734
siege of Geroldseck, 638
siege of Rhodes, 306, 439, 675, 705, 713
student uprisings at Bologna, 77, 490f.; *Maluicii*, xxvi, 77
Wars: Archduke Sigismund vs. Venetians, 112, 712, 519, 743
Burgundian wars, xxiii, 269, 280, 356, 386f., 434, 701, 712, 749, 762, 778
captivity of Maximilian at Bruges and Flemish campaign, 138, 140, 514, 538, 540
civil and foreign wars in Italy 1478, 17, 423f.
Florence vs. Sixtus IV, Venice and Siena, 424
France vs. Milan, 424
France vs. Italians, 436
Franco-Prussian War, xxii, 377
Friedrich III vs. Matthias I of Hungary, 80, 493, 553
Innocent VIII vs. Naples and Hungary, 409
Lombards vs. Swiss, 363, 506, 786f.,
Thirty Years War, 784
Turks, 439f., 675, 712
Venice vs. Ferrara 1482, 458
World War II, xxii, 378, 663
Zürich and allies vs. Lombards, 363, 786f.
Höwen, Heinrich von, *see* Hewen
Hrabanus Maurus, 9(?), 499f., 635, 748
Hrotsvitha, 765
Hub (baths), 165, 564f.
Hugo, bishop of Constance, 741
Hugo, Johann, 394
Hugonis, Jacob, 709
humanism and humanists, xi, xii, xiii, xxv, xxviii, 34, 71, 105, 106, 121, 133, 155, 164, 191, 201, 363, 369f., 393, 423, 435, 439, 458, 482, 484, 500, 644, 650, 655, 658, 659, 670, 685, 701, 705, 712, 720, 725, 730, 732, 740, 745, 747, 748, 750, 751, 752, 766
humanistic gymnasium, 370
humanistic training, 755
humanistic societies: Augsburg, 699; Buda, 729; Schlettstadt, 732; Strassburg, 369, 725; Wittenberg, 729
Hund, Florentinus, 394
Hungary, 493f., 532, 574, 648, 653, 704, 707, 729, 732
king of, 80, 190, 279, *see* Hunyadi (Matthias), Emperor Sigismund, Vladislaus
Hungarian language, 763
Huns, 481, 669
Huntington, Henry E., Library and Art Gallery, x, xiv, xv, 19, 98
Hunyadi, János, 732, 740
Hunyadi, Matthias (Corvinus), 80 (*Pannoniorum Rege*), 190 (*Ungarum Regem*), 279, 406, 439, 449, 492ff., 583f., 648, 653, 707, 710, 727, 732, 740
Hupfuff, Mathias (printer), xix, xx, 372, 375, 376, 732f.
Hürnheim family, 700
Hus, John, 640, 648, 759, 802
Hussites, 44, 118, 120f., 260, 270, 272f., 458 (N. 379), 523, 525f., 647, 648, 653, 745, 759, 802
Hybleis (Hyblaeis), 303
Hymetus, 332
hymns, correcting of, 484

Iachum (Bacchus), 267, 646
Ida, Mt., 332
Idalium (city on Cyprus), 346
idololatrae, idolatrae, 133, 248, 533, 630
Ilium, 191
Ill (river), 368, 572, 601
illegitimate children of priests, 236f., 238, 625f.
illness, *see* medical references
Im Giessen (Strassburg watercourse), 637
"Imitaciunculae," *see* Luc., aphorisms
Imitatio Christi, xxxi, 413f., 735, 752
Immaculate Conception of the Virgin Mary, 577, 644, 673f.
Immaculists, 674
Imola (Italian town), 733
Imola, Alexander de (glossator), 242
Imola, Hieronymus de (Riario), 140, 174, 424, 540, 573, 732, 733
Imola, Iohannes de, 241, 243
in forma pauperum(-is), 34, 35, 36, 448, 450

865

India, 159, 559
indiction, 383, 419, 420 (explanation)
Indos (people of India), 289
indulgences, 215, 216, 380, 454, 515, 618, 735, 747
Ingold, Jacob, 755, 810
Ingolstadt, university of, 62, 473, 501, 716, 725, 750, 751, 765, 766
Ingweiler (Alsatian town), 752, 769
Inn (river), 719
Innocent III (pope, glossator), 221, 228, 243, 245, 246, 258, 512, 543, 803
Innocent IV (pope), 408f., 489, 728
Innocent VI (pope), 183, 578, 748
Innocent VIII (pope), 11, 86, 87, 88-90, 91, 176, 177, 186-188, 198, 216(?), 257, 383, 390, 409ff., 419, 491, 494, 498ff., 502, 544, 575, 580, 591, 598, 604, 619, 628, 637, 701, 703, 708, 711, 712, 714, 719, 729, 731, 733, 736, 747, 748
Innocentius (glossator), see Innocent III
inns: *ad auratum Leonem*, 311, 678, 708
ad Lunam, 149
St. Christopher, 149
zur Huoben, 165, 564f.
zum Rohraffen, 606
zum Ungemach, 114, 521
Innsbruck (city), 703, 727, 745
irreverence, acts of, *see* abuses
Isabella of Portugal, 712
Isenburg, Diether von, 213 (*Archiepiscopus*), 432, 515, 613f., 733f.
Isny (town), 744
Isocrates, 18, 29, 427, 439, 441, 483, 514
Italian language, 364, 704
Italian nation at the university of Bologna, 395f., 490
Italian(s), xxviii, 9, 25, 71, 188, 303, 304, 482, 647, 655, 670, 671, 682
Italy, xxv, xxvi, xxviii, xxxi, 10, 17, 22, 364, 367, 368, 370, 372, 381, 382, 392, 397, 399, 406, 415, 418, 421, 422, 423, 424, 425, 427, 428, 429, 439f., 457, 483, 516, 537, 538, 593, 610, 634, 649, 650, 655, 668, 670, 671, 675, 677, 679, 682, 683, 684, 695, 703, 705, 722, 743, 750, 769, 802
Ithaci vagi (Ulysses), 295, 297
Iuncensis (Jungingen?, adj.), 60
Iunonis pestifere (planet Venus?), 198, 592
stella Iunonis (planet Venus), 592
Iupiter, 267, 645
planet of, 299 (*sydus Iouis*), 668
ius precium primarium, 408

Jacob, *Markgraf* of Baden (Müller's charge, heir apparent of Baden), 50, 51, 60, 61, 62, 65, 66, 68, 69, 80, 95, 104, 111, 112, 113, 196, 424, 430, 463, 464, 470f., 472, 475, 479, 480, 492, 512, 519, 520f., 536, 557, 564, 589f., 609, 703f., 743f.
Jacob, chaplain to *Markgraf* Christoph of Baden, 66; *see* Keller, Jacob
Jacob I, *Markgraf* of Baden, 702
Jacob, *Magister*, prior of Knights of St. John, 173, 572
Jacob Minor, *Pater*, 139, 538f.
Janua (Genoa), 786
Jason, 648
Jenuowe (Genoa), 787
Jerusalem, 658, 675, 705
Jesuits, 544; college of, 730
Jezebel, 652
Joannes de Aragonia, *see* Aragonia
Johann (husband of Elizabeth), 103, 512
Johann, canon of Eichstätt, 43, 457
Johann, duke of Bavaria (son of Albrecht II), 704
Johann, duke of Bavaria (Johann VI, *praepositus* of Strassburg grand chapter), 49, 463, 478, 705
Johann, messenger, 110, 517
Johann, protégé of Schott, 107, 112, 515
Johann Friburgensis, *see* Teutonicus
Johann von Pfalz, 747
Johann von (de) Strassburg, *see* Teutonicus
Johann Teutonicus, *see* Teutonicus
Johannes, bishop of Basel, 385
Johannes Germanicus, 305, 672
Johannes *titulus Sanctae Sabine*

presbiter, 176, *see* Aragonia, Johannes de
John VIII (pope), 465
John XXII (pope), 578
John XXIII (deposed pope), 640
John the Fearless, duke of Burgundy, 261 (*Principis potentissimi*), 640, 712, 724
John the Good, duke of Burgundy, 712, 751
Jörger, Johann (Hans), 60, 471, 734, 739, 758
Jörger, Nicolaus, 728
jubilee year, 216, 515, 619
Judas Iscariot, 734
Julianus, victory over *Alemannii*, 368
Julius II (pope), 409, 712, 730
Jung, Sebastian, 808
Jungingen (town), 471
  church of, 60, 471, 739
Juno, 271, 301, 648, 669, 672
Jupiter Capitolinus, 489
Justinian, emperor, 14, 24, 422, 588
Juvenal, 99, 102, 128, 290, 291, 293 297, 509, 511, 530, 662, 663, 665, 667

Kagen, Nicholaus, Pater, 201, 595, 734f.
Kaiserstuhl (mountain), 717
Kalocsa, archbishop of, 763
Kammerer, Wolff, 193, 587
Kaniel, Emericus de, *see* Kemel, Emerich
Karl III (the Fat), emperor, 465
Karl I, *Markgraf* of Baden, 702, 703, 749
Karl, *Markgraf* of Baden, bishop of Utrecht, 703, 749
Karl, *Markgraf* of Baden, *custos* of Strassburg grand chapter, 165, 427, 565, 704
Katherine of Lorraine, 702
Katzenellenbogen, Ottilie von, 703
Kauffman, Johann, 143, 545
Kaysersberg (Alsatian town), 385, 444, 721, 757, 771
Keller, Jacob, 66, 113, 476, 520f., 735
Keller, Johann, 152, 553
Kemel, Emerich, xiii, xxvii, 39f., 76, 204, 205ff., 401, 423, 453f., 489, 573, 599-608, 615, 633, 714, 735, 738
Kempen (town on the Yssel), 735
Kempis, Thomas à, xxx, 262, 392f., 411, 413f., 639, 641, 715, 735
Kerer, Johann, 95, 114; (*Doctor Friburgensis*) 29, 30, 146; 366, 408, 442, 443, 444, 507, 520, 521, 547, 550, 735f., 739
Kessler, Nicolaus (Basel printer), 413
Kestler, Bartolomeus (printer), 481
Kilianus Herbipolensis, 20, 21, 429
Kistler, Bartolomeus (Strassburg printer, same as Kestler?), 725
Klein, Johann, 51, 68, 75, 76 (*pro illo*), 79, 465, 479, 488f., 491f., 736
Klein-Arnsberg, castle of, 699
kleiner Rat, 385
Kleingeroldseck, castle of, 638
Klingenthal (town), 713
Klitsch von Rixingen, Johann, 77 (*pueri mei?*), 85, 107, 112, 160, 162, 207, 406f., 490, 498, 515, 519f., 560f., 562, 608, 736
Kniebs, Nicolaus, 370
Knights of St. John the Baptist of Jerusalem, Order of, 173, 201, 202, 454, 572, 596, 675, 717 (*tutores*), 723, 725, 735, 759
  Strassburg monastery, 279 (*templo*), 572
Knights of St. William of Aquitania, Order of, 492
Knobloch, Barbara von, 465
Knoblochtzer, Heinrich (printer), 481
Knoblouch, Johann (printer), 413, 718
Koburger, Anton (Nürnberg printer), 541, 617, 702
Koelhoff, J. (Cologne printer), 413
Kolb, Matthias, 60, 66, 69, 113, 198, 471, 478, 480, 521, 592, 736f.
Kolbeck von Freisingen, Christian, 408
Kölle (Cöllen), Katharina, 714
Königreichen (dramas), 608
Königsbach, *also* Künigsbach, Melchior, *see* Kungsbach
Konrad, bishop of Strassburg, 637
Krakow, university of, 751
Krebs von Anspach, 389
Kreutzer, Johann, 543, 713
Kuhn, Nicolaus, 408

Kulm (Silesian town), 393
Kungsbach, Melchior, 112?, 171, 173, 520, 571, 572, 701, 737
Kuttolsheim (Alsatian village), 718

Labyrinthus, 192
Lacene (Helen), 302
Lachesis (a Fate), 44
Laci- (*Lati-*, adj.), 267, 271, 304, 308, 310
    Lacium, 268
    laciare, 304
Lactantius, 322, 683, 686
lacunae, *see* Greek typography
Ladislaus of Veszprém, 28, 34, 189, 191, 207 (Amicus N.), 398, 399, 440, 441, 448, 458, 490, 582f., 608f., 729, 737
Laelius, 647
Laflo (Dutch town), 700
Lahr (village), 638
Lampacher, *also* Lamparter, Lamperthen, Lampertius, Thomas, *see* Lampertheim
Lampertheim, Thomas, 56f., 85 (*Magistrum Thomam?*), 468, 498, 547, 616, 737f., 763, 764
Landau (town), 385
Landeck, Johann, 154, 554
Landsperg, Heradis von, 754
Lang, Rudolph, 613
Langen, Hans, 256, 636
Laodomia, 302
Lapicida, *also* Lapicida de Argentina, Gangolphus, *see* Steinmetz
Lapide, Johann à, *see* Heylin
Larentalia, 666
lares, 309
Last Sacrament for condemned, *see* case of
Latin, xi, xxf., xxivf., xxviii, xxx, 18, 71, 107, 282, 313, 333, 363, 655f., 671, 689, 704, 720, 722, 732, 738, 745, 754, 760, 765, 766, 771, 810
Latium, 367, 646, 701
Lauber, Jakob (printer), 732
Laudenburg, Johann, 12 (Sartoris?), 40, 158, 421, 484, 558, 722, 738
Laudenburg, Peter Boland, 673
Lauffen (on the Neckar), 716
Lauingen (on the Danube), 701
Laurencius, 24, 46, *see* Grave

Laurencius (the subject of a barbed elegiac), 304f.
Laurentius (possibly L. Hell), 79, 491f.
Lauri von Vingen, Martin, 34, 35, 36, 37, 215 (*plebanus Sancti Thome?*), 448, 449, 450
"laus Gersonis," *see Luc.*, eulogy of Gerson
law, canon and civil, *see* advice, case, opinion, question, testimonials, Strassburg laws
League Decapolis, 385
League of 1474, 385 (N. 72), 449, 455f., 471, 583, 585
legal problems, *see* law
Leimer, Georg, 808
Leipzig, 377, 753; university of, 501, 716, 725, 731
Leli (Laelius), 270, 647
Lent, xxvi, 242, 358, 433f., 438, 544, 628, 635, 694, 701, 778, 805
    Lenten foods, xxvi, 22, 433, 701
    see fasting, *also* fat and lard
Leo (constellation), 533, 648
Leo IX (pope), 403
Leonardus, 82, *see* Sturm, Leonard
Leonhardus, magister, 132, 133, *see* Wirt
Leonora of Portugal, 727
Leontarius, *also* Leontorius, Conrad, xiv, 146, 311, 373, 416, 432, 548, 673, 679, 702, 738
Letter(s), bearers of, 440, 490
    Geiler to Trachenfels, 806
    Hassenstein to Geiler (1507), 802
    Hassenstein to Sslechta, 415f.
    in *Epithoma*, 332
    in *Luc.*, XXIIf. (alphabetical list)
    manuscript letters, 363, 365, 776-778, 780-783
    of same content to same person, 490f.
    Sforza letters, 363f., 785-790
    to Anna, xi, 357f., 364f., 374, 377, 684, 694ff., 775-779
Leyden, *see* Louvain
Lhuillier, Johannes, 474
Liber (Bacchus), 272, 648
Liber de homine, 194, 588
Liber rerum memorabilium, 25, 436
library: (1) of fifteenth century:
    at Bologna, xxx, 597
    at Buda, 732, 740

at New St. Peter, 377, 403
at Old St. Peter, 377, 403
at monastery of Strassburg Dominicans, 578
at monastery of Strassburg Knights of St. John of Jerusalem, xxii, 572, 779
at Spires cathedral, 500
at Strassburg cathedral, 377, 410
Geiler's, 377, 722
Hassenstein's, 473, 729, 748;
Heynlin's, 732
Paul Munthart's, 744
Rusch's, 597,
Simmler's, 759
Jacob Sturm's, 761
Thomas Wolf, Sr.'s, 768
(2) of later centuries:
Strassburg city Library (before 1870), 365, 377, 754, 779
see Vatican Library, Uppsala university library
Licaonius custos, 307 (here, perhaps Ursa Minor)
Lichtenberg, nobles of, 752, 761
Liechtenstein, counts of, 719
Liechtenwerth (town), 719
Liége (town), 712, 746; university of, 761
Ligia, Paulus de (glossator), 243
Linage, *see* Lyningen
Lindenfelser, Johann, 808
Linz (Austrian town), 727
Lipsius, Iustus, 432, 434
Livy, 10 (*Historie Vates*), 202, 418, 514, 597
Löbel, Peter, 752
Locher, Jacob, 676
Lombard, Peter, xxx, 557, 578, 588, 764
Lombards, 363, 506, 786f.
London, 761
Longovico, Helisabet von, 764
Lorraine, 385, 386, 387, 738
duke of, *see* Charles I, Nicholas, Reinhardt
Lothar, 449
Lotharingia, *also* Lothoringia (Lorraine), 190, 386, 562
Louis XI king of France (*Rex Francorum*), xxix, 53, 54, 55f., 363, 385, 386f., 427, 466ff., 717, 719, 738, 749, 751, 758
Louis XIV, king of France, 368, 388
Louis, duke of Orléans, 640, 712
Louvain, 370

university of, 700, 726
Löwenberg (town), 738
Lowlands, 392, 448, 498, 520, 538, 608, 623, 708, 727, 736
Lübeck, 735
Lubkovitz, Bohuslaus von, *see* Hassenstein
Lucan, 99, 102, 103, 265, 271 (*Annei Vatis*), 280, 303 (*Asirei Vatis?*), 393, 509, 511, 643, 644, 648, 653f., 670, 671
Lucelsteinus, Gangolyphus, *see* Steinmetz
Lucian, 483, 648
Lucretius, 342, 348, 352, 690, 691, 692, 693
Lucubraciunculae (Luc.), frontispiece, xxi, xxii, xxiii, xxv, xxvii, 365, 366, 367, 370ff., 380, 381f., 385, 401, 413, 416, 418, 420, 425, 431, 433, 452, 493, 496, 613, 649, 673, 675, 679, 685, 686, 687, 710, 738, 767, 775, 783, 784f.
alphabetical index according to category, XXIIff.
aphorisms from Geiler's sermons ("imitaciunculae"), xv, xxvii, 262-266 (text), 401, 444, 527, 529, 641-644, 722
canon and civil law items, list of, XXIVf.
dialogue between Biel and Schott, 249ff. (text), 632f.
eulogy of Gerson ("laus Gersonis"), xxx, 11, 258-261 (text), 412f.
Hassenstein-Schott items, chronological list of, XXf.
letters, list of, XXIIf.
orations, list of, XXV
petitions, list of, XXV
poems

(1) Hassenstein-Schott
Hassenstein in defense of Schott, 308f., 676f.
Hassenstein lamenting Schott's departure, 309f., 677f.
Hassenstein on his illness, 44, 438
Hassenstein on his love for Schott, 310f., 676
Hassenstein on Schott's return to Strassburg, 310, 678

869

Hassenstein to a rival of Schott, 307f., 676
Hassenstein to Schott, 267, 646; 270ff., 647ff.
Schott to Hassenstein, 267, 645; 267ff., 646f.; 298 (*re:* *Epithoma*), 668

(2) for Strassburg schoolboys, xxviii, 281-298, 655-667
asclepiad to St. Peter on Maximilian's captivity, 295ff., 667
elegiac for end of year 1487, xxxi, 292f., 664f.
elegiac for end of year 1488, 293f., 665
elegiac for schoolboys of Sts. Peter and Michael, 281f., 655f.
elegiac on harshness of man's lot, 283, 675
elegiac on inconstancy of human affairs, 285f., 658
elegiac to Friedrich von Zollern (1485), 286f., 685f.
elegiac to St. Nicholas, 282f., 656
elegiac to St. Peter (1486), 287, 659
elegiac to St. Peter (1487), 249f., 665f.
elegiac written in Hagenau, 295, 666
encomium to Strassburg, xxxi, 287ff. (text), 415, 659f., 683
prophetic poem, 283f., 657
to Friedrich von Zollern (1486), 292, 664
to St. Nicholas (1485), 284f., 657f.

(3) other poems by Schott
an abusive elegiac, 303f., 671
"de tribus Iohannibus," xii, xxxi, 11, 273f. 274ff. (text), 278f. 367, 374, 412, 415, 444, 448, 585, 649ff.
distich against threats, 304, 671
distich on death, 307, 676
elegiac against a German-Italian, 303, 670
elegiac against vices of the Germans, 304f., 671f.
elegiac on death of Agricola, 281, 654f.
elegiac to a certain Johannes, 305, 672
elegiac to Bartolomaeus Favensis, 305, 672

elegiac to Wimpheling, 280, 653f., 784
epithalamium for Matthias of Hungary and Beatrice of Naples, 279, 653
first poem (Latin version of Dringenberg's proverb), 266, 644
hexastich on Wimphelling's poem to the Virgin, 306, 672ff.
lines composed for a poor lad to Heinrich von Hennenberg, 150, 551
lines following collophon, 325, 687
on the collapse of the temple of St. Ulrich, 288f., 669
on the siege of Rhodes, 306, 675
riddles for Rusch, 150, 550f.
sapphic in response to Heinrich, 301ff., 670
tetrastich (against an enemy), 304, 671
tetrastich against an Italianized German, 304, 671
tetrastich against a shameful epigram (*re:* Galeotus Marcius) 305f., 672
tetrastich on Death, 307, 676
tetrastich on Death speaking to man, 307, 675f.
tetrastich on the eight fruits of the virtuous soul, 306, 674f.
to Georg Erlebach, 298f., 668f.

(4) poems by others
an old proverb, 321, 685
distich by Wimpheling, 10f., 418; 11, 418; 321f., 685f.
elegiac by Gallus on the death of Schott, 313f., 681
elegiac by Wernher on canonical hours, 321, 685
epitaph for Schoot by Wimpheling, 10, 418
poetic invitation to Schott by Reuchlin, 311, 678f.
sapphic to Schott by Heinrich, 300, 669f.

quotable passages from *Luc.*, 811
registrum operis, 325ff.
table of contents, 3ff.
text, 9-325
treatise on Christian life (*opusculum de vita Christiana*),

870

xxvf., 121-130 (text), 322, 399, 401, 527-531, 644, 686, 689, 729, 761, 784
Ludersheim (village near Nürnberg), 751
Ludovicus Aquilanus Episcopus, 176, see Burses, Ludovicus de
Ludovicus de Roma (glossator), 223
Ludovicus, Doctor, 151, 552
Ludwig of Mainz (*principis Bauarij*), 107, 515
Ludwig, duke of Bavaria and count of Veldenz, 515
Ludwig, *Graf* von Zweybrücken, 478
Ludwig, son of Philipp II of Palatine, 765
Lugdunensis (Lyons, adj.), 261
Lullus, Raymond, 641
Luna (moon), 133, 442, 533
  ad Lunam (inn), 149
Lupercalia, feast of, 666
Luscinius, Ottmar, 406
Luther, Martin, 606, 695, 706, 729
Lutheran(s), 381, 404, 411, 544, 714, 722
Lützelstein, Gangolph, see Steinmetz
Luxembourg, 386, 703
  ruling family of, 758
Luzern, canton of, 434; city of, 455
Lybiaeque (Libya), 711
Lycambeo sanguine, 304
Lydius, 289
Lyei (Bacchus), 287, 289, 661
Lyningen, counts of, xxix, 53, 54, 55, 56, 57. 467f., 505, 738
  Friedrich (+ 1470), 738
  Friedrich (*fl.* 1669), 738
  Han, 55, 738f.
  Johann, 738
  Wecker, 55, 738f.
Lyons, 577, 722; archlishop of, 260, 412f., 641, 762
Lysippus, 150, 281, 551, 655f.

Maas (river), 747
Macedonia, 647, 678
Maculists, 674
Maeler von Memmingen, Vitus, xxv, xxx, 20f., 23f., 25f., 28, 31f., 34f., 36, 39, 45f., 48f., 50, 51, 60f., 64f., 67f., 69, 75, 76, 78f., 81, 82, 83, 84, 94f., 103ff., 108f., 110, 111, 137f., 139f., 145, 156f., 198, 199ff., 209 (#191)?, 398, 401, 411, 423, 428, 429, 431, 435, 436ff., 440, 443, 445f., 448f., 450, 452, 453, 454, 459f., 464f., 471f., 472, 475, 478, 479, 480, 488f., 491, 494ff., 506, 512f., 515f., 518f., 536, 537, 540, 549, 557, 575, 586f., 593ff., 600, 610, 686, 712, 724, 739, 765
Maenads, 670
Magdalena veterana, 60, 471
Magdalenes, 401, 722, 759
Mage, Peter, see Müg, Peter
magister scabinorum (mayor), 196, 384, 416, 575
Magisterciuium (mayor), 176
Magunciacum (Mainz), 158
Mahomethei Imperij sedem, 159
Maichingen (town in Württemberg), 445, 766
Maifeld (in the Eifel), 614
  monastery of (*Magnensiae*), 614
  Minstermeyfelt, 213
Mainz, 77, 107, 158, 216, 372, 474, 489, 561, 613, 619, 706, 738, 731, 733, 734, 748, 771; archbishop-elector of, 499, 673, aee Adolf I of Nassau, Albrecht Ernst of Saxony, Berthold von Hennenberg, Diether von Isenburg, Gerhardt, Hrabanus Maurus
  cathedral of, 614
  canon of, 703, 731, 733
  chapter of, 499f., 673
  preaching chair of, 474, 543, 706, 758
  diocese of, 213, 614
  university of, 733
Mäler, Veit, see Maeler, Vitus
Malleolus, Paul, 160, 161f., 560f., 562, 739f., 741
Malleolus, Thomas, see Kempis
Mals (town), 703
Malvezzi family, 549; conspiracy of, see hostilities
Malvezzi, Giovanni, 549
Malvezzi de Medici, Josepho Maria, 491
Malvezziis, Pyrro de, 491
Malvicijs, see hostilities, student uprising
Mamotrectus, 194, 588
Manfredi, Frederico, 740

871

Manfredi, Galeotti, 140 (*alterum Fauenciae*), 540, 740
Manilius, M., *Astronomicon*, 648, 677, 691
Manlius, Antonius, xxv, 79f., 83, 95, 392, 405, 492ff., 506, 592, 740
Mantua, 305
  university of, 740
Marcius, Galeotus, 305f., 588, 740
Margaretha, wife of Philipp II of Palatine, 760
Margarita Jacoba, Domina, 26, 437 730
Margarita facetiarum, Geiler author of, 444
Margarita Pavonis (university of Pavia), 25
Marienthal (in the Rheingau), 393, 706; (in Alsace), 734
Maronem (Vergil), 267, 282 (*Maronis*), 305 (*Marone*)
Marpesian rock, 429
marriage, case of dispensation or consanguinity, *see* case
Mars, 95, 121, 130, 268, 288, 294, 295, 297, 388
Mars, Peter, 740
Marseilles, 722
Martial, 103, 208, 441, 511, 512, 610, 648, 654
Martin V (pope), 453, 640, 713
Martinus, Magister, 215, 616
Martius (*also* Marzi, Marzio), Galeottus, *see* Marcius
Mary, duchess of Burgundy, 386f., 537, 727
Mary Magdalene, Petrarch's poem to, 375, 722, 784
  Zasius' poem to, 375
masks, 145, 287, 288, 602, 607, 659, 660
Mater Ecclesia, 181, 577
Mater Fridrichen, 41, 456
Mathias, *Magister*, 198; *see* Kolb, Mathias
Matho (Medone, Methoni, Modon), 559, 577
  bishop of, 181, 182, 185, 746; *see* Ortwin
  Mathonensis (Matho, adj.)
Matthias I, king of Hungary, *see* Hunyadi, Matthias
Matugliano, Anthonius de (*Mercator*), of Bologna, 193, 587
  brother of, in Venice, 193, 587

Maulbronn (Württemberg), monastery and abbot of, 738
Maykon, François de, 641
Maximilian I, king of the Romans, later emperor, xxiv, 90 (*Regie Maiestatis*), 137, 138, 139, 140, 148, 167, 168, 169, 170, 295ff., 386f., 391, 393, 402, 406, 408, 477, 502ff., 516, 520, 537, 538, 549f., 567, 568, 582, 589, 598, 667, 702, 710, 727, 731, 732, 736, 739, 742, 747, 750, 754, 760, 769, 770, 771, 810, 812, captivity at Bruges, 138, 140, 295ff., 537f., 540, 667, 703, 705, 722, 725
  coronation as king of the Romans at Aachen, 502, 503f., 750, 770
Meandros (*Maeandros*), 268
Mechinger, Johann, *see* Widmann
Medea, 669
medical references
  arthritis, 74f.
  bath regimen, 425f. (dangers of, medical supervision of, medical tracts on)
  bleeding, xxxi, 73 (hepatic and cephalic veins), 114, 172, 487, 521
  fever, 40, 312f., 711
  health and astrological phenomena, 29, 133, 198, 442, 533, 592
  hydratiform moles and miscarriage, 96, 131, 508, 531
  illness, 31, 38, 41, 42, 44, 47, 48, 49, 69, 72-76 (*passim*), 84, 96, 110, 113, 114, 131, 132, 133, 135, 136, 137, 149, 151, 156, 160, 161, 163, 165, 168, 169, 172, 189, 198, 208, 214, 312f., 392, 454, 458, 461f., 463, 464, 496f., 517, 521, 531, 536, 550f., 554, 556, 560, 563, 564f., 569, 582f., 609, 616, 680, 717
  kidney or bladder stones, 131, 135, 156
  medical profession likened to a treadmill, 164, 563
  midwives organized, 766
  physicians, *see* Hieronymus Brunschwig, Andreas Oudorp, Johann Widmann, Leonhard Wirt
  works on curative properties

872

of spa waters, 425f.
on plague, 766
on surgery, 711
on syphilis, 710, 766
plague, xxvi, xxvii, xxxi, 17, 21, 27, 44, 45, 67, 171, 197, 198, 283, 284, 313, 381, 382f., 397, 402, 405, 415, 423f., 427f., 430, 438, 459, 477, 478, 542, 544, 560, 565, 566, 569, 570, 571f., 584, 591, 593, 674, 681, 710, 720, 728, 759, 765, 766, 805, 810
  medication for, 166, 565
  plague powders, 169 (*puluere Materno*), 198, 566, 591
  symptoms of, 172, 572
purging, 114, 132, 136, 426, 521, 537
sanitation reform urged in Strassburg, 766
sympathetic medicine: birth charms, 74, 131, 486, 487f., 531, 537, 556
  prayer beads, 156, 161, 163, 556, 561, 563
  apple, 162, 563
  walnut, 141, 541f.
syphilitic patients excluded from hospitals, 602
tertian fever, 48, 72ff., 76, 84, 132f., 464f, 468f., 488, 489, 496f., 531ff.
  prescription for, 132, 532
  symptoms of, 73, 486f.
typhus, 114 (?), 521
see herbology
Medici, 424, 491, 733; Julian, 733; Lorenzo, 733
Medone, Methoni, Modon, *see* Matho
Medos, 289
Medusa, 267, 646
Meier, Johann, 394
Meiger, Johann, 95, 741
Meissen (town), 197, 591
Melchior, *Magister*, 112, 520
Melchior, baron of Limberg, 725
Meisterlin, Sisgismund, 725
Meler *or* Meller, *see* Maeler
Melethei (Homer), 271
Melanchthon, Philipp, 729, 760, 761
Melk, monastery of, 724
Memmingen (Bavarian town), 740, 765
Menala (*Maenala*), 102

Meneciades (Patroclus), 309, 677
Menelae, 273
Menin (Flemish town), 726
menses ordinarius (*or ordinariorum*) and *menses papales*, 66, 76, 198, 204, 409 (defined)
Mentelin (Mentel), Johann, 371, 695, 718, 752, 755
Mentelin, Salome, 752, 755, 808
Mentorei calices (cups made by the artist Mentor), 333, 688
Meonia (*Maeonia*, Lydian), 295, 296
  Meonides (Homer), 268, 280, 296, 309, 646, 677
Mercurius, 271, 296, 299, 647
  ad diem Mercurij Iouisue, 114
Merseburg (town), 719
Merswin, Jacob, 706
Merswin, Rulmann, 572
messenger (*nuntius*), 103, 111, 141, 169, 171, 195, *see* Letter(s), bearers of
Messinger, Jacob, 492
Metz, 711; diocese of, 467, 735
Meuchinger, Johann, *see* Widmann
Meyer, Jacob, 370
Meyger, Johann, 12, 421, 741
Meyger, Johann, 95 (Meiger), 162, 561, 562, 741
Michael (messenger), 117, 524
Mieg, *see* Müg
Milan, 363f., 424
  cathedral of, 364, 788f.
  fabrica of cathedral, 364
  Sforza letters from, *see* Letter(s)
  university of, 705
miles auratus, *see* eques auratus
Minerva, 144, 268, 271, 280, 281, 303, 654, 762
Mingelheim (Mindelheim, town), 719
ministra tua, 67, *see* Elisabeth
Minor, *Pater* Jacob, 139, 538f.
minor canons, 408, 451
Minstermeyfelt, 213, *see* Maifeld
Misnensis (Meissen, adj.), 197
Mittelhain (village near Wiesbaden), 720
Mnestheus, 291
Möchinger, Johann, *see* Widmann
Modena (Italian town), 764
Moguncia (Mainz)
  Moguntinensis (adj.), 210
Mohammed II, sultan, 439f., 675

873

Mohammedan, 675
Molitor(is), Johann, see Müller
Mollisheym (town), 10
Molossi, 150
Monaco (Munich), Christoph von and Wolfgang von, 138; see Christoph and Wolfgang, dukes of Bavaria
money (currency), 12, 29, 32, 34, 35, 36, 37, 39, 40, 46, 49, 51, 65, 68, 69, 75, 77, 78, 104 (*per cambium*), 105, 107, 108, 112, 113, 134, 135, 136, 143, 152, 156, 158f., 162f., 163 (weights), 165, 171, 188 (false weights), 193, 194, 196, 198, 200, 206, 216, 217, 226, 232, 247, 262, 386f., 390, 392, 394, 396, 397, 402, 403, 404, 416, 434, 446, 448, 449, 458, 460, 465, 476, 480, 490, 512, 513, 515, 519, 535, 536, 553, 554, 560, 563, 565, 566, 568, 590, 591, 595, 603, 619f., 622ff., 663, 712, 730, 734, 735, 747, 751, 757, 759, 771, 808
  bursaries, 736, 739
  Franciscans' use of money, 158, 558
  regular rate of interest 21%, 227
  Strassburg money and its relative value, 812
Monita Joannis Geileri ad Fridericum, comitem de Zollern, 428, 433, 527, 529, 530, 626, 644, 722, 791-795 (text)
Morat, 654
Mosbach, Johann von, 502
Moser, Heinrich, xxv, 106f., 300ff.(?), 398, 399, 448, 514, 669, 741
Mount Agnes (near Zwolle), 393
Mug, see Müg
Müg, Daniel, 459, 755, 810
Müg, Florencius, 85, 105 (*hos fratres*), 188, 255, 256, 459, 498, 514, 582, 636, 741f., 755, 810
Müg, Florencius, Jr., 755, 810
Müg, Jakob, Jr., 741, 755, 765, 810
Müg, Jakob, Sr., 171, 571, 714, 741f., 765
Müg, Ludovicus (Ludwig), 85, 105 (*hos fratres*), 498, 582, 742, 810
Müg, Maria, 755, 810
Müg, Matthäus, 741, 742

Müg, Peter (son of Florencius, Sr.), 459, 755, 810
Müg, Peter, Jr., 171, 571, 742
Müg, Peter, Sr., 613, 741
Müg, Veronica, 755, 810
Mülhausen (town), 216f. (*Mulhusen*), 385, 619, 741, 742
Müllenheim, Theobald von, 390, 744
Müller, Johann, von Rastetten, xxiv, xxvi, xxvii, xxx, xxxi, 12, 13, 17f., 20, 24, 29, 35, 36, 46, 47, 49, 50, 51, 59, 61, 62, 65, 68, 69, 76, 78, 79, 80, 82, 83, 84, 92, 91, 92, 94, 95, 104, 111, 112f., 137, 138, 139, 140, 151, 157, 165, 166-168, 169, 171, 193, 194, 195, 196, 197, 199, 315, 357, 363, 368, 382, 391, 394, 395, 396f., 404, 405, 408, 409f., 411, 420ff., 424, 425ff., 429, 435, 436, 440, 441, 443, 449, 450, 453, 454, 459f., 461, 462f., 464, 470f., 464, 470f., 472f., 475ff., 479f., 489, 491, 492, 494ff., 502, 503, 504f., 507, 512, 516, 519, 520f., 537, 538, 539, 540, 551, 557, 560, 564-568, 569-572, 587-592, 593, 598, 672, 682, 683, 695, 703, 709, 713, 728, 734, 736, 741, 742ff., 749, 751, 760, 777, 780, 781, 782
  benefice, 477 (N. 527)
  canonicate at Old St. Peter, 165-172, 564-568, 569-572
  nephew, 66, 475, 476
  treatment by Christoph I of Baden, 476f. (N. 526)
Mülnheim, Theobald (Diebolt) von, 133, 533, 744
Münster (city), 385
Munthart, Conrad, 48 (*Prepositum*), 462, 464, 744, 753
Munthart, Jacob, 744
Munthart, Paul, 409, 744, 753
Murner, Thomas, 425, 606, 707
Murrho, Sebastian, 394
Musée de l'oeuvre de Notre Dame, 364, 387f., 663
Muse(s), 267, 269, 271, 295, 300, 305, 306, 310, 311, 332, 646, 647, 650, 654, 667, 669, 672, 678, 679, 688
music, xxiv, 48, 237f. (singing in choir, French style), 281 (3-part harmony), 462, 604, 607,

626f., 656, 661
Myra, bishop of, 288, 658, see St. Nicholas
Myrensis (Myra, adj.)
mysticism, 259f., 261, 638

Naaman, 321, 686
Nachtigal, Ottomar, 493
Nancy, 69 (*Nanseyum*), 480
　battle of, xxviii, 387, 432, 645, 647, 653, 654, 736, 758
Naples, 409, 424, 653
　king of, see Ferdinand of Aragon
　Beatrice of, see Beatrice of Aragon
Narni (Italian town), 740
Nassau, Adolf von, see Adolf von Nassau
nations, university students' associations, 710
　see *Alemannia* nation and German nation
Navarre (la) college at Paris, 724
Nazareth, 159, 559
Near East, xxv, 366, 399, 559, 710, 729
Neckar (river), 426, 598
Neguiler, Johann, 69f., 480ff., 744
Nemesis, 271, 647, 648
Nemetensis (Spires, adj.), 332, 771
Nemi (lake), 647
Nerea Delphin, 289
Nestor, 648
Netherlands, 447
Neuberg (town), 756
Neumünster (church in Würzburg), 720
Neusatz valley (Baden), 565
Neustadt an der Hardt, 759, 765
Newberry Library, x, xiii, xiv, xv, 324, 418
New St. Peter, collegiate church of (Strassburg), plate 8, xxvii, 43, 46 (*collegii nostri*), 50, 118, 215, 313, 366, 369, 376, 377, 378, 383, 401ff., 408, 409, 410, 415, 417, 419, 454, 457, 459, 462, 463f., 470, 498, 507, 572, 573, 577, 583, 587, 598, 618f., 637, 681, 717, 719, 725, 726, 727, 728, 730, 731, 737, 741, 744, 750, 753, 769, 809
　cloister renovated, 768
　fabrica, 215, 618f.

library, 377, 404
officers, 403f.
reconstruction, 404
school, 406
Zorn chapel, xxxi, 378, 403, 415, 717, 728, 809
　restoration of, 378, 637
Nexemberger, Johannes, 364
Nicholas V (pope), 409, 502, 590, 727, 763
Nicholas, duke of Lorraine and Calabria, 386, 738
Nicholas (Geiler's *famulus*), 30, 139, 154, 443, 554
Nicholaus barbitonsor, 26, see Barbitonsor, Nicholaus
Nicolaus von Siegen, 747
Nicolavi de Rixingen, Johannes, 736
Nictelij Dei (Bacchus), 309, 677
Nider, Johann, 246, 630, 713, 744f.
Niesenberger, Johannes, 364
nigri antra ducis (Hades), 310, 678
Nigri, Johann, 33 (*Prior Ratisponensis*), 44, 116, 447, 523, 745
Nilum (Nile), 711
　Niloticus (adj.), 136
Nisus, 270, 298, 677
nobles, loss of power in Strassburg, 368, 383, 662, 717
　restricting cathedral canonicates to, see case of restricting...
nominalism, 427, 706, 758
Noricorum ciuitatem (Vienna), 80
Norway, 747
Numidique leones, 267
Nürnberg, 80, 115, 215, 413, 458, 493, 524, 581, 617, 702, 706, 720, 745, 751, 765
N... Tag, 449
Nycholaus, *Dominus noster*, 196, see Zeis, Nicholaus

Oberbaden (Swiss town), 455f.
Obernai (Alsatian town), 385
Obersteigen (Alsatian village), 93, 505, 506, 714, 737
Obwalden (village), 718
Occam, William, 251, 632, 706
Occeanus, 307, 310, 678 (*Oceanus*)
Occo, Adolf, xxviii, 155, 163, 406, 448, 497, 555, 563, 564, 700, 701, 738, 745
　projected history of German achievement, xxviii, 164, 563

875

Odyssey, 297, 671
Oebalio... genus (Gemini), 271, 648
Oedipus, 150
Oettingen (town), 706
Offenburg (town), 715, 744
Officium manuale, 77, 491
Old St. Peter, collegiate church of (Strassburg), xxx, 68, 160, 165, 166, 169, 170, 171, 281, 377, 403, 408, 410, 411, 477, 481, 500, 504, 520, 560, 564f., 566f., 569ff., 587, 589, 598, 655, 711, 742, 743, 749, 767f., 807, 809
Olerin, Wibelina, 759
Olmütz, bishopric of, 680, 707, 719, 729
Olympia, 684
Olympus, 44
Ondorp, Andreas, *see* Oudorp
Onheim, Johann Hell, *see* Hell (Onheim), Johann
opinion on a marriage contract, xxix, 255, 635f.
opinion on moral and legal questions concerning clerics, 236ff., 625ff.
opinion on the producing of witnesses, 256f., 636f.
opinion on questions concerning clerics' hair (style of tonsure and covering the head), 246ff., 626f.
Oppenheim (town), 163 (Oppenheym), 563, 582, 756
orations, list of, XXV
Orator Apostolicus, 160, 161, 162; *see* Peraudi, Raymund
Orci Dominus, 301
orders, 543, 547, 600; *see* Augustinians, Benedictines, Brethren of the Common Life, Carmelites, Carthusians, Celestines, Cistercians, Dominicans, Franciscans, Knights of St. John, Hermits of St. William, Premonstratensians
Orestes, 646, 647, 668, 677
Orient, walnut from, 542
Orion (constellation), 299, 668
Orléans, 427, 470, 743
    duke of, 538
    university of, 61 (*Aurelianensem Academiam*), 427, 472, 589, 703, 750
Orpheus, 282, 300, 646, 647, 649, 669, 670, 677

Orta and Civita Castellana, (suffragan) bishop of, 711
Ortenberg, Barbara, 702
Ortenburg (town), 700
Ortwin, Johann, 181, 182, 185, 423, 506, 577ff., 604, 745f.
Osiander, *see* Hoffmann, Crato
Osnabrück, diocese of, 763
Osterhausen (Frisian town), 745
Ostiensis, 217, 144; *see* Hostiensis
Other, Jacob, 401
Otilia (housekeeper?, sister of Johann Hell [Onheim]?), 38, 452, 730
Otmar, Johann (printer), xix, xx, 746
Otronto (Italian town), 439
Ottenburn, *see* Ottobeuren
Ottenheim (town), 638
Otto the Great, emperor, 669
Otto, duke of Bavaria, 701
Otto von Neumarkt, duke of Bavaria, 502
Ottobeuren, abbey of (Bavaria), 463
    abbot of, 48, 51, 65, 68, 463, 475, 479, 751; *see* case of abbot of O...
Oudorp, Andreas, 135, 136, 536, 746
Ovid, 99, 102, 268, 271, 296, 315, 393, 509, 511, 527, 643, 646, 647, 648, 654, 666, 667, 671, 672, 683

Pactolus (river), 333
Paderborn (town), 715
Padua, 519, 746
    university of, 18, 111, 427f., 593, 703, 707, 709, 740, 743, 746, 763, 766
Padus (Po), 310, 678
Paeonijs (Macedonian), 282
Paion, 647
Palaemon, Remnius, 647
Palatinate, 582, 638, 662, 700, 759
    count of (*Pfalzgraf*), 258; *see* Friedrich I, Philipp II, Rupert, Ruprecht
Palemon, 268, 647
Palestine, xxv; *see* Holy Land
Pallade (Pallas Athene), 268, 305
Pallantius, *see* Spangel
Paludi, Petrus de (glossator), 246
Pannonij (Hungarians), 80, 194, 272
    János Panonius, 732

876

Panormitanus (glossator), 228, 229, 232, 253
Paphos, 346
Papinius, 280, 653f.
Paris (son of Priam), 279 (*Priamidis*), 297, 302, 653, 670
Paris (city), xv, 50, 51, 59, 76, 69, 104, 162, 196, 198, 372, 392, 405, 412, 413, 423, 432, 464, 467, 470, 472, 475, 480, 492, 520f., 560, 562, 588ff., 608, 640, 645, 674, 712, 725, 731, 736, 743, 745
  university of, xxv, xxvii, xxix, 15f., 61, 62, 63, 65, 68, 80, 82, 84, 160, 161, 199, 258, 260, 316f., 383, 392, 395, 396, 397f., 405, 417, 423, 424, 427, 430, 474, 475f., 512, 561, 575, 589, 593, 608, 638f., 640, 645, 682, 683, 700, 701, 702, 703, 705, 708, 709, 710, 715, 724, 731, 736, 739, 742f.,, 745, 749, 750, 751, 752, 757, 760, 761,
Parnassus, 310, 332, 346, 688
Paros, 429
Parrhasis ursa (Ursa Major), 307
Parthenope (Naples), 279
Parthus, 332
Parvus, Johann (printer), 413
Pasyphe, 302, 352, 670
Patauia, 18, 112; *see* Padua
Pater Wilhelmitarum Prouincialis, 79, 492
Patroclum, 273, 647, 677, 678
Paul II (pope), 439, 619, 704, 712
Pauli, Johannes, 369, 401
Paulus de Castro (Cachensis), 746
Paulus Iurisconsultus, 201, 596, 746
Paulus Julius, 746
Pavia (Pafye, Papia), 786, 787; university of, 25, 428, 437, 482, 490, 700, 705, 739, 766
Pavo, Jacob, 394
Payens *or* Payns (Mohammedan name), 675
Pazzi family, 424
  conspiracy, 424
Peana (Paeana) veste, 302
Peancius heros (Philoctetes), 270, 298, 647
Pegasides (Muses), 271
Pegasus, 646
Pelagianorum heresi (Pelagianism), 260, 640
  Pelagius, 640

Peliaco robore (Argo), 272, 648
Pelican, Conrad, 721
Pella (Macedonia), 647
  Pellei (Alexandrian) *Triumphi*, 270, 647
Pelligno (Ovidian) *carmine*, 280
  Peligni, 305
Pelopennesus, 559, 577, 748
penates, 299, 310
Penelope, 12, 421
Pentaselea, 302
Peonis (Paion), 269, 303, 647
Peraudi, Raymund (Raimund), 160 (*oratori apostolico*), 161, 162, 391, 515, 561, 562, 618, 746f.
Pergama, 280, 299, 302
Perithous (Pirithous), 298
Perler, Hieronymus, 705
Persius, 117, 192, 289, 429, 487, 524, 661
Petersthal, church at, 739
petitions, list of, XXV
Petrarch, 375, 393, 722, 784
Petrus (glossator), 245; *see* Paludi
Petrus (messenger), 44, 854
Peutinger, Conrad, 483, 699, 750
Pfalz (former Strassburg city hall), 377, 807
Pfefferkorn, Johann, 750
Pfennigturm (former Strassburg Treasury), 384, 606, 661, 663, 808
Pfirt (town), 386
Pforzheim (town), 49, 213, 462f., 476, 615, 674, 743, 749, 766
Phaedra, 669f.
Phaeton, 678
  Phaetontei, 310
Phariam, 280
Phebi (*Phoebus*), 271, 307, 310
Pheidios of Syracuse, 647
Philadelphia, Free Library of, x, xix, xx, 375
Philip the Bold, duke of Burgundy, 712
Philip the Fair, duke of Flanders, 537f., 727
Philip the Good, duke of Burgundy, 386, 712
Philip the Long, duke of Burgundy, 470
Philipp II, *Pfalzgraf*, 258 (*comitis Rheni Palatini*), 502, 597, 638, 662, 699, 701, 706, 720, 731, 734, 745, 747, 750, 758, 765, 770

Philipp, *Markgraf* of Baden, 703
Philipp, von Ravenstein, *see* Ravenstein
Philoctetes, 646, 647
phoebigene (Aesculapian), 282
Phoebus, 150; 163 (*phoebarum*), 271 (*Phebi*), 272, 283, 300, 307, 310, 669
Phoedra (Phaedra), 302
Phoenissus Pater (Cadmus), 269,l647
Phorcensis (Pforzheim, adj.), 18
Phormio the Peripatetic, 117, 524
Phrixus, 648
Phrysij (Frisian), 701
Piacenza (Italian city), 711
Pibra, Johann de, 526
Piccardy (province), 387
Piccolomini, Aeneas Silvio (Silvius), 369, 457, 613, 702, 725, 727, 744; *see* Pius II
Pierijs aquis, 296
Pilades (Pylades), 270, 272, 298
Pilio hero (Nestor), 272, 648
Pindar, 273
Pirckheimer, Willibald, 699
Pirithous, 648
Pisa (city), 770
Pisana (Bartholomeus of San Concordio, glossator), 233 (*autor summe pisane*), 246
Pisces (constellation), 648
Piso, Stephan, 118, 120, 194 (*Pannonium virum*), 525, 559, 588, 747f.
Pistor (Becker), Anthon, 557
Pistor, Maternus, 769
Pius II (pope), 43, 457, 473, 713, 733f., 748; *see* Piccolomini
Pius III (pope), 712
Pius IX (pope), 674
Place Broglie and Place Kléber (Strassburg), 370
plague, *see* medical references
plappardi (*blaffardus, plappert, plaphardus*), 135, 536, 812
Plato, 117, 192, 315, 319, 585, 671, 682, 683, 684, 729
  editions available in Strassburg, 523
  translations by a Florentine, 117
  by Agricola, 483
Plautus, 85, 293, 497, 586, 595, 662, 665
Plebanus (of New St. Peter), 172, 173
Pleningen, Dietrich von, 701, 720

Plienswiler, *see* Blienswiler
Pliny, 669
Plutarch, 418
Po (river), 646, 678
Poenitenciaria Apostolica, 104, 512
poetry, 10f., 44, 102, 121, 150, 192, 266-311, 313f., 321, 325, 332f., 375, 386, 420, 426, 493, 497, 606, 607, 654f., 659f., 663, 675f., 685, 686, 701, 711, 720, 722, 723, 724, 734, 745, 754, 757, 768, 769, 770; *see Luc., Epithoma*
Poitiers, university of, 750
Poland, 393; king of, *see* Casimir
Poli, 10 (*Polos*), 267, 272, 307, 309, 310 (*polum*),
Pollion, Simphorien, 544
Pollux, 299, 668
Ponsa, Johann, *see* Teutonicus
Pont des Corbeaux (Strassburg bridge), 601
Ponte, Valentinus de, 43, 457
Pontum (Black Sea), 272
poor scholars, 607
pope, 46, 198, 216, 239ff., 248, 250, 543, 547, 627f., 748
  see Alexander VI, Benedict XI, Benedict XIII, Boniface VIII, Boniface IX, Clement V, Clement VI, Clement XIV, Felix V (antipope), Gregory IX, Gregory XII, Honorius III, Innocent III, Innocent IV, Innocent VI, Innocent VIII, John VIII, John XXII, John XXIII (deposed), Julius II, Leo IX, Martin V, Nicholas V, Paul II, Pius II, Pius III, Pius IX, Sixtus IV
portarius, duties of, 404
Poseidon, 648, 670
Posen (Silesian city), 521, 736
praeceptor, 508 (meanings)
Praedicatores, also *Predicatores*, *see* Dominicans
praepositus, duties of, 403
Praepositus of Baden-Baden, 195, 589f.
  of New St. Peter, 48, 49; *see* Munthart, Conrad
  of St. Thomas, 38, 200, 209; *see* Christoph von Uttenheim
  of Surburg, 194; *see* Dedinger, Jacob
Prague, 680, 729; compact of, 648

878

university of, 501
prayer beads, 156, 161, 162, 556, 561, 563
prebend, 405 (meaning)
preces primae (*primariae, regales*), 90, 91, 113, 165, 166, 167, 168, 169, 170, 171, 195, 203, 204, 408f. (defined), 411, 477, 502, 504, 520, 540, 557, 565ff., 570f., 588f., 598, 782
Prechter, Clara, 755, 810
Premonstratensians, 211f., 612f., 666, 716, 725
    Hagenau monastery dedicated to B. M. V., Sts. Paul and Nicholaus, 612
    Prémontré (in Aisne), 613
Pressburg, 729
    bishop of, 763
    cathedral canon of, 737
Priamidis (Paris), 279
priest, demanding profession of, 163f.
    training of, 405
    see clergy
Principis philosophorum (Aristotle), 191
Printers, see J. Amerbach, M. Brant, H. Eggestan, M. Flach, H. Grau, M. Hupfuff, N. Kessler, B. Kestler, B. Kistler, H. Knoblochtzer, J. Knoblouch, A. Koburger, J. Koelhoff, J. Mentelin, Nürnberg Augustinians, J. Otmar, J. Parvus, J. Pruss, "R" printer, F. Reynault, A. Rusch, W. Schencker, J. Schott, M. Schott, A. Schurer, J. Speyer, W. Speyer, Strassburg Carthusians, G. Stuchs, P. Vischer, P. Wagner, G. Zainer, K. Zeninger
Printing, xiiiff., xixf., 370ff., 411ff., 702, 750, 752
    at Paris, 731
    at Strassburg, 411ff.,
    at Venice, 440
    dispute over inventor of moveable, 564
    see *contrafaçon*, Greek typography, xylography
Prior Celestinus, 261; see Gerson, Johann
Prior of Colmar Dominicans, 156, 157, 557
Prior of the Knights of St. John, 173, 572
Prior Ratisponensis, 33, 44, 116; see Nigri, Johann
Prioress of St. Agnes, later of Sts. Margaret and Agnes, 357, 358; see Zorn, Anna von
Priorissa Conventus sancti Nycholai in Undis, 211, 611
Priscian, 100, 101, 352, 371, 509ff., 690, 692
Procris, 670
procurator capituli, duties of, 404
procurator fabrice, 41, 455
Proserpine, 442, 647
prosody
    general rules for syllable quantity, 333ff.
    common syllables (short vowel plus mute or liquid), 97-101, 333, 509ff.
    examples from classical poets, 102f.
    explained by Diomedes, 100f.; by Priscian, 101; by Quintillian, 101
    compounds, 334f.
    derivatives, 334
    diphthongs, 333
    effect of accent, 334
    first syllable of verbs, 335
    position, 333 (defined)
    two vowels, 333f.
    special rules
        final syllables, 351-354
        initial syllables, 336-344
        middle syllables, 344-351
    writings about prosody, 117, 298, 331-354, 376
Protestant(s), 377, 544
Prothonotarius, 178, 576
proverbs, xxiv, 30, 43, 45, 58, 65, 69, 71, 73, 88, 89, 103, 108, 110, 122, 132, 130, 137, 138, 139, 141, 142, 144, 191, 197, 205, 220, 261, 263, 265, 266, 288, 305, 316, 321, 358, 456, 469, 482, 487, 512, 528, 539, 542, 591, 643, 644, 662, 669, 671f., 685
Prouincialis Conuentus Argentinensis (Franciscans), 61; see Summer, Georg
Prouincialis Predicatorum, 214; see Sprenger, Jacob
Prouincialem Vuilhelmitarum, 79, 492
provisio, 408, 409

provisor provinciae, 396, 683, 758
Pruschenk *or* Prueschenk, Sigismund, *see* Bruschenckner
Prüss, Johann (Strassburg printer), 412f., 747
Prussia, 747
Ptolemy, 289, 368, 671, 740
Püller von Hohenburg, Richard, 41 (*negocio illo turbatissimo*), 190f. (*iniuriam nostris a Thuricensibus*), 449, 455f., 585
Pyeridum (Muses), 267, 305, 310
Pylades, 298, 646, 647, 668
Pyrithous (Pirithous), 270
Pytagoricum Ypsylon, 158; *see* Samian letter

quarta canonica, 253, 634
 quarta funerum, 634
quaternio, quaternus, 535
quarter days, 623
quendam Phisicum, 73; *see* Wirt
question on right of bishop to declare war, 258, 637f.
question on powers of absolution, 252
 reply by Rot, 252f., 633f.
question whether demons (and angels) can perceive man's thought, 181-186, 577-580
Quinckener von Saarburg, Gottfried, 165 (*Cancellario*), 565, 748
quinternus, 24, 435
Quintillian, 10, 70, 97, 101, 315, 319, 418, 482, 484, 485, 508f., 511, 586, 683, 684
Qwincker, Geoffrey, *see* Quinckener

"R" printer, 752
Rabanus, bishop of Spires, 86, 417, 499f., 748f.
Rabenbrücke(Strassburg bridge),601
Radewyns, Florentius, 393
radicibus mese, 132, 532
Ramstein, count of, 739
Rappoltstein, counts of, 710, 737
Rastatt (town), 78, 491, 742
Rastetten, *see* Rastatt
Rateln, *Markgraf* of, 713
Ratis, also *Ratispona*, *see* Regensburg
 Ratisponensis (adj.)
Ratzemhusen, Dorothea von, abbess of St. Stephan, 449
Rausch, Adolf, *see* Rusch
Ravensburg (town), 724
Ravenstein, Philipp von, 138 (Dominus de R.), 538, 749
Raymond, Benedict, 641
Raymundus (glossator), 228, 229, 245
Rectorem Friburgensem, 29, *passim*; *see* Kerer, Johann
reform of convents and monasteries, 53ff., 61, 239-242, 390, 469, 471f., 745; *see* Clingenthal sisters
Reformation, 369, 370, 377, 380f., 393, 394, 404, 421, 452, 604, 663, 761f.
Regensburg, 287 (*Ratispona*), 288, 291, 659, 662, 663, 668, 701, 704, 745
 bridge, 663
Reiffsteck, Jacob, 160, 163, 165, 166, 168, 170, 455, 560, 563, 564f., 727, 749
Reiffsteck, Peter, 160, 161, 560, 561f., 749
Rein, Caspar de, bishop of Basel, 190, 749, 764
Reinhardt (René, Renatus), duke of Lorraine, 190, 385, 386f., 738
Reisner, Nicolaus, 560
Reno, Caspar de, *see* Rein
restitution of goods distributed to benefice holders, 236, 237, 625ff.
Reuchlin, Johann, xiii, xv, 17, 18, 311, 372f., 376, 381, 426, 427, 484, 486, 500, 655, 699, 701, 702, 708, 709, 738, 745, 748, 749f., 760, 764, 765, 769, 769, 784
 poetic invitation, xv, 311, 678f., 706
Reutlingen, 746; convent at, 737,
Reynault, Franciscus (printer), 413
Rhamnusia (Nemesis), 44
Rhein, Caspar zu, *see* Rein
Rheinau (town), 411, 750
Rheinbischoffsheim (town in Baden), 410
Rhenanus, Antonius, 750
Rhenanus, Beatus, xxix, 369, 394, 407, 723, 750, 760, 769
Rhenish Palatinate, *see* Palatinate
Rhentingen (village), 53, 56, 59, 466, 468f., 506, 739

880

Rhenus, 29, 202, 267, 284, 287, 310; see Rhine
Rhesijs equis (horses of Rhesus, king of Thrace), 302
Rhine (river), 368, 385, 386, 390, 393, 442, 447, 481, 490, 520, 584, 597, 646, 659, 678, 760; see *Rhenus*
Rhineland, 623
Rhine confederation, see confederation of Rhine cities
Rhodes, 439, 675, 705, 712; poem on siege of, 306
Rhodopeius heros (Orpheus), 269, 300, 669
Riario, Girolamo, see Imola, Hieronymus de
Riario, Raphael, 733
Ribysen, Theodoricus, 77, 169, 407, 489f., 568, 750
Richardis, empress, 465
Richardus (glossator), 245
riddles, 149f., 550f.
Riedner, Johann, 62, 472f., 751
Rimini (Italian city), 640
Ringmann, Matthias, 762
Ripheus nimbus (Rhipaean mountains), 310, 678
Rixingen (Alsatian town), 736
robber knights, 446, 638, 738f.
Roche, Alain de la, see Rupe
Rochefort, Guillaume de, xxix, 52ff., 54, 56, 466ff., 751
Röchlin, Johann, see Reuchlin
Roeslin, Nicolaus, abbot of Ottobeuren, 48, 51, 68, 463, 751
Rohraffe, 206, 388, 599, 604ff.
Rohraffen, 604f., 663
Rohrtal (valley in Upper Alsace), 758
Roman antiquities, 713, 762, 769
Roman law, 635f., 727, 746
Romans, 368, 388, 425, 426, 485, 542, 647, 662, 666, 677
Rome, xv, xxv, xxvi, 12, 21, 23, 24, 27, 28, 35, 39, 45, 65, 76, 79, 82, 84, *passim*
national churches with hostels in, 515f.
pilgrims to, 82, 108, 495, 515
university of, 437, 711, 739
Romulides (son of Romulus), 269
Romulus, 297
rosary, 556; see prayer beads; *confraternitas* of, 556, 760
Rossheim (town), 385

Rostock, 393
university of, 501, 751
Rot, Johann, the cleric, 15ff., 24f., 36, 38, 66, 95, 110, 112, 113, 114, 134, 143, 158, 161, 162, 188, 195, 196, 200, 209 (*Amico N.* of #192), 226 (author of 213), 236 (author of #216?), 252 (*Vicarium Episcopi*), 266, 382, 396, 405, 406, 410, 422, 423, 429, 436, 449f., 451f., 460, 504, 507, 520, 521, 522, 534f., 542, 558, 560f., 562, 575, 582, 583, 588f., 593ff., 611, 622ff., 625, 629, 633f., 645, 710, 723, 725, 738, 743, 751f.
Schott's tribute to, 200
Rot, Johann, the procurator, 176-181, 463, 574ff., 716, 752
Rouen, "butter" towers of, 434
Roumanian language, 763
Rubiacensis (Ruffach, adj.), 313
Rudesheim, Rudolph von, 726
Rudolf von Hapsburg, 388
Ruffach (town), 720
Rufus, Mutianus, 712
Rupe, Alanus de, 556, 760
Rupefort, Guillermus de, see Rochefort
Rupert, *Pfalzgraf* (son of Philipp II), 747
Ruprecht, bishop of Strassburg, 385, 409, 455, 543, 544, 738, 803f.
Ruprecht, *Pfalzgraf*, 748
Rusch, Adolf (Ruscus, Adelphys), xiii, xxx, 25, 69, 71, 84f., 136f., 140f., 149ff., 153, 202, 281, 411, 414, 425, 436, 444, 448, 480, 483, 497, 537, 541, 550f., 553, 596f., 612, 613, 654, 718, 752, 755
Russ, Johann, 492
Russell, Bertrand, 633
Rutuli (Turnus), 272, 648
Ryne, Béatrice van den, 726
Ryssel, Alanus von, 640

Sabeus (Sabaeus), 332
Säckingen (town), 758
sacrilege, see abuses
Sagittarius (constellation), 648
SS *Mart. Marcellini et Petri, monasterium* (Strassburg?), 365
St. Amand, 768

881

St. Ambrose, 793
St. André (church in Strassburg), 700
St. Andreas (church in Andlau), 737
St. Andrew, poem to, 365, 419
St. Anthony, 127, 529
St. Augustine, 90, 130, 185, 247, 260, 503, 530, 579, 580, 630f., 640, 686, 702
St. Aurelia, 481
St. Bernard, 120, 140?, 143, 526, 529, 541
  chapel of (Rohrtal), 758
St. Bonaventura, 261
St. Bruno, 561
St. Christian abbey (Strassburg), 406
St. Christopher inn, 149
St. Colombo hospital (Strassburg), 403
St. Dominic, 357, 556, 694, 695, 777
  tomb of, 357, 695, 777
St. Donatien (church in Bruges), 724
St. Elizabeth (church in Pressburg), 737
St. Etienne (church in Strassburg), 384
St. Florentius (church in Haslach), 711
St. Georg (church in Ruprechtsau), 715
St. Georg (church in Strassburg), 732
St. Gertrudis (church in Augsburg?), 699
St. Gertrud (church in Cologne), 760
St. Jean-en-Grève (church in Paris), 724
St. Jerome, 13, 22, 48, 322, 434, 686, 702, 792
St. John the Baptist, 11, 274, 275 (*De tribus Iohannibus*), 278, 279, 419, 650f., 652
St. John Chrysostom, 11, 215 (book), 261, 274, 277-278 (*De tribus Iohannibus*), 411, 419, 617, 640, 650ff.
St. John the Evangelist, 11, 276-277 (*De tribus Iohannibus*), 278, 279, 419, 632, 650f., 652
St. Leonhard (church in Basel), 732
St. Mark (convent in Strassburg), 765
St. Martin (church in Colmar), 769
St. Martin (church in Memmingen), 739
St. Martin (church in Strassburg), 601, 758, 807
St. Maternus, 411
St. Michael, xxix, 165, 282 (*Aliger*), 565, 656
St. Michael (church in Rheinau), 377
St. Moritz (church in Augsburg), 460, 497, 534, 739
St. Moritz (church in Mainz diocese), 213
St. Nicholas, bishop of Myra, 281, 282, 284, 285, 288, 295, 612, 656, 657f., 666
St. Nicholaus (church in Strassburg), 761
St. Nicholaus *in Undis* (convent in Strassburg), 211, 423, 611f., 714, 737, 760
  paintings in church of, 757
St. Nicolaus im Metzgergiessen (chapel in Strassburg), 257, 637
St. Norbert, archbishop of Magdeburg, 613
St. Odile, 449
St. Paul, 247ff., 295, 358, 612, 630f., 639, 666, 791; see *Apostolus*
St. Peter, xxix, 165, 282 (*Claviger*), 283, 287, 294, 295f., 297, 565, 632, 656, 659, 665f., 669
St. Peter (church in Fritzlar), 213, 614
St. Peter (church in Rome), 746
St. Praxedis, 410
St. Pol, count of, 749
St. Remigius, 388
St. Richardis (convent in Andlau), 51, 68, 75, 465, 507
St. Severus of Valeria, 614
St. Stephan (convent in Strassburg), 34, 35, 36, 448
St. Thomas, see Aquinas, Thomas
St. Thomas, collegiate church of (Strassburg), 38, 166, 167, 173, 200, 209, 215, 367, 369, 370, 403, 408, 409, 410, 451f., 457, 461, 481, 491f., 565, 566f., 594, 598, 611, 618, 711, 714, 715, 720, 726, 728, 730, 731, 737, 738, 742, 744, 749, 753, 759, 761, 764, 768, 807
St. Ulrich (Udalricus), 143, 299, 545, 669
  church in Augsburg, 299f.

(poem on the collapse of), 669
St. Ursula, 69, 480f.
  skiff (*navicula, Schifflein*) of, 69, 481, 725
St. Vincent de Ferrara, 365, 779
St. Vitus (church in Freising), 64, 76, 81, 82, 94, 475, 739
St. William of Aquitania, 492
St. William of Maleval, 492
(La) Sainte Baume, cave at, 412, 722
Sts. Einbeth, Worbet and Vilbeth, 481
Sts. Margaret and Agnes (convent in Strassburg), xxii, xxiv, 358, 371, 384, 390f., 695, 696, 715, 771, 778, 808
  St. Agnes (before union), 715, 745, 754, 771, 779
  St. Margaret (before union), 810
Sts. Mary, Paul and Nicholas (church at Hagenau), 295, 666
Sts. Michael and Peter (church in Strassburg), *see* Old St. Peter
Sts. Peter and Paul (church at Weissenau), 725
Sala, Johann Gaspar (Giovanni Gaspara della Sala), 77, 194(?), 400, 490, 588, 753
Säldner, Konrad, 725
Saler, Jerome, *see* Brunschwig
Salicetus, *see* Widmann
Salome (mother of St. John the Evangelist), 651
Samian letter (Pythagorean Ypsylon), 20 (*Samij ramum*), 158, 429, 558
San Dominico (church in Bologna), 695
San Petronia (church in Bologna), canon of, 740
sancta mater Ecclesia, 181, 577
Santa Clara (convent near Ulm), 471
Santa Maria de Anima ("Anima"), German national church in Rome, 515f., 708, 711, 716, 719, 720, 724, 734, 737, 739, 743, 753
Santa Maria de Araceli (head church of Franciscans, in Rome), 76, 489, 735
Santa Maria in Capitolo (church in Rome), 489
Santa Maria in Obersteigen (*Steyga superiori*), 93, 505, 506, 714
Santa Maria super Minerva (church in Rome), 724
Sapidus, Johann, 394
Saracenus, 58
Sarbonenses (Sorbonne), 66
Sardanapalus, king of Assyria, 802
Sartoris, Johannes, 12, 421, 738; *see* Laudenburg, Johann
Sator, 310 (here, God)
Saturn, 295
  Saturnalia, 666
  Saturnia bruma (winter solstice), 287
Saverne, *see* Zabern
scabini, 385
Schaffhausen (city on Rhine), 721
Scharffenecker, Sixtus, 408
Schedel, Hermann, 725
Schefflen (river), 598
Schencker, Wolfgang (Erfurt printer), xix, 753
Schiller, Friedrich, *Wilhelm Tell*, 387, 723
Schimpfele, Ole, 543f., 804
Schindbrücke (Strassburg bridge), 601
Schism, the Great, 260, 409, 640
Schlegel, Lucas, 411
Schlettstadt, xxiv, 9, 10, 180, 385, 393ff., 417, 418, 427, 576, 715, 742, 744, 750, 766
  Latin school of, xxivf., 168, 392, 393ff., 417, 569, 631, 644, 702, 708, 709, 715, 720, 732, 742, 749, 750, 766
Schöffen, 385
Schola Palatina, 437
scholasticism, 181ff. (philosophical argument), 259, 577ff., 638, 706
scholasticus, duties of, 404
Schönleben, Heinrich, 81, 494, 753
schoolmaster(s), xxiv, xxxi, 281, 292ff., 393f., 607, 656, 664f.
schools, 735, 765
  of Brethren of the Common Life, 392f.
  see education, Schlettstadt Latin school, Strassburg schools, universities
Schott, family, xxiii, 383f., 416, 456, 461, 488, 536, 567, 753ff., 808ff.
  coat-of-arms, 324, 371, 391, 753, 775, 808, 809f.
  genealogical table, 810
  home, xxvi, xxvii, 153, 161,

883

209, 214, 553f., 610, 616
Schott, Anna, xi, xxi, xxiv, xxvii, 357f., 364f., 374, 377, 384, 390f., 684, 694ff., 753f., 771, 776ff., 808, 810
Schott, Ansel, 808
Schott, Augustin, 384, 554
Schott, Brigitta, 808
Schott, Claus (*floruit ca.* 1400), xxiii
Schott, Claus, 29 (*Vetterclaus*), 384, 441f., 443, 754
Schott, Conrad, xxiii, 401
Schott, Einbetha, 808
Schott, Friedrich, engraver and sculptor, 753, 755
Schott, Gertrud, 808
Schott, Jacob, 416 (*also* wife Ottilia), 416, 756, 810
Schott, Johann (Strassburg printer), xix, xx, 354, 689, 752, 754f., 808
Schott, Laurentius, 808
Schott, Margareth, 808
Schott, Margred, xxiv, 391, 741, 755, 810
Schott, Maria (Merga), xxiv, 459, 498, 741, 755, 808, 810
Schott, Martin (Strassburg printer), xiii, xiv, xx, xxiii, 323, 324, 371f., 419, 431, 687, 752, 754, 755f.
  collophon of, 323ff., 687
Schott, Odele, 384, 391
Schott, Ottilia, xxiv, 60, 96, 118, 120, 131, 135, 203, 366, 371, 450, 471, 507f., 525, 531, 536, 597, 699, 700, 714, 756, 760, 808, 809, 810
Schott, Peter, of Ghent, 363
Schott, Peter, Jr., xiff., xxii, 714, 718, 720, 721-725 *passim*, 727, 729, 734, 736, 739, 740, 741, 742, 743, 745, 746, 747, 750, 751, 754, 756, 757, 760, 761, 769, 771, 778, 784, 785, 809, 810
  assistance to Schott, Sr., 401 (N. 113)
  benefice (canon of New St. Peter), xxvii, 9, 11, 39f., 43, 80, 82, 173-175, 401f., 404, 453f., 495, 553f., 573f., 700, 711
  letters soliciting support for, 39f., 173-175
  biographical data, xxii-xxxi, 315-320 (Hassenstein's oration), XVI (chronology of life)
  age, dates of birth and death, 378-382
  cause of death, 380ff.
  education, xxiv, xxv, 316ff., 394f., 396ff.
  health and parental concern for, 391 (N. 87)
  ordination and first mass, 38, 43, 45, 46, 404, 460f.
  plan to live and work with Hassenstein, 477 (N. 302)
  predilection for quiet life, xxvi, xxvii, 391 (N. 86), 438f. (N. 255)
  predilection for theology, xxvii, 405 (N. 121)
  epitaph, xxii, xxxi, 366, 371, 378ff., 415, 808
  parents, xxiiif., xxvi, 9, 17, 21, 25, 26, 29, 37, 38, 42, 46, 48, 49, 59, 60, 63, 64, 65, 69, 74, 80, 84, 91, 96, 106, 107, 112, 113, 115, 118, 120, 135, 139, 142, 147, 149, 159, 160, 166, 170, 171, 190, 192, 195, 196, 197, 199, 215, 312, 320, 322, 366, 392, 405, 416, 417, 423, 430, 435, 437, 441, 445, 447, 470, 476, 479, 496f., 507, 513, 525, 550, 554, 559, 560, 561, 578, 591, 610, 618, 680, 684, 686, 723, 743, 780, 781; see Cöllen, Susanna von, *also* Schott, Peter, Sr.
  patriotism, xxviii, 406 (N. 124)
  provisor of *Alemmania* nation at Paris, 317, 683f.
  sister(s), 36, 47, 320, 450, 461, 684; *see* Anna, Margred, Maria, Ottilia
  works, 363f.
    editions, xxx, 157, 215, 411-414, 557f., 617
    lost works, xi, 365
    translations, 363f., Appendices E *and* F
Schott, Peter, Sr., xxiiif., xxv, xxvi, xxvii, 9, 11-14, 21, 25, 26, 27, 29, 31, 33, 35, 36, 40, 41, 48, 50, 52, 62, 64, 74, 91, 117, 131, 132, 133, 135, 136, 151, 152, 153, 156, 161, 163, 166, 171, 189, 190, 203, 204, 210, 214, 310, 315, 317, 358, 363f.,

365, 366, 370, 371, 379, 381, 383, 385, 386, 387, 389f., 391, 392, 401, 405, 416, 417, 420ff., 423, 424, 430, 431, 438, 447, 449, 450, 454, 455, 504, 523, 524, 531, 533, 534, 536, 543f., 553, 554, 556, 563, 565, 571, 582ff., 590, 599, 611, 616, 662, 681f., 694, 696, 700, 706, 718, 722, 741, 753, 755, 756f., 778, 790, 808, 809, 810
Schott, Sebastian, 384, 808
Schreiber, Johann, *see* Scriptor
Schürer, Lazarus (printer), 750
Schürer, Mathias (printer), 372, 413
Schüttern, abbot of, 638
  monastery of, 706
Schwabach (town), 720
Schwarzau, convent at, 737
Schwitz (canton), 434
Schwörbrief, xxiii, 368, 385, 388
Scintilla, *see* Funck
Scipiades (Scipio Africanus), 270
Scipio Africanus, 647, 680
Scironian Rocks, 677
Scommata, Geiler author of, 444
Scorpius (constellation), 272, 648
Scotus, Johannes Duns (*Doctor subtilis*), 9, 59, 63, 181, 182, 183, 185, 194, 222, 232, 235, 245, 247, 251, 369, 417, 470, 474, 577ff., 588, 621, 631, 632, 641, 674
Scriba, Vitus, 115, 522
Scriptor von Kaysersberg, Johann, xxv, 63f., 66, 198, 405, 406, 424, 470, 474f., 476, 592f., 684, 757f.
Scriptoris, Johannes of Ulm, 757
Scythia, 678
Sebastian (apothecary), 169, 569
Sebastian, *Frater* (hermit), 110, 518, 722, 758
Seckingen, Johann von, 106, 514, 638, 711, 728, 758
Sedulius, 334
seed, contract for sale of, 255f., 636
Seltz (town), 385
Semeca, Johann, *see* Teutonicus
Semites, 686
Seneca, 363, 434, 528
Senis, Fridericus de (glossator), 232, 242
Septimus Severus, 746
seres (people of Eastern Asia), 332
Serpens (constellation), 648

Servius Honoratus, Maurus, 72, 291, 293, 294, 296, 482, 661, 663, 665, 667, 668, 670
sexprebendarius, 77, 500, 750
sexternio, *sexternus*, 134, 143, 535
Sforza, Bona, duchess of Milan, 363f., 786f.
Sforza, Giovanni Galeaz Maria, duke of Milan, 363f., 786f., 788f., 790
Sforza, Lodovic Maria, duke of Milan, 731
Sforza, Maria (wife of Maximilian I), 703
Sforza, Catherine, 733
Sforza letters, *see* letters
Shem, 321, 686
Sicily, 684
Sickingen, Johann von, *see* Seckingen
Siculus iuuencus (bull of Phalarus), 278, 650, 652
Siebenbürgen (Hungary), 747
Siena, 424, 739, 746
Sifrid, Johann, 96, 210, 508, 611, 758
Sigismund, emperor, 272, 648, 708, 729, 758f.
Sigismund, archduke of Austria, 60, 83, 112, 190, 272, 385, 386f., 471, 496, 502, 506, 519, 713, 716, 718, 719, 725, 727f., 736, 739, 745
Sigismund, duke of Bavaria, 704
Silberina, 368
Silbermann, André, 389
Silberstadt, 368
Silesia, 393
Simmler, Georg, 759
Simmler, Johann, dean of St. Thomas, xxxi, 38, 134, 143, 165, 166, 170, 171, 172, 188, 200, 209, 210, 215, 227ff., 233, 235, 236, 238, 253, 313, 410, 416, 425, 452, 520, 535, 542, 544, 564f., 569f., 572, 582, 595, 603, 617f., 621, 622, 624, 627, 629, 634, 681, 701, 723, 759
Simmler, Johann, cantor of Old St. Peter (nephew of above), 759
Simmler, Walter, 759
Siracusij viri (Archimedes), 269, 647
Siria (Syria), 159
Sirius, 271, 309, 442, 648, 677
Sixtus IV (pope), xxix, 39, 40, 56-59, 86f., 173, 174, 175, 176,

885

177, 198, 390, 407, 424, 434, 435, 439, 453, 454, 459, 460, 468f., 471, 491, 498f., 502, 544, 547, 556, 558, 573f., 581, 592, 626, 633, 674, 675, 701, 702, 704, 711, 712, 713, 714, 733, 735, 736, 748, 771
Sleida (Eifel), 370
Sletstatinum (Schlettstadt), 9, 10
  Sletstatensis, Sletstatinus (adj.), 9, 97, *passim*
Smyrna, 712
Socrates, 22, 272 (*Cecropio seni*), 648, 683, 684
Sorbonne, 66, 474, 476, 736 (*socius Sorbonicus*), 758
Sororius, 40, 454
Soultz-les-Bains, *also* Soultz, 10, 417, 418, 686, 766, 767
source material, loss of, xxii, 377f., 369
Spain, 675
Spangel, Pallas, 157f., 414, 557, 759f.
Spanheim, monastery of, 674, 764
  abbot of, *see* Trithemius
Speculator (glossator), 217, 218, 241
spelling, xviiif., 72, 133, 158
Sperlin, Georgius, abbot of Hirsau, 706
Speyer, Johann von (Venetian printer), 440
Speyer, Wendelin von, (Venetian printer), 440
Sphinga, 150
Spiegel, Jacob, 393, 394, 732
Spires, xxix, 139, 148, 484, 489, 498, 508, 541, 549, 629, 637, 705, 706, 708, 734, 760, 766f., 771; *Spirensis* (adj.), 77
  bishop of, xxix, 242, 258, 407, 720f., 734, 748
  see Helmstadt, Ludwig von; Rabanus
  cathedral, 86, 750
    chapter of, 499f., 541, 673, 767
    canon of, 731, 739
    prebendarius of, 133
    sexprebendarius of, 77, 500, 750
    vicar of, 88
    library, 140, 500, 541
    preaching chair, 500, 543, 721, 767
  diocese of, 78, 169, 242, 491, 628, 638, 771
Sprenger, Jacob, 214 (*Prouincialis*), 556, 611, 707, 760

Spreu, Paulus, abbot of Hirsau, 706
Sselnberck, Johann, 559
Sslechta, Johann, 415f., 677, 685
Staedlin, Christopf, 808
Stanton, Johann, 743
Statius, 296 (*Stacius*), 667
Stein, Eitelwolf von, 394
Stein (town), 731
Steinach (town), 720
Steinmetz von Lützelstein, Gangolf, xxvii, xxix, 65, 66, 69, 160, 162, 195, 196, 197f. (*puerum meum*), 375, 406f., 475f., 479f., 560f., 562, 589ff., 760
Stephan, 118, 120; *see* Piso
Stettenfels, castle of, 700
Stettmeister, 384 (defined)
Steudlin, Wilhelm, 751
Steyga superiori, 93; *see* Obersteigen
stigias, 309; *Stigieque*, 44; *stigios*, 271; *stigius*, 299; *see Styga*
Stoica sentencia, 22, 434
Storck, Elisabeth, 808
Strabo, Walfrid, 541, 752
Strassburg, plate 5, xiii, 368f., *passim*
  banners of, 288, 291, 663
  banquets and arms preferred to letters in, 80, 493
  bishop(s) of, xxvi, xxviii, 22, 46, 51, 68, 75, 92, 165, 190, 214, 218, 219, 220, 701, 710, 734, 738, 768, 812
    see Albrecht von Bayern, Konrad, Ruprecht, Walter von Geroldseck, Wilhelm von Diest, Wilhelm von Honstein,
  cathedral de Notre Dame, xxiiif., 158, 206, 288, 364, 368, 377, 387ff., 402, 403, 407, 429, 476, 477, 479, 491, 504, 505, 506, 507, 522, 541, 580, 590f., 591, 594, 604ff., 608, 625, 658, 663, 709, 711, 728, 736, 738, 751, 757, 761, 782, 788f., 804, 807
    abuse of: buying and selling at doors, 207
    celebration of dedication, 602
    mayor holding audience in, 206, 606
    traffic through, 207, 607
    see abuses, *Rohraffe*
    chapter of, 34, 36, 134, 186, 449, 463, 465, 478, 534, 542, 544, 547, 565, 580f., 627, 701,

886

708, 727, 804, 806
  dean of, *see* Zollern, Friedrich von; Brandis, Johann von; Barby-Mulingen, Hieronymus von
  fabrica of, xxiiif., 41, 134, 387f., 455, 473, 535, 543, 611, 717, 722, 727, 749, 757, 790
  library of, 377, 410, 727, 757, 759
  organ of, xxiii, 206, 389, 604ff., 663, 727, 757
  preaching chair of, 143, 144, 366, 389, 407, 434, 444, 504, 534f., 542ff., 545ff., 621, 757
  charter for, 543f., 711, 803ff. (text)
  pulpit, xxiii, 389, 543, 605, 757
  spire, 364, 388, 661
  St. Catherine chapel of, 602, 723
  St. Laurentius chapel of, 389, 429, 477, 478, 558, 575, 757
  altar of, 389, 543, 751
  mural of, 158, 558f., 752
  parish of, 805
city hall (*Pfalz*), 377, 807; city treasury, *see Pfennigturm*
coat-of-arms, Plate 6, 663
constitution, *see Schwörbrief*
diocese, 76, 166, 404, 405, 436, 448f., 455, 467, 469, 575, 601, 604, 702, 736, 737, 744, 748, 761, 765
economic conditions, *see* economic conditions, 856
fair, 113, 521
fire of 1870, xii, 369, 377
government, 384f.
  city council, xxiii, 382, 384, 387, 402, 543, 574ff., 576, 706, 708, 709, 717, 741, 754, 756, 758, 759, 761, 762
  magistracy, 173, 174, 175, 177, 205, 384, 401, 402, 454, 492, 493, 573, 574, 576, 601f., 604, 608, 620, 636, 739, 752, 756, 762
  nobles' loss of power in, 368, 383, 662, 717
  guilds, 383, 384f., 636, 662, 709, 718, 726
    furrier guild, 756
    goldsmith guild, 718 (printers members of)
    grain guild, 754, 756
hostilities, *see* hostilities (864):

Burgundian Wars, captivity of Maximilian, Franco-Prussian War, French Revolution, World War II; *also* Püller von Hohenburg, Reformation
humanism and humanists, xi, xiii, xxv, 369
humanistic gymansium, xiii, 370, 461
humanistic society, 369
law(s), 206ff., 208, 214, 255, 599, 601f., 603f., 606, 608, 609f., 616
  breaking Sabbath, 207, 608
  foreign baker's restricted license, 207, 608
  loss of inheritance on entering orders, 206, 603
  mayor holding audience in cathedral, *see* abuse of cathedral
  mishandling of wills, allowed by 206, 603f., 746, 759
  preferential treatment of citizens over foreigners in assault, mayhem, 206, 603
  prohibition against money willed to religious institutions, 206, 603f.
  protection of wildlife, 208, 610
  public market on holy days, 207
  safe conduct to law evaders, 206, 604
  taxation of clergy, 206, 604
  see case of Last Sacrament, testimonials in sale of seed
merchants, 188, 440
money, 812
motto, 663
museum, *see Musée de l'oeuvre de Notre Dame*
Order of Free Masons founded at, 363, 388
patron saint of, *see* Virgin Mary
praise of, 199, 287ff. (encomium), 315, 593, 659f., 681
schools, xiii, xxviii, 369f., 401, 403, 406, 461, 470, 707, 719
  Johann Sturm humanistic gymnasium, xiii, 370, 761
  university, 547
seal, 663
Strassburgers, 369, 420, 441, 479, 521, 534f., 541, 548, 681, 682
Strassburg, Johann de, *see* Teutonicus

Strassburg, Thomas von, *see* Lampertheim, Thomas, *and* Thomas von Strassburg
Strassburg, Udalricus von, *see* Udalricus Argentinensis
Strateburgum, 368
Strimonis (Strymon, river), 310, 677f.
Stromayr, *also* Stromeyer, *see* Stromeiger
Stromeiger, Udalrich, Jr., 52, 465f., 576, 761
Stromeiger, Udalrich, Sr., 178 (*protonotarius*)?, 465, 576, 760f.
Stubach, Jacob von, 469, 713
Stubenweg, Reimbold, 257, 637, 761
Stüblin, Caspar, 394
Stuchs, Georg, 413, 617
Stuckmann, Gregorius, 69 (*decrepitus*), 78, 477, 491, 761
students, Brant's admonitions to, 684
 fare of, 198, 592
Studium Curiae, 437
Sturm, Heinrich, 761
Sturm, Jacob, viii, xxiv, 365, 366, 370, 399, 406, 470, 715, 761f., 767, 784
Sturm, Johann, of Sleida, 370, 461
Sturm, Leonard, 82, 83, 94, 495f.
Sturm, Ludwig, 762
Sturm, Margredt, 391
Sturm, Martin, xxiv, 60, 471, 525, 715, 761, 762
Sturm, Otto (Othon), 149, 762
Sturm, Philip, 752, 755, 808
Stuttgart, 750, 766
Styga, 102, 282
Styria and Carinthia, duke of, 727
Suetonius, 393
Suffragan bishops' titles, 577
Suitenses (Swiss), 191
Sulce (Soultz), 10
Sulpicius, 334
Summer, Georg, 61, 472, 762
summissarius, duties of, 404
Sundgau (province), 386
Surburg, 715
Sutor, Johann, *see* Brockingen
Swabia, 393, 481, 484, 542, 701, 719
 Swabian spirits, 699
Sweden, 747, 784
 Swedes, 377
Swiss, 191 (*Suitenses*), 385, 386, 434, 471, 613, 728, 751

Switzerland, 426, 598, 718, 722
sydus Iouis (planet Jupiter), 299, 668
Syfridus, *see* Sifrid
syllable quantity, *see* prosody
Symphorien, Ole, *see* Schimpfele
Symplegades (islands), 648
Syrenarum (sirens), 91
Syriam, 711
syrupi acetosi, 132, 532

Taborities, 525
Tacitus, 647, 750
Tagi (Tagus, river), 272, 333, 648
Talaru, Amadeus de, archbishop of Lyons, 261, 413, 641, 763
Tambachensis (Dambach, adj.), 24
Tamina (river), 426
Tartareus, 282
Tarsus, university of, 666
Tauler, Johann, 641
Taurus, 648
Tegeaticus volucer (Mercury), 271, 648
Temarensis, *see* Wernher, Adam
Temple Neuf (Strassburg), 370, 746
tenebrae, syllable quantity of, 508ff.
Terence, 27, 194, 290, 299, 439, 460, 588, 661, 662, 665, 740, 752
 "Terence stage," 439
testimonials in sale of seed, 255f., 374, 636
Tethios (Tethys), 310, 678
Teutonicus, Johann, 9, 417, 762f.
Texery, Bartholomeus, 713
Textor, Wilhelm, 731
textual difficulties, xvi, 39, 88, 130, 161, 174, 198, 213, 268, 342, 347, 350, 351, 452f. (N. 342), 501, 504, 531, 561, 562, 573, 614, 646, 690, 691, 692
Thalia, 150, 308
Thebas, 280, 648, 649
 Theban, 315
Theess *or* Thess, Georgius, *see* Georgius Ungarus
Themar (town on the Werra), 765
Theodoricus *Argentine*, *Magister*, 169; *see* Ribysen
thesaurarius, duties of, 403
Theseo, 301
 Theseum, 298
 Theseus, 646, 648, 668, 670
Thessala, 299

Thessalonians, 668f.
Thetze, Georg, *see* Georgius Ungarus
Theutonici, 305
Theutonico, 304
Thierstein, Oswald von, *see* Dyrstein
Thirty Years War, 784
Thomas (glossator), 245
Thomas the Abbot, 127, 529
Thomas, *abbas Mauriniancensis*, 529
Thomas, canon, 262, *see* Kempis, Thomas à
Thomas, *Magister*, 85, 498
Thomas Argentinensis, *also* Thomas de Argentina, xxx, 9, 157; *see* Thomas von Strassburg, *also* Lampertheim
Thomas von Strassburg, xxx, 9, 157, 414, 417, 557, 579, 763
Thracie, 301
Thubingen (Tübingen), 72
Thumb von Neuberg, Conrad, 700
Thumb von Neuberg, Hans, 700
Thuricensibus (people of Zürich), 189, 191
Thuricensium, 190
Thüringen, 765
Thurni (Turnus), 280
Tiber, 289, 677, 740
Tiberius, 610
Tibullus, 271, 647
Tirium (Tyrian), 271, 648
Titan (sun), 272, 648
Tito, Sebastian, *see* Brant
Tityrus, 119, 525
Tonantis (here, God), 44
tonsure, xxvi, 32, 246ff., 445, 630ff.
Torrentinus, Johann, 394
Torrentinus, Hermann, 393
Tortellius, Johann Arretinus, 202, 597, 763
Trachenfels, Maternus, 601, 806
Traci Vati (Orpheus), 302; *Tracius*, 310
translations of items, passages, xii, xxiv, xxviiif., xxxi, 367, 407, 654, 659f., 664, 665
treatise on Christian life, *see Luc.*
Trens, Hans, 255, 256, 636
Trent, bishop of, 719, 729
diocese of, 460, 497, 719, 727, 739
Tribaces, 368
Tribochi, 368, 388

Tribores, 368
Trier, 386, 704, 756, 762, 764
archbishop-elector of, 477, 499, 703, 734, 748, 770; *see* Friedrich, *Markgraf* of Baden
cathedral chapter, 499f.
canon of, 703, 733
diet of, 762
diocese of, 213, 434, 614
Trithemius, Johann, xxiii, 11, 365, 373, 380f., 381, 411, 413, 419, 420, 455, 604, 623, 674, 675, 706, 718, 720, 763, 764
excerpt from *Cathalogus*, 419; from *Liber*, 11, 419
Trittenheim (on the Moselle), 764
Troianorum, 191
Troie, 302
Troy, 668, 670
Truchsess, Thomas, 500
Tübingen, 72, 96, 132, 151, 153, 155, 156, 366, 426, 471, 488, 508, 533, 555, 556, 655, 746, 758
university of, 132, 136, 149, 160, 161, 162, 486, 501, 545, 554f., 706, 713, 720, 725, 731, 746, 750, 758, 766, 769
Tudeschi, Nicolas de (Abbas siculus, glossator), 588
Tullio (Cicero), 319; *Tullianis*, 686
Türckheim, 385, 706
Turk(s), xxv, xxix, 27, 58, 439f., 454, 577, 653, 675, 702, 704, 708, 712, 735. 747
Turnus, 648
Tuscus fluens (Tiber), 309, 677
Tybris (Tiber), 289
Tygrides (Tigris), 301
Tyndareus, 668
Tyria, 267, 646, 648
Tyrol, 728
Tytiros (Tityrus), 119

Überlingen (town), 434, 758
Udalricus Argentinensis, 9, 417, 764
Udenheim, *see* Uttenheim
Ulm, 135, 180, 471f., 576, 725, 757, 762, 765
Ulmensis (adj.), 61 (*Ulmensium*)
Ulrich I, duke of Württemberg, 597, 700, 716, 750, 766, 769
ultimum vale, 543, 634; *see quarta canonica*

889

Ultramontani, 395f., 490
Ulysses, 421, 647, 667
    see *Vlixem*
universities, 395f., 403, 405
    university nations, 400; see *Alemannia* nation, German nation
Untergruppenbach (village), 699
Uppsala, XII, 377, 784
    university library (*Carolina Rediviva*), XII, 784
Uracensis (Urach, adj.), 153, 249
Urach (town), 706
Urals, 678
Uranienses (people of Uri), 786
    Urei (Uri, Swiss canton), 786, 787
Urceus, Antonius Codrus, xxv, 764
Ursa Major, 648
    Ursa Minor, 648
usage, questions of, 71f., 96ff., 158, 215, 484-486, 508-512, 617
usury, xxvii, 227ff. (case of grain loans), 406, 622, 624
Utenheim, see Uttenheim
Utraquists, 525
Utrecht, bishop of, 703, 749
Uttenheim, Christian von, 535
Uttenheim, Christoph von (*prepositus Sancti Thome*), 38, 200, 209, 452, 506, 535, 595, 701, 714, 722, 723, 749, 764
Uttenheim, Johann, 369

Valentinus de Ponte, 43, 457
Valerius Maximus, 22, 147, 289, 433, 661, 752
Valtbrun, 31, 445
Vangiones, 368
Varius, 18
Varro Atacinus, 588
Varro, Marcus, Terentius, 119, 192, 297, 319, 586, 667
Vates Historie (Livy?), 10
Vatican Library, XII, 372, 377, 412 (first librarian of), 763
Velusine (*ve-Luscine*, Homer?), 305
Vendenheim (town), 745
Veneciae (Venice), 312
Venedig von Emrebach, Hans, see, Amerbach, Johann
Venetians, war with Archduke Sigismund, 506
Venetos (Venetians), 44, 112, 193, 194

Venetus, Johann de, see Amerbach, Johann
Venice, xxvi, 28, 32, 33, 159, 193, 194, 312, 400, 440 (book mart), 446, 458, 519, 584, 587, 617, 672, 677, 678, 679, 680, 703, 716, 729, 733, 740
Venus, 301, 442, 602, 648, 653, 669, 762
    planet, 592, 668
Vergil, 18, 20, 99, 100, 102, 150, 191f., 268, 271, 280, 282, 289, 291, 293, 294, 297, 305, 338, 346, 350, 352, 411, 414, 458, 482, 509ff., 525f., 550f., 551, 559, 585, 617, 646, 653f., 655, 661, 662, 663, 665, 667, 668, 670, 672, 676, 679, 688, 690, 691, 692, 693, 752, 765
Veronica Friderichen, 456
Veszprém, cathedral of, 737
    diocese of, 609, 729, 737
Veszprém, Ladislaus de, see Ladislaus of Veszprém
Veterbuda, Ladislaus, see Ladislaus of Veszprém
Vetterclaus, 29; see Schott, Claus
via appellacionis, 239ff.
    delegacionis, 243f.
    iurisiurandi, 255f.
    prorogacionis, 244ff.
    querelae, 239ff.
Vicar noster, 214, 219; see Hartmann von Eppingen, Andreas
Vicarium Episcopi in poenitencialibus, 252; see Rot, Johann
Vicedecanus sancti Petri senioris, 170, 570
Vicentius (glossator), 243, 256
Vienna, 372, 493, 724, 729, 763
    concordat of, 727
    university of, 501, 725, 745
Villa Dei, Alexander de, see Alexander de Villa Dei
Villingen (town), 707
Villinger, Jacob, 732
Vincenzi, Thomas, 711
Virbius (Hippolytus), 282, 301, 303, 656, 670
Virgin Mary, 44 (*genitrix Tonantis, diva parens*), 275, 284 (*genitrix tua*), 292, 295, 306, 612f., 666, 672, 678
    immaculate conception of, 577, 644, 673f.
    patroness of Strassburg, 284

(*refouente patrona*), 288, 291f.,
  657, 660, 663
  image on Strassburg coat-of-
    arms, plate 6, 663
  pregnant image of, *see* folklore:
    birth charms
Wimpheling's poem to, 306, 672f.
Virgin Islands, 481
Virgins (11,000) of Cologne and St.
  Ursula, 480f., 545
Virgo (constellation), 272, 442, 648
Vischer, Peter (Nürnberg printer),
  617
Vladislaus II, king of Bohemia, 122
  (*Regis*), 192 (*Vratislao*), 494,
  523, 586, 707, 729, 732
Vlixem (Ulysses), 12
  Vlixis, 268, 270
Vocabularium Grecarum dictionum,
  194, 587
Vocabulary of names of instru-
  ments and implements, *see*
  *Codicillum...nomina instru-
  mentorum*
Voeltsch, Eucharius, 171, 571, 765
Voeltsch, Reimboltz, 601?, 765
Vogler, Daniel, 808
Vogt, Conrad, 364
Voleau, Petrus, 758
Völkerwanderung, 368
Völtsch *or* Voltz, Eucharius, *see*
  Voeltsch, Eucharius
Voltz, Rudolf, 455
Vosges (mountains), 368, 565, 598,
  699, 721
Vratislaus, 192; *see* Vladislaus II,
  king of Bohemia
Vuimpinensis (Wimpfen, adj.), 203
Vulgate, references to, 11, 20, 23,
  24, 26, 33, 44, 52, 65, 67, 83,
  87, 91, 110, 112, 115, 117, 120,
  121, 122, 123, 124, 126, 128,
  129, 130, 144, 145, 146, 148,
  164, 191, 199, 200, 216, 223,
  247, 249, 258, 262, 265, 275,
  276, 282, 323, 357, 420, 428,
  429, 435, 436, 438, 447, 459,
  465, 475, 479, 496, 501, 503,
  518, 520, 523, 524, 526, 527,
  528, 529, 530, 531. 535, 542,
  546, 547, 549, 564, 585, 593,
  594, 619, 622, 630, 631, 632,
  639, 643, 644. 651. 654, 656,
  657, 659, 664, 687, 695, 734,
  754, 777f., 791
Vuormacia (Worms), 50

Vuormaciensis (adj.), 38, 42

Wagner, Peter (Nürnberg printer),
  617
Waldenses, sect of, 434
Walter von Geroldseck, 387
war(s), *see* hostilities
  right of bishop to declare,
    xxix, 258, 637f.
Wasselone *or* Wasselnheim, castle
  of, 203, 366, 506, 699, 714
Wedels, Hans, 256, 636
Wegeraufft, Johann, 711
Weissenburg (Alsatian town), 385,
  589 (monastery of), 756
Welker, Johann, *see* Amerbach,
  Johann
Wellen Peter, 745
Werdenberg, Agnes von, 456, 770
Werdenberg, Hugo von, 770
Werdenberg, Johann von, 477, 483,
  502, 745, 770, 782
Werdenberg, Heinrich von, 383,
  402, 411, 770
Werner, Adam, 321; *see* Wernher
Wernher, Adam, 321, 673, 685, 700,
  765
Wertheim (town on the Tauber),
  444, 735
Weschbach, Johann, 21, 26, 52, 61,
  65, 76, 79, 82, 83, 398, 430,
  437, 465, 492, 494f., 765
Wesmail, Heinrich von, 369
Wickgram, Conrad, 370
Wickgram, Peter, 370, 401, 444,
  544
Wideman, Johann, *see* Widmann
Widmann, Johann, 30f., 40f., 47,
  49, 72ff., 96, 131ff., 135, 136,
  149, 151, 153, 154f., 155f., 160,
  161, 162f., 169 (*Doctor Thubingensis*), 208 (#190)?, 426, 443,
  444f., 454, 461, 471, 486f., 488,
  497, 507f., 531ff., 536f., 550,
  551, 552, 553, 554, 555f., 560,
  561f., 563, 568, 609f., 714, 749,
  758, 765f., 769
  wife of, 74, 96, 131, 132, 133,
    135, 136, 149, 151, 156, 161,
    163, 486f., 507, 531, 536f., 552,
    556, 561, 563, 765f.
  relative of, 73, 131, 487, 531, 533
Widmanns, 554
Wiedman, Johann, *see* Widmann
Wigersheim, Albrecht, 408

wild Weib von Geispoltzheim, 602
Wildbad, spa of, 30, 31 (*Valtbrun*), 33, 62, 149, 366, 426, 441, 443, 444, 445, 447, 473, 488, 507f., 550, 745, 766
Wildersheim (diocese of Osnabrück), 763
Wilhelm, bishop of Strassburg (+ 1438), 738; *see* Diest
Wilhelm IV, duke of Bavaria, 704
Wilhelm von Honstein, bishop of Strassburg, *see* Honstein
wills, breaking of, 603f.
   Ortwin's will, 746
   Simmler's will, 759
Wilstett (town), 480
Wimpfen (on the Neckar), 598, 699, 700, 759
   cathedral chapter of, 500,
   praepositus of, 366, 599, 700
   sexprebendarius of, 500,
"Wimpheling Codex," 363f., 377, 654, 673, 734, 761, 784f., 786f., 788, 790
Wimpheling, Jacob, xiii, xiv, xv, xix, xx, xxiii, xxiv, xxviii, xxix, xxx, xxxi, 9, 10, 11, 88ff., 96-103, 133, 139, 140f., 280, 306, 311, 313, 321f., 322, 332, 369, 372f., 374, 376, 380, 381, 383, 392, 393, 394f., 399, 406, 409, 410, 413, 416, 417, 418, 419, 431, 432, 442, 444, 448, 461, 469, 470, 484, 499, 500, 501, 508ff., 533, 540, 541, 542, 572, 602, 604, 605, 613, 629, 630, 653f., 663, 672ff., 676, 679, 681, 685ff., 701, 702, 707, 720, 721, 722, 723, 725, 734, 738, 752, 760, 761, 762, 764, 765, 766f., 769, 771, 784, 798ff.
Wimpheling, Ulrich, 418, 766
Windesheim (town), 393, 490, 520
wine, 29, 172 (part of income from benefice), 190, 368, 441, 572, 584, 657, 658, 749
Wirt, Leonardus, 73 (*quendam Phisicam*), 132, 133, 487, 531f., 767
witches, persecution of, 760
witnesses, opinion on producing of, *see* opinion
Wittelsbach faction, 502
Wittenberg, 729
Witz, Hans, *see* Sapidus
Wolf, Andreas, 768
Wolf, Johann, dean of Old St. Peter, 52 (*pater illius?*), 160, 161, 560, 767, 768
Wolf, Johann, son of Thomas, Sr., 768
Wolf, Kilian, 736, 766
Wolf, Thomas, Jr., 38 (*Thome nostri*), 42, 61, 62, 81, 82, 94, 104, 111, 193 (case of litigation), 369, 431, 451, 456f., 461f, 465f., 472, 473f., 494ff., 506, 513, 518, 567, 576, 586, 711, 717, 719, 726, 730, 761, 767, 768f. *see* case of litigation, Funck vs. Wolf
Wolf, Thomas, Sr., 37, 42, 45, 46, 47, 50, 61, 62, 68, 71, 81, 84, 85, 94, 104, 110, 111, 193, 194, 369, 402, 404, 408, 431, 451f., 456f., 460, 461f., 464, 471, 472, 473f., 483, 494, 496f., 508, 513, 518, 521, 567, 586f., 588, 610, 626, 730, 749, 768
Wolfart, Johann, 745
Wolff, Kammerer (*Mercator* in Venice), 193, 587
Wolfgang, duke of Bavaria, 138, 502, 538, 704, 705
words not found in Latin dictionaries consulted: *mysticacio*, 79; *preconus*, 176; *saciacio*, 160; *sexternio*, 134
World War II, *see* hostilities
Worms, 50, 451, 456, 459, 461, 462, 473, 610, 662, 756, 765, 769 (diet of)
   bishop of, 700, 747, 760
   cathedral of, 462
   canon of, 38, 42, 46, 47, 62
   diocese of 711, 738
Württemberg, 426, 508, 531, 582, 706, 716, 724, 732, 769
   see Eberhard V, *Graf* (later Eberhard I, duke); Eberhard II, duke; Heinrich, *Graf*; Ulrich I, duke
Würzburg, 444
   cathedral canon, 716
   cathedral preaching chair, 543, 721
   diocese, 735
Wycliff, 640, 802

Xanten (cathedral), 747
Xenophon, 436
xylography, 372, 376

Ypsylon, Pytagoricum, 158; see Samian letter
Yssel (river), 735

Zabern (seat of Strassburg bishop), 165, 434, 565f., 598, 638, 699, 701, 737, 759
  episcopal palace at, 434
Zabernia Montana (town), 172, 572
Zainer, Günther (printer), 695
Zamometiĭ, Andreas, archbishop of Carniola, 454, 735
Zanctivis, Hieronymous de, 77, 400, 490, 618, 769
Zanctivis, Tommaso de, 769
Zanetini, Hieronymus, see Zanctivis
Zasius, Ulrich, 375
Zeis, Nicholas, 66, 195 (*Praepositus Badensis?*), 196, 478, 589f.
Zellerbad (spa), 169 (*Cellense balneum*), 426, 539f., 564, 569f.
Zellweiler (Alsatian town), 736
Zemecke, Johann, see Teutonicus
Zeninger, Konrad (Nürnberg printer), 617
Zephyri, 299
Zeus, 647, 648, 668
Zierer, Johann, 674
Zierotin, Sophia von, 728
Zoilus, 309, 677
Zollern, Friedrich von, dean of Strassburg cathedral and bishop of Augsburg, xiii, xxx, 52, 66, 67, 90f., 110, 114ff., 134, 141f., 143, 147, 154, 195 (*aelectum Augustensem*), 196, 215, 286, 292, 363, 366, 407, 408, 409, 411, 426, 428, 433, 456, 465, 477f., 479, 500, 502ff., 517f., 520, 521f., 527, 534ff., 538, 541, 542, 543, 548f., 555, 575, 580f., 588ff., 618, 626, 658ff., 664, 699, 708, 719, 731, 745, 751, 764, 770f., 780ff., 791ff.
Zollern, Friedrich von (uncle of the above), 770
Zollern, Jodocus Niklas von, 770
(*Des*) *Zollers Kapelle im Giessen*, 637
Zorn, Anna von, 357 (*muter Priorin*), 358 (*muter priorin*), 391, 695, 771, 777, 778
Zorn von Bulach, Caspar, 755, 810
Zorn chapel, see New St. Peter
Zuber, Anna, 41 (*matrem tuam*), 67 (*genitricis*), 134 (*Matri tue*), 143 (*Matrem tuam*), 442, 444, 445, 456, 478, 534f., 544f., 721, 771
Zug, canton of, 434
zum elenden Kreuz (Strassburg chapel), 601, 807
zum Ungemach (inn), 114, 521
zur Huoben (inn), 165, 564f.
Zürich, 189 (*Thuricensibus*), 190 (*Thuricensium*), 191 (*Thuricensibus*), 363, 385, 455f., 583, 585, 603, 713, 741, 756, 786f.
  cathedral canon of, 734
Zwig (*also* Zwick), Johann, 332, 668, 771
Zwolle (town), 393, 520, 715, 735, 736
Zwinglian, 544

www.ingramcontent.com/pod-product-compliance
Lightning Source LLC
Chambersburg PA
CBHW021756220426
43662CB00006B/80